GO!

Premium Media Site

Improve your grade with hands-on tools and resources!

- Master *Key Terms* to expand your vocabulary.
- Assess your knowledge with fun *Crossword Puzzles* and *Flipboards*, which let you flip through the definitions of the key terms and match them with the correct term.
- Prepare for exams by taking practice quizzes in the *Online Chapter Review*.
- Download *Student Data Files* for the application projects in each chapter.
- Answer matching and multiple choice questions to test what you learned in each chapter.

And for even more tools, you can access the following Premium Resources using your Access Code. Register now to get the most out of *GO!*.

- *Student Training Videos* for each Objective have been created by the author - a real instructor teaching the same types of courses that you take.*
- *GO! to Work* videos are short interviews with workers showing how they use Office in their job.*
- *GO! for Job Success* videos related to the projects in the chapter cover such important topics as Dressing for Success, Time Management, and Making Ethical Choices.*

*Access code required for these premium resources

Your Access Code is:

GMEC-PPRIL-FARCI-TRONA-ABBOT-WISES

Note: If there is no silver foil covering the access code, it may already have been redeemed, and therefore may no longer be valid. In that case, you can purchase online access using a major credit card or PayPal account. To do so, go to **www.pearsonhighered.com/go**, select your book cover, click on "Buy Access" and follow the on-screen instructions.

To Register:

- To start you will need a valid email address and this access code.
- Go to **www.pearsonhighered.com/go** and scroll to find your text book.
- Once you've selected your text, on the Home Page for the book, click the link to access the Student Premium Content.
- Click the Register button and follow the on-screen instructions.
- After you register, you can sign in any time via the log-in area on the same screen.

System Requirements

Windows 7 Ultimate Edition; IE 8
Windows Vista Ultimate Edition SP1; IE 8
Windows XP Professional SP3; IE 7
Windows XP Professional SP3; Firefox 3.6.4
Mac OS 10.5.7; Firefox 3.6.4
Mac OS 10.6; Safari 5

Technical Support

http://247pearsoned.custhelp.com

GO!

with Microsoft®

Excel 2013

Comprehensive

GO!

with Microsoft®

Excel 2013

Comprehensive

Shelley Gaskin, Alicia Vargas, and Debra Geoghan

PEARSON

Boston   Columbus   Indianapolis   New York   San Francisco   Upper Saddle River
Amsterdam   Cape Town   Dubai   London   Madrid   Milan   Munich   Paris   Montréal   Toronto
Delhi   Mexico City   São Paulo   Sydney   Hong Kong   Seoul   Singapore   Taipei   Tokyo

Editor in Chief: Michael Payne
Executive Acquisitions Editor: Jenifer Niles
Editorial Project Manager: Carly Prakapas
Product Development Manager: Laura Burgess
Development Editor: Ginny Munroe
Editorial Assistant: Andra Skaalrud
Director of Marketing: Maggie Leen
Marketing Manager: Brad Forrester
Marketing Coordinator: Susan Osterlitz
Marketing Assistant: Darshika Vyas
Managing Editor: Camille Trentacoste
Senior Production Project Manager: Rhonda Aversa

Operations Specialist: Maura Zaldivar-Garcia
Senior Art Director: Jonathan Boylan
Cover Photo: © photobar/Fotolia
Associate Director of Design: Blair Brown
Director of Media Development: Taylor Ragan
Media Project Manager, Production: Renata Butera
Full-Service Project Management: PreMediaGlobal
Composition: PreMediaGlobal
Printer/Binder: Webcrafters, Inc.
Cover Printer: Lehigh-Phoenix Color/Hagerstown
Text Font: MinionPro

Credits and acknowledgments borrowed from other sources and reproduced, with permission, in this textbook appear on the appropriate page within text. Microsoft and/or its respective suppliers make no representations about the suitability of the information contained in the documents and related graphics published as part of the services for any purpose. All such documents and related graphics are provided "as is" without warranty of any kind.

Microsoft and/or its respective suppliers hereby disclaim all warranties and conditions with regard to this information, including all warranties and conditions of merchantability, whether express, implied or statutory, fitness for a particular purpose, title and non-infringement. In no event shall Microsoft and/or its respective suppliers be liable for any special, indirect or consequential damages or any damages whatsoever resulting from loss of use, data or profits, whether in an action of contract, negligence or other tortious action, arising out of or in connection with the use or performance of information available from the services.

The documents and related graphics contained herein could include technical inaccuracies or typographical errors. Changes are periodically added to the information herein. Microsoft and/or its respective suppliers may make improvements and/or changes in the product(s) and/or the program(s) described herein at any time.

Microsoft® and Windows® are registered trademarks of the Microsoft Corporation in the U.S.A. and other countries. This book is not sponsored or endorsed by or affiliated with the Microsoft Corporation.

Many of the designations by manufacturers and sellers to distinguish their products are claimed as trademarks. Where those designations appear in this book, and the publisher was aware of a trademark claim, the designations have been printed in initial caps or all caps.

Library of Congress Cataloging-in-Publication Data

Gaskin, Shelley.
 Go! with Microsoft Excel 2013 : comprehensive / Shelley Gaskin, Alicia Vargas, and Debra Geoghan.
     pages cm
 Includes index.
 ISBN-13: 978-0-13-341733-3 (alk. paper)
 ISBN-10: 0-13-341733-6 (alk. paper)
 1. Microsoft Excel (Computer file)   2. Business—Computer programs.   3. Electronic spreadsheets.   I. Vargas, Alicia.   II. Geoghan, Debra.   III. Title.
 2. Business—Computer programs.   I. Title.
 HF5548.4.M523G3767 2014
 005.54—dc23

                                                                                      2013009156

10 9 8 7 6 5 4 3

ISBN 10: 0-13-341733-6
ISBN 13: 978-0-13-341733-3

Brief Contents

Table of Contents

Excel Introduction to Microsoft Excel 2013   **49**

Chapter 1   Creating a Worksheet and Charting Data **51**

Chapter 9   Using Macros and Visual Basic for Applications 507

About the Authors

Shelley Gaskin, Series Editor, is a professor in the Business and Computer Technology Division at Pasadena City College in Pasadena, California. She holds a bachelor's degree in Business Administration from Robert Morris College (Pennsylvania), a master's degree in Business from Northern Illinois University, and a doctorate in Adult and Community Education from Ball State University (Indiana). Before joining Pasadena City College, she spent 12 years in the computer industry, where she was a systems analyst, sales representative, and director of Customer Education with Unisys Corporation. She also worked for Ernst & Young on the development of large systems applications for their clients. She has written and developed training materials for custom systems applications in both the public and private sector, and has also written and edited numerous computer application textbooks.

This book is dedicated to my students, who inspire me every day.

Alicia Vargas is a faculty member in Business Information Technology at Pasadena City College. She holds a master's and a bachelor's degree in business education from California State University, Los Angeles, and has authored several textbooks and training manuals on Microsoft Word, Microsoft Excel, and Microsoft PowerPoint.

This book is dedicated with all my love to my husband Vic, who makes everything possible; and to my children Victor, Phil, and Emmy, who are an unending source of inspiration and who make everything worthwhile.

Debra Geoghan is a professor in the Science, Technology, Engineering, and Mathematics (STEM) Department at Bucks County Community College in Pennsylvania where she is coordinator of the Computer Science area. Deb teaches computer classes ranging from basic computer literacy to cybercrime, computer forensics, and networking. She holds a B.S. in Secondary Science Education from Temple University and an M.A. in Computer Science Education from Arcadia University, and has earned certifications from Microsoft, CompTIA, and Apple. Deb has taught at the college level since 1996 and also spent 11 years in the high school classroom.

Throughout her teaching career Deb has worked with educators to integrate technology across the curriculum. At Bucks she serves on many technology committees, presents technology workshops for faculty, and runs a summer workshop for local K-12 teachers interested in using technology in their classrooms. Deb is an avid user of technology, which has earned her the nickname "gadget lady."

This book is dedicated to my husband Joe, and my sons Joe and Mike, whose love and support have made this project possible.

GO! with Excel 2013

GO! with Excel 2013 is the right solution for you and your students in today's fast-moving, mobile environment. The GO! Series content focuses on the real-world job skills students need to succeed in the workforce. They learn Office by working step-by-step through practical job-related projects that put the core functionality of Office in context. And as has always been true of the GO! Series, students learn the important concepts when they need them, and they never get lost in instruction, because the GO! Series uses Microsoft procedural syntax. Students learn how and learn why—at the teachable moment.

After completing the instructional projects, students are ready to apply the skills in a wide variety of progressively challenging projects that require them to solve problems, think critically, and create projects on their own. And, for those who want to go beyond the classroom and become certified, GO! provides clear MOS preparation guidelines so students know what is needed to ace the Core exam!

What's New

New Design reflects the look of Windows 8 and Office 2013 and enhances readability.

Enhanced Chapter Opener now includes a deeper introduction to the A and B instructional projects and more highly defined chapter Objectives and Learning Outcomes.

New Application Introductions provide a brief overview of the application and put the chapters in context for students.

Coverage of New Features of Office 2013 ensures that students are learning the skills they need to work in today's job market.

New Application Capstone Projects ensure that students are ready to move on to the next set of chapters. Each Application Capstone Project can be found on the Instructor Resource Center and is also a Grader project in MyITLab.

More Grader Projects based on the E, F, and G mastering-level projects, both homework and assessment versions! These projects are written by our GO! authors, who are all instructors in colleges like yours!

New Training and Assessment Simulations are now written by the authors to match the book one-to-one!

New MOS Map on the Instructor Resource Site and in the Annotated Instructor's Edition indicates clearly where each required MOS Objective is covered.

Three Types of Videos help students understand and succeed in the real world:

- *Student Training Videos* are broken down by Objective and created by the author—a real instructor teaching the same types of courses that you do. Real personal instruction.
- *GO! to Work* videos are short interviews with workers showing how they use Office in their jobs.
- *GO! for Job Success* videos relate to the projects in the chapter and cover important career topics such as *Dressing for Success, Time Management,* and *Making Ethical Choices.* **Available for Chapters 1–3 only.**

New GO! Learn It Online section at the end of the chapter indicates where various student learning activities can be found, including multiple choice and matching activities.

New Styles for In-Text Boxed Content: Another Way, Notes, More Knowledge, Alerts, and **new *By Touch* instructions** are included in line with the instruction and not in the margins so that the student is more likely to read this information.

Clearly Indicated Build from Scratch Projects: GO! has always had many projects that begin "from scratch," and now we have an icon to really call them out!

New Visual Summary focuses on the four key concepts to remember from each chapter.

New Review and Assessment Guide summarizes the end-of-chapter assessments for a quick overview of the different types and levels of assignments and assessments for each chapter.

New Skills and Procedures Summary Chart (online at the Instructor Resource Center) summarizes all of the shortcuts and commands covered in the chapter.

New End-of-Chapter Key Term Glossary with Definitions for each chapter, plus a comprehensive end-of-book glossary.

New Flipboards and Crossword Puzzles enable students to review the concepts and key terms learned in each chapter by completing online challenges.

Teach the Course You Want in Less Time

A Microsoft® Office textbook designed for student success!

- **Project-Based** – Students learn by creating projects that they will use in the real world.

- **Microsoft Procedural Syntax** – Steps are written to put students in the right place at the right time.

- **Teachable Moment** – Expository text is woven into the steps—at the moment students need to know it—not chunked together in a block of text that will go unread.

- **Sequential Pagination** – Students have actual page numbers instead of confusing letters and abbreviations.

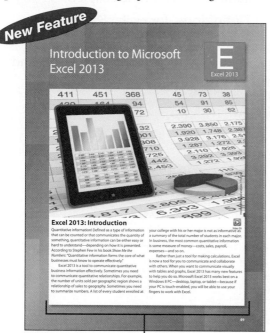

New Feature

New Application Introductions – Provide an overview of the application to prepare students for the upcoming chapters.

Student Outcomes and Learning Objectives – Objectives are clustered around projects that result in student outcomes.

New Design – Provides a more visually appealing and concise display of important content.

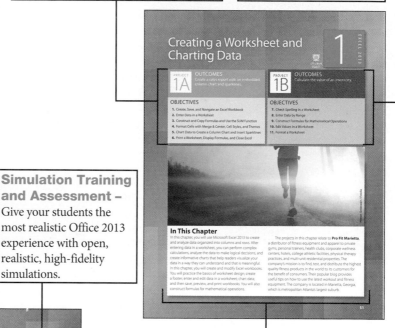

Simulation Training and Assessment – Give your students the most realistic Office 2013 experience with open, realistic, high-fidelity simulations.

Scenario – Each chapter opens with a job-related scenario that sets the stage for the projects the student will create.

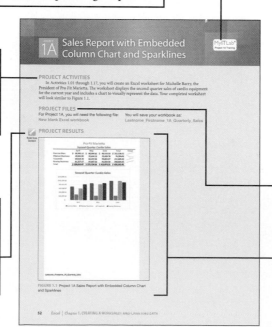

Project Activities – A project summary stated clearly and quickly.

New Build from Scratch Icons – Enable you to easily see all the projects that the student builds from scratch.

Project Files – Clearly shows students which files are needed for the project and the names they will use to save their documents.

Project Results – Shows students what successful completion looks like.

In-Text Features

Another Way, Notes, More Knowledge, Alerts, and By Touch Instructions

Microsoft Procedural Syntax – Steps are written to put the student at the right place at the right time.

Color Coding – Each chapter has two instructional projects, which is less overwhelming for students than one large chapter project. The two projects are differentiated by different colored numbering and headings.

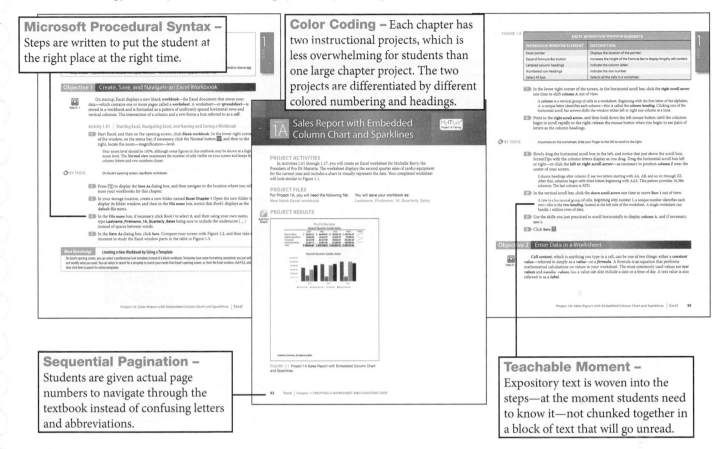

Sequential Pagination – Students are given actual page numbers to navigate through the textbook instead of confusing letters and abbreviations.

Teachable Moment – Expository text is woven into the steps—at the moment students need to know it—not chunked together in a block of text that will go unread.

End-of-Chapter

Content-Based Assessments – Assessments with defined solutions.

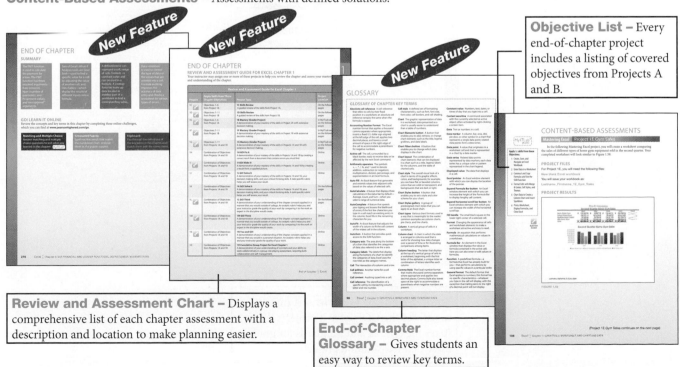

Objective List – Every end-of-chapter project includes a listing of covered objectives from Projects A and B.

Review and Assessment Chart – Displays a comprehensive list of each chapter assessment with a description and location to make planning easier.

End-of-Chapter Glossary – Gives students an easy way to review key terms.

End-of-Chapter

Content-Based Assessments – Assessments with defined solutions. (continued)

Grader Projects – Each chapter has six MyITLab Grader projects—three homework and three assessment—clearly indicated by the MyITLab logo.

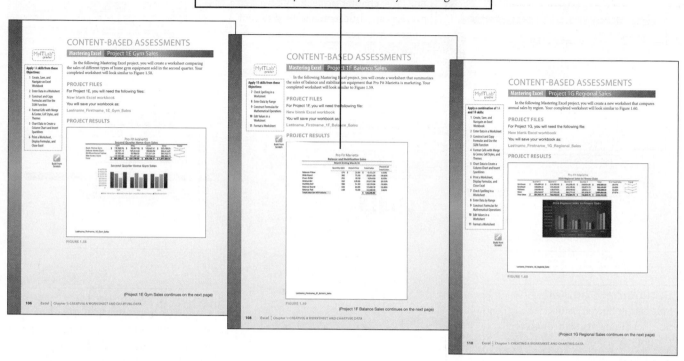

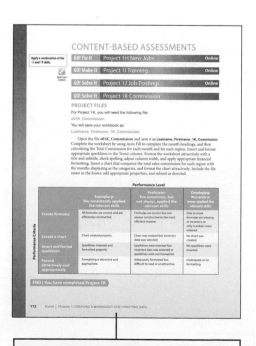

Task-Specific Rubric – A matrix specific to the GO! Solve It projects that states the criteria and standards for grading these defined-solution projects.

End-of-Chapter

Outcomes-Based Assessments – Assessments with open-ended solutions.

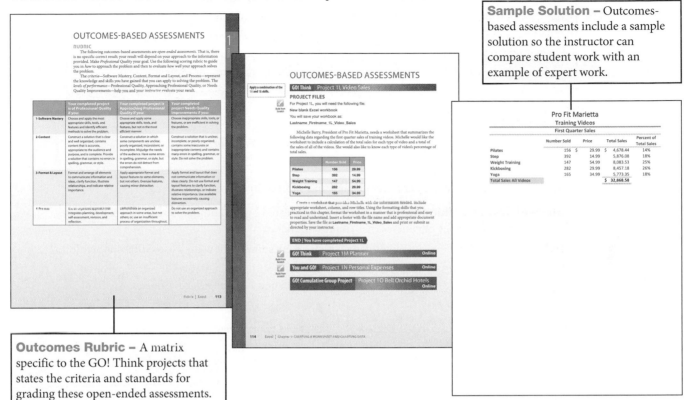

Sample Solution – Outcomes-based assessments include a sample solution so the instructor can compare student work with an example of expert work.

Outcomes Rubric – A matrix specific to the GO! Think projects that states the criteria and standards for grading these open-ended assessments.

GO! with Microsoft Office 365 – A collaboration project for each chapter teaches students how to use the cloud-based tools of Office 365 to communicate and collaborate from any device, anywhere. **Available for Chapters 1–3 only**.

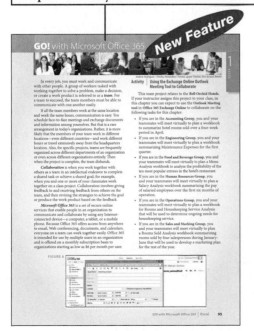

Office Web Apps – For each instructional project, students can create the same or similar result in the corresponding Office Web Apps - 24 projects in all! **Available for Chapters 1–3 only**.

Student Materials

Student Data Files – All student data files are available to all on the companion website: www.pearsonhighered.com/go.

3 Types of Videos help students understand and succeed in the real world:

- **Student Training Videos** are by Objective and created by the author—a real instructor teaching the same types of courses that you teach.
- *GO! to Work* videos are short interviews with workers showing how they use Office in their job.
- *GO! for Job Success* videos related to the projects in the chapter cover important career topics such as *Dressing for Success*, *Time Management*, and *Making Ethical Choices*. **Available for Chapters 1–3 only**.

Flipboards and crossword puzzles provide a variety of review options for content in each chapter.
Available on the companion website using the access code included with your book.
pearsonhighered.com/go

All Instructor and Student materials available at pearsonhighered.com/go

Instructor Materials

Annotated Instructor Edition – An instructor tool includes a full copy of the student textbook and a guide to implementing your course in three different ways, depending on the emphasis you want to place on digital engagement. Also included are teaching tips, discussion topics, and other useful pieces for teaching each chapter.

Student Assignment Tracker (previously called Assignment Sheets) – Lists all the assignments for the chapter. Just add the course information, due dates, and points. Providing these to students ensures they will know what is due and when.

Scripted Lectures – A script to guide your classroom lecture of each instructional project.

Annotated Solution Files – Coupled with the scorecards, these create a grading and scoring system that makes grading easy and efficient.

PowerPoint Lectures – PowerPoint presentations for each chapter.

Audio PowerPoints – Audio versions of the PowerPoint presentations for each chapter.

Scoring Rubrics – Can be used either by students to check their work or by you as a quick check-off for the items that need to be corrected.

Syllabus Templates – For 8-week, 12-week, and 16-week courses.

MOS Map – Provided at the Instructor Resource Center site and in the Annotated Instructor's Edition, showing where each required MOS Objective is covered either in the book or via additional instructional material provided.

Test Bank – Includes a variety of test questions for each chapter.

Companion Website – Online content such as the Online Chapter Review, Glossary, and Student Data Files are all at www.pearsonhighered.com/go.

Reviewers

GO! Focus Group Participants

Kenneth Mayer	Heald College
Carolyn Borne	Louisiana State University
Toribio Matamoros	Miami Dade College
Lynn Keane	University of South Carolina
Terri Hayes	Broward College
Michelle Carter	Paradise Valley Community College

GO! Reviewers

Abul Sheikh	Abraham Baldwin Agricultural College
John Percy	Atlantic Cape Community College
Janette Hicks	Binghamton University
Shannon Ogden	Black River Technical College
Karen May	Blinn College
Susan Fry	Boise State University
Chigurupati Rani	Borough of Manhattan Community College / CUNY
Ellen Glazer	Broward College
Kate LeGrand	Broward College
Mike Puopolo	Bunker Hill Community College
Nicole Lytle-Kosola	California State University, San Bernardino
Nisheeth Agrawal	Calhoun Community College
Pedro Diaz-Gomez	Cameron
Linda Friedel	Central Arizona College
Gregg Smith	Central Community College
Norm Cregger	Central Michigan University
Lisa LaCaria	Central Piedmont Community College
Steve Siedschlag	Chaffey College
Terri Helfand	Chaffey College
Susan Mills	Chambersburg
Mandy Reininger	Chemeketa Community College
Connie Crossley	Cincinnati State Technical and Community College
Marjorie Deutsch	City University of New York - Queensborough Community College
Mary Ann Zlotow	College of DuPage
Christine Bohnsak	College of Lake County
Gertrude Brier	College of Staten Island
Sharon Brown	College of The Albemarle
Terry Rigsby	Columbia College
Vicki Brooks	Columbia College
Donald Hames	Delgado Community College
Kristen King	Eastern Kentucky University
Kathie Richer	Edmonds Community College
Gary Smith	Elmhurst College
Wendi Kappersw	Embry-Riddle Aeronautical University
Nancy Woolridge	Fullerton College
Abigail Miller	Gateway Community & Technical College
Deep Ramanayake	Gateway Community & Technical College
Gwen White	Gateway Community & Technical College
Debbie Glinert	Gloria K School
Dana Smith	Golf Academy of America
Mary Locke	Greenville Technical College
Diane Marie Roselli	Harrisburg Area Community College
Linda Arnold	Harrisburg Area Community College - Lebanon
Daniel Schoedel	Harrisburg Area Community College - York Campus
Ken Mayer	Heald College
Xiaodong Qiao	Heald College
Donna Lamprecht	Hopkinsville Community College
Kristen Lancaster	Hopkinsville Community College
Johnny Hurley	Iowa Lakes Community College
Linda Halverson	Iowa Lakes Community College
Sarah Kilgo	Isothermal Community College
Chris DeGeare	Jefferson College
David McNair	Jefferson College
Diane Santurri	Johnson & Wales University
Roland Sparks	Johnson & Wales University
Ram Raghuraman	Joliet Junior College
Eduardo Suniga	Lansing Community College
Kenneth A. Hyatt	Lone Star College - Kingwood
Glenn Gray	Lone Star College - North Harris
Gene Carbonaro	Long Beach City College
Betty Pearman	Los Medanos College
Diane Kosharek	Madison College
Peter Meggison	Massasoit Community College
George Gabb	Miami Dade College
Lennie Alice Cooper	Miami Dade College
Richard Mabjish	Miami Dade College
Victor Giol	Miami Dade College
John Meir	Midlands Technical College
Greg Pauley	Moberly Area Community College
Catherine Glod	Mohawk Valley Community College
Robert Huyck	Mohawk Valley Community College
Kevin Engellant	Montana Western
Philip Lee	Nashville State Community College
Ruth Neal	Navarro College
Sharron Jordan	Navarro College
Richard Dale	New Mexico State University
Lori Townsend	Niagara County Community College
Judson Curry	North Park University
Mary Zegarski	Northampton Community College
Neal Stenlund	Northern Virginia Community College
Michael Goeken	Northwest Vista College
Mary Beth Tarver	Northwestern State University
Amy Rutledge	Oakland University
Marcia Braddock	Okefenokee Technical College
Richard Stocke	Oklahoma State University - OKC
Jane Stam	Onondaga Community College
Mike Michaelson	Palomar College
Kungwen (Dave) Chu	Purdue University Calumet
Wendy Ford	City University of New York - Queensborough Community College
Lewis Hall	Riverside City College
Karen Acree	San Juan College
Tim Ellis	Schoolcraft College
Dan Combellick	Scottsdale Community College
Pat Serrano	Scottsdale Community College
Rose Hendrickson	Sheridan College
Kit Carson	South Georgia College
Rebecca Futch	South Georgia State College
Brad Hagy	Southern Illinois University Carbondale
Mimi Spain	Southern Maine Community College
David Parker	Southern Oregon University
Madeline Baugher	Southwestern Oklahoma State University
Brian Holbert	St. Johns River State College
Bunny Howard	St. Johns River State College
Stephanie Cook	State College of Florida
Sharon Wavle	Tompkins Cortland Community College
George Fiori	Tri-County Technical College
Steve St. John	Tulsa Community College
Karen Thessing	University of Central Arkansas
Richard McMahon	University of Houston-Downtown
Shohreh Hashemi	University of Houston-Downtown
Donna Petty	Wallace Community College
Julia Bell	Walters State Community College
Ruby Kowaney	West Los Angeles College
Casey Thompson	Wiregrass Georgia Technical College
DeAnnia Clements	Wiregrass Georgia Technical College

Introduction to Microsoft Office 2013 Features

PROJECT 1A

OUTCOMES
Create, save, and print a Microsoft Office 2013 document.

PROJECT 1B

OUTCOMES
Use the ribbon and dialog boxes to perform commands in Microsoft Office 2013.

OBJECTIVES

1. Use File Explorer to Download, Extract, and Locate Files and Folders
2. Use Start Search to Locate and Start a Microsoft Office 2013 Desktop App
3. Enter, Edit, and Check the Spelling of Text in an Office 2013 Program
4. Perform Commands from a Dialog Box
5. Create a Folder and Name and Save a File
6. Insert a Footer, Add Document Properties, Print a File, and Close a Desktop App

OBJECTIVES

7. Open an Existing File and Save It with a New Name
8. Sign In to Office and Explore Options for a Microsoft Office Desktop App
9. Perform Commands from the Ribbon and Quick Access Toolbar
10. Apply Formatting in Office Programs
11. Compress Files and Use the Microsoft Office 2013 Help System
12. Install Apps for Office and Create a Microsoft Account

etse1112/Fotolia

In This Chapter

In this chapter, you will use File Explorer to navigate the Windows folder structure, create a folder, and save files in Microsoft Office 2013 programs. You will also practice using features in Microsoft Office 2013 that work similarly across Word, Excel, Access, and PowerPoint. These features include managing files, performing commands, adding document properties, signing in to Office, applying formatting, and using Help. You will also practice compressing files and installing Apps for Office from the Office Store. In this chapter, you will also learn how to set up a free Microsoft account so that you can use SkyDrive.

The projects in this chapter relate to **Skyline Metro Grill**, which is a chain of 25 casual, full-service restaurants based in Boston. The Skyline Metro Grill owners are planning an aggressive expansion program. To expand by 15 additional restaurants in Chicago, San Francisco, and Los Angeles by 2018, the company must attract new investors, develop new menus, develop new marketing strategies, and recruit new employees, all while adhering to the company's quality guidelines and maintaining its reputation for excellent service. To succeed, the company plans to build on its past success and maintain its quality elements.

Note Form

PROJECT
1A

MyITLab®
Project 1A Training

PROJECT ACTIVITIES

In Activities 1.01 through 1.09, you will create a note form using Microsoft Word, save it in a folder that you create by using File Explorer, and then print the note form or submit it electronically as directed by your instructor. Your completed note form will look similar to Figure 1.1.

PROJECT FILES

For Project 1A, you will need the following file: You will save your file as:

New blank Word document   Lastname_Firstname_1A_Note_Form

PROJECT RESULTS

Build from
Scratch

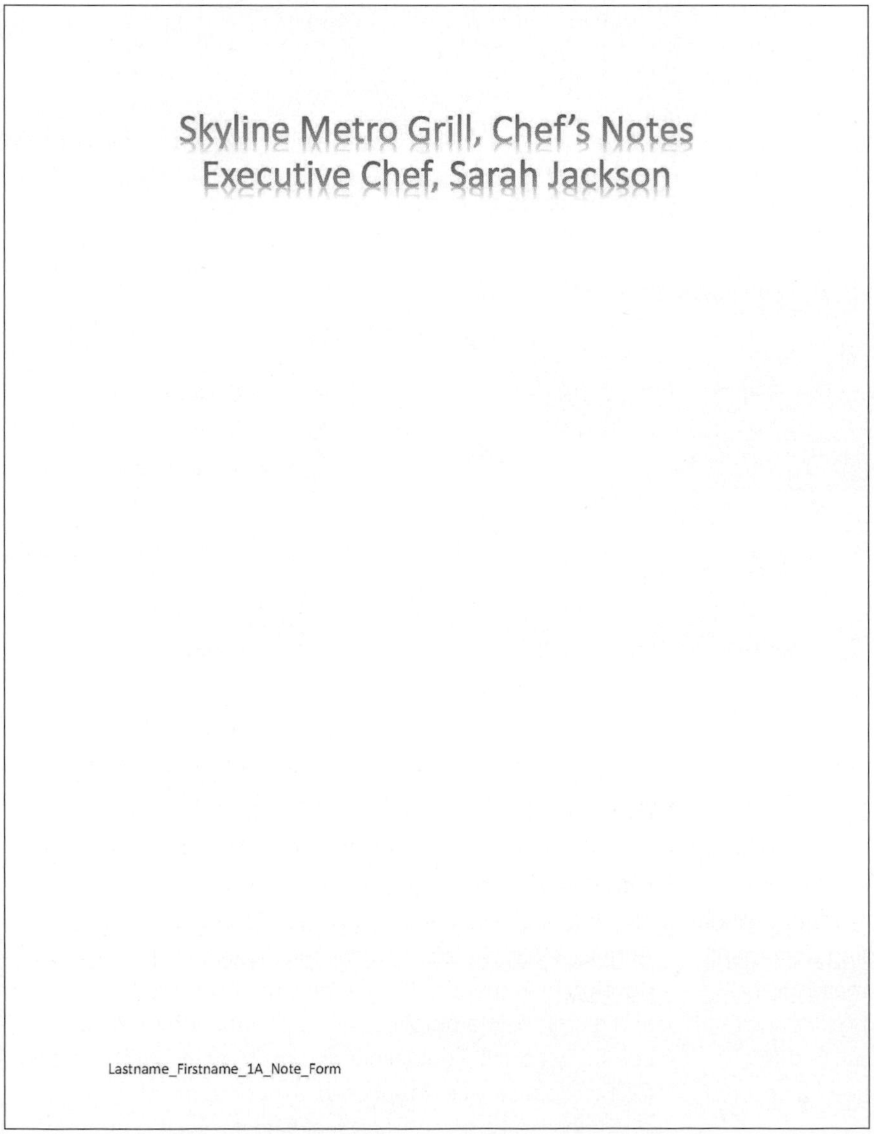

Skyline Metro Grill, Chef's Notes
Executive Chef, Sarah Jackson

Lastname_Firstname_1A_Note_Form

FIGURE 1.1 Project 1A Note Form

<table>
<tr><td>**NOTE**</td><td>**If You Are Using a Touchscreen**</td></tr>
</table>

- Tap an item to click it.
- Press and hold for a few seconds to right-click; release when the information or commands displays.
- Touch the screen with two or more fingers and then pinch together to zoom in or stretch your fingers apart to zoom out.
- Slide your finger on the screen to scroll—slide left to scroll right and slide right to scroll left.
- Slide to rearrange—similar to dragging with a mouse.
- Swipe from edge: from right to display charms; from left to expose open apps, snap apps, or close apps; from top or bottom to show commands or close an app.
- Swipe to select—slide an item a short distance with a quick movement to select an item and bring up commands, if any.

Objective 1 — Use File Explorer to Download, Extract, and Locate Files and Folders

Video OF1-1

A *file* is a collection of information stored on a computer under a single name, for example, a Word document or a PowerPoint presentation. A file is stored in a *folder*—a container in which you store files—or a *subfolder*, which is a folder within a folder. The Windows operating system stores and organizes your files and folders, which is a primary task of an operating system.

You *navigate*—explore within the organizing structure of Windows—to create, save, and find your files and folders by using the *File Explorer* program. File Explorer displays the files and folders on your computer and is at work anytime you are viewing the contents of files and folders in a *window*. A window is a rectangular area on a computer screen in which programs and content appear; a window can be moved, resized, minimized, or closed.

Activity 1.01 | Using File Explorer to Download, Extract, and Locate Files and Folders

<table>
<tr><td>**ALERT!**</td><td>**You Will Need a USB Flash Drive**</td></tr>
</table>

You will need a USB flash drive for this activity to download the Student Data Files for this chapter. If your instructor is providing the files to you, for example by placing the files at your learning management system, be sure you have downloaded them to a location where you can access the files and then skip to Activity 1.02.

<table>
<tr><td>**NOTE**</td><td>**Creating a Microsoft Account**</td></tr>
</table>

Use a free Microsoft account to sign in to Windows 8 and Office 2013 so that you can work on different PCs and use your SkyDrive. You need not use the Microsoft account as your primary email address unless you want to do so. To create a Microsoft account, go to **www.outlook.com**.

1 ▶ Sign in to Windows 8 with your Microsoft account—or the account provided by your instructor—to display the Windows 8 **Start screen**, and then click the **Desktop** tile. Insert a **USB flash drive** in your computer; **Close** ☒ any messages or windows that display.

The *desktop* is the screen in Windows that simulates your work area. A *USB flash drive* is a small data storage device that plugs into a computer USB port.

2 ▶ On the taskbar, click **Internet Explorer** 🅮. Click in the **address bar** to select the existing text, type **www.pearsonhighered.com/go** and press Enter. Locate and click the name of this textbook, and then click the **STUDENT DATA FILES tab**.

The *taskbar* is the area along the lower edge of the desktop that displays buttons representing programs—also referred to as desktop apps. In the desktop version of Internet Explorer 10, the *address bar* is the area at the top of the Internet Explorer window that displays, and where you can type, a *URL—Uniform Resource Locator*—which is an address that uniquely identifies a location on the Internet.

3 On the list of files, move your mouse pointer over—*point* to—**Office Features Chapter 1** and then *click*—press the left button on your mouse pointing device one time.

4 In the **Windows Internet Explorer** dialog box, click **Save As**.

A *dialog box* is a small window that contains options for completing a task.

5 In the **Save As** dialog box, on the left, locate the **navigation pane**, and point to the vertical **scroll bar**.

The Save As dialog box is an example of a *common dialog box*; that is, this dialog box looks the same in Excel and in PowerPoint and in most other Windows-based desktop applications—also referred to as programs.

Use the *navigation pane* on the left side of the Save As dialog box to navigate to, open, and display favorites, libraries, folders, saved searches, and an expandable list of drives. A *pane* is a separate area of a window.

A *scroll bar* displays when a window, or a pane within a window, has information that is not in view. You can click the up or down scroll arrows—or the left and right scroll arrows in a horizontal scroll bar—to scroll the contents up and down or left and right in small increments.

You can also drag the *scroll box*—the box within the scroll bar—to scroll the window or pane in either direction.

This is a *compressed folder*—also called a *zipped folder*—which is a folder containing one or more files that have been reduced in size. A compressed folder takes up less storage space and can be transferred to other computers faster.

NOTE | **Comparing Your Screen with the Figures in This Textbook**

Your screen will match the figures shown in this textbook if you set your screen resolution to 1280 × 768. At other resolutions, your screen will closely resemble, but not match, the figures shown. To view your screen's resolution, on the desktop, right-click in a blank area, and then click Screen resolution.

---

6 In the **navigation pane**, if necessary, on the scroll bar click ⌄ to scroll down. If necessary, to the left of **Computer**, click ▷ to expand the list. Then click the name of your **USB flash drive**.

7 With *Office_Features* displayed in the **File name** box, in the lower right corner click **Save**.

At the bottom of your screen, the *Notification bar* displays information about pending downloads, security issues, add-ons, and other issues related to the operation of your computer.

8 In the **Notification bar**, when the download is complete, click **Open folder** to display the folder window for your **USB flash drive**.

A *folder window* displays the contents of the current location—folder, library, or drive—and contains helpful parts so that you can navigate within the file organizing structure of Windows.

9 With the compressed **Office_Features** folder selected, on the ribbon, click the **Extract tab** to display the **Compressed Folder Tools**, and then click **Extract all**.

The *ribbon* is a user interface in both Office 2013 and Windows 8 that groups the commands for performing related tasks on tabs across the upper portion of a window.

In the dialog box, you can *extract*—decompress or pull out—files from a compressed folder.

You can navigate to some other location by clicking the Browse button and navigating within your storage locations.

10 In the **Extract Compressed (Zipped) Folders** dialog box, click to the right of the selected text, and then press ⌨Backspace until only the drive letter of your USB and the colon following it display—for example G:—and then click **Extract**. Notice that a progress bar indicates the progress of the extract process, and that when the extract is complete, the **Office_Features** folder displays on the file list of your **USB flash drive**.

In a dialog box or taskbar button, a ***progress bar*** indicates visually the progress of a task such as a download or file transfer.

The ***address bar*** in File Explorer displays your current location in the folder structure as a series of links separated by arrows, which is referred to as the ***path***—a sequence of folders that leads to a specific file or folder.

By pressing ⌨Backspace in the Extract dialog box, you avoid creating an unneeded folder level.

11 Because you no longer need the compressed (zipped) version of the folder, be sure it is selected, click the **Home tab**, and then click **Delete**. In the upper right corner of the **USB drive** folder window, click **Close** ⊠. **Close** ⊠ the **Internet Explorer** window and in the Internet Explorer message, click **Close all tabs**.

Your desktop redisplays.

Objective 2   Use Start Search to Locate and Start a Microsoft Office 2013 Desktop App

Video OF1-2

The term ***desktop app*** commonly refers to a computer program that is installed on your computer and requires a computer operating system such as Microsoft Windows or Apple OS to run. The programs in Microsoft Office 2013 are considered to be desktop apps. Apps that run from the *device software* on a smartphone or a tablet computer—for example, iOS, Android, or Windows Phone—or apps that run from *browser software* such as Internet Explorer, Safari, Firefox, or Chrome on a desktop PC or laptop PC are referred to simply as ***apps***.

Activity 1.02 | **Using Start Search to Locate and Start a Microsoft Office 2013 Desktop App**

The easiest and fastest way to search for an app is to use the ***Start search*** feature—simply display the Windows 8 Start screen and start typing. By default, Windows 8 searches for apps; you can change it to search for files or settings.

1 With your desktop displayed, press ⊞ to display the Windows 8 **Start screen**, and then type **word 2013** With *word 2013* bordered in white in the search results, press ⌨Enter to return to the desktop and open Word. If you want to do so, in the upper right corner, sign in with your Microsoft account, and then compare your screen with Figure 1.2.

Documents that you have recently opened, if any, display on the left. On the right, you can select either a blank document or a ***template***—a preformatted document that you can use as a starting point and then change to suit your needs.

 BY TOUCH

Swipe from the right edge of the screen to display the charms, and then tap Search. Tap in the Apps box, and then use the onscreen keyboard that displays to type *word 2013*. Tap the selected Word 2013 app name to open Word.

FIGURE 1.2

Recently opened documents, if any, display here

Start a blank document here

User signed in; this is optional

Templates to start different types of documents

2 Click **Blank document**. Compare your screen with Figure 1.3, and then take a moment to study the description of these screen elements in the table in Figure 1.4.

NOTE | **Displaying the Full Ribbon**

If your full ribbon does not display, click any tab, and then at the right end of the ribbon, click 📌 to pin the ribbon to keep it open while you work.

FIGURE 1.3

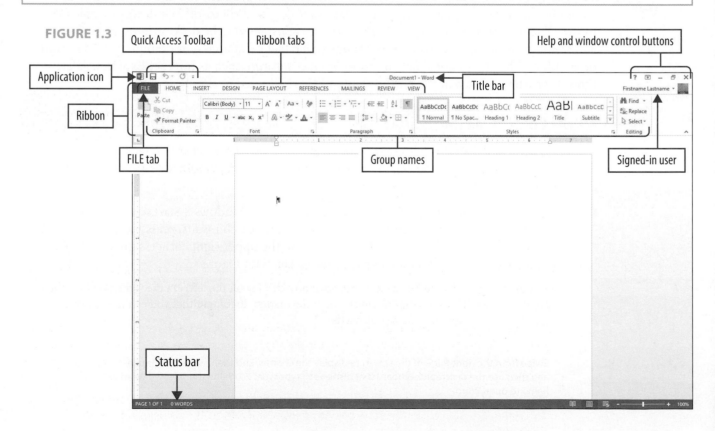

Quick Access Toolbar

Ribbon tabs

Help and window control buttons

Application icon

Title bar

Ribbon

FILE tab

Group names

Signed-in user

Status bar

FIGURE 1.4

MICROSOFT OFFICE SCREEN ELEMENTS	
SCREEN ELEMENT	**DESCRIPTION**
FILE tab	Displays Microsoft Office Backstage view, which is a centralized space for all of your file management tasks such as opening, saving, printing, publishing, or sharing a file—all the things you can do *with* a file.
Group names	Indicate the names of the groups of related commands on the displayed tab.
Help and window control buttons	Display Word Help and Full Screen Mode and enable you to Minimize, Restore Down, or Close the window.
Application icon	When clicked, displays a menu of window control commands including Restore, Minimize, and Close.
Quick Access Toolbar	Displays buttons to perform frequently used commands and use resources with a single click. The default commands include Save, Undo, and Redo. You can add and delete buttons to customize the Quick Access Toolbar for your convenience.
Ribbon	Displays a group of task-oriented tabs that contain the commands, styles, and resources you need to work in an Office 2013 desktop app. The look of your ribbon depends on your screen resolution. A high resolution will display more individual items and button names on the ribbon.
Ribbon tabs	Display the names of the task-oriented tabs relevant to the open program.
Status bar	Displays file information on the left; on the right displays buttons for Read Mode, Print Layout, and Web Layout views; on the far right displays Zoom controls.
Title bar	Displays the name of the file and the name of the program. The Help and window control buttons are grouped on the right side of the title bar.
Signed-in user	Name of the Windows 8 signed-in user.

Objective 3 Enter, Edit, and Check the Spelling of Text in an Office 2013 Program

Video OF1-3

All of the programs in Office 2013 require some typed text. Your keyboard is still the primary method of entering information into your computer. Techniques to enter text and to *edit*—make changes to—text are similar among all of the Office 2013 programs.

Activity 1.03 | Entering and Editing Text in an Office 2013 Program

1 On the ribbon, on the HOME tab, in the Paragraph group, if necessary, click Show/Hide ¶ so that it is active—shaded. If necessary, on the VIEW tab, in the Show group, select the Ruler check box so that rulers display below the ribbon and on the left side of your window.

The *insertion point*—a blinking vertical line that indicates where text or graphics will be inserted—displays. In Office 2013 programs, the mouse *pointer*—any symbol that displays on your screen in response to moving your mouse device—displays in different shapes depending on the task you are performing and the area of the screen to which you are pointing.

When you press Enter, Spacebar, or Tab on your keyboard, characters display to represent these keystrokes. These screen characters do not print and are referred to as *formatting marks* or *nonprinting characters*.

2 Type **Skyline Grille Info** and notice how the insertion point moves to the right as you type. Point slightly to the right of the letter *e* in *Grille* and click to place the insertion point there. Compare your screen with Figure 1.5.

A *paragraph symbol* (¶) indicates the end of a paragraph and displays each time you press Enter. This is a type of formatting mark and does not print.

FIGURE 1.5

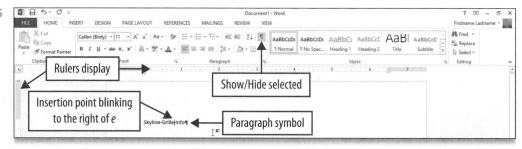

3 On your keyboard, locate and then press the Backspace key to delete the letter *e*.

Pressing Backspace removes a character to the left of the insertion point.

4 Press → one time to place the insertion point to the left of the *I* in *Info*. Type **Chef's** and then press Spacebar one time.

By *default*, when you type text in an Office program, existing text moves to the right to make space for new typing. Default refers to the current selection or setting that is automatically used by a program unless you specify otherwise.

5 Press Del four times to delete *Info* and then type **Notes**

Pressing Del removes a character to the right of the insertion point.

6 With your insertion point blinking after the word *Notes*, on your keyboard, hold down the Ctrl key. While holding down Ctrl, press ← three times to move the insertion point to the beginning of the word *Grill*.

This is a *keyboard shortcut*—a key or combination of keys that performs a task that would otherwise require a mouse. This keyboard shortcut moves the insertion point to the beginning of the previous word.

A keyboard shortcut is commonly indicated as Ctrl + ← (or some other combination of keys) to indicate that you hold down the first key while pressing the second key. A keyboard shortcut can also include three keys, in which case you hold down the first two and then press the third. For example, Ctrl + Shift + ← selects one word to the left.

7 With the insertion point blinking at the beginning of the word *Grill*, type **Metro** and press Spacebar.

8 Press Ctrl + End to place the insertion point after the letter *s* in *Notes*, and then press Enter one time. With the insertion point blinking, type the following and include the spelling error: **Exective Chef, Madison Dunham**

9 With your mouse, point slightly to the left of the *M* in *Madison*, hold down the left mouse button, and then ***drag***—hold down the left mouse button while moving your mouse—to the right to select the text *Madison Dunham* but not the paragraph mark following it, and then release the mouse button. Compare your screen with Figure 1.6.

The ***mini toolbar*** displays commands that are commonly used with the selected object, which places common commands close to your pointer. When you move the pointer away from the mini toolbar, it fades from view.

Selecting refers to highlighting, by dragging or clicking with your mouse, areas of text or data or graphics so that the selection can be edited, formatted, copied, or moved. The action of dragging includes releasing the left mouse button at the end of the area you want to select.

The Office programs recognize a selected area as one unit to which you can make changes. Selecting text may require some practice. If you are not satisfied with your result, click anywhere outside of the selection, and then begin again.

BY TOUCH   Tap once on *Madison* to display the gripper—small circle that acts as a handle—directly below the word. This establishes the start gripper. If necessary, with your finger, drag the gripper to the beginning of the word. Then drag the gripper to the end of Dunham to select the text and display the end gripper.

FIGURE 1.6

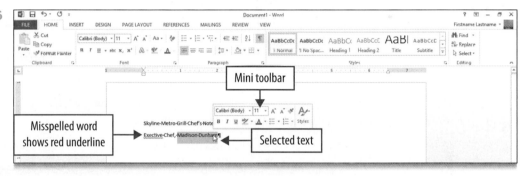

10 With the text *Madison Dunham* selected, type **Sarah Jackson**

In any Windows-based program, such as the Microsoft Office 2013 programs, selected text is deleted and then replaced when you begin to type new text. You will save time by developing good techniques for selecting and then editing or replacing selected text, which is easier than pressing the Del key numerous times to delete text.

Activity 1.04 | Checking Spelling

Office 2013 has a dictionary of words against which all entered text is checked. In Word and PowerPoint, words that are not in the dictionary display a wavy red line, indicating a possible misspelled word or a proper name or an unusual word—none of which are in the Office 2013 dictionary.

In Excel and Access, you can initiate a check of the spelling, but red underlines do not display.

1 Notice that the misspelled word *Exective* displays with a wavy red underline.

2 Point to *Exective* and then ***right-click***—click your right mouse button one time.

A ***shortcut menu*** displays, which displays commands and options relevant to the selected text or object. These are ***context-sensitive commands*** because they relate to the item you right-clicked. These types of menus are also referred to as ***context menus***. Here, the shortcut menu displays commands related to the misspelled word.

BY TOUCH   Tap and hold a moment to select the misspelled word, then release your finger to display the shortcut menu.

3 Press [Esc] to cancel the shortcut menu, and then in the lower left corner of your screen, on the **status bar**, click the **Proofing** icon ▣, which displays an *X* because some errors are detected. Compare your screen with Figure 1.7.

> The Spelling pane displays on the right. Here you have many more options for checking spelling than you have on the shortcut menu. The suggested correct word, *Executive*, is highlighted.
>
> You can click the speaker icon to hear the pronunciation of the selected word. You can also see some synonyms for *Executive*. Finally, if you have not already installed a dictionary, you can click *Get a Dictionary*—if you are signed in to Office with a Microsoft account—to find and install one from the online Office store; or if you have a dictionary app installed, it will display here and you can search it for more information.
>
> In the Spelling pane, you can ignore the word one time or in all occurrences, change the word to the suggested word, select a different suggestion, or add a word to the dictionary against which Word checks.

FIGURE 1.7

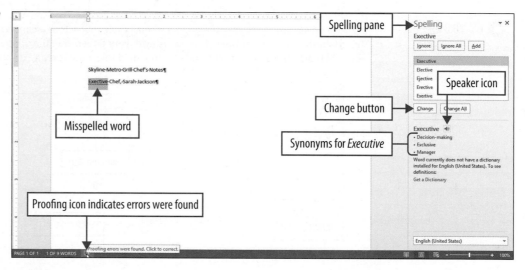

🔄 **ANOTHER WAY**   Press [F7] to display the Spelling pane; or, on the Review tab, in the Proofing group, click Spelling & Grammar.

4 In the **Spelling** pane, click **Change** to change the spelling to *Executive*. In the message box that displays, click **OK**.

Objective 4   Perform Commands from a Dialog Box

Video OF1-4

In a dialog box, you make decisions about an individual object or topic. In some dialog boxes, you can make multiple decisions in one place.

Activity 1.05 │ Performing Commands from a Dialog Box

1 On the ribbon, click the **DESIGN tab**, and then in the **Page Background group**, click **Page Color**.

2 At the bottom of the menu, notice the command **Fill Effects** followed by an **ellipsis** (...). Compare your screen with Figure 1.8.

> An *ellipsis* is a set of three dots indicating incompleteness. An ellipsis following a command name indicates that a dialog box will display when you click the command.

FIGURE 1.8

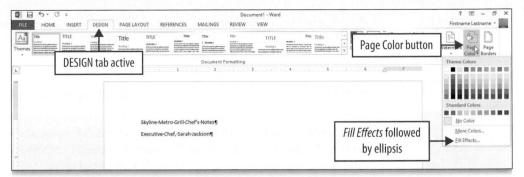

Page Color button

DESIGN tab active

Fill Effects followed by ellipsis

3 ▶ Click **Fill Effects** to display the **Fill Effects** dialog box. Compare your screen with Figure 1.9.

Fill is the inside color of a page or object. The Gradient tab is active. In a ***gradient fill***, one color fades into another. Here, the dialog box displays a set of tabs across the top from which you can display different sets of options. Some dialog boxes display the option group names on the left.

FIGURE 1.9

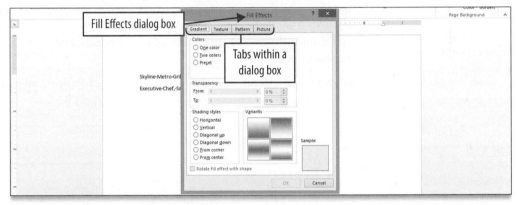

Fill Effects dialog box

Tabs within a dialog box

4 ▶ Under **Colors,** click the **One color** option button.

The dialog box displays settings related to the One color option. An ***option button*** is a round button that enables you to make one choice among two or more options.

5 ▶ Click the **Color 1 arrow**—the arrow under the text *Color 1*—and then in the third column, point to the second color to display the ScreenTip *Gray-25%, Background 2, Darker 10%.*

A ***ScreenTip*** displays useful information about mouse actions, such as pointing to screen elements or dragging.

6 ▶ Click **Gray-25%, Background 2, Darker 10%,** and then notice that the fill color displays in the **Color 1** box. In the **Dark Light** bar, click the **Light arrow** as many times as necessary until the scroll box is all the way to right. Under **Shading styles,** click the **Diagonal down** option button. Under **Variants,** click the upper right variant. Compare your screen with Figure 1.10.

FIGURE 1.10

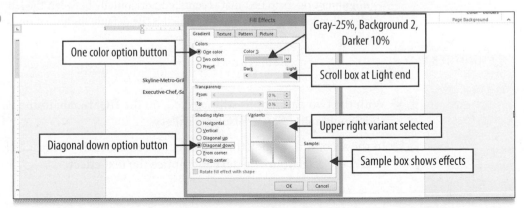

Gray-25%, Background 2, Darker 10%

One color option button

Scroll box at Light end

Diagonal down option button

Upper right variant selected

Sample box shows effects

7 At the bottom of the dialog box, click **OK**, and notice the subtle page color.

In Word, the gray shading page color will not print—even on a color printer—unless you set specific options to do so. However a subtle background page color is effective if people will be reading the document on a screen. Microsoft's research indicates that two-thirds of people who open Word documents never edit them; they only read them.

Activity 1.06 │ Using Undo

1 Point to the *S* in *Skyline*, and then drag down and to the right to select both paragraphs of text and include the paragraph marks. On the mini toolbar, click **Styles,** and then *point to* but do not click **Title**. Compare your screen with Figure 1.11.

A *style* is a group of *formatting* commands, such as font, font size, font color, paragraph alignment, and line spacing that can be applied to a paragraph with one command. Formatting is the process of establishing the overall appearance of text, graphics, and pages in an Office file—for example, in a Word document.

Live Preview is a technology that shows the result of applying an editing or formatting change as you point to possible results—before you actually apply it.

FIGURE 1.11

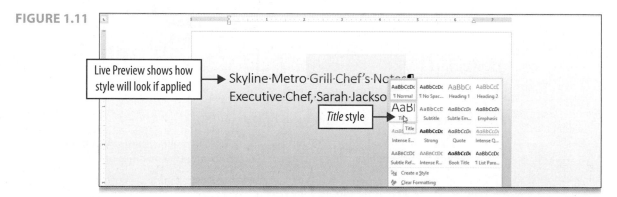

2 In the **Styles** gallery, click **Title**.

A *gallery* is an Office feature that displays a list of potential results.

3 On the ribbon, on the **HOME tab**, in the **Paragraph group**, click **Center** ≣ to center the two paragraphs.

Alignment refers to the placement of paragraph text relative to the left and right margins. *Center alignment* refers to text that is centered horizontally between the left and right margins. You can also align text at the left margin, which is the default alignment for text in Word, or at the right.

4 With the two paragraphs still selected, on the **HOME tab**, in the **Font Group**, click **Text Effects and Typography** A ⋅ to display a gallery.

5 In the second row, click the first effect—**Gradient Fill – Gray**. Click anywhere to *deselect*—cancel the selection—the text and notice the text effect.

6 Because this effect might be difficult to read, in the upper left corner of your screen, on the **Quick Access Toolbar**, click **Undo** ↺.

> The **Undo** command reverses your last action.

↻ ANOTHER WAY   Press [Ctrl] + [Z] as the keyboard shortcut for the Undo command.

7 Display the **Text Effects and Typography** gallery again, and then in the second row, click the second effect—**Gradient Fill – Blue, Accent 1, Reflection**. Click anywhere to deselect the text and notice the text effect. Compare your screen with Figure 1.12.

> As you progress in your study of Microsoft Office, you will practice using many dialog boxes and applying interesting effects such as this to your Word documents, Excel worksheets, Access database objects, and PowerPoint slides.

FIGURE 1.12

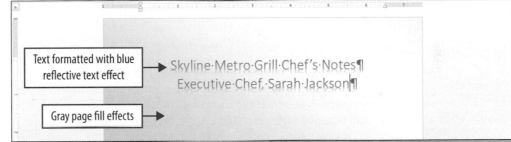

Text formatted with blue reflective text effect → Skyline·Metro·Grill·Chef's·Notes¶
Executive·Chef,·Sarah·Jackson¶

Gray page fill effects →

Objective 5   Create a Folder and Name and Save a File

Video OF1-5

A *location* is any disk drive, folder, or other place in which you can store files and folders. Where you store your files depends on how and where you use your data. For example, for your college classes, you might decide to store on a removable USB flash drive so that you can carry your files to different locations and access your files on different computers.

If you do most of your work on a single computer, for example your home desktop system or your laptop computer that you take with you to school or work, then you can store your files in one of the Libraries—Documents, Music, Pictures, or Videos—that the Windows 8 operating system creates on your hard drive.

The best place to store files if you want them to be available anytime, anywhere, from almost any device is on your *SkyDrive*, which is Microsoft's free *cloud storage* for anyone with a free Microsoft account. Cloud storage refers to online storage of data so that you can access your data from different places and devices. *Cloud computing* refers to applications and services that are accessed over the Internet, rather than to applications that are installed on your local computer.

Because many people now have multiple computing devices—desktop, laptop, tablet, smartphone—it is common to store data *in the cloud* so that it is always available. *Synchronization*, also called *syncing*—pronounced SINK-ing—is the process of updating computer files that are in two or more locations according to specific rules. So if you create and save a Word document on your SkyDrive using your laptop, you can open and edit that document on your tablet. And then when you close the document again, the file is properly updated to reflect your changes.

You need not be connected to the Internet to access documents stored on SkyDrive because an up-to-date version of your content is synched to your local system and available on SkyDrive. You must, however, be connected to the Internet for the syncing to occur. Saving to SkyDrive will keep the local copy on your computer and the copy in the cloud synchronized for as long as you need it. If you open and edit on a different computer, log into the SkyDrive website, and then edit using Office 2013, Office 2010, or the *Office Web Apps*, you can save any changes back to SkyDrive. Office Web Apps are the free online companions to Microsoft Word, Excel, PowerPoint, Access, and OneNote. These changes will be synchronized back to any of your computers that run the SkyDrive for Windows application, which you get for free simply by logging in with your Microsoft account at skydrive.com.

The Windows operating system helps you to create and maintain a logical folder structure, so always take the time to name your files and folders consistently.

Activity 1.07 | Creating a Folder and Naming and Saving a File

A Word document is an example of a file. In this activity, you will create a folder on your USB flash drive in which to store your files. If you prefer to store on your SkyDrive or in the Documents library on your hard drive, you can use similar steps.

1 If necessary, insert your **USB flash drive** into your computer.

As the first step in saving a file, determine where you want to save the file, and if necessary, insert a storage device.

2 At the top of your screen, in the title bar, notice that *Document1 – Word* displays.

The Blank option on the opening screen of an Office 2013 program displays a new unsaved file with a default name—*Document1, Presentation1*, and so on. As you create your file, your work is temporarily stored in the computer's memory until you initiate a Save command, at which time you must choose a file name and a location in which to save your file.

3 In the upper left corner of your screen, click the **FILE tab** to display **Backstage** view. Compare your screen with Figure 1.13.

Backstage view is a centralized space that groups commands related to *file* management; that is why the tab is labeled *FILE*. File management commands include opening, saving, printing, publishing, or sharing a file. The *Backstage tabs*—*Info, New, Open, Save, Save As, Print, Share, Export*, and *Close*—display along the left side. The tabs group file-related tasks together.

Here, the *Info tab* displays information—*info*—about the current file, and file management commands display under Info. For example, if you click the Protect Document button, a list of options that you can set for this file that relate to who can open or edit the document displays.

On the right, you can also examine the *document properties*. Document properties, also known as *metadata*, are details about a file that describe or identify it, such as the title, author name, subject, and keywords that identify the document's topic or contents. To close Backstage view and return to the document, you can click ⊛ in the upper left corner or press Esc.

FIGURE 1.13

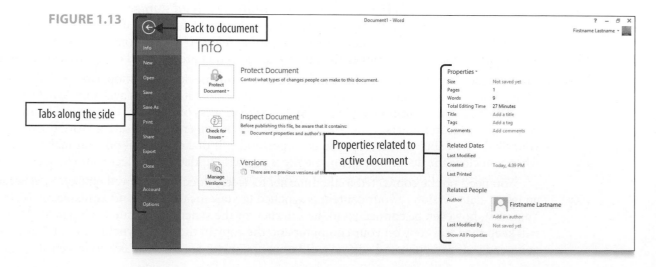

4 On the left, click **Save As**, and notice that the default location for storing Office files is your **SkyDrive** if you arc signed in. Compare your screen with Figure 1.14.

> When you are saving something for the first time, for example a new Word document, the Save and Save As commands are identical. That is, the Save As commands will display if you click Save or if you click Save As.

FIGURE 1.14

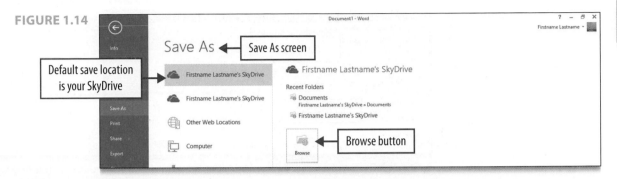

N O T E   **Saving after Your File Is Named**

After you name and save a file, the Save command on the Quick Access Toolbar saves any changes you make to the file without displaying Backstage view. The Save As command enables you to name and save a *new* file based on the current one—in a location that you choose. After you name and save the new document, the original document closes, and the new document—based on the original one—displays.

---

5 To store your Word file on your **USB flash drive**—instead of your SkyDrive—click the **Browse** button to display the **Save As** dialog box. On the left, in the navigation pane, scroll down, and then under **Computer**, click the name of your **USB flash drive**. Compare your screen with Figure 1.15.

> In the Save As dialog box, you must indicate the name you want for the file and the location where you want to save the file. When working with your own data, it is good practice to pause at this point and determine the logical name and location for your file.

> In the Save As dialog box, a **toolbar** displays. This is a row, column, or block of buttons or icons, that usually displays across the top of a window and that contains commands for tasks you perform with a single click.

FIGURE 1.15

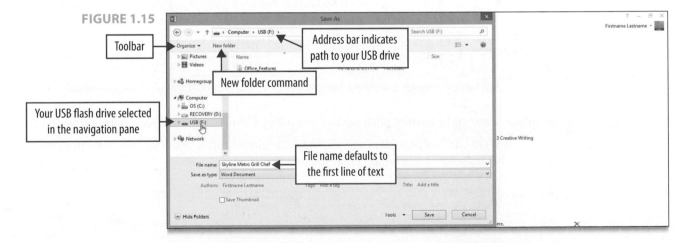

6 ▶ On the toolbar, click **New folder**.

In the file list, Word creates a new folder, and the text *New folder* is selected.

7 ▶ Type **Office Features Chapter 1** and press Enter. Compare your screen with Figure 1.16.

In Windows-based programs, the Enter key confirms an action.

FIGURE 1.16

8 ▶ In the **file list**, double-click the name of your new folder to open it and display its name in the **address bar**.

9 ▶ In the lower portion of the dialog box, click in the **File name** box to select the existing text. Notice that Office inserts the text at the beginning of the document as a suggested file name.

10 ▶ On your keyboard, locate the hyphen ⊟ key. Notice that the Shift of this key produces the underscore character. With the text still selected and using your own name, type **Lastname_Firstname_1A_Note_Form** and then compare your screen with Figure 1.17.

You can use spaces in file names, however, some people prefer not to use spaces. Some programs, especially when transferring files over the Internet, may insert the extra characters *%20* in place of a space. This can happen in ***SharePoint***, so using underscores instead of spaces can be a good habit to adopt. SharePoint is Microsoft's collaboration software with which people in an organization can set up team sites to share information, manage documents, and publish reports for others to see. In general, however, unless you encounter a problem, it is OK to use spaces. In this textbook, underscores are used instead of spaces in file names.

FIGURE 1.17

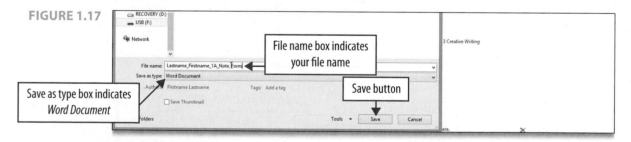

11 ▶ In the lower right corner, click **Save** or press Enter. Compare your screen with Figure 1.18.

The Word window redisplays and your new file name displays in the title bar, indicating that the file has been saved to a location that you have specified.

FIGURE 1.18

12 In the first paragraph, click to place the insertion point after the word *Grill* and type , (a comma). In the upper left corner of your screen, on the **Quick Access Toolbar**, click **Save** 🔲.

> After a document is named and saved in a location, you can save any changes you have made since the last Save operation by using the Save command on the Quick Access Toolbar. When working on a document, it is good practice to save your changes from time to time.

Objective 6 | Insert a Footer, Add Document Properties, Print a File, and Close a Desktop App

Video OF1-6

For most of your files, especially in a workplace setting, it is useful to add identifying information to help in finding files later. You might also want to print your file on paper or create an electronic printout. The process of printing a file is similar in all of the Office applications.

Activity 1.08 | Inserting a Footer, Inserting Document Info, and Adding Document Properties

1 On the ribbon, click the **INSERT tab**, and then in the **Header & Footer group**, click **Footer**.

2 At the bottom of the list, click **Edit Footer**. On the ribbon, notice that the **HEADER & FOOTER TOOLS** display.

> The *Header & Footer Tools Design* tab displays on the ribbon. The ribbon adapts to your work and will display additional tabs like this one—referred to as ***contextual tabs***—when you need them.
>
> A ***footer*** is a reserved area for text or graphics that displays at the bottom of each page in a document. Likewise, a ***header*** is a reserved area for text or graphics that displays at the top of each page in a document. When the footer (or header) area is active, the document area is dimmed, indicating it is unavailable.

3 On the ribbon, under **HEADER & FOOTER TOOLS**, on the **DESIGN tab**, in the **Insert group**, click **Document Info**, and then click **File Name** to insert the name of your file in the footer, which is a common business practice. Compare your screen with Figure 1.19.

> Ribbon commands that display ▼ will, when clicked, display a list of options for the command.

FIGURE 1.19

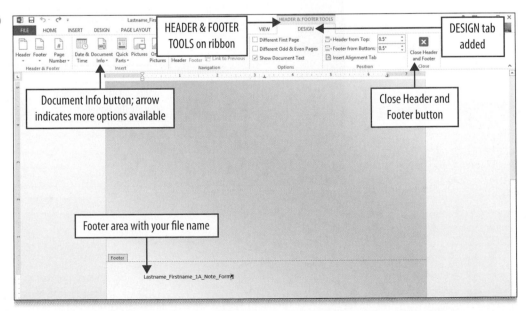

Document Info button; arrow indicates more options available

HEADER & FOOTER TOOLS on ribbon

DESIGN tab added

Close Header and Footer button

Footer area with your file name

Lastname_Firstname_1A_Note_Form

4 At the right end of the ribbon, click **Close Header and Footer**.

ANOTHER WAY   Double-click anywhere in the dimmed document to close the footer.

5 Click the **FILE tab** to display **Backstage** view. On the right, at the bottom of the **Properties** list, click **Show All Properties**.

ANOTHER WAY   Click the arrow to the right of Properties, and then click Show Document Panel to show and edit properties at the top of your document window.

6 On the list of **Properties**, click to the right of **Tags** to display an empty box, and then type **chef, notes, form**

> *Tags*, also referred to as ***keywords***, are custom file properties in the form of words that you associate with a document to give an indication of the document's content. Adding tags to your documents makes it easier to search for and locate files in File Explorer and in systems such as Microsoft SharePoint document libraries.

BY TOUCH   Tap to the right of Tags to display the Tags box and the onscreen keyboard.

7 Click to the right of **Subject** to display an empty box, and then type your course name and section #; for example *CIS 10, #5543*.

8 Under **Related People**, be sure that your name displays as the author. If necessary, right-click the author name, click Edit Property, type your name, click outside of the Edit person dialog box, and then click OK. Compare your screen with Figure 1.20.

FIGURE 1.20

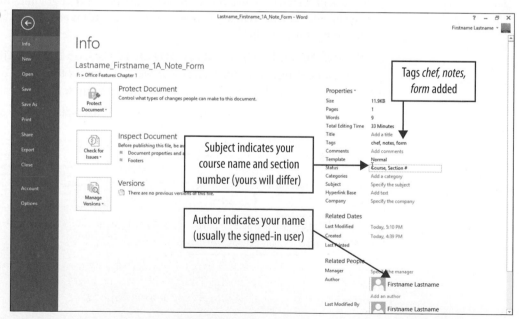

Activity 1.09 | Printing a File and Closing a Desktop App

1 On the left, click **Print**, and then compare your screen with Figure 1.21.

Here you can select any printer connected to your system and adjust the settings related to how you want to print. On the right, the **Print Preview** displays, which is a view of a document as it will appear on paper when you print it.

At the bottom of the Print Preview area, in the center, the number of pages and page navigation arrows with which you can move among the pages in Print Preview display. On the right, the Zoom slider enables you to shrink or enlarge the Print Preview. **Zoom** is the action of increasing or decreasing the viewing area of the screen.

⟳ ANOTHER WAY   From the document screen, press Ctrl + P or Ctrl + F2 to display Print in Backstage view.

FIGURE 1.21

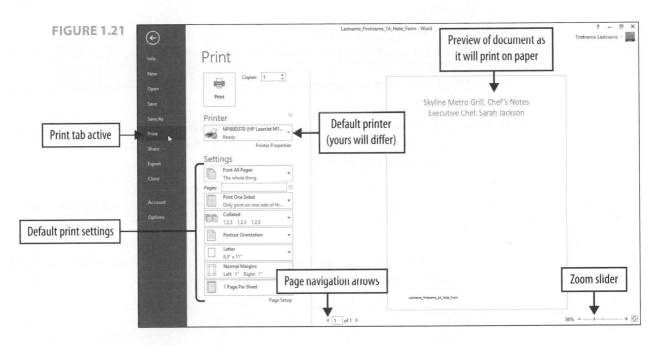

2 To submit your file electronically, skip this step and continue to Step 3. To print your document on paper using the default printer on your system, in the upper left portion of the screen, click the **Print** button.

The document will print on your default printer; if you do not have a color printer, the blue text will print in shades of gray. The gray page color you applied to the document does not display in Print Preview nor does it print unless you specifically adjust some of Word's options. Backstage view closes and your file redisplays in the Word window.

3 To create an electronic file, on the left click **Export**. On the right, click the **Create PDF/XPS** button to display the **Publish as PDF or XPS** dialog box.

PDF stands for **Portable Document Format**, which is a technology that creates an image that preserves the look of your file. This is a popular format for sending documents electronically, because the document will display on most computers.

XPS stands for **XML Paper Specification**—a Microsoft file format that also creates an image of your document and that opens in the XPS viewer.

4 On the left in the **navigation pane**, if necessary expand ▷ Computer, and then navigate to your **Office Features Chapter 1** folder on your **USB flash drive**. Compare your screen with Figure 1.22.

FIGURE 1.22

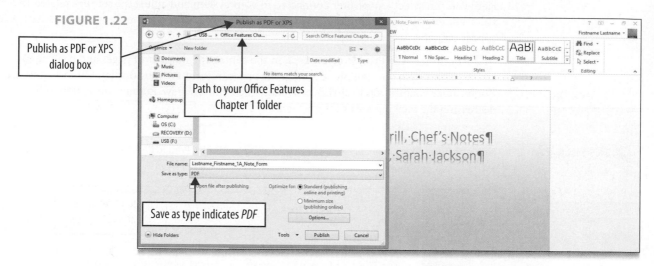

Publish as PDF or XPS dialog box

Path to your Office Features Chapter 1 folder

Save as type indicates *PDF*

5 In the lower right corner of the dialog box, click **Publish**; if your Adobe Acrobat or Adobe Reader program displays your PDF, in the upper right corner, click Close ❌. Notice that your document redisplays in Word.

 **ANOTHER WAY**   In Backstage view, click Save As, navigate to the location of your Chapter folder, click the Save as type arrow, on the list click PDF, and then click Save.

6 Click the **FILE tab** to redisplay **Backstage** view. On the left, click **Close**, if necessary click Save, and then compare your screen with Figure 1.23.

FIGURE 1.23

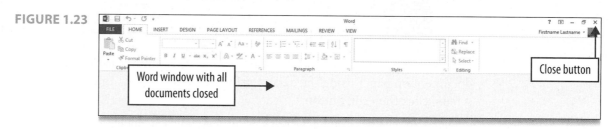

Word window with all documents closed

Close button

7 In the upper right corner of the Word window, click **Close** ❌. If directed by your instructor to do so, submit your paper or electronic file.

END | You have completed Project 1A

PROJECT ACTIVITIES

In Activities 1.10 through 1.21, you will open, edit, and then compress a Word file. You will also use the Office Help system and install an app for Office. Your completed document will look similar to Figure 1.24.

PROJECT FILES

For Project 1B, you will need the following file:

of01B_Rehearsal_Dinner

You will save your file as:

Lastname_Firstname_1B_Rehearsal_Dinner

PROJECT RESULTS

Skyline Metro Grill

TO: Sarah Jackson, Executive Chef

FROM: Laura Mabry Hernandez, General Manager

DATE: February 17, 2016

SUBJECT: Wedding Rehearsal Dinners

In the spring and summer months, wedding rehearsal dinners provide a new marketing opportunity for Skyline Metro Grill at all of our locations. A rehearsal dinner is an informal meal following a wedding rehearsal at which the bride and groom typically thank those who have helped them make their wedding a special event.

Our smaller private dining rooms with sweeping city views are an ideal location for a rehearsal dinner. At each of our locations, I have directed the Sales and Marketing Coordinator to partner with local wedding planners to promote Skyline Metro Grill as a relaxed yet sophisticated venue for rehearsal dinners. The typical rehearsal dinner includes the wedding party, the immediate family of the bride and groom, and out-of-town guests.

Please develop six menus—in varying price ranges—to present to local wedding planners so that they can easily promote Skyline Metro Grill to couples who are planning a rehearsal dinner. In addition to a traditional dinner, we should also include options for a buffet-style dinner and a family-style dinner.

This marketing effort will require extensive communication with our Sales and Marketing Coordinators and with local wedding planners. Let's meet to discuss the details and the marketing challenges, and to create a promotional piece that begins something like this:

Skyline Metro Grill for Your Rehearsal Dinner

Lastname_Firstname_1B_Rehearsal_Dinner

FIGURE 1.24 Project 1B Memo

Video OF1-7

In any Office program, you can display the **Open dialog box**, from which you can navigate to and then open an existing file that was created in that same program.

The Open dialog box, along with the Save and Save As dialog boxes, is a common dialog box. These dialog boxes, which are provided by the Windows programming interface, display in all Office programs in the same manner. So the Open, Save, and Save As dialog boxes will all look and perform the same regardless of the Office program in which you are working.

Activity 1.10 | Opening an Existing File and Saving It with a New Name

In this activity, you will display the Open dialog box, open an existing Word document, and then save it in your storage location with a new name.

1   Sign in to your computer, and then on the Windows 8 Start screen, type **word 2013** Press ⏎ to open Word on your desktop. If you want to do so, on the taskbar, right-click the **Word icon**, and then click **Pin this program to taskbar** to keep the Word program available from your desktop.

2   On Word's opening screen, on the left, click **Open Other Documents**. Under **Open**, click **Computer**, and then on the right click **Browse**.

3   In the **Open** dialog box, on the left in the **navigation pane**, scroll down, if necessary expand ▷ Computer, and then click the name of your **USB flash drive**. In the **file list**, double-click the **Office_Features** folder that you downloaded.

4   Double-click **of01B_Rehearsal_Dinner**. If **PROTECTED VIEW** displays at the top of your screen, in the center click **Enable Editing**.

> In Office 2013, a file will open in **Protected View** if the file appears to be from a potentially risky location, such as the Internet. Protected View is a security feature in Office 2013 that protects your computer from malicious files by opening them in a restricted environment until you enable them. **Trusted Documents** is another security feature that remembers which files you have already enabled.

> You might encounter these security features if you open a file from an email or download files from the Internet; for example, from your college's learning management system or from the Pearson website. So long as you trust the source of the file, click Enable Editing or Enable Content—depending on the type of file you receive—and then go ahead and work with the file.

5   With the document displayed in the Word window, be sure that **Show/Hide** is active; if necessary, on the HOME tab, in the Paragraph group, click Show/Hide to activate it. Compare your screen with Figure 1.25.

FIGURE 1.25

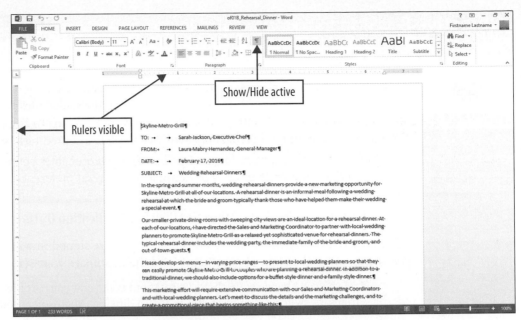

Show/Hide active

Rulers visible

6 ▶ Click the **FILE tab** to display **Backstage** view, and then on the left, click **Save As**. On the right, click the folder under **Current Folder** to open the **Save As** dialog box. Notice that the current folder is the **Office_Features** folder you downloaded.

ANOTHER WAY   Press F12 to display the Save As dialog box.

7 ▶ In the upper left corner of the **Save As** dialog box, click the **Up** button ↑ to move up one level in the File Explorer hierarchy. In the **file list**, double-click your **Office Features Chapter 1** folder to open it.

8 ▶ Click in the **File name** box to select the existing text, and then, using your own name, type **Lastname_Firstname_1B_Rehearsal_Dinner** Compare your screen with Figure 1.26.

FIGURE 1.26

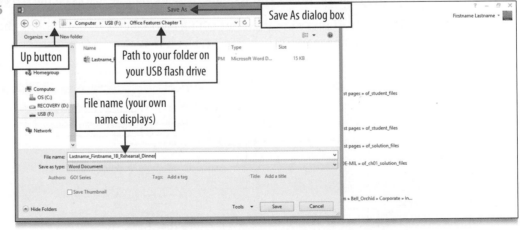

Save As dialog box

Up button

Path to your folder on your USB flash drive

File name (your own name displays)

9 ▶ Click **Save** or press Enter; notice that your new file name displays in the title bar.

The original document closes, and your new document, based on the original, displays with the name in the title bar.

More Knowledge   **Read-Only**

Some files might display **Read-Only** in the title bar, which is a property assigned to a file that prevents the file from being modified or deleted; it indicates that you cannot save any changes to the displayed document unless you first save it with a new name.

Video OF1-8

If you sign in to Windows 8 with a Microsoft account, you may notice that you are also signed in to Office. This enables you to save files to and retrieve files from your SkyDrive and to *collaborate* with others on Office files when you want to do so. To collaborate means to work with others as a team in an intellectual endeavor to complete a shared task or to achieve a shared goal.

Within each Office application, an *Options dialog box* enables you to select program settings and other options and preferences. For example, you can set preferences for viewing and editing files.

Activity 1.11 | Signing In to Office and Viewing Application Options

1 In the upper right corner of your screen, if you are signed in with a Microsoft account, click the arrow to the right of your name, and then compare your screen with Figure 1.27.

Here you can change your photo, go to About me to edit your profile, examine your Account settings, or switch accounts to sign in with a different Microsoft account.

FIGURE 1.27

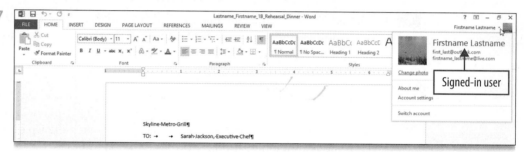

2 Click the **FILE tab** to display **Backstage** view. On the left, click the last tab—**Options**.

3 In the **Word Options** dialog box, on the left, click **Display**, and then on the right, locate the information under **Always show these formatting marks on the screen**.

4 Under **Always show these formatting marks on the screen**, be sure the last check box, **Show all formatting marks**, is selected—select it if necessary. Compare your screen with Figure 1.28.

FIGURE 1.28

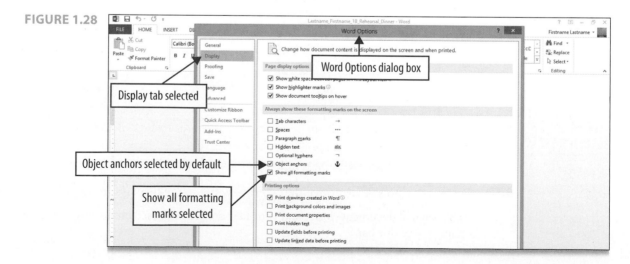

5 In the lower right corner of the dialog box, click **OK**.

Video OF1-9

The ribbon that displays across the top of the program window groups commands in a manner that you would most logically use them. The ribbon in each Office program is slightly different, but all contain the same three elements: *tabs*, *groups*, and *commands*.

Tabs display across the top of the ribbon, and each tab relates to a type of activity; for example, laying out a page. Groups are sets of related commands for specific tasks. Commands—instructions to computer programs—are arranged in groups and might display as a button, a menu, or a box in which you type information.

You can also minimize the ribbon so only the tab names display, which is useful when working on a smaller screen such as a tablet computer where you want to maximize your screen viewing area.

Activity 1.12 | Performing Commands from and Customizing the Ribbon and the Quick Access Toolbar

1 Take a moment to examine the document on your screen. If necessary, on the ribbon, click the VIEW tab, and then in the Show group, click to place a check mark in the Ruler check box. Compare your screen with Figure 1.29.

> This document is a memo from the General Manager to the Executive Chef regarding a new restaurant promotion for wedding rehearsal dinners.
>
> When working in Word, display the rulers so that you can see how margin settings affect your document and how text and objects align. Additionally, if you set a tab stop or an indent, its location is visible on the ruler.

FIGURE 1.29

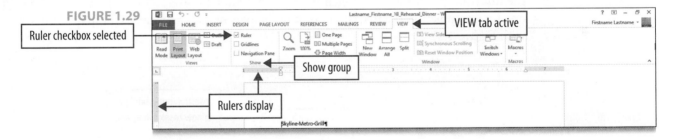

2 In the upper left corner of your screen, above the ribbon, locate the **Quick Access Toolbar**.

> Recall that the Quick Access Toolbar contains commands that you use frequently. By default, only the commands Save, Undo, and Redo display, but you can add and delete commands to suit your needs. Possibly the computer at which you are working already has additional commands added to the Quick Access Toolbar.

3 At the end of the **Quick Access Toolbar**, click the **Customize Quick Access Toolbar** button ☐, and then compare your screen with Figure 1.30.

> A list of commands that Office users commonly add to their Quick Access Toolbar displays, including New, Open, Email, Quick Print, and Print Preview and Print. Commands already on the Quick Access Toolbar display a check mark. Commands that you add to the Quick Access Toolbar are always just one click away.
>
> Here you can also display the More Commands dialog box, from which you can select any command from any tab on the ribbon to add to the Quick Access Toolbar.

 BY TOUCH   Tap once on Quick Access Toolbar commands.

FIGURE 1.30

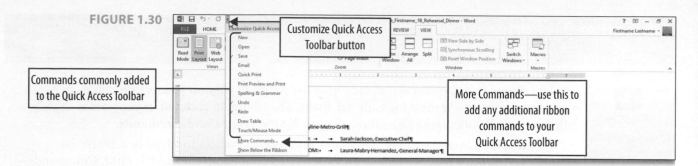

4 ▶ On the list, click **Print Preview and Print**, and then notice that the icon is added to the **Quick Access Toolbar**. Compare your screen with Figure 1.31.

> The icon that represents the Print Preview command displays on the Quick Access Toolbar. Because this is a command that you will use frequently while building Office documents, you might decide to have this command remain on your Quick Access Toolbar.

🔄 **ANOTHER WAY**   Right-click any command on the ribbon, and then on the shortcut menu, click Add to Quick Access Toolbar.

FIGURE 1.31

5 ▶ In the first line of the document, if necessary, click to the left of the *S* in *Skyline* to position the insertion point there, and then press Enter one time to insert a blank paragraph. Press ↑ one time to position the insertion point in the new blank paragraph. Compare your screen with Figure 1.32.

FIGURE 1.32

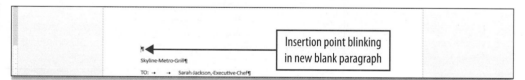

6 ▶ On the ribbon, click the **INSERT tab**. In the **Illustrations group**, *point* to the **Online Pictures** button to display its ScreenTip.

> Many buttons on the ribbon have this type of *enhanced ScreenTip*, which displays useful descriptive information about the command.

7 ▶ Click **Online Pictures**, and then compare your screen with Figure 1.33.

> In the Insert Pictures dialog box you can search for online pictures using Microsoft's Clip Art collection. *Clip art* refers to royalty-free photos and illustrations you can download from Microsoft's Office.com site.

> Here you can also search for images using the Bing search engine, and if you are signed in with your Microsoft account, you can also find images on your SkyDrive or on your computer by clicking Browse. At the bottom, you can click the Flickr logo and download pictures from your Flickr account if you have one.

FIGURE 1.33

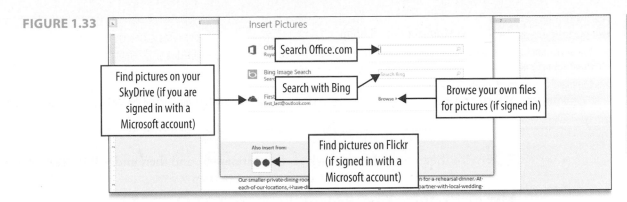

8 ▶ Click **Office.com Clip Art** and in the box that displays to the right, type **salad in a bowl** and press Enter. As shown in Figure 1.34, point to the illustration of the salad bowl to display its keywords.

> You can use various keywords to find clip art that is appropriate for your documents.

FIGURE 1.34

9 ▶ Click the illustration of the salad to select it, and then in the lower right corner, click **Insert**. In the upper right corner of the picture, point to the **Layout Options** button 🖾 to display its ScreenTip, and then compare your screen with Figure 1.35. If you cannot find the image, select a similar image, and then drag one of the corner sizing handles to match the approximate size shown in the figure.

> Inserted pictures anchor—attach to—the paragraph at the insertion point location—as indicated by the anchor symbol. *Layout Options* enable you to choose how the *object*—in this instance an inserted picture—interacts with the surrounding text. An object is a picture or other graphic such as a chart or table that you can select and then move and resize.

> When a picture is selected, the PICTURE TOOLS become available on the ribbon. Additionally, *sizing handles*—small squares that indicate an object is selected—surround the selected picture.

FIGURE 1.35

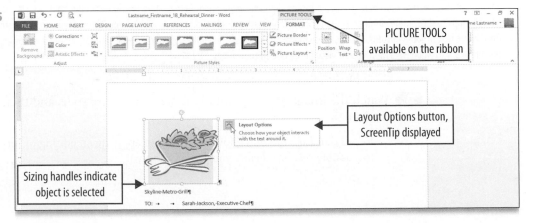

10 With the image selected, click **Layout Options** 🖼, and then under **With Text Wrapping**, in the second row, click the first layout—**Top and Bottom**.

11 Point to the image to display the 🖎 pointer, hold down the left mouse button to display a green line at the left margin, and then drag the image to the right and slightly upward until a green line displays in the center of the image and at the top of the image, as shown in Figure 1.36, and then release the left mouse button. If you are not satisfied with your result, on the Quick Access Toolbar, click Undo 🔄 and begin again.

> *Alignment Guides* are green lines that display to help you align objects with margins or at the center of a page.

FIGURE 1.36

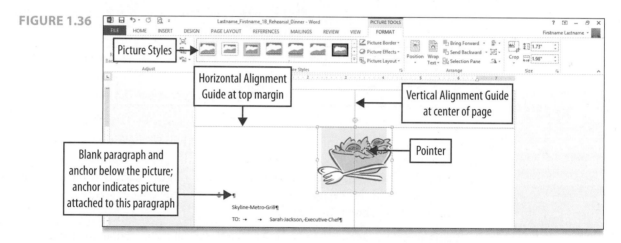

12 On the ribbon, in the **Picture Styles group**, point to the first style to display the ScreenTip *Simple Frame, White,* and notice that the image displays with a white frame.

13 Watch the image as you point to the second picture style, and then to the third, and then to the fourth.

> Recall that Live Preview shows the result of applying an editing or formatting change as you point to possible results—*before* you actually apply it.

14 In the **Picture Styles group**, click the second style—**Beveled Matte, White**—and then click anywhere outside of the image to deselect it. Notice that the *PICTURE TOOLS* no longer display on the ribbon. Compare your screen with Figure 1.37.

Contextual tabs on the ribbon display only when you need them.

FIGURE 1.37

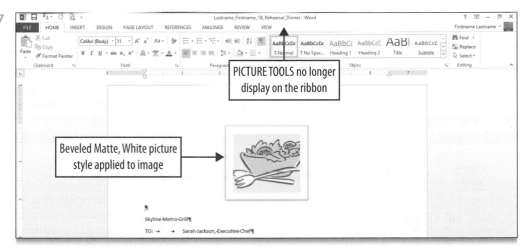

15 On the **Quick Access Toolbar**, click **Save** 🔲 to save the changes you have made.

Activity 1.13 | Minimizing and Using the Keyboard to Control the Ribbon

Instead of a mouse, some individuals prefer to navigate the ribbon by using keys on the keyboard.

1 On your keyboard, press Alt, and then on the ribbon, notice that small labels display. Press N to activate the commands on the **INSERT tab**, and then compare your screen with Figure 1.38.

Each label represents a *KeyTip*—an indication of the key that you can press to activate the command. For example, on the INSERT tab, you can press F to open the Online Pictures dialog box.

FIGURE 1.38

2 Press Esc to redisplay the KeyTips for the tabs. Then, press Alt or Esc again to turn off keyboard control of the ribbon.

3 Point to any tab on the ribbon and right-click to display a shortcut menu.

Here you can choose to display the Quick Access Toolbar below the ribbon or collapse the ribbon to maximize screen space. You can also customize the ribbon by adding, removing, renaming, or reordering tabs, groups, and commands, although this is not recommended until you become an expert Office user.

4 Click **Collapse the Ribbon**. Notice that only the ribbon tabs display. Click the **HOME tab** to display the commands. Click anywhere in the document, and notice that the ribbon goes back to the collapsed display.

5 Right-click any ribbon tab, and then click **Collapse the Ribbon** again to remove the check mark from this command.

Many expert Office users prefer the full ribbon display.

6 Point to any tab on the ribbon, and then on your mouse device, roll the mouse wheel. Notice that different tabs become active as you roll the mouse wheel.

You can make a tab active by using this technique instead of clicking the tab.

Objective 10 | Apply Formatting in Office Programs

Video OF1-10

Activity 1.14 | **Changing Page Orientation and Zoom Level**

In this activity, you will practice common formatting techniques used in Office applications.

1 On the ribbon, click the **PAGE LAYOUT tab**. In the **Page Setup group**, click **Orientation**, and notice that two orientations display—*Portrait* and *Landscape*. Click **Landscape**.

In ***portrait orientation***, the paper is taller than it is wide. In ***landscape orientation***, the paper is wider than it is tall.

2 In the lower right corner of the screen, locate the **Zoom slider**.

Recall that to zoom means to increase or decrease the viewing area. You can zoom in to look closely at a section of a document, and then zoom out to see an entire page on the screen. You can also zoom to view multiple pages on the screen.

3 Drag the **Zoom slider** to the left until you have zoomed to approximately *60%*. Compare your screen with Figure 1.39.

FIGURE 1.39

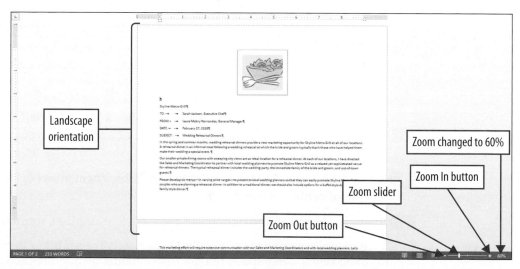

BY TOUCH Drag the Zoom slider with your finger.

4 Use the technique you just practiced to change the **Orientation** back to **Portrait**.

The default orientation in Word is Portrait, which is commonly used for business documents such as letters and memos.

5 In the lower right corner, click the **Zoom In** button ➕ as many times as necessary to return to the **100%** zoom setting.

> Use the zoom feature to adjust the view of your document for editing and for your viewing comfort.

⟳ ANOTHER WAY   You can also control Zoom from the ribbon. On the VIEW tab, in the Zoom group, you can control the Zoom level and also zoom to view multiple pages.

6 On the **Quick Access Toolbar**, click **Save** 🖫.

More **Knowledge**	**Zooming to Page Width**

Some Office users prefer Page Width, which zooms the document so that the width of the page matches the width of the window. Find this command on the VIEW tab, in the Zoom group.

Activity 1.15 | Formatting Text by Using Fonts, Alignment, Font Colors, and Font Styles

1 If necessary, on the right side of your screen, drag the vertical scroll box to the top of the scroll bar. To the left of *Skyline Metro Grill*, point in the margin area to display the 🔖 pointer and click one time to select the entire paragraph. Compare your screen with Figure 1.40.

> Use this technique to select complete paragraphs from the margin area—drag downward to select multiple-line paragraphs—which is faster and more efficient than dragging through text.

FIGURE 1.40

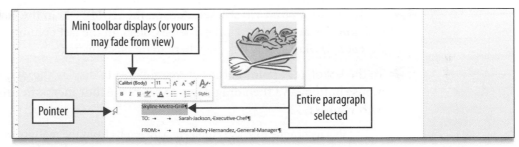

2 On the ribbon, click the **HOME tab**, and then in the **Paragraph group**, click **Center** ☰ to center the paragraph.

3 On the **HOME tab**, in the **Font group**, click the **Font button arrow** `Calibri (Body) ▾`. On the alphabetical list of font names, scroll down and then locate and *point to* **Cambria**.

> A *font* is a set of characters with the same design and shape. The default font in a Word document is Calibri, which is a *sans serif* font—a font design with no lines or extensions on the ends of characters.

> The Cambria font is a *serif font*—a font design that includes small line extensions on the ends of the letters to guide the eye in reading from left to right.

> The list of fonts displays as a gallery showing potential results. For example, in the Font gallery, you can point to see the actual design and format of each font as it would look if applied to text.

4 Point to several other fonts and observe the effect on the selected text. Then, scroll back to the top of the **Font** gallery. Under **Theme Fonts**, click **Calibri Light**.

> A *theme* is a predesigned combination of colors, fonts, line, and fill effects that look good together and is applied to an entire document by a single selection. A theme combines two sets of fonts—one for text and one for headings. In the default Office theme, Calibri Light is the suggested font for headings.

5 With the paragraph *Skyline Metro Grill* still selected, on the **HOME tab**, in the **Font group**, click the **Font Size button arrow** 11 ⌄, point to **36**, and then notice how Live Preview displays the text in the font size to which you are pointing. Compare your screen with Figure 1.41.

FIGURE 1.41

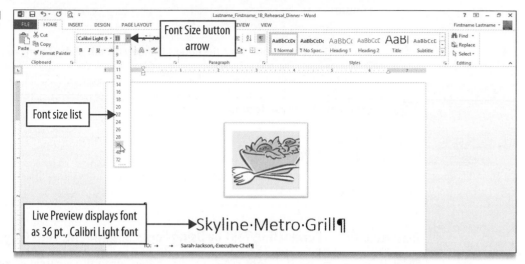

6 On the list of font sizes, click **20**.

> Fonts are measured in *points*, with one point equal to 1/72 of an inch. A higher point size indicates a larger font size. Headings and titles are often formatted by using a larger font size. The word *point* is abbreviated as *pt*.

7 With *Skyline Metro Grill* still selected, on the **HOME tab**, in the **Font group**, click the **Font Color button arrow** ▲ ⌄. Under **Theme Colors**, in the last column, click the last color—**Green, Accent 6, Darker 50%**. Click anywhere to deselect the text.

8 To the left of *TO:*, point in the left margin area to display the 🖅 pointer, hold down the left mouse button, and then drag down to select the four memo headings. Compare your screen with Figure 1.42.

> Use this technique to select complete paragraphs from the margin area—drag downward to select multiple paragraphs—which is faster and more efficient than dragging through text.

BY TOUCH　　Tap once on TO: to display the gripper, then with your finger, drag to the right and down to select the four paragraphs.

FIGURE 1.42

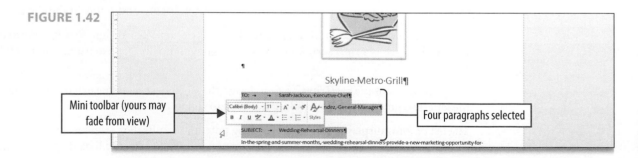

9 With the four paragraphs selected, on the mini toolbar, click the **Font Color** button A ▾, and notice that the text color of the four paragraphs changes.

The font color button retains its most recently used color—Green, Accent 6, Darker 50%. As you progress in your study of Microsoft Office, you will use other buttons that behave in this manner; that is, they retain their most recently used format. This is commonly referred to as *MRU*—most recently used.

Recall that the mini toolbar places commands that are commonly used for the selected text or object close by so that you reduce the distance that you must move your mouse to access a command. If you are using a touchscreen device, most commands that you need are close and easy to touch.

10 On the right, drag the vertical scroll box down slightly to position more of the text on the screen. Click anywhere in the paragraph that begins *In the spring*, and then *triple-click*—click the left mouse button three times—to select the entire paragraph. If the entire paragraph is not selected, click in the paragraph and begin again.

11 With the entire paragraph selected, on the mini toolbar, click the **Font Color button arrow** A ▾, and then under **Theme Colors**, in the sixth column, click the last color— **Orange, Accent 2, Darker 50%**.

12 In the memo headings, select the guide word *TO:* and then on the mini toolbar, click **Bold** B and **Italic** I .

Font styles include bold, italic, and underline. Font styles emphasize text and are a visual cue to draw the reader's eye to important text.

13 On the mini toolbar, click **Italic** I again to turn off the Italic formatting.

A *toggle button* is a button that can be turned on by clicking it once, and then turned off by clicking it again.

Activity 1.16 | Using Format Painter

Use the Format Painter to copy the formatting of specific text or of a paragraph and then apply it in other locations in your document.

1 With *TO:* still selected, on the mini toolbar, click **Format Painter** . Then, move your mouse under the word *Sarah*, and notice the ▲I mouse pointer. Compare your screen with Figure 1.43.

The pointer takes the shape of a paintbrush, and contains the formatting information from the paragraph where the insertion point is positioned. Information about the Format Painter and how to turn it off displays in the status bar.

FIGURE 1.43

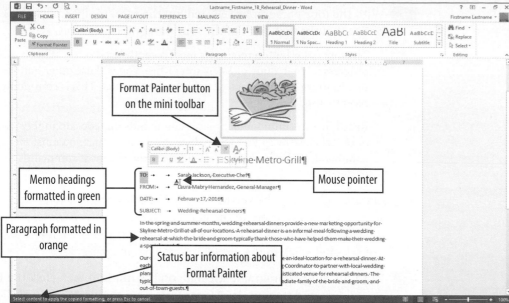

Format Painter button on the mini toolbar

Memo headings formatted in green

Mouse pointer

Paragraph formatted in orange

Status bar information about Format Painter

2 With the pointer, drag to select the guide word *FROM:* and notice that Bold formatting is applied. Then, point to the selected text *FROM:* and on the mini toolbar, *double-click* **Format Painter** .

3 Select the guide word *DATE:* to copy the Bold formatting, and notice that the pointer retains the shape.

> When you *double-click* the Format Painter button, the Format Painter feature remains active until you either click the Format Painter button again, or press Esc to cancel it—as indicated on the status bar.

4 With Format Painter still active, select the guide word *SUBJECT:*, and then on the ribbon, on the **HOME tab**, in the **Clipboard group**, notice that **Format Painter** is selected, indicating that it is active. Compare your screen with Figure 1.44.

FIGURE 1.44

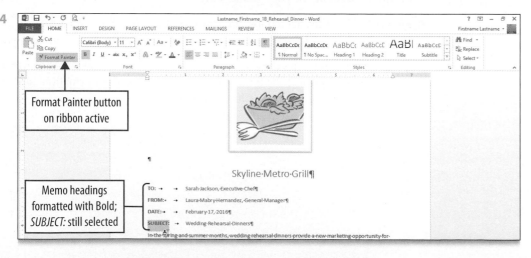

Format Painter button on ribbon active

Memo headings formatted with Bold; *SUBJECT:* still selected

5 On the ribbon, click **Format Painter** to turn the command off.

ANOTHER WAY   Press Esc to turn off Format Painter.

6 ▶ In the paragraph that begins *In the spring*, triple-click again to select the entire paragraph. On the mini toolbar, click **Bold** B and **Italic** I . Click anywhere to deselect.

7 ▶ On the **Quick Access Toolbar**, click **Save** 🖫 to save the changes you have made to your document.

Activity 1.17 | Using Keyboard Shortcuts and Using the Clipboard to Copy, Cut, and Paste

The *Clipboard* is a temporary storage area that holds text or graphics that you select and then cut or copy. When you *copy* text or graphics, a copy is placed on the Clipboard and the original text or graphic remains in place. When you *cut* text or graphics, a copy is placed on the Clipboard, and the original text or graphic is removed—cut—from the document.

After copying or cutting, the contents of the Clipboard are available for you to *paste*—insert—in a new location in the current document, or into another Office file.

1 ▶ Hold down [Ctrl] and press [Home] to move to the beginning of your document, and then take a moment to study the table in Figure 1.45, which describes similar keyboard shortcuts with which you can navigate quickly in a document.

FIGURE 1.45

KEYBOARD SHORTCUTS TO NAVIGATE IN A DOCUMENT	
TO MOVE	**PRESS**
To the beginning of a document	[Ctrl] + [Home]
To the end of a document	[Ctrl] + [End]
To the beginning of a line	[Home]
To the end of a line	[End]
To the beginning of the previous word	[Ctrl] + [←]
To the beginning of the next word	[Ctrl] + [→]
To the beginning of the current word (if insertion point is in the middle of a word)	[Ctrl] + [←]
To the beginning of the previous paragraph	[Ctrl] + [↑]
To the beginning of the next paragraph	[Ctrl] + [↓]
To the beginning of the current paragraph (if insertion point is in the middle of a paragraph)	[Ctrl] + [↑]
Up one screen	[PgUp]
Down one screen	[PgDn]

2 ▶ To the left of *Skyline Metro Grill*, point in the left margin area to display the ⌐⃗ pointer, and then click one time to select the entire paragraph. On the **HOME tab**, in the **Clipboard group**, click **Copy** 🗎 .

> Because anything that you select and then copy—or cut—is placed on the Clipboard, the Copy command and the Cut command display in the Clipboard group of commands on the ribbon. There is no visible indication that your copied selection has been placed on the Clipboard.

🔁 **ANOTHER WAY**   Right-click the selection, and then click Copy on the shortcut menu; or, use the keyboard shortcut [Ctrl] + [C].

3 On the **HOME tab**, in the **Clipboard group**, to the right of the group name *Clipboard*, click the **Dialog Box Launcher** button 🔲, and then compare your screen with Figure 1.46.

> The Clipboard pane displays with your copied text. In any ribbon group, the *Dialog Box Launcher* displays either a dialog box or a pane related to the group of commands. It is not necessary to display the Clipboard in this manner, although sometimes it is useful to do so.

FIGURE 1.46

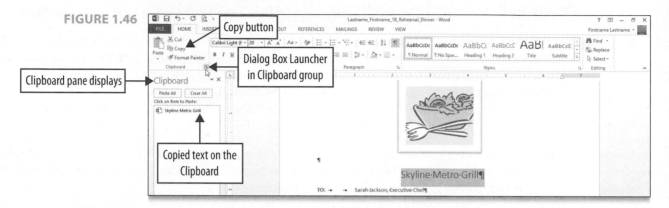

4 In the upper right corner of the **Clipboard** pane, click **Close** ☒.

5 Press Ctrl + End to move to the end of your document. Press Enter one time to create a new blank paragraph. On the **HOME tab**, in the **Clipboard group**, point to **Paste**, and then click the *upper* portion of this split button.

> The Paste command pastes the most recently copied item on the Clipboard at the insertion point location. If you click the lower portion of the Paste button, a gallery of Paste Options displays. A *split button* is divided into two parts; clicking the main part of the button performs a command, and clicking the arrow displays a list or gallery with choices.

 **ANOTHER WAY** Right-click, on the shortcut menu under Paste Options, click the desired option button; or, press Ctrl + V.

6 Below the pasted text, click **Paste Options** 📋 as shown in Figure 1.47.

> Here you can view and apply various formatting options for pasting your copied or cut text. Typically you will click Paste on the ribbon and paste the item in its original format. If you want some other format for the pasted item, you can choose another format from the *Paste Options gallery*.
>
> The Paste Options gallery provides a Live Preview of the various options for changing the format of the pasted item with a single click. The Paste Options gallery is available in three places: on the ribbon by clicking the lower portion of the Paste button—the Paste button arrow; from the Paste Options button that displays below the pasted item following the paste operation; or on the shortcut menu if you right-click the pasted item.

FIGURE 1.47

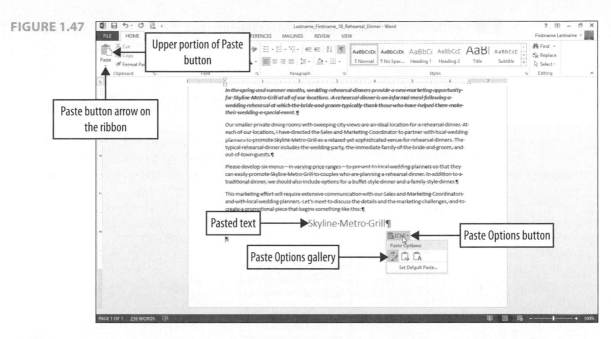

7 ▶ In the **Paste Options** gallery, *point* to each option to see the Live Preview of the format that would be applied if you clicked the button.

The contents of the Paste Options gallery are contextual; that is, they change based on what you copied and where you are pasting.

8 ▶ Press Esc to close the gallery; the button will remain displayed until you take some other screen action.

9 ▶ Press Ctrl + Home to move to the top of the document, and then click the **salad image** one time to select it. While pointing to the selected image, right-click, and then on the shortcut menu, click **Cut**.

Recall that the Cut command cuts—removes—the selection from the document and places it on the Clipboard.

🔄 ANOTHER WAY   On the HOME tab, in the Clipboard group, click the Cut button; or, use the keyboard shortcut Ctrl + X.

10 ▶ Press Del one time to remove the blank paragraph from the top of the document, and then press Ctrl + End to move to the end of the document.

11 ▶ With the insertion point blinking in the blank paragraph at the end of the document, right-click, and notice that the **Paste Options** gallery displays on the shortcut menu. Compare your screen with Figure 1.48.

FIGURE 1.48

12 On the shortcut menu, under **Paste Options**, click the first button—**Keep Source Formatting**.

13 Point to the picture to display the pointer, and then drag to the right until the center green **Alignment Guide** displays and the blank paragraph is above the picture, as shown in Figure 1.49. Release the left mouse button.

🔄 **BY TOUCH** Drag the picture with your finger to display the Alignment Guide.

FIGURE 1.49

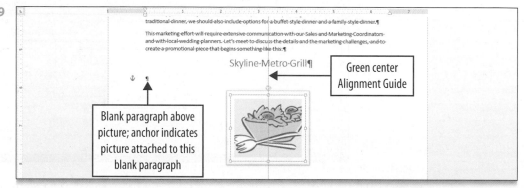

Blank paragraph above picture; anchor indicates picture attached to this blank paragraph

Skyline·Metro·Grill¶

Green center Alignment Guide

14 Above the picture, click to position the insertion point at the end of the word *Grill*, press [Spacebar] one time, type **for Your Rehearsal Dinner** and then **Save** 🖫 your document. Compare your screen with Figure 1.50.

FIGURE 1.50

New heading → Skyline·Metro·Grill·for·Your·Rehearsal·Dinner¶

15 On the **INSERT tab**, in the **Header & Footer group**, click **Footer**. At the bottom of the list, click **Edit Footer,** and then with the **HEADER & FOOTER Design tab** active, in the **Insert group**, click **Document Info**. Click **File Name** to add the file name to the footer.

16 On the right end of the ribbon, click **Close Header and Footer**.

17 On the **Quick Access Toolbar**, point to the **Print Preview and Print icon** 🔍 you placed there, right-click, and then click **Remove from Quick Access Toolbar**.

If you are working on your own computer and you want to do so, you can leave the icon on the toolbar; in a lab setting, you should return the software to its original settings.

18 Click **Save** 🖫 and then click the **FILE tab** to display **Backstage** view. With the **Info tab** active, in the lower right corner click **Show All Properties**. As **Tags**, type **weddings, rehearsal dinners, marketing**

19 As the **Subject**, type your course name and number—for example *CIS 10, #5543*. Under **Related People**, be sure your name displays as the author (edit it if necessary), and then on the left, click **Print** to display the Print Preview. Compare your screen with Figure 1.51.

FIGURE 1.51

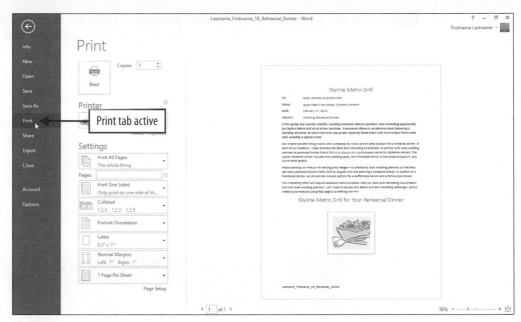

20 On the left side of **Backstage** view, click **Save**. As directed by your instructor, print or submit your file electronically as described in Project 1A, and then in the upper right corner of the Word window, click **Close** ⏹ ✕ ⏹.

21 If a message indicates *Would you like to keep the last item you copied?* click **No**.

> This message displays if you have copied some type of image to the Clipboard. If you click Yes, the items on the Clipboard will remain for you to use in another program or document.

Objective 11 | Compress Files and Use the Microsoft Office 2013 Help System

Video OF1-11

A *compressed file* is a file that has been reduced in size. Compressed files take up less storage space and can be transferred to other computers faster than uncompressed files. You can also combine a group of files into one compressed folder, which makes it easier to share a group of files.

Within each Office program, the Help feature provides information about all of the program's features and displays step-by-step instructions for performing many tasks.

Activity 1.18 | Compressing Files

In this activity, you will combine the two files you created in this chapter into one compressed file.

1 On the Windows taskbar, click **File Explorer** 📁. On the left, in the **navigation pane**, navigate to your **USB flash drive**, and then open your **Office Features Chapter 1** folder. Compare your screen with Figure 1.52.

FIGURE 1.52

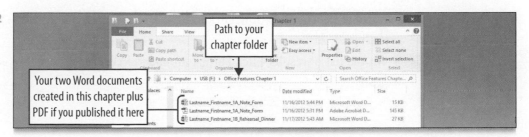

2 In the **file list**, click your **Lastname_Firstname_1A_Note_Form** Word file one time to select it. Then, hold down Ctrl, and click your **Lastname_Firstname_1B_Rehearsal_Dinner** file to select the files in the list.

> In any Windows-based program, holding down Ctrl while selecting enables you to select multiple items.

3 On the **File Explorer** ribbon, click **Share**, and then in the **Send group**, click **Zip**. Compare your screen with Figure 1.53.

> Windows creates a compressed folder containing a *copy* of each of the selected files. The folder name is selected—highlighted in blue—so that you can rename it.

🔄 **BY TOUCH**   Tap the ribbon commands.

FIGURE 1.53

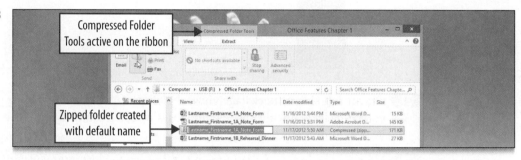

🔄 **ANOTHER WAY**   Point to the selected files in the File List, right-click, point to Send to, and then click Compressed (zipped) folder.

4 Using your own name, type **Lastname_Firstname_Office_Features_Chapter_1** and press Enter.

> The compressed folder is ready to attach to an email or share in some other format.

5 In the upper right corner of the folder window, click **Close** ❌.

Activity 1.19 | Using the Microsoft Office 2013 Help System in Excel

In this activity, you will use the Microsoft Help feature to find information about formatting numbers in Excel.

1 Press ⊞ to display the Windows 8 **Start screen**, and then type **excel 2013** Press Enter to open the Excel desktop app.

2 On Excel's opening screen, click **Blank workbook**, and then in the upper right corner, click **Microsoft Excel Help** ⊘.

🔄 **ANOTHER WAY**   Press F1 to display Help in any Office program.

3 In the **Excel Help** window, click in the **Search online help** box, type **formatting numbers** and then press Enter.

4 On the list of results, click **Format numbers as currency**. Compare your screen with Figure 1.54.

FIGURE 1.54

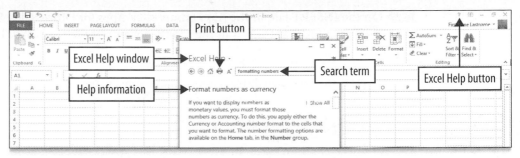

5 If you want to do so, at the top of the **Excel Help** window, click Print 🖨 to print a copy of this information for your reference.

6 In the upper right corner of the Help window, click **Close** ⊠.

7 Leave Excel open for the next activity.

Objective 12   Install Apps for Office and Create a Microsoft Account

ALERT!	Working with Web-Based Applications and Services

Computer programs and services on the web receive continuous updates and improvements. Thus, the steps to complete the following web-based activities may differ from the ones shown. You can often look at the screens and the information presented to determine how to complete the activity.

Video OF1-12

Apps for Office 2013 and SharePoint 2013 are a collection of downloadable apps that enable you to create and view information within your familiar Office programs. Some of these apps are developed by Microsoft, but many more are developed by specialists in different fields. As new apps are developed, they will be available from the online Office Store.

An **app for Office** is a webpage that works within one of the Office applications, such as Excel, that you download from the Office Store. Office apps combine cloud services and web technologies within the user interface of Office and SharePoint. For example, in Excel, you can use an app to look up and gather search results for a new apartment by placing the information in an Excel worksheet, and then use maps to determine the distance of each apartment to work and to family members.

Activity 1.20 | Installing Apps for Office

ALERT!	You Must Be Signed In to Office with a Microsoft Account to Complete This Activity

To download an Office app, you must be signed in to Office with a free Microsoft account. If you do not have a Microsoft account, refer to the next activity to create one by using Microsoft's outlook.com email service, which includes free SkyDrive cloud storage.

1 On the Excel ribbon, click the **INSERT tab**. In the **Apps group**, click the **Apps for Office** arrow, and then click **See All**.

2 Click **FEATURED APPS**, and then on the right, click in the **Search for apps on the Office Store** box, type **Bing Maps** and press Enter.

3 Click the **Bing logo**, and then click the **Add** button, and then if necessary, click Continue.

4 **Close** ⊠ Internet Explorer, and then **Close** ⊠ the **Apps for Office** box.

5 On the **INSERT tab**, in the **Apps group**, click **Apps for Office**, click **See All**, click **MY APPS**, click the **Bing Map**s app, and then in the lower right corner, click **Insert**.

6 On the Welcome message, click **Insert Sample Data**.

> Here, the Bing map displays information related to the sample data. Each state in the sample data displays a small pie chart that represents the two sets of data. Compare your screen with Figure 1.55.
>
> This is just one example of many apps downloadable from the Office store.

FIGURE 1.55

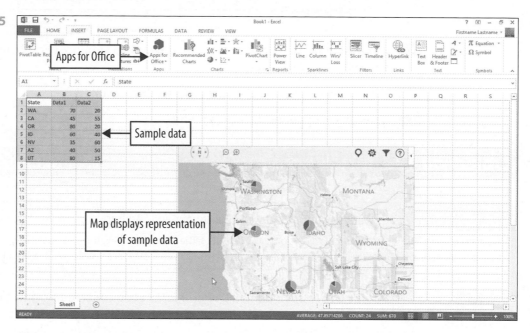

7 **Close** ☒ Excel without saving.

Activity 1.21 | Creating a Microsoft Account

In Windows 8, you can create a Microsoft account, and then use that account to sign in to *any* Windows 8 PC. Signing in with a Microsoft account is recommended because you can:

- Download Windows 8 apps from the Windows Store.
- Get your online content—email, social network updates, updated news—automatically displayed in an app on the Windows 8 Start screen when you sign in.
- Synch settings online to make every Windows 8 computer you use look and feel the same.
- Sign in to Office so that you can store documents on your SkyDrive and download Office apps.

1 Open Internet Explorer 🅔, and then go to **www.outlook.com**

2 Locate and click **Sign up now** to display a screen similar to Figure 1.56. Complete the form to create your account.

FIGURE 1.56

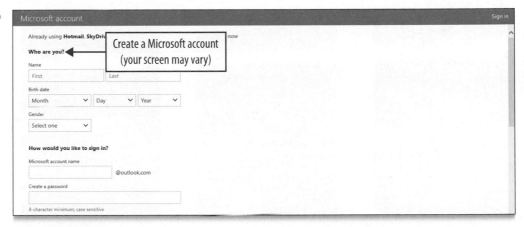

3 **Close** ☒ Internet Explorer.

END | You have completed Project 1B

END OF CHAPTER

SUMMARY

Many Office features and commands, such as the Open and Save As dialog boxes, performing commands from the ribbon and from dialog boxes, and using the Clipboard are the same in all Office desktop apps.

A desktop app is installed on your computer and requires a computer operating system such as Microsoft Windows or Apple OS to run. The programs in Microsoft Office 2013 are considered to be desktop apps.

Apps that run on a smartphone or tablet computer—for example, iOS, Android, or Windows Phone—or apps that run from browser software such as Internet Explorer or Chrome on a PC, are referred to as apps.

Within each Office app, you can install additional Apps for Office from the Office Store. You must have a Microsoft account, which includes free SkyDrive storage, to download Windows 8 or Office apps.

GO! LEARN IT ONLINE

Review the concepts and key terms in this chapter by completing these online challenges, which you can find at **www.pearsonhighered.com/go**.

Matching and Multiple Choice: Answer matching and multiple choice questions to test what you learned in this chapter. MyITLab®

Crossword Puzzle: Spell out the words that match the numbered clues, and put them in the puzzle squares.

Flipboard: Flip through the definitions of the key terms in this chapter and match them with the correct term.

GLOSSARY

GLOSSARY OF CHAPTER KEY TERMS

Address bar (Internet Explorer) The area at the top of the Internet Explorer window that displays, and where you can type, a URL—Uniform Resource Locator—which is an address that uniquely identifies a location on the Internet.

Address bar (Windows) The bar at the top of a folder window with which you can navigate to a different folder or library, or go back to a previous one.

Alignment The placement of text or objects relative to the left and right margins.

Alignment guides Green lines that display when you move an object to assist in alignment.

App The term that commonly refers to computer programs that run from the device software on a smartphone or a tablet computer—for example, iOS, Android, or Windows Phone—or computer programs that run from the browser software on a desktop PC or laptop PC—for example Internet Explorer, Safari, Firefox, or Chrome.

App for Office A webpage that works within one of the Office applications, such as Excel, and that you download from the Office Store.

Apps for Office 2013 and SharePoint 2013 A collection of downloadable apps that enable you to create and view information within your familiar Office programs.

Backstage tabs The area along the left side of Backstage view with tabs to display screens with related groups of commands.

Backstage view A centralized space for file management tasks; for example, opening, saving, printing, publishing, or sharing a file. A navigation pane displays along the left side with tabs that group file-related tasks together.

Center alignment The alignment of text or objects that is centered horizontally between the left and right margins.

Click The action of pressing and releasing the left button on a mouse pointing device one time.

Clip art Downloadable predefined graphics available online from Office.com and other sites.

Clipboard A temporary storage area that holds text or graphics that you select and then cut or copy.

Cloud computing Refers to applications and services that are accessed over the Internet, rather than to applications that are installed on your local computer.

Cloud storage Online storage of data so that you can access your data from different places and devices.

Collaborate To work with others as a team in an intellectual endeavor to complete a shared task or to achieve a shared goal.

Commands An instruction to a computer program that causes an action to be carried out.

Common dialog boxes The set of dialog boxes that includes Open, Save, and Save As, which are provided by the Windows programming interface, and which display and operate in all of the Office programs in the same manner.

Compressed file A file that has been reduced in size and thus takes up less storage space and can be transferred to other computers quickly.

Compressed folder A folder that has been reduced in size and thus takes up less storage space and can be transferred to other computers quickly; also called a *zipped* folder.

Context menus Menus that display commands and options relevant to the selected text or object; also called *shortcut menus*.

Context-sensitive commands Commands that display on a shortcut menu that relate to the object or text that you right-clicked.

Contextual tabs Tabs that are added to the ribbon automatically when a specific object, such as a picture, is selected, and that contain commands relevant to the selected object.

Copy A command that duplicates a selection and places it on the Clipboard.

Cut A command that removes a selection and places it on the Clipboard.

Default The term that refers to the current selection or setting that is automatically used by a computer program unless you specify otherwise.

Deselect The action of canceling the selection of an object or block of text by clicking outside of the selection.

Desktop In Windows, the screen that simulates your work area.

Desktop app The term that commonly refers to a computer program that is installed on your computer and requires a computer operating system like Microsoft Windows or Apple OS to run.

Dialog box A small window that contains options for completing a task.

Dialog Box Launcher A small icon that displays to the right of some group names on the ribbon, and which opens a related dialog box or pane providing additional options and commands related to that group.

Document properties Details about a file that describe or identify it, including the title, author name, subject, and keywords that identify the document's topic or contents; also known as *metadata*.

Drag The action of holding down the left mouse button while moving your mouse.

Edit The process of making changes to text or graphics in an Office file.

Ellipsis A set of three dots indicating incompleteness; an ellipsis following a command name indicates that a dialog box will display if you click the command.

Enhanced ScreenTip A ScreenTip that displays more descriptive text than a normal ScreenTip.

Extract To decompress, or pull out, files from a compressed form.

File A collection of information stored on a computer under a single name, for example, a Word document or a PowerPoint presentation.

File Explorer The program that displays the files and folders on your computer, and which is at work anytime you are viewing the contents of files and folders in a window.

Fill The inside color of an object.

Folder A container in which you store files.

Folder window In Windows, a window that displays the contents of the current folder, library, or device, and contains helpful parts so that you can navigate the Windows file structure.

Font A set of characters with the same design and shape.

Font styles Formatting emphasis such as bold, italic, and underline.

Footer A reserved area for text or graphics that displays at the bottom of each page in a document.

Formatting The process of establishing the overall appearance of text, graphics, and pages in an Office file—for example, in a Word document.

Formatting marks Characters that display on the screen, but do not print, indicating where the Enter key, the Spacebar, and the Tab key were pressed; also called *nonprinting characters*.

Gallery An Office feature that displays a list of potential results instead of just the command name.

Gradient fill A fill effect in which one color fades into another.

Groups On the Office ribbon, the sets of related commands that you might need for a specific type of task.

Header A reserved area for text or graphics that displays at the top of each page in a document.

Info tab The tab in Backstage view that displays information about the current file.

Insertion point A blinking vertical line that indicates where text or graphics will be inserted.

Keyboard shortcut A combination of two or more keyboard keys, used to perform a task that would otherwise require a mouse.

KeyTip The letter that displays on a command in the ribbon and that indicates the key you can press to activate the command when keyboard control of the ribbon is activated.

Keywords Custom file properties in the form of words that you associate with a document to give an indication of the document's content; used to help find and organize files. Also called *tags*.

Landscape orientation A page orientation in which the paper is wider than it is tall.

Layout Options A button that displays when an object is selected and that has commands to choose how the object interacts with surrounding text.

Live Preview A technology that shows the result of applying an editing or formatting change as you point to possible results—*before* you actually apply it.

Location Any disk drive, folder, or other place in which you can store files and folders.

Metadata Details about a file that describe or identify it, including the title, author name, subject, and keywords that identify the document's topic or contents; also known as *document properties*.

Mini toolbar A small toolbar containing frequently used formatting commands that displays as a result of selecting text or objects.

MRU Acronym for *most recently used*, which refers to the state of some commands that retain the characteristic most recently applied; for example, the Font Color button retains the most recently used color until a new color is chosen.

Navigate The process of exploring within the organizing structure of Windows.

Navigation pane In a folder window, the area on the left in which you can navigate to, open, and display favorites, libraries, folders, saved searches, and an expandable list of drives.

Nonprinting characters Characters that display on the screen, but do not print, indicating where the Enter key, the Spacebar, and the Tab key were pressed; also called *formatting marks*.

Notification bar An area at the bottom of an Internet Explorer window that displays information about pending downloads, security issues, add-ons, and other issues related to the operation of your computer.

Object A text box, picture, table, or shape that you can select and then move and resize.

Office Web Apps The free online companions to Microsoft Word, Excel, PowerPoint, Access, and OneNote.

Open dialog box A dialog box from which you can navigate to, and then open on your screen, an existing file that was created in that same program.

Option button In a dialog box, a round button that enables you to make one choice among two or more options.

Options dialog box A dialog box within each Office application where you can select program settings and other options and preferences.

Pane A separate area of a window.

Paragraph symbol The symbol ¶ that represents the end of a paragraph.

Paste The action of placing text or objects that have been copied or cut from one location to another location.

Paste Options gallery A gallery of buttons that provides a Live Preview of all the Paste options available in the current context.

Path A sequence of folders that leads to a specific file or folder.

PDF The acronym for Portable Document Format, which is a file format that creates an image that preserves the look of your file; this is a popular format for sending documents electronically because the document will display on most computers.

Point The action of moving your mouse pointer over something on your screen.

Pointer Any symbol that displays on your screen in response to moving your mouse.

Points A measurement of the size of a font; there are 72 points in an inch.

Portable Document Format A file format that creates an image that preserves the look of your file, but that cannot be easily changed; a popular format for sending documents electronically, because the document will display on most computers.

Portrait orientation A page orientation in which the paper is taller than it is wide.

Print Preview A view of a document as it will appear when you print it.

Progress bar In a dialog box or taskbar button, a bar that indicates visually the progress of a task such as a download or file transfer.

Protected View A security feature in Office 2013 that protects your computer from malicious files by opening them in a restricted environment until you enable them; you might encounter this feature if you open a file from an email or download files from the Internet.

pt The abbreviation for *point*; for example, when referring to a font size.

Quick Access Toolbar In an Office program window, the small row of buttons in the upper left corner of the screen from which you can perform frequently used commands.

Read-Only A property assigned to a file that prevents the file from being modified or deleted; it indicates that you cannot save any changes to the displayed document unless you first save it with a new name.

Ribbon A user interface in both Office 2013 and File Explorer that groups the commands for performing related tasks on tabs across the upper portion of the program window.

Right-click The action of clicking the right mouse button one time.

Sans serif font A font design with no lines or extensions on the ends of characters.

ScreenTip A small box that that displays useful information when you perform various mouse actions such as pointing to screen elements or dragging.

Scroll bar A vertical or horizontal bar in a window or a pane to assist in bringing an area into view, and which contains a scroll box and scroll arrows.

Scroll box The box in the vertical and horizontal scroll bars that can be dragged to reposition the contents of a window or pane on the screen.

Selecting Highlighting, by dragging with your mouse, areas of text or data or graphics, so that the selection can be edited, formatted, copied, or moved.

Serif font A font design that includes small line extensions on the ends of the letters to guide the eye in reading from left to right.

SharePoint Collaboration software with which people in an organization can set up team sites to share information, manage documents, and publish reports for others to see.

Shortcut menu A menu that displays commands and options relevant to the selected text or object; also called a *context menu*.

Sizing handles Small squares that indicate a picture or object is selected.

SkyDrive Microsoft's free cloud storage for anyone with a free Microsoft account.

Split button A button divided into two parts and in which clicking the main part of the button performs a command and clicking the arrow opens a menu with choices.

Start search The search feature in Windows 8 in which, from the Start screen, you can begin to type and by default, Windows 8 searches for apps; you can adjust the search to search for files or settings.

Status bar The area along the lower edge of an Office program window that displays file information on the left and buttons to control how the window looks on the right.

Style A group of formatting commands, such as font, font size, font color, paragraph alignment, and line spacing that can be applied to a paragraph with one command.

Subfolder A folder within a folder.

Synchronization The process of updating computer files that are in two or more locations according to specific rules—also called *syncing*.

Syncing The process of updating computer files that are in two or more locations according to specific rules—also called *synchronization*.

Tabs (ribbon) On the Office ribbon, the name of each activity area.

Tags Custom file properties in the form of words that you associate with a document to give an indication of the document's content; used to help find and organize files. Also called *keywords*.

Taskbar The area along the lower edge of the desktop that displays buttons representing programs.

Template A preformatted document that you can use as a starting point and then change to suit your needs.

Theme A predesigned combination of colors, fonts, and effects that look good together and is applied to an entire document by a single selection.

Title bar The bar at the top edge of the program window that indicates the name of the current file and the program name.

Toggle button A button that can be turned on by clicking it once, and then turned off by clicking it again.

Toolbar In a folder window, a row of buttons with which you can perform common tasks, such as changing the view of your files and folders or burning files to a CD.

Triple-click The action of clicking the left mouse button three times in rapid succession.

Trusted Documents A security feature in Office that remembers which files you have already enabled; you might encounter this feature if you open a file from an email or download files from the Internet.

Uniform Resource Locator An address that uniquely identifies a location on the Internet.

URL The acronym for Uniform Resource Locator, which is an address that uniquely identifies a location on the Internet.

USB flash drive A small data storage device that plugs into a computer USB port.

Window A rectangular area on a computer screen in which programs and content appear, and which can be moved, resized, minimized, or closed.

XML Paper Specification A Microsoft file format that creates an image of your document and that opens in the XPS viewer.

XPS The acronym for XML Paper Specification—a Microsoft file format that creates an image of your document and that opens in the XPS viewer.

Zipped folder A folder that has been reduced in size and thus takes up less storage space and can be transferred to other computers quickly; also called a *compressed* folder.

Zoom The action of increasing or decreasing the size of the viewing area on the screen.

Introduction to Microsoft Excel 2013

E
Excel 2013

mcdern financial analysis / Fotolia

Excel 2013: Introduction

Quantitative information! Defined as a type of information that can be counted or that communicates the quantity of something, quantitative information can be either easy or hard to understand—depending on how it is presented. According to Stephen Few in his book *Show Me the Numbers*: "Quantitative information forms the core of what businesses must know to operate effectively."

Excel 2013 is a tool to communicate quantitative business information effectively. Sometimes you need to communicate quantitative relationships. For example, the number of units sold per geographic region shows a relationship of sales to geography. Sometimes you need to summarize numbers. A list of every student enrolled at your college with his or her major is not as informative as a summary of the total number of students in each major. In business, the most common quantitative information is some measure of money—costs, sales, payroll, expenses—and so on.

Rather than just a tool for making calculations, Excel is now a tool for you to communicate and collaborate with others. When you want to communicate visually with tables and graphs, Excel 2013 has many new features to help you do so. Microsoft Excel 2013 works best on a Windows 8 PC—desktop, laptop, or tablet—because if your PC is touch-enabled, you will be able to use your fingers to work with Excel.

Video EA

Creating a Worksheet and Charting Data

PROJECT 1A

OUTCOMES
Create a sales report with an embedded column chart and sparklines.

OBJECTIVES

1. Create, Save, and Navigate an Excel Workbook
2. Enter Data in a Worksheet
3. Construct and Copy Formulas and Use the SUM Function
4. Format Cells with Merge & Center, Cell Styles, and Themes
5. Chart Data to Create a Column Chart and Insert Sparklines
6. Print a Worksheet, Display Formulas, and Close Excel

PROJECT 1B

OUTCOMES
Calculate the value of an inventory.

OBJECTIVES

7. Check Spelling in a Worksheet
8. Enter Data by Range
9. Construct Formulas for Mathematical Operations
10. Edit Values in a Worksheet
11. Format a Worksheet

Warren Goldswain / Fotolia

In This Chapter

In this chapter, you will use Microsoft Excel 2013 to create and analyze data organized into columns and rows. After entering data in a worksheet, you can perform complex calculations, analyze the data to make logical decisions, and create informative charts that help readers visualize your data in a way they can understand and that is meaningful. In this chapter, you will create and modify Excel workbooks. You will practice the basics of worksheet design; create a footer; enter and edit data in a worksheet; chart data; and then save, preview, and print workbooks. You will also construct formulas for mathematical operations.

The projects in this chapter relate to **Pro Fit Marietta**, a distributor of fitness equipment and apparel to private gyms, personal trainers, health clubs, corporate wellness centers, hotels, college athletic facilities, physical therapy practices, and multi-unit residential properties. The company's mission is to find, test, and distribute the highest quality fitness products in the world to its customers for the benefit of consumers. Their popular blog provides useful tips on how to use the latest workout and fitness equipment. The company is located in Marietta, Georgia, which is metropolitan Atlanta's largest suburb.

Sales Report with Embedded Column Chart and Sparklines

MyITLab®
Project 1A Training

PROJECT ACTIVITIES

In Activities 1.01 through 1.17, you will create an Excel worksheet for Michelle Barry, the President of Pro Fit Marietta. The worksheet displays the second quarter sales of cardio equipment for the current year and includes a chart to visually represent the data. Your completed worksheet will look similar to Figure 1.1.

PROJECT FILES

For Project 1A, you will need the following file:

New blank Excel workbook

You will save your workbook as:

Lastname_Firstname_1A_Quarterly_Sales

Build from Scratch

PROJECT RESULTS

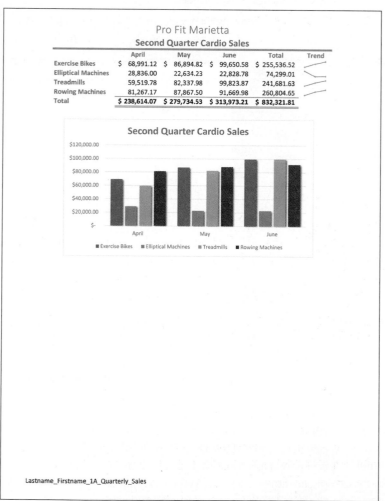

FIGURE 1.1 Project 1A Sales Report with Embedded Column Chart and Sparklines

- Tap an item to click it.
- Press and hold for a few seconds to right-click; release when the information or commands displays.
- Touch the screen with two or more fingers and then pinch together to zoom in or stretch your fingers apart to zoom out.
- Slide your finger on the screen to scroll—slide left to scroll right and slide right to scroll left.
- Slide to rearrange—similar to dragging with a mouse.
- Swipe from edge: from right to display charms; from left to expose open apps, snap apps, or close apps; from top or bottom to show commands or close an app.
- Swipe to select—slide an item a short distance with a quick movement—to select an item and bring up commands, if any.

Objective 1 Create, Save, and Navigate an Excel Workbook

Video F1-1

On startup, Excel displays a new blank **workbook**—the Excel document that stores your data—which contains one or more pages called a **worksheet**. A worksheet—or **spreadsheet**—is stored in a workbook and is formatted as a pattern of uniformly spaced horizontal rows and vertical columns. The intersection of a column and a row forms a box referred to as a **cell**.

Activity 1.01 | Starting Excel, Navigating Excel, and Naming and Saving a Workbook

1 Start Excel, and then on the opening screen, click **Blank workbook**. In the lower right corner of the window, on the status bar, if necessary, click the Normal button 🔳, and then to the right, locate the zoom—magnification—level.

Your zoom level should be 100%, although some figures in this textbook may be shown at a higher zoom level. The **Normal view** maximizes the number of cells visible on your screen and keeps the column letters and row numbers closer.

BY TOUCH On Excel's opening screen, tap Blank workbook.

2 Press F12 to display the **Save As** dialog box, and then navigate to the location where you will store your workbooks for this chapter.

3 In your storage location, create a new folder named **Excel Chapter 1** Open the new folder to display its folder window, and then in the **File name** box, notice that *Book1* displays as the default file name.

4 In the **File name** box, if necessary click *Book1* to select it, and then using your own name, type **Lastname_Firstname_1A_Quarterly_Sales** being sure to include the underscore (_) instead of spaces between words.

5 In the **Save As** dialog box, click **Save**. Compare your screen with Figure 1.2, and then take a moment to study the Excel window parts in the table in Figure 1.3.

More **Knowledge**   **Creating a New Workbook by Using a Template**

On Excel's opening screen, you can select a professional-look template instead of a blank workbook. Templates have some formatting completed; you just add and modify what you want. You can select or search for a template to match your needs from Excel's opening screen; or, from the Excel window, click FILE, and then click New to search for online templates.

FIGURE 1.2

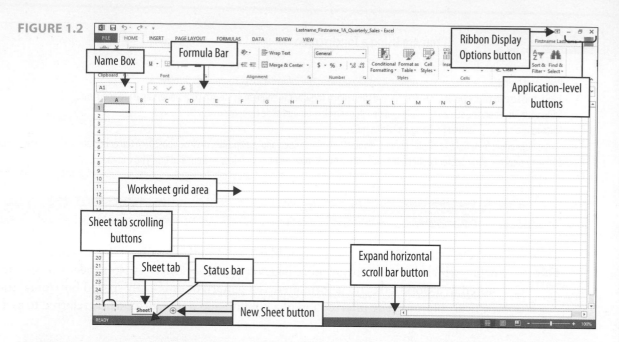

FIGURE 1.3

PARTS OF THE EXCEL WINDOW	
WINDOW PART	**DESCRIPTION**
Expand horizontal scroll bar button	Increases the width of the horizontal scroll bar.
Formula Bar	Displays the value or formula contained in the active cell; also permits entry or editing.
Sheet tab	Identifies the worksheet in the workbook.
New sheet button	Inserts an additional worksheet.
Name Box	Displays the name of the selected cell, table, chart, or object.
Sheet tab scrolling buttons	Display sheet tabs that are not in view when there are numerous sheet tabs.
Status bar	Displays the current cell mode, page number, worksheet information, view and zoom buttons, and for numerical data, common calculations such as Sum and Average.
Application-level buttons	Minimize, close, or restore the previous size of the displayed workbook.
Ribbon Display Options button	Displays various ways you can display the ribbon—the default is Show Tabs and Commands.
Worksheet grid area	Displays the columns and rows that intersect to form the worksheet's cells.

6 Take a moment to study Figure 1.4 and the table in Figure 1.5 to become familiar with the Excel workbook window.

FIGURE 1.4

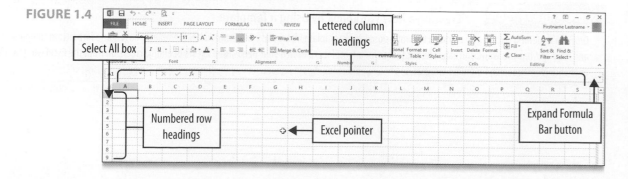

FIGURE 1.5

EXCEL WORKBOOK WINDOW ELEMENTS	
WORKBOOK WINDOW ELEMENT	**DESCRIPTION**
Excel pointer	Displays the location of the pointer.
Expand Formula Bar button	Increases the height of the Formula Bar to display lengthy cell content.
Lettered column headings	Indicate the column letter.
Numbered row headings	Indicate the row number.
Select All box	Selects all the cells in a worksheet.

7 ▶ In the lower right corner of the screen, in the horizontal scroll bar, click the **right scroll arrow** one time to shift **column A** out of view.

A *column* is a vertical group of cells in a worksheet. Beginning with the first letter of the alphabet, *A*, a unique letter identifies each column—this is called the *column heading*. Clicking one of the horizontal scroll bar arrows shifts the window either left or right one column at a time.

8 ▶ Point to the **right scroll arrow**, and then hold down the left mouse button until the columns begin to scroll rapidly to the right; release the mouse button when you begin to see pairs of letters as the column headings.

🔄 **BY TOUCH**   Anywhere on the worksheet, slide your finger to the left to scroll to the right.

9 ▶ Slowly drag the horizontal scroll box to the left, and notice that just above the scroll box, ScreenTips with the column letters display as you drag. Drag the horizontal scroll box left or right—or click the **left or right scroll arrow**—as necessary to position **column Z** near the center of your screen.

Column headings after column Z use two letters starting with AA, AB, and so on through ZZ. After that, columns begin with three letters beginning with AAA. This pattern provides 16,384 columns. The last column is XFD.

10 ▶ In the vertical scroll bar, click the **down scroll arrow** one time to move **Row 1** out of view.

A *row* is a horizontal group of cells. Beginning with number 1, a unique number identifies each row—this is the *row heading*, located at the left side of the worksheet. A single worksheet can handle 1 million rows of data.

11 ▶ Use the skills you just practiced to scroll horizontally to display **column A**, and if necessary, **row 1**.

12 ▶ Click **Save** 🔲.

Objective 2   Enter Data in a Worksheet

Video E1-2

Cell content, which is anything you type in a cell, can be one of two things: either a *constant value*—referred to simply as a *value*—or a *formula*. A formula is an equation that performs mathematical calculations on values in your worksheet. The most commonly used values are *text values* and *number values*, but a value can also include a date or a time of day. A text value is also referred to as a *label*.

A text value usually provides information about number values in other worksheet cells. For example, a title such as Second Quarter Cardio Sales gives the reader an indication that the data in the worksheet relates to information about sales of cardio equipment during the three-month period April through June.

1 Point to and then click the cell at the intersection of **column A** and **row 1** to make it the *active cell*—the cell is outlined in black and ready to accept data.

The intersecting column letter and row number form the *cell reference*—also called the *cell address*. When a cell is active, its column letter and row number are highlighted. The cell reference of the selected cell, *A1*, displays in the Name Box.

2 With cell **A1** as the active cell, type the worksheet title **Pro Fit Marietta** and then press Enter. Compare your screen with Figure 1.6.

Text or numbers in a cell are referred to as *data*. You must confirm the data you type in a cell by pressing Enter or by some other keyboard movement, such as pressing Tab or an arrow key. Pressing Enter moves the active cell to the cell below.

FIGURE 1.6

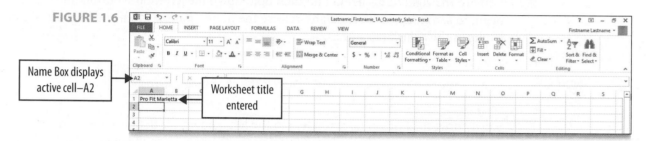

Name Box displays active cell–A2

Worksheet title entered

3 In cell **A1**, notice that the text does not fit; the text extends into cell **B1** to the right.

If text is too long for a cell and cells to the right are empty, the text will display. If the cells to the right contain other data, only the text that will fit in the cell displays.

4 In cell **A2**, type the worksheet subtitle **Second Quarter Cardio Sales** and then press Enter. Compare your screen with Figure 1.7.

FIGURE 1.7

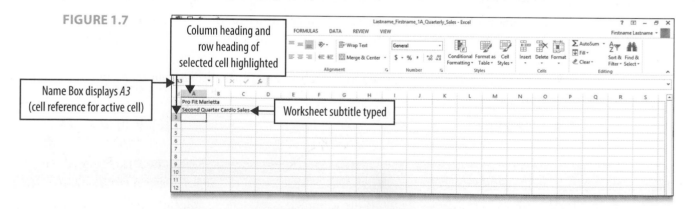

Column heading and row heading of selected cell highlighted

Name Box displays *A3* (cell reference for active cell)

Worksheet subtitle typed

5 Above **column A**, click in the **Name Box** to select the cell reference *A3*, and then type **a4** Press Enter to make cell **A4** the active cell. In cell **A4**, type **Exercise Bikes** to form the first row title, and then press Enter.

The text characters that you typed align at the left edge of the cell—referred to as *left alignment*—and cell A5 becomes the active cell. Left alignment is the default for text values. You can type a cell address in the Name Box and press Enter to move to a specific cell quickly.

6 In cell **A5**, type **E** and notice the text from the previous cell displays.

> If the first characters you type in a cell match an existing entry in the column, Excel fills in the remaining characters for you. This feature, called **AutoComplete**, assists only with alphabetic values.

7 Continue typing the remainder of the row title **lliptical Machines** and press [Enter].

> The AutoComplete suggestion is removed when the entry you are typing differs from the previous value.

8 In cell **A6**, type **Treadmills** and press [Enter]. In cell **A7**, type **Rowing Machines** and press [Enter]. In cell **A8**, type **Total** and press [Enter]. On the **Quick Access Toolbar**, click **Save** 🔲.

ANOTHER WAY   Use the keyboard shortcut [Ctrl] + [S] to save changes to your workbook.

Activity 1.03 | Using Auto Fill and Keyboard Shortcuts

1 Click cell **B3**. Type **A** and notice that when you begin to type in a cell, on the **Formula Bar**, the **Cancel** and **Enter** buttons become active, as shown in Figure 1.8.

FIGURE 1.8

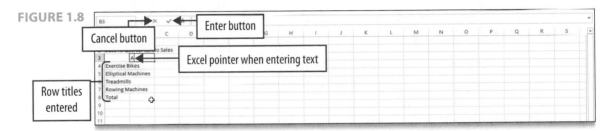

2 Continue to type **pril** On the **Formula Bar**, notice that values you type in a cell also display there. Then, on the **Formula Bar**, click **Enter** ✔ to confirm the entry and keep cell **B3** active.

3 With cell **B3** active, locate the small square in the lower right corner of the selected cell.

> You can drag this **fill handle**—the small square in the lower right corner of a selected cell—to adjacent cells to fill the cells with values based on the first cell.

4 Point to the **fill handle** until the ➕ pointer displays, hold down the left mouse button, drag to the right to cell **D3**, and as you drag, notice the ScreenTips *May* and *June*. Release the mouse button.

5 Under the text that you just filled, click the **Auto Fill Options** button ⊞ that displays, and then compare your screen with Figure 1.9.

> **Auto Fill** generates and extends a *series* of values into adjacent cells based on the value of other cells. A series is a group of things that come one after another in succession; for example, *April, May, June*.
>
> The Auto Fill Options button displays options to fill the data; options vary depending on the content and program from which you are filling, and the format of the data you are filling.
>
> *Fill Series* is selected, indicating the action that was taken. Because the options are related to the current task, the button is referred to as being **context sensitive**.

FIGURE 1.9

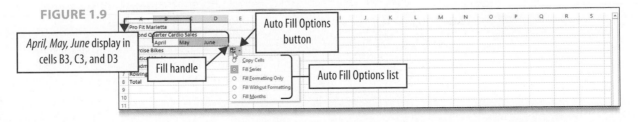

6 ▶ Click in any cell to cancel the display of the list.

The list no longer displays; the button will display until you perform some other screen action.

7 ▶ Press `Ctrl` + `Home`, which is the keyboard shortcut to make cell **A1** active.

8 ▶ On the **Quick Access Toolbar**, click **Save** 💾 to save the changes you have made to your workbook.

9 ▶ Take a moment to study the table in Figure 1.10 to become familiar with keyboard shortcuts with which you can navigate the Excel worksheet.

FIGURE 1.10

KEYBOARD SHORTCUTS TO NAVIGATE THE EXCEL WINDOW	
TO MOVE THE LOCATION OF THE ACTIVE CELL:	**PRESS:**
Up, down, right, or left one cell	`↑`, `↓`, `→`, `←`
Down one cell	`Enter`
Up one cell	`Shift` + `Enter`
Up one full screen	`PageUp`
Down one full screen	`PageDown`
To column A of the current row	`Home`
To the last cell in the last column of the active area (the rectangle formed by all the rows and columns in a worksheet that contain entries)	`Ctrl` + `End`
To cell A1	`Ctrl` + `Home`
Right one cell	`Tab`
Left one cell	`Shift` + `Tab`
To the cell one worksheet window to the right	`Alt` + `PageDown`
To the cell one worksheet window to the left	`Alt` + `PageUp`
To the cell containing specific content that you enter in the Find and Replace dialog box	`Shift` + `F5`
To the cell that corresponds with the cell reference you enter in the Go To dialog box	`F5`

Activity 1.04 | **Aligning Text and Adjusting the Size of Columns**

1 ▶ In the **column heading area**, point to the vertical line between **column A** and **column B** to display the ✛ pointer, press and hold down the left mouse button, and then compare your screen with Figure 1.11.

A ScreenTip displays information about the width of the column. The default width of a column is 64 *pixels*. A pixel, short for *picture element*, is a point of light measured in dots per square inch. Sixty-four pixels equal 8.43 characters, which is the average number of characters that will fit in a cell using the default font. The default font in Excel is Calibri and the default font size is 11.

FIGURE 1.11

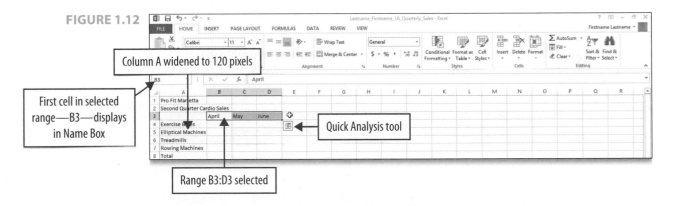

Column heading area

ScreenTip

Mouse pointer

2 Drag to the right, and when the number of pixels indicated in the ScreenTip reaches **120 pixels**, release the mouse button. If you are not satisfied with your result, click Undo ⤾ on the Quick Access Toolbar and begin again.

> This width accommodates the longest row title in cells A4 through A8—*Elliptical Machines*. The worksheet subtitle in cell A2 spans more than one column and still does not fit in column A.

3 Point to cell **B3** and then drag across to select cells **B3**, **C3**, and **D3**. Compare your screen with Figure 1.12; if you are not satisfied with your result, click anywhere and begin again.

> The three cells, B3 through D3, are selected and form a *range*—two or more cells on a worksheet that are adjacent (next to each other) or nonadjacent (not next to each other). This range of cells is referred to as *B3:D3*. When you see a colon (:) between two cell references, the range includes all the cells between the two cell references.

> A range of cells you select this way is indicated by a dark border, and Excel treats the range as a single unit so you can make the same changes to more than one cell at a time. The selected cells in the range are highlighted except for the first cell in the range, which displays in the Name Box.

> When you select a range of data, the *Quick Analysis tool* displays in the lower right corner of the selected range with which you can analyze your data by using Excel tools such as charts, color-coding, and formulas.

FIGURE 1.12

Column A widened to 120 pixels

First cell in selected range—B3—displays in Name Box

Quick Analysis tool

Range B3:D3 selected

↻ **BY TOUCH**   To select a range, tap and hold the first cell, and then when the circular gripper displays, drag it to the right, or to the right and down, to define the beginning and end of a range.

4 With the range **B3:D3** selected, point anywhere over the selected range, right-click, and then on the mini toolbar, click **Center** ≡. On the **Quick Access Toolbar**, click **Save** 🖫.

> The column titles *April*, *May*, *June* align in the center of each cell.

Activity 1.05 | Entering Numbers

To type number values, use either the number keys across the top of your keyboard or the numeric keypad if you have one—laptop computers may not have a numeric keypad.

1 Under *April*, click cell **B4**, type **68991.12** and then on the **Formula Bar**, click **Enter** ☑ to maintain cell **B4** as the active cell. Compare your screen with Figure 1.13.

By default, *number* values align at the right edge of the cell. The default *number format*—a specific way in which Excel displays numbers—is the *general format*. In the default general format, whatever you type in the cell will display, with the exception of trailing zeros to the right of a decimal point. For example, in the number 237.50 the *0* following the *5* is a trailing zero and will not display.

Data that displays in a cell is the *displayed value*. Data that displays in the Formula Bar is the *underlying value*. The number of digits or characters that display in a cell—the displayed value—depends on the width of the column. Calculations on numbers will always be based on the underlying value, not the displayed value.

FIGURE 1.13

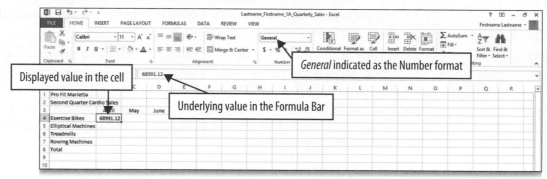

2 Press ⟨Tab⟩ to make cell **C4** active. Type **86894.82** and then press ⟨Tab⟩ to move to cell **D4**. Type **99650.58** and then press ⟨Enter⟩ to move to cell **B5** in the next row. Then, by using the same technique, enter the remaining sales numbers as shown:

	APRIL	MAY	JUNE
Elliptical Machines	28836	22634.23	22828.78
Treadmills	59519.78	82337.98	99823.87
Rowing Machines	81267.17	87867.50	91669.98

3 Compare the numbers you entered with Figure 1.14, and then **Save** 💾 your workbook.

In the default General format, trailing zeros to the right of a decimal point will not display. For example, when you type *87867.50*, the cell displays 87867.5 instead.

FIGURE 1.14

Values entered for each category in each month

Video E1-3

A cell contains either a constant value (text or numbers) or a formula. A formula is an equation that performs mathematical calculations on values in other cells, and then places the result in the cell containing the formula. You can create formulas or use a *function*—a prewritten formula that looks at one or more values, performs an operation, and then returns a value.

Activity 1.06 | Constructing a Formula and Using the SUM Function

In this activity, you will practice three different ways to sum a group of numbers in Excel.

1 Click cell **B8** to make it the active cell and type **=**

The equal sign (=) displays in the cell with the insertion point blinking, ready to accept more data.

All formulas begin with the = sign, which signals Excel to begin a calculation. The Formula Bar displays the = sign, and the Formula Bar Cancel and Enter buttons display.

2 At the insertion point, type **b4** and then compare your screen with Figure 1.15.

A list of Excel functions that begin with the letter *B* may briefly display—as you progress in your study of Excel, you will use functions of this type. A blue border with small corner boxes surrounds cell B4, which indicates that the cell is part of an active formula. The color used in the box matches the color of the cell reference in the formula.

FIGURE 1.15

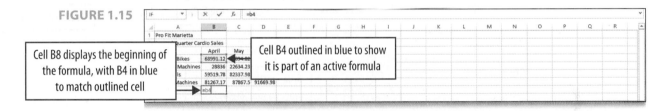

Cell B8 displays the beginning of the formula, with B4 in blue to match outlined cell

Cell B4 outlined in blue to show it is part of an active formula

3 At the insertion point, type **+** and then type **b5**

A border of another color surrounds cell B5, and the color matches the color of the cell reference in the active formula. When typing cell references, it is not necessary to use uppercase letters.

4 At the insertion point, type **+b6+b7** and then press Enter.

The result of the formula calculation—*238614.1*—displays in the cell. Recall that in the default General format, trailing zeros do not display.

5 Click cell **B8** again, look at the **Formula Bar**, and then compare your screen with Figure 1.16.

The formula adds the values in cells B4 through B7, and the result displays in cell B8. In this manner, you can construct a formula by typing. Although cell B8 displays the *result* of the formula, the formula itself displays in the Formula Bar. This is referred to as the **underlying formula**.

Always view the Formula Bar to be sure of the exact content of a cell—*a displayed number may actually be a formula.*

FIGURE 1.16

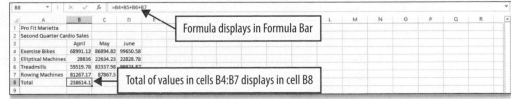

Formula displays in Formula Bar

Total of values in cells B4:B7 displays in cell B8

6 Click cell **C8** and type **=** to signal the beginning of a formula. Then, point to cell **C4** and click one time.

The reference to the cell C4 is added to the active formula. A moving border surrounds the referenced cell, and the border color and the color of the cell reference in the formula are color coded to match.

7 At the insertion point, type **+** and then click cell **C5**. Repeat this process to complete the formula to add cells **C6** and **C7**, and then press Enter.

The result of the formula calculation—*279734.5*—displays in the cell. This method of constructing a formula is the ***point and click method***.

8 Click cell **D8**. On the **HOME tab**, in the **Editing group**, click **AutoSum** Σ AutoSum ˅ , and then compare your screen with Figure 1.17.

SUM is an Excel function—a prewritten formula. A moving border surrounds the range D4:D7 and *=SUM(D4:D7)* displays in cell D8.

The = sign signals the beginning of a formula, *SUM* indicates the type of calculation that will take place (addition), and *(D4:D7)* indicates the range of cells on which the sum calculation will be performed. A ScreenTip provides additional information about the action.

FIGURE 1.17

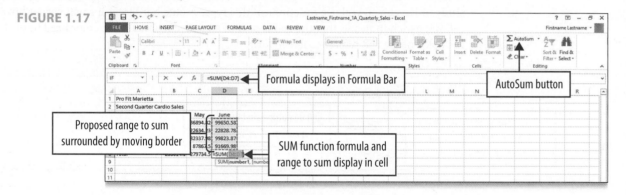

ANOTHER WAY   Use the keyboard shortcut Alt + = ; or, on the Formulas tab, in the Function Library group, click the AutoSum button.

9 Look at the **Formula Bar**, and notice that the formula also displays there. Then, look again at the cells surrounded by the moving border.

When you activate the ***Sum function***, Excel first looks *above* the active cell for a range of cells to sum. If no range is above the active cell, Excel will look to the *left* for a range of cells to sum. If the proposed range is not what you want to calculate, you can select a different group of cells.

10 Press Enter to construct a formula by using the prewritten SUM function.

Your total is *313973.2*. Because the Sum function is frequently used, it has its own button in the Editing group on the Home tab of the ribbon. A larger version of the button also displays on the FORMULAS tab in the Function Library group. This button is also referred to as ***AutoSum***.

11 Notice that the totals in the range **B8:D8** display only one decimal place. Click **Save** 🖫.

Number values that are too long to fit in the cell do *not* spill over into the unoccupied cell to the right in the same manner as text values. Rather, Excel rounds the number to fit the space.

Rounding is a procedure that determines which digit at the right of the number will be the last digit displayed and then increases it by one if the next digit to its right is 5, 6, 7, 8, or 9.

You have practiced three ways to create a formula—by typing, by using the point-and-click technique, and by using a Function button from the ribbon. You can also copy formulas. When you copy a formula from one cell to another, Excel adjusts the cell references to fit the new location of the formula.

1 Click cell **E3**, type **Total** and then press (Enter).

> The text in cell E3 is centered because the centered format continues from the adjacent cell.

2 With cell **E4** as the active cell, hold down (Alt), and then press (=). Compare your screen with Figure 1.18.

> (Alt) + (=) is the keyboard shortcut for the Sum function. Recall that Excel first looks above the selected cell for a proposed range of cells to sum, and if no data is detected, Excel looks to the left and proposes a range of cells to sum.

FIGURE 1.18

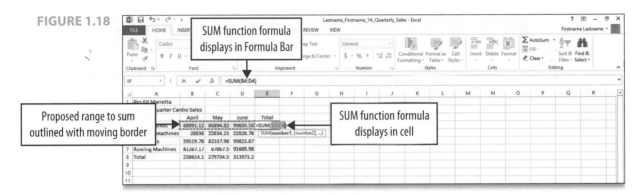

3 On the **Formula Bar**, click **Enter** ✓ to display the result and keep cell **E4** active.

> The total dollar amount of *Exercise Bikes* sold in the quarter is *255536.5*. In cells E5:E8, you can see that you need a formula similar to the one in E4, but formulas that refer to the cells in row 5, row 6, and so on.

4 With cell **E4** active, point to the **fill handle** in the lower right corner of the cell until the ➕ pointer displays. Then, drag down through cell **E8**; if you are not satisfied with your result, on the Quick Access Toolbar, click Undo ↺ and begin again. Compare your screen with Figure 1.19.

FIGURE 1.19

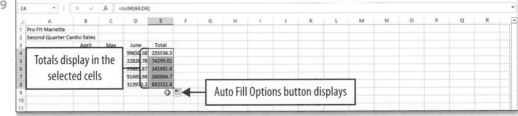

5 Click cell **E5**, look at the **Formula Bar**, and notice the formula *=SUM(B5:D5)*. Click cell **E6**, look at the **Formula Bar**, and then notice the formula *=SUM(B6:D6)*.

> In each row, Excel copied the formula but adjusted the cell references *relative to* the row number. This is called a ***relative cell reference***—a cell reference based on the relative position of the cell that contains the formula and the cells referred to in the formula.

> The calculation is the same, but it is performed on the cells in that particular row. Use this method to insert numerous formulas into spreadsheets quickly.

6 Click cell **F3**, type **Trend** and then press (Enter). **Save** 💾 your workbook.

Video E1-4

Format—change the appearance of—cells to make your worksheet attractive and easy to read.

Activity 1.08 | Using Merge & Center and Applying Cell Styles

1 Select the range **A1:F1**, and then in the **Alignment group**, click **Merge & Center**. Then, select the range **A2:F2** and click **Merge & Center**.

The *Merge & Center* command joins selected cells into one larger cell and centers the contents in the merged cell; individual cells in the range B1:F1 and B2:F2 can no longer be selected—they are merged into cell A1 and A2 respectively.

ANOTHER WAY   Select the range, right-click over the selection, and then on the mini toolbar, click the Merge & Center button.

2 Click cell **A1**. In the **Styles group**, click **Cell Styles**, and then compare your screen with Figure 1.20.

A *cell style* is a defined set of formatting characteristics, such as font, font size, font color, cell borders, and cell shading.

FIGURE 1.20

3 In the displayed gallery, under **Titles and Headings**, click **Title** and notice that the row height adjusts to accommodate the larger font size.

4 Click cell **A2**, display the **Cell Styles** gallery, and then under **Titles and Headings**, click **Heading 1**.

Use cell styles to maintain a consistent look in a worksheet and across worksheets in a workbook.

5 Select the horizontal range **B3:F3**, hold down **Ctrl**, and then select the vertical range **A4:A8** to select the column titles and the row titles.

Use this technique to select two or more ranges that are nonadjacent—not next to each other.

6 Display the **Cell Styles** gallery, click **Heading 4** to apply this cell style to the column titles and row titles, and then **Save** 🖫 your workbook.

1 Select the range **B4:E4**, hold down Ctrl, and then select the range **B8:E8**.

This range is referred to as *b4:e4,b8:e8* with a comma separating the references to the two nonadjacent ranges.

ANOTHER WAY In the Name Box type b4:e4,b8:e8 and then press Enter.

2 On the **HOME tab**, in the **Number group**, click **Accounting Number Format** $ ▾. Compare your screen with Figure 1.21.

The *Accounting Number Format* applies a thousand comma separator where appropriate, inserts a fixed U.S. dollar sign aligned at the left edge of the cell, applies two decimal places, and leaves a small amount of space at the right edge of the cell to accommodate a parenthesis when negative numbers are present. Excel widens the columns to accommodate the formatted numbers.

At the bottom of your screen, in the status bar, Excel displays the results for some common calculations that might be made on the range; for example, the Average of the numbers selected and the Count—the number of items selected.

FIGURE 1.21

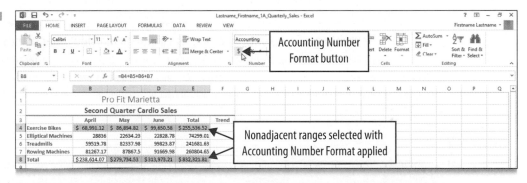

ANOTHER WAY Display the Cell Styles gallery, and under Number Format, click Currency.

3 Select the range **B5:E7**, and then in the **Number group**, click **Comma Style** ▸.

The *Comma Style* inserts a thousand comma separator where appropriate and applies two decimal places. Comma Style also leaves space at the right to accommodate a parenthesis when negative numbers are present.

When preparing worksheets with financial information, the first row of dollar amounts and the total row of dollar amounts are formatted in the Accounting Number Format; that is, with thousand comma separators, dollar signs, two decimal places, and space at the right to accommodate a parenthesis for negative numbers, if any. Rows that are *not* the first row or the total row should be formatted with the Comma Style.

4 Select the range **B8:E8**. In the **Styles group**, display the **Cell Styles** gallery, and then under **Titles and Headings**, click **Total**. Click any blank cell to cancel the selection, and then compare your screen with Figure 1.22.

This is a common way to apply borders to financial information. The single border indicates that calculations were performed on the numbers above, and the double border indicates that the information is complete. Sometimes financial documents do not display values with cents; rather, the values are rounded up. You can do this by selecting the cells, and then clicking the Decrease Decimal button two times.

FIGURE 1.22

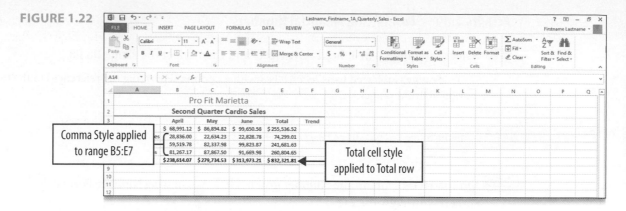

Comma Style applied to range B5:E7

Total cell style applied to Total row

Activity 1.10 | Changing the Workbook Theme

A *theme* is a predefined set of colors, fonts, lines, and fill effects that coordinate for an attractive look.

1 Click the **PAGE LAYOUT tab**, and then in the **Themes group**, click **Themes**.

2 Click the **Retrospect** theme, and notice that the cell styles change to match the new theme. Click **Save** 🖫.

More Knowledge | **Formatting a Cell's Font, Style, Size, or Color with Individual Commands**

Instead of using Cell Styles, you could use a combination of individual commands to format a cell. For example, on the HOME tab, in the Font group, you can change a cell's font by clicking the Font arrow and selecting a different font. You can change the font size by clicking the Font Size arrow and selecting a size. From the same group, you can apply various styles to the cell—such as Bold or Italic or Underline. To change a cell's font color, in the Font Group, click the Font Color arrow and select a different color.

Objective 5 | Chart Data to Create a Column Chart and Insert Sparklines

Video E1-5

A *chart* is a graphic representation of data in a worksheet. Data in a chart is easier to understand than a table of numbers. *Sparklines* are tiny charts embedded in a cell that give a visual trend summary alongside your data. A sparkline makes a pattern more obvious to the eye.

Activity 1.11 | Charting Data and Using Recommended Charts to Select and Insert a Column Chart

Recommended Charts is an Excel feature that displays a customized set of charts that, according to Excel's calculations, will best fit your data based on the range of data that you select. In this activity, you will create a *column chart* showing the monthly sales of cardio equipment by category during the second quarter. A column chart is useful for illustrating comparisons among related numbers. The chart will enable the company president, Michelle Barry, to see a pattern of overall monthly sales.

1 Select the range **A3:D7**.

> When charting data, typically you should *not* include totals—include only the data you want to compare.

2 With the data that you want to compare selected, click the **INSERT tab**, and then in the **Charts group**, click **Recommended Charts**. Compare your screen with Figure 1.23.

> The Insert Chart dialog box displays a list of recommended charts on the left and a preview of the first chart, which is selected, on the right. The second tab of the Insert Chart dialog box includes all chart types—even those that are not recommended by Excel for this type of data.
>
> By using different *chart types*, you can display data in a way that is meaningful to the reader—common examples are column charts, pie charts, and line charts.

FIGURE 1.23

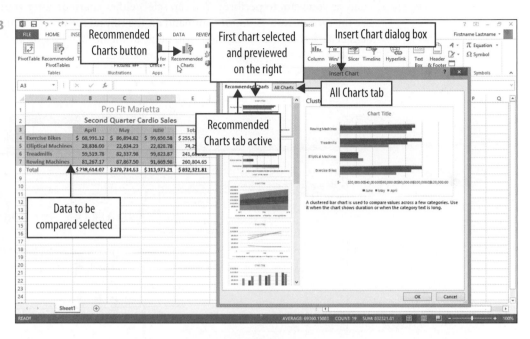

3 In the **Insert Chart** dialog box, use the scroll bar to scroll down about one-third of the way, and then click the second Clustered Column chart. Compare your screen with Figure 1.24.

> Here, *each type of cardio equipment* displays its *sales for each month*. A clustered column chart is useful to compare values across a few categories, especially if the order of categories is not important.

FIGURE 1.24

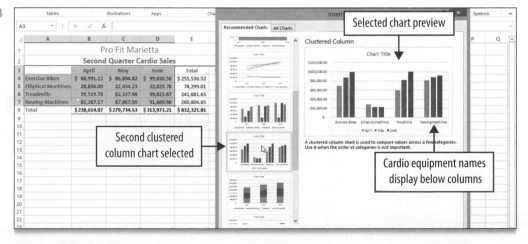

4 In the **Insert Chart** dialog box, click the chart directly above the selected chart—the first clustered column chart. Compare your screen with Figure 1.25.

In this clustered column chart, *each month* displays its *sales for each type of cardio equipment.* When constructing a chart, you can switch the row and column data in this manner to display the data in a way that is most useful to the reader. Here, the president of Pro Fit Marietta wants to compare sales of each type of equipment by month to detect patterns.

The comparison of data—either by month or by type of equipment—depends on the type of analysis you want to perform. You can select either chart, or, after your chart is complete, you can use the *Switch/Row Column* command on the ribbon to swap the data over the axis; that is, data being charted on the vertical axis will move to the horizontal axis and vice versa.

FIGURE 1.25

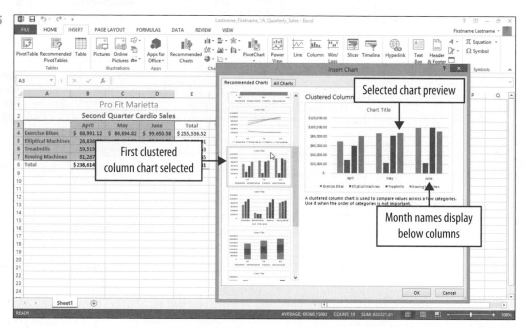

5 In the lower right corner of the **Insert Chart** dialog box, click **OK** to insert the selected chart into the worksheet. Compare your screen with Figure 1.26.

Your selected column chart displays in the worksheet, and the charted data is bordered by colored lines. Because the chart object is selected—surrounded by a border and displaying sizing handles—contextual tools named *CHART TOOLS* display and add contextual tabs next to the standard tabs on the ribbon.

FIGURE 1.26

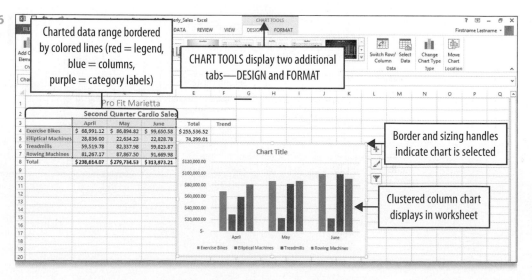

Activity 1.12 | Using the Chart Tools to Apply Chart Styles

1 On the ribbon, locate the contextual tabs under **CHART TOOLS—DESIGN** and **FORMAT**.

When a chart is selected, CHART TOOLS become available and these two tabs provide commands for working with the chart.

Based on the data you selected in your worksheet and the chart you selected in the Insert Chart dialog box, Excel constructs a column chart and adds *category labels*—the labels that display along the bottom of the chart to identify the category of data. This area is referred to as the *category axis* or the *x-axis*.

Depending on which arrangement of row and column data you select in the Insert Chart dialog box, Excel arranges either the row titles or the column titles as the category names. Here, based on your selection, the column titles that form the category labels are bordered in purple, indicating the cells that contain the category names.

On the left side of the chart, Excel includes a numerical scale on which the charted data is based; this is the *value axis* or the *y-axis*. Along the lower edge of the chart, a *legend*, which is a chart element that identifies the patterns or colors that are assigned to the categories in the chart, displays. Here, the row titles are bordered in red, indicating the cells containing the legend text.

2 To the right of the chart, notice the three buttons, and then point to each button to display its ScreenTip, as shown in Figure 1.27.

The *Chart Elements button* enables you to add, remove, or change chart elements such as the title, legend, gridlines, and data labels.

The *Chart Styles button* enables you to set a style and color scheme for your chart.

The *Chart Filters button* enables you to change which data displays in the chart—for example, to see only the data for *May* and *June* or only the data for *Treadmills* and *Rowing Machines*.

FIGURE 1.27

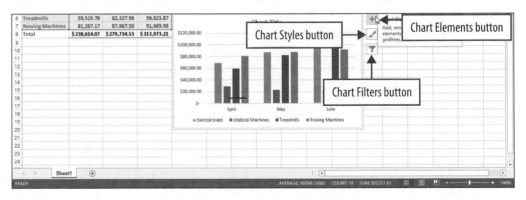

3 In the worksheet data, locate the group of cells bordered in blue.

Each of the twelve cells bordered in blue is referred to as a *data point*—a value that originates in a worksheet cell. Each data point is represented in the chart by a *data marker*—a column, bar, area, dot, pie slice, or other symbol in a chart that represents a single data point.

Related data points form a *data series*; for example, there is a data series for *April*, for *May*, and for *June*. Each data series has a unique color or pattern represented in the chart legend.

4 On the **DESIGN tab**, in the **Chart Layouts group**, click **Quick Layout**, and then compare your screen with Figure 1.28.

In the Quick Layout gallery, you can change the overall layout of the chart by selecting a predesigned *chart layout*—a combination of chart elements, which can include a title, legend, labels for the columns, and the table of charted cells.

FIGURE 1.28

5 *Point* to several different layouts to see how Live Preview displays the effect on your chart, and then click the **Quick Layout** button again *without* changing the layout.

6 In the chart, click anywhere in the text *Chart Title* to select the title box, watch the **Formula Bar** as you begin to type **Second** and notice that AutoComplete fills in the subtitle for you. Press Enter at any point to insert the subtitle as the chart title.

7 Click in a white area just slightly *inside* the chart border to deselect the chart title but keep the chart selected. To the right of the chart, click **Chart Styles** ✎, and then at the top of the **Chart Styles** gallery, be sure that **Style** is selected. Compare your screen with Figure 1.29.

The ***Chart Styles gallery*** displays an array of pre-defined ***chart styles***—the overall visual look of the chart in terms of its colors, backgrounds, and graphic effects such as flat or shaded columns. You can also select Chart Styles from the Chart Styles group on the ribbon, but having the gallery closer to the chart makes it easier to use a touch gesture on a touch device to format a chart.

FIGURE 1.29

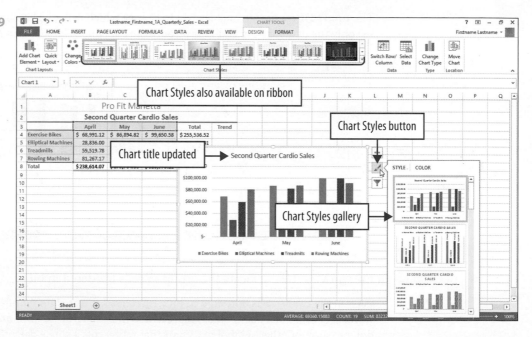

8 On the right side of the **Style** gallery, scroll down about halfway, and then by using the ScreenTips as your guide, locate and click **Style 6**.

This style uses a white background, formats the columns with theme colors, and applies a slight shadowed effect to the columns. With this clear visual representation of the data, the president can see the sales of all product categories in each month, and can see that the sale of exercise bikes and treadmills has risen markedly during the quarter.

9 At the top of the gallery, click **COLOR**. Under **Colorful**, point to the third row of colors to display the ScreenTip *Color 3*, and then click to apply the **Color 3** variation of the theme colors.

10 Point to the top border of the chart to display the ⬚ pointer, and then drag the upper left corner of the chart just inside the upper left corner of cell **A10**, approximately as shown in Figure 1.30.

FIGURE 1.30

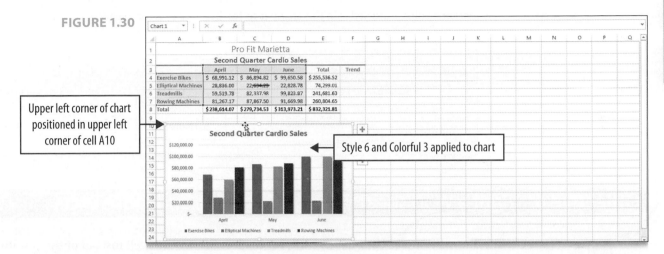

Upper left corner of chart positioned in upper left corner of cell A10

Style 6 and Colorful 3 applied to chart

11 Click any cell to deselect the chart, and notice that the chart buttons no longer display to the right of the chart and the CHART TOOLS no longer display on the ribbon. Click **Save** 🖫.

Contextual tabs display when an object is selected and then are removed from view when the object is deselected.

Activity 1.13 | Creating and Formatting Sparklines

By creating sparklines, you provide a context for your numbers. Your readers will be able to see the relationship between a sparkline and its underlying data quickly.

1 Select the range **B4:D7**, which represents the monthly sales figures for each product and for each month. Click the **INSERT tab**, and then in the **Sparklines group**, click **Line**. In the displayed **Create Sparklines** dialog box, notice that the selected range *B4:D7* displays as the Data Range.

2 With the insertion point blinking in the **Location Range** box, type **f4:f7** which is the range of cells where you want the sparklines to display. Compare your screen with Figure 1.31.

FIGURE 1.31

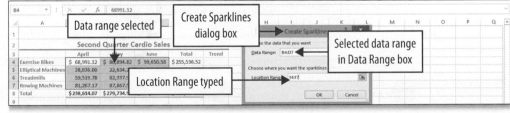

Data range selected

Create Sparklines dialog box

Selected data range in Data Range box

Location Range typed

 ANOTHER WAY   In the worksheet, select the range F4:F7 to insert it into the Location Range box.

3 Click **OK** to insert the sparklines in the range **F4:F7**, and then on the **DESIGN tab**, in the **Show group**, click the **Markers** check box to select it.

Alongside each row of data, the sparkline provides a quick visual trend summary for sales of each cardio item over the three-month period. For example, you can see instantly that of the four items, only Elliptical Machines had declining sales for the period.

4 On the **DESIGN tab**, in the **Style group**, click **More** ⏷. In the second row, click the fourth style—**Sparkline Style Accent 4, Darker 25%**. Press [Ctrl] + [Home] to deselect the range and make cell **A1** the active cell. Click **Save** 🖫, and then compare your screen with Figure 1.32.

Use markers, colors, and styles in this manner to further enhance your sparklines.

FIGURE 1.32

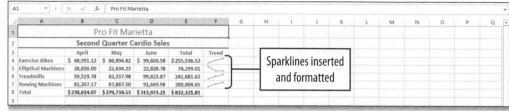

Objective 6 | Print a Worksheet, Display Formulas, and Close Excel

Video E1-6

Use the Show Formulas command to display the formula in each cell instead of the resulting value. Use the commands on the PAGE LAYOUT tab to prepare for printing.

Activity 1.14 | Creating a Footer and Centering a Worksheet

For each Excel project in this textbook, you will create a footer containing the file name, which includes your name and the project name. You will also center the data horizontally on the page to create an attractive result if your worksheet is printed.

1 If necessary, click cell **A1** to deselect the chart. Click the **PAGE LAYOUT tab**, and then in the **Page Setup group**, click **Margins**. At the bottom of the **Margins** gallery, click **Custom Margins**, to display the **Page Setup** dialog box. Compare your screen with Figure 1.33.

FIGURE 1.33

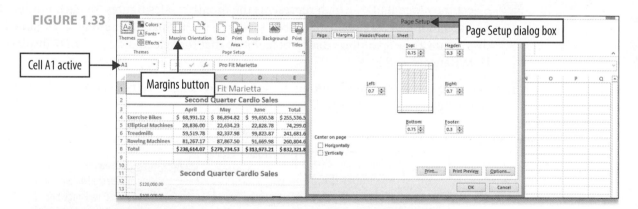

2 On the **Margins tab**, under **Center on page**, select the **Horizontally** check box.

This action will center the data and chart horizontally on the page, as shown in the Preview area.

3 Click the **Header/Footer tab**, and then in the center of the dialog box, click **Custom Footer**. In the **Footer** dialog box, with your insertion point blinking in the **Left section**, on the row of buttons, click **Insert File Name** 📄. Compare your screen with Figure 1.34.

&[File] displays in the Left section. Here you can type or insert information from the row of buttons into the left, middle, or right section of the footer. The Custom Header button displays a similar screen to enter information in the header of the worksheet.

FIGURE 1.34

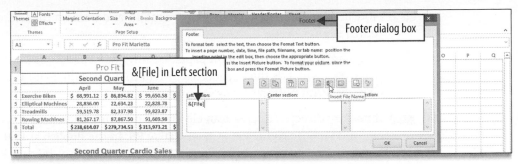

4 Click **OK** two times.

The vertical dotted line between columns indicates that as currently arranged, only the columns to the left of the dotted line will print on the first page. The exact position of the vertical line may depend on your default printer setting.

ANOTHER WAY Deselect the chart. On the INSERT tab, in the Text group, click Header & Footer to display Page Layout view. Click in the Left section of the displayed footer, and then in the Header & Footer Elements group, click File Name. Click any cell in the workbook to deselect the footer area, and then on the status bar, click the Normal button to return to Normal view.

Activity 1.15 | Adding Document Properties and Printing a Workbook

1 In the upper left corner of your screen, click the **FILE tab** to display **Backstage** view. In the lower right corner, click **Show All Properties**.

2 As the **Tags**, type **cardio sales** In the **Subject** box, type your course name and section number. Be sure your name displays as the author and edit if necessary.

3 On the left, click **Print** to view the **Print Preview**. Compare your screen with Figure 1.35.

FIGURE 1.35

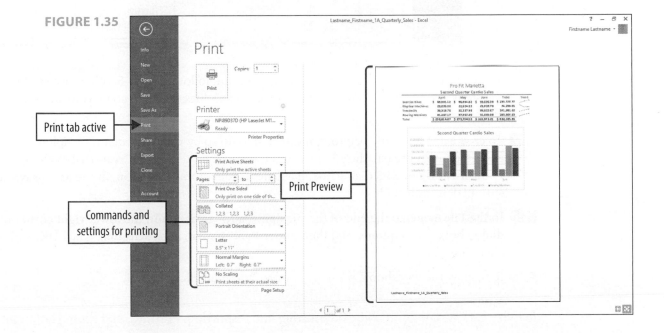

4 Note any adjustments that need to be made, and then on the left, click **Save** to save and return to the workbook.

5 If you are directed to print on paper, be sure that a printer is available to your system. Press Ctrl + F2, which is the keyboard shortcut to display the **Print Preview**, and then under **Print**, click the **Print** button.

6 If you are directed to create an electronic printout, click the **FILE tab**, on the left click **Export**, and then on the right, click **Create PDF/XPS**. In the **Publish as PDF or XPS** dialog box, navigate to your storage location, in the **Save as type** box, be sure **PDF** is indicated, and then click **Publish** to create the PDF file.

Activity 1.16 | Printing a Section of the Worksheet

From Backstage view, you can print only the portion of the worksheet that you select, and there are times you might want to do this.

1 Select the range **A2:F5** to select only the subtitle and the data for *Exercise Bikes* and *Elliptical Machines* and the column titles

2 Press Ctrl + F2 to display **Print Preview**, and then under **Settings**, click the first arrow, which currently displays *Print Active Sheets*. On the list that displays, click **Print Selection**, and then compare your screen with Figure 1.36.

FIGURE 1.36

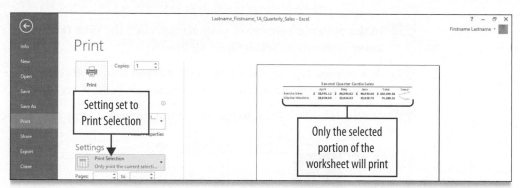

3 To print on paper or create an electronic printout, follow Steps 3-5; otherwise read through the steps and move to Step 6. To print on paper, if directed to do so by your instructor, click **Print**.

4 To create an electronic printout, if directed to do so by your instructor, complete this step and Step 5. On the left click **Export**, and then on the right, click **Create PDF/XPS**. In the **Publish as PDF or XPS** dialog box, navigate to your storage location, in the **Save as type** box, be sure **PDF** is indicated.

5 In the **File name**, to the end of the file name, add **_selection** In the lower right corner of the dialog box, click **Options**, and then under **Publish what**, click **Selection**. Click **OK**, and then click **Publish**.

6 Redisplay the workbook, press Ctrl + Home, and then click **Save** 🔲.

Activity 1.17 | Changing Page Orientation and Displaying, Printing, and Hiding Formulas

When you type a formula in a cell, the cell displays the *results* of the formula calculation. Recall that this value is called the displayed value. You can view and print the underlying formulas in the cells. When you do so, a formula often takes more horizontal space to display than the result of the calculation.

1 If necessary, redisplay your worksheet. Because you will make some temporary changes to your workbook, on the **Quick Access Toolbar**, click **Save** 🖫 to be sure your work is saved up to this point.

2 On the **FORMULAS tab**, in the **Formula Auditing group**, click **Show Formulas**.

🔁 **ANOTHER WAY**   Hold down Ctrl, and then press ~ (usually located below Esc).

3 In the **column heading area**, point to the **column A** heading to display the ↓ pointer, hold down the left mouse button, and then drag to the right to select columns **A:F**. Compare your screen with Figure 1.37.

FIGURE 1.37

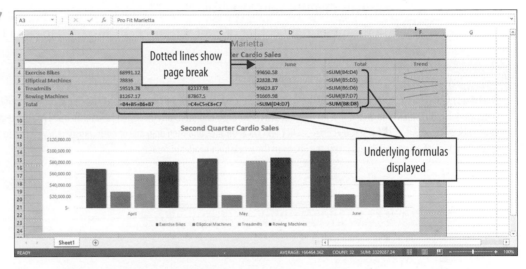

NOTE   **Turning the Display of Formulas On and Off**

The Show Formulas button is a toggle button. Clicking it once turns the display of formulas on—the button will be shaded. Clicking the button again turns the display of formulas off.

---

4 Point to the column heading boundary between any two of the selected columns to display the ↔ pointer, and then double-click to AutoFit the selected columns.

AutoFit adjusts the width of a column to fit the cell content of the *widest* cell in the column.

🔁 **ANOTHER WAY**   With the columns selected, on the HOME tab, in the Cells group, click Format, and then click AutoFit Column Width.

5 On the **PAGE LAYOUT tab**, in the **Page Setup group**, click **Orientation**, and then click **Landscape**. In the **Scale to Fit** group, click the **Width arrow**, and then click **1 page** to scale the data to fit onto one page.

Scaling shrinks the width or height of the printed worksheet to fit a maximum number of pages, and is convenient for printing formulas. Although it is not always the case, formulas frequently take up more space than the actual data.

🔁 **ANOTHER WAY**   In the Scale to Fit group, click the Dialog Box Launcher button to display the Page tab of the Page Setup dialog box. Then, under Scaling, click the Fit to option button.

6 In the **Page Setup group**, click **Margins**, click **Custom Margins**, and then on the **Margins tab**, under **Center on page**, be sure the **Horizontally** check box is selected—select it if necessary.

7 Click **OK** to close the dialog box. Check to be sure your chart is centered below the data and the left and right edges are slightly inside column A and column F—use the ⬚ pointer to drag a chart edge and then deselect the chart if necessary.

8 Click any cell so that the chart is not selected, and then press Ctrl + F2 to display the **Print Preview**. Under **Settings**, if necessary switch back to the option to **Print Active Sheets**. If directed to do so by your instructor, print on paper or click Save As and name the worksheet **Lastname_Firstname_1A_Quarterly_Sales_fomulas**

9 On the left, click **Close**, and when prompted, click **Don't Save** so that you do *not* save the changes you made—displaying formulas, changing column widths and orientation, and scaling—to print your formulas.

10 In the upper right corner of your screen, click **Close** ☒ to close Excel.

More Knowledge   **Inserting a Watermark**

Excel does not have a watermark feature like the watermark in Word, but there are two ways you can achieve the same effect. To use WordArt to mimic a watermark, on the INSERT tab, in the Text group, click Insert WordArt, and then click the style you want to use. Type the text and resize as necessary. Then, right-click the WordArt, click Format Text Effects, click Text Fill & Outline, and then drag one or both transparency sliders to the percentage you want. Or, simply create an image of a watermark and insert the image in the worksheet header or footer.

END | You have completed Project 1A

Objective	**Create** a Sales Report with an Embedded Column Chart Using the Excel Web App

If you are working on a computer that does not have Microsoft Office installed, you can still create new workbooks in your web browser by using the Excel Office Web App.

> **ALERT!** **Working with Web-Based Applications and Services**
>
> Computer programs and services on the web receive continuous updates and improvements, so the steps to complete this web-based activity may differ from the ones shown. You can often look at the screens and the information presented to determine how to complete the activity.

Activity | **Creating a Sales Report with Embedded Column Chart Using the Excel Web App**

In this activity, you will use the Excel Web App to create a sales report and chart similar to the one you created in Project 1A.

1 Start Excel, open a new blank workbook, and then if necessary, in the upper right corner, log into Office with your Microsoft account. In cell **A1**, type **Pro Fit Marietta** press Enter, and then click the **FILE tab**. On the left, click **Save As**, and then on the right, click the name of your SkyDrive—the path to your GO! Web Projects folder on the SkyDrive may display under Recent Folders and if so, you can click there.

2 In the **Save As** dialog box for your SkyDrive, if necessary open your **GO! Web Projects** folder, and then save the file as **Lastname_Firstname_EX_1A_Web** Close Excel, launch Internet Explorer, go to http://skydrive.com, sign in, and then from your **GO! Web Projects** folder, open the file you just saved there.

3 To help you create this project quickly and to eliminate extra typing, you will import the data from a Word table. From the taskbar, open **File Explorer**, navigate to the student data files that accompany this textbook, and then open the Word document **e01_1A_Web**. Press Ctrl + A to select all of the text, right-click anywhere over the

selection, and then click **Copy**. **Close** ☒ Word and **Close** ☒ File Explorer.

4 Click cell **A2**, on the Excel Web App ribbon, in the **Clipboard group**, click the upper portion of the **Paste** button; if necessary click **Allow access**. Notice that number symbols display when numeric data is too wide for the cell.

5 Select column headings **A:E**, point to the border between any two selected column headings to display the ⟷ pointer, and then double-click to resize all the columns to display all data.

6 Drag to select the range **A1:E1**, and then in the **Alignment group**, click **Merge & Center** ▦▾. Merge and center the worksheet's subtitle in the same manner. Select the range **A1:A2**, and then in the **Font group**, apply **Bold** B and change the **Font Color** A ▾ to **Dark Blue**.

7 Select the range **B4:E4**. In the **Number group**, click the **Number Format arrow**, and then click **Currency**. Apply the same format to the range **B8:E8**.

FIGURE A

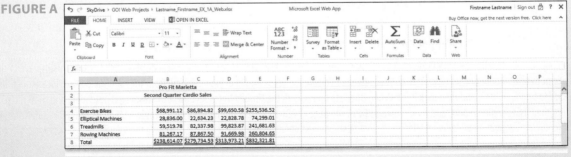

	A	B	C	D	E
1	Pro Fit Marietta				
2	Second Quarter Cardio Sales				
3					
4	Exercise Bikes	$68,991.12	$86,894.82	$99,650.58	$255,536.52
5	Elliptical Machines	28,836.00	22,634.23	22,828.78	74,299.01
6	Treadmills	59,519.78	82,337.98	99,823.87	241,681.63
7	Rowing Machines	81,267.17	87,867.50	91,669.98	260,804.65
8	Total	$238,614.07	$279,734.53	$313,973.21	$832,321.81

(GO! with Office Web Apps continues on the next page)

8 Select the range **B7:E7**, and then in the **Font group**, click **Underline** $\underline{\text{U}}$ ▾. Select the range **B8:E8**, and then in the **Font group** click **Double Underline**. Click any empty cell, and then compare your screen with Figure A.

9 Click cell **B3**, type **April** and press ⏎, and then click the cell **B3** again. Drag the fill handle to select cells **C3:D3** to complete the series. In cell **E3** type **Total** Select these four column titles and apply **Center** ▤ and **Bold** **B**.

10 Select the range **A3:D7**—the data without the totals. On the **INSERT tab**, in the **Charts group**, click **Column**, and then click the first chart type—**Clustered Column**. In the **Data group**, click **Switch Row/Column**.

11 Drag the chart so that the upper left corner of the chart is inside the upper left portion of cell **A9**. From

the **Labels group**, add a **Chart Title** in the **Above Chart** position with the text **2nd Quarter Cardio Sales**

12 Click cell **A1**, and then compare your screen with Figure B.

In the Excel Web App, you do not have the same set of features available that you have in the full version of Office; for example, you do not have Cell Styles, sparklines, and chart styles. But you can still create the data and chart in a meaningful way.

13 If you are instructed to submit your file, use one of the methods outlined in the Note box below. Then, on the ribbon, click the **FILE tab** and click **Exit**. In the Excel Web App, there is no Save button because your workbook is being saved automatically. Sign out of your SkyDrive and close Internet Explorer.

FIGURE B

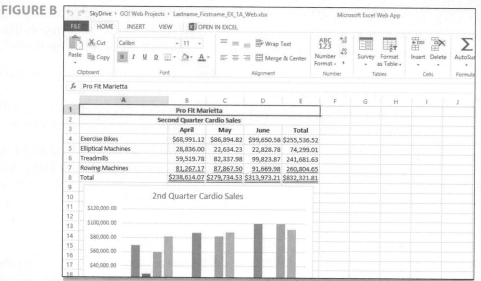

Inventory Valuation

PROJECT ACTIVITIES

In Activities 1.18 through 1.27 you will create a workbook for Josh Feingold, Operations Manager, which calculates the retail value of an inventory of plyometric training products. Your completed worksheet will look similar to Figure 1.38.

PROJECT FILES

For Project 1B, you will need the following file:

New blank Excel workbook

You will save your workbook as:

Lastname_Firstname_1B_Plyo_Products

PROJECT RESULTS

Pro Fit Marietta
Plyometric Products Inventory Valuation
As of September 30

	Warehouse Location	Quantity in Stock	Retail Price	Total Retail Value	Percent of Total Retail Value
Power Hurdle	Atlanta	125	$ 32.95	$ 4,118.75	1.41%
Speed Hurdle	Atlanta	995	59.95	59,650.25	20.37%
Stackable Steps	Marietta	450	251.59	113,215.50	38.65%
Pro Jump Rope	Marietta	1,105	49.95	55,194.75	18.84%
Plyometric Box Set	Marietta	255	158.05	40,302.75	13.76%
Plyometric Mat	Atlanta	215	94.99	20,422.85	6.97%
Total Retail Value for All Products				$ 292,904.85	

Lastname_Firstname_1B_Plyo_Products

FIGURE 1.38 Project 1B Inventory Valuation

Video E1-7

In Excel, the spelling checker performs similarly to the other Microsoft Office programs.

Activity 1.18 | Checking Spelling in a Worksheet

1 ▶ **Start** Excel and display a new blank workbook. In cell **A1**, type **Pro Fit Marietta** and press Enter. In cell **A2**, type **Plyometric Products Inventory** and press Enter.

2 ▶ Press F12 to display the **Save As** dialog box, and then navigate to your **Excel Chapter 1** folder. As the **File name**, using your own name, type **Lastname_Firstname_1B_Plyo_Products** and then click **Save**.

3 ▶ Press Tab to move to cell **B3**, type **Quantity** and press Tab. In cell **C3**, type **Average Cost** and press Tab. In cell **D3**, type **Retail Price** and press Tab.

4 ▶ Click cell **C3**, and then look at the **Formula Bar**. Notice that in the cell, the displayed value is cut off; however, in the **Formula Bar**, the entire text value—the underlying value—displays. Compare your screen with Figure 1.39.

> Text that is too long to fit in a cell extends into cells on the right only if they are empty. If the cell to the right contains data, the text in the cell to the left is truncated—cut off. The entire value continues to exist, but is not completely visible.

FIGURE 1.39

Entire contents of C3 display in Formula Bar

Cell C3 active; text cut off

5 ▶ Click cell **E3**, type **Total Retail Value** and press Tab. In cell **F3**, type **Percent of Total Retail Value** and press Enter.

6 ▶ Click cell **A4**. *Without* correcting the spelling error, type **Powr Hurdle** and then press Enter. In the range **A5:A10**, type the remaining row titles shown below. Then compare your screen with Figure 1.40.

Speed Hurdle
Stackable Steps
Pro Jump Rope
Plyometric Box Set
Plyometric Mat
Total Retail Value for All Products

FIGURE 1.40

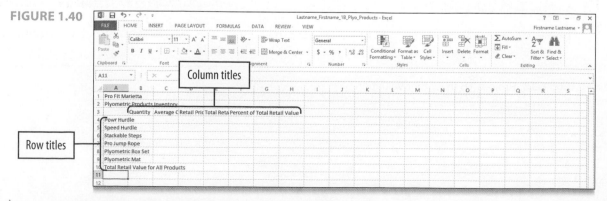

Column titles

Row titles

7 In the **column heading area**, point to the right boundary of **column A** to display the ✛ pointer, and then drag to the right to widen **column A** to **215** pixels.

8 Select the range **A1:F1**, **Merge & Center** the text, and then from the **Cell Styles** gallery, apply the **Title** style.

9 Select the range **A2:F2**, **Merge & Center** the text, and then from the **Cell Styles** gallery, apply the **Heading 1** style. Press [Ctrl] + [Home] to move to the top of your worksheet.

10 With cell **A1** as the active cell, click the **REVIEW tab**, and then in the **Proofing group**, click **Spelling**. Compare your screen with Figure 1.41.

FIGURE 1.41

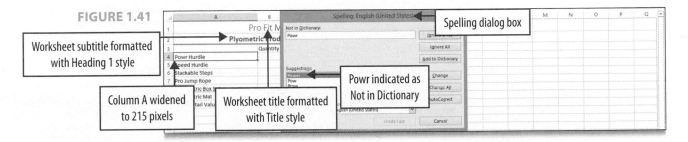

Worksheet subtitle formatted with Heading 1 style

Spelling dialog box

Column A widened to 215 pixels

Worksheet title formatted with Title style

Powr indicated as Not in Dictionary

ANOTHER WAY   Press [F7], which is the keyboard shortcut for the Spelling command.

---

11 In the **Spelling** dialog box, under **Not in Dictionary**, notice the word *Powr*.

The spelling tool does not have this word in its dictionary. Under *Suggestions*, Excel provides a list of suggested spellings.

12 Under **Suggestions**, click **Power**, and then click **Change**.

Powr, a typing error, is changed to *Power*. A message box displays *Spell check complete. You're good to go!*—unless you have additional unrecognized words. Because the spelling check begins its checking process starting with the currently selected cell, it is good practice to return to cell A1 before starting the Spelling command.

13 Correct any other errors you may have made. When the message displays, *Spell check complete. You're good to go!*, click **OK**. **Save** 💾 your workbook.

Objective 8   Enter Data by Range

Video E1-8

You can enter data by first selecting a range of cells. This is a time-saving technique, especially if you use the numeric keypad to enter the numbers.

Activity 1.19 | Entering Data by Range

1 Select the range **B4:D9**, type **125** and then press [Enter].

The value displays in cell B4, and cell B5 becomes the active cell.

2 With cell **B5** active in the range, and pressing [Enter] after each entry, type the following, and then compare your screen with Figure 1.42:

1125
450
1105
255
215

After you enter the last value and press [Enter], the active cell moves to the top of the next column within the selected range. Although it is not required to enter data in this manner, you can see that selecting the range before you enter data saves time because it confines the movement of the active cell to the selected range. When you select a range of data, the Quick Analysis button displays.

FIGURE 1.42

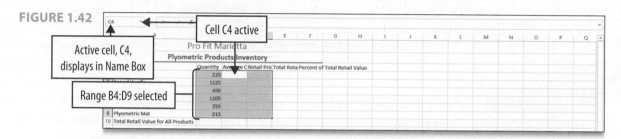

3 With the selected range still active, from the following table, beginning in cell **C4** and pressing [Enter] after each entry, enter the data for the **Average Cost** column and then the **Retail Price** column. If you prefer, deselect the range to enter the values—typing in a selected range is optional.

AVERAGE COST	RETAIL PRICE
15.50	32.95
29.55	59.95
125.95	251.59
18.75	49.95
85.25	159.05
49.95	94.99

Recall that the default number format for cells is the *General* number format, in which numbers display exactly as you type them and trailing zeros do not display, even if you type them.

4 Click any blank cell, and then compare your screen with Figure 1.43. Correct any errors you may have made while entering data, and then click **Save** [💾].

FIGURE 1.43

Objective 9 | Construct Formulas for Mathematical Operations

Video E1-9

Operators are symbols with which you can specify the type of calculation you want to perform in a formula.

Activity 1.20 | Using Arithmetic Operators

1 Click cell **E4**, type **=b4*d4** and notice that the two cells are outlined as part of an active formula. Then press Enter.

> The *Total Retail Value* of all *Power Hurdle* items in inventory—*4118.75*—equals the *Quantity* (125) times the *Retail Price* (selling price) of 32.95. In Excel, the asterisk (*) indicates multiplication.

2 Take a moment to study the symbols you will use to perform basic mathematical operations in Excel as shown in the table in Figure 1.44, which are referred to as **arithmetic operators**.

FIGURE 1.44

SYMBOLS USED IN EXCEL FOR ARITHMETIC OPERATORS	
OPERATOR SYMBOL	**OPERATION**
+	Addition
–	Subtraction (also negation)
*	Multiplication
/	Division
%	Percent
^	Exponentiation

3 Click cell **E4**.

> You can see that in cells E5:E9, you need a formula similar to the one in E4, but one that refers to the cells in row 5, row 6, and so forth. Recall that you can copy formulas and the cell references will change *relative to* the row number.

4 With cell **E4** selected, position your pointer over the fill handle in the lower right corner of the cell until the ➕ pointer displays. Then, drag down through cell **E9** to copy the formula.

5 Select the range **B4:B9**, and then on the **HOME tab**, in the **Number group**, click **Comma Style** ,. In the **Number group**, click **Decrease Decimal** two times to remove the decimal places from these values.

> Comma Style formats a number with two decimal places; because these are whole numbers referring to quantities, no decimal places are necessary.

ANOTHER WAY Select the range, display the Cell Styles gallery, and then under Number Format, click Comma [0].

6 Select the range **E4:E9**, and then at the bottom of your screen, in the status bar, notice the displayed values for **Average**, **Count**, and **Sum**—*50158.89167, 6* and *300953.35*.

> When you select a range of numerical data, Excel's *AutoCalculate* feature displays three calculations in the status bar by default—Average, Count, and Sum. Here, Excel indicates that if you averaged the selected values, the result would be *50158.89167*, there are 6 cells in the selection that contain values, and that if you added the values the result would be *300953.35*.

> You can display three additional calculations to this area by right-clicking the status bar and selecting them—Numerical Count, Minimum, and Maximum.

Activity 1.21 | Using the Quick Analysis Tool

Recall that the Quick Analysis button displays when you select a range of data. Quick Analysis is convenient because it keeps common commands close to your mouse pointer and also displays commands in a format that is easy to touch with your finger if you are using a touchscreen device.

1 In the lower right corner of the selected range, click **Quick Analysis** 📊, and then in the displayed gallery, click **TOTALS**. *Point to*, but do not click, the first **Sum** button, which shows blue cells at the bottom. Compare your screen with Figure 1.45.

Here, the shaded cells on the button indicate what will be summed and where the result will display, and a preview of the result displays in the cell bordered with a gray shadow.

FIGURE 1.45

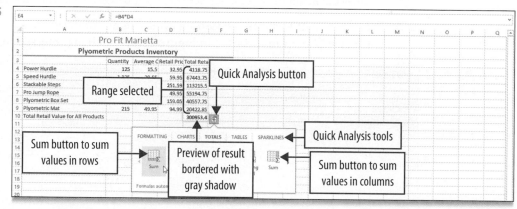

2 Click the first **Sum** button to display the column total *300953.4* formatted in Bold.

Sums calculated using the Quick Analysis tool are formatted in Bold.

3 Select the range **C5:E9** and apply the **Comma Style** �’; notice that Excel widens the columns to accommodate the data.

4 Select the range **C4:E4**, hold down Ctrl, and then click cell **E10**. Release Ctrl, and then apply the **Accounting Number Format** $ ▾. Notice that Excel widens the columns as necessary.

5 Click cell **E10**, and then in the **Cell Styles** gallery, apply the **Total** style. Click any blank cell, **Save** 💾 your workbook, and then compare your screen with Figure 1.46.

FIGURE 1.46

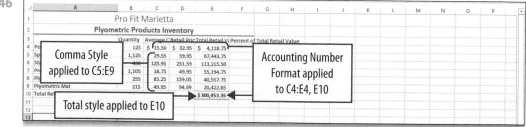

Activity 1.22 | Copying Formulas Containing Absolute Cell References

In a formula, a relative cell reference refers to a cell by its position *relative to* the cell that contains the formula. An **absolute cell reference**, on the other hand, refers to a cell by its *fixed* position in the worksheet, for example, the total in cell E10.

A relative cell reference automatically adjusts when a formula is copied. In some calculations, you do *not* want the cell reference to adjust; rather, you want the cell reference to remain the same when the formula is copied.

1 Click cell **F4**, type **=** and then click cell **E4**. Type **/** and then click cell **E10**.

The formula =E4/E10 indicates that the value in cell E4 will be *divided* by the value in cell E10. Why? Because Mr. Feingold wants to know the percentage by which each product's Total Retail Value makes up the Total Retail Value for All Products.

Arithmetically, the percentage is computed by dividing the *Total Retail Value* for each product by the *Total Retail Value for All Products*. The result will be a percentage expressed as a decimal.

2 Press Enter. Click cell **F4** and notice that the formula displays in the **Formula Bar**. Then, point to cell **F4** and double-click.

The formula, with the two referenced cells displayed in color and bordered with the same color, displays in the cell. This feature, called the *range finder*, is useful for verifying formulas because it visually indicates which workbook cells are included in a formula calculation.

3 Press Enter to redisplay the result of the calculation in the cell, and notice that .013686, which is approximately 1% of the total retail value of the inventory, is made up of Power Hurdles.

4 Click cell **F4** again, and then drag the fill handle down through cell **F9**. Compare your screen with Figure 1.47.

Each cell displays an error message—*#DIV/0!* and a green triangle in the upper left corner of each cell indicates that Excel detects an error.

Like a grammar checker, Excel uses rules to check for formula errors and flags errors in this manner. Additionally, the Auto Fill Options button displays, from which you can select formatting options for the copied cells.

FIGURE 1.47

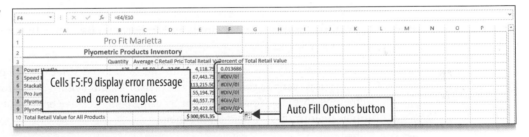

5 Click cell **F5**, and to the left of the cell, point to the **Error Checking** button ⬦ ▾ to display its ScreenTip—*The formula or function used is dividing by zero or empty cells.*

In this manner, Excel suggests the cause of an error.

6 Look at the **Formula Bar** and examine the formula.

The formula is =E5/E11. The cell reference to E5 is correct, but the cell reference following the division operator (/) is *E11*, and E11 is an *empty* cell.

7 Click cell **F6**, point to the **Error Checking** button ⬦ ▾, and in the **Formula Bar** examine the formula.

Because the cell references are relative, Excel builds the formulas by increasing the row number for each equation. But in this calculation, the divisor must always be the value in cell E10—the *Total Retail Value for All Products*.

8 Point to cell **F4**, and then double-click to place the insertion point within the cell.

9 Within the cell, use the arrow keys as necessary to position the insertion point to the left of *E10*, and then press F4. Compare your screen with Figure 1.48.

Dollar signs ($) display, which changes the reference to cell E10 to an absolute cell reference. The use of the dollar sign to denote an absolute reference is not related in any way to whether or not the values you are working with are currency values. It is simply the symbol that Excel uses to denote an absolute cell reference.

FIGURE 1.48

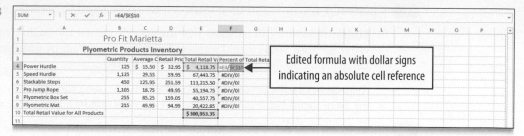
Edited formula with dollar signs indicating an absolute cell reference

ANOTHER WAY   Edit the formula so that it indicates =E4/$E$10.

10 On the **Formula Bar**, click **Enter** ✓ so that **F4** remains the active cell. Then, drag the fill handle to copy the new formula down through cell **F9**. Compare your screen with Figure 1.49.

FIGURE 1.49

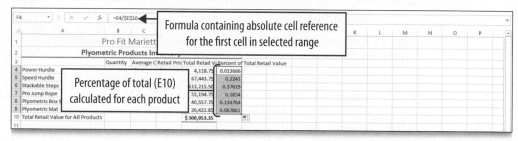
Formula containing absolute cell reference for the first cell in selected range

Percentage of total (E10) calculated for each product

11 Click cell **F5**, examine the formula in the **Formula Bar**, and then examine the formulas for cells **F6**, **F7**, **F8**, and **F9**.

For each formula, the cell reference for the *Total Retail Value* of each product changed relative to its row; however, the value used as the divisor—*Total Retail Value for All Products* in cell E10—remained absolute. You can see that by using either relative or absolute cell references, it is easy to duplicate formulas without typing them.

12 Save 🖫 your workbook.

More Knowledge   **Calculate a Percentage if You Know the Total and the Amount**

Using the equation *amount/total = percentage*, you can calculate the percentage by which a part makes up a total—with the percentage formatted as a decimal. For example, if on a test you score 42 points correctly out of 50, your percentage of correct answers is 42/50 = 0.84 or 84%.

Objective 10   Edit Values in a Worksheet

Video E1-10

Excel performs calculations on numbers; that is why you use Excel. If you make changes to the numbers, Excel automatically *re*-calculates the results. This is one of the most powerful and valuable features of Excel.

Activity 1.23   Editing Values in a Worksheet

You can edit text and number values directly within a cell or in the Formula Bar.

86   **Excel** | Chapter 1: CREATING A WORKSHEET AND CHARTING DATA

1 In cell **E10**, notice the column total *$300,953.35*. Then, click cell **B5**, and to change its value type **995** Watch cell **E5** and press [Enter].

> Excel formulas *re-calculate* if you change the value in a cell that is referenced in a formula. It is not necessary to delete the old value in a cell; selecting the cell and typing a new value replaces the old value with your new typing.

> The *Total Retail Value* of all *Speed Hurdle* items recalculates to *59,650.25* and the total in cell E10 recalculates to *$293,159.85*. Additionally, all of the percentages in column F recalculate.

2 Point to cell **D8**, and then double-click to place the insertion point within the cell. Use the arrow keys to move the insertion point to left or right of 9, and use either [Del] or [Backspace] to delete 9 and then type **8** so that the new Retail Price is *158.05*.

3 Watch cell **E8** and **E10** as you press [Enter], and then notice the recalculation of the formulas in those two cells.

> Excel recalculates the value in cell E8 to *40,302.75* and the value in cell E10 to *$292,904.85*. Additionally, all of the percentages in column F recalculate because the *Total Retail Value for All Products* recalculated.

4 Point to cell **A2** so that the ✛ pointer is positioned slightly to the right of the word *Inventory*, and then double-click to place the insertion point in the cell. Edit the text to add the word **Valuation** pressing [Spacebar] as necessary, and then press [Enter].

5 Click cell **B3**, and then in the **Formula Bar**, click to place the insertion point after the letter *y*. Press [Spacebar] one time, type **in Stock** and then on the **Formula Bar**, click **Enter** ✓. Click **Save** 🖫, and then compare your screen with Figure 1.50.

> Recall that if text is too long to fit in the cell and the cell to the right contains data, the text is truncated—cut off—but the entire value still exists as the underlying value.

FIGURE 1.50

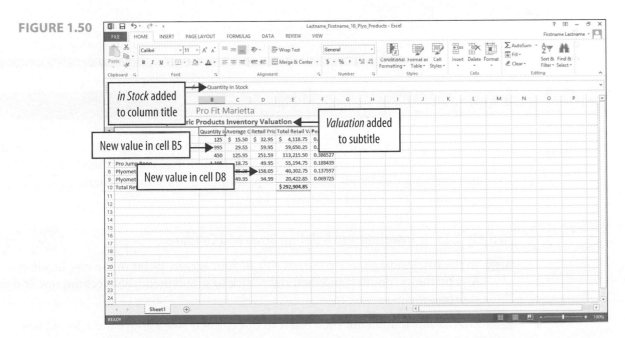

Activity 1.24 | Formatting Cells with the Percent Style

A percentage is part of a whole expressed in hundredths. For example, 75 cents is the same as 75 percent of one dollar. The Percent Style button formats the selected cell as a percentage rounded to the nearest hundredth.

1 ▶ Click cell **F4**, and then in the **Number group**, click **Percent Style** 🔲.

Your result is 1%, which is *0.014062* rounded to the nearest hundredth and expressed as a percentage. Percent Style displays the value of a cell as a percentage.

2 ▶ Select the range **F4:F9**, right-click over the selection, and then on the mini toolbar, click **Percent Style** 🔲, click **Increase Decimal** 🔲 two times, and then click **Center** 🔲.

Percent Style may not offer a percentage precise enough to analyze important financial information—adding additional decimal places to a percentage makes data more precise.

3 ▶ Click any cell to cancel the selection, **Save** 🔲 your workbook, and then compare your screen with Figure 1.51.

FIGURE 1.51

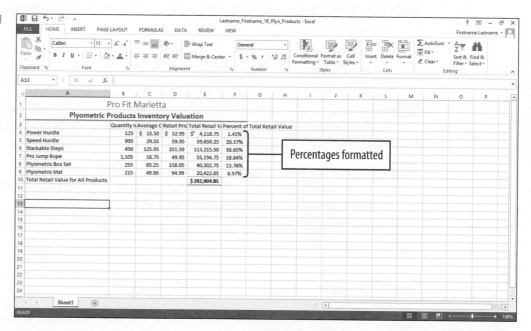

Objective 11 Format a Worksheet

Video E1-11

Formatting refers to the process of specifying the appearance of cells and the overall layout of your worksheet. Formatting is accomplished through various commands on the ribbon, for example, applying Cell Styles, and also from commands on shortcut menus, using keyboard shortcuts, and in the Format Cells dialog box.

Activity 1.25 │ Inserting and Deleting Rows and Columns

1 ▶ In the **row heading area** on the left side of your screen, point to the row heading for **row 3** to display the ➡ pointer, and then right-click to simultaneously select the row and display a shortcut menu.

2 ▶ On the shortcut menu, click **Insert** to insert a new **row 3** above the selected row.

The rows below the new row 3 move down one row, and the Insert Options button displays. By default, the new row uses the formatting of the row *above*.

 **ANOTHER WAY**   Select the row, on the Home tab, in the Cells group, click the Insert button arrow, and then click Insert Sheet Rows. Or, select the row and click the Insert button—the default setting of the button inserts a new sheet row above the selected row.

3 Click cell **E11**. On the **Formula Bar**, notice that the range changed to sum the new range **E5:E10**. Compare your screen with Figure 1.52.

> If you move formulas by inserting additional rows or columns in your worksheet, Excel automatically adjusts the formulas. Excel adjusted all of the formulas in the worksheet that were affected by inserting this new row.

FIGURE 1.52

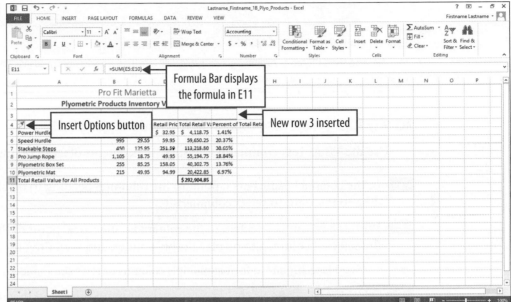

4 Click cell **A3**, type **As of September 30** and then on the **Formula Bar**, click **Enter** ✓ to maintain **A3** as the active cell. **Merge & Center** the text across the range **A3:F3**, and then apply the **Heading 2** cell style.

5 In the **column heading area**, point to **column B** to display the ↓ pointer, right-click, and then click **Insert**.

> A column is inserted to the left of column B. By default, the new column uses the formatting of the column to the *left*.

 ANOTHER WAY   Select the column, on the Home tab, in the Cells group, click the Insert button arrow, and then click Insert Sheet Columns. Or, select the column and click the Insert button—the default setting of the button inserts a new sheet column to the right of the selected column.

6 Click cell **B4**, type **Warehouse Location** and then press Enter.

7 In cell **B5**, type **Atlanta** and then type **Atlanta** again in cells **B6** and **B10**. Use AutoComplete to speed your typing by pressing Enter as soon as the AutoComplete suggestion displays. In cells **B7**, **B8**, and **B9**, type **Marietta**

8 In the **column heading area**, point to **column D**, right-click, and then click **Delete**.

> The remaining columns shift to the left, and Excel adjusts all the formulas in the worksheet accordingly. You can use a similar technique to delete a row in a worksheet.

9 Compare your screen with Figure 1.53, and then **Save** 🖫 your workbook.

FIGURE 1.53

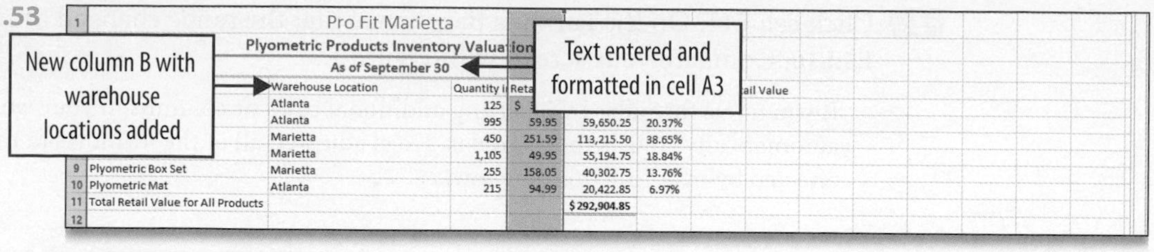

	Pro Fit Marietta				
1	Plyometric Products Inventory Valuation				
	As of September 30				
	Warehouse Location	Quantity i	Reta		ail Value
	Atlanta	125	$		
	Atlanta	995	59.95	59,650.25	20.37%
	Marietta	450	251.59	113,215.50	38.65%
	Marietta	1,105	49.95	55,194.75	18.84%
9 Plyometric Box Set	Marietta	255	158.05	40,302.75	13.76%
10 Plyometric Mat	Atlanta	215	94.99	20,422.85	6.97%
11 Total Retail Value for All Products				$ 292,904.85	
12					

New column B with warehouse locations added

Text entered and formatted in cell A3

More Knowledge — **Hiding Rows and Columns**

To hide a row or column from view, select the row or column, right-click, and then click Hide. A border displays to indicate that data is hidden from view. To unhide, select the rows above and below—or the adjacent columns—right-click, and then click Unhide.

Activity 1.26 | Adjusting Column Widths and Wrapping Text

Use the Wrap Text command to display the contents of a cell on multiple lines.

1 In the **column heading area**, point to the **column B** heading to display the ↓ pointer, and then drag to the right to select **columns B:F**.

2 With the columns selected, in the **column heading area**, point to the right boundary of any of the selected columns to display the ┿ pointer, and then drag to set the width to **95 pixels**.

Use this technique to format multiple columns or rows simultaneously.

3 Select the range **B4:F4** that comprises the column titles, and then on the **HOME tab**, in the **Alignment group**, click **Wrap Text** . Notice that the row height adjusts to display the titles on multiple lines.

4 With the range **B4:F4** still selected, in the **Alignment group**, click **Center** and **Middle Align** . With the range **B4:F4** still selected, apply the **Heading 4** cell style.

The Middle Align command aligns text so that it is centered between the top and bottom of the cell.

5 Select the range **B5:B10**, right-click, and then on the mini toolbar, click **Center** . Click cell **A11**, and then from the **Cell Styles** gallery, under **Themed Cell Styles**, click **40% - Accent1**. **Save** your workbook.

Activity 1.27 | Changing Theme Colors

You can change only the Theme colors of a workbook—without changing the theme fonts or effects.

1 On the **PAGE LAYOUT tab**, in the **Themes group**, click the **Colors arrow**, and then click **Green** to change the theme color. Click any blank cell, and then compare your screen with Figure 1.54.

FIGURE 1.54

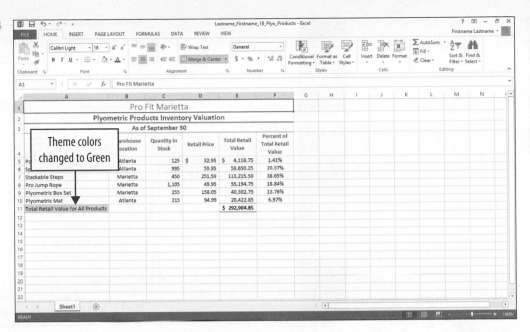

2 On the **PAGE LAYOUT tab**, in the **Page Setup group**, click **Margins**, and then click **Custom Margins**.

3 In the **Page Setup** dialog box, on the **Margins tab**, under **Center on page**, select the **Horizontally** check box.

This action will center the data and chart horizontally on the page, as shown in the Preview area.

4 In the displayed **Page Setup** dialog box, click the **Header/Footer tab**, and then in the center of the dialog box, click **Custom Footer**. In the **Footer** dialog box, with your insertion point blinking in the **Left section**, on the row of buttons, click **Insert File Name**.

&[File] displays in the Left section. Here you can type or insert information from the row of buttons into the left, middle, or right section of the footer. The Custom Header button displays a similar screen to enter information in the header of the worksheet.

5 Click **OK** two times.

6 Click the **FILE tab** to display **Backstage** view, and then in the lower right corner, click **Show All Properties**.

7 As the **Tags**, type **plyo products, inventory** and as the **Subject**, type your course name and section number. Be sure your name displays as the author.

8 On the left, click **Print** to view the **Print Preview**. At the bottom of the **Print Preview**, click **Next Page**, and notice that as currently formatted, the worksheet occupies two pages.

9 Under **Settings**, click **Portrait Orientation**, and then click **Landscape Orientation**. Compare your screen with Figure 1.55.

You can change the orientation on the Page Layout tab, or here, in Print Preview. Because it is in the Print Preview that you will often see adjustments that need to be made, commonly used settings display on the Print tab in Backstage view.

FIGURE 1.55

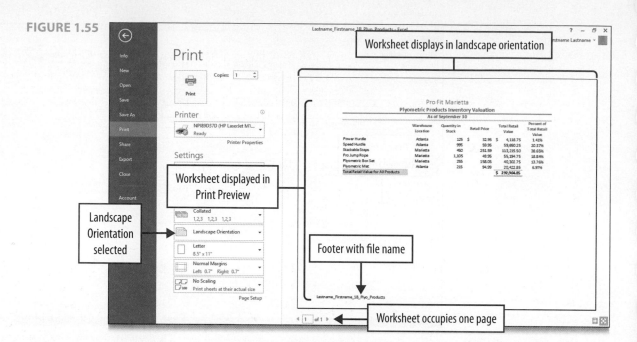

10 By using the techniques you practiced in Project 1A, print or submit electronically as directed by your instructor. If required by your instructor, print or create an electronic version of your worksheet with formulas displayed.

11 Close your workbook and Close Excel.

END | You have completed Project 1B

Objective Calculate the Value of an Inventory in the Excel Web App

If you are working on a computer that does not have Microsoft Office installed, you can still create new workbooks in your web browser by using the Excel Office Web App.

ALERT! **Working with Web-Based Applications and Services**

Computer programs and services on the web receive continuous updates and improvements, so the steps to complete this web-based activity may differ from the ones shown. You can often look at the screens and the information presented to determine how to complete the activity.

Activity | Creating an Inventory Valuation Report in the Excel Web App

In this activity, you will use the Excel Web App to create an inventory valuation similar to the one you created in Project 1B.

1 From the desktop, start Internet Explorer. Navigate to **http://skydrive.com**, and then sign in to your Microsoft account. Open your **GO! Web Projects** folder—or create and then open this folder if necessary.

2 Near the top of the screen, click **Create**, and then click **Excel workbook**. Using your own name, as the file name type **Lastname_Firstname_EX_1B_Web** and then click **Create**.

3 To help you create this project quickly and to eliminate extra typing, you will import the data from a Word table. From the taskbar, open **File Explorer**, navigate to the student data files that accompany this textbook, and then open the Word document **e01_1B_Web**. Press Ctrl + A to select all of the text, right-click anywhere over the selection, and then click **Copy**. **Close** Word and File Explorer.

4 With cell **A1** selected, on the Excel Web App ribbon, in the **Clipboard group**, click the upper portion of the **Paste** button; if necessary click **Allow access**.

5 Select column headings **A:D**, point to the border between any two selected column headings to display the pointer, and then double-click to resize the selected columns to display all the data.

6 In cell **E3** type **Total Retail Value** and press Enter. Select the range **B3:E3**, and then in the **Alignment group**, click **Center**, **Middle Align**, and **Wrap Text**. Widen **column E** so that *Total Retail* is on one line and *Value* is on the second line.

7 Click cell **E4** and type **=c4*d4** to create the formula and press Enter; your result is *4118.75*. Click cell **E4** again, and then drag the fill handle down through cell **E9** to calculate each row. Compare your screen with Figure A.

FIGURE A

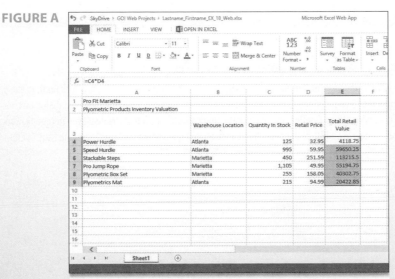

(GO! with Office Web Apps continues on the next page)

8 Click cell **E10**, and then in the **Formulas group**, click **AutoSum** and press [Enter] to total the column.

9 In cell **F3** type **Percent of Total Retail Value** and then apply **Center** ☰, **Middle Align** ☰, and **Wrap Text** 📄. Widen the column to display the column title on three lines. In cell **F4** type the formula to calculate the percent of total value **=e4/e10** and press [Enter], and then copy the formula down through cell **F9**. With the range **F4:F9** still selected, from the **Number Format arrow**, click **Percentage**.

10 Select the range **E4:E10** and then from the **Number Format arrow**, apply **Currency** format. Click cell **E9**, and then in the **Font group**, click **Underline**. Click cell **E10**, and then in the **Font group**, click **Double Underline**.

11 Select the range **A1:F1**, and then in the **Alignment group**, click **Merge & Center**. Merge and center the worksheet's subtitle in the same

manner. Select the range **A1:A2**, and then in the **Font group**, apply **Bold** 🅱 and change the **Font Color** 🅰 ▾ to **Orange, Darker 50%**.

12 Click cell **B3**, and then adjust the width of **column B** so that the column title displays on two lines. Click cell **C3** and adjust in the same manner.

13 In cell **A10** type **Total Retail Value for All Products** and then AutoFit **column A**.

14 Click cell **A1**, and then compare your screen with Figure B.

15 If you are instructed to submit your file, use one of the methods outlined in the Note box below. Then, on the ribbon, click the **FILE tab** and click **Exit**. Recall that in the Excel Web App, there is no Save button because your workbook is being saved automatically. Sign out of your SkyDrive and close Internet Explorer.

FIGURE B

EXCEL

Andrew Rodriguez / Fotolia; FotolEdhar/ Fotolia; apops/ Fotolia; Yuri Arcurs/ Fotolia

In every job, you must work and communicate with other people. A group of workers tasked with working together to solve a problem, make a decision, or create a work product is referred to as a *team*. For a team to succeed, the team members must be able to communicate with one another easily.

If all the team members work at the same location and work the same hours, communication is easy. You schedule face-to-face meetings and exchange documents and information among yourselves. But that is a rare arrangement in today's organizations. Rather, it is more likely that the members of your team work in different locations—even different countries—and work different hours or travel extensively away from the headquarters location. Also, for specific projects, teams are frequently organized across different departments of an organization or even across different organizations entirely. Then when the project is complete, the team disbands.

Collaboration is when you work together with others as a team in an intellectual endeavor to complete a shared task or achieve a shared goal; for example, when you and one or more of your classmates work together on a class project. Collaboration involves giving feedback to and receiving feedback from others on the team, and then revising the strategies to achieve the goal or produce the work product based on the feedback.

Microsoft Office 365 is a set of secure online services that enable people in an organization to communicate and collaborate by using any Internet-connected device—a computer, a tablet, or a mobile phone. Because Office 365 offers access from anywhere to email, Web conferencing, documents, and calendars, everyone on a team can work together easily. Office 365 is intended for use by multiple users in an organization and is offered on a monthly subscription basis to organizations starting as low as $6 per month per user.

Activity | Using the Exchange Online Outlook Meeting Tool to Collaborate

This team project relates to the **Bell Orchid Hotels**. If your instructor assigns this project to your class, in this chapter you can expect to use the **Outlook Meeting tool** in **Office 365 Exchange Online** to collaborate on the following tasks for this chapter:

- If you are in the **Accounting Group**, you and your teammates will meet virtually to plan a workbook to summarize hotel rooms sold over a four-week period in April.
- If you are in the **Engineering Group**, you and your teammates will meet virtually to plan a workbook summarizing Maintenance Expenses for the first quarter.
- If you are in the **Food and Beverage Group**, you and your teammates will meet virtually to plan a Menu Analysis workbook to analyze the profitability of the ten most popular entrees in the hotel's restaurant.
- If you are in the **Human Resources Group**, you and your teammates will meet virtually to plan a Salary Analysis workbook summarizing the pay of salaried employees over the first six months of operation.
- If you are in the **Operations Group**, you and your teammates will meet virtually to plan a workbook for Rooms and Housekeeping Service Analysis that will be used to determine ongoing needs for housekeeping service.
- If you are in the **Sales and Marking Group**, you and your teammates will meet virtually to plan a Rooms Sold Analysis workbook summarizing rooms sold by four salespersons during January-June that will be used to develop a marketing plan for the rest of the year.

FIGURE A

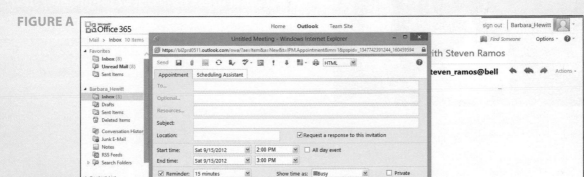

END OF CHAPTER

SUMMARY

In Excel, you work with worksheets that are contained in a workbook. A worksheet is formatted as a pattern of uniformly spaced horizontal rows and vertical columns, the intersection of which forms a cell.

A cell can contain a constant value—referred to as a value—or a formula, which is an equation that performs mathematical calculations on the values in your worksheet. Common values are text and numbers.

You can insert sparklines in an Excel worksheet, which are tiny charts embedded in a cell that give a visual trend summary alongside your data. A sparkline makes a pattern more obvious to the eye.

Charts provide a graphic representation of data in a worksheet. Use the Recommended Charts feature to display customized charts that, according to Excel's calculations, will best represent your data.

GO! LEARN IT ONLINE

Review the concepts and key terms in this chapter by completing these online challenges, which you can find at **www.pearsonhighered.com/go**.

Matching and Multiple Choice:
Answer matching and multiple choice questions to test what you learned in this chapter. MyITLab®

Crossword Puzzle:
Spell out the words that match the numbered clues, and put them in the puzzle squares.

Flipboard:
Flip through the definitions of the key terms in this chapter and match them with the correct term.

GO! FOR JOB SUCCESS

Video: Dress to Impress

Your instructor may assign this video to your class, and then ask you to think about, or discuss with your classmates, these questions:

FotolEdhar / Fotolia

If you were interviewing people for your company, what would you look for in terms of their dress and personal presentation?

What might you want to change about your personal dress for work or for an interview?

Do you feel that it's right to "judge a book by its cover"? Why or why not?

END OF CHAPTER
REVIEW AND ASSESSMENT GUIDE FOR EXCEL CHAPTER 1

Your instructor may assign one or more of these projects to help you review the chapter and assess your mastery and understanding of the chapter.

	Review and Assessment Guide for Excel Chapter 1		
Project	**Apply Skills from These Chapter Objectives**	**Project Type**	**Project Location**
1C	Objectives 1–6 from Project 1A	**1C Skills Review** A guided review of the skills from Project 1A.	On the following pages
1D	Objectives 7–11 from Project 1B	**1D Skills Review** A guided review of the skills from Project 1B.	On the following pages
1E	Objectives 1–6 from Project 1A	**1E Mastery (Grader Project)** A demonstration of your mastery of the skills in Project 2A with extensive decision making.	In MyITLab and on the following pages
1F	Objectives 7–11 from Project 1B	**1F Mastery (Grader Project)** A demonstration of your mastery of the skills in Project 1B with extensive decision making.	In MyITLab and on the following pages
1G	Objectives 1–11 from Projects 1A and 1B	**1G Mastery (Grader Project)** A demonstration of your mastery of the skills in Projects 1A and 1B with extensive decision making.	In MyITLab and on the following pages
1H	Combination of Objectives from Projects 1A and 1B	**1H GO! Fix It** A demonstration of your mastery of the skills in Projects 1A and 1B by creating a correct result from a document that contains errors you must find.	Online
1I	Combination of Objectives from Projects 1A and 1B	**1I GO! Make It** A demonstration of your mastery of the skills in Projects 1A and 1B by creating a result from a supplied picture.	Online
1J	Combination of Objectives from Projects 1A and 1B	**1J GO! Solve It** A demonstration of your mastery of the skills in Projects 1A and 1B, your decision-making skills, and your critical thinking skills. A task-specific rubric helps you self-assess your result.	Online
1K	Combination of Objectives from Projects 1A and 1B	**1K GO! Solve It** A demonstration of your mastery of the skills in Projects 1A and 1B, your decision-making skills, and your critical thinking skills. A task-specific rubric helps you self-assess your result.	On the following pages
1L	Combination of Objectives from Projects 1A and 1B	**1L GO! Think** A demonstration of your understanding of the chapter concepts applied in a manner that you would outside of college. An analytic rubric helps you and your instructor grade the quality of your work by comparing it to the work an expert in the discipline would create.	On the following pages
1M	Combination of Objectives from Projects 1A and 1B	**1M GO! Think** A demonstration of your understanding of the chapter concepts applied in a manner that you would outside of college. An analytic rubric helps you and your instructor grade the quality of your work by comparing it to the work an expert in the discipline would create.	Online
1N	Combination of Objectives from Projects 1A and 1B	**1N You and GO!** A demonstration of your understanding of the chapter concepts applied in a manner that you would in a personal situation. An analytic rubric helps you and your instructor grade the quality of your work.	Online
1O	Combination of Objectives from Projects 1A and 1B	**1O Cumulative Group Project for Excel Chapter 1** A demonstration of your understanding of concepts and your ability to work collaboratively in a group role-playing assessment, requiring both collaboration and self-management.	Online

GLOSSARY

Absolute cell reference A cell reference that refers to cells by their fixed position in a worksheet; an absolute cell reference remains the same when the formula is copied.

Accounting Number Format The Excel number format that applies a thousand comma separator where appropriate, inserts a fixed U.S. dollar sign aligned at the left edge of the cell, applies two decimal places, and leaves a small amount of space at the right edge of the cell to accommodate a parenthesis for negative numbers.

Active cell The cell, surrounded by a black border, ready to receive data or be affected by the next Excel command.

Arithmetic operators The symbols +, −, *, /, %, and ^ used to denote addition, subtraction (or negation), multiplication, division, percentage, and exponentiation in an Excel formula.

Auto Fill An Excel feature that generates and extends values into adjacent cells based on the values of selected cells.

AutoCalculate A feature that displays three calculations in the status bar by default—Average, Count, and Sum—when you select a range of numerical data.

AutoComplete A feature that speeds your typing and lessens the likelihood of errors; if the first few characters you type in a cell match an existing entry in the column, Excel fills in the remaining characters for you.

AutoFit An Excel feature that adjusts the width of a column to fit the cell content of the widest cell in the column.

AutoSum A button that provides quick access to the SUM function.

Category axis The area along the bottom of a chart that identifies the categories of data; also referred to as the x-axis.

Category labels The labels that display along the bottom of a chart to identify the categories of data; Excel uses the row titles as the category names.

Cell The intersection of a column and a row.

Cell address Another name for a cell reference.

Cell content Anything typed into a cell.

Cell reference The identification of a specific cell by its intersecting column letter and row number.

Cell style A defined set of formatting characteristics, such as font, font size, font color, cell borders, and cell shading.

Chart The graphic representation of data in a worksheet; data presented as a chart is usually easier to understand than a table of numbers.

Chart Elements button A button that enables you to add, remove, or change chart elements such as the title, legend, gridlines, and data labels.

Chart Filters button A button that enables you to change which data displays in the chart.

Chart layout The combination of chart elements that can be displayed in a chart such as a title, legend, labels for the columns, and the table of charted cells.

Chart style The overall visual look of a chart in terms of its graphic effects, colors, and backgrounds; for example, you can have flat or beveled columns, colors that are solid or transparent, and backgrounds that are dark or light.

Chart Styles button A button that enables you to set a style and color scheme for your chart.

Chart Styles gallery A group of predesigned chart styles that you can apply to an Excel chart.

Chart types Various chart formats used in a way that is meaningful to the reader; common examples are column charts, pie charts, and line charts.

Column A vertical group of cells in a worksheet.

Column chart A chart in which the data is arranged in columns and that is useful for showing how data changes over a period of time or for illustrating comparisons among items.

Column heading The letter that displays at the top of a vertical group of cells in a worksheet; beginning with the first letter of the alphabet, a unique letter or combination of letters identifies each column.

Comma Style The Excel number format that inserts thousand comma separators where appropriate and applies two decimal places; Comma Style also leaves space at the right to accommodate a parenthesis when negative numbers are present.

Constant value Numbers, text, dates, or times of day that you type into a cell.

Context sensitive A command associated with the currently selected or active object; often activated by right-clicking a screen item.

Data Text or numbers in a cell.

Data marker A column, bar, area, dot, pie slice, or other symbol in a chart that represents a single data point; related data points form a data series.

Data point A value that originates in a worksheet cell and that is represented in a chart by a data marker.

Data series Related data points represented by data markers; each data series has a unique color or pattern represented in the chart legend.

Displayed value The data that displays in a cell.

Excel pointer An Excel window element with which you can display the location of the pointer.

Expand Formula Bar button An Excel window element with which you can increase the height of the Formula Bar to display lengthy cell content.

Expand horizontal scroll bar button An Excel window element with which you can increase the width of the horizontal scroll bar.

Fill handle The small black square in the lower right corner of a selected cell.

Format Changing the appearance of cells and worksheet elements to make a worksheet attractive and easy to read.

Formula An equation that performs mathematical calculations on values in a worksheet.

Formula Bar An element in the Excel window that displays the value or formula contained in the active cell; here you can also enter or edit values or formulas.

Function A predefined formula—a formula that Excel has already built for you—that performs calculations by using specific values in a particular order.

General format The default format that Excel applies to numbers; this format has no specific characteristics—whatever you type in the cell will display, with the exception that trailing zeros to the right of a decimal point will not display.

Label Another name for a text value, and which usually provides information about number values.

Left alignment The cell format in which characters align at the left edge of the cell; this is the default for text entries and is an example of formatting information stored in a cell.

Legend A chart element that identifies the patterns or colors that are assigned to the categories in the chart.

Lettered column headings The area along the top edge of a worksheet that identifies each column with a unique letter or combination of letters.

Merge & Center A command that joins selected cells in an Excel worksheet into one larger cell and centers the contents in the merged cell.

Name Box An element of the Excel window that displays the name of the selected cell, table, chart, or object.

Normal view A screen view that maximizes the number of cells visible on your screen and keeps the column letters and row numbers close to the columns and rows.

Number format A specific way in which Excel displays numbers in a cell.

Number values Constant values consisting of only numbers.

Numbered row headings The area along the left edge of a worksheet that identifies each row with a unique number.

Operators The symbols with which you can specify the type of calculation you want to perform in an Excel formula.

Page Layout view A screen view in which you can use the rulers to measure the width and height of data, set margins for printing, hide or display the numbered row headings and the lettered column headings, and change the page orientation; this view is useful for preparing your worksheet for printing.

Picture element A point of light measured in dots per square inch on a screen; 64 pixels equals 8.43 characters, which is the average number of characters that will fit in a cell in an Excel worksheet using the default font.

Pixel The abbreviated name for a picture element.

Point and click method The technique of constructing a formula by pointing to and then clicking cells; this method

is convenient when the referenced cells are not adjacent to one another.

Quick Analysis tool A tool that displays in the lower right corner of a selected range with which you can analyze your data by using Excel tools such as charts, color-coding, and formulas.

Range Two or more selected cells on a worksheet that are adjacent or nonadjacent; because the range is treated as a single unit, you can make the same changes or combination of changes to more than one cell at a time.

Range finder An Excel feature that outlines cells in color to indicate which cells are used in a formula; useful for verifying which cells are referenced in a formula.

Recommended Charts An Excel feature that displays a customized set of charts that, according to Excel's calculations, will best fit your data based on the range of data that you select.

Relative cell reference In a formula, the address of a cell based on the relative positions of the cell that contains the formula and the cell referred to in the formula.

Rounding A procedure in which you determine which digit at the right of the number will be the last digit displayed and then increase it by one if the next digit to its right is 5, 6, 7, 8, or 9.

Row A horizontal group of cells in a worksheet.

Row heading The numbers along the left side of an Excel worksheet that designate the row numbers.

Scaling The process of shrinking the width and/or height of printed output to fit a maximum number of pages.

Select All box A box in the upper left corner of the worksheet grid that, when clicked, selects all the cells in a worksheet.

Series A group of things that come one after another in succession; for example, January, February, March, and so on.

Sheet tab scrolling buttons Buttons to the left of the sheet tabs used to display Excel sheet tabs that are not in view; used when there are more sheet tabs than will display in the space provided.

Sheet tabs The labels along the lower border of the Excel window that identify each worksheet.

Show Formulas A command that displays the formula in each cell instead of the resulting value.

Sparkline A tiny chart in the background of a cell that gives a visual trend summary alongside your data; makes a pattern more obvious.

Spreadsheet Another name for a worksheet.

Status bar The area along the lower edge of the Excel window that displays, on the left side, the current cell mode, page number, and worksheet information; on the right side, when numerical data is selected, common calculations such as Sum and Average display.

SUM function A predefined formula that adds all the numbers in a selected range of cells.

Switch Row/Column A charting command to swap the data over the axis— data being charted on the vertical axis will move to the horizontal axis and vice versa.

Text values Constant values consisting of only text, and which usually provide information about number values; also referred to as labels.

Theme A predefined set of colors, fonts, lines, and fill effects that coordinate with each other.

Underlying formula The formula entered in a cell and visible only on the Formula Bar.

Underlying value The data that displays in the Formula Bar.

Value Another name for a constant value.

Value axis A numerical scale on the left side of a chart that shows the range of numbers for the data points; also referred to as the Y-axis.

Workbook An Excel file that contains one or more worksheets.

Workbook-level buttons Buttons at the far right of the ribbon tabs that minimize or restore a displayed workbook.

Worksheet The primary document that you use in Excel to work with and store data, and which is formatted as a pattern of uniformly spaced horizontal and vertical lines.

Worksheet grid area A part of the Excel window that displays the columns and rows that intersect to form the worksheet's cells.

X-axis Another name for the horizontal (category) axis.

Y-axis Another name for the vertical (value) axis.

CHAPTER REVIEW

Apply 1A skills from these Objectives:

1 Create, Save, and Navigate an Excel Workbook

2 Enter Data in a Worksheet

3 Construct and Copy Formulas and Use the SUM Function

4 Format Cells with Merge & Center, Cell Styles, and Themes

5 Chart Data to Create a Column Chart and Insert Sparklines

6 Print a Worksheet, Display Formulas, and Close Excel

Skills Review | Project 1C Step Sales

In the following Skills Review, you will create a new Excel worksheet with a chart that summarizes the first quarter sales of fitness equipment for step training. Your completed worksheet will look similar to Figure 1.56.

PROJECT FILES

For Project 1C, you will need the following file:

New blank Excel workbook

You will save your workbook as:

Lastname_Firstname_1C_Step_Sales

PROJECT RESULTS

Build from Scratch

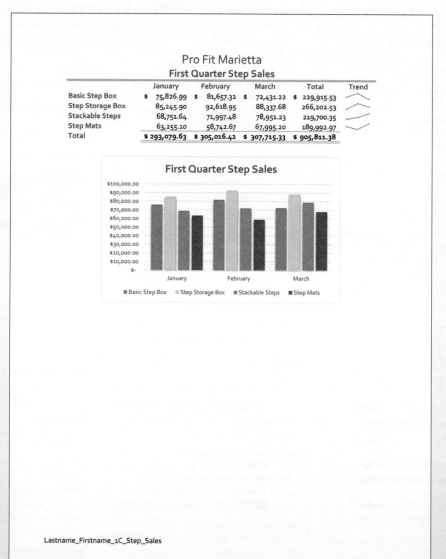

FIGURE 1.56

(Project 1C Step Sales continues on the next page)

CHAPTER REVIEW

1 **Start** Excel and open a new blank workbook. Click the **FILE tab** to display **Backstage** view, click **Save As**, and then navigate to your **Excel Chapter 1** folder. In the **File name** box, using your own name, type **Lastname_Firstname_1C_Step_Sales** and then press Enter.

a. With cell **A1** as the active cell, type the worksheet title **Pro Fit Marietta** and then press Enter. In cell **A2**, type the worksheet subtitle **First Quarter Step Sales** and then press Enter.

b. Leave row 3 blank, click in cell **A4**, type **Basic Step Box** and then press Enter. In cell **A5**, type **Step Storage Box** and then press Enter. In cell **A6**, type **Stackable Steps** and then press Enter. In cell **A7**, type **Step Mats** and then press Enter. In cell **A8**, type **Total** and then press Enter.

c. Click cell **B3**. Type **January** and then in the **Formula Bar**, click **Enter** to keep cell **B3** the active cell. With **B3** as the active cell, point to the **fill handle** in the lower right corner of the selected cell, drag to the right to cell **D3**, and then release the mouse button to enter the text *February* and *March*.

d. Press Ctrl + Home to make cell **A1** the active cell. In the **column heading area**, point to the vertical line between **column A** and **column B** to display the ⊞ pointer, hold down the left mouse button, and drag to the right to increase the column width to **130 pixels**.

e. Point to cell **B3**, and then drag across to select cells **B3** and **C3** and **D3**. With the range **B3:D3** selected, point anywhere over the selected range, right-click, and then on the mini toolbar, click **Center**.

f. Click cell **B4**, type **75826.99** and press Tab to make cell **C4** active. Enter the remaining values, as shown below in **Table 1**, pressing Tab to move across the rows and Enter to move down the columns.

TABLE 1

	January	February	March
Basic Step Box	75826.99	81657.32	72431.22
Step Storage Rack	85245.90	92618.95	88337.68
Stackable Steps	68751.64	71997.48	78951.23
Step Mats	63255.10	58742.67	67995.20

2 Click cell **B8** to make it the active cell and type **=**

a. At the insertion point, type **b4** and then type **+** Type **b5** and then type **+b6+b7** Press Enter. Your result is *293079.6*.

b. Click in cell **C8**. Type **=** and then click cell **C4**. Type **+** and then click cell **C5**. Repeat this process to complete the formula to add cells **C6** and **C7** to the formula, and then press Enter. Your result is *305016.4*.

c. Click cell **D8**. On the **HOME tab**, in the **Editing group**, click **AutoSum**, and then press Enter to construct a formula by using the SUM function. Your result is *307715.3*.

d. In cell **E3** type **Total** and press Enter. With cell **E4** as the active cell, hold down Alt, and then press =. On the **Formula Bar**, click **Enter** to display the result and keep cell **E4** active.

e. With cell **E4** active, point to the **fill handle** in the lower right corner of the cell. Drag down through cell **E8**, and then release the mouse button to copy the formula with relative cell references down to sum each row.

3 Click cell **F3**. Type **Trend** and then press Enter.

a. Select the range **A1:F1**, and then on the **HOME tab**, in the **Alignment group**, click **Merge & Center**. Select the range **A2:F2** and **Merge & Center** the selection.

b. Click cell **A1**. In the **Styles group**, click **Cell Styles**. Under **Titles and Headings**, click **Title**. Click cell **A2**, display the **Cell Styles** gallery, and then click **Heading 1**.

c. Select the range **B3:F3**, hold down Ctrl, and then select the range **A4:A8**. From the **Cell Styles** gallery, click **Heading 4** to apply this cell style to the column and row titles.

d. Select the range **B4:E4**, hold down Ctrl, and then select the range **B8:E8**. On the **HOME tab**, in the **Number group**, click **Accounting Number Format**. Select the range **B5:E7**, and then in the **Number group**, click **Comma Style**. Select the range **B8:E8**. From the **Styles group**, display the **Cell Styles** gallery, and then under **Titles and Headings**, click **Total**.

e. On the ribbon, click the **PAGE LAYOUT tab**, and then in the **Themes group**, click **Themes** to display the **Themes** gallery. Click the **Basis** theme. (This theme widens the columns slightly). On the **Quick Access Toolbar**, click **Save**.

(Project 1C Step Sales continues on the next page)

CHAPTER REVIEW

4 Select the range **A3:D7**, which includes the row titles, the column titles and the data without the totals. Click the **INSERT tab**, and then in the **Charts group**, click **Recommended Charts**. In the **Insert Chart** dialog box, scroll down and click the fifth recommended chart—a **Clustered Column** chart in which *each month* displays its *sales for each type of step training equipment*. Click **OK**.

a. In the chart, click anywhere in the text *Chart Title* to select the text box. Watch the **Formula Bar** as you type **First** and then let AutoComplete complete the title by pressing Enter.

b. Click in a white area just slightly *inside* the chart border to deselect the chart title but keep the chart selected. To the right of the chart, click the second button—the **Chart Styles** button. Be sure the **STYLE** tab is selected. Use the scroll bar to scroll down, and then by using the ScreenTips, locate and click **Style 6**.

c. At the top of the gallery, click **COLOR**. Under **Colorful**, point to the fourth row of colors to display the ScreenTip *Color 4*, and then click to apply the **Color 4** variation of the theme colors.

d. Point to the top border of the chart to display the pointer, and then drag the upper left corner of the chart just to the center of cell **A10** to visually center it below the data.

5 Select the range **B4:D7**. Click the **INSERT tab**, and then in the **Sparklines group**, click **Line**. In the **Create Sparklines** dialog box, in the **Location Range** box, type **f4:f7** and then click **OK** to insert the sparklines.

a. On the **DESIGN tab**, in the **Show group**, select the **Markers** check box to display markers in the sparklines.

b. On the **DESIGN tab**, in the **Style group**, click **More** and then in the second row, click the fourth style—**Sparkline Style Accent 4, Darker 25%**.

6 Click cell **A1** to deselect the chart. Click the **PAGE LAYOUT tab**, and then in the **Page Setup group**, click **Margins**. At the bottom, click **Custom Margins** to display the **Page Setup** dialog box, and then on the **Margins tab**, under **Center on page**, select the **Horizontally** check box.

a. In the dialog box, click the **Header/Footer tab**, and then click **Custom Footer**. With your insertion point in the **Left section**, click **Insert File Name**. Click **OK** two times.

b. Click the **FILE tab** to display **Backstage** view. In the lower right corner, click **Show All Properties**. As the **Tags**, type **step sales, 1st quarter** In the **Subject** box, type your course name and section number. Be sure your name displays as the Author—edit if necessary.

c. On the left, click **Save**.

d. Print or submit your workbook electronically as directed by your instructor. If required by your instructor, print or create an electronic version of your worksheet with formulas displayed by using the instructions in Project 1A. **Close** Excel without saving so that you do not save the changes you made to print formulas.

END | You have completed Project 1C

CHAPTER REVIEW

Apply 1B skills from these Objectives:

7 Check Spelling in a Worksheet
8 Enter Data by Range
9 Construct Formulas for Mathematical Operations
10 Edit Values in a Worksheet
11 Format a Worksheet

Skills Review Project 1D Band and Tubing Inventory

In the following Skills Review, you will create a worksheet that summarizes the inventory of band and tubing exercise equipment. Your completed worksheet will look similar to Figure 1.57.

Build from Scratch

PROJECT FILES

For Project 1D, you will need the following file:

New blank Excel workbook

You will save your workbook as:

Lastname_Firstname_1D_Band_Inventory

PROJECT RESULTS

Pro Fit Marietta

Band and Tubing Inventory

As of June 30

	Material	Quantity in Stock	Retail Price	Total Retail Value	Percent of Total Retail Value
Super Strength Bands	Latex	225	$ 48.98	$ 11,020.50	25.16%
Medium Tubing	Rubber	198	27.95	5,534.10	12.64%
Resistance Band, Average	Latex	165	42.95	7,086.75	16.18%
Mini Bands, Medium	Latex	245	25.95	6,357.75	14.52%
Mini Bands, Heavy	Rubber	175	32.95	5,766.25	13.17%
Heavy Tubing	Latex	187	42.95	8,031.65	18.34%
Total Retail Value for All Products				$ 43,797.00	

Lastname_Firstname_1D_Band_Inventory

FIGURE 1.57

(Project 1D Band and Tubing Inventory continues on the next page)

CHAPTER REVIEW

1 **Start** Excel and display a new blank workbook. **Save** the workbook in your **Excel Chapter 1** folder as **Lastname_Firstname_1D_Band_Inventory** In cell **A1** type **Pro Fit Marietta** and in cell **A2** type **Band and Tubing Inventory**

a. Click cell **B3**, type **Quantity in Stock** and press Tab. In cell **C3** type **Average Cost** and press Tab. In cell **D3**, type **Retail Price** and press Tab. In cell **E3**, type **Total Retail Value** and press Tab. In cell **F3** type **Percent of Total Retail Value** and press Enter.

b. Click cell **A4**, type **Super Strength Bands** and press Enter. In the range **A5:A10**, type the remaining row titles as shown below, including any misspelled words.

   Medium Tubing

   Resistnce Band, Average

   Mini Bands, Medium

   Mini Bands, Heavy

   Heavy Tubing

   Total Retail Value for All Products

c. Press Ctrl + Home to move to the top of your worksheet. On the **REVIEW tab**, in the **Proofing group**, click **Spelling**. Correct *Resistnce* to **Resistance** and any other spelling errors you may have made, and then when the message displays, *Spell check complete. You're good to go!* click **OK**.

d. In the **column heading area**, point to the right boundary of **column A** to display the ⊞ pointer, and then drag to the right to widen **column A** to **225 pixels**.

e. In the **column heading area**, point to the **column B** heading to display the ⬇ pointer, and then drag to the right to select **columns B:F**. With the columns selected, in the **column heading area**, point to the right boundary of any of the selected columns, and then drag to the right to set the width to **100 pixels**.

f. Select the range **A1:F1**. On the **HOME tab**, in the **Alignment group**, click **Merge & Center**, and then in the **Cell Styles** gallery, apply the **Title** style. Select the range **A2:F2**. **Merge & Center** the text across the selection, and then in the **Cell Styles** gallery, apply the **Heading 1** style.

2 On the **PAGE LAYOUT tab**, in the **Themes group**, change the **Colors** to **Blue Green**. Select the empty range **B4:D9**. With cell **B4** active in the range, type **225** and then press Enter.

a. With cell **B5** active in the range, and pressing Enter after each entry, type the following data in the *Quantity in Stock* column:

   198

   265

   245

   175

   187

b. With the selected range still active, from the following table, beginning in cell **C4** and pressing Enter after each entry, enter the following data for the **Average Cost** column and then the **Retail Price** column. If you prefer, type without selecting the range first; recall that this is optional.

Average Cost	Retail Price
22.75	48.98
15.95	27.95
26.90	42.95
12.95	25.95
18.75	32.95
26.90	42.95

3 In cell **E4**, type **=b4*d4** and then press Enter to construct a formula that calculates the *Total Retail Value* of the *Super Strength Bands* (Quantity in Stock × Retail Price).

a. Click cell **E4**, position your pointer over the fill handle, and then drag down through cell **E9** to copy the formula with relative cell references.

b. Select the range **B4:B9**, and then on the **HOME tab**, in the **Number group**, click **Comma Style**. Then, in the **Number group**, click **Decrease Decimal** two times to remove the decimal places from these non-currency values.

c. To calculate the *Total Retail Value for All Products*, select the range **E4:E9**, and then in the lower right corner of the selected range, click the **Quick Analysis** button 🔲.

(Project 1D Band and Tubing Inventory continues on the next page)

CHAPTER REVIEW

d. In the gallery, click **TOTALS**, and then click the *first* **Sum** button, which visually indicates that the column will be summed with a result at the bottom of the column.

e. Select the range **C5:E9** and apply the **Comma Style**. Select the range **C4:E4**, hold down Ctrl, and then click cell **E10**. With the nonadjacent cells selected, apply the **Accounting Number Format**. Click cell **E10**, and then from the **Cell Styles** gallery, apply the **Total** style.

f. Click cell **F4**, type = and then click cell **E4**. Type / and then click cell **E10**. Press F4 to make the reference to cell *E10* absolute, and then on the **Formula Bar**, click ✓ so that cell **F4** remains the active cell. Drag the **fill handle** to copy the formula down through cell **F9**.

g. Point to cell **B6**, and then double-click to place the insertion point within the cell. Use the arrow keys to move the insertion point to the left or right of *2*, and use either Delete or Backspace to delete *2*, and then type **1** and press Enter so that the new *Quantity in Stock* is *165*. Notice the recalculations in the worksheet.

4 Select the range **F4:F9**, right-click over the selection, and then on the mini toolbar, click **Percent Style**. Click **Increase Decimal** two times, and then **Center** the selection.

a. In the **row heading area** on the left side of your screen, point to **row 3** to display the ➡ pointer, and then right-click to simultaneously select the row and display a shortcut menu. On the shortcut menu, click **Insert** to insert a new **row 3**.

b. Click cell **A3**, type **As of June 30** and then on the **Formula Bar**, click ✓ to keep cell **A3** as the active cell. **Merge & Center** the text across the range **A3:F3**, and then apply the **Heading 2** cell style.

5 In the **column heading area**, point to **column B**. When the ⬇ pointer displays, right-click, and then click **Insert** to insert a new column.

a. Click cell **B4**, type **Material** and then press Enter. In cell **B5**, type **Latex** and then press Enter. In cell **B6**, type **Rubber** and then press Enter.

b. Using AutoComplete to speed your typing by pressing Enter as soon as the AutoComplete suggestion displays, in cells **B7**, **B8**, and **B10** type **Latex** and in cell **B9** type **Rubber**

c. In the **column heading area**, point to the right boundary of **column B**, and then drag to the left and set the width to **90 pixels**. In the **column heading area**, point to **column D**, right-click, and then click **Delete**.

d. Select the column titles in the range **B4:F4**, and then on the **HOME tab**, in the **Alignment group**, click **Wrap Text**, **Center**, and **Middle Align**. With the range still selected, apply the **Heading 4** cell style.

e. Click cell **A11**, and then in the **Cell Styles** gallery, under **Themed Cell Styles**, click **40% - Accent1**.

6 Click the **PAGE LAYOUT tab**, in the **Page Setup** group, click **Margins**, and then click **Custom Margins**. In the **Page Setup** dialog box, on the **Margins tab**, under **Center on page**, select the **Horizontally** check box.

a. Click the **Header/Footer tab**, and then click **Custom Footer**. With your insertion point in the **Left section**, click **Insert File Name**. Click **OK** two times.

b. In the **Page Setup group**, click **Orientation**, and then click **Landscape**.

c. Click the **FILE tab** to display **Backstage** view. In the lower right corner, click **Show All Properties**. As the **Tags**, type **bands, tubing, inventory** In the **Subject** box, type your course name and section number. Be sure your name displays as the author—edit if necessary.

d. On the left, click **Save** to be sure that you have saved your work up to this point.

e. Print or submit your workbook electronically as directed by your instructor. If required by your instructor, print or create an electronic version of your worksheet with formulas displayed by using the instructions in Project 1A. **Close** Excel without saving so that you do not save the changes you made to print formulas.

END | You have completed Project 1D

CONTENT-BASED ASSESSMENTS

Mastering Excel   Project 1E Gym Sales

In the following Mastering Excel project, you will create a worksheet comparing the sales of different types of home gym equipment sold in the second quarter. Your completed worksheet will look similar to Figure 1.58.

Apply 1A skills from these Objectives:

1 Create, Save, and Navigate an Excel Workbook

2 Enter Data in a Worksheet

3 Construct and Copy Formulas and Use the SUM Function

4 Format Cells with Merge & Center, Cell Styles, and Themes

5 Chart Data to Create a Column Chart and Insert Sparklines

6 Print a Worksheet, Display Formulas, and Close Excel

PROJECT FILES

For Project 1E, you will need the following files:

New blank Excel workbook

You will save your workbook as:

Lastname_Firstname_1E_Gym_Sales

PROJECT RESULTS

Build from Scratch

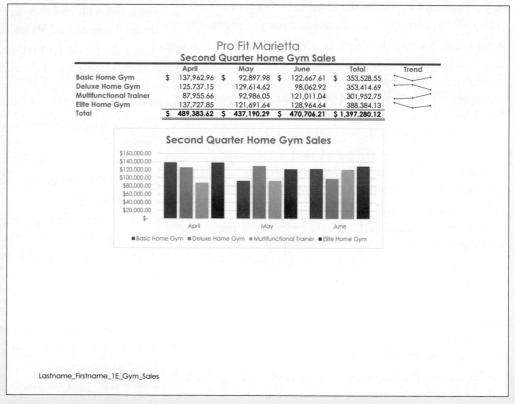

FIGURE 1.58

(Project 1E Gym Sales continues on the next page)

1 Start Excel and display a new blank workbook. In cell **A1**, type **Pro Fit Marietta** and in cell **A2**, type **Second Quarter Home Gym Sales** Change the **Theme** to **Wisp**, and then **Save** the workbook in your **Excel Chapter 1** folder as **Lastname_Firstname_1E_Gym_Sales**

2 In cell **B3**, type **April** and then fill the months *May* and *June* in the range **C3:D3**. In cell **E3**, type **Total** and in cell **F3**, type **Trend**

3 **Center** the column titles in the range **B3:F3**. **Merge & Center** the title across the range **A1:F1**, and apply the **Title** cell style. **Merge & Center** the subtitle across the range **A2:F2**, and then apply the **Heading 1** cell style.

4 Widen **column A** to **180 pixels**, and then in the range **A4:A8**, type the following row titles:

> **Basic Home Gym**
>
> **Deluxe Home Gym**
>
> **Multifunctional Trainer**
>
> **Elite Home Gym**
>
> **Total**

5 Widen columns **B:F** to **115 pixels**, and then in the range **B4:D7**, enter the monthly sales figures for each type of gym, as shown in the table below:

	April	May	June
Basic Home Gym	137962.96	92897.98	122667.61
Deluxe Home Gym	125737.15	129614.62	98062.92
Multifunctional Trainer	87955.66	92986.05	121011.04
Elite Home Gym	137727.85	121691.64	128964.64

6 Select the range that represents April sales, and then on the **HOME tab**, in the **Editing group**, click **AutoSum**. Copy the formula across to cells **C8:D8**. Select the range that represents the sales of the *Basic Home Gym*, and then on the **HOME tab**, in the **Editing group**, click **AutoSum**. Copy the formula down to cells **E5:E8**.

7 Apply the **Heading 4** cell style to the row titles and the column titles. Apply the **Total** cell style to the totals in the range **B8:E8**. Apply the **Accounting Number Format** to the first row of sales figures and to the total row. Apply the **Comma Style** to the remaining sales figures.

8 To compare the monthly sales of each product visually, select the range that represents the sales figures for the three months, including the month names and the product names—do not include any totals in the range. With this data selected, use **Recommended Charts** to insert a **Clustered Column** chart with the month names displayed on the category axis and the product names displayed in the legend.

9 Drag the center right sizing handle to widen the chart slightly so that all the legend items display on one line, and then position the chart so that it is visually centered below the data with its top edge aligned with the top edge of row 10 approximately as shown in Figure 1.58. Apply **Chart Style 6** and **Color 2** under **Colorful**. Change the **Chart Title** to **Second Quarter Home Gym Sales**

10 In the range **F4:F7**, insert **Line** sparklines that compare the monthly data. Do not include the totals. Show the sparkline **Markers** and apply **Sparkline Style Accent 2, Darker 50%**.

11 Center the worksheet **Horizontally** on the page, and then insert a **Footer** with the **File Name** in the **Left section**. Change the **Orientation** to **Landscape**. Display the document properties, and then as the **Tags** type **home gym, sales** As the **Subject**, type your course name and section number. Be sure your name displays as the author. Check your worksheet by previewing it in **Print Preview**, and then make any necessary corrections.

12 **Save** your workbook, and then print or submit electronically as directed. If required by your instructor, print or create an electronic version of your worksheet with formulas displayed by using the instructions in Project 1A. **Close** Excel without saving so that you do not save the changes you made to print formulas.

END | You have completed Project 1E

CONTENT-BASED ASSESSMENTS

MyITLab® grader

Mastering Excel | Project 1F Balance Sales

Apply 1B skills from these Objectives:

7 Check Spelling in a Worksheet
8 Enter Data by Range
9 Construct Formulas for Mathematical Operations
10 Edit Values in a Worksheet
11 Format a Worksheet

In the following Mastering Excel project, you will create a worksheet that summarizes the sales of balance and stabilization equipment that Pro Fit Marietta is marketing. Your completed worksheet will look similar to Figure 1.59.

PROJECT FILES

For Project 1F, you will need the following file:

New blank Excel workbook

You will save your workbook as:

Lastname_Firstname_1F_Balance_Sales

PROJECT RESULTS

Build from Scratch

Pro Fit Marietta

Balance and Stabilization Sales

Month Ending March 31

	Quantity Sold	Retail Price	Total Sales	Percent of Total Sales
Balance Pillow	275	$ 22.95	$ 6,311.25	5.43%
Slide Board	382	75.50	28,841.00	24.82%
Foam Roller	251	39.50	9,914.50	8.53%
Rebounder	162	139.95	22,671.90	19.51%
Stability Ball	380	51.50	19,570.00	16.84%
Balance Board	206	84.95	17,499.70	15.06%
Balance Pad	150	75.99	11,398.50	9.81%
Total Sales for All Products			$ 116,206.85	

Lastname_Firstname_1F_Balance_Sales

FIGURE 1.59

(Project 1F Balance Sales continues on the next page)

CONTENT-BASED ASSESSMENTS

1 Start Excel and display a new blank workbook. **Save** the workbook in your **Excel Chapter 1** folder as **Lastname_Firstname_1F_Balance_Sales** In cell **A1**, type **Pro Fit Marietta** In cell **A2**, type **Balance and Stabilization Sales** and then **Merge & Center** the title and the subtitle across **columns A:F**. Apply the **Title** and **Heading 1** cell styles respectively.

2 Beginning in cell **B3**, type the following column titles: **Product Number** and **Quantity Sold** and **Retail Price** and **Total Sales** and **Percent of Total Sales**

3 Beginning in cell **A4**, type the following row titles, including misspelled words:

> **Balance Pillow**
> **Silde Board**
> **Foam Roller**
> **Rebounder**
> **Stability Ball**
> **Balance Board**
> **Balance Pad**
> **Total Sales for All Products**

4 Make cell **A1** the active cell, and then check spelling in your worksheet. Correct *Silde* to **Slide**, and make any other necessary corrections. Widen **column A** to **180 pixels** and **columns B:F** to **95 pixels**.

5 In the range **B4:D10**, type the following data:

	Product Number	Quantity Sold	Retail Price
Balance Pillow	BP-3	275	22.95
Slide Board	SB-8	382	99.95
Foam Roller	FR-2	251	39.50
Rebounder	RB-4	162	139.95
Stability Ball	SB-5	380	51.50
Balance Board	BB-6	206	84.95
Balance Pad	BP-8	220	75.99

6 In cell **E4**, construct a formula to calculate the *Total Sales* of the *Balance Pillow* by multiplying the *Quantity Sold* times the *Retail Price*. Copy the formula down for the remaining products. Select the range **E4:E10**, and then use the **Quick Analysis tool** to **Sum** the *Total Sales for All Products*, which will be formatted in **Bold**. To the total in cell **E11**, apply the **Total** cell style.

7 Using absolute cell references as necessary so that you can copy the formula, in cell **F4**, construct a formula to calculate the *Percent of Total Sales* for the first product. Copy the formula down for the remaining products. To the computed percentages, apply **Percent Style** with two decimal places, and then **Center** the percentages.

8 Apply the **Comma Style** with no decimal places to the *Quantity Sold* figures. To cells **D4**, **E4**, and **E11** apply the **Accounting Number Format**. To the range **D5:E10**, apply the **Comma Style**.

9 Change the *Retail Price* of the *Slide Board* to **75.50** and the *Quantity Sold* of the *Balance Pad* to **150** Delete **column B**, and then **Insert** a new **row 3**. In cell **A3**, type **Month Ending March 31** and then **Merge & Center** the text across the range **A3:E3**. Apply the **Heading 2** cell style. To cell **A12**, apply the **20%-Accent1** cell style. Select the four column titles, apply **Wrap Text**, **Middle Align**, and **Center** formatting, and then apply the **Heading 3** cell style.

10 Center the worksheet **Horizontally** on the page, and then insert a **Footer** with the **File Name** in the **Left section**. Display the document properties, and then as the **Tags**, type **balance, stability, sales** In the **Subject** box, add your course name and section number. Be sure your name displays as the author.

11 **Save** your workbook, and then print or submit electronically as directed. If required by your instructor, print or create an electronic version of your worksheet with formulas displayed by using the instructions in Project 1A. **Close** Excel without saving so that you do not save the changes you made to print formulas.

END | You have completed Project 1F

CONTENT-BASED ASSESSMENTS

MyITLab®
grader

In the following Mastering Excel project, you will create a new worksheet that compares annual sales by region. Your completed worksheet will look similar to Figure 1.60.

Apply a combination of 1A and 1B skills:

1 Create, Save, and Navigate an Excel Workbook

2 Enter Data in a Worksheet

3 Construct and Copy Formulas and Use the SUM Function

4 Format Cells with Merge & Center, Cell Styles, and Themes

5 Chart Data to Create a Column Chart and Insert Sparklines

6 Print a Worksheet, Display Formulas, and Close Excel

7 Check Spelling in a Worksheet

8 Enter Data by Range

9 Construct Formulas for Mathematical Operations

10 Edit Values in a Worksheet

11 Format a Worksheet

PROJECT FILES

For Project 1G, you will need the following file:

New blank Excel workbook

You will save your workbook as:

Lastname_Firstname_1G_Regional_Sales

PROJECT RESULTS

Build from Scratch

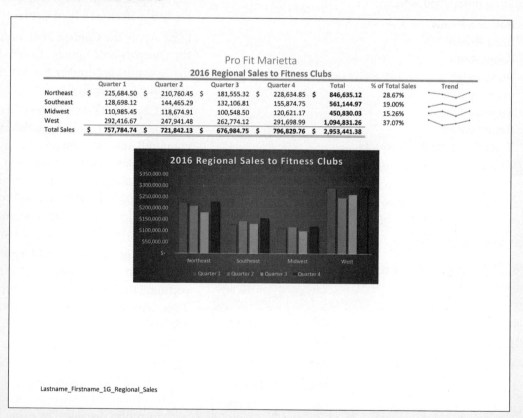

FIGURE 1.60

(Project 1G Regional Sales continues on the next page)

1 Start Excel and display a new blank workbook. Change the **Theme** to **Retrospect**. In cell **A1**, type **Pro Fit Marietta** In cell **A2**, type **2016 Regional Sales to Fitness Clubs** and then **Save** the workbook in your **Excel Chapter 1** folder as **Lastname_Firstname_1G_Regional_Sales**

2 In cell **B3**, type **Quarter 1** and fill *Quarter 2*, *Quarter 3*, and *Quarter 4* in the range **C3:E3**. In cell **F3**, type **Total** In cell **G3**, type **% of Total Sales** and in cell **H3**, type **Trend**

3 In the range **A4:A7**, type the following row titles: **Northeast** and **Southeast** and **West** and **Total Sales**

4 Set the width of **column A** to **80 pixels** and the width of columns **B:H** to **110 pixels**. **Merge & Center** the title across the range **A1:H1**, and then apply the **Title** cell style. **Merge & Center** the subtitle across the range **A2:H2**, and then apply the **Heading 1** cell style. Select the seven column titles, apply **Center** formatting, and then apply the **Heading 4** cell style.

5 In the range **B4:E6**, enter the sales values for each Quarter as shown below.

	Quarter 1	Quarter 2	Quarter 3	Quarter 4
Northeast	225684.50	210760.45	181555.32	228634.85
Southeast	128698.12	144465.29	132106.81	155874.75
West	292416.67	247941.48	262774.12	291698.99

6 By using the **Quick Analysis tool**, **Sum** the *Quarter 1* sales, and then copy the formula across for the remaining Quarters. By using the **Quick Analysis tool**, **Sum** the sales for the *Northeast* region, and then copy the formula down through cell **F7**. Recall that the **Quick Analysis tool** formats sums in **Bold**. Apply the **Accounting Number Format** to the first row of sales figures and to the total row, and apply the **Comma Style** to the remaining sales figures. Format the totals in **row 7** with the **Total** cell style.

7 Insert a new **row 6** with the row title **Midwest** and the following sales figures for each quarter: **110985.45**

and **118674.91** and **100548.50** and **120621.17** Copy the formula in cell **F5** down to cell **F6** to sum the new row.

8 Using absolute cell references as necessary so that you can copy the formula, in cell **G4** construct a formula to calculate the *Percent of Total Sales* for the first region. Copy the formula down for the remaining regions. To the computed percentages, apply **Percent Style** with two decimal places, and then **Center** the percentages.

9 Insert **Line** sparklines in the range **H4:H7** that compare the quarterly data. Do not include the totals. Show the sparkline **Markers** and apply the second style in the second row—**Sparkline Style Accent 2, Darker 25%**.

10 **Save** your workbook. To compare the quarterly sales of each region visually, select the range that represents the sales figures for the four quarters, including the quarter names and each region—do not include any totals in the range. With this data selected, by using **Recommended Charts**, insert a **Clustered Column** with the regions as the category axis and the Quarters as the legend.

11 Apply **Chart Style 8** and **Color 3** under **Colorful**. Position the top edge of the chart in **row 10** and visually center it below the worksheet data. Change the **Chart Title** to **2016 Regional Sales to Fitness Clubs**

12 Deselect the chart. Change the page **Orientation** to **Landscape**, center the worksheet **Horizontally** on the page, and then insert a footer with the file name in the Left section.

13 Show the document properties. As the **Tags**, type **fitness clubs, sales** In the **Subject** box, type your course name and section number. Be sure your name displays as the author.

14 **Save** your workbook, and then print or submit electronically as directed. If required by your instructor, print or create an electronic version of your worksheet with formulas displayed by using the instructions in Project 1A. **Close** Excel without saving so that you do not save the changes you made to print formulas.

END | You have completed Project 1G

CONTENT-BASED ASSESSMENTS

GO! Fix It	Project 1H Team Sales	Online

GO! Make It	Project 1I Agility Sales	Online

GO! Solve It	Project 1J Kettlebell Sales	Online

GO! Solve It	Project 1K Commission	

PROJECT FILES

For Project 1K, you will need the following file:

e01K_Commission

You will save your workbook as:

Lastname_Firstname_1K_Commission

Open the file **e01K_Commission** and save it as **Lastname_Firstname_1K_Commission** Complete the worksheet by using Auto Fill to complete the month headings, and then calculating the Total Commission for each month and for each region. Insert and format appropriate sparklines in the Trend column. Format the worksheet attractively with a title and subtitle, check spelling, adjust column width, and apply appropriate financial formatting. Insert a chart that compares the total sales commission for each region with the months displaying as the categories, and format the chart attractively. Include the file name in the footer, add appropriate properties, and submit as directed.

Performance Level

	Exemplary: You consistently applied the relevant skills	Proficient: You sometimes, but not always, applied the relevant skills	Developing: You rarely or never applied the relevant skills
Create formulas	All formulas are correct and are efficiently constructed.	Formulas are correct but not always constructed in the most efficient manner.	One or more formulas are missing or incorrect, or only numbers were entered.
Create a chart	Chart created properly.	Chart was created but incorrect data was selected.	No chart was created.
Insert and format sparklines	Sparklines inserted and formatted properly.	Sparklines were inserted but incorrect data was selected or sparklines were not formatted.	No sparklines were inserted.
Format attractively and appropriately	Formatting is attractive and appropriate.	Adequately formatted but difficult to read or unattractive.	Inadequate or no formatting.

Performance Criteria

END | You have completed Project 1K

OUTCOMES-BASED ASSESSMENTS

RUBRIC

The following outcomes-based assessments are *open-ended assessments*. That is, there is no specific correct result; your result will depend on your approach to the information provided. Make *Professional Quality* your goal. Use the following scoring rubric to guide you in *how* to approach the problem and then to evaluate *how well* your approach solves the problem.

The *criteria*—Software Mastery, Content, Format and Layout, and Process—represent the knowledge and skills you have gained that you can apply to solving the problem. The *levels of performance*—Professional Quality, Approaching Professional Quality, or Needs Quality Improvements—help you and your instructor evaluate your result.

	Your completed project is of Professional Quality if you:	Your completed project is Approaching Professional Quality if you:	Your completed project Needs Quality Improvements if you:
1-Software Mastery	Choose and apply the most appropriate skills, tools, and features and identify efficient methods to solve the problem.	Choose and apply some appropriate skills, tools, and features, but not in the most efficient manner.	Choose inappropriate skills, tools, or features, or are inefficient in solving the problem.
2-Content	Construct a solution that is clear and well organized, contains content that is accurate, appropriate to the audience and purpose, and is complete. Provide a solution that contains no errors in spelling, grammar, or style.	Construct a solution in which some components are unclear, poorly organized, inconsistent, or incomplete. Misjudge the needs of the audience. Have some errors in spelling, grammar, or style, but the errors do not detract from comprehension.	Construct a solution that is unclear, incomplete, or poorly organized; contains some inaccurate or inappropriate content; and contains many errors in spelling, grammar, or style. Do not solve the problem.
3-Format & Layout	Format and arrange all elements to communicate information and ideas, clarify function, illustrate relationships, and indicate relative importance.	Apply appropriate format and layout features to some elements, but not others. Overuse features, causing minor distraction.	Apply format and layout that does not communicate information or ideas clearly. Do not use format and layout features to clarify function, illustrate relationships, or indicate relative importance. Use available features excessively, causing distraction.
4-Process	Use an organized approach that integrates planning, development, self-assessment, revision, and reflection.	Demonstrate an organized approach in some areas, but not others; or, use an insufficient process of organization throughout.	Do not use an organized approach to solve the problem.

OUTCOMES-BASED ASSESSMENTS

GO! Think   Project 1L Video Sales

PROJECT FILES

For Project 1L, you will need the following file:

New blank Excel workbook

You will save your workbook as:

Lastname_Firstname_1L_Video_Sales

Michelle Barry, President of Pro Fit Marietta, needs a worksheet that summarizes the following data regarding the first quarter sales of training videos. Michelle would like the worksheet to include a calculation of the total sales for each type of video and a total of the sales of all of the videos. She would also like to know each type of video's percentage of total sales.

	Number Sold	Price
Pilates	156	29.99
Step	392	14.99
Weight Training	147	54.99
Kickboxing	282	29.99
Yoga	165	34.99

Create a worksheet that provides Michelle with the information needed. Include appropriate worksheet, column, and row titles. Using the formatting skills that you practiced in this chapter, format the worksheet in a manner that is professional and easy to read and understand. Insert a footer with the file name and add appropriate document properties. Save the file as **Lastname_Firstname_1L_Video_Sales** and print or submit as directed by your instructor.

END | You have completed Project 1L

Build from Scratch

GO! Think   Project 1M Planner   **Online**

Build from Scratch

You and GO!   Project 1N Personal Expenses   **Online**

GO! Cumulative Group Project   Project 1O Bell Orchid Hotels

Online

Using Functions, Creating Tables, and Managing Large Workbooks

2

PROJECT 2A

OUTCOMES

Analyze inventory by applying statistical and logical calculations to data and by sorting and filtering data.

PROJECT 2B

OUTCOMES

Summarize the data on multiple worksheets.

OBJECTIVES

1. Use Flash Fill and the SUM, AVERAGE, MEDIAN, MIN, and MAX Functions
2. Move Data, Resolve Error Messages, and Rotate Text
3. Use COUNTIF and IF Functions and Apply Conditional Formatting
4. Use Date & Time Functions and Freeze Panes
5. Create, Sort, and Filter an Excel Table
6. View, Format, and Print a Large Worksheet

OBJECTIVES

7. Navigate a Workbook and Rename Worksheets
8. Enter Dates, Clear Contents, and Clear Formats
9. Copy and Paste by Using the Paste Options Gallery
10. Edit and Format Multiple Worksheets at the Same Time
11. Create a Summary Sheet with Column Sparklines
12. Format and Print Multiple Worksheets in a Workbook

In This Chapter

In this chapter, you will use the Statistical functions to calculate the average of a group of numbers and use other Logical and Date & Time functions. Excel's statistical functions are useful for common calculations that you probably encounter frequently. You will also use Excel's new Flash Fill to automatically fill in values, use the counting functions, and apply different types of conditional formatting to make data easy to visualize. You will create a table to organize related information and analyze the table's information by sorting and filtering. You will summarize a workbook that contains multiple worksheets.

The projects in this chapter relate to **Rosedale Landscape and Garden**, which grows and sells trees and plants suitable for all areas of North America. Throughout its 75 year history, the company has introduced many new plants for the enjoyment of home gardeners. The company has nurseries and stores in the major metropolitan areas in the United States and Canada. In addition to high-quality plants and trees, Rosedale sells garden tools and outdoor furniture. Rosedale also offers professional landscape design and installation for both commercial and residential clients. The company headquarters is in Pasadena, California.

Inventory Status Report

PROJECT ACTIVITIES

In Activities 2.01 through 2.20 you will edit a worksheet for Holman Hill, President, detailing the current inventory of trees at the Pasadena nursery. Your completed worksheet will look similar to Figure 2.1.

PROJECT FILES

For Project 2A, you will need the following file:

e02A_Tree_Inventory

You will save your workbook as:

Lastname_Firstname_2A_Tree_Inventory

PROJECT RESULTS

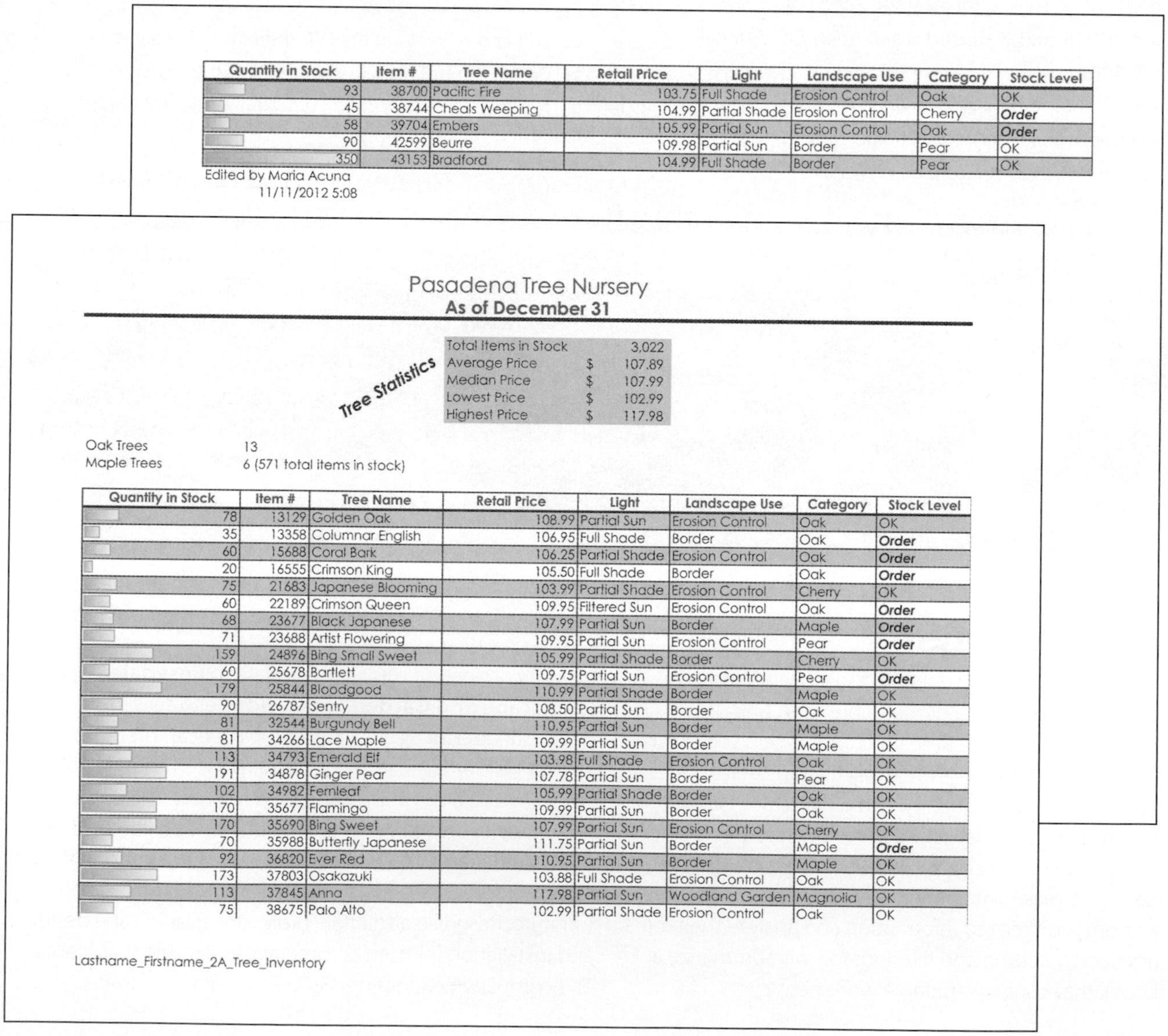

Quantity in Stock	Item #	Tree Name	Retail Price	Light	Landscape Use	Category	Stock Level
93	38700	Pacific Fire	103.75	Full Shade	Erosion Control	Oak	OK
45	38744	Cheals Weeping	104.99	Partial Shade	Erosion Control	Cherry	Order
58	39704	Embers	105.99	Partial Sun	Erosion Control	Oak	Order
90	42599	Beurre	109.98	Partial Sun	Border	Pear	OK
350	43153	Bradford	104.99	Full Shade	Border	Pear	OK

Edited by Maria Acuna
11/11/2012 5:08

Pasadena Tree Nursery
As of December 31

Tree Statistics		
Total Items in Stock		3,022
Average Price	$	107.89
Median Price	$	107.99
Lowest Price	$	102.99
Highest Price	$	117.98

Oak Trees   13
Maple Trees   6 (571 total items in stock)

Quantity in Stock	Item #	Tree Name	Retail Price	Light	Landscape Use	Category	Stock Level
78	13129	Golden Oak	108.99	Partial Sun	Erosion Control	Oak	OK
35	13358	Columnar English	106.95	Full Shade	Border	Oak	Order
60	15688	Coral Bark	106.25	Partial Shade	Erosion Control	Oak	Order
20	16555	Crimson King	105.50	Full Shade	Border	Oak	Order
75	21683	Japanese Blooming	103.99	Partial Shade	Erosion Control	Cherry	OK
60	22189	Crimson Queen	109.95	Filtered Sun	Erosion Control	Oak	Order
68	23677	Black Japanese	107.99	Partial Sun	Border	Maple	Order
71	23688	Artist Flowering	109.95	Partial Sun	Erosion Control	Pear	Order
159	24896	Bing Small Sweet	105.99	Partial Shade	Border	Cherry	OK
60	25678	Bartlett	109.75	Partial Sun	Erosion Control	Pear	Order
179	25844	Bloodgood	110.99	Partial Shade	Border	Maple	OK
90	26787	Sentry	108.50	Partial Sun	Border	Oak	OK
81	32544	Burgundy Bell	110.95	Partial Sun	Border	Maple	OK
81	34266	Lace Maple	109.99	Partial Sun	Border	Maple	OK
113	34793	Emerald Elf	103.98	Full Shade	Erosion Control	Oak	OK
191	34878	Ginger Pear	107.78	Partial Sun	Border	Pear	OK
102	34982	Femleaf	105.99	Partial Shade	Border	Oak	OK
170	35677	Flamingo	109.99	Partial Sun	Border	Oak	OK
170	35690	Bing Sweet	107.99	Partial Sun	Erosion Control	Cherry	OK
70	35988	Butterfly Japanese	111.75	Partial Sun	Border	Maple	Order
92	36820	Ever Red	110.95	Partial Sun	Border	Maple	OK
173	37803	Osakazuki	103.88	Full Shade	Erosion Control	Oak	OK
113	37845	Anna	117.98	Partial Sun	Woodland Garden	Magnolia	OK
75	38675	Palo Alto	102.99	Partial Shade	Erosion Control	Oak	OK

Lastname_Firstname_2A_Tree_Inventory

FIGURE 2.1 Project 2A Inventory Status Report

Video E2-1

Flash Fill recognizes a pattern in your data, and then automatically fills in values when you enter examples of the output that you want. Use Flash Fill to split data from two or more cells or to combine data from two cells.

A *function* is the name given to a predefined formula—a formula that Excel has already built for you—that performs calculations by using specific values that you insert in a particular order or structure. *Statistical functions*, which include the AVERAGE, MEDIAN, MIN, and MAX functions, are useful to analyze a group of measurements.

Activity 2.01 | Using Flash Fill

1 Start Excel, and then in the lower left corner of Excel's opening screen, click **Open Other Workbooks**.

🔄 **ANOTHER WAY**   Press Ctrl + F12 to display the Open dialog box.

2 Navigate to the student files that accompany this textbook, and then locate and open **e02A_Tree_Inventory**. Press F12 to display the **Save As** dialog box, and then navigate to the location where you are storing your projects for this chapter.

3 Create a new folder named **Excel Chapter 2** and open the new folder. In the **File name** box, using your own name, type **Lastname_Firstname_2A_Tree_Inventory** and click **Save** or press Enter.

4 Scroll down. Notice that the worksheet contains data related to types of trees in inventory, including information about the *Quantity in Stock*, *Item #/Category*, *Tree Name*, *Retail Price*, *Light*, and *Landscape Use*.

5 In the **column heading area**, point to **column C** to display the ↓ pointer, and then drag to the right to select **columns C:D**. On the **HOME tab**, in the **Cells group**, click the **Insert button arrow**, and then click **Insert Sheet Columns**.

New columns for C and D display and the remaining columns move to the right.

🔄 **ANOTHER WAY**   Select the columns, right-click anywhere over the selected columns, and then on the shortcut menu, click Insert.

6 Click cell **C11**, type **13129** and then on the **Formula Bar**, click ✓ to confirm the entry and keep **C11** as the active cell.

7 On the **HOME tab**, in the **Editing group**, click **Fill**, and then click **Flash Fill**. Compare your screen with Figure 2.2.

Use this technique to split a column of data based on what you type. Flash Fill looks to the left and sees the pattern you have established, and then fills the remaining cells in the column with only the Item #. The Flash Fill Options button displays.

FIGURE 2.2

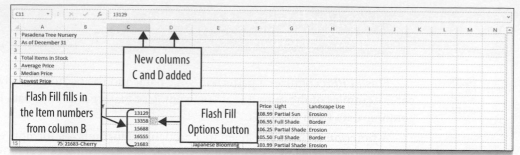

8 ▸ Near the lower right corner of cell **C11**, click the **Flash Fill Options** button, and notice that here you can *Undo Flash Fill*, *Accept suggestions*, or *Select all 28 changed cells*, for example, to apply specific formatting. Click the button again to close it.

> If Excel is not sure what pattern to use, it suggests a pattern by filling with pale gray characters, and then you can use the Accept suggestions command to accept or start again.

9 ▸ Click cell **D11**, type **Oak** On the **Formula Bar**, click ✓ to confirm the entry and keep **D11** as the active cell, and then press Ctrl + E, which is the keyboard shortcut for Flash Fill.

> Flash Fill extracts the text from the *Item#/Category* column and also inserts *Category* as the column name. Now that *Item #* and *Category* are in two separate columns, Mr. Hill can sort and filter by both Item # and Category.

10 ▸ Select **column B**, and then in the **Cells group**, click the **Delete button arrow**. Click **Delete Sheet Columns**. On the Quick Access Toolbar, click **Save** 🖫.

🔁 **ANOTHER WAY**   Select the column, right-click anywhere over the selected column, and then on the shortcut menu, click Delete.

Activity 2.02 | Moving a Column

1 ▸ In cell **B10** type **Item #** and press Enter. Select **column C**, and then on the **HOME tab**, in the **Clipboard group**, click **Cut** ✂. Notice that the column is surrounded by a moving border. Click cell **H1**, and then in the **Clipboard group**, click the upper portion of the **Paste** button.

🔁 **ANOTHER WAY**   Press Ctrl + X to cut and Ctrl + V to paste.

2 ▸ Select and then delete **column C**. Select **columns A:G**. In the **Cells group**, click **Format**, and then click **AutoFit Column Width**.

🔁 **ANOTHER WAY**   Select the columns, in the column heading area point to any of the column borders to display the ✛ pointer, and then double-click to AutoFit the columns.

3 ▸ Press Ctrl + Home to deselect and make cell **A1** the active cell.

4 ▸ **Merge & Center** cell **A1** across the range **A1:H1**, and then apply the **Title** cell style. **Merge & Center** cell **A2** across the range **A2:H2**, and apply the **Heading 1** cell style. Compare your screen with Figure 2.3. **Save** 🖫 your workbook.

FIGURE 2.3

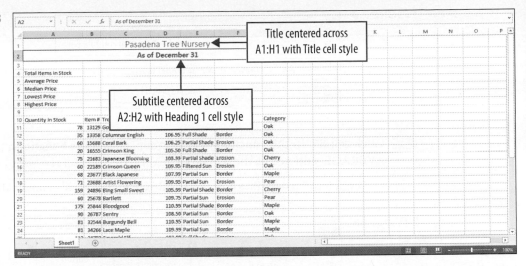

Title centered across A1:H1 with Title cell style

Subtitle centered across A2:H2 with Heading 1 cell style

Activity 2.03 | Using the SUM and AVERAGE Functions

Mr. Hill has a worksheet with information about the inventory of trees currently in stock at the Pasadena nursery. In this activity, you will use the SUM and AVERAGE functions to gather information about the product inventory.

1 Click cell **B4**. Click the **FORMULAS tab**, and then in the **Function Library group**, click the upper portion of the **AutoSum** button. Compare your screen with Figure 2.4.

The ***SUM function*** that you have used is a predefined formula that adds all the numbers in a selected range of cells. Because it is frequently used, there are several ways to insert the function. For example, you can insert the function from the HOME tab's Editing group, or by using the keyboard shortcut Alt + =, or from the Function Library group on the Formulas tab, or from the Math & Trig button in that group.

FIGURE 2.4

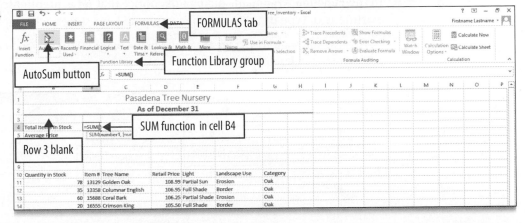

FORMULAS tab

Function Library group

AutoSum button

SUM function in cell B4

Row 3 blank

2 With the insertion point blinking in the function, type the cell range **a11:a39** to sum all the values in the **Quantity in Stock** column, and then press Enter; your result is *3022*.

3 Click cell **B4**, look at the **Formula Bar**, and then compare your screen with Figure 2.5.

SUM is the name of the function. The values in parentheses are the ***arguments***—the values that an Excel function uses to perform calculations or operations. In this instance, the argument consists of the values in the range A11:A39.

FIGURE 2.5

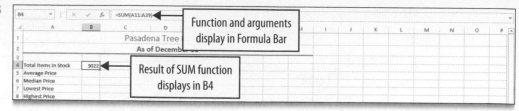

4 ▶ Click cell **B5**. In the **Function Library group**, click **More Functions**, point to **Statistical**, point to **AVERAGE**, and notice the ScreenTip. Compare your screen with Figure 2.6.

The ScreenTip describes how the AVERAGE function will compute the calculation.

FIGURE 2.6

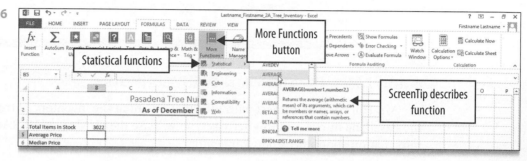

5 ▶ Click **AVERAGE**, and then if necessary, drag the title bar of the **Function Arguments** dialog box down and to the right so you can view the **Formula Bar** and cell **B5**.

The ***AVERAGE function*** adds a group of values, and then divides the result by the number of values in the group. In the cell, the Formula Bar, and the dialog box, Excel proposes to average the value in cell B4. Recall that Excel functions will propose a range if there is data above or to the left of a selected cell.

6 ▶ In the **Function Arguments** dialog box, notice that *B4* is highlighted. Press Del to delete the existing text, type **d11:d39** and then compare your screen with Figure 2.7.

Because you want to average the values in the range D11:D39—and not cell B4—you must edit the proposed range.

FIGURE 2.7

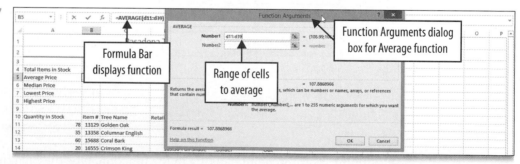

7 ▶ In the **Function Arguments** dialog box, click **OK**, and then click **Save** 🔲.

The result indicates that the average Retail Price of all products is *107.89*.

Activity 2.04 | Using the MEDIAN Function

The ***MEDIAN function*** is a statistical function that describes a group of data—it is commonly used to describe the price of houses in a particular geographical area. The MEDIAN function finds the middle value that has as many values above it in the group as are below it. It differs from

AVERAGE in that the result is not affected as much by a single value that is greatly different from the others.

1 Click cell **B6**. In the **Function Library group**, click **More Functions**, display the list of **Statistical** functions, scroll down as necessary, and then click **MEDIAN**.

2 Press Del to delete the text in the **Number1** box, and then type **d11:d39** Compare your screen with Figure 2.8.

> When indicating which cells you want to use in the function's calculation—known as *defining the arguments*—you can either select the values with your mouse or type the range of values, whichever you prefer.

FIGURE 2.8

3 Click **OK** to display *107.99* in cell **B6**. Click **Save** 🖫, and then compare your screen with Figure 2.9.

> In the range of prices, 107.99 is the middle value. Half of all trees in inventory are priced *above* 107.99 and half are priced *below* 107.99.

FIGURE 2.9

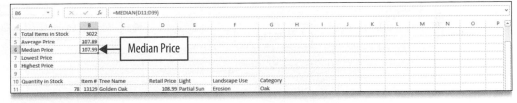

Activity 2.05 | Using the MIN and MAX Functions

The statistical *MIN function* determines the smallest value in a selected range of values. The statistical *MAX function* determines the largest value in a selected range of values.

1 Click cell **B7**. On the **FORMULAS tab**, in the **Function Library group**, click **More Functions**, display the list of **Statistical** functions, scroll as necessary, and then click **MIN**.

2 Press Del, and then in the **Number1** box, type **d11:d39** Click **OK**.

> The lowest Retail Price is *102.99*.

3 Click cell **B8**, and then by using a similar technique, insert the **MAX** function to determine the highest **Retail Price**, then check to see that your result is *117.98*.

4 Press Ctrl + Home. Point to cell **B4**, right-click, and then on the mini toolbar, click **Comma Style** 🔻 one time and **Decrease Decimal** two times.

5 Select the range **B5:B8**, apply the **Accounting Number Format** $ ▾, click **Save** 🖫, and then compare your screen with Figure 2.10.

FIGURE 2.10

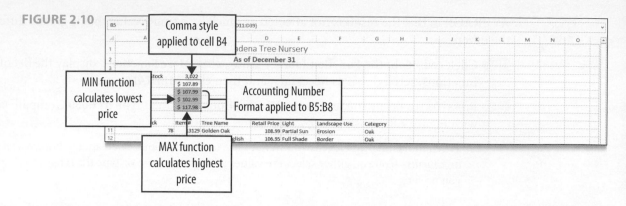

Objective 2 Move Data, Resolve Error Messages, and Rotate Text

Video E2-2

When you move a formula, the cell references within the formula do not change, no matter what type of cell reference you use.

If you move cells into a column that is not wide enough to display number values, Excel will display a message so that you can adjust as necessary.

You can reposition data within a cell at an angle by rotating the text.

Activity 2.06 │ Moving Data and Resolving a # # # # # Error Message

1 ▸ Select **column E** and set the width to **50 pixels**. Select the range **A4:B8**. Point to the right edge of the selected range to display the ⬚ pointer, and then compare your screen with Figure 2.11.

FIGURE 2.11

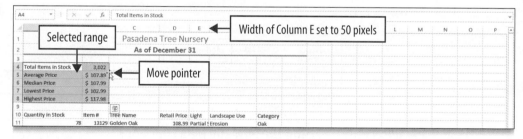

2 ▸ Drag the selected range to the right until the ScreenTip displays *D4:E8*, release the mouse button, and then notice that a series of # symbols displays in **column E**. Point to any of the cells that display # symbols, and then compare your screen with Figure 2.12.

Using this technique, cell contents can be moved from one location to another; this is referred to as *drag and drop*.

If a cell width is too narrow to display the entire number, Excel displays the ##### message, because displaying only a portion of a number would be misleading. The underlying values remain unchanged and are displayed in the Formula Bar for the selected cell. An underlying value also displays in the ScreenTip if you point to a cell containing # symbols.

FIGURE 2.12

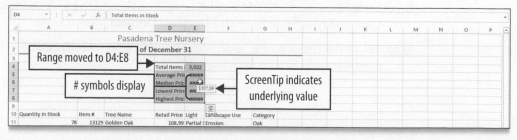

3 Select **column E** and widen it to **60** pixels, and notice that four cells are still not wide enough to display the cell contents.

4 Select **columns D:E**, and then in the **column heading area**, point to the right boundary of **column E** to display the ✛ pointer. Double-click to AutoFit the column to accommodate the widest entry.

5 Select the range **D4:E8**. On the **HOME tab**, in the **Styles group**, display the **Cell Styles** gallery. Under **Themed Cell Styles**, click **20%-Accent1**. Click **Save** 💾.

Activity 2.07 | Rotating Text

1 In cell **C6**, type **Tree Statistics** Select the range **C4:C8**, right-click over the selection, and then on the shortcut menu, click **Format Cells**.

2 In the **Format Cells** dialog box, click the **Alignment tab**. Under **Text control**, select the **Merge cells** check box.

3 Under **Orientation**, click in the **Degrees** box, select the existing text, type **30** and then compare your screen with Figure 2.13.

ANOTHER WAY   In the upper right portion of the dialog box, under Orientation, point to the red diamond, and then drag the diamond upward until the Degrees box indicates 30.

FIGURE 2.13

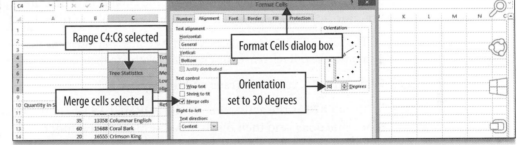

4 In the lower right corner of the **Format Cells** dialog box, click **OK**.

5 With the merged cell still selected, on the **HOME tab**, in the **Font group**, change the **Font Size** `11 ▾` to **14**, and then apply **Bold** B and **Italic** I. Click the **Font Color arrow** A ▾, and then in the fifth column, click the first color—**Blue, Accent 1**.

6 In the **Alignment group**, apply **Align Right** ≡. Press `Ctrl` + `Home`, **Save** 💾 your workbook, and then compare your screen with Figure 2.14.

FIGURE 2.14

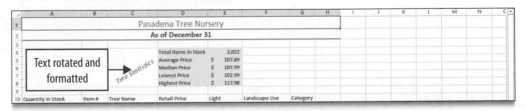

7 In the **row heading area**, point to **row 9** and right-click to select the row and display the shortcut menu. Click **Insert**, and then press `F4` two times to repeat the last action and insert three blank rows.

> `F4` is useful to repeat commands in Microsoft Office programs. Most commands can be repeated in this manner.

8 ▶ From the **row heading area**, select **rows 9:11**. On the **HOME tab**, in the **Editing group**, click **Clear** 🖉 and then click **Clear Formats** to remove the blue accent color in columns D and E from the new rows. Click **Save** 🖫.

When you insert rows or columns, formatting from adjacent rows or columns repeats in the new cells.

Objective 3 | Use COUNTIF and IF Functions and Apply Conditional Formatting

Video E2-3

Recall that statistical functions analyze a group of measurements. Another group of Excel functions, referred to as *logical functions*, test for specific conditions. Logical functions typically use conditional tests to determine whether specified conditions—called *criteria*—are true or false.

Activity 2.08 | Using the COUNT and COUNTIF Functions

The *Count function* counts the number of cells in a range that contain numbers. The **COUNTIF function** is a statistical function that counts the number of cells within a range that meet the given condition—the criteria that you provide. The COUNTIF function has two arguments—the range of cells to check and the criteria.

The trees of Rosedale Landscape and Garden will be featured on an upcoming segment of a TV gardening show. In this activity, you will use the COUNTIF function to determine the number of *Oak* trees currently available in inventory that can be featured in the TV show.

1 ▶ Click cell **E4**, look at the **Formula Bar**, and then notice that the arguments of the **SUM** function adjusted and refer to the appropriate cells in rows 14:42.

The referenced range updates to *A14:A42* after you insert the three new rows. In this manner, Excel adjusts the cell references in a formula relative to their new locations.

2 ▶ Click cell **A10**, type **Oak Trees** and then press [Tab].

3 ▶ With cell **B10** as the active cell, on the **FORMULAS tab**, in the **Function Library group**, click **More Functions**, and then display the list of **Statistical** functions. Click **COUNTIF**.

The COUNTIF function counts the number of cells within a range that meet the given condition.

4 ▶ In the **Range** box, type **g14:g42** Click in the **Criteria** box, type **Oak** and then compare your screen with Figure 2.15.

FIGURE 2.15

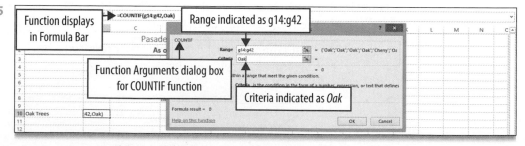

5 ▶ In the lower right corner of the **Function Arguments** dialog box, click **OK**.

There are *13* different *Oak* trees available to feature on the TV show.

6 ▶ On the **HOME tab**, in the **Alignment group**, click **Align Left** 🗏 to place the result closer to the row title. **Save** 🖫 your workbook.

A *logical test* is any value or expression that you can evaluate as being true or false. The *IF function* uses a logical test to check whether a condition is met, and then returns one value if true, and another value if false.

For example, *C14=228* is an expression that can be evaluated as true or false. If the value in cell C14 is equal to 228, the expression is true. If the value in cell C14 is not 228, the expression is false.

In this activity, you will use the IF function to determine the inventory levels and determine if more products should be ordered.

1 Click cell **H13**, type **Stock Level** and then press Enter.

2 In cell **H14**, on the **FORMULAS tab**, in the **Function Library group**, click **Logical**, and then in the list, click **IF**. Drag the title bar of the **Function Arguments** dialog box up or down to view **row 14** on your screen.

3 With the insertion point in the **Logical_test** box, type **a14 < 75**

This logical test will look at the value in cell A14, which is *78*, and then determine if the number is less than 75. The expression *<75* includes the < *comparison operator*, which means *less than*. Comparison operators compare values.

4 Examine the table in Figure 2.16 for a list of comparison operator symbols and their definitions.

FIGURE 2.16

COMPARISON OPERATORS	
COMPARISON OPERATORS	**SYMBOL DEFINITION**
=	Equal to
>	Greater than
<	Less than
>=	Greater than or equal to
<=	Less than or equal to
<>	Not equal to

5 Press Tab to move the insertion point to the **Value_if_true** box, and then type **Order**

If the result of the logical test is true—the Quantity in Stock is less than 75—cell H14 will display the text *Order* indicating that additional trees must be ordered.

6 Press Tab to move to the **Value_if_false** box, type **OK** and then compare your screen with Figure 2.17.

If the result of the logical test is false—the Quantity in Stock is *not* less than 75—then Excel will display *OK* in the cell.

FIGURE 2.17

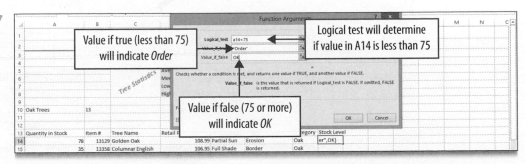

7 ▶ Click **OK** to display the result *OK* in cell **H14**.

8 ▶ Using the fill handle, copy the function in cell **H14** down through cell **H42**. Then scroll as necessary to view cell **A18**, which contains the value *75*. Look at cell **H18** and notice that the **Stock Level** is indicated as *OK*. **Save** 💾 your workbook. Compare your screen with Figure 2.18.

> The comparison operator indicated <75 (less than 75) and therefore a value of *exactly* 75 is indicated as OK.

FIGURE 2.18

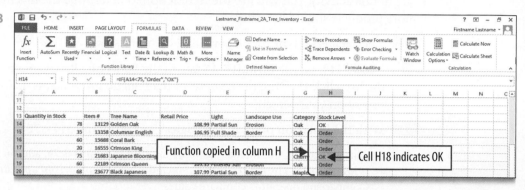

Activity 2.10 | Applying Conditional Formatting by Using Highlight Cells Rules and Data Bars

A *conditional format* changes the appearance of a cell based on a condition—a criteria. If the condition is true, the cell is formatted based on that condition; if the condition is false, the cell is *not* formatted. In this activity, you will use conditional formatting as another way to draw attention to the Stock Level of trees.

1 ▶ Be sure the range **H14:H42** is selected. On the **HOME tab**, in the **Styles group**, click **Conditional Formatting**. In the list, point to **Highlight Cells Rules**, and then click **Text that Contains**.

2 ▶ In the **Text That Contains** dialog box, with the insertion point blinking in the first box, type **Order** and notice that in the selected range, the text *Order* displays with the default format—Light Red Fill with Dark Red Text.

3 ▶ In the second box, click the **arrow**, and then in the list, click **Custom Format**.

> Here, in the Format Cells dialog box, you can select any combination of formats to apply to the cell if the condition is true. The custom format you specify will be applied to any cell in the selected range if it contains the text *Order*.

4 ▶ On the **Font tab**, under **Font style**, click **Bold Italic**. Click the **Color arrow**, and then under **Theme Colors**, in the last column, click the first color—**Green, Accent 6**. Click **OK**. Compare your screen with Figure 2.19.

> In the range, if the cell meets the condition of containing *Order*, the font color will change to Bold Italic, Green, Accent 6.

FIGURE 2.19

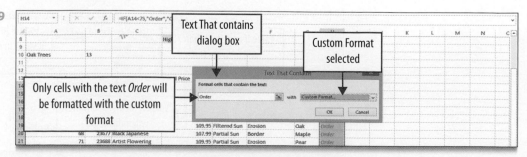

5 In the **Text That Contains** dialog box, click **OK**.

6 Select the range **A14:A42**. In the **Styles group**, click **Conditional Formatting**. Point to **Data Bars**, and then under **Gradient Fill**, click **Orange Data Bar**. Click anywhere to cancel the selection, click **Save** 🖫, and then compare your screen with Figure 2.20.

A *data bar* provides a visual cue to the reader about the value of a cell relative to other cells. The length of the data bar represents the value in the cell. A longer bar represents a higher value and a shorter bar represents a lower value. Data bars are useful for identifying higher and lower numbers quickly within a large group of data, such as very high or very low levels of inventory.

FIGURE 2.20

Activity 2.11 | Using Find and Replace

The **Find and Replace** feature searches the cells in a worksheet—or in a selected range—for matches, and then replaces each match with a replacement value of your choice.

Comments from customers on the company's blog indicate that using the term *Erosion Control* would be clearer than *Erosion* when describing the best landscape use for specific trees. Therefore, all products of this type will be re-labeled accordingly. In this activity, you will replace all occurrences of *Erosion* with *Erosion Control*.

1 Select the range **F14:F42**.

Restrict the find and replace operation to a specific range in this manner, especially if there is a possibility that the name occurs elsewhere.

2 On the **HOME tab**, in the **Editing group**, click **Find & Select**, and then click **Replace**.

3 Type **Erosion** to fill in the **Find what** box. In the **Replace with** box, type **Erosion Control** and then compare your screen with Figure 2.21.

FIGURE 2.21

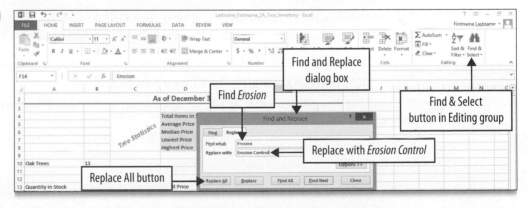

4 Click **Replace All**. In the message box, notice that 13 replacements were made, and then click **OK**. In the lower right corner of the **Find and Replace** dialog box, click **Close**. Click **Save** 🖫.

Video E2-4

Excel can obtain the date and time from your computer's calendar and clock and display this information on your worksheet.

By freezing or splitting panes, you can view two areas of a worksheet and lock rows and columns in one area. When you freeze panes, you select the specific rows or columns that you want to remain visible when scrolling in your worksheet.

Activity 2.12 Using the NOW Function to Display a System Date

The *NOW function* retrieves the date and time from your computer's calendar and clock and inserts the information into the selected cell. The result is formatted as a date and time.

1 To the left of the **Formula Bar**, click in the **Name Box**, type **a44** and then press Enter. Notice that cell **A44** is the active cell. In cell **A44**, type **Edited by Maria Acuna** and then press Enter.

2 With cell **A45** as the active cell, on the **FORMULAS tab**, in the **Function Library group**, click **Date & Time**. In the list of functions, click **NOW**. Compare your screen with Figure 2.22.

FIGURE 2.22

3 Read the description in the **Function Arguments** dialog box, and notice that this result is *Volatile*.

The Function Arguments dialog box displays a message indicating that this function does not require an argument. It also states that this function is *volatile*, meaning the date and time will not remain as entered, but rather the date and time will automatically update each time you open this workbook.

4 In the **Function Arguments** dialog box, click **OK** to close the dialog box and display the current date and time in cell **A45**. **Save** 💾 your workbook.

More Knowledge **NOW Function Recalculates Each Time a Workbook Opens**

The NOW function updates each time the workbook is opened. With the workbook open, you can force the NOW function to update by pressing F9, for example, to update the time.

Activity 2.13 Freezing and Unfreezing Panes

In a large worksheet, if you scroll down more than 25 rows or scroll beyond column O (the exact row number and column letter varies, depending on your screen resolution), you will no longer see the top rows or first column of your worksheet where identifying information about the data is usually placed. You will find it easier to work with your data if you can always view the identifying row or column titles.

The *Freeze Panes* command enables you to select one or more rows or columns and then freeze (lock) them into place. The locked rows and columns become separate panes. A *pane* is a portion of a worksheet window bounded by and separated from other portions by vertical or horizontal bars.

1 Press `Ctrl` + `Home` to make cell **A1** the active cell. Scroll down until **row 21** displays at the top of your Excel window, and notice that all of the identifying information in the column titles is out of view.

2 Press `Ctrl` + `Home` again, and then from the **row heading area**, select **row 14**. Click the **VIEW tab**, and then in the **Window group**, click **Freeze Panes**. In the list, click **Freeze Panes**. Click any cell to deselect the row, and then notice that a line displays along the upper border of **row 14**.

By selecting row 14, the rows above—rows 1–13—are frozen in place and will not move as you scroll down.

3 Watch the row numbers below **row 13**, and then begin to scroll down to bring **row 21** into view again. Notice that rows 1:13 are frozen in place. Compare your screen with Figure 2.23.

The remaining rows of data continue to scroll. Use this feature when you have long or wide worksheets.

FIGURE 2.23

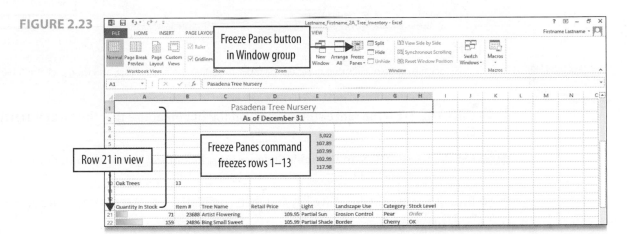

4 In the **Window group**, click **Freeze Panes**, and then click **Unfreeze Panes** to unlock all rows and columns. **Save** 💾 your workbook.

More Knowledge | **Freeze Columns or Freeze Both Rows and Columns**

You can freeze columns that you want to remain in view on the left. Select the column to the right of the column(s) that you want to remain in view while scrolling to the right, and then click the Freeze Panes command. You can also use the command to freeze both rows and columns; click a *cell* to freeze the rows *above* the cell and the columns to the *left* of the cell.

Objective 5 | Create, Sort, and Filter an Excel Table

Video E2-5

To analyze a group of related data, you can convert a range of cells to an *Excel table*. An Excel table is a series of rows and columns that contains related data that is managed independently from the data in other rows and columns in the worksheet.

Activity 2.14 | Creating an Excel Table and Applying a Table Style

1 Be sure that you have applied the Unfreeze Panes command—no rows on your worksheet are locked.

2 Click any cell in the data below row 13. Click the **INSERT tab**. In the **Tables group**, click **Table**. In the **Create Table** dialog box, if necessary, click to select the My table has headers check box, and then compare your screen with Figure 2.24.

The column titles in row 13 will form the table headers. By clicking in a range of contiguous data, Excel will suggest the range as the data for the table. You can adjust the range if necessary.

FIGURE 2.24

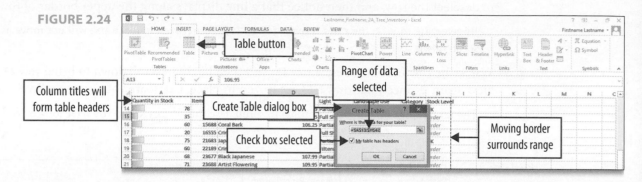

🔄 **ANOTHER WAY**   Select the range of cells that make up the table, including the header row, and then click the Table button.

3 Click **OK**. With the range still selected, on the ribbon notice that the **TABLE TOOLS** are active.

4 On the **DESIGN tab**, in the **Table Styles group**, click **More** ⬇, and then under **Light**, locate and click **Table Style Light 16**.

5 Press Ctrl + Home. Click **Save** 🖫, and then compare your screen with Figure 2.25.

Sorting and filtering arrows display in the table's header row.

FIGURE 2.25

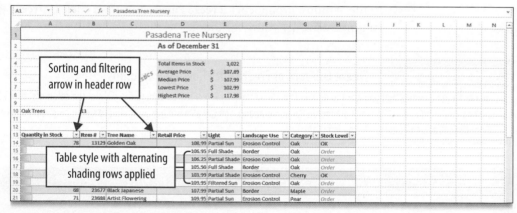

Activity 2.15 | Sorting an Excel Table

You can **sort** tables—arrange all the data in a specific order—in ascending or descending order.

1 In the header row of the table, click the **Retail Price arrow**, and then on the menu, click **Sort Smallest to Largest**. Next to the arrow, notice the small **up arrow** indicating an ascending (smallest to largest) sort.

This action sorts the rows in the table from the lowest retail price to highest retail price.

2 In the table's header row, click the **Category arrow**. On the menu, click **Sort A to Z**. Next to the arrow, notice the small **up arrow** indicating an ascending (A to Z) sort.

> This action sorts the rows in the table alphabetically by Category, and within a Category, sorts the rows from smallest to largest by Retail Price.

3 Click the **Category arrow** again, and then sort from **Z to A**.

> This action sorts the rows in the table in reverse alphabetic order by Category name, and the small arrow points downward, indicating a descending (Z to A) sort. The Retail Price continues to be sorted from smallest to largest within each category.

Activity 2.16 | Filtering an Excel Table and Displaying a Total Row

You can *filter* tables—display only a portion of the data based on matching a specific value—to show only the data that meets the criteria that you specify.

1 Click the **Category arrow** again. On the menu, click the **(Select All)** check box to clear all the check boxes. Click to select only the **Maple** check box, and then click **OK**. Compare your screen with Figure 2.26.

> Only the rows containing *Maple* in the Category column display—the remaining rows are hidden from view. A small funnel—the filter icon—indicates that a filter is applied to the data in the table. Additionally, the row numbers display in blue to indicate that some rows are hidden from view. A filter hides entire rows in the worksheet.

FIGURE 2.26

Funnel indicates filter applied

ScreenTip indicates Equals "Maple"

Blue row numbers indicate some rows hidden

Only products in Maple category display

2 Point to the funnel icon to the right of *Category*, and notice that *Equals "Maple"* displays to indicate the filter criteria.

3 Click any cell in the table so that the table is selected. On the ribbon, click the **DESIGN tab**, and then in the **Table Style Options group**, select the **Total Row** check box.

> *Total* displays in cell A43. In cell H43, the number 6 indicates that six rows currently display.

4 Click cell **A43**, click the **arrow** that displays to the right of cell **A43**, and then in the list, click **Sum**.

> Excel sums only the visible rows in Column A, and indicates that 571 products in the Maple category are in stock. In this manner, you can use an Excel table to quickly find information about a group of data.

5 Click cell **A11**, type **Maple Trees** and press [Tab]. In cell **B11**, type **6 (571 total items in stock)** and then press [Enter].

6 In the table header row, click the **Category arrow**, and then on the menu, click **Clear Filter From "Category"**.

> All the rows in the table redisplay. The Z to A sort on Category remains in effect.

More Knowledge | **Band Rows and Columns in a Table**

You can band rows to format even rows differently from odd rows making them easier to read. To band rows or columns, on the DESIGN tab, in the Table Style Options group, select the Banded Rows or Banded Columns check box.

7 Click the **Landscape Use arrow**, click the (**Select All**) check box to clear all the check boxes, and then click to select the **Erosion Control** check box. Click **OK**.

8 Click the **Category arrow**, click the (**Select All**) check box to clear all the check boxes, and then click the **Oak** check box. Click **OK**, **Save**  your workbook, and then compare your screen with Figure 2.27.

By applying multiple filters, Mr. Hill can determine quickly that eight tree names identified with a *Landscape Use* of *Erosion Control* are in the *Oak* tree category with a total of 710 such trees in stock.

FIGURE 2.27

Activity 2.17 | Clearing Filters and Converting a Table to a Range of Data

When you are finished answering questions about the data in a table by sorting, filtering, and totaling, you can convert the table into a normal range. Doing so is useful if you want to use the Table feature only to apply a Table Style to a range. For example, you can insert a table, apply a Table Style, and then convert the table to a normal range of data but keep the formatting.

1 Click the **Category arrow**, and then click **Clear Filter From "Category"**. Use the same technique to remove the filter from the **Landscape Use** column.

2 In the table header row, click the **Item # arrow**, and then click **Sort Smallest to Largest**, which will apply an ascending sort to the data using the *Item #* column.

3 Click anywhere in the table to activate the table and display the **TABLE TOOLS** on the ribbon. Click the **DESIGN tab**, and then in the **Table Style Options group**, click the **Total Row** check box to clear the check mark and remove the Total row from the table.

4 On the **DESIGN tab**, in the **Tools group**, click **Convert to Range**. In the message box, click **Yes**. Click **Save** , and then compare your screen with Figure 2.28.

FIGURE 2.28

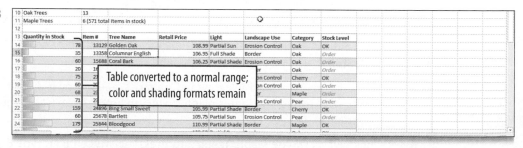

 ANOTHER WAY   With any table cell selected, right-click, point to Table, and then click Convert to Range.

Objective 6   View, Format, and Print a Large Worksheet

Video E2-6

You can magnify or shrink the view of a worksheet on your screen to either zoom in to view specific data or zoom out to see the entire worksheet. You can also split a worksheet window into panes to view different parts of a worksheet at the same time.

A worksheet might be too wide, too long—or both—to print on a single page. Use Excel's *Print Titles* and *Scale to Fit* commands to create pages that are attractive and easy to read.

The Print Titles command enables you to specify rows and columns to repeat on each printed page. Scale to Fit commands enable you to stretch or shrink the width, height, or both, of printed output to fit a maximum number of pages.

Activity 2.18 | Modifying and Shrinking the Worksheet View

1 Press Ctrl + Home to display the top of your worksheet. On the **VIEW tab**, in the **Zoom group**, click **Zoom**.

2 In the **Zoom** dialog box, click the **75%** option button, and then click **OK**. Notice that by zooming out in this manner, you can see additional rows of your worksheet on the screen.

3 In the lower right corner of your worksheet, in the status bar, click the **Zoom In** button until the worksheet redisplays at 100%.

Activity 2.19 | Splitting a Worksheet Window into Panes

The *Split* command splits the window into multiple resizable panes that contain views of your worksheet. This is useful to view multiple distant parts of your worksheet at one time.

1 Click cell **F9**. On the **VIEW tab**, in the **Window group**, click **Split**.

Horizontal and vertical split bars display. You can drag the split bars to view any four portions of the worksheet.

2 Notice on the right that separate vertical scroll bars display for the upper and lower panes and at the bottom, separate horizontal scroll bars display for the left and right panes.

3 Drag the lower vertical scroll box down to the bottom of the scroll bar to view **line 44**. Compare your screen with Figure 2.29.

Here it could be useful to isolate the Tree Statistics at the top and then scroll to the bottom to browse the inventory items or to make a note about who edited the original worksheet.

FIGURE 2.29

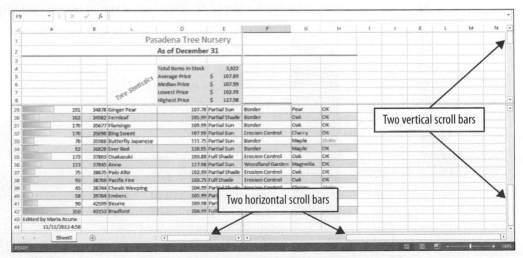

4 On the **VIEW tab**, click **Split** again to remove the split bars.

5 Press Ctrl + Home to display the top of your worksheet. On the **PAGE LAYOUT tab**, in the **Themes group**, click **Themes**, and then click **Slice**.

6 Select the range **A13:H13**. On the **HOME tab**, from the **Styles group**, apply the **Heading 4** cell style, and then apply **Center** ⊟. Click cell **A1**.

1 Click the **PAGE LAYOUT tab**, and then in the **Page Setup group**, click **Margins**. At the bottom of the gallery, click **Custom Margins** to display the **Page Setup** dialog box. Under **Center on page**, select the **Horizontally** check box.

2 Click the **Header/Footer tab**, and then in the center of the dialog box, click **Custom Footer**. In the **Footer** dialog box, with your insertion point blinking in the **Left section**, on the row of buttons, click **Insert File Name**. Click **OK** two times.

3 In the **Page Setup group**, click **Orientation**, and then click **Landscape**.

The dotted line indicates that as currently formatted, column H will not fit on one page.

4 Press Ctrl + F2 to display the **Print Preview**. At the bottom of the **Print Preview**, click **Next Page** ▶.

As currently formatted, the worksheet will print on four pages, and the columns will span multiple pages. Additionally, after Page 1, no column titles are visible to identify the data in the columns.

5 Click **Next Page** ▶ two times to display **Page 4**, and notice that one column moves to an additional page.

6 In the upper left corner of **Backstage** view, click **Back** ← to return to the worksheet. In the **Page Setup group**, click **Print Titles**. Under **Print titles**, click in the **Rows to repeat at top** box, and then at the right, click **Collapse Dialog**.

7 From the **row heading area**, select **row 13**, and then in the **Page Setup - Rows to repeat at top** dialog box, click **Expand Dialog**. Click **OK** to print the column titles in row 13 at the top of every page.

You can collapse and then expand dialog boxes on your screen to enable a better view of your data.

8 Press Ctrl + F2 to display the **Print Preview** again. At the bottom of the **Settings group**, click the **No Scaling arrow**, and then on the displayed list, point to **Fit All Columns on One Page**. Compare your screen with Figure 2.30.

This action will shrink the width of the printed output to fit all the columns on one page. You can make adjustments like this on the Page Layout tab, or here, in the Print Preview.

FIGURE 2.30

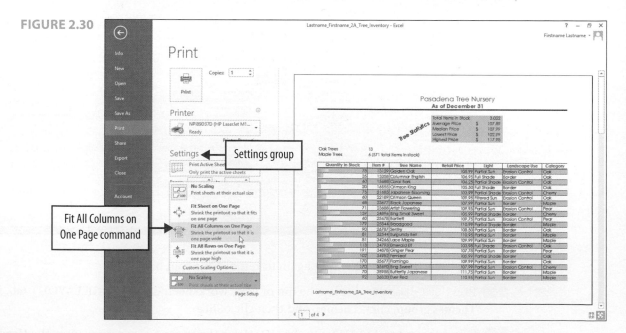

9 Click **Fit All Columns on One Page**. Notice in the **Print Preview** that all the columns display on one page.

 **ANOTHER WAY**   With the worksheet displayed, on the Page Layout tab, in the Scale to Fit group, click the Width button arrow, and then click 1 page.

10 At the bottom of the **Print Preview**, click **Next Page** ▶ one time. Notice that the output will now print on two pages and that the column titles display at the top of **Page 2**. Compare your screen with Figure 2.31.

FIGURE 2.31

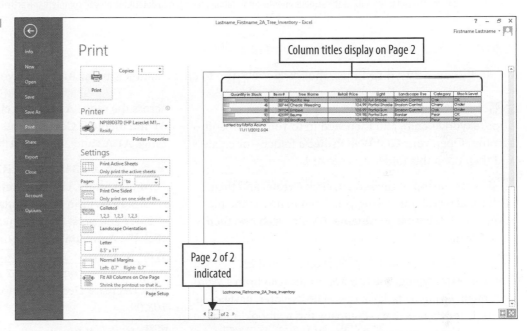

11 On the left, click **Info**, and then click **Show All Properties**. As the **Tags**, type **tree inventory, Pasadena** As the **Subject**, type your course name and section number. Be sure your name displays as the author; edit if necessary.

12 On the left, click **Save**. By using the techniques you practiced in Project 1A, print or submit electronically as directed by your instructor. If required by your instructor, print or create an electronic version of your worksheet with formulas displayed.

13 Close your workbook and close Excel.

More **Knowledge**   **Scaling for Data That Is Slightly Larger Than the Printed Page**

For data just a little too large to fit on a page, you can scale the worksheet to make it fit. Scaling reduces the width and height of the printed data to a percentage of its original size or by the number of pages that you specify. On the Page Layout tab, in the Scale to Fit group, click the Scale arrows to select a percentage.

END | You have completed Project 2A

Objective | Sort, Filter, and Use Functions in a Table in Excel Web App

If you are working on a computer that does not have Microsoft Office installed, you can still create new workbooks with tables in your web browser by using the Excel Office Web App.

ALERT!	Working with Web-Based Applications and Services

Computer programs and services on the web receive continuous updates and improvements, so the steps to complete this web-based activity may differ from the ones shown. You can often look at the screens and the information presented to determine how to complete the activity.

Activity | Sort, Filter, and Use Functions in a Table

In this activity, you will use the Excel Web App to create a table similar to the one you created in Project 2A.

1 Launch your web browser, navigate to **http://skydrive.com**, and then sign in to your Microsoft account. Open your **GO! Web Projects** folder—or create and then open this folder if necessary.

2 Near the top of the screen, click **Create**, and then click **Excel workbook**. Using your own name, as the file name type **Lastname_Firstname_EX_2A_Web** and then click **Create**.

3 To help you create this project quickly and to eliminate extra typing, you will import the data from a Word document. From the taskbar, open **File Explorer**, navigate to the student data files that accompany this textbook, and then open the Word document **e02_2A_Web**. Press Ctrl + A to select all of the text, right-click anywhere over the selection, and then click **Copy**. Close **×** Word and if necessary Close **-×** the folder window.

4 With cell **A1** selected, on the Excel Web App ribbon, in the **Clipboard group**, click **Paste**; if necessary click Allow access.

5 Select column headings **A:H**, point to the border between any two selected column headings to display the ⬌ pointer, and then double-click to resize all the columns to display all data.

6 Click cell **A1**, type **Pasadena Nursery: Tree Inventory** Press Enter and then **Merge & Center** the text

across the range **A1:H1**. In cell **A2**, type **As of December 31** and **Merge & Center** across the range **A2:H2**. Select the range **A1:A2** and apply **Bold** B.

7 Click cell **B4**. On the **HOME tab**, in the **Formulas group**, click the **AutoSum arrow** and then click **Sum**. Within the formula's parentheses, type **a13:a67** and press Enter for a result of *7085*. In cell **B5**, click the **AutoSum arrow** again, and then click **Average**. With *B4* selected, press Backspace one time, and then within the parentheses type **d13:d67** and press Enter. If necessary, click Decrease Decimal ⬇.00 two times for a result of *108.09*.

8 With cell **B6** selected, click the **INSERT tab**, and then click **Function**. Click the **Pick a category arrow**, click **Statistical**, and then scroll down and click **MEDIAN**. Click OK. Type **d13:d67)** and press Enter for a result of *106.98*.

9 In cell **B7**, click **Function**, from the **Commonly Used** group click **MIN**, click OK, type **d13:d67)** and press Enter for a result of *79.99*. In cell **B8**, use the same technique to compute the Highest Price for a result of *131.78*.

10 In cell **B9**, display the list of **Commonly Used** functions, scroll down, click **COUNTIF**, and then click OK. Type **g13:g67,"Oak")** and press Enter. Compare your screen with Figure A.

FIGURE A

	A	B
1	Pasadena Nursery: Tree Inventory	
2	As of December 31	
3		
4	Total Items in Stock	7085
5	Average Price	108.09
6	Median Price	106.98
7	Lowest Price	79.99
8	Highest Price	131.78
9	Oak Trees:	20
10	Magnolia Trees:	
11		

(GO! with Office Web Apps continues on the next page)

11 Click cell **H13**. From the **Commonly Used** list of functions, insert **IF**, and then type **a13<75,"Order","OK")** and press Enter. Copy this formula down through cell **H67**, which you will have to do in sections due to the way the Excel Web App scrolls on your screen.

12 Scroll up and click cell **A12**, hold down Shift, drag the vertical scroll box down to view **row 67**, and then click cell **H67** to select the entire range of the table data. On the **INSERT tab**, click **Table**, and then click **OK**. Drag the scroll box back to the top of the vertical scroll bar.

13 Sort the **Retail Price** column in **Ascending** order. Click the **Category arrow**, click **Filter**, and then filter on **Magnolia**.

14 Scroll as necessary to view all the rows in the filtered table, click the **HOME tab**, and then in the **Tables**

group, click the **Format as Table arrow**. On the list, click **Toggle Total Row**. Notice that a total row displays and indicates *8* different types of Magnolia trees. In cell **B10** type **8 types** and press Enter.

15 Click any cell in the table. Click **Format as Table** again, and then click **Toggle Total Row** to turn it off. Click the **Category arrow**, and then clear the filter. Press Ctrl + Home, and then compare your screen with Figure B.

16 If you are instructed to submit your file, use one of the methods outlined in the Note box below. Then, on the ribbon, click the **FILE tab** and click **Exit**. In the Excel Web App, there is no Save button because your workbook is being saved automatically. Sign out of your SkyDrive and close Internet Explorer.

NOTE | **Printing or Creating an Electronic File from the Excel Web App**

To print on paper, click the FILE tab, click Print, click the Print button, and then click Print. In the Print preview display, click Print. In the displayed Print dialog box, click Print to print on the printer connected to your system. To create an electronic file of your printout, from the Print dialog box, locate the printer labeled *Send to OneNote 2013*, and then click Print. When OneNote opens, click the Unfiled Notes section of the displayed notebook, and then click OK. On the ribbon, click the FILE tab, click Export, and then create a PDF of the page. A PDF created in this manner may include a blank Page 1. Close OneNote.

FIGURE B

1			Pasadena Nursery: Tree Inventory					
2			As of December 31					
3								
4	Total Items in Stock	7085						
5	Average Price	108.0944						
6	Median Price	106.98						
7	Lowest Price	79.99						
8	Highest Price	131.78						
9	Oak Trees:	20						
10	Magnolia Trees:	8 types						
11								
12	Quantity in Stock	Item #	Tree Name	Retail Price	Light	Landscape Use	Category	Stock Level
13	20	43625	Petite Red	79.99	Partial Shade	Hedge	Oak	Order
14	120	55255	Canadian Boxwood	89.99	Partial Sun	Hedge	Oak	OK
15	190	46532	Bold Box	100.95	Partial Sun	Erosion	Maple	OK
16	140	78655	Honey Oak	102.78	Filtered Sun	Erosion	Oak	OK
17	75	38675	Palo Alto	102.99	Partial Shade	Erosion	Oak	OK
18	250	54635	Kagiri	102.99	Partial Shade	Border	Maple	OK

Sheet1

Weekly Sales Summary

PROJECT ACTIVITIES

In Activities 2.21 through 2.35, you will edit an existing workbook for the Sales Director, Mariam Daly. The workbook summarizes the online and in-store sales of products during a one-week period in April. The worksheets of your completed workbook will look similar to Figure 2.32.

PROJECT FILES

For Project 2B, you will need the following file:

e02B_Weekly_Sales

You will save your workbook as:

Lastname_Firstname_2B_Weekly_Sales

PROJECT RESULTS

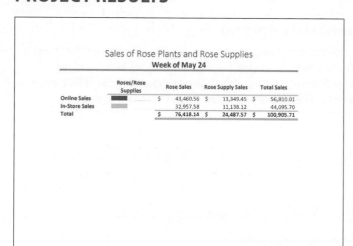

Sales of Rose Plants and Rose Supplies
Week of May 24

	Roses/Rose Supplies	Rose Sales	Rose Supply Sales	Total Sales
Online Sales		$ 43,460.56	$ 13,349.45	$ 56,810.01
In-Store Sales		32,957.58	11,138.12	44,095.70
Total		$ 76,418.14	$ 24,487.57	$ 100,905.71

Rose Plants and Rose Supplies: Weekly Online Sales
Week of May 24

Day	Climbing Roses	Patio Roses	Tea Roses	Total Rose Sales	Rose Supply Sales	Total Sales
Sun	$ 1,911.51	$ 2,026.46	$ 2,033.47	$ 5,971.44	$ 1,926.49	$ 7,897.93
Mon	2,310.49	2,313.85	1,782.64	6,406.98	1,526.03	7,933.01
Tue	1,942.37	2,402.99	2,030.08	6,375.44	1,853.82	8,229.26
Wed	2,185.89	1,992.29	2,253.98	6,432.16	1,922.36	8,354.52
Thu	2,003.53	1,825.79	2,340.34	6,169.66	1,973.73	8,143.39
Fri	1,931.46	1,946.92	1,966.92	5,845.30	2,121.47	7,966.77
Sat	2,047.23	1,978.23	2,234.12	6,259.58	2,025.55	8,285.13
Total	$ 14,332.48	$ 14,486.53	$ 14,641.55	$ 43,460.56	$ 13,349.45	$ 56,810.01

Recorded on:
6/3/16

Reviewed on:
6/7/16

Rose Plants and Rose Supplies: Weekly In-Store Sales
Week of May 24

Day	Climbing Roses	Patio Roses	Tea Roses	Total Rose Sales	Rose Supply Sales	Total Sales
Sun	$ 1,493.21	$ 1,681.92	$ 1,594.22	$ 4,769.35	$ 1,626.59	$ 6,395.94
Mon	1,689.37	1,552.58	1,624.44	4,866.39	1,483.69	6,350.08
Tue	1,271.12	1,709.58	1,386.26	4,366.96	1,693.82	6,060.78
Wed	1,410.88	1,584.02	1,596.72	4,591.62	1,778.94	6,370.56
Thu	1,558.58	1,526.63	1,735.51	4,820.72	1,416.37	6,237.09
Fri	1,483.62	1,486.91	1,656.56	4,627.09	1,645.24	6,272.33
Sat	1,605.58	1,783.64	1,526.23	4,915.45	1,493.47	6,408.92
Total	$ 10,512.36	$ 11,325.28	$ 11,119.94	$ 32,957.58	$ 11,138.12	$ 44,095.70

Recorded on:
6/3/16

Reviewed on:
6/7/16

FIGURE 2.32 Project 2B Weekly Sales Summary

Video E2-7

Use multiple worksheets in a workbook to organize data in a logical arrangement. When you have more than one worksheet in a workbook, you can *navigate* (move) among worksheets by clicking the *sheet tabs*. Sheet tabs identify each worksheet in a workbook and display along the lower left edge of the window. When you have more worksheets than can display in the sheet tab area, use the sheet tab scrolling buttons to move sheet tabs into and out of view.

Activity 2.21 | Navigating Among Worksheets, Renaming Worksheets, and Changing the Tab Color of Worksheets

Excel names the first worksheet in a workbook *Sheet1* and each additional worksheet that you add in order—*Sheet2*, *Sheet3*, and so on. Most Excel users rename their worksheets with meaningful names. In this activity, you will navigate among worksheets, rename worksheets, and change the tab color of sheet tabs.

1 Start Excel, and then in the lower left corner of Excel's opening screen, click **Open Other Workbooks**.

🔁 **ANOTHER WAY**   Press Ctrl + F12 to display the Open dialog box.

2 Navigate to the student files that accompany this textbook, and then locate and open **e02B_Weekly_Sales**. Press F12 to display the **Save As** dialog box, and then navigate to your **Excel Chapter 2** folder. In the **File name** box, using your own name, type **Lastname_Firstname_2B_Weekly_Sales** and click **Save** or press Enter

In this workbook, two worksheets display into which some data has already been entered. For example, on the first worksheet, the days of the week and sales data for the one-week period displays.

3 Along the bottom of the Excel window, point to and then click the **Sheet2 tab**.

The second worksheet in the workbook displays and becomes the active worksheet. *Sheet2* displays in bold.

4 In cell **A1**, notice the text *In-Store*—this worksheet will contain data for in-store sales.

5 Click the **Sheet1 tab**. Then, point to the **Sheet1 tab**, and double-click to select the sheet tab name. Type **Online Sales** and press Enter.

The first worksheet becomes the active worksheet, and the sheet tab displays *Online Sales*.

6 Point to the **Sheet2 tab**, right-click, and then from the shortcut menu, click **Rename**. Type **In-Store Sales** and press Enter. Compare your screen with Figure 2.33.

You can use either of these methods to rename a sheet tab.

More Knowledge   **Copying a Worksheet**

To copy a worksheet to the same workbook, right-click the sheet tab, on the shortcut menu click Move or Copy, click the sheet before which you want to insert the copied sheet, select the Create a copy check box, and then click OK. To copy to a different workbook, in the Move or Copy dialog box, click the To book arrow, and then select the workbook into which you want to insert the copy.

FIGURE 2.33

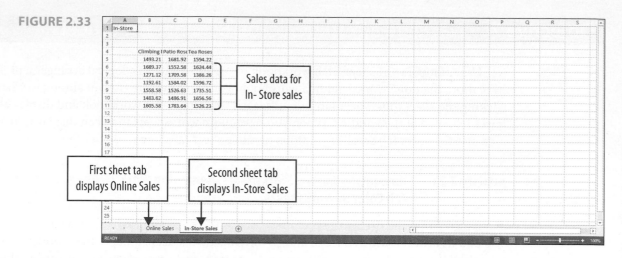

> **7** Point to the **In-Store Sales sheet tab** and right-click. Point to **Tab Color**, and then in the last column, click the first color—**Green, Accent 6**.

 **ANOTHER WAY**   On the Home tab, in the Cells group, click the Format button, and then on the displayed list, point to Tab Color.

> **8** Using the technique you just practiced, change the tab color of the **Online Sales sheet tab** to **Blue, Accent 5**—in the next to last column, the first color. **Save** 🖫 your workbook.

Objective 8   Enter Dates, Clear Contents, and Clear Formats

Video E2-8

Dates represent a type of value that you can enter in a cell. When you enter a date, Excel assigns a serial value—a number—to the date. This makes it possible to treat dates like other numbers. For example, if two cells contain dates, you can find the number of days between the two dates by subtracting the older date from the more recent date.

Activity 2.22 | Entering and Formatting Dates

In this activity, you will examine the various ways that Excel can format dates in a cell. Date values entered in any of the following formats will be recognized by Excel as a date:

Format	Example
m/d/yy	7/4/2016
d-mmm	4-Jul
d-mmm-yy	4-Jul-16
mmm-yy	Jul-12

On your keyboard, ⊟ (the hyphen key) and ⊘ (the forward slash key) function identically in any of these formats and can be used interchangeably. You can abbreviate the month name to three characters or spell it out. You can enter the year as two digits, four digits, or even leave it off. When left off, the current year is assumed but does not display in the cell.

A two-digit year value of 30 through 99 is interpreted by the Windows operating system as the four-digit years of 1930 through 1999. All other two-digit year values are assumed to be in the 21st century. If you always type year values as four digits, even though only two digits may display in the cell, you can be sure that Excel interprets the year value as you intended. Examples are shown in Figure 2.34.

FIGURE 2.34

HOW EXCEL INTERPRETS DATES	
DATE TYPED AS:	**COMPLETED BY EXCEL AS:**
7/4/15	7/4/2015
7/4/98	7/4/1998
7/4	4-Jul (current year assumed)
7-4	4-Jul (current year assumed)
July 4	4-Jul (current year assumed)
Jul 4	4-Jul (current year assumed)
Jul/4	4-Jul (current year assumed)
Jul-4	4-Jul (current year assumed)
July 4, 1998	4-Jul-98
July 2012	Jul-12 (first day of month assumed)
July 1998	Jul-98 (first day of month assumed)

1 On the **Online Sales** sheet, click cell **A16** and notice that the cell displays *6/3*. In the **Formula Bar**, notice that the full date of June 3, 2016 displays in the format *6/3/2016*.

2 With cell **A16** selected, on the **HOME tab**, in the **Number group**, click the **Number Format arrow**. At the bottom, click **More Number Formats** to display the **Number tab** of the **Format Cells** dialog box.

Under Category, *Date* is selected, and under Type, *3/14* is selected. Cell A16 uses this format type; that is, only the month and day display in the cell.

3 In the displayed dialog box, under **Type**, click several other date types and watch the **Sample** area to see how applying the selected date format will format your cell. When you are finished, click the **3/14/12** type, and then compare your screen with Figure 2.35.

FIGURE 2.35

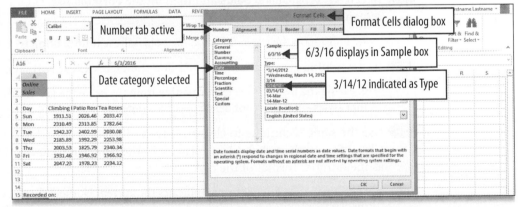

4 At the bottom of the dialog box, click **OK**. Click cell **A19**, type **6-7-16** and then press Enter.

Cell A19 has no special date formatting applied, and displays in the default date format *6/7/2016*.

ALERT! **The Date Does Not Display as 6/7/2016?**

Settings in your Windows operating system determine the default format for dates. If your result is different, it is likely that the formatting of the default date was adjusted on the computer at which you are working.

5 Click cell **A19** again. Hold down [Ctrl] and press [;] (semicolon) on your keyboard. Press [Enter] to confirm the entry.

> Excel enters the current date, obtained from your computer's internal calendar, in the selected cell using the default date format. [Ctrl] + [;] is a quick method to enter the current date.

6 Click cell **A19** again, type **6/7/16** and then press [Enter].

> Because the year *16* is less than 30, Excel assumes a 21st century date and changes *16* to *2016* to complete the four-digit year. Typing *98* would result in *1998*. For two-digit years that you type that are between 30 and 99, Excel assumes a 20th century date.

7 Click cell **A16**, and then on the **HOME tab**, in the **Clipboard group**, click **Format Painter** 🖌. Click cell **A19**, and notice that the date format from cell **A16** is copied to cell **A19**. **Save** 💾 your workbook.

Activity 2.23 | Clearing Cell Contents and Formats

A cell has *contents*—a value or a formula—and a cell may also have one or more *formats* applied, for example bold and italic font styles, fill color, font color, and so on. You can choose to clear—delete—the *contents* of a cell, the *formatting* of a cell, or both.

Clearing the contents of a cell deletes the value or formula typed there, but it does *not* clear formatting applied to a cell. In this activity, you will clear the contents of a cell and then clear the formatting of a cell that contains a date to see its underlying content.

1 In the **Online Sales** worksheet, click cell **A1**. In the **Editing group**, click **Clear** 🧹, and then click **Clear Contents**. Notice that the text is cleared, but the green formatting remains.

2 Click cell **A2**, and then press [Delete].

> You can use either of these two methods to delete the *contents* of a cell. Deleting the contents does not, however, delete the formatting of the cell; you can see that the green fill color format applied to the two cells still displays.

3 In cell **A1**, type **Online Sales** and then on the **Formula Bar**, click **Enter** ✓ so that cell **A1** remains the active cell.

> In addition to the green fill color, the bold italic text formatting remains with the cell.

4 In the **Editing group**, click **Clear** 🧹, and then click **Clear Formats**.

> Clearing the formats deletes formatting from the cell—the green fill color and the bold and italic font styles—but does not delete the cell's contents.

5 Use the same technique to clear the green fill color from cell **A2**. Click cell **A16**, click **Clear** 🧹, and then click **Clear Formats**. In the **Number group**, notice that *General* displays as the number format of the cell.

> The box in the Number group indicates the current Number format of the selected cell. Clearing the date formatting from the cell displays the date's serial number. The date, June 3, 2016, is stored as a serial number that indicates the number of days since January 1, 1900. This date is the 42,524th day since the reference date of January 1, 1900.

6 On the Quick Access Toolbar, click **Undo** ↺ to restore the date format. **Save** 💾 your workbook, and then compare your screen with Figure 2.36.

FIGURE 2.36

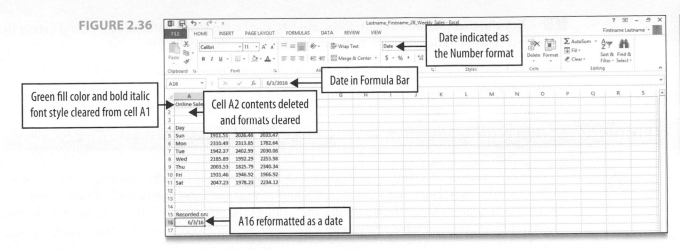

Date indicated as the Number format

Date in Formula Bar

Green fill color and bold italic font style cleared from cell A1

Cell A2 contents deleted and formats cleared

A16 reformatted as a date

More **Knowledge** **Clearing an Entire Worksheet**

To clear an entire worksheet, in the upper left corner of the worksheet, click the Select All button, and then on the Home tab, in the Editing group, click Clear, and then click Clear All.

Objective 9 Copy and Paste by Using the Paste Options Gallery

Video E2-9

Data in cells can be copied to other cells in the same worksheet, to other sheets in the same workbook, or to sheets in another workbook. The action of placing cell contents that have been copied or moved to the Clipboard into another location is called *paste*.

Activity 2.24 | Copying and Pasting by Using the Paste Options Gallery

Recall that the Clipboard is a temporary storage area maintained by your Windows operating system. When you select one or more cells, and then perform the Copy command or the Cut command, the selected data is placed on the Clipboard. From the Clipboard storage area, the data is available for pasting into other cells, other worksheets, other workbooks, and even into other Office programs. When you paste, the *Paste Options gallery* displays, which includes Live Preview to preview the Paste formatting that you want.

1 With the **Online Sales** worksheet active, select the range **A4:A19**.

A range of cells identical to this one is required for the *In-Store Sales* worksheet.

2 Right-click over the selection, and then click **Copy** to place a copy of the cells on the Clipboard. Notice that the copied cells display a moving border.

3 At the bottom of the workbook window, click the **In-Store Sales sheet tab** to make it the active worksheet. Point to cell **A4**, right-click, and then on the shortcut menu, under **Paste Options**, *point* to the first button—**Paste**. Compare your screen with Figure 2.37.

Live Preview displays how the copied cells will be placed in the worksheet if you click the Paste button. In this manner, you can experiment with different paste options, and then be sure you are selecting the paste operation that you want. When pasting a range of cells, you need only point to or select the cell in the upper left corner of the *paste area*—the target destination for data that has been cut or copied using the Clipboard.

FIGURE 2.37

Paste Options (6 option buttons)

4 ▶ Click the first button, **Paste**. In the status bar, notice the message that displays, indicating that your selected range remains available on the Office Clipboard.

5 ▶ Display the **Online Sales** worksheet. Press [Esc] to cancel the moving border. **Save** 🖫 your workbook.

The status bar no longer displays the message.

Objective 10 Edit and Format Multiple Worksheets at the Same Time

Video E2-10

You can enter or edit data on several worksheets at the same time by selecting and grouping multiple worksheets. Data that you enter or edit on the active sheet is reflected in all selected sheets. If you apply color to the sheet tabs, the name of the sheet tab will be underlined in the color you selected. If the sheet tab displays with a background color, you know the sheet is not selected.

Activity 2.25 | Grouping Worksheets for Editing

1 ▶ With the **Online Sales** sheet active, press [Ctrl] + [Home] to make cell **A1** the active cell. Point to the **Online Sales sheet tab**, right-click, and then click **Select All Sheets**.

2 ▶ At the top of your screen, notice that *[Group]* displays in the title bar. Compare your screen with Figure 2.38.

Both worksheets are selected, as indicated by *[Group]* in the title bar and the sheet tab names underlined. Data that you enter or edit on the active sheet will also be entered or edited in the same manner on all the selected sheets in the same cells.

FIGURE 2.38

[Group] displays in title bar

3 ▶ Select **columns A:G**, and then set their width to **85 pixels**.

4 ▶ Click cell **A2**, type **Week of May 24** and then on the **Formula Bar**, click **Enter** ✓ to keep cell **A2** as the active cell. **Merge & Center** 🖭▾ the text across the range **A2:G2**, and then apply the **Heading 1** cell style.

5 ▶ Click cell **E4**, type **Total Rose Sales** and then press [Tab]. In cell **F4**, type **Rose Supply Sales** and then press [Tab]. In cell **G4**, type **Total Sales** and then press [Enter].

6 ▶ Select the range **A4:G4**, and then apply the **Heading 3** cell style. In the **Alignment group**, click **Center** 🖹, **Middle Align** 🖹, and **Wrap Text**. **Save** 🖫 your workbook.

7 ▶ Display the **In-Store Sales** worksheet to cancel the grouping, and then compare your screen with Figure 2.39.

As soon as you select a single sheet, the grouping of the sheets is canceled and *[Group]* no longer displays in the title bar. Because the sheets were grouped, the same new text and formatting were applied to both sheets. In this manner, you can make the same changes to all the sheets in a workbook at one time.

More Knowledge **Hide Worksheets**

You can hide any worksheet in a workbook to remove it from view using this technique:
Select the sheet tabs of the worksheets you want to hide, right-click any of the selected sheet tabs, and then click Hide.

FIGURE 2.39

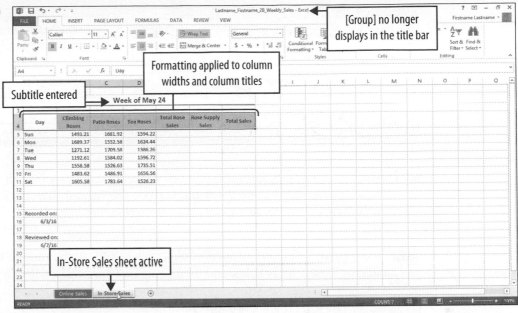

ANOTHER WAY   Right-click any sheet tab, and then click Ungroup Sheets.

Activity 2.26 | Formatting and Constructing Formulas on Grouped Worksheets

Recall that formulas are equations that perform calculations on values in your worksheet and that a formula starts with an equal sign (=). Operators are the symbols with which you specify the type of calculation that you want to perform on the elements of a formula. In this activity, you will enter and calculate sales for Rose Supply items from both Online and In-Store sales.

1 Display the **Online Sales** worksheet. Verify that the sheets are not grouped—*[Group]* does *not* display in the title bar.

2 Click cell **A1**, replace *Online Sales* by typing **Rose Plants and Rose Supplies: Weekly Online Sales** and then on the **Formula Bar**, click **Enter** ✔ to keep cell **A1** as the active cell. **Merge & Center** the text across the range **A1:G1**, and then apply the **Title** cell style.

3 In the column titled *Rose Supply Sales*, click cell **F5**, in the range **F5:F11**, type the following data for Rose Supply Sales, and then compare your screen with Figure 2.40.

	ROSE SUPPLY SALES
Sun	1926.49
Mon	1526.03
Tue	1853.82
Wed	1922.36
Thu	1973.73
Fri	2121.47
Sat	2025.55

FIGURE 2.40

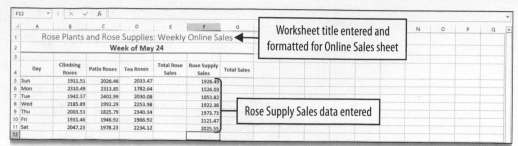

Worksheet title entered and
formatted for Online Sales sheet

Rose Supply Sales data entered

4 Display the **In-Store Sales** sheet. In cell **A1**, replace *In-Store* by typing **Rose Plants and Rose Supplies: Weekly In-Store Sales** and then on the **Formula Bar**, click **Enter** ☑ to keep cell **A1** as the active cell. **Merge & Center** the text across the range **A1:G1**, and then apply the **Title** cell style.

5 In the column titled *Rose Supply Sales*, click cell **F5**, in the range **F5:F11**, type the following data for Rose Supply Sales, and then compare your screen with Figure 2.41.

ROSE SUPPLY SALES	
Sun	1626.59
Mon	1483.69
Tue	1693.82
Wed	1778.94
Thu	1416.37
Fri	1645.24
Sat	1493.47

FIGURE 2.41

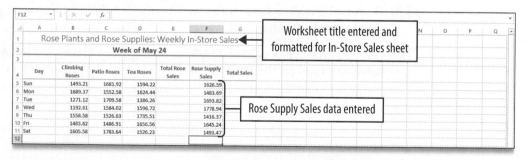

Worksheet title entered and
formatted for In-Store Sales sheet

Rose Supply Sales data entered

6 Save 🖫 your workbook. Right-click the **Online Sales sheet tab**, and then click **Select All Sheets**.

The first worksheet becomes the active sheet, and the worksheets are grouped. *[Group]* displays in the title bar, and the sheet tabs are underlined in the tab color to indicate they are selected as part of the group. Recall that when grouped, any action that you perform on the active worksheet is *also* performed on any other selected worksheets.

7 With the sheets *grouped* and the **Online Sales** sheet active, click cell **E5**. On the **HOME tab**, in the **Editing group**, click **AutoSum**. Compare your screen with Figure 2.42.

Recall that when you enter the SUM function, Excel looks first above and then left for a proposed range of cells to sum.

FIGURE 2.42

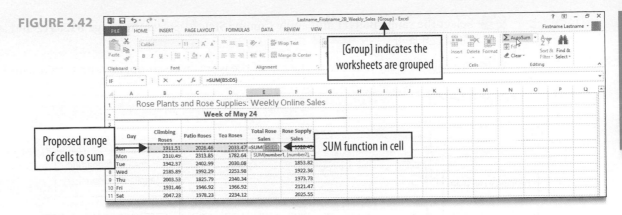

8 Press Enter to display Total Rose Sales for Sunday, which is *5971.44*.

9 Click cell **E5**, and then drag the fill handle down to copy the formula through cell **F11**.

10 Click cell **G5**, type **=** click cell **E5**, type **+** click cell **F5**, and then compare your screen with Figure 2.43.

> Using the point-and-click technique to construct this formula is only one of several techniques you can use. Alternatively, you could use any other method to enter the SUM function to add the values in these two cells.

FIGURE 2.43

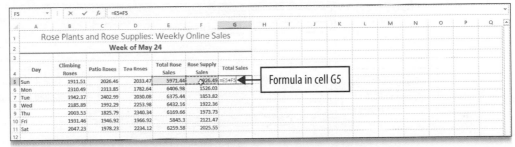

11 Press Enter to display the result *7897.93*, and then copy the formula down through cell **G11**.

Activity 2.27 | Determining Multiple Totals at the Same Time

You can select a contiguous range of cells adjacent to rows or columns of numbers and then click the Sum button—or use Alt + =—to enter the a SUM function for each row or column.

1 Save 💾 your workbook. With the two worksheets still grouped, in cell **A12**, type **Total** and then select the range **B5:G12**, which is all of the sales data and the empty cells at the bottom of each column of sales data.

2 With the range **B5:G12** selected, hold down Alt and press = to enter the **SUM** function in each empty cell. Click **Save** 💾.

> Selecting a range in this manner and then clicking the SUM button, or entering the SUM function with the keyboard shortcut Alt = =, places the Sum function in the empty cells at the bottom of each column.

Activity 2.28 | Formatting Grouped Worksheets

1 With the two worksheets still grouped, select the range **A5:A12**, and then apply the **Heading 4** cell style.

2 To apply financial formatting to the worksheets, select the range **B5:G5**, hold down Ctrl, and then select the range **B12:G12**. With the nonadjacent ranges selected, apply the **Accounting Number Format** $ ▾.

3 Select the range **B6:G11** and apply **Comma Style** ⟨,⟩. Select the range **B12:G12** and apply the **Total** cell style.

4 Press ⌈Ctrl⌉ + ⌈Home⌉ to move to the top of the worksheet; compare your screen with Figure 2.44.

FIGURE 2.44

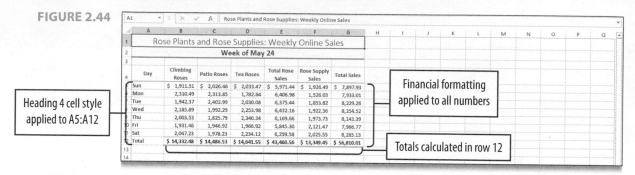

Activity 2.29 | Ungrouping Worksheets

1 Click the **In-Store Sales sheet tab** to cancel the grouping and display the second worksheet. Click **Save** ⌈🖫⌉, and then compare your screen with Figure 2.45.

With your worksheets grouped, the calculations and formatting on the first worksheet were also added on the second worksheet. As soon as you click a single sheet tab, the grouping is canceled.

FIGURE 2.45

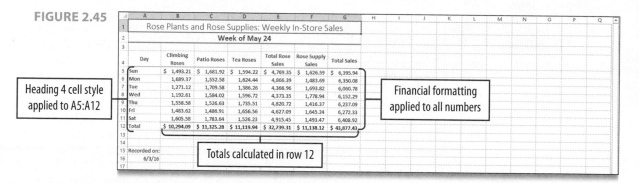

Objective 11   Create a Summary Sheet with Column Sparklines

Video E2-11

A **summary sheet** is a worksheet where totals from other worksheets are displayed and summarized. Recall that sparklines are tiny charts within a single cell that show a data trend.

Activity 2.30 | Inserting a Worksheet

1 To the right of the **In-Store Sales** sheet tab, click **New sheet** ⊕.

2 Rename the new worksheet tab **Summary** and change its **Tab Color** to **Gold, Accent 4**.

3 Widen **columns A:E to 110 pixels**. In cell **A1**, type **Sales of Rose Plants and Rose Supplies Merge & Center** the title across the range **A1:E1**, and then apply the **Title** cell style.

4 In cell **A2**, type **Week of May 24** and then **Merge & Center** across **A2:E2**; apply the **Heading 1** cell style.

5 Leave **row 3** blank. To form column titles, in cell **B4**, type **Roses/Rose Supplies** and press ⌈Tab⌉. In cell **C4**, type **Rose Sales** and press ⌈Tab⌉. In cell **D4**, type **Rose Supply Sales** and press ⌈Tab⌉. In cell **E5**, type **Total Sales** Press ⌈Enter⌉.

6 Select the range **B4:E4**. Apply the **Heading 3** cell style. In the **Alignment group**, click **Center** ☰, **Middle Align** ☰, and **Wrap Text**.

7 To form row titles, in cell **A5**, type **Online Sales** In cell **A6**, type **In-Store Sales** Save 🖫, and then compare your screen with Figure 2.46.

FIGURE 2.46

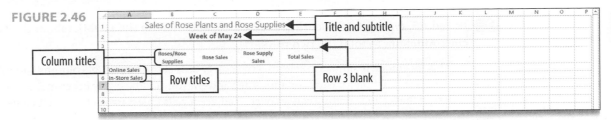

Activity 2.31 | Constructing Formulas That Refer to Cells in Another Worksheet

In this activity, you will construct formulas in the Summary worksheet to display the total sales for both online sales and in-store sales that will update the Summary worksheet whenever changes are made to the other worksheet totals.

1 Click cell **C5**. Type **=** Click the **Online Sales sheet tab**. On the **Online Sales** worksheet, click cell **E12**, and then press ⏎ to redisplay the **Summary** worksheet and insert the total **Rose Sales** amount of *$43,460.56*.

2 Click cell **C5** to select it again. Look at the **Formula Bar**, and notice that instead of a value, the cell contains a formula that is equal to the value in another cell in another worksheet. Compare your screen with Figure 2.47.

> The value in this cell is equal to the value in cell E12 of the *Online Sales* worksheet. The Accounting Number Format applied to the referenced cell is carried over. By using a formula of this type, changes in cell E12 on the *Online Sales* worksheet will be automatically updated in this *Summary* worksheet.

FIGURE 2.47

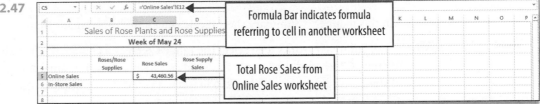

3 Click cell **D5**. Type **=** and then click the **Online Sales sheet tab**. Click cell **F12**, and then press ⏎ to redisplay the **Summary** worksheet and insert the total **Rose Supply Sales** amount of *$13,349.45*.

4 By using the techniques you just practiced, in cells **C6** and **D6** insert the total **Rose Sales** and **Rose Supply Sales** data from the **In-Store Sales** worksheet. Click Save 🖫, and then compare your screen with Figure 2.48.

FIGURE 2.48

Activity 2.32 | Changing Values in a Detail Worksheet to Update a Summary Worksheet

The formulas in cells C5:D6 display the totals from the other two worksheets. Changes made to any of the other two worksheets—sometimes referred to as *detail sheets* because the details of the information are contained there—that affect their totals will display on this Summary worksheet. In this manner, the Summary worksheet accurately displays the current totals from the other worksheets.

1 In cell **A7**, type **Total** Select the range **C5:E6**, and then on the **HOME tab**, in the **Editing group**, click **AutoSum** to total the two rows.

This technique is similar to selecting the empty cells at the bottom of columns and then inserting the SUM function for each column. Alternatively, you could use any other method to sum the rows. Recall that cell formatting carries over to adjacent cells unless two cells are left blank.

2 Select the range **C5:E7**, and then click **AutoSum** to total the three columns. Compare your screen with Figure 2.49.

FIGURE 2.49

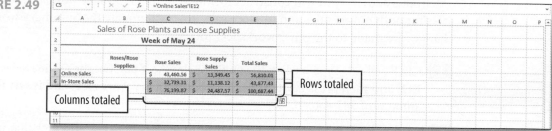

3 In cell **C6**, notice that total **Rose Sales** for **In-Store** Sales is *$32,739.31*, and in cell **C7**, notice the total of *$76,199.87*.

4 Display the **In-Store Sales** worksheet, click cell **B8**, type **1410.88** and then press Enter. Notice that the formulas in the worksheet recalculate.

5 Display the **Summary** worksheet, and notice that in the **Rose Sales** column, both the total for the *In-Store Sales* and the *Total* were recalculated.

In this manner, a Summary sheet recalculates any changes made in the other worksheets.

6 On the **Summary** worksheet, select the range **C6:E6** and change the format to **Comma Style**. Select the range **C7:E7**, and then apply the **Total** cell style. Select the range **A5:A7** and apply the **Heading 4** cell style. **Save** 💾 your workbook. Click cell **A1**, and then compare your screen with Figure 2.50.

FIGURE 2.50

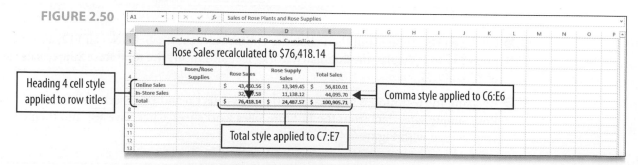

Activity 2.33 | Inserting Column Sparklines

In this activity, you will insert column sparklines to visualize the ratio of Rose sales to Rose Supply sales for both Online and In-Store.

1 On the **Summary** worksheet, click cell **B5**. On the **INSERT tab**, in the **Sparklines group**, click **Column**. In the **Create Sparklines** dialog box, with the insertion point blinking in the **Data Range** box, type **c5:d5** and then compare your screen with Figure 2.51.

FIGURE 2.51

2 ▶ Click **OK**. Click cell **B6**, and then **INSERT** a **Column Sparkline** for the range **c6:d6** In the **Style group**, apply **Sparkline Style Accent 4, (no dark or light)**—in the third row, the fourth style. Press Ctrl + Home, click **Save** 🖫, and then compare your screen with Figure 2.52.

> You can see, at a glance, that for both Online and In-Store sales, Rose sales are much greater than Rose Supply sales.

FIGURE 2.52

Column sparklines compare sales of Roses to Rose Supplies in both Online and In-Store

---

Objective 12 Format and Print Multiple Worksheets in a Workbook

Video E2-12

Each worksheet within a workbook can have different formatting, for example different headers or footers. If all the worksheets in the workbook will have the same header or footer, you can select all the worksheets and apply formatting common to all of the worksheets; for example, you can set the same footer in all of the worksheets.

Activity 2.34 | Moving a Worksheet, Repeating Footers, and Formatting Multiple Worksheets in a Workbook

In this activity, you will move the Summary sheet to become the first worksheet in the workbook. Then you will format and prepare your workbook for printing. The three worksheets containing data can be formatted simultaneously.

1 ▶ Point to the **Summary sheet tab**, hold down the left mouse button to display a small black triangle—a caret—and then notice that a small paper icon attaches to the mouse pointer.

2 ▶ Drag to the left until the caret and mouse pointer are to the left of the **Online Sales sheet tab**, as shown in Figure 2.53, and then release the left mouse button.

> Use this technique to rearrange the order of worksheets within a workbook.

FIGURE 2.53

Caret moved to the left

Mouse pointer with paper icon attached

3 ▶ Be sure the **Summary** worksheet is the active sheet, point to its sheet tab, right-click, and then click **Select All Sheets** to display *[Group]* in the title bar.

4 ▶ Click the **PAGE LAYOUT tab**. In the **Page Setup group**, click **Margins**, and then at the bottom of the gallery, click **Custom Margins** to display the **Page Setup** dialog box.

5 In the **Page Setup** dialog box, on the **Margins tab**, under **Center on page**, select the **Horizontally** check box.

6 Click the **Header/Footer tab**, and then in the center of the dialog box, click **Custom Footer**. In the **Footer** dialog box, with your insertion point blinking in the **Left section**, on the row of buttons, click **Insert File Name** 🖼️.

7 Click **OK** two times.

The dotted line indicates the page break as currently formatted.

8 Press [Ctrl] + [Home]; verify that *[Group]* still displays in the title bar.

By selecting all sheets, you can apply the same formatting to all the worksheets at the same time, for example to repeat headers or footers.

9 Click the **FILE tab** to display **Backstage** view, and then click **Show All Properties**. As the **Tags**, type **weekly sales, online, in-store, rose plants, rose supplies** In the **Subject** box, type your course name and section number. Be sure your name displays as the author.

10 On the left, click **Print** to display the **Print Preview**, and then compare your screen with Figure 2.54.

By grouping, you can view all sheets in Print Preview. If you do not see *1 of 3* at the bottom of the Preview, redisplay the workbook, select all the sheets again, and then redisplay Print Preview.

FIGURE 2.54

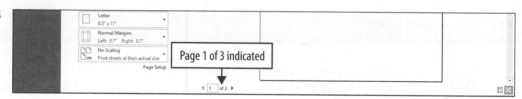

11 At the bottom of the **Print Preview**, click **Next Page** ▶ as necessary and take a moment to view each page of your workbook.

Activity 2.35 | Printing All or Individual Worksheets in a Workbook

1 In **Backstage** view, click **Save** to save your workbook before printing. In the displayed workbook, right-click the **Summary sheet tab**, and then click **Ungroup Sheets**.

2 Press [Ctrl] + [F2] to display **Print Preview**, and then at the bottom of the window, notice that *1 of 1* is indicated.

Because the worksheets are no longer grouped, only the active sheet is available for printing.

3 On the left, under **Settings**, click **Print Active Sheets**, and then click **Print Entire Workbook**.

At the bottom of the window, *1 of 3* is indicated. By default, Excel prints only the active worksheet; however, you can use this command to print an entire workbook.

4 By using the techniques you practiced in Project 1A, print or submit electronically as directed by your instructor. If required by your instructor, print or create an electronic version of your worksheet with formulas displayed.

5 Close your workbook and close Excel.

END | You have completed Project 2B

GO! with Office Web Apps

Objective   Summarize the Data on Multiple Worksheets in Excel Web App

If you are working on a computer that does not have Microsoft Office installed, you can still create new workbooks in your web browser by using the Excel Office Web App.

> **ALERT!**   **Working with Web-Based Applications and Services**
>
> Computer programs and services on the web receive continuous updates and improvements, so the steps to complete this web-based activity may differ from the ones shown. You can often look at the screens and the information presented to determine how to complete the activity.

Activity | Creating an Inventory Valuation Report in the Excel Web App

In this activity, you will use the Excel Web App to add a worksheet to a workbook created in Excel.

1 Launch your web browser, navigate to **http://skydrive.com**, and then sign in to your Microsoft account. Open your **GO! Web Projects** folder—or create and then open this folder if necessary.

2 In the SkyDrive menu bar, click **Upload**. Navigate to your student data files, click the Excel file **e02_2B_Web**, and then click **Open**.

3 Point to the uploaded file **e02_2B_Web**, and then right-click. On the shortcut menu, scroll as necessary, and then click **Rename**. Using your own name, type **Lastname_Firstname_EX_2B_Web** and then press Enter to rename the file.

4 Click the file you just renamed to open it in the Excel Web App.

5 At the bottom of the workbook, at the right end of the sheet tabs, click **New sheet** ⊕. Double-click the **Sheet4 tab**, and then name the worksheet tab **TV Sales**

6 To help you create this project quickly and to eliminate extra typing, you will import the data from a Word table. From the taskbar, open **File Explorer**,

navigate to the student data files that accompany this textbook, and then open the Word document **e02_2B_TV_Sales**. Press Ctrl + A to select all of the text, right-click anywhere over the selection, and then click **Copy**. **Close** Word and the folder window.

7 With cell **A1** selected, on the Excel Web App ribbon, in the **Clipboard group**, click **Paste**; if necessary click Allow access. Notice that # symbols display when numeric data is too wide for the cell.

8 Select the range **A1:G1**, and then in the **Alignment group**, click **Merge & Center**. Merge and center the worksheet's subtitle in the same manner. Select the range **A1:A2**, and then in the **Font group**, apply **Bold**.

9 Select column headings **A:G**, point to the border between any two selected column headings to display the ⊹ pointer, and then double-click to resize all the columns to display all data.

10 Select the range **B5:G12**, and then in the **Formulas group**, click the upper portion of the **AutoSum** button to total all the columns. Compare your screen with Figure A.

FIGURE A

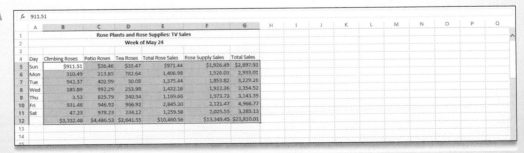

(GO! with Office Web Apps continues on the next page)

11 Display the **Summary** worksheet. Click cell **A7**, and then in the **Cells group**, click the **Insert button arrow**, and then click **Insert Rows**. In the new cell **A7**, type **TV Sales** and then press `Tab` two times to make cell **C7** active.

12 Type **='TV Sales'!E12** and press `Enter` for a result of *$10,460.56*. Notice that you cannot use the `=` plus `Enter` method in the Excel Web App, but you can simply type the command.

13 Click cell **C7** and drag the fill handle to the right to cell **E7**. Compare your screen with Figure B. Notice that Excel copies the formula and adjusts the cell references

to record the Rose Supply Sales and the Total Sales from the TV Sales worksheet. Also, the sparkline is filled in. The TV Sales had higher sales of Rose Supplies than Rose plants.

14 If you are instructed to submit your file, use one of the methods outlined in the Note box below. Then, on the ribbon, click the **FILE tab** and click **Exit**. Recall that in the Excel Web App, there is no Save button because your workbook is being saved automatically. Sign out of your SkyDrive and close Internet Explorer.

NOTE **Printing or Creating an Electronic File from the Excel Web App**

To print on paper, click the FILE tab, click Print, click the Print button, and then click Print. In the Print preview display, click Print. In the displayed Print dialog box, click Print to print on the printer connected to your system. To create an electronic file of your printout, from the Print dialog box, locate the printer labeled *Send to OneNote 2013*, and then click Print. When OneNote opens, click the Unfiled Notes section of the displayed notebook, and then click OK. On the ribbon, click the FILE tab, click Export, and then create a PDF of the page. A PDF created in this manner may include a blank Page 1. Close OneNote.

FIGURE B

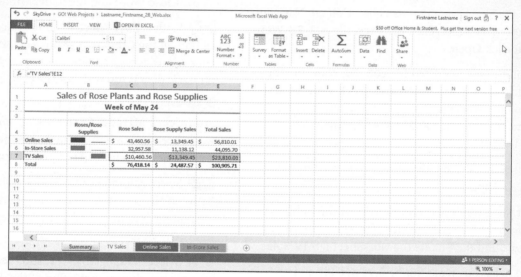

Andrew Rodriguez / Fotolia; FotolEdhar/ Fotolia; apops/ Fotolia; Yuri Arcurs/ Fotolia

Office 365 includes business-class security and is backed by Microsoft. For an organization, what does that mean?

When you and a few classmates work together on a class project, you are not concerned about the security of your data. You probably use free personal email services such as Hotmail, Gmail, or Yahoo Mail to exchange documents, or perhaps you post your documents to free services such as Google Docs.

Organizations, on the other hand—even small ones with only two or three employees—must be concerned with the privacy and security of their data. Organizations cannot entrust their data and confidential communications to free services that may change frequently or that have no legal responsibility for the security of the data.

Organizations must provide each employee with a company email address rather than having each employee use his or her own personal free email address for business communications. Organizations must provide a central storage location for its data rather than having employees store data on flash drives or local hard drives with no control or oversight.

An organization must have a *secure environment*, which is a system that uses controlled *servers*—computers that provide services on a network such as an email server or a file server—to ensure the security and privacy of email, to control the storage and use of information, and to protect against the loss of confidential data.

Most small organizations cannot afford to hire the people with the skills necessary to install and maintain servers. So to establish and maintain a secure environment, many small organizations contract with and rely on small IT—the acronym for *Information Technology*—hosting companies to host their email communications and to provide secure storage.

Activity | Using Lync to Collaborate by Using a Video Call

This group project relates to the **Bell Orchid Hotels**. If your instructor assigns this project to your class, you can expect to use **Lync** in **Office 365** to collaborate on the following tasks for this chapter:

- If you are in the **Accounting Group**, you and your teammates will conduct a video call to discuss and agree on a workbook to summarize hotel rooms sold over a four-week period in April.

- If you are in the **Engineering Group**, you and your teammates will conduct a video call to discuss and agree on a workbook summarizing Maintenance Expenses for the first quarter.

- If you are in the **Food and Beverage Group**, you and your teammates will conduct a video call to discuss and agree on a Menu Analysis workbook to analyze the profitability of the ten most popular entrees in the hotel's restaurant.

- If you are in the **Human Resources Group**, you and your teammates will conduct a video call to discuss and agree on a Salary Analysis workbook summarizing the pay of salaried employees over the first six months of operation.

- If you are in the **Operations Group**, you and your teammates will conduct a video call to discuss and agree on a workbook for Rooms and Housekeeping Service Analysis that will be used to determine ongoing needs for housekeeping service.

- If you are in the **Sales and Marking Group**, you and your teammates will conduct a video call to discuss and agree on a Rooms Sold Analysis workbook summarizing rooms sold by four salespersons during January-June that will be used to develop a marketing plan for the rest of the year.

FIGURE A

END OF CHAPTER

SUMMARY

Use Flash Fill to recognize a pattern in data and automatically fill in values when you enter examples of desired output. Flash Fill can split data from two or more cells or combine data from two cells.

Functions are formulas that Excel provides and that perform calculations by using specific values in a particular order or structure. Statistical functions are useful to analyze a group of measurements.

You can navigate among worksheets in a workbook by clicking the sheet tabs, which identify each worksheet in a workbook. Use multiple worksheets in a workbook to organize data in a logical arrangement.

Dates are a value you can enter in a cell to which Excel assigns a serial value—a number—so that you can treat dates like other numbers. For example, you can find the number of days between two dates.

GO! LEARN IT ONLINE

Review the concepts and key terms in this chapter by completing these online challenges, which you can find at **www.pearsonhighered.com/go**.

Matching and Multiple Choice:
Answer matching and multiple choice questions to test what you learned in this chapter. MyITLab®

Crossword Puzzle:
Spell out the words that match the numbered clues, and put them in the puzzle squares.

Flipboard:
Flip through the definitions of the key terms in this chapter and match them with the correct term.

GO! FOR JOB SUCCESS

Video: Customer Service

Your instructor may assign this video to your class, and then ask you to think about, or discuss with your classmates, these questions:

FotolEdhar / Fotolia

How could Lee have been more helpful to the customer?

What did the supervisor, Christine, do to calm the customer?

What might SunTel do on a company-wide basis to create a better customer service experience?

END OF CHAPTER
REVIEW AND ASSESSMENT GUIDE FOR EXCEL CHAPTER 2

Your instructor may assign one or more of these projects to help you review the chapter and assess your mastery and understanding of the chapter.

	Review and Assessment Guide for Excel Chapter 2		
Project	**Apply Skills from These Chapter Objectives**	**Project Type**	**Project Location**
2C	Objectives 1-6 from Project 2A	**2C Skills Review** A guided review of the skills from Project 2A.	On the following pages
2D	Objectives 7-12 from Project 2B	**2D Skills Review** A guided review of the skills from Project 2B.	On the following pages
2E	Objectives 1-6 from Project 2A	**2E Mastery (Grader Project)** A demonstration of your mastery of the skills in Project 2A with extensive decision making.	In MyITLab and on the following pages
2F	Objectives 7-12 from Project 2B	**2F Mastery (Grader Project)** A demonstration of your mastery of the skills in Project 2B with extensive decision making.	In MyITLab and on the following pages
2G	Objectives 1-12 from Projects 2A and 2B	**2G Mastery (Grader Project)** A demonstration of your mastery of the skills in Projects 2A and 2B with extensive decision making.	In MyITLab and on the following pages
2H	Combination of Objectives from Projects 2A and 2B	**2H GO! Fix It** A demonstration of your mastery of the skills in Projects 2A and 2B by creating a correct result from a document that contains errors you must find.	Online
2I	Combination of Objectives from Projects 2A and 2B	**2I GO! Make It** A demonstration of your mastery of the skills in Projects 2A and 2B by creating a result from a supplied picture.	Online
2J	Combination of Objectives from Projects 2A and 2B	**2J GO! Solve It** A demonstration of your mastery of the skills in Projects 2A and 2B, your decision-making skills, and your critical thinking skills. A task-specific rubric helps you self-assess your result.	Online
2K	Combination of Objectives from Projects 2A and 2B	**2K GO! Solve It** A demonstration of your mastery of the skills in Projects 2A and 2B, your decision-making skills, and your critical thinking skills. A task-specific rubric helps you self-assess your result.	On the following pages
2L	Combination of Objectives from Projects 2A and 2B	**2L GO! Think** A demonstration of your understanding of the chapter concepts applied in a manner that you would outside of college. An analytic rubric helps you and your instructor grade the quality of your work by comparing it to the work an expert in the discipline would create.	On the following pages
2M	Combination of Objectives from Projects 2A and 2B	**2M GO! Think** A demonstration of your understanding of the chapter concepts applied in a manner that you would outside of college. An analytic rubric helps you and your instructor grade the quality of your work by comparing it to the work an expert in the discipline would create.	Online
2N	Combination of Objectives from Projects 2A and 2B	**2N You and GO!** A demonstration of your understanding of the chapter concepts applied in a manner that you would in a personal situation. An analytic rubric helps you and your instructor grade the quality of your work.	Online
2O	Combination of Objectives from Projects 2A and 2B	**2O Cumulative Group Project for Excel Chapter 2** A demonstration of your understanding of concepts and your ability to work collaboratively in a group role-playing assessment, requiring both collaboration and self-management.	Online

GLOSSARY

GLOSSARY OF CHAPTER KEY TERMS

Arguments The values that an Excel function uses to perform calculations or operations.

AVERAGE function An Excel function that adds a group of values, and then divides the result by the number of values in the group.

Comparison operators Symbols that evaluate each value to determine if it is the same (=), greater than (>), less than (<), or in between a range of values as specified by the criteria.

Conditional format A format that changes the appearance of a cell—for example, by adding cell shading or font color—based on a condition; if the condition is true, the cell is formatted based on that condition, and if the condition is false, the cell is *not* formatted.

COUNT A statistical function that counts the number of cells in a range that contain numbers.

COUNTIF function A statistical function that counts the number of cells within a range that meet the given condition and that has two arguments—the range of cells to check and the criteria.

Criteria Conditions that you specify in a logical function.

Data bar A cell format consisting of a shaded bar that provides a visual cue to the reader about the value of a cell relative to other cells; the length of the bar represents the value in the cell—a longer bar represents a higher value and a shorter bar represents s lower value.

Detail sheets The worksheets that contain the details of the information summarized on a summary sheet.

Drag and drop The action of moving a selection by dragging it to a new location.

Excel table A series of rows and columns that contains related data that is managed independently from the data in other rows and columns in the worksheet.

Filter The process of displaying only a portion of the data based on matching a specific value to show only the data that meets the criteria that you specify.

Find and replace A command that searches the cells in a worksheet—or in a selected range—for matches and then replaces each match with a replacement value of your choice.

Flash Fill Recognizes a pattern in your data, and then automatically fills in values when you enter examples of the output that you want. Use it to split data from two or more cells or to combine data from two cells.

Formula AutoComplete An Excel feature that, after typing an = (equal sign) and the beginning letter or letters of a function name, displays a list of function names that match the typed letter(s), and from which you can insert the function by pointing to its name and pressing the Tab key or double-clicking.

Freeze Panes A command that enables you to select one or more rows or columns and freeze (lock) them into place; the locked rows and columns become separate panes.

Function A predefined formula—a formula that Excel has already built for you—that performs calculations by using specific values in a particular order or structure.

IF function A function that uses a logical test to check whether a condition is met, and then returns one value if true, and another value if false.

Logical functions A group of functions that test for specific conditions and that typically use conditional tests to determine whether specified conditions are true or false.

Logical test Any value or expression that can be evaluated as being true or false.

MAX function An Excel function that determines the largest value in a selected range of values.

MEDIAN function An Excel function that finds the middle value that has as many values above it in the group as are below it; it differs from AVERAGE in that the result is not affected as much by a single value that is greatly different from the others.

MIN function An Excel function that determines the smallest value in a selected range of values.

Navigate The process of moving within a worksheet or workbook.

NOW function An Excel function that retrieves the date and time from your computer's calendar and clock and inserts the information into the selected cell.

Pane A portion of a worksheet window bounded by and separated from other portions by vertical and horizontal bars.

Paste The action of placing cell contents that have been copied or moved to the Clipboard into another location.

Paste area The target destination for data that has been cut or copied using the Office Clipboard.

Paste Options gallery A gallery of buttons that provides a Live Preview of all the Paste options available in the current context.

Print Titles An Excel command that enables you to specify rows and columns to repeat on each printed page.

Scale to Fit Excel commands that enable you to stretch or shrink the width, height, or both, of printed output to fit a maximum number of pages.

Sheet tabs The labels along the lower border of the workbook window that identify each worksheet.

Sort The process of arranging data in a specific order based on the value in each field.

Split Splits the window into multiple resizable panes that contain views of your worksheet. This is useful to view multiple distant parts of your worksheet at one time.

Statistical functions Excel functions, including the AVERAGE, MEDIAN, MIN, and MAX functions, which are useful to analyze a group of measurements.

SUM function A predefined formula that adds all the numbers in a selected range of cells.

Summary sheet A worksheet where totals from other worksheets are displayed and summarized.

Volatile A term used to describe an Excel function that is subject to change each time the workbook is reopened; for example the NOW function updates itself to the current date and time each time the workbook is opened.

CHAPTER REVIEW

Skills Review Project 2C Roses

Apply 2A skills from these Objectives:

1. Use Flash Fill and the SUM, AVERAGE, MEDIAN, MIN, and MAX Functions
2. Move Data, Resolve Error Messages, and Rotate Text
3. Use COUNTIF and IF Functions and Apply Conditional Formatting
4. Use Date & Time Functions and Freeze Panes
5. Create, Sort, and Filter an Excel Table
6. View, Format, and Print a Large Worksheet

In the following Skills Review, you will edit a worksheet detailing the current inventory of Roses at the Pasadena nursery. Your completed workbook will look similar to Figure 2.55.

PROJECT FILES

For Project 2C, you will need the following file:

e02C_Roses

You will save your workbook as:

Lastname_Firstname_2C_Roses

PROJECT RESULTS

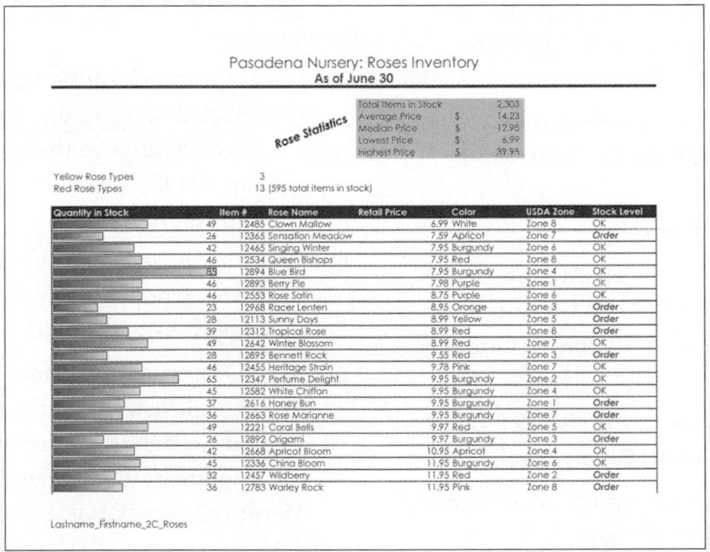

Pasadena Nursery: Roses Inventory

As of June 30

Rose Statistics

Total Items in Stock		2,303
Average Price	$	14.23
Median Price	$	12.95
Lowest Price	$	6.99
Highest Price	$	39.95

Yellow Rose Types 3

Red Rose Types 13 (595 total items in stock)

Quantity in Stock	Item #	Rose Name	Retail Price	Color	USDA Zone	Stock Level
49	12485	Clown Mallow	6.99	White	Zone 8	OK
26	12365	Sensation Meadow	7.59	Apricot	Zone 7	Order
42	12465	Singing Winter	7.95	Burgundy	Zone 6	OK
46	12534	Queen Bishops	7.95	Red	Zone 8	OK
85	12894	Blue Bird	7.95	Burgundy	Zone 4	OK
46	12893	Berry Pie	7.98	Purple	Zone 1	OK
46	12553	Rose Satin	8.75	Purple	Zone 6	OK
23	12968	Racer Lenten	8.95	Orange	Zone 3	Order
28	12113	Sunny Days	8.99	Yellow	Zone 5	Order
39	12312	Tropical Rose	8.99	Red	Zone 8	Order
49	12642	Winter Blossom	8.99	Red	Zone 7	OK
28	12895	Bennett Rock	9.55	Red	Zone 3	Order
46	12455	Heritage Strain	9.78	Pink	Zone 7	OK
65	12347	Perfume Delight	9.95	Burgundy	Zone 2	OK
45	12582	White Chiffon	9.95	Burgundy	Zone 4	OK
37	2616	Honey Bun	9.95	Burgundy	Zone 1	Order
36	12663	Rose Marianne	9.95	Burgundy	Zone 7	Order
49	12221	Coral Bells	9.97	Red	Zone 5	OK
26	12892	Origami	9.97	Burgundy	Zone 3	Order
42	12668	Apricot Bloom	10.95	Apricot	Zone 4	OK
45	12336	China Bloom	11.95	Burgundy	Zone 6	OK
32	12457	Wildberry	11.95	Red	Zone 2	Order
36	12783	Warley Rock	11.95	Pink	Zone 8	Order

Lastname_Firstname_2C_Roses

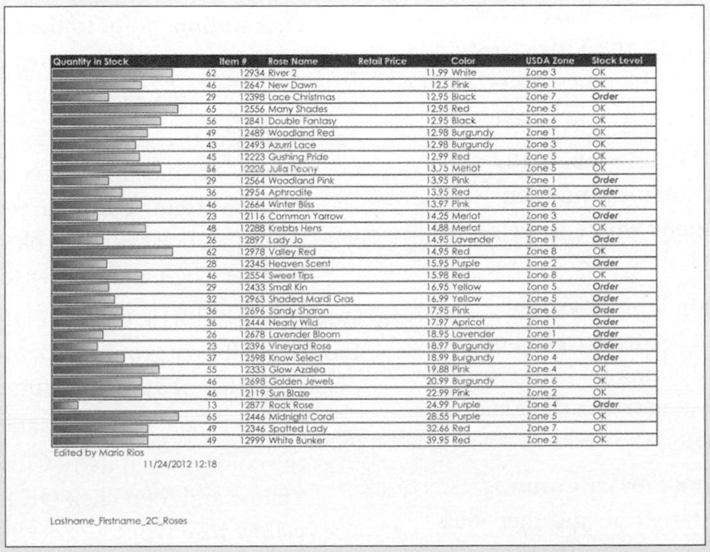

Quantity in Stock	Item #	Rose Name	Retail Price	Color	USDA Zone	Stock Level
62	12934	River 2	11.99	White	Zone 3	OK
46	12647	New Dawn	12.5	Pink	Zone 1	OK
29	12398	Lace Christmas	12.95	Black	Zone 7	Order
65	12556	Many Shades	12.95	Red	Zone 5	OK
56	12841	Double Fantasy	12.95	Black	Zone 6	OK
49	12489	Woodland Red	12.98	Burgundy	Zone 1	OK
43	12493	Azurri Lace	12.98	Burgundy	Zone 3	OK
45	12223	Gushing Pride	12.99	Red	Zone 5	OK
56	12225	Julia Peony	13.75	Merlot	Zone 5	OK
29	12564	Woodland Pink	13.95	Pink	Zone 1	Order
36	12954	Aphrodite	13.95	Red	Zone 2	Order
46	12664	Winter Bliss	13.97	Pink	Zone 6	OK
23	12116	Common Yarrow	14.25	Merlot	Zone 3	Order
48	12288	Krebbs Hens	14.88	Merlot	Zone 5	OK
26	12897	Lady Jo	14.95	Lavender	Zone 1	Order
62	12978	Valley Red	14.95	Red	Zone 8	OK
28	12345	Heaven Scent	15.95	Purple	Zone 2	Order
46	12554	Sweet Tips	15.98	Red	Zone 8	OK
29	12433	Small Kin	16.95	Yellow	Zone 5	Order
32	12963	Shaded Mardi Gras	16.99	Yellow	Zone 5	Order
36	12696	Sandy Sharon	17.95	Pink	Zone 6	Order
36	12444	Nearly Wild	17.97	Apricot	Zone 1	Order
26	12678	Lavender Bloom	18.95	Lavender	Zone 1	Order
23	12396	Vineyard Rose	18.97	Burgundy	Zone 7	Order
37	12598	Know Select	18.99	Burgundy	Zone 4	Order
55	12333	Glow Azalea	19.88	Pink	Zone 4	OK
46	12698	Golden Jewels	20.99	Burgundy	Zone 6	OK
46	12119	Sun Blaze	22.99	Pink	Zone 2	OK
13	12877	Rock Rose	24.99	Purple	Zone 4	Order
65	12446	Midnight Coral	28.55	Purple	Zone 5	OK
49	12346	Spotted Lady	32.66	Red	Zone 7	OK
49	12999	White Bunker	39.95	Red	Zone 2	OK

Edited by Mario Rios

11/24/2012 12:18

Lastname_Firstname_2C_Roses

FIGURE 2.55

(Project 2C Roses continues on the next page)

CHAPTER REVIEW

1 Start Excel. From your student files, locate and open **e02C_Roses**. Save the file in your **Excel Chapter 2** folder as **Lastname_Firstname_2C_Roses**

a. In the **column heading area**, point to **column C** to display the ↓ pointer, and then drag to the right to select **columns C:D**. On the **HOME tab**, in the **Cells group**, click the **Insert button arrow**, and then click Insert **Sheet Columns**.

b. Click cell **C14**, type **12113** and then on the **Formula Bar**, click **Enter** to confirm the entry and keep cell **C14** as the active cell. On the **HOME tab**, in the **Editing group**, click **Fill**, and then click **Flash Fill**.

c. Click cell **D14**, type **Zone 5** On the **Formula Bar**, click **Enter** to confirm the entry and keep the cell active. Press Ctrl + E, which is the keyboard shortcut for Flash Fill.

d. Select **column B**, and then in the **Cells group**, click the **Delete button arrow**. Click **Delete Sheet Columns**.

2 In cell **B13** type **Item #** and press Enter.

a. Select **column C**, and then on the **HOME tab**, in the **Clipboard group**, click **Cut**. Click cell **G1**, and then in the **Clipboard group**, click the upper portion of the **Paste** button.

b. Select and then delete **column C**. In cell **F13** type **USDA Zone** and in cell **G13** type **Stock Level**

c. Select columns **A:G**. In the **Cells group**, click **Format**, and then click **AutoFit Column Width**.

d. Press Ctrl + Home. **Merge & Center** cell **A1** across the range **A1:G1**, and then apply the **Title** cell style. **Merge & Center** cell **A2** across the range **A2:G2**, and then apply the **Heading 1** cell style. Click **Save**.

3 Click cell **B4**. On the **FORMULAS tab**, in the **Function Library group**, click **AutoSum**, and then within the parentheses, type **a14:a68** which is the range containing the quantities for each item.

a. Click cell **B5**, in the **Function Library group**, click **More Functions**. Point to **Statistical**, click **AVERAGE**, and then in the **Number1** box, type **d14:d68** which is the range containing the *Retail Price* for each item. Click **OK**.

b. Click cell **B6**. In the **Function Library group**, click **More Functions**, point to **Statistical**, and then click

MEDIAN. In the **Function Arguments** dialog box, to the right of the **Number1** box, click **Collapse Dialog** 🔳, and then select the range **D14:D68**. Click **Expand Dialog** 🔳, and then click **OK**. Recall that you can select or type a range and that you can collapse the dialog box to make it easier to view your selection.

c. Click cell **B7**, and then by typing or selecting, insert the **MIN** function to determine the lowest **Retail Price**. Click cell **B8**, and then insert the **MAX** function to determine the highest **Retail Price**.

4 Select cell **B4**. On the **HOME tab**, apply **Comma Style**, and then click **Decrease Decimal** two times. Select the range **B5:B8**, and then apply the **Accounting Number Format**.

a. Select the range **A4:B8**. Point to the right edge of the selected range to display the 🔭 pointer. Drag the selected range to the right until the ScreenTip displays *D4:E8*, and then release the mouse button. AutoFit **column D**.

b. With the range **D4:E8** selected, on the **HOME tab**, in the **Styles group**, display the **Cell Styles** gallery, and then apply **20%—Accent1**.

c. In cell **C6**, type **Rose Statistics** Select the range **C4:C8**, right-click over the selection, and then click **Format Cells**. In the **Format Cells** dialog box, click the **Alignment tab**. Under **Text control**, select the **Merge cells** check box.

d. In the upper right portion of the dialog box, under **Orientation**, point to the **red diamond**, and then drag the diamond upward until the **Degrees** box indicates *20*. Click **OK**.

e. With the merged cell still selected, change the **Font Size** to 14, and then apply **Bold** and **Italic**. Click the **Font Color button arrow**, and then in the fifth column, click the first color—**Blue, Accent 1**. Apply **Middle Align** and **Center** to the cell.

5 Click cell **B10**. On the **FORMULAS tab**, in the **Function Library group**, click **More Functions**, and then display the list of **Statistical** functions. Click **COUNTIF**.

a. As the range, type **e14:e68** which is the range with the color of each item. Click in the **Criteria** box, type **Yellow** and then click **OK** to calculate the number of yellow rose types.

(Project 2C Roses continues on the next page)

b. Click cell **G14**. On the **FORMULAS tab**, in the **Function Library group**, click **Logical**, and then on the list, click **IF**. If necessary, drag the title bar of the **Function Arguments** dialog box up or down so that you can view **row 14** on your screen.

c. With the insertion point in the **Logical_test** box, click cell **A14**, and then type **<40** Press Tab to move the insertion point to the **Value_if_true** box, and then type **Order** Press Tab to move the insertion point to the **Value_if_false** box, type **OK** and then click **OK**. Using the fill handle, copy the function in cell **G14** down through cell **G68**.

6 With the range **G14:G68** selected, on the **HOME tab**, in the **Styles group**, click **Conditional Formatting**. In the list, point to **Highlight Cells Rules**, and then click **Text that Contains**.

a. In the **Text That Contains** dialog box, with the insertion point blinking in the first box, type **Order** and then in the second box, click the arrow. On the list, click **Custom Format**.

b. In the **Format Cells** dialog box, on the **Font tab**, under **Font style**, click **Bold Italic**. Click the **Color arrow**, and then under **Theme Colors**, in the fourth column, click the first color—**Blue-Gray, Text 2**. Click **OK** two times to apply the font color, bold, and italic to the cells that contain the word *Order*.

c. Select the range **A14:A68**. In the **Styles group**, click **Conditional Formatting**. In the list, point to **Data Bars**, and then under **Gradient Fill**, click **Red Data Bar**. Click anywhere to cancel the selection.

d. Select the range **E14:E68**. On the **HOME tab**, in the **Editing group**, click **Find & Select**, and then click **Replace**. In the **Find and Replace** dialog box, in the **Find what** box, type **Deep Burgundy** and then in the **Replace with** box type **Burgundy** Click **Replace All** and then click **OK**. In the lower right corner of the **Find and Replace** dialog box, click **Close**.

e. Scroll down as necessary, and then click cell **A70**. Type **Edited by Maria Rios** and then press Enter. With cell **A71** as the active cell, on the **FORMULAS tab**, in the **Function Library group**, click **Date & Time**. In the list of functions, click **NOW**, and then click **OK** to enter the current date and time. **Save** your workbook.

7 Click any cell in the data below row 13. Click the **INSERT tab**, and then in the **Tables group**, click **Table**. In the **Create Table** dialog box, be sure the **My table has headers** check box is selected, and then click **OK**. On the **DESIGN tab**, in the **Table Styles group**, click **More** ▾ and then under **Light**, locate and click **Table Style Light 9**.

a. In the header row of the table, click the **Retail Price arrow**, and then from the menu, click **Sort Smallest to Largest**. Click the **Color arrow**. On the menu, click the **(Select All)** check box to clear all the check boxes. Scroll as necessary and then select only the **Red** check box. Click OK.

b. Click anywhere in the table. On the **DESIGN tab**, in the **Table Style Options group**, select the **Total Row** check box. Click cell **A69**, click the arrow that displays to the right of cell **A69**, and then click **Sum**. In cell **B11**, type the result **13** and then press Tab. In cell **C11**, type **(595 total items in stock)** and then press Enter.

c. In the header row of the table, click the **Color arrow** and then click **Clear Filter From "Color"** to redisplay all of the data. Click anywhere in the table. Click the **DESIGN tab**, in the **Table Style Options group**, clear the **Total Row** check box, and then in the **Tools group**, click **Convert to Range**. Click **Yes**.

8 On the **PAGE LAYOUT tab**, in the **Themes group**, click **Themes** and then click the **Ion** theme. Change the **Orientation** to **Landscape**.

a. In the **Page Setup group**, click **Margins**, and then click **Custom Margins** to display the **Page Setup** dialog box.

b. On the **Margins tab**, under **Center on page**, select the **Horizontally** check box. On the **Header/Footer tab**, display the **Custom Footer**, and then in the **Left section**, insert the file name. Click **OK** two times.

c. In the **Page Setup** group, click **Print Titles** to redisplay the **Page Setup** dialog box. Under **Print titles**, click in the **Rows to repeat at top** box, and then at the right, click **Collapse Dialog**. From the **row heading area**, select **row 13**, and then click **Expand Dialog**. Click **OK** to print the column titles in row 13 at the top of every page.

d. Press Ctrl + F2 to display the **Print Preview**. At the bottom of the **Settings group**, click **No Scaling**, and

(Project 2C Roses continues on the next page)

CHAPTER REVIEW

then on the displayed list, point to **Fit All Columns on One Page**.

e. On the left, click **Info**, and then in the lower right corner, click **Show All Properties**. As the **Tags**, type **inventory, Pasadena, roses** In the **Subject** box, type your course name and section number. Be sure your name displays as the author.

END | You have completed Project 2C

9 **Save** your workbook. Print or submit electronically as directed by your instructor. If required by your instructor, print or create an electronic version of your worksheets with formulas displayed by using the instructions in Excel Project 1A, and then Close Excel without saving so that you do not save the changes you made to print formulas.

CHAPTER REVIEW

Skills Review   Project 2D Canada

Apply 2B skills from these Objectives:

7 Navigate a Workbook and Rename Worksheets

8 Enter Dates, Clear Contents, and Clear Formats

9 Copy and Paste by Using the Paste Options Gallery

10 Edit and Format Multiple Worksheets at the Same Time

11 Create a Summary Sheet with Column Sparklines

12 Format and Print Multiple Worksheets in a Workbook

In the following Skills Review, you will edit a workbook that summarizes sales in the Eastern and Western region of Canada. Your completed workbook will look similar to Figure 2.56.

PROJECT FILES

For Project 2D, you will need the following file:

e02D_Canada

You will save your workbook as:

Lastname_Firstname_2D_Canada

PROJECT RESULTS

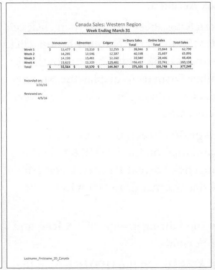

FIGURE 2.56

(Project 2D Canada continues on the next page)

CHAPTER REVIEW

1 ▶ Start Excel. From your student files, locate and open **e02D_Canada**. Save the file in your **Excel Chapter 2** folder as **Lastname_Firstname_2D_Canada**

a. Point to the **Sheet1 tab**, and then double-click to select the sheet tab name. Type **Western Sales** and then press Enter.

b. Point to the **Sheet2 tab**, right-click, and then from the shortcut menu, click **Rename**. Type **Eastern Sales** and press Enter.

c. Point to the **Western Sales sheet tab** and right-click. On the shortcut menu, point to **Tab Color**, and then in the last column, click the first color—**Green, Accent 6**. Change the **Tab Color** of the **Eastern Sales sheet tab** to **Blue, Accent 5**.

d. Click the **Western Sales sheet tab**, and then click cell **A13**. On the **HOME tab**, in the **Number group**, click the **Number Format arrow**. At the bottom of the list, click **More Number Formats** to display the **Number tab** of the **Format Cells** dialog box. Click the **3/14/12** type, and then click **OK**.

e. Click cell **A16**, type **4/5/16** and then press Enter. Click cell **A13**, and then on the **HOME tab**, in the **Clipboard group**, click **Format Painter**. Click cell **A16** to copy the date format from cell **A13** to cell **A16**.

f. Click cell **A1**. In the **Editing group**, click **Clear**, and then click **Clear Formats**.

g. Select the range **A5:A16**. On the **HOME tab**, in the **Clipboard group**, click **Copy**. At the bottom of the workbook window, click the **Eastern Sales sheet tab** to make it the active worksheet. Right-click cell **A5**, and then under **Paste Options**, click the first button—**Paste**. Display the **Western Sales** sheet. Press Esc to cancel the moving border.

2 ▶ With the **Western Sales** sheet active, make cell **A1** the active cell. Point to the sheet tab, right-click, and then on the shortcut menu, click **Select All Sheets**. Verify that *[Group]* displays in the title bar.

a. **Merge & Center** the text in cell **A1** across the range **A1:G1**, and then apply the **Title** cell style. Select **columns A:G**, and then set their widths to **100 pixels**.

b. Click cell **A2**, type **Week Ending March 31** and then on the **Formula Bar**, click the **Enter** button to keep cell **A2** as the active cell. **Merge & Center**

the text across the range **A2:G2**, and then apply the **Heading 1** cell style.

c. Select the range **B4:G4**, and then apply the **Heading 3** cell style. In the **Alignment group**, click **Center**, **Middle Align**, and **Wrap Text**.

d. With the sheets still grouped and the **Western Sales** sheet active, click cell **E5**. On the **HOME tab**, in the **Editing group**, click **AutoSum**, and then press Enter. Click cell **E5**, and then drag the fill handle down to copy the formula through cell **E8**.

e. Click cell **G5**, type = click cell **E5**, type + click cell **F5**, and then press Enter. Copy the formula down through cell **G8**. In cell **A9**, type **Total** Select the range **B5:G9**, and then hold down Alt and press = to enter the SUM function for all the columns. Select the range **A5:A9**, and then apply the **Heading 4** cell style.

f. Select the range **B5:G5**, hold down Ctrl, and then select the range **B9:G9**. Apply the **Accounting Number Format** and decrease the decimal places to zero. Select the range **B6:G8**, and then apply **Comma Style** with zero decimal places. Select the range **B9:G9**, and then apply the **Total** cell style.

3 ▶ Click the **Eastern Sales sheet tab** to cancel the grouping and display the second worksheet.

a. To the right of the **Eastern Sales sheet tab**, click the **New sheet** button. **Rename** the new worksheet tab **Summary** and then change the **Tab Color** to **Gold, Accent 4**.

b. Widen **columns A:E to 150** pixels. In cell **A1**, type **Canadian Sales** and then **Merge & Center** the title across the range **A1:E1**. Apply the **Title** cell style. In cell **A2**, type **Week Ending March 31** and then **Merge & Center** the text across the range **A2:E2**. Apply the **Heading 1** cell style. In cell **A5**, type **Western Sales** and in cell **A6**, type **Eastern Sales**

c. In cell **B4**, type **In-Store/Online Sales** and in cell **C4**, type **In-Store Sales** In cell **D4**, type **Online Sales** and in cell **E4**, type **Total Sales** Select the range **B4:E4**, apply the **Heading 3** cell style, and then **Center** these column titles.

d. Click cell **C5**. Type = and then click the **Western Sales sheet tab**. In the **Western Sales** worksheet, click cell **E9**, and then press Enter. Click cell **D5**. Type = and

(Project 2D Canada continues on the next page)

CHAPTER REVIEW

then click the **Western Sales sheet tab**. Click cell **F9**, and then press Enter.

e. By using the same technique, in cells **C6** and **D6**, insert the total **In-Store Sales** and **Online Sales** data from the **Eastern Sales** worksheet.

f. Select the range **C5:E6**, and then click **AutoSum** to total the two rows. In cell **A7**, type **Total** Select the range **C5:E6** again. In the lower right corner of the selection, click the **Quick Analysis** button, click **Totals**, and then click the first **Sum** button. Recall there are many ways to sum a group of cells.

g. Select the nonadjacent ranges **C5:E5** and **C7:E7**, and then apply **Accounting Number Format** with zero decimal places. Select the range **C6:E6**, and then apply **Comma Style** with zero decimal places. Select the range **C7:E7**, and then apply the **Total** cell style. Select the range **A5:A7** and apply the **Heading 4** cell style.

h. Click cell **B5**. On the **INSERT tab**, in the **Sparklines group**, click **Column**. In the **Create Sparklines** dialog box, with the insertion point blinking in the **Data Range** box, select the range **C5:D5** and then click **OK**.

i. Click cell **B6**, and then insert a **Column Sparkline** for the range **C6:D6**. With the **Eastern Sales** sparkline selected, in the **Style group**, click More ▼. Apply the second style in the third row—**Sparkline Style Accent 2, (no dark or light)**.

4 Point to the **Summary sheet tab**, hold down the left mouse button to display a small black triangle, and drag to the left until the triangle and mouse pointer are to the left of the **Western Sales sheet tab**, and then release the left mouse button to move the sheet to the first position in the workbook.

a. Be sure the **Summary** worksheet is the active sheet, and then press Ctrl + Home to move to cell **A1**. Point to the **Summary sheet tab**, right-click, and then click **Select All Sheets** to display [Group] in the title bar. On the **PAGE LAYOUT tab**, in the **Page Setup group**, click **Margins**, and then click **Custom Margins** to display the **Page Setup** dialog box. On the **Margins tab**, center the worksheets **Horizontally**. On the **Header/Footer tab**, insert the file name in the **left section** of the footer.

b. Display the **Print Preview** of the worksheets. Under **Settings**, click **No Scaling**, and then click **Fit All Columns on One Page**. Use the **Next** button to view all three worksheets.

c. On the left, click **Info**, and then in the lower right corner of the screen, click **Show All Properties**. As the **Tags**, type **Canada, sales** In the **Subject** box, type your course name and section number. Be sure your name displays as the author.

d. On the left, click **Save**. Print or submit electronically as directed by your instructor. If required by your instructor, print or create an electronic version of your worksheets with formulas displayed by using the instructions in Excel Project 1A, and then **Close** Excel without saving so that you do not save the changes you made to print formulas.

END | You have completed Project 2D

CONTENT-BASED ASSESSMENTS

Mastering Excel   Project 2E Plants

Apply 2A skills from these Objectives:

1 Use Flash Fill and the SUM, AVERAGE, MEDIAN, MIN, and MAX Functions

2 Move Data, Resolve Error Messages, and Rotate Text

3 Use COUNTIF and IF Functions and Apply Conditional Formatting

4 Use Date & Time Functions and Freeze Panes

5 Create, Sort, and Filter an Excel Table

6 View, Format, and Print a Large Worksheet

In the following project, you will edit a worksheet detailing the current inventory of plants at the Pasadena facility. Your completed worksheet will look similar to Figure 2.57.

PROJECT FILES

For Project 2E, you will need the following file:

e02E_Plants

You will save your workbook as:

Lastname_Firstname_2E_Plants

PROJECT RESULTS

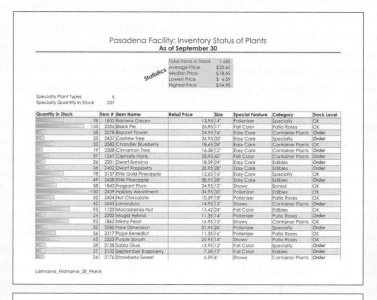

FIGURE 2.57

(Project 2E Plants continues on the next page)

CONTENT-BASED ASSESSMENTS

1 Start Excel. From your student files, locate and open **e02E_Plants**, and then **Save** the file in your **Excel Chapter 2** folder as **Lastname_Firstname_2E_Plants**

2 To the right of **column B**, insert two new columns to create **new blank columns C and D**. By using **Flash Fill** in the two new columns, split the data in **column B** into a column for *Item #* in **column C** and *Category* in **column D**. As necessary, type **Item #** as the column title in **column C** and **Category** as the column title in **column D**.

3 Delete **column B**. By using the **Cut** and **Paste** commands, cut **column C**—*Category*—and paste it to **column H**, and then delete the empty **column C**. Apply **AutoFit** to **columns A:G**.

4 In cell **B4**, insert a function to calculate the **Total Items in Stock** by summing the **Quantity in Stock** data, and then apply **Comma Style** with zero decimal places to the result. In each cell in the range **B5:B8**, insert functions to calculate the Average, Median, Lowest, and Highest retail prices, and then apply the **Accounting Number Format** to each result.

5 Move the range **A4:B8** to the range **D4:E8**, apply the **40%—Accent4** cell style to the range, and then select **columns D:E** and **AutoFit**. In cell **C6**, type **Statistics** and then select the range **C4:C8**. In the **Format Cells** dialog box, merge the selected cells, and change the text **Orientation** to **25 Degrees**. Format the cell with **Bold**, a **Font Size** of **14 pt**, and then change the **Font Color** to **Blue-Gray, Text 2**. Apply **Middle Align** and **Align Right**.

6 In the **Category** column, **Replace All** occurrences of **Vine Roses** with **Patio Roses** In cell **B10**, use the **COUNTIF** function to count the number of **Specialty** plant types in the **Category** column.

7 In cell **H13**, type **Stock Level** In cell **H14**, enter an **IF** function to determine the items that must be ordered. If the **Quantity in Stock** is less than **50** the **Value_if_true**

is **Order** Otherwise the **Value_if_false** is **OK** Fill the formula down through cell **H42**. Apply **Conditional Formatting** to the **Stock Level** column so that cells that contain the text *Order* are formatted with **Bold Italic** and with a **Color** of **Green, Accent 6**. Apply conditional formatting to the **Quantity in Stock** column by applying a **Gradient Fill Green Data Bar**.

8 Format the range **A13:H42** as a **Table** with headers, and apply the style **Table Style Light 20**. Sort the table from A to Z by **Item Name**, and then filter on the **Category** column to display the **Specialty** types. Display a **Total Row** in the table, and then in cell **A43**, **Sum** the **Quantity in Stock** for the **Specialty** items. Type the result in cell **B11**. Click in the table, and then on the **DESIGN tab**, remove the total row from the table. Clear the **Category** filter, and convert the table to a range.

9 **Merge & Center** the title and subtitle across **columns A:H**, and apply **Title** and **Heading 1** styles respectively. Change the theme to **Mesh**, and then select and **AutoFit** all the columns. Set the orientation to **Landscape**. In the **Page Setup** dialog box, center the worksheet **Horizontally**, insert a custom footer in the **left section** with the file name, and set **row 13** to repeat at the top of each page. Display the **Print Preview**. Apply the **Fit All Columns on One Page** setting.

10 As the **Tags**, type **plants inventory, Pasadena** As the **Subject**, type your course name and section number. Be sure your name displays as the **Author**. In Backstage view, on the left click **Save**, and then print or submit electronically as directed. If required by your instructor, print or create an electronic version of your worksheet with formulas displayed by using the instructions in Project 1A, and then close Excel without saving so that you do not save the changes you made to print formulas.

END | You have completed Project 2E

CONTENT-BASED ASSESSMENTS

In the following project, you will edit a workbook that summarizes the compensation for the commercial salespersons who qualified for bonuses in the Western and Eastern Canadian regions. Your completed worksheets will look similar to Figure 2.58.

Apply 2B skills from these Objectives:

7 Navigate a Workbook and Rename Worksheets

8 Enter Dates, Clear Contents, and Clear Formats

9 Copy and Paste by Using the Paste Options Gallery

10 Edit and Format Multiple Worksheets at the Same Time

11 Create a Summary Sheet with Column Sparklines

12 Format and Print Multiple Worksheets in a Workbook

PROJECT FILES

For Project 2F, you will need the following file:

e02F_Bonus

You will save your workbook as:

Lastname_Firstname_2F_Bonus

PROJECT RESULTS

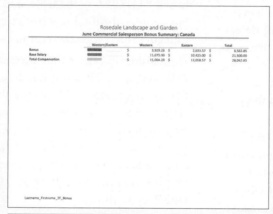

FIGURE 2.58

(Project 2F Bonus continues on the next page)

CONTENT-BASED ASSESSMENTS

1 **Start** Excel. From your student files, open **e02F_Bonus**, and then save the file in your **Excel Chapter 2** folder as **Lastname_Firstname_2F_Bonus**

2 Rename **Sheet1** as **Western** and change the **Tab Color** to **Brown, Accent 2**. Rename **Sheet2** as **Eastern** and change the **Tab Color** to **Orange, Accent 1**.

3 Click the **Western sheet tab** to make it the active sheet, and then group the worksheets. In cell **A1**, type **Rosedale Landscape and Garden** and then **Merge & Center** the text across the range **A1:F1**. Apply the **Title** cell style. **Merge & Center** the text in cell **A2** across the range **A2:F2**, and then apply the **Heading 3** cell style.

4 With the sheets still grouped, in cell **D5** calculate the **Bonus** for *Reid* by multiplying the **Sales Eligible for Bonus** times the **Bonus Rate**. Copy the formula down through cell **D8**. In cell **F5**, calculate **Total Compensation** by summing the **Bonus** and **Base Salary** for *Reid*. Copy the formula down through the cell **F8**.

5 In **row 9**, sum the columns for **Sales Eligible for Bonus**, **Bonus**, **Base Salary**, and **Total Compensation**. Apply the **Accounting Number Format** with two decimal places to the appropriate cells in **row 5** and **row 9** (do not include the percentages). Apply the **Comma Style** with two decimal places to the appropriate cells in **rows 6:8** (do not include the percentages). Apply the **Total** cell style to the appropriate cells in the Total row.

6 Click the **Eastern** sheet tab to ungroup the sheets, and then insert a new worksheet. Change the sheet name to **Summary** and then change the **Tab Color** to **Brown, Text 2**. Widen **column A** to **210** pixels, widen **columns B:E** to **155** pixels, and then move the **Summary** sheet so that it is the first sheet in the workbook. In cell **A1** of the **Summary** sheet, type **Rosedale Landscape and Garden** and then **Merge & Center** the title across the range **A1:E1**. Apply the **Title** cell style. In cell **A2**, type **June Commercial Salesperson Bonus Summary: Canada** and then **Merge & Center** the text across the range **A2:E2**. Apply the **Heading 1** cell style.

7 In the range **A5:A7**, type the following row titles and then apply the **Heading 4** cell style:

> Bonus

> Base Salary

> Total Compensation

8 In the range **B4:E4**, type the following column titles, and then **Center** and apply the **Heading 3** cell style.

> Western/Eastern

> Western

> Eastern

> Total

9 In cell **C5**, enter a formula that references cell **D9** in the **Western** worksheet so that the total bonus amount for the Western region displays in **C5**. Create similar formulas to enter the total **Base Salary** for the Western region in cell **C6**. Using the same technique, enter formulas in the range **D5:D6** so that the **Eastern** totals display.

10 Sum the **Bonus** and **Base Salary** rows, and then calculate **Total Compensation** for the **Western**, **Eastern**, and **Total** columns.

11 In cell **B5**, insert a **Column Sparkline** for the range **C5:D5**. In cells **B6** and **B7**, insert **Column** sparklines for the appropriate ranges to compare Western totals with Eastern totals. To the sparkline in cell **B5**, apply the second style in the third row—**Sparkline Style Accent 2**, (**no dark or light**). To the sparkline in cell **B6**, apply the first style in the fifth row—**Sparkline Style Dark #1**. To the sparkline in cell **B7**, apply the first style in the fourth row—**Sparkline Style Accent 1, Lighter 40%**.

12 **Group** the three worksheets, and then in the **Page Setup** dialog box, center the worksheets **Horizontally** on the page, and insert a **Custom Footer** in the **left section** with the file name. Change the **Orientation** to **Landscape**.

13 As the **Tags**, type **June, bonus, compensation** As the **Subject**, type your course name and section number. Be sure your name displays as the **Author**. Click **Save**, and then print or submit your workbook electronically as directed. If required by your instructor, print or create an electronic version of your worksheets with formulas displayed by using the instructions in Project 1A, and then close Excel without saving so that you do not save the changes you made to print formulas.

END | You have completed Project 2F

Apply a combination of 2A and 2B skills:

1 Use Flash Fill and the SUM, AVERAGE, MEDIAN, MIN, and MAX Functions

2 Move Data, Resolve Error Messages, and Rotate Text

3 Use COUNTIF and IF Functions and Apply Conditional Formatting

4 Use Date & Time Functions and Freeze Panes

5 Create, Sort, and Filter an Excel Table

6 View, Format and Print a Large Worksheet

7 Navigate a Workbook and Rename Worksheets

8 Enter Dates, Clear Contents, and Clear Formats

9 Copy and Paste by Using the Paste Options Gallery

10 Edit and Format Multiple Worksheets at the Same Time

11 Create a Summary Sheet with Column Sparklines

12 Format and Print Multiple Worksheets in a Workbook

In the following project, you will edit a worksheet that summarizes the inventory of bulbs and trees at the Pasadena facility. Your completed workbook will look similar to Figure 2.59.

PROJECT FILES

For Project 2G, you will need the following file:

e02G_Inventory

You will save your workbook as

Lastname_Firstname_2G_Inventory

PROJECT RESULTS

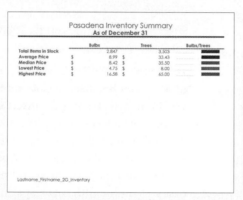

FIGURE 2.59

(Project 2G Inventory continues on the next page)

CONTENT-BASED ASSESSMENTS

1 Start Excel. From your student files, open **e02G_Inventory**. Save the file in your **Excel Chapter 2** folder as **Lastname_Firstname_2G_Inventory.**

2 Change the **Theme** to **Slice**. Rename **Sheet1** as **Bulbs** and **Sheet2** as **Trees** Click the **Bulbs sheet tab** to make it the active sheet.

3 To the right of **column B**, insert two new columns to create **new blank columns C and D**. By using **Flash Fill** in the two new columns, split the data in **column B** into a column for *Item #* in **column C** and *Category* in **column D**. As necessary, type **Item #** as the column title in **column C** and **Category** as the column title in **column D**.

4 Delete **column B**. By using the **Cut** and **Paste** commands, cut **column C**—*Category*—and paste it to **column G**, and then delete the empty **column C**. Apply **AutoFit** to **columns A:F**.

5 Display the **Trees** worksheet, and then repeat Steps 3 and 4 on this worksheet.

6 Make the following calculations in each of the two worksheets *without* grouping the sheets:

- In cell **B4**, enter a function to sum the **Quantity in Stock** data, and then apply **Comma Style** with zero decimal places to the result.

- In cells **B5:B8**, enter formulas to calculate the Average, Median, Lowest, and Highest retail prices, and then apply the **Accounting Number Format**.

7 In each of the two worksheets, make the following calculations *without* grouping the sheets:

- In cell **B10**, enter a COUNTIF function to determine how many different types of **Tulips** are in stock on the **Bulbs** sheet and how many different types of **Evergreens** are in stock on the **Trees** worksheet.

- In cell **G14** type **Stock Level** In cell **G15**, enter an **IF** function to determine the items that must be ordered. If the **Quantity in Stock** is less than **75** the **Value_if_true** is **Order** Otherwise the **Value_if_false** is **OK** Fill the formula down through all the rows.

- Apply **Conditional Formatting** to the **Stock Level** column so that cells that contain the text *Order* are formatted with **Bold Italic** with a **Font Color** of **Dark Blue, Text 2**. Apply **Gradient Fill Blue Data Bars** to the **Quantity in Stock** column.

8 In the **Bulbs** sheet, format the range **A14:G42** as a table with headers and apply **Table Style Light 20**. Insert a **Total Row**, filter by **Category** for **Tulips**, and then **Sum** the **Quantity in Stock** column. Record the result in cell **B11**.

9 Select the table, clear the filter, **Sort** the table on the **Item Name** column from **A to Z**, remove the **Total Row**, and then convert the table to a range. On the **Page Layout tab**, set **Print Titles** so that **row 14** repeats at the top of each page.

10 In the **Trees** sheet, format the range **A14:G42** as a table with headers and apply **Table Style Light 19**. Insert a **Total Row**, filter by **Category** for **Evergreens**, and then **Sum** the **Quantity in Stock** column. Record the result in cell **B11**.

11 Select the table, clear the filter, **Sort** the table on the **Item Name** column from **A to Z**, remove the **Total Row**, and then convert the table to a range.

12 On the **Page Layout tab**, set **Print Titles** so that **row 14** repeats at the top of each page, and then **Save** your workbook. **Group** the two worksheets. Center the title in cell **A1** across the range **A1:G1** and apply the **Title** cell style. Center the subtitle in cell **A2** across the range **A2:G2** and apply the **Heading 1** cell style. **Center** the worksheets **Horizontally**, change the **Orientation** to **Landscape**, display the **Print Preview**, and then change the **Settings** to **Fit All Columns on One Page**.

13 In **Backstage** view, on the left click **Save**, and then click the **Trees sheet tab** to cancel the grouping. Insert a new worksheet. Change the sheet name to **Summary** and then widen **columns A:D** to **170** pixels. Move the **Summary** sheet so that it is the first sheet in the workbook. In cell **A1**, type **Pasadena Inventory Summary** and then **Merge & Center** the title across **A1:D1**. Apply the **Title** cell style. In cell **A2**, type **As of December 31** and then **Merge & Center** the text across the range **A2:D2**. Apply the **Heading 1** cell style.

14 On the **Bulbs sheet**, **Copy** the range **A4:A8**. Display the **Summary sheet** and **Paste** the selection to cell **A5**. Apply the **Heading 4** cell style to the selection. In the **Summary sheet**, in cell **B4**, type **Bulbs** In cell **C4** type **Trees** In cell **D4** type **Bulbs/Trees** and then **Center** the column titles. Apply the **Heading 3** cell style.

(Project 2G Inventory continues on the next page)

CONTENT-BASED ASSESSMENTS

15 In cell **B5**, enter a formula that references cell **B4** in the **Bulbs sheet** so that the **Bulbs Total Items in Stock** displays in **B5**. Create similar formulas to enter the **Average Price**, **Median Price**, **Lowest Price**, and **Highest Price** from the **Bulbs sheet** into the **Summary** sheet in the range **B6:B9**. Enter formulas in the range **C5:C9** that reference the appropriate cells in the **Trees** worksheet.

16 To the range **B5:C5**, apply **Comma Style** with zero decimal places, and to the range **B6:C9**, apply **Accounting Number Format**. In cells **D5**, **D6**, **D7**, **D8**, and **D9**, insert **Column** sparklines using the values in the *Bulbs* and *Trees* columns. Format each sparkline using the first five Sparkline styles in the first row.

17 Center the **Summary** worksheet **Horizontally** and change the **Orientation** to **Landscape**. **Group** the worksheets and insert a footer in the left section with the **File Name**. As the **Tags**, type **Pasadena inventory** As the **Subject**, type your course name and section number. Be sure your name displays as the **Author**.

18 In **Backstage** view, on the left click **Save**, and then print or submit electronically as directed. If required by your instructor, print or create an electronic version of your worksheet with formulas displayed by using the instructions in Project 1A, and then close Excel without saving so that you do not save the changes you made to print formulas.

END | You have completed Project 2G

CONTENT-BASED ASSESSMENTS

Apply a combination of the 2A and 2B skills.

GO! Fix It	Project 2H Planters	Online

GO! Make It	Project 2I Salary	Online

GO! Solve It	Project 2J Sod	Online

GO! Solve It	Project 2K Products	

PROJECT FILES

For Project 2K, you will need the following file:

e02K_Products

You will save your workbook as:

Lastname_Firstname_2K_Products

From your student data files, open the file e02K_Products and save it as **Lastname_Firstname_2K_Products** This workbook contains two worksheets: one for U.S. sales data by product and one for Canadian sales data by product. Complete the two worksheets by calculating totals by product and by month. Then calculate the Percent of Total for all products by dividing the Product Total by the Monthly Total, using absolute cell references as necessary. Format the percentages with two decimal places and center in the cells. Format the worksheets attractively and apply financial formatting. Insert a new worksheet that summarizes the monthly totals for the U.S. and Canada. Enter the months as the column titles and the countries as the row titles. Include a Product Total column and a column for sparklines titled **April/May/June** Format the Summary worksheet attractively with a title and subtitle, insert column sparklines that compare the months, and apply financial formatting. Include the file name in the footer, add appropriate document properties, and submit as directed.

(Project 2K Products continues on the next page)

Performance Level

Performance Criteria		Exemplary: You consistently applied the relevant skills	Proficient: You sometimes, but not always, applied the relevant skills	Developing: You rarely or never applied the relevant skills
	Create formulas	All formulas are correct and are efficiently constructed.	Formulas are correct but not always constructed in the most efficient manner.	One or more formulas are missing or incorrect; or only numbers were entered.
	Create Summary worksheet	Summary worksheet created properly.	Summary worksheet was created but the data, sparklines, or formulas were incorrect.	No Summary worksheet was created.
	Format attractively and appropriately	Formatting is attractive and appropriate.	Adequately formatted but difficult to read or unattractive.	Inadequate or no formatting.

END | You have completed Project 2K

OUTCOMES-BASED ASSESSMENTS

RUBRIC

The following outcomes-based assessments are open-ended assessments. That is, there is no specific correct result; your result will depend on your approach to the information provided. Make Professional Quality your goal. Use the following scoring rubric to guide you in how to approach the problem and then to evaluate how well your approach solves the problem.

The *criteria*—Software Mastery, Content, Format and Layout, and Process—represent the knowledge and skills you have gained that you can apply to solving the problem. The *levels of performance*—Professional Quality, Approaching Professional Quality, or Needs Quality Improvements—help you and your instructor evaluate your result.

	Your completed project is of Professional Quality if you:	Your completed project is Approaching Professional Quality if you:	Your completed project Needs Quality Improvements if you:
1-Software Mastery	Choose and apply the most appropriate skills, tools, and features and identify efficient methods to solve the problem.	Choose and apply some appropriate skills, tools, and features, but not in the most efficient manner.	Choose inappropriate skills, tools, or features, or are inefficient in solving the problem.
2-Content	Construct a solution that is clear and well organized, contains content that is accurate, appropriate to the audience and purpose, and is complete. Provide a solution that contains no errors in spelling, grammar, or style.	Construct a solution in which some components are unclear, poorly organized, inconsistent, or incomplete. Misjudge the needs of the audience. Have some errors in spelling, grammar, or style, but the errors do not detract from comprehension.	Construct a solution that is unclear, incomplete, or poorly organized; contains some inaccurate or inappropriate content; and contains many errors in spelling, grammar, or style. Do not solve the problem.
3-Format & Layout	Format and arrange all elements to communicate information and ideas, clarify function, illustrate relationships, and indicate relative importance.	Apply appropriate format and layout features to some elements, but not others. Overuse features, causing minor distraction.	Apply format and layout that does not communicate information or ideas clearly. Do not use format and layout features to clarify function, illustrate relationships, or indicate relative importance. Use available features excessively, causing distraction.
4-Process	Use an organized approach that integrates planning, development, self-assessment, revision, and reflection.	Demonstrate an organized approach in some areas, but not others; or, use an insufficient process of organization throughout.	Do not use an organized approach to solve the problem.

OUTCOMES-BASED ASSESSMENTS

Apply a combination of the 2A and 2B skills.

GO! Think   Project 2L Palms

PROJECT FILES

For Project 2L, you will need the following file:

e02L_Palms

You will save your workbook as:

Lastname_Firstname_2L_Palms

Melanie Castillo, Product Manager for Rosedale Landscape and Garden, has requested a worksheet that summarizes the palm tree inventory data for the month of March. Melanie would like the worksheet to include the total Quantity in Stock and Number of Items for each of the four categories of palm trees, and she would like the items to be sorted from lowest to highest retail price. She would also like a separate column for Item # and for Category.

Edit the workbook to provide Melanie with the information requested, and use the Table feature to find the data requested. Format the worksheet titles and data and include an appropriately formatted table so that the worksheet is professional and easy to read and understand. Insert a footer with the file name and add appropriate document properties. Save the file as **Lastname_Firstname_2L_Palms** and print or submit as directed by your instructor.

END | You have completed Project 2L

GO! Think   Project 2M Contracts   **Online**

Build from Scratch

You and GO!   Project 2N Annual Expenses   **Online**

GO! Cumulative Group Project   Project 2O Bell Orchid Hotels   **Online**

Analyzing Data with Pie Charts, Line Charts, and What-If Analysis Tools

GO! to Work
Video E3

PROJECT 3A

OUTCOMES
Present fund data in a pie chart.

OBJECTIVES

1. Chart Data with a Pie Chart
2. Format a Pie Chart
3. Edit a Workbook and Update a Chart
4. Use Goal Seek to Perform What-If Analysis

PROJECT 3B

OUTCOMES
Make projections by using what-if analysis and present projections in a line chart.

OBJECTIVES

5. Design a Worksheet for What-If Analysis
6. Answer What-If Questions by Changing Values in a Worksheet
7. Chart Data with a Line Chart

In This Chapter

In this chapter, you will work with two different types of commonly used charts that make it easy to visualize data. You will create a pie chart in a separate chart sheet to show how the parts of a fund contribute to a total fund. Pie charts are one type of chart you can use to show part-to-whole relationships. You will also practice by using parentheses in a formula, calculate the percentage rate of an increase, answer what-if questions, and then chart data in a line chart to show the flow of data over time and the flow of one value to the next. In this chapter, you will also practice formatting the axes in a line chart.

The projects in this chapter relate to the city of **Pacifica Bay**, a coastal city south of San Francisco. The city's access to major transportation provides both residents and businesses an opportunity to compete in the global marketplace. The city's mission is to create a more beautiful and more economically viable community for its residents. Each year the city welcomes a large number of tourists who enjoy exploring the rocky coastline and seeing the famous landmarks in San Francisco. The city encourages best environmental practices and partners with cities in other countries to promote sound government at the local level.

PROJECT ACTIVITIES

In Activities 3.01 through 3.12, you will edit a worksheet for Michael Larsen, City Manager, that reports the adjusted figures for Enterprise Fund Expenditures for the next fiscal year, and then present the data in a pie chart. Your completed worksheets will look similar to Figure 3.1.

PROJECT FILES

For Project 3A, you will need the following file:

e03A_Enterprise_Fund

You will save your workbook as:

Lastname_Firstname_3A_Enterprise_Fund

PROJECT RESULTS

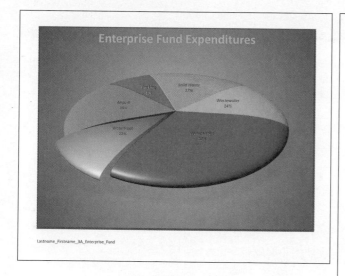

Lastname_Firstname_3A_Enterprise_Fund

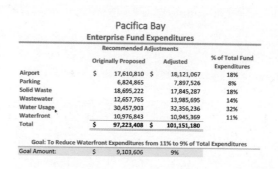

Pacifica Bay
Enterprise Fund Expenditures

	Recommended Adjustments		
	Originally Proposed	Adjusted	% of Total Fund Expenditures
Airport	$ 17,610,810	$ 18,121,067	18%
Parking	6,824,865	7,897,526	8%
Solid Waste	18,695,222	17,845,287	18%
Wastewater	12,657,765	13,985,695	14%
Water Usage	30,457,903	32,356,236	32%
Waterfront	10,976,843	10,945,369	11%
Total	$ 97,223,408	$ 101,151,180	

Goal: To Reduce Waterfront Expenditures from 11% to 9% of Total Expenditures

Goal Amount:	$ 9,103,606	9%

Lastname_Firstname_3A_Enterprise_Fund

FIGURE 3.1 Project 3A Enterprise Fund Pie Chart

Video E3-1

A *pie chart* shows the relationship of each part to a whole. The size of each pie slice is equal to its value compared to the total value of all the slices. The pie chart style charts data that is arranged in a single column or single row, and shows the size of items in a single data series proportional to the sum of the items. Whereas a column or bar chart can have two or more data series in the chart, a pie chart can have only one data series.

Consider using a pie chart when you have only one data series to plot, you do not have more than seven categories, and the categories represent parts of a total value.

Activity 3.01 | Calculating Values for a Pie Chart

A *fund* is a sum of money set aside for a specific purpose. In a municipal government like the city of Pacifica Bay, the *general fund* is money set aside for the normal operating activities of the city, such as police, fire, and administering the everyday functions of the city.

Municipal governments also commonly establish an *enterprise fund* to report income and expenditures related to municipal services for which a fee is charged in exchange for goods or services. For example, Pacifica Bay receives income from airport landing fees, parking fees, water usage fees, and rental fees along public beaches, but there are costs—expenditures—related to building and maintaining these facilities and services from which income is received.

1 Start Excel. From the student files that accompany this textbook, open **e03A_Enterprise_Fund**. From **Backstage** view, display the **Save As** dialog box. Navigate to the location where you are storing your projects for this chapter.

2 Create a new folder named **Excel Chapter 3** and open the new folder. In the **File name** box, using your name, type **Lastname_Firstname_3A_Enterprise_Fund** Click **Save** or press Enter.

> The worksheet indicates the originally proposed and adjusted expenditures from the Enterprise Fund for the next fiscal year.

3 Click cell **D5**, and then type **=** to begin a formula.

4 Click cell **C5**, which is the first value that is part of the total Fund Expenditures, to insert it into the formula. Type **/** to indicate division, and then click cell **C11**, which is the total adjusted expenditures.

> Recall that to determine the percentage by which a value makes up a total, you must divide the value by the total. The result will be a percentage expressed as a decimal.

5 Press F4 to make the reference to the value in cell **C11** absolute, which will enable you to copy the formula. Compare your screen with Figure 3.2.

> Recall that an *absolute cell reference* refers to a cell by its fixed position in the worksheet—the cell reference will not change when you copy the formula. The reference to cell C5 is a *relative cell reference*, because when you copy the formula, you want the reference to change *relative* to its row. Recall also that dollar signs display to indicate that a cell reference is absolute.

FIGURE 3.2

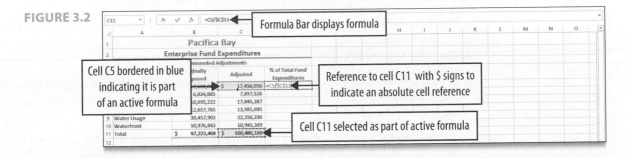

6 On the **Formula Bar**, click **Enter** ✓ to confirm the entry and to keep cell **D5** the active cell. Copy the formula down through cell **D10**, and then compare your screen with Figure 3.3.

FIGURE 3.3

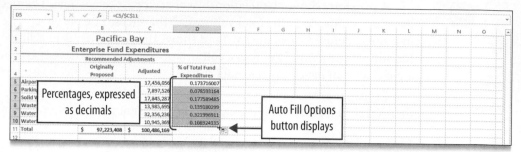

7 With the range **D5:D10** still selected, right-click over the selection, and then on the mini toolbar, click **Percent Style** 🔲 and **Center** 🔲. Click cell **A1** to cancel the selection, and then **Save** 🔲 your workbook. Compare your screen with Figure 3.4.

FIGURE 3.4

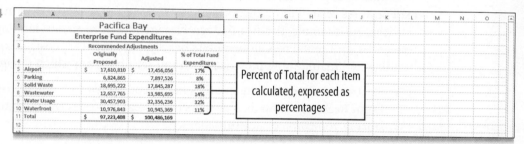

Activity 3.02 | Creating a Pie Chart in a Chart Sheet

1 Select the range **A5:A10**, hold down [Ctrl], and then select the range **C5:C10** to select the nonadjacent ranges with the item names and the adjusted expenditure for each item.

> To create a pie chart, you must select two ranges. One range contains the labels for each slice of the pie chart, and the other range contains the values that add up to a total. The two ranges must have the same number of cells and the range with the values should *not* include the cell with the total.

> The item names (Airport, Parking, and so on) are the category names and will identify the slices of the pie chart. Each projected expenditure is a ***data point***—a value that originates in a worksheet cell and that is represented in a chart by a ***data marker***. In a pie chart, each pie slice is a data marker. Together, the data points form the ***data series***—related data points represented by data markers—and determine the size of each pie slice.

2 With the nonadjacent ranges selected, click the **INSERT tab**, and then in the **Charts group**, click **Insert Pie or Doughnut Chart** 🔵 ▾. Under 3-D Pie, click the chart **3-D Pie** to create the chart on your worksheet and to display the **CHART TOOLS** on the ribbon.

3 On the **DESIGN tab**, at the right end of the ribbon in the **Location group**, click **Move Chart**. In the **Move Chart** dialog box, click the **New sheet** option button.

4 In the **New sheet** box, replace the highlighted text *Chart1* by typing **Expenditures Chart** and then click **OK** to display the chart on a separate worksheet in your workbook. Compare your screen with Figure 3.5.

> The pie chart displays on a separate new sheet in your workbook, and a ***legend*** identifies the pie slices. Recall that a legend is a chart element that identifies the patterns or colors assigned to the categories in the chart.

> A ***chart sheet*** is a workbook sheet that contains only a chart; it is useful when you want to view a chart separately from the worksheet data. The sheet tab indicates *Expenditures Chart*.

FIGURE 3.5

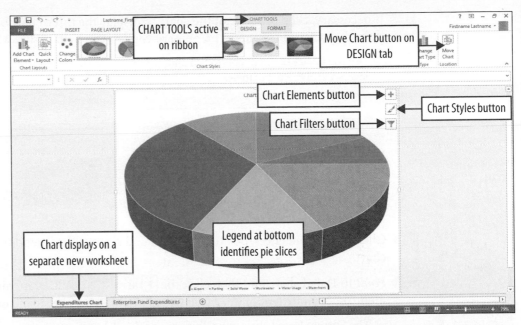

Objective 2 | Format a Pie Chart

Video E3-2

Activity 3.03 | Formatting a Chart Title by Applying a WordArt Style and Changing Font Size

1 Click the text *Chart Title* to surround it with selection handles, and then watch the **Formula Bar** as you type **Enterprise Fund Expenditures** Press Enter to create the new chart title in the box.

2 Click the **FORMAT tab**, and then in the **WordArt Styles group**, click **More** ⊡. In the first row, click the last style—**Fill – Gold, Accent 4, Soft Bevel**.

3 With the I pointer, drag to select the chart title text, and then on the mini toolbar, change the **Font Size** to **32**. Click the edge of the chart to deselect the title, and then compare your screen with Figure 3.6.

FIGURE 3.6

Chart Title text typed, WordArt Style applied, Font Size 32 → Enterprise Fund Expenditures

Activity 3.04 | Formatting Chart Elements by Removing a Legend and Adding and Formatting Data Labels

In your worksheet, for each budget item, you calculated the percent of the total in column D. These percentages can also be calculated by the Chart feature and added to the pie slices as labels.

1 If necessary, click the edge of the chart to display the three chart buttons on the right, and then click **Chart Elements** ➕. Compare your screen with Figure 3.7.

> Use the Chart Elements button to add, remove, or change chart elements such as the chart title, the legend, and the data labels.

FIGURE 3.7

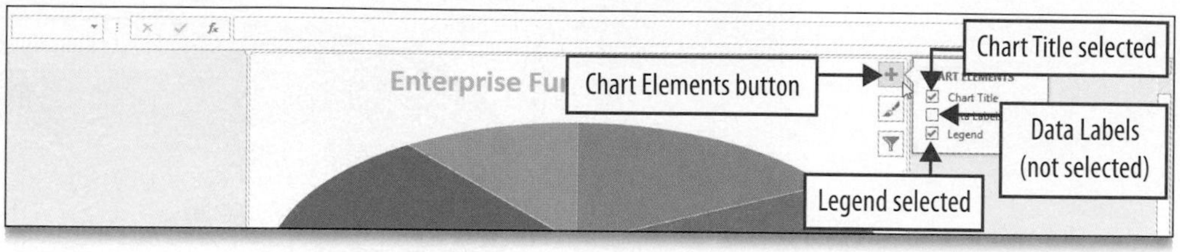

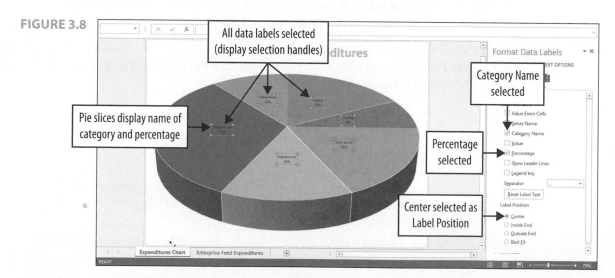

2 Click the **Legend** check box to deselect it and remove the legend from the bottom of the chart.

3 *Point* to **Data Labels**, and then click the ▶ arrow to display a menu. At the bottom of the menu, click **More Options** to display the **Format Data Labels** pane on the right.

> The Format Data Labels pane displays and data labels representing the values display on each pie slice.

4 In the **Format Data Labels** pane, under **LABEL OPTIONS**, click as necessary to select the **Category Name** and **Percentage** check boxes. Click to *clear* any other check boxes in this group. Under **Label Position**, click the **Center** option button. Compare your screen with Figure 3.8.

> All of the data labels are selected and display both the category name and the percentage. In the worksheet, you calculated the percent of the total in column D. Here, the percentage will be calculated by the Chart feature and added to the chart as a label.

FIGURE 3.8

5 Point to any of the selected data labels, right-click to display a shortcut menu, and then click **Font** to display the **Font** dialog box.

6 In the **Font** dialog box, on the **Font tab**, click the **Font style arrow**, and then click **Bold Italic**. In the **Size** box, drag to select 9 and type **11** Compare your screen with Figure 3.9.

FIGURE 3.9

Font dialog box

Font Size set to 11

Font style set to Bold Italic

7 ▶ Click **OK** to close the dialog box and apply the formatting to the data labels. In the upper right corner of the **Format Data Labels** pane, click **Close** ✕.

Activity 3.05 | Formatting a Data Series with 3-D Effects

3-D, which is short for *three-dimensional*, refers to an image that appears to have all three spatial dimensions—length, width, and depth.

1 ▶ In any pie slice, point anywhere outside of the selected label, and then double-click to display the **Format Data Series** pane on the right.

🔄 **ANOTHER WAY**   Right-click outside the label of any pie slice, and then click Format Data Series to display the Format Data Series pane. Or, on the FORMAT tab, in the Current Selection group, click the Chart Elements arrow, click Series 1, and then click Format Selection.

2 ▶ In the **Format Data Series** pane, under **SERIES OPTIONS**, click **Effects** ⬠, and then click **3-D FORMAT**. Compare your screen with Figure 3.10.

FIGURE 3.10

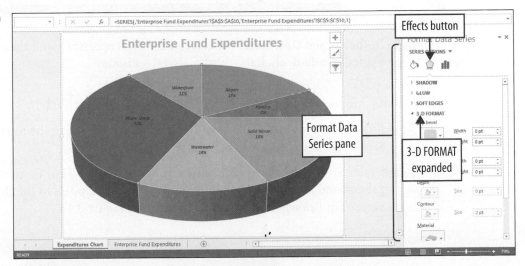

Effects button

Format Data Series pane

3-D FORMAT expanded

3 ▶ Click the **Top bevel arrow**, and then in the gallery, under **Bevel**, click the first bevel—**Circle**—as shown in Figure 3.11.

Bevel is a shape effect that uses shading and shadows to make the edges of a shape appear to be curved or angled.

FIGURE 3.11

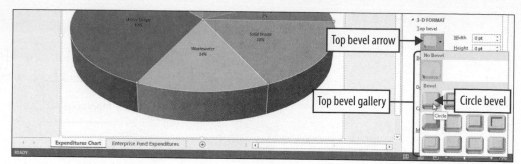

4 ▶ Under **Top bevel**, in the **Width** box, select the existing text and type **512 pt** Use the same technique to change the **Height** to **512 pt**

5 ▶ Under **Bottom bevel**, use the technique you just practiced to apply a **Circle** bevel with **Width** of **512 pt** and **Height** of **512 pt** Compare your screen with Figure 3.12.

FIGURE 3.12

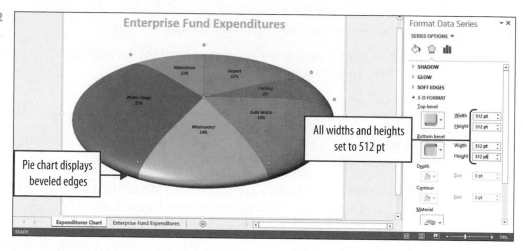

6 ▶ In the **Format Data Series** pane, scroll down as necessary, and then click the **Material arrow**. Under **Standard**, click the third material—**Plastic**.

Activity 3.06 │ Formatting a Data Series with a Shadow Effect

1 ▶ If necessary, in the **Format Data Series** pane, scroll back to the top of the pane, and then click **SHADOW** to expand the options for this effect.

2 ▶ Under **SHADOW**, click the **Presets arrow**, use the scroll bar to move to the bottom of the gallery, and then under **Perspective**, in the first row, point to the third effect to display the ScreenTip *Below*. Compare your screen with Figure 3.13.

FIGURE 3.13

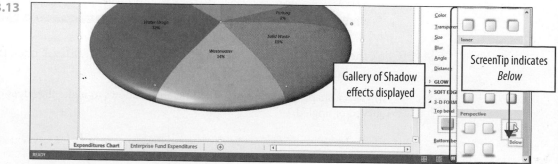

3 ▶ Click **Below** to apply the shadow to the chart.

Activity 3.07 | Rotating a Pie Chart by Changing the Angle of the First Slice

The order in which the data series in pie charts are plotted in Excel is determined by the order of the data on the worksheet. To gain a different view of the chart, you can rotate the chart within the 360 degrees of the circle of the pie shape to present a different visual perspective of the chart.

1 Notice the position of the **Water Usage** and **Waterfront** slices in the chart. Then, with the pie chart still selected—sizing handles surround the pie—in the **Format Data Series** pane, under **SERIES OPTIONS**, click **Series Options** ◨.

2 Under **Angle of first slice**, in the box to the right, drag to select **0°**, type **250** and then press Enter to rotate the chart 250 degrees to the right.

🔄 **ANOTHER WAY**   Drag the slider to 250°, or click the spin box up arrow as many times as necessary.

3 Click **Save** 🖫, and then compare your screen with Figure 3.14.

Rotating the chart can provide a better perspective to the chart. Here, rotating the chart in this manner emphasizes that Water Usage is the largest enterprise fund expenditure.

FIGURE 3.14

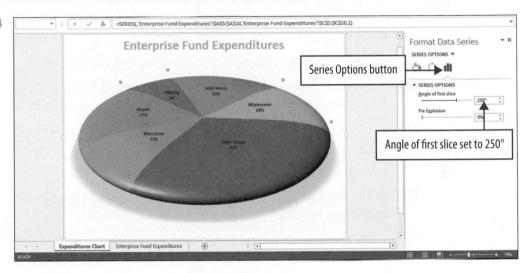

Activity 3.08 | Exploding and Coloring a Pie Slice

You can pull out—*explode*—one or more slices of a pie chart to emphasize a specific slice or slices.

1 In the **Format Data Series** pane, under **SERIES OPTIONS**, notice the slider and box for *Pie Explosion*.

When all the pie slices are selected, as they currently are, you can use this command to explode *all* of the pie pieces away from the center by varying degrees to emphasize all the individual slices of the pie chart. An exploded pie chart visualizes the contribution of each value to the total, while at the same time emphasizing individual values.

2 On the pie chart, click the green **Waterfront** slice to select only that slice, and then on the right, notice that the **Format Data Point** pane displays.

Excel adjusts the pane, depending on what you have selected, so that the commands you need are available.

3 In the **Format Data Point** pane, in the **Point Explosion** box, select the existing text, type **10%** and then press Enter.

4 With the **Waterfront** slice still selected, in the **Format Data Point** pane, under **SERIES OPTIONS**, click **Fill & Line** ◇, and then click **FILL** to expand its options.

5 Click the **Gradient fill** option button, click the **Preset gradients arrow**, and then in the fourth row, click the last gradient—**Bottom Spotlight – Accent 6**. Click **Save** 🖫, and then compare your screen with Figure 3.15.

FIGURE 3.15

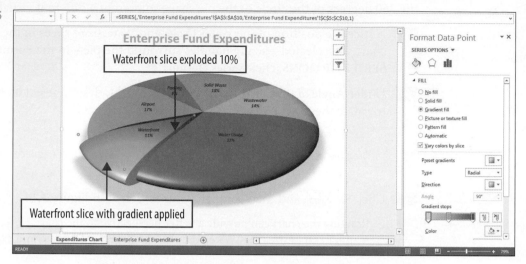

Activity 3.09 | Formatting the Chart Area

The entire chart and all of its elements comprise the ***chart area***.

1 Point to the white area just inside the border of the chart to display the ScreenTip *Chart Area*. Click one time, and notice that on the right, the **Format Chart Area** pane displays.

2 Under **CHART OPTIONS**, click **Fill & Line** 🖾, and be sure the **FILL** options are still displayed.

3 Click the **Gradient fill** option button, click the **Preset gradients arrow**, and then in the fourth row, click the first gradient—**Bottom Spotlight – Accent 1**.

4 In the **Format Chart Area** pane, click **FILL** to collapse the options, and then click **BORDER** to expand its options.

5 Under **Border**, click **Solid line**, click the **Color arrow** to display the Outline colors, and then in the fourth column, click the first color—**Blue – Gray, Text 2**. In the **Width** box, drag to select the existing width, and then type **5 pt**

6 **Close** 🗙 the **Format Chart Area** pane, and then click outside of the Chart Area to deselect the chart. Click **Save** 🖫, and then compare your screen with Figure 3.16.

FIGURE 3.16

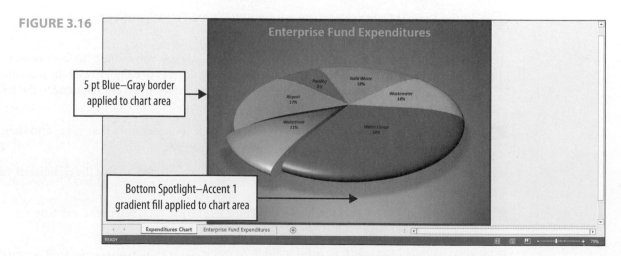

Video E3-3

Activity 3.10 | Editing a Workbook and Updating a Chart

If you edit the data in your worksheet, the chart data markers—in this instance the pie slices—will adjust automatically to accurately represent the new values.

1 On the pie chart, notice that *Airport* represents 17% of the total projected expenses.

2 In the sheet tab area at the bottom of the workbook, click the **Enterprise Fund Expenditures tab** to redisplay the worksheet.

3 Click cell **C5**, type **18121067** and then press Enter. Notice that the Accounting Number Format is retained in the cell.

♺ ANOTHER WAY   Double-click the cell to position the insertion point in the cell and edit.

4 Notice that the total in cell **C11** is recalculated to *$101,151,180* and the percentages in **column D** are also recalculated.

5 Display the **Expenditures Chart** sheet. Notice that the pie slices adjust to show the recalculation—*Airport* is now *18%* of the adjusted expenditures. Click **Save** 🖫, and then compare your screen with Figure 3.17.

FIGURE 3.17

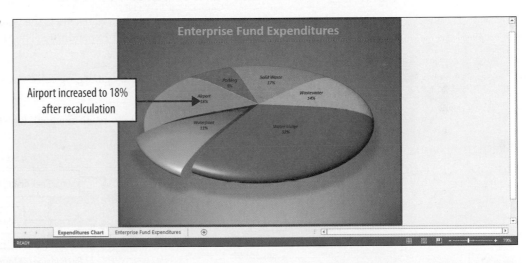

Video E3-4

Activity 3.11 | Using Goal Seek to Perform What-If Analysis

The process of changing the values in cells to see how those changes affect the outcome of formulas in your worksheet is referred to as *what-if analysis*. One what-if analysis tool in Excel is *Goal Seek*, which finds the input needed in one cell to arrive at the desired result in another cell.

1 Click the **Enterprise Fund Expenditures sheet tab** to redisplay the worksheet. In cell **A13**, type **Goal: To Reduce Waterfront Expenditures from 11% to 9% of Total Expenditures** **Merge & Center** the text across the range **A13:D13**, and then apply the **Heading 3** Cell Style.

2 In cell **A14**, type **Goal Amount:** and press Enter.

3 Select the range **C10:D10**, right-click over the selection, and then click **Copy**. Point to cell **B14**, right-click, and then under **Paste Options**, click **Paste** 🗋.

4 Press [Esc] to cancel the moving border, click cell **C14**, and then compare your screen with Figure 3.18.

FIGURE 3.18

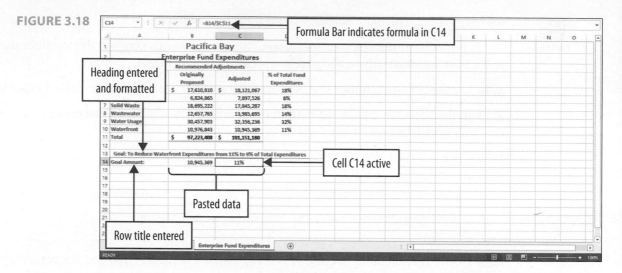

5 Be sure cell **C14** is the active cell. On the **DATA tab**, in the **Data Tools group**, click **What-If Analysis**, and then click **Goal Seek**.

6 In the **Goal Seek** dialog box, notice that the active cell, **C14**, is indicated in the **Set cell** box. Press [Tab] to move to the **To value** box, and then type **9%**

C14 is the cell in which you want to set a specific value; 9% is the percentage of the total expenditures that is your goal for the Waterfront Expenditure. The Set cell box contains the formula that calculates the information you seek.

7 Press [Tab] to move the insertion point to the **By changing cell** box, and then click cell **B14**. Compare your screen with Figure 3.19.

Cell B14 contains the value that Excel changes to reach the goal. Excel formats this cell as an absolute cell reference.

FIGURE 3.19

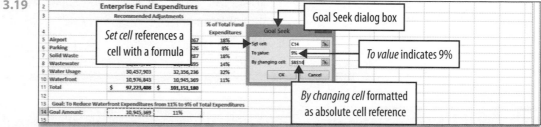

8 Click **OK**. In the displayed **Goal Seek Status** dialog box, click **OK**.

9 Select the range **A14:C14**. On the **HOME tab**, display the **Cell Styles** gallery. Under **Themed Cell Styles**, apply **20% - Accent1**.

10 Click cell **B14**, display the **Cell Styles** gallery again, and then at the bottom, under **Number Format**, click **Currency [0]**.

Use this cell style when you want to apply currency formatting with no decimal places quickly.

11 ▶ Press ⌃Ctrl⌄ + ⌃Home⌄, click **Save** 🖫, and then compare your screen with Figure 3.20.

Excel calculates that the city must budget for *$9,103,606* in Waterfront expenditures in order for this item to become 9% of the total projected budget.

FIGURE 3.20

Activity 3.12 | Preparing and Printing a Workbook with a Chart Sheet

1 ▶ Click the **PAGE LAYOUT tab**. In the **Page Setup group**, click **Margins**, and then click **Custom Margins**.

2 ▶ In the **Page Setup** dialog box, on the **Margins tab**, under **Center on page**, select the **Horizontally** check box.

3 ▶ Click the **Header/Footer tab**, and then in the center of the dialog box, click **Custom Footer**. In the **Footer** dialog box, with your insertion point blinking in the **Left section**, on the row of buttons, click **Insert File Name** 🗐.

4 ▶ Click **OK** two times.

The dotted line indicates the page break as currently formatted.

5 ▶ Display the **Expenditures Chart**, which must have its footer formatted separately. In the **Page Setup group**, click the **Dialog Box Launcher** 🖳.

Chart sheets are automatically centered on the page.

6 ▶ Click the **Header/Footer tab**, and then in the center of the dialog box, click **Custom Footer**. In the **Footer** dialog box, with your insertion point blinking in the **Left section**, on the row of buttons, click **Insert File Name** 🗐.

7 ▶ Click **OK** two times. Click the **FILE tab**, and then click **Show All Properties**. As the **Tags**, type **enterprise fund, expenditures** As the **Subject**, type your course name and section number. Be sure your name displays as the author.

8 ▶ On the left, click **Save**. Right-click the **Expenditures Chart sheet tab**, and then click **Select All Sheets**. Verify that *[Group]* displays in the title bar.

Recall that by selecting all sheets, you can view all of the workbook pages in Print Preview.

9 ▶ Press ⌃Ctrl⌄ + ⌃F2⌄ to display the **Print Preview**. Examine the first page, and then at the bottom of the **Print Preview**, click **Next Page** ▶ to view the second page of your workbook.

NOTE | **Printing a Chart Sheet Uses More Toner**

Printing a chart that displays on a chart sheet will use more toner or ink than a small chart that is part of a worksheet. If you are printing your work, check with your instructor to verify whether or not you should print the chart sheet.

---

10 ▸ On the left, click **Save** to redisplay the workbook.

11 ▸ By using the techniques you practiced in Project 1A, print or submit electronically as directed by your instructor. If required by your instructor, print or create an electronic version of your worksheet with formulas displayed.

12 ▸ **Close** your workbook and close **Excel**.

END | You have completed Project 3A

GO! with Office Web Apps

Objective	Create a JPEG Photo of a Chart and Upload to a OneNote Web App Notebook

Recall that **OneNote** is a Microsoft application with which you can create a digital notebook that gives you a single location where you can gather and organize information in the form of notes. The OneNote Web App enables you to share your OneNote notebooks on the web.

A L E R T !	**Working with Web-Based Applications and Services**

Computer programs and services on the web receive continuous updates and improvements, so the steps to complete this web-based activity may differ from the ones shown. You can often look at the screens and the information presented to determine how to complete the activity.

Activity | **Creating a JPEG Photo of a Chart and Uploading It to a OneNote Web App Notebook**

In this activity, you will create a JPEG image of a chart, and then upload the image to a OneNote Web App notebook.

1 From File Explorer, navigate to your **Excel Chapter 3** folder, and then open your file **Lastname_Firstname_3A_ Enterprise_Fund** workbook. Display the **Expenditures Chart** worksheet.

2 Display the **Start** screen and type **snipping** Click the **Snipping Tool** program to start it.

3 In the Snipping Tool dialog box, click the **New arrow**, and then click **Rectangular Snip**. With the pointer, point to the upper left corner of the chart, hold down the left mouse button, and then drag down to the lower right corner of the chart to create a red rectangle around the chart. Release the mouse button. Compare your screen with Figure A.

4 On the **Snipping Tool** mark-up window toolbar, click **Save Snip** 🖫. In the **Save As** dialog box, navigate to your **Excel Chapter 3** folder. Be sure the **Save as type** box displays **JPEG file**. In the **File name** box, type **Lastname_Firstname_EX_3A_Web** and then click **Save**. **Close** ☒ the **Snipping Tool** window and **Close** ☒ Excel.

5 Launch Internet Explorer, navigate to **www.skydrive.com** and then sign in to your **Microsoft** account. Click your **GO! Web Projects** folder to open it; if necessary, create this folder.

FIGURE A

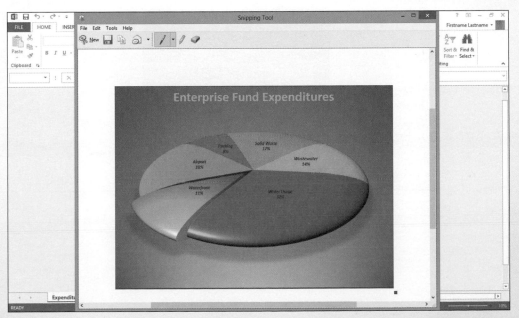

(GO! with Office Web Apps continues on the next page)

6 In the SkyDrive menu bar, click **Create**, and then click **OneNote notebook** to create a new notebook. In the **Name** box, using your own name, type **Lastname_Firstname_EX_3A_Web** and then click **Create**.

7 Point to the text *Untitled Section*, right-click, and then click **New Section**. As the **Section Name**, type **Fund Reports**, and then click **OK**.

8 With the insertion point blinking at the top of the notebook page, type **Chart of Enterprise Fund Expenditures** and press Enter. With the insertion point in the blank page, on the ribbon, click the **INSERT tab**, and then in the **Pictures group**, click **Picture**.

9 In the **Choose File to Upload** dialog box, navigate to your **Excel Chapter 3** folder, and then click the **EX_3A_ Web** JPEG file that you created with the Snipping Tool. Click **Open**.

Use this technique to insert a picture to store in a OneNote notebook.

10 With the insertion point blinking below the inserted picture, click the **HOME tab**, and then in the **Tags group**,

click **Tag** to display a list of tags. Click **Important**. Below the picture, click to the right of the tag—a gold star—to position the insertion point there. Type **Attention Council Members: The expenditures from the Enterprise Fund will be discussed at the August City Council meeting.** Compare your screen with Figure B.

A note tag can help you locate specific information quickly. A note tag is both a descriptive term representing a category, such as *Important* or *To Do*, and a related icon that can be associated with a specific note. When this notebook on the SkyDrive is shared with all of the City Council members, each will be able to view the chart and see that it is important.

11 If you are instructed to submit your file, use one of the methods outlined in the Note box below. Then, on the ribbon, click the **FILE tab** and click **Exit**. In the OneNote Web App, there is no Save button because your notebook is being saved automatically.

12 Sign out of your Microsoft account, and then close all windows.

N O T E	**Printing or Creating an Electronic File of a Web App OneNote Page**

You can use Snipping Tool to create an electronic file or to paste the snip into a document to save and print. In the Office OneNote app, in which you can open this page, you can print pages directly to a printer.

FIGURE B

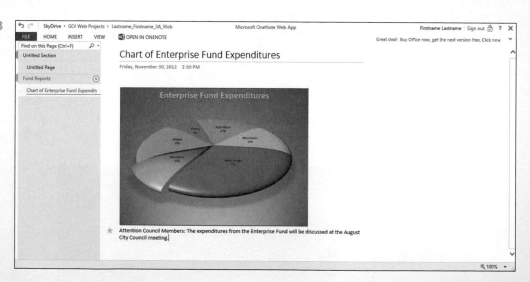

Tourism Spending Projection with Line Chart

PROJECT ACTIVITIES

In Activities 3.13 through 3.20, you will assist Michael Larsen, City Manager, in creating a worksheet to estimate future tourism spending based on two possible growth rates. You will also create a line chart to display past visitor spending. Your resulting worksheet and chart will look similar to Figure 3.21.

PROJECT FILES

Build from Scratch

For Project 3B, you will need the following files:

New blank Excel file
e03B_Surfers

You will save your workbook as:

Lastname_Firstname_3B_Tourism

PROJECT RESULTS

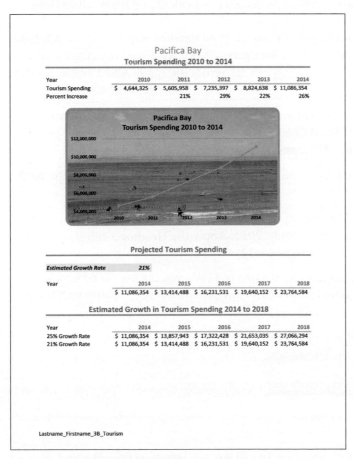

FIGURE 3.21 Project 3B Tourism Spending Projection with Line Chart

Objective 5 Design a Worksheet for What-If Analysis

Video E3-5

If you change the value in a cell referenced in a formula, Excel automatically recalculates the result of the formula. This means that you can change cell values to see *what* would happen *if* you tried different values. Recall that this process of changing the values in cells to see how those changes affect the outcome of formulas in your worksheet is referred to as what-if analysis.

Activity 3.13 | Using Parentheses in a Formula to Calculate a Percentage Rate of Increase

Mr. Larsen has the city's tourism spending figures for the recent 5-year period. In each year, tourism spending has increased. In this activity, you will construct a formula to calculate the *percentage rate of increase*—the percent by which one number increases over another number—for each year since 2010. From this information, future tourism spending growth can be estimated.

Excel follows a set of mathematical rules called the *order of operations*, which has four basic parts:

- Expressions within parentheses are processed first.
- Exponentiation, if present, is performed before multiplication and division.
- Multiplication and division are performed before addition and subtraction.
- Consecutive operators with the same level of precedence are calculated from left to right.

1 Start Excel and open a new blank workbook. In cell **A1**, type **Pacifica Bay** and in cell **A2**, type **Tourism Spending 2010 to 2014** and then **Merge & Center** ⊞▾ cell **A1** across the range **A1:F1** and apply the **Title** cell style. **Merge & Center** ⊞▾ cell **A2** across the range **A2:F2** and apply the **Heading 1** cell style.

2 Widen **column A** to **150 pixels** and widen **columns B:F** to **90 pixels**. Press F12 to display the **Save As** dialog box. Navigate to your **Excel Chapter 3** folder, and then in the **File name** box, using your own name, type **Lastname_Firstname_3B_Tourism** Click **Save** or press Enter.

3 Leave **row 3** blank, and then click cell **A4**. Type **Year** and then press Tab. In cell **B4**, type **2010** and then press Tab.

4 In cell **C4**, type **2011** and then press Tab. Select the range **B4:C4**, and then drag the fill handle to the right through cell **F4** to extend the series to *2014*. Apply the **Heading 3** cell style to the selected range. Compare your screen with Figure 3.22.

By establishing a pattern of 1-year intervals with the first two cells, you can use the fill handle to continue the series. The AutoFill feature will do this for any pattern that you establish with two or more cells.

FIGURE 3.22

5 In cell **A5**, type **Tourism Spending** and press Enter. In cell **A6**, type **Percent Increase** and press Enter.

6 Click cell **B5**, and then beginning in cell **B5** and pressing ⌨Tab to move across the row, enter the following values for tourism spending in the years listed:

2010	2011	2012	2013	2014
4644325	5605958	7235397	8824638	11086354

7 Click cell **C6**. Being sure to include the parentheses, type **=(c5-b5)/b5** and then on the **Formula Bar**, click **Enter** ✔ to keep cell **C6** active; your result is *0.207055492*. Compare your screen with Figure 3.23.

> Recall that as you type, a list of Excel functions that begin with the letter *C* and *B* may briefly display. This is *Formula AutoComplete*, an Excel feature which, after typing an = (equal sign) and the beginning letter or letters of a function name, displays a list of function names that match the typed letter(s). In this instance, the letters represent cell references, *not* the beginning of a function name.

FIGURE 3.23

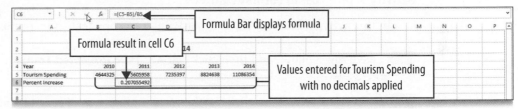

8 With cell **C6** selected, drag the fill handle to the right to copy the formula through cell **F6**.

> Because this formula uses relative cell references—that is, for each year, the formula is the same but the values used are relative to the formula's location—you can copy the formula in this manner. For example, the result for 2012 uses the 2011 value as the base, the result for 2013 uses the 2012 value as the base, and the result for 2014 uses the 2013 value as the base.

9 Select the range **B5:F5**, right-click, on the mini toolbar, click **Accounting Number Format** $ ▾, and then click **Decrease Decimal** ⁰⁰→ two times. Select the range **C6:F6**, right-click, and then apply **Percent Style** %. Click cell **C6** and look at the **Formula Bar**.

> The mathematical formula *rate = amount of increase/base* is used to calculated the percentage rate of tourism spending increase from 2010 to 2011. The formula is applied as follows:

> First, determine the *amount of increase* by subtracting the *base*—the starting point represented by the 2010 tourism spending—from the 2011 tourism spending. Therefore, the *amount of increase* = $5,605,958 – $4,644,325 or $961,633. Between 2010 and 2011 tourism spending increased by $961,633. In the formula, this calculation is represented by *C5-B5*.

> Second, calculate the *rate*—what the amount of increase ($961,633) represents as a percentage of the base (2010's tourism spending of $4,644,325). Determine this by dividing the amount of increase ($961,633) by the base ($4,644,325). Therefore $961,633 divided by $4,644,325 is equal to *0.207055492* or, when formatted as a percent and rounded up, 21%.

10 In the **Formula Bar**, locate the parentheses enclosing *C5-B5*.

> Recall that Excel follows a set of mathematical rules called the order of operations, in which expressions within parentheses are processed first, multiplication and division are performed before addition and subtraction, and consecutive operators with the same level of precedence are calculated from left to right.

11 **Save** 💾 your workbook, and then compare your screen with Figure 3.24.

FIGURE 3.24

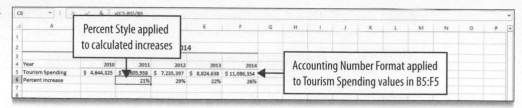

Percent Style applied to calculated increases

Accounting Number Format applied to Tourism Spending values in B5:F5

More Knowledge   **Use of Parentheses in a Formula**

When writing a formula in Excel, use parentheses to specify the order in which the operations should occur. For example, to average three test scores of 100, 50, and 90 that you scored on three different tests, you would add the test scores and then divide by the number of test scores in the list. If you write this formula as =100+50+90/3, the result would be 180, because Excel would first divide 90 by 3 and then add 100+50+30. Excel would do so because the order of operations states that multiplication and division are calculated *before* addition and subtraction.

The correct way to write this formula is =(100+50+90)/3. Excel will add the three values, and then divide the result by 3, or 240/3 resulting in a correct average of 80. Parentheses play an important role in ensuring that you get the correct result in your formulas.

Activity 3.14 | Using Format Painter

In this activity, you will use Format Painter to copy text (non-numeric) formats.

1 Leave **row 7** blank, and then click cell **A8**. Type **Projected Tourism Spending** and then press Enter.

2 Point to cell **A2**, right-click, on the mini toolbar, click **Format Painter** 🖌, and then click cell **A8** to copy the format.

> The format of cell **A2** is *painted*—applied to—cell **A8**, including the merging and centering of the text across the range **A8:F8**.

🔄 **BY TOUCH**   On the Home tab, in the Clipboard group, tap the Format Painter button.

3 Leave **row 9** blank, and then click cell **A10**. Type **Estimated Growth Rate** and then press Tab.

4 In cell **B10**, type **25%** and press Enter. Select the range **A10:B10**, right-click over the selection, and then from the mini toolbar, apply **Bold** B and **Italic** I.

5 Leave **row 11** blank. Click cell **A12**, type **Year** and then press Tab. In cell **B12**, type **2014** and press Tab. In cell **C12**, type **2015** and press Tab.

6 Select the range **B12:C12**, and then drag the fill handle through cell **F12** to extend the pattern of years to *2018*. Apply the **Heading 3** cell style to the selected range.

7 Point to cell **F5**, right-click, and then click **Copy**. Point to cell **B13**, right-click, and then click **Paste** 📋. Compare your screen with Figure 3.25, and then **Save** 💾 your workbook.

FIGURE 3.25

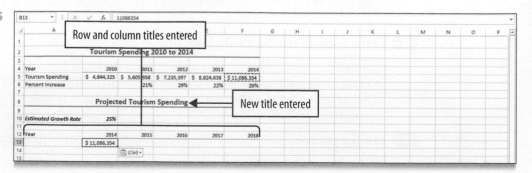

Row and column titles entered

New title entered

More Knowledge | **Percentage Calculations**

When you type a percentage into a cell—for example *25%*—the percentage format, without decimal points, displays in both the cell and the Formula Bar. Excel will, however, use the decimal value of *0.25* for actual calculations.

Activity 3.15 | Calculating a Value After an Increase

A growth in tourism spending means that the city can plan for additional revenues and also plan more hotel and conference space to accommodate the increasing number of visitors. Therefore, city planners in Pacifica Bay want to estimate how much tourism spending will increase in the future. The calculations you made in the previous activity show that tourism spending has increased at varying rates during each year from 2010 to 2014, ranging from a low of 21% to a high of 29% per year.

Economic data suggests that future growth will trend close to that of the recent past. To plan for the future, Mr. Larsen wants to prepare a forecast of tourism spending based on the percentage increase halfway between the high of 29% and the low of 21%; that is, for 25%. In this activity, you will calculate the tourism spending that would result from a 25% increase.

1 ► Click cell **C13**. Type **=b13*(100%+b10)** and then on the **Formula Bar**, click **Enter** ✓ to display a result of *13857942.5*. Point to cell **B13**, right-click, click **Format Painter** 💅, and then click cell **C13** to copy the format. Compare your screen with Figure 3.26.

This formula calculates what tourism spending will be in the year 2015 assuming an increase of 25% over 2014's tourism spending. Use the mathematical formula ***value after increase = base × percent for new value*** to calculate a value after an increase as follows:

First, establish the *percent for new value*. The ***percent for new value = base percent + percent of increase***. The *base percent* of 100% represents the base tourism spending and the *percent of increase*—in this instance is 25%. Therefore, the tourism spending will equal 100% of the base year plus 25% of the base year. This can be expressed as 125% or 1.25. In this formula, you will use 100% + the rate in cell **B10**, which is 25%, to equal 125%.

Second, enter a reference to the cell that contains the *base*—the tourism spending in 2014. The base value resides in cell **B13**—*$11,086,354*.

Third, calculate the *value after increase*. Because in each future year the increase will be based on 25%—an absolute value located in cell **B10**—this cell reference can be formatted as absolute by typing dollar signs.

FIGURE 3.26

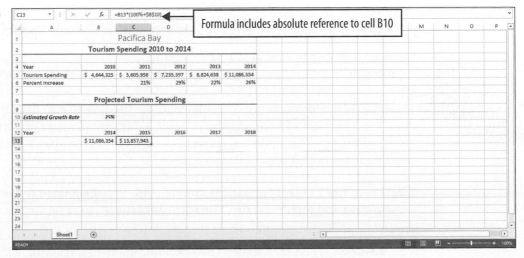

Formula includes absolute reference to cell B10

2 With cell **C13** as the active cell, drag the fill handle to copy the formula to the range **D13:F13**. Click an empty cell to cancel the selection, click **Save** 🔲 and then compare your screen with Figure 3.27.

> This formula uses a relative cell address—B13—for the *base*; the tourism spending in the year is used in each of the formulas in cells D13:F13 as the *base* value. Because the reference to the *percent of increase* in cell B10 is an absolute reference, each *value after increase* is calculated with the value from cell B10.
>
> The tourism spending projected for 2015—*$13,857,943*—is an increase of 25% over the spending in 2014. The projected spending in 2016—*$17,322,428*—is an increase of 25% over the spending in 2015, and so on.

FIGURE 3.27

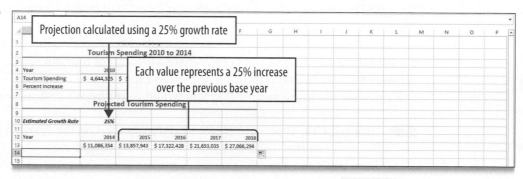

Objective 6   Answer What-If Questions by Changing Values in a Worksheet

Video E3-6

If a formula depends on the value in a cell, you can see what effect it will have if you change the value in that cell. Then, you can copy the value computed by the formula and paste it into another part of the worksheet where you can compare it to other values.

Activity 3.16 │ Answering What-If Questions and Using Paste Special

A growth rate of 25% in tourism spending in each year will result in tourism spending of approximately $27 million by 2018. The city planners will likely ask: *What if* tourism spending grows at the lowest rate of 21%?

Because the formulas are constructed to use the growth rate displayed in cell **B10**, Mr. Larsen can answer that question quickly by entering a different percentage into that cell. To keep the results of the new calculation so it can be compared, you will paste the results of the what-if question into another area of the worksheet.

1 Leave **row 14** blank, and then click cell **A15**. Type **Estimated Growth in Tourism Spending 2014 to 2018** and then press Enter. Use **Format Painter** 🖌 to copy the format from cell **A8** to cell **A15**.

2 Select the range **A10:B10**, right-click to display the mini toolbar, click the **Fill Color button arrow** 🎨 ▾, and then under **Theme Colors**, in the first column, click the third color—**White, Background 1, Darker 15%**.

3 Leave **row 16** blank, and then in the range **A17:A19**, type the following row titles:

Year

25% Growth Rate

21% Growth Rate

4 Select the range **B12:F12**, right-click over the selection, and then on the shortcut menu, click **Copy**.

ANOTHER WAY   Press Ctrl + C ; or, on the Home tab, in the Clipboard group, click the Copy button.

5 Point to cell **B17**, right-click, and then on the shortcut menu, under **Paste Options**, click **Paste** 📋.

> Recall that when pasting a group of copied cells to a target range, you need only point to or select the first cell of the range.

6 Select and **Copy** the range **B13:F13**, and then **Paste** it beginning in cell **B18**.

7 Click cell **C18**. On the **Formula Bar**, notice that the *formula* was pasted into the cell, as shown in Figure 3.28.

> This is *not* the desired result. The actual *calculated values*—not the formulas—are needed in the range.

FIGURE 3.28

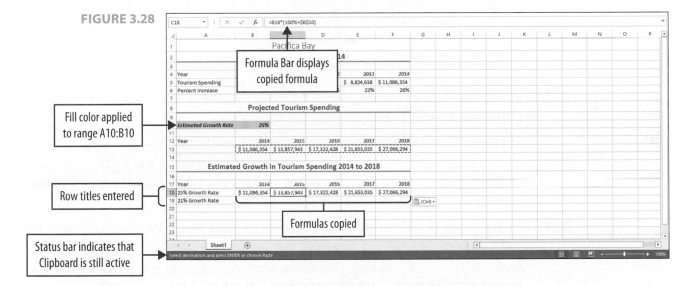

8 On the **Quick Access Toolbar**, click **Undo** ↺. With the range **B13:F13** still copied to the Clipboard—as indicated by the message in the status bar and the moving border—point to cell **B18**, and then right-click to display the shortcut menu.

9 Under **Paste Options**, point to **Paste Special** to display another gallery, and then under **Paste Values**, point to **Values & Number Formatting** 📋 to display the ScreenTip as shown in Figure 3.29.

> The ScreenTip *Values & Number Formatting (A)* indicates that you can paste the calculated values that result from the calculation of formulas along with the formatting applied to the copied cells. *(A)* is the keyboard shortcut for this command.

FIGURE 3.29

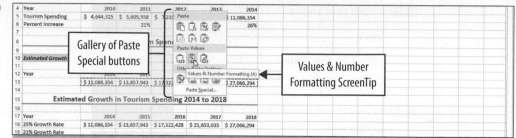

10 ▶ Click **Values & Number Formatting** 🗒, click cell **C18** and notice on the **Formula Bar** that the cell contains a *value*, not a formula. Press Esc to cancel the moving border. Compare your screen with Figure 3.30.

The calculated estimates based on a 25% growth rate are pasted along with their formatting.

FIGURE 3.30

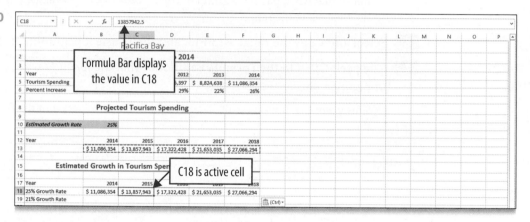

11 ▶ Click cell **B10**. Type **21** and then watch the values in **C13:F13** *recalculate* as, on the **Formula Bar**, you click **Enter** ✓.

The value *21%* is the lowest percent increase for the past 5-year period.

12 ▶ Select and **Copy** the new values in the range **B13:F13**. Point to cell **B19**, right-click, and then on the shortcut menu, point to **Paste Special**. Under **Paste Values**, click **Values & Number Formatting** 🗒.

13 ▶ Press Esc to cancel the moving border, click cell **A1**, click **Save** 💾, and then compare your screen with Figure 3.31.

With this information, Mr. Larsen can answer what-if questions about the projected increase in tourism spending based on the rates of increase over the past 5 years.

FIGURE 3.31

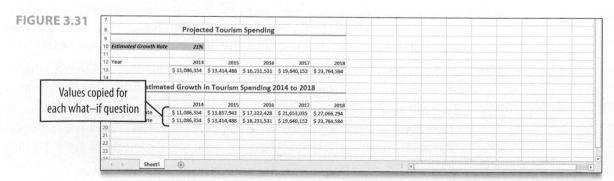

Video E3-7

A *line chart* displays trends over time. Time is displayed along the bottom axis and the data point values connect with a line. The curve and direction of the line make trends obvious to the reader.

The columns in a column chart and the pie slices in a pie chart emphasize the distinct values of each data point. A line chart, on the other hand, emphasizes the flow from one data point value to the next.

Activity 3.17 | Inserting Multiple Rows and Creating a Line Chart

So that City Council members can see how tourism spending has increased over the past five years, in this activity, you will chart the actual tourism spending from 2010 to 2014 in a line chart.

1 Click the **PAGE LAYOUT tab**. In the **Themes group**, click the **Colors arrow**, and then change the **Theme Colors** to **Orange**.

2 In the **row header area**, point to **row 8** to display the → pointer, and then drag down to select **rows 8:24**. Right-click over the selection, and then click **Insert** to insert the same number of blank rows as you selected. Compare your screen with Figure 3.32.

Use this technique to insert multiple rows quickly.

FIGURE 3.32

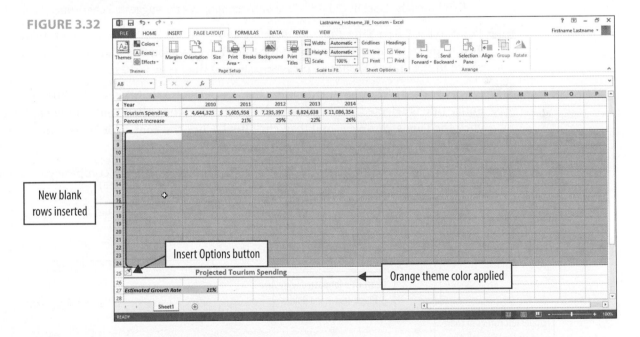

New blank rows inserted

Insert Options button

Projected Tourism Spending

Orange theme color applied

Estimated Growth Rate   21%

3 Near **row 25**, click **Insert Options**, and then click the **Clear Formatting** option button to clear any formatting from these rows.

You will use this blank area to position your line chart.

4 Press Ctrl + Home to deselect the rows and move to the top of your worksheet. Select the range **A5:F5**. On the **INSERT tab**, in the **Charts group**, click **Insert Line Chart**.

5 In the gallery of line charts, in the second row, point to the first chart type to display the ScreenTip *Line with Markers*. Compare your screen with Figure 3.33.

FIGURE 3.33

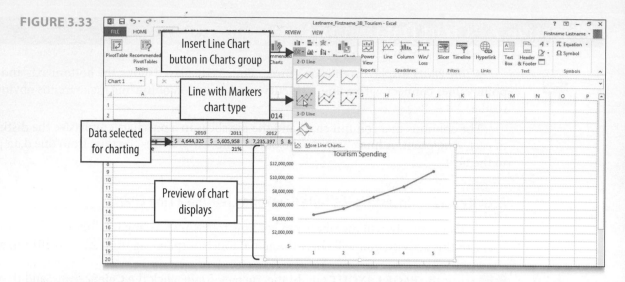

6 Click the **Line with Markers** chart type to create the chart as an embedded chart in the worksheet.

7 Point to the border of the chart to display the 🔼 pointer, and then drag the chart so that its upper left corner is positioned in cell **A8**, aligned approximately under the *t* in the word *Percent* above.

Excel uses the label in cell A5—*Tourism Spending*—as the suggested chart title.

8 Point to the **Chart Title** *Tourism Spending* and right-click. On the shortcut menu, click **Edit Text** to place the insertion point in the title. Type **Pacifica Bay** and press Enter. Press End to move to the end of *Spending*, press Spacebar, and then type **2010 to 2014**

9 Click the dashed border surrounding the **Chart Title** so that it is a solid line, indicating the entire title is selected. Right-click over the title, and then click **Font**. In the **Font** dialog box, click the **Font style arrow**, and then click **Bold**. Click the **Font color arrow**, and then in the second column, click the first color—**Black, Text 1**. Click **OK**.

10 On the right side of the chart, click **Chart Elements** ➕, and then compare your screen with Figure 3.34.

Three of the available chart elements are included for this chart by default—the axes, the chart title, and the gridlines.

FIGURE 3.34

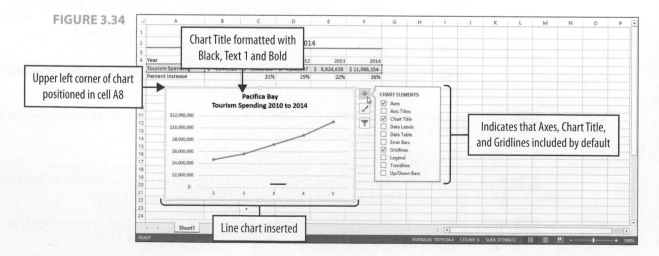

Activity 3.18 | Formatting Axes in a Line Chart

An *axis* is a line that serves as a frame of reference for measurement; it borders the chart *plot area*. The plot area is the area bounded by the axes, including all the data series. Recall that the area along the bottom of a chart that identifies the categories of data is referred to as the *category axis* or the *x-axis*. Recall also that the area along the left side of a chart that shows the range of numbers for the data points is referred to as the *value axis* or the *y-axis*.

In this activity, you will change the category axis to include the years 2010 to 2014 and adjust the numeric scale of the value axis.

1 Be sure the chart is still selected. At the bottom of the chart, point to any of the numbers *1* through *5* to display the ScreenTip *Horizontal (Category) Axis*, and then right-click. On the shortcut menu, click **Select Data**.

🔄 **BY TOUCH**   On the ribbon, tap the DESIGN tab, and then in the Data group, tap Select Data.

2 On the right side of the **Select Data Source** dialog box, under **Horizontal (Category) Axis Labels**, locate **Edit**, as shown in Figure 3.35.

Here you can change the labels on the category axis to the years that are represented in the chart.

FIGURE 3.35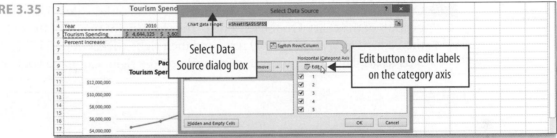

3 In the right column, click **Edit**. If necessary, drag the title bar of the **Axis Labels** dialog box to the right of the chart so that it is not blocking your view of the data, and then select the years in the range **B4:F4**. Compare your screen with Figure 3.36.

FIGURE 3.36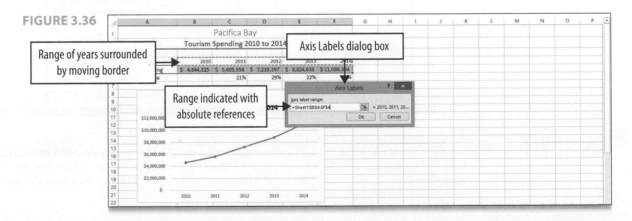

4 In the **Axis Labels** dialog box, click **OK**, and notice that in the right column of the **Select Data Source** dialog box, the years display as the category labels. Click **OK** to close the **Select Data Source** dialog box. Compare your screen with Figure 3.37.

FIGURE 3.37

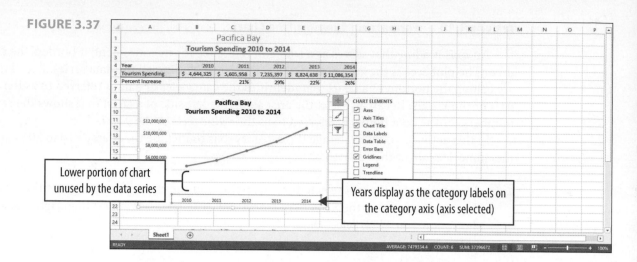

Lower portion of chart unused by the data series

Years display as the category labels on the category axis (axis selected)

5 With the **Horizontal (Category) Axis** still selected, click the **Chart Elements** button ⊞, point to **Axes**, click the ▶ **arrow**, and then click **More Options** to display the **Format Axis** pane.

6 Under **AXIS OPTIONS**, click **Fill & Line** 🖌, if necessary click **LINE** to expand the options, and then click the **No line** option button so that the line can become a gridline at the bottom of the chart when you format the plot area. **Close** ☒ the **Format Axis** pane.

7 On the chart, notice that the orange line—the data series—does not display in the lower portion of the chart. On the left side of the chart, point to any of the dollar values to display the ScreenTip *Vertical (Value) Axis*, and then right-click. On the shortcut menu, click **Format Axis** to display the **Format Axis** pane again on the right. Compare your screen to Figure 3.38.

FIGURE 3.38

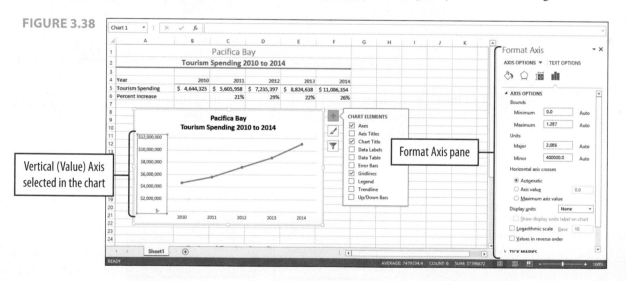

Vertical (Value) Axis selected in the chart

Format Axis pane

ANOTHER WAY
On the FORMAT tab, in the Current Selection group, click the Chart Elements arrow, click Vertical (Value) Axis, and then click Format Selection. Or, click the Chart Elements button, point to Axes, click the arrow, click More Options, and then in the Format Axis pane, click the AXIS OPTIONS arrow. On the displayed list, click Vertical (Value) Axis.

8 In the **Format Axis** pane, under **Bounds**, click in the **Minimum** box, select the existing text *0.0*, and then type **4000000**

Because none of the spending figures are under $4,000,000, changing the Minimum number to $4,000,000 will enable the data series to occupy more of the plot area.

9 Under **Units**, in the **Major** box, select the text *2.0E6*, type **2000000** and press Enter. Click **Save** 🔲, and then compare your screen with Figure 3.39.

> The *Major unit* value determines the spacing between the gridlines in the plot area. By default, Excel started the values at zero and increased in increments of $2,000,000. By setting the Minimum value on the value axis to $4,000,000 and changing the Major unit to $2,000,000, the line chart shows a clearer and more pronounced trend in tourism spending.

> Numbers that display E + a number are expressed by Excel in the Scientific format, which displays a number in exponential notation.

FIGURE 3.39

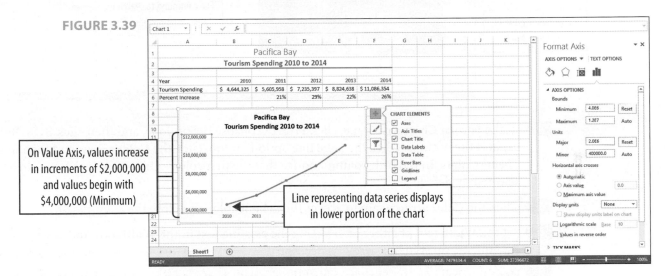

Activity 3.19 | Formatting the Chart Area in a Line Chart

An Excel chart has two background elements—the plot area and the chart area—which, by default display a single fill color. To add visual appeal to a chart, you can insert a graphic image as the background.

1 Near the top of the **Format Axis** pane, click the **AXIS OPTIONS arrow**, and then click **Chart Area** to display the **Format Chart Area** pane. Then click **Fill & Line** 🖎.

> When formatting chart elements, Excel provides multiple ways to display the panes that you need. You can right-click the area you want to format and choose a command on the shortcut menu. You can use an existing pane to move to a different pane. And you can use the FORMAT tab on the ribbon to navigate among various chart elements in the Current Selection group. Use whatever method is easiest for you.

ANOTHER WAY On the FORMAT tab, in the Current Selection group, click the Chart Elements arrow, click Chart Area, and then click Format Selection. Or, right-click slightly inside the chart to display the shortcut menu, and then click Format Chart Area.

2 In the **Format Chart Area** pane, click **FILL** to expand the options, and then click the **Picture or texture fill** option button.

> A default texture displays in the chart area.

3 In the **Format Chart Area** pane, under **Insert picture from**, click **File**. In the **Insert Picture** dialog box, navigate to the student data files that accompany this textbook, and then click **e03B_Surfers**. Click **Insert**. Compare your screen with Figure 3.40.

FIGURE 3.40

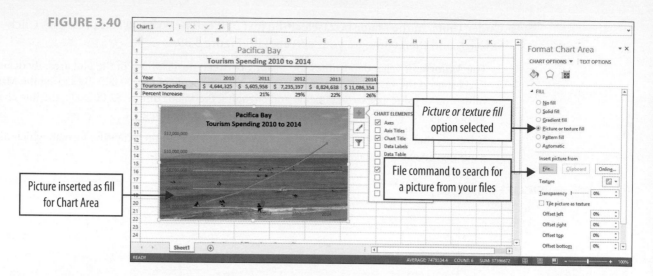

Picture inserted as fill for Chart Area

Picture or texture fill option selected

File command to search for a picture from your files

4 In the **Format Chart Area** pane, click **FILL** to collapse the options, and then click **BORDER** to expand the options. Click the **Solid line** option button, click the **Color arrow**, and then under **Theme Colors**, in the fifth column, notice that the first color—**Orange, Accent 1**—is already selected by default.

5 Click the **Color arrow** again to accept the default color and close the color palette.

6 Set the **Width** to **4 pt** either by selecting the existing text in the Width box and typing or by clicking the up spin box arrow as necessary.

7 Use the scroll bar on the right side of the **Format Chart Area** pane if necessary to scroll to the bottom of the pane, and then select the **Rounded corners** check box. On the **Quick Access Toolbar**, click **Save** 🖫, and then compare your screen with Figure 3.41.

FIGURE 3.41

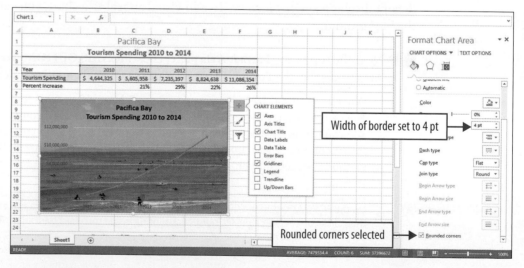

Width of border set to 4 pt

Rounded corners selected

Activity 3.20 | Formatting the Plot Area Gridlines and Axis Fonts in a Line Chart

1 To the right of the chart, if necessary click **Chart Elements** ➕ to display the list of elements, point to **Gridlines**, click the **arrow**, and then click **More Options** to display the **Format Major Gridlines** pane. Compare your screen with Figure 3.42.

FIGURE 3.42

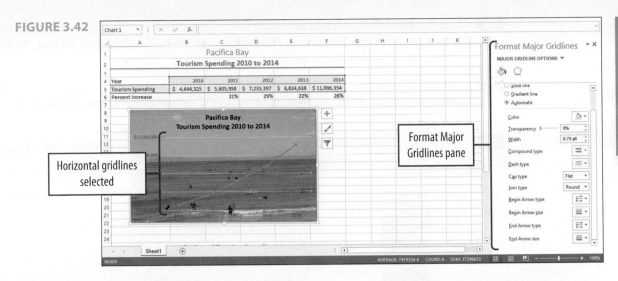

Horizontal gridlines selected

Format Major Gridlines pane

2 ▸ If necessary, in the pane, scroll to the top and click to expand **LINE**. Click the **Solid line** option button. Click the **Color arrow**, and be sure that **Orange, Accent 1**—in the fifth column, the first color—is selected.

3 ▸ Set the **Width** to **1 pt**.

4 ▸ In the chart, point to any of the dollar values on the **Vertical (Value) Axis**, right-click, and then click **Font**.

5 ▸ In the **Font** dialog box, change the **Font style** to **Bold**, and then change the **Font color** to **Black, Text 1**—in the second column, the first color. Click **OK**.

6 ▸ Use the same technique to format the font of the **Horizontal (Category) Axis** to **Bold** with **Black, Text 1**.

7 ▸ **Close** ✖ the **Format Axis** pane. Click cell **A1** to deselect the chart. Click **Save** 🔲, and then compare your screen with Figure 3.43.

FIGURE 3.43

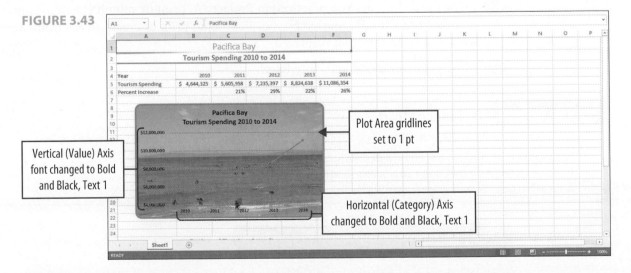

Vertical (Value) Axis font changed to Bold and Black, Text 1

Plot Area gridlines set to 1 pt

Horizontal (Category) Axis changed to Bold and Black, Text 1

8 ▸ Click the **PAGE LAYOUT tab**. In the **Page Setup group**, click **Margins**, and then click **Custom Margins**.

9 ▸ In the **Page Setup** dialog box, on the **Margins tab**, under **Center on page**, select the **Horizontally** check box.

10 ▶ Click the **Header/Footer tab**, and then in the center of the dialog box, click **Custom Footer**. In the **Footer** dialog box, with your insertion point blinking in the **Left section**, on the row of buttons, click **Insert File Name** 🔲.

11 ▶ Click **OK** two times. Click the **FILE tab**, and then click **Show All Properties**. As the **Tags**, type **tourism spending** As the **Subject**, type your course name and section number. Be sure your name displays as the author.

12 ▶ On the left, click **Print** to display the **Print Preview**, and then compare your screen with Figure 3.44. If necessary return to the worksheet and make any corrections.

FIGURE 3.44

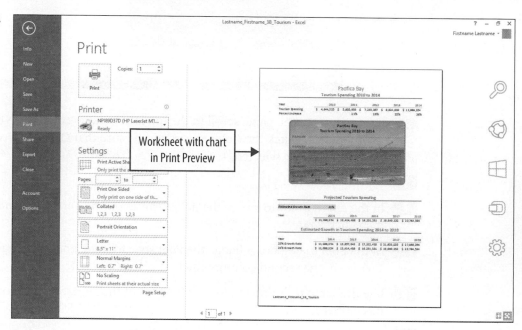

13 ▶ On the left, click **Save** to redisplay the workbook.

14 ▶ Using the techniques you practiced in Project 1A, print or submit electronically as directed by your instructor. If required by your instructor, print or create an electronic version of your worksheet with formulas displayed.

15 ▶ Close your workbook and close Excel.

More Knowledge   **Resizing a Chart**

To resize a chart, on the CHART TOOLS FORMAT tab, in the Size group, type the dimensions in the Shape Height or Shape Width box. Or:

- To change the width of a chart, drag a left or right sizing handle.
- To change the height of a chart, drag a top or bottom sizing handle.
- To size a chart proportionately, drag a corner sizing handle.

END | You have completed Project 3B

Objective   Convert an Excel Worksheet to a Google Docs Spreadsheet with a Chart

Google Docs is Google's free, web-based word processor, spreadsheet, slide show, and form service that, along with free data storage, is known as *Google Drive*. You can convert an Excel worksheet to a Google Docs spreadsheet. Google Drive and Google Docs are similar to SkyDrive and Office Web Apps—both are free, cloud-based productivity tools.

> **ALERT!**   **Working with Web-Based Applications and Services**
>
> Computer programs and services on the web receive continuous updates and improvements, so the steps to complete this web-based activity may differ from the ones shown. You can often look at the screens and the information presented to determine how to complete the activity.

Activity | Converting an Excel Worksheet to a Google Docs Spreadsheet with a Chart

In this activity, you will convert an Excel worksheet to a Google Docs spreadsheet and create a column chart.

1 If you do *not* have a Google account, skip to Step 2. Start Internet Explorer, in the address bar, type **http://docs.google.com** and then press Enter. Sign in to your Google account and display the Google docs page. Now skip to Step 3.

2 From the desktop, start Internet Explorer. In the address bar, type **http://docs.google.com** and then press Enter. Locate and click the button to sign up for a new account, and then complete the information. As your email address, you can use your Microsoft account or other email address. Sign in to your new Google account.

3 Locate and click **CREATE**, and then click **Spreadsheet**. Under **Untitled spreadsheet**, click **File**, and then click **Import**. Under **Upload file**, click **Browse**, and then in the **Choose File to Upload** dialog box, navigate

to your student data files and click **e03_3B_Web**. In the lower right corner of the dialog box, click **Open**, and then click **Import**.

4 When the screen indicates that the file was imported successfully, click **Open now**. Compare your screen with Figure A.

5 Drag to select the years and values in the range **A4:F5**, and then on the menu bar, click **Insert**. On the menu, click **Chart**.

6 On the **Chart Editor** screen, under **Recommended charts**, click the second chart—the **Column chart**, and then on the left above *Recommended charts*, click to select the first check box—**Switch rows/columns**, and then the second check box **Use column A as headers**, and then the third check box, **Use row 4 as labels**.

FIGURE A

(GO! with Office Web Apps continues on the next page)

7 Click **Insert**. If necessary, click one time in the white space on the worksheet to display the chart. In the upper right corner, click the down arrow and then click **Move to own sheet**.

8 On the displayed chart, click the text *Chart title*. In the box that displays, select the existing text, and then using your own name, type **2010 – 2014 Tourism Spending Prepared by Firstname Lastname** Press [Enter].

9 In the upper right corner of the chart, click the small square labeled *Tourism Spending*, and then click one time to edit the legend. In the toolbar that displays above, click **Right**, and then on the displayed list, click **None**. Compare your screen with Figure B.

10 In the upper right, click **Save image**, and then in the **Notification bar** at the bottom, click the **Save arrow**. Click **Save as**, and then in the **Save As** dialog box, navigate to your **Excel Chapter 3** folder. In the **File name** box, using your own name, type **Lastname_Firstname_EX_3B_Web** and then press [Enter].

11 In the upper right corner, click your Google name, and then click **Sign out**. Close Internet Explorer.

It is not necessary to save your spreadsheet, because Google Drive saves your work automatically. Your image is saved as a *.png* file, which is the file extension for an image in the *Portable Network Graphics* format. This format, like JPEG, is commonly used for graphics on the web.

12 Submit your .png image file to your instructor as directed.

FIGURE B

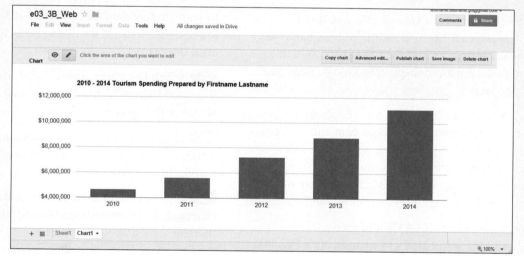

Andrew Rodriguez / Fotolia; FotolEdhar/ Fotolia; apops/ Fotolia; Yuri Arcurs/ Fotolia

The advantage of using Office 365 is that your organization does not have to purchase and install server hardware and software for sophisticated business applications and does not need a full-time IT person or staff just to manage the technology your teams need.

By using Office 365, you are able to have business-class services for your employees without investing in expensive hardware, software, and personnel. However, at least one person in an organization must be designated as the *Office 365 Administrator*—the person who creates and manages the account, adds new users, sets up the services your organization wants to use, sets permission levels, and manages the SharePoint team sites. You can have more than one Administrator if you want to share these tasks with others.

Microsoft provides easy-to-use instructions and videos to get you started, and you might also have contact with a Microsoft representative. You will probably find, however, that subscribing to and setting up the account, adding users, and activating services is a straightforward process that requires little or no assistance.

After purchasing the required number of licenses, you will add each team member as a user that includes his or her email address.

The Office 365 Administrator can manage the team sites, as shown in Figure A. On the left there are links to manage the site pages in the Office 365 account. Here the administrator can manage permissions, specifying which users can access and edit which team sites. The administrator can also manage and modify the look and feel of the team site.

Activity | Using a Team Site to Collaborate

This group project relates to the **Bell Orchid Hotels**. If your instructor assigns this project to your class, you can expect to use **Lync** in **Office 365** to collaborate on the following tasks for this chapter:

- If you are in the **Accounting Group**, you and your teammates will finalize the workbook to summarize hotel rooms sold over a four-week period in April and post it to your team site.

- If you are in the **Engineering Group**, you and your teammates will finalize your workbook summarizing Maintenance Expenses for the first quarter and post it to your team site.

- If you are in the **Food and Beverage Group**, you and your teammates will finalize your workbook to analyze the profitability of the ten most popular entrees in the hotel's restaurant and post it to your team site.

- If you are in the **Human Resources Group**, you and your teammates will finalize your workbook summarizing the pay of salaried employees over the first six months of operation and post it to your team site.

- If you are in the **Operations Group**, you and your teammates will finalize your workbook for Rooms and Housekeeping Service Analysis that will be used to determine ongoing needs for housekeeping service and post it to your team site.

- If you are in the **Sales and Marketing Group**, you and your teammates will finalize your Rooms Sold Analysis workbook summarizing rooms sold by four salespersons during January-June that will be used to develop a marketing plan for the rest of the year and post it to your team site.

FIGURE A

END OF CHAPTER

SUMMARY

Use pie charts when you want to show the relationship of each part to a whole. Consider using a pie chart when you have only one data series to plot and you do not have more than seven categories.

To create a pie chart, you must select two ranges. One range contains the labels for each pie slice; the other contains the values that add up to a total. Both ranges must have the same number of cells.

In formulas, Excel follows rules called the order of operations; expressions within parentheses are processed first, and multiplication and division are performed before addition and subtraction.

Use a line chart when you want to show trends over time. Time displays along the bottom axis and the data point values connect with a line. The curve and direction of the line make trends obvious.

GO! LEARN IT ONLINE

Review the concepts and key terms in this chapter by completing these online challenges, which you can find at **www.pearsonhighered.com/go**.

Matching and Multiple Choice:
Answer matching and multiple choice questions to test what you learned in this chapter. MyITLab®

Crossword Puzzle:
Spell out the words that match the numbered clues, and put them in the puzzle squares.

Flipboard:
Flip through the definitions of the key terms in this chapter and match them with the correct term.

GO! FOR JOB SUCCESS

Video: Planning and Managing Your Career

Your instructor may assign this video to your class, and then ask you to think about, or discuss with your classmates, these questions:

FotolEdhar / Fotolia

When did you start career planning and what were the main steps you took to plan your career?

What have been your best sources for networking?

What advice would you give to others about how to stay employable throughout your career?

Your instructor may assign one or more of these projects to help you review the chapter and assess your mastery and understanding of the chapter.

Project	Apply Skills from These Chapter Objectives	Project Type	Project Location
3C	Objectives 1-4 from Project 3A	**3C Skills Review** A guided review of the skills from Project 3A.	On the following pages
3D	Objectives 5-7 from Project 3B	**3D Skills Review** A guided review of the skills from Project 3B.	On the following pages
3E	Objectives 1-4 from Project 3A	**3E Mastery (Grader Project)** A demonstration of your mastery of the skills in Project 3A with extensive decision making.	In MyITLab and on the following pages
3F	Objectives 5-7 from Project 3B	**3F Mastery (Grader Project)** A demonstration of your mastery of the skills in Project 3B with extensive decision making.	In MyITLab and on the following pages
3G	Objectives 1-7 from Projects 3A and 3B	**3G Mastery (Grader Project)** A demonstration of your mastery of the skills in Projects 3A and 3B with extensive decision making.	In MyITLab and on the following pages
3H	Combination of Objectives from Projects 3A and 3B	**3H GO! Fix It** A demonstration of your mastery of the skills in Projects 3A and 3B by creating a correct result from a document that contains errors you must find.	Online
3I	Combination of Objectives from Projects 3A and 3B	**3I GO! Make It** A demonstration of your mastery of the skills in Projects 3A and 3B by creating a result from a supplied picture.	Online
3J	Combination of Objectives from Projects 3A and 3B	**3J GO! Solve It** A demonstration of your mastery of the skills in Projects 3A and 3B, your decision-making skills, and your critical thinking skills. A task-specific rubric helps you self-assess your result.	Online
3K	Combination of Objectives from Projects 3A and 3B	**3K GO! Solve It** A demonstration of your mastery of the skills in Projects 3A and 3B, your decision-making skills, and your critical thinking skills. A task-specific rubric helps you self-assess your result.	On the following pages
3L	Combination of Objectives from Projects 3A and 3B	**3L GO! Think** A demonstration of your understanding of the chapter concepts applied in a manner that you would outside of college. An analytic rubric helps you and your instructor grade the quality of your work by comparing it to the work an expert in the discipline would create.	On the following pages
3M	Combination of Objectives from Projects 3A and 3B	**3M GO! Think** A demonstration of your understanding of the chapter concepts applied in a manner that you would outside of college. An analytic rubric helps you and your instructor grade the quality of your work by comparing it to the work an expert in the discipline would create.	Online
3N	Combination of Objectives from Projects 3A and 3B	**3N You and GO!** A demonstration of your understanding of the chapter concepts applied in a manner that you would in a personal situation. An analytic rubric helps you and your instructor grade the quality of your work.	Online
3O	Combination of Objectives from Projects 3A and 3B	**3O Cumulative Group Project for Excel Chapter 3** A demonstration of your understanding of concepts and your ability to work collaboratively in a group role-playing assessment, requiring both collaboration and self-management.	Online
Capstone Project for Excel Chapters 1-3	Combination of Objectives from Projects 1A, 1B, 2A, 2B, 3A, and 3B	A demonstration of your mastery of the skills in Chapters 1-3 with extensive decision making. **(Grader Project)**	In MyITLab and online

GLOSSARY

GLOSSARY OF CHAPTER KEY TERMS

3-D The shortened term for *three-dimensional*, which refers to an image that appears to have all three spatial dimensions—length, width, and depth.

Absolute cell reference A cell reference that refers to cells by their fixed position in a worksheet; an absolute cell reference remains the same when the formula is copied.

Axis A line that serves as a frame of reference for measurement and which borders the chart plot area.

Base The starting point when you divide the amount of increase by it to calculate the rate of increase.

Bevel A shape effect that uses shading and shadows to make the edges of a shape appear to be curved or angled.

Category axis The area along the bottom of a chart that identifies the categories of data; also referred to as the x-axis.

Chart area The entire chart and all of its elements.

Chart sheet A workbook sheet that contains only a chart.

Data marker A column, bar, area, dot, pie slice, or other symbol in a chart that represents a single data point; related data points form a data series.

Data point A value that originates in a worksheet cell and that is represented in a chart by a data marker.

Data series Related data points represented by data markers; each data series has a unique color or pattern represented in the chart legend.

Enterprise fund A municipal government fund that reports income and expenditures related to municipal services for which a fee is charged in exchange for goods or services.

Explode The action of pulling out one or more pie slices from a pie chart for emphasis.

Formula AutoComplete An Excel feature which, after typing an = (equal sign) and the beginning letter or letters of a function name, displays a list of function names that match the typed letter(s).

Fund A sum of money set aside for a specific purpose.

General fund The term used to describe money set aside for the normal operating activities of a government entity such as a city.

Goal Seek A what-if analysis tool that finds the input needed in one cell to arrive at the desired result in another cell.

Google Docs Google's free, web-based word processor, spreadsheet, slide show, and form service, that along with free data storage, is known as Google Drive.

Google Drive Google's free web-based word processor, spreadsheet, slide show, and form service, that includes free data storage.

Legend A chart element that identifies the patterns or colors that are assigned to the categories in the chart.

Line chart A chart type that displays trends over time; time displays along the bottom axis and the data point values are connected with a line.

Major unit The value in a chart's value axis that determines the spacing between tick marks and between the gridlines in the plot area.

Order of operations The mathematical rules for performing multiple calculations within a formula.

Percent for new value = base percent + percent of increase The formula for calculating a percentage by which a value increases by adding the base percentage—usually 100%—to the percent increase.

Percentage rate of increase The percent by which one number increases over another number.

Pie chart A chart that shows the relationship of each part to a whole.

Plot area The area bounded by the axes of a chart, including all the data series.

Rate = amount of increase/base The mathematical formula to calculate a rate of increase.

Relative cell reference In a formula, the address of a cell based on the relative position of the cell that contains the formula and the cell referred to.

Value after increase = base x percent for new value The formula for calculating the value after an increase by multiplying the original value—the base—by the percent for new value (see the *Percent for new value* formula).

Value axis A numerical scale on the left side of a chart that shows the range of numbers for the data points; also referred to as the Y-axis.

What-if analysis The process of changing the values in cells to see how those changes affect the outcome of formulas in a worksheet.

x-axis Another name for the category axis.

y-axis Another name for the value axis.

CHAPTER REVIEW

Skills Review | Project 3C Parks

Apply 3A skills from these Objectives:

1. Chart Data with a Pie Chart
2. Format a Pie Chart
3. Edit a Workbook and Update a Chart
4. Use Goal Seek to Perform What-If Analysis

In the following Skills Review, you will edit a worksheet for Jerry Silva, City Parks Manager, which details the revenue generated from city parks and structures. Your completed worksheets will look similar to Figure 3.45.

PROJECT FILES

For Project 3C, you will need the following file:

e03C_Parks

You will save your workbook as:

Lastname_Firstname_3C_Parks

PROJECT RESULTS

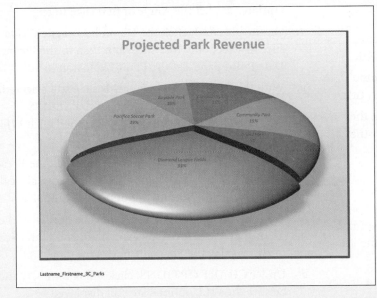

City of Pacifica Bay
Fee and Rental Revenue from City Parks
Projection for Next Fiscal Year Budget

	Current Year Revenue	Projected Revenue for Next Fiscal Year	% of Total Projected Budget
Community Park	$ 2,510,980	$ 2,536,529	14%
Grand Park	1,245,730	1,395,218	8%
Diamond League Fields	3,385,050	5,896,360	33%
Pacifica Soccer Park	2,231,050	3,423,515	19%
Bayside Park	1,907,890	1,812,297	10%
Community Center	2,582,340	2,711,459	15%
Total	$ 13,863,040	$ 17,775,378	

Goal: To Increase Revenue at Grand Park from 8% to 10%

| Goal Amount: | $ 1,777,538 | 10% |

Lastname_Firstname_3C_Parks

FIGURE 3.45

(Project 3C Parks continues on the next page)

CHAPTER REVIEW

1 ▶ Start Excel. From your student data files, open the file **e03C_Parks**. Save the file in your **Excel Chapter 3** folder as **Lastname_Firstname_3C_Parks**

a. Click cell **D5**, and then type **=** to begin a formula. Click cell **C5**, type **/** and then click cell **C11**. Press [F4] to make the reference to the value in cell **C11** absolute. On the **Formula Bar**, click **Enter**, and then fill the formula down through cell **D10**.

b. With the range **D5:D10** selected, right-click over the selection, and then on the mini toolbar, click **Percent Style** and **Center**.

2 ▶ Select the nonadjacent ranges **A5:A10** and **C5:C10** to select the park names and the projected revenue. Click the **INSERT tab**, and then in the **Charts group**, click **Insert Pie or Doughnut Chart**. Under **3-D Pie**, click the chart type **3-D Pie**.

a. On the **DESIGN tab**, in the **Location group**, click **Move Chart**. In the **Move Chart** dialog box, click the **New sheet** option button. In the **New sheet** box, replace the highlighted text *Chart1* by typing **Projected Park Revenue Chart** and then click **OK**.

b. Click the text *Chart Title*, and then type **Projected Park Revenue** Press [Enter] to create the new chart title.

c. With the title selected, on the **FORMAT tab**, in the **WordArt Styles group**, click **More** [▾] to display the gallery. In the second row, select the fifth style—**Fill – Olive Green, Accent 3, Sharp Bevel**. Drag to select the chart title text, and then on the mini toolbar, change the **Font Size** to **32**.

d. Click in a white area of the chart to deselect the chart title. Click **Chart Elements** [+], and then click the **Legend** check box to remove the legend.

e. In the list of **CHART ELEMENTS**, point to **Data Labels**, click the **arrow** that displays, and then click **More Options**. In the **Format Data Labels** pane on the right, under **LABEL OPTIONS**, select the **Category Name** and **Percentage** check boxes, and *clear* all other check boxes. Under **Label Position**, click **Center**.

f. Point to any of the selected labels, right-click to display a shortcut menu, and then click **Font**. In the **Font** dialog box, on the **Font tab**, change the **Font style** to **Bold Italic** and change the **Size** to **11** Click **OK**.

3 ▶ In any pie slice, point anywhere outside the selected label, and then double-click to display the **Format Data Series** pane. Under **SERIES OPTIONS**, click **Effects** [⬠], and then click **3-D FORMAT**.

a. Click the **Top bevel arrow**, and then under **Bevel**, click the first button—**Circle**. Apply the **Circle** bevel to the **Bottom bevel**.

b. Set the **Width** and **Height** of both the **Top bevel** and the **Bottom bevel** to **512 pt**

c. Scroll down, click the **Material arrow**, and then under **Standard**, click the third material—**Plastic**.

d. Scroll to the top of the **Format Data Series** pane, click **SHADOW**, and then click the **Presets arrow**. Scroll down, and then under **Perspective**, in the first row, click the third effect—**Below**.

e. In the **Format Data Series** pane, under **SERIES OPTIONS**, click the third button—**Series Options** [▮]. Set the **Angle of first slice** to **50**

f. On the pie chart, click the **Diamond League Fields** slice to select only that slice, and then in the **Format Data Point** pane, set the Point Explosion to **10%**

g. With the **Diamond League Fields** slice still selected, in the **Format Data Point** pane, under **SERIES OPTIONS**, click **Fill & Line** [◇], and then click **FILL** to expand the options.

h. Click the **Gradient fill** option button, click the **Preset gradients arrow**, and then in the fourth row, click the third gradient—**Bottom Spotlight – Accent 3**.

4 ▶ Point to the white area just inside the border of the chart to display the ScreenTip *Chart Area*, and then click one time to display the **Format Chart Area** pane.

a. Under **CHART OPTIONS**, click **Fill & Line** [◇], and be sure the **FILL** options are still displayed.

b. Click the **Gradient fill** option button, click the **Preset gradients arrow**, and then in the first row, click the fifth gradient—**Light Gradient – Accent 5**.

c. In the **Format Chart Area** pane, click **FILL** to collapse the options, and then click **BORDER** to expand the options.

d. Click the **Solid line** option button, click the **Color arrow**, and then in the fifth column, click the last color—**Ice Blue, Accent 1, Darker 50%**. Set the **Width** of the border to **5 pt** Close the pane, and then **Save** your workbook.

(Project 3C Parks continues on the next page)

5 In the sheet tab area at the bottom of the workbook, click the **Sheet1 tab**. In cell **A13**, type **Goal: To Increase Revenue at Grand Park from 8% to 10%** and then **Merge & Center** the text across the range **A13:D13**. Apply the **Heading 3** cell style.

a. In cell **A14**, type **Goal Amount:** and press Enter. Select the range **C6:D6**, right-click over the selection, and then click **Copy**. Point to cell **B14**, right-click, and then under **Paste Options**, click **Paste**. Press Esc to cancel the moving border.

b. Click cell **C14**. On the **DATA tab**, in the **Data Tools group**, click **What-If Analysis**, and then click **Goal Seek**. In the **Goal Seek** dialog box, press Tab to move to the **To value** box, and then type **10%**

c. Press Tab to move the insertion point to the **By changing cell** box, and then click cell **B14**. Click **OK**. In the displayed **Goal Seek Status** dialog box, click **OK**.

d. Select the range **A14:C14**. From the **HOME tab**, display the **Cell Styles** gallery. Under **Themed Cell Styles**, apply **20% - Accent6**. Click cell **B14**, and then from the **Cell Styles** gallery, under **Number Format**, apply the **Currency [0]** cell style.

6 With your worksheet displayed, in the sheet tab area, double-click *Sheet1* to select the text, and then type **Projected Park Revenue Data** and press Enter.

END | You have completed Project 3C

a. Click the **PAGE LAYOUT tab**. In the **Page Setup Group**, click **Margins**, click **Custom Margins**, and then in the **Page Setup** dialog box, on the **Margins tab**, under **Center on page**, select the **Horizontally** check box.

b. Click the **Header/Footer tab**, click **Custom Footer**, and then with your insertion point in the **Left section**, on the row of buttons, click **Insert File Name**. Click **OK** two times.

c. Display the **Projected Park Revenue Chart**—recall a chart sheet must have its footer formatted separately. Display the **Page Setup** dialog box.

d. Click the **Header/Footer tab**, click **Custom Footer**, and then in the **Left section**, click the **Insert File Name** button. Click **OK** two times.

e. Click the **FILE tab**, and then click **Show All Properties**. As the **Tags**, type **park revenue** As the **Subject**, type your course name and section number. Be sure your name displays as the **Author**.

f. On the left, click **Save**. Right-click the **Projected Park Revenue Chart sheet tab**, and then click **Select All Sheets**. Print or submit electronically as directed by your instructor. If required by your instructor, print or create an electronic version with formulas displayed by using the instructions in Project 1A. Close Excel without saving so that you do not save the changes you made to print formulas.

CHAPTER REVIEW

Skills Review Project 3D Housing Permits

In the following Skills Review, you will edit a worksheet that forecasts the revenue from new housing permits that the City of Pacifica Bay expects to collect in the five-year period 2014–2018. Your completed worksheet will look similar to Figure 3.46.

PROJECT FILES

For Project 3D, you will need the following files:

Build from Scratch

New blank workbook

e03D_Housing

You will save your workbook as:

Lastname_Firstname_3D_Housing

PROJECT RESULTS

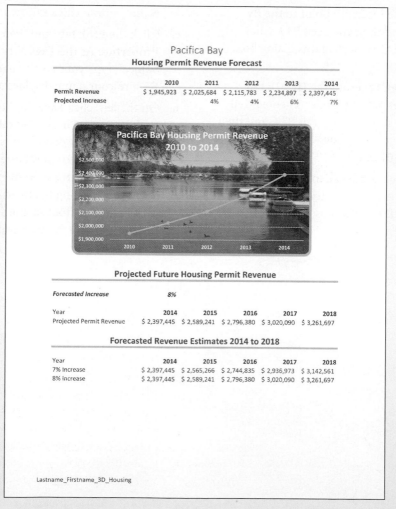

FIGURE 3.46

(Project 3D Housing Permits continues on the next page)

CHAPTER REVIEW

1 Start Excel and display a new blank workbook. By using your own name, save the file in your **Excel Chapter 3** folder as **Lastname_Firstname_3D_Housing**

a. In cell **A1**, type **Pacifica Bay** and in cell **A2** type **Housing Permit Revenue Forecast**

b. **Merge & Center** the title and subtitle across **columns A:F**. To **A1** apply the **Title** cell style and to **A2** apply the **Heading 1** cell style.

c. Widen **column A** to **175 pixels**, and widen **columns B:F** to **80 pixels**.

d. In cell **A5**, type **Permit Revenue** and in cell **A6** type **Projected Increase** Apply the **Heading 4** cell style to both cells. In cell **B4**, type **2010** Press Tab, and then in **C4**, type **2011** Use the fill handle to fill the remaining years through **column F** so that the last year that displays is 2014. Apply the **Heading 3** cell style to the years.

e. In the range **B5:F5**, type the values **1945923** and **2025684** and **2115783** and **2234897** and **2397445** Select the values you just typed, display the **Cell Styles** gallery, and then at the bottom, apply the **Currency [0]** cell style.

2 Click cell **C6**. Being sure to include the parentheses, type **=(c5-b5)/b5** and then press Enter. Select cell **C6**, and then apply **Percent Style**.

a. With cell **C6** selected, drag the fill handle to the right through cell **F6**.

b. In cell **A8**, type **Projected Future Housing Permit Revenue** and then press Enter. Point to cell **A2**, right-click, on the mini toolbar, click **Format Painter**, and then click cell **A8**. In cell **A10**, type **Forecasted Increase** leave row 11 blank, and then in cell **A12**, type **Year**

c. In cell **A13**, type **Projected Permit Revenue** and then in cell **B12**, type **2014** and press Tab. In cell **C12**, type **2015** and then press Tab. Select the range **B12:C12**, and then drag the fill handle through cell **F12** to extend the pattern of years to *2018*. Apply **Bold** to the selection.

d. Right-click cell **F5**, and then click **Copy**. Right-click over cell **B13**, and then click **Paste**.

e. In cell **B10**, type **7%** which is the percent of increase from 2013 to 2014. Select the range **A10:B10**, and then from the mini toolbar, apply **Bold** and **Italic**.

3 Click cell **C13**. Type **=b13*(100%+b10)** and then on the **Formula Bar**, click **Enter** to keep the cell active. With cell **C13** as the active cell, drag the fill handle to copy the formula to the range **D13:F13**.

a. Point to cell **B13**, right-click, click **Format Painter**, and then select the range **C13:F13**.

b. Click cell **A15**. Type **Forecasted Revenue Estimates 2014 to 2018** and then press Enter. Use **Format Painter** to copy the format from cell **A8** to cell **A15**.

c. In the range **A17:A19**, type the following row titles:

Year

7% Increase

8% Increase

4 Select the range **B12:F12**, right-click over the selection, and then on the shortcut menu, click **Copy**. **Paste** the selection to the range **B17:F17**.

a. Select the range **B13:F13**, right-click over the selection, and then on the shortcut menu, click **Copy**. Point to cell **B18**, right-click, and then from the shortcut menu, point to **Paste Special**. Under **Paste Values**, click the second button—**Values & Number Formatting**. Press Esc to cancel the moving border.

b. Click cell **B10**. Type **8** and then press Enter. Copy the new values in the range **B13:F13**. Point to cell **B19**, right-click, and then point to **Paste Special**. Under **Paste Values**, click **Values & Number Formatting**. **Save** your workbook.

5 In the **row header area**, point to **row 8** to display the pointer, and then drag down to select **rows 8:24**. Right-click over the selection, and then click **Insert** to insert the same number of blank rows as you selected. Under the selection area near cell **A25**, click **Insert Options**, and then click the **Clear Formatting** option button to clear any formatting from these rows.

a. On the **PAGE LAYOUT tab**, in the **Themes group**, click the **Colors arrow**, and then click **Yellow**. Select the range **A5:F5**. On the **INSERT tab**, in the **Charts group**, click **Insert Line Chart**. In the displayed gallery of line charts, in the second row, click the **Line with Markers** chart type to create the chart as an embedded chart in the worksheet.

b. Point to the border of the chart to display the pointer, and then drag the chart so that its upper left corner is positioned in cell **A9**, aligned approximately under the *c* in the word *Projected* above.

(Project 3D Housing Permits continues on the next page)

CHAPTER REVIEW

c. Point to the Chart Title *Permit Revenue* and right-click. On the shortcut menu, click **Edit Text** so that the insertion point is positioned before the word *Permit*. Type **Pacifica Bay Housing** and then press [Spacebar]. Press [End] and then press [Enter] to create a second line. Type **2010 to 2014**

6 At the bottom of the chart, point to any of the numbers *1* through *5*, and then right-click. On the shortcut menu, click **Select Data**. On the right side of the **Select Data Source** dialog box, click **Edit**. In the worksheet, select the years in the range **B4:F4**, and then click **OK** two times to enter the years as the category labels.

a. With the **Horizontal (Category) Axis** still selected, click **Chart Elements** [+], point to **Axes**, click the [▶] **arrow**, and then click **More Options**. In the **Format Axis** pane, under **AXIS OPTIONS**, click **Fill & Line** [◇], if necessary click **LINE** to expand the options, and then click the **No line** option button. **Close** the **Format Axis** pane.

b. On the left side of the chart, point to any of the dollar values, right-click, and then click **Format Axis**. In the **Format Axis** pane, under **Bounds**, select the text in the **Minimum** box, and then type **1900000**

c. Under **Units**, in the **Major** box, select the existing text, and then type **100000**

d. Near the top of the **Format Axis** pane, click the **AXIS OPTIONS arrow**, and then click **Chart Area** to display the **Format Chart Area** pane. Then, click **Fill & Line** [◇].

e. In the **Format Chart Area** pane, click **FILL** to expand the options, and then click the **Picture or texture fill** option button. Under **Insert picture from**, click **File**. In the **Insert Picture** dialog box, navigate to your student data files, and then click **e03D_Housing**. Click **Insert**.

f. In the **Format Chart Area** pane, click **FILL** to collapse the options, and then click **Border** to expand the options. Click the **Solid line** option button, click the **Color arrow**, and then under **Theme Colors**, in the fifth column, click the first color—**Gold Accent 1**. Set the **Width** to **4 pt** Scroll to the bottom of the pane, and then select the **Rounded corners** check box

g. Right-click the chart title, and then on the shortcut menu, click **Font**. In the **Font** dialog box, change the **Font style** to **Bold**, change the **Size** to **16**, and change the **Font color** to **White, Background 1**—in the first column, the first color. Click **OK**.

7 To the right of the chart, click **Chart Elements** [+], point to **Gridlines**, click the **arrow**, and then click **More Options** to display the **Format Major Gridlines** pane.

a. Under **LINE**, click the **Solid line** option button. Click the **Color arrow**, and be sure that **Gold, Accent 1** is the selected color. Set the **Width** to **1 pt**

b. In the chart, point to any of the dollar values on the **Vertical (Value) Axis**, right-click, and then click **Font**. In the **Font** dialog box, change the **Font style** to **Bold**, and then change the **Font color** to **White, Background 1**—in the first column, the first color. Click **OK**.

c. By using the same technique, format the **Font** of the **Horizontal (Category) Axis** to **Bold** with **White, Background 1** as the font color.

d. **Close** the **Format Axis** pane, and then click cell **A1** to deselect the chart. Click the **PAGE LAYOUT tab**. In the **Page Setup group**, click **Margins**, and then click **Custom Margins**. In the **Page Setup** dialog box, on the **Margins tab**, select the **Horizontally** check box. Click the **Header/Footer tab**, click **Custom Footer**, and then in the **Left section**, insert the file name. Click **OK** two times.

e. Click the **FILE tab**, and then click **Show All Properties**. As the **Tags**, type **housing permit revenue, forecast** In the **Subject** box, type your course name and section number. Be sure your name displays as the **Author**.

f. View the **Print Preview**, and then **Save** your workbook. Print or submit electronically as directed by your instructor. If required by your instructor, print or create an electronic version of your worksheet with formulas displayed by using the instructions in Project 1A, and then **Close** Excel without saving so that you do not save the changes you made to print formulas.

END | You have completed Project 3D

Mastering Excel Project 3E Revenue

In the following project, you will edit a worksheet that summarizes the revenue budget for the City of Pacifica Bay. Your completed worksheets will look similar to Figure 3.47.

PROJECT FILES

For Project 3E, you will need the following file:

e03E_Revenue

You will save your workbook as:

Lastname_Firstname_3E_Revenue

PROJECT RESULTS

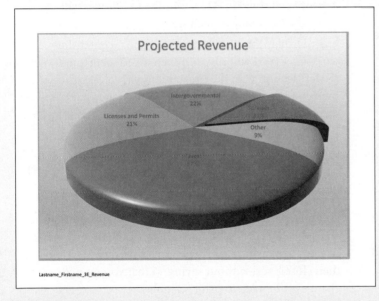

FIGURE 3.47

(Project 3E Revenue continues on the next page)

CONTENT-BASED ASSESSMENTS

1 Start Excel. From your student data files, locate and open **e03E_Revenue**. **Save** the file in your **Excel Chapter 3** folder as **Lastname_Firstname_3E_Revenue**

2 In cells **B10** and **C10**, enter formulas to calculate totals for each column. In cell **D5**, construct a formula to calculate the **% of Total Projected Revenue** from **Taxes** by dividing the **Projected Revenue for Next Fiscal Year** for **Taxes** by the **Total Projected Revenue for Next Fiscal Year**. Use absolute cell references as necessary, format the result in **Percent Style**, and **Center** the percentage. Fill the formula down through cell **D9**.

3 Select the nonadjacent ranges **A5:A9** and **C5:C9** as the data for a pie chart, and then insert a **3-D Pie** chart. Move the chart to a **New sheet** named **Projected Revenue Chart** As the text for the **Chart Title** element, type **Projected Revenue** Format the **Chart Title** by using the **WordArt Style Fill – Aqua, Accent 1, Shadow**—in the first row, the second style and a **Font Size** of **32**.

4 Remove the **Legend** chart element, and then add the **Data Labels** chart element formatted so that only the **Category Name** and **Percentage** display positioned in the **Center**. Format the data labels with a **Font style** of **Bold** and a **Font Size** of **14**.

5 Format the **Data Series** by using a **3-D Format** effect. Change the **Top bevel** and **Bottom bevel** to **Art Deco**. Set the **Top bevel Width** and **Height** to **350 pt** and then set the **Bottom bevel Width** and **Height** to **0 pt** Change the **Material** to the second **Special Effect—Soft Edge**.

6 Display the **Series Options**, and then set the **Angle of first slice** to **115** so that the **Taxes** slice is in the front of the pie. Select the **Services** slice, and then explode the slice **10%**. Change the **Fill Color** of the **Services** slice to a **Solid fill** by using **Gray-50%, Accent 4**—in the eighth column, the first color.

7 Format the **Chart Area** by applying a **Gradient fill** by using the **Preset gradients Light Gradient – Accent 4**.

Format the **Border** of the **Chart Area** by applying a **Solid line** border by using **Gray-50%, Accent 4** and a **5 pt Width**. Close any panes that are open on the right.

8 Display the **Page Setup** dialog box, and then for this chart sheet, insert a **Custom Footer** in the **left section** with the file name.

9 Display **Sheet1** and rename the sheet as **Revenue Sources** Click in any blank cell to cancel any selections. In cell **A12**, type **Goal: Increase Intergovernmental Revenue** and then **Merge & Center** the text across the range **A12:D12**. Apply the **Heading 3** cell style. In cell **A13**, type **Goal Amount**

10 Copy the range **C7:D7** to the range **B13:C13**. Click cell **C13**, and then use **Goal Seek** to determine the projected amount of Intergovernmental Revenue in cell **B13** if the value in **C13** is **25%**

11 Select the range **A13:C13**, and then apply the **20% - Accent4** cell style. In **B13**, from the **Cell Styles** gallery, apply the **Currency [0]** cell style.

12 Display the **Page Setup** dialog box, center the worksheet **Horizontally**, and then insert a custom footer in the **left section** with the file name. Select all the sheets, and then click the **FILE tab** to display **Backstage** view. Show all the properties, and then as the **Tags**, type **revenue sources** As the **Subject**, type your course name and section number. Be sure your name displays as the **Author**. On the left, click **Print** to display the **Print Preview**, and note any necessary changes or corrections. In **Backstage** view, on the left click **Save**, and then print or submit electronically as directed. If required by your instructor, print or create an electronic version of your worksheet with formulas displayed by using the instructions in Project 1A, and then close Excel without saving so that you do not save the changes you made to print formulas.

END | You have completed Project 3E

Mastering Excel   Project 3F Streets

MyITLab®
grader

Apply 3B skills from these Objectives:

5 Design a Worksheet for What-If Analysis

6 Answer What-If Questions by Changing Values in a Worksheet

7 Chart Data with a Line Chart

Build from Scratch

In the following project, you will create a worksheet that the City of Pacifica Bay Facilities Director will use to prepare a five-year forecast of the costs associated with street maintenance. Your completed worksheet will look similar to Figure 3.48.

PROJECT FILES

For Project 3F, you will need the following file:

New blank Excel workbook

You will save your workbook as:

Lastname_Firstname_3F_Streets

PROJECT RESULTS

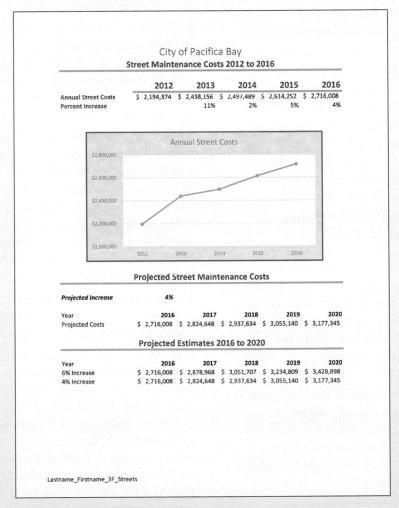

City of Pacifica Bay
Street Maintenance Costs 2012 to 2016

	2012	2013	2014	2015	2016
Annual Street Costs	$ 2,194,374	$ 2,438,156	$ 2,497,489	$ 2,614,252	$ 2,716,008
Percent Increase		11%	2%	5%	4%

Projected Street Maintenance Costs

Projected Increase	4%				
Year	2016	2017	2018	2019	2020
Projected Costs	$ 2,716,008	$ 2,824,648	$ 2,937,634	$ 3,055,140	$ 3,177,345

Projected Estimates 2016 to 2020

Year	2016	2017	2018	2019	2020
6% Increase	$ 2,716,008	$ 2,878,968	$ 3,051,707	$ 3,234,809	$ 3,428,898
4% Increase	$ 2,716,008	$ 2,824,648	$ 2,937,634	$ 3,055,140	$ 3,177,345

Lastname_Firstname_3F_Streets

FIGURE 3.48

(Project 3F Streets continues on the next page)

CONTENT-BASED ASSESSMENTS

1 Start Excel and display a new Blank workbook. Change the **Theme Colors** to **Paper**, and then **Save** the file in your **Excel Chapter 3** folder as **Lastname_Firstname_3F_Streets**

2 In cell **A1**, type the title **City of Pacifica Bay** and then in cell **A2** type the subtitle **Street Maintenance Costs 2012 to 2016** Merge & Center both the title and the subtitle across **columns A:F**, and then apply the **Title** and **Heading 1** cell styles respectively.

3 In the range **B4:F4**, fill the year range with the values 2012 through 2016. In cell **A5** type **Annual Street Costs** and in cell **A6** type **Percent Increase** Change the width of **column A** to **150 pixels**, and then change the width of **columns B:F** to **85 pixels**. In the range **B5:F5** type **2194374** and **2438156** and **2497489** and **2614252** and **2716008**

4 Apply the **Currency [0]** cell style to the values in **B5:F5**. Apply the **Heading 1** cell style to the years, and apply the **Heading 4** cell style to the range **A5:A6**.

5 In cell **C6**, construct a formula to calculate the percent of increase in annual street maintenance costs from 2012 to 2013. Format the result with the **Percent Style** and then fill the formula through cell **F6** to calculate the percent of increase in each year.

6 In cell **A8**, type **Projected Street Maintenance Costs** and then use **Format Painter** to copy the formatting from cell **A2** to cell **A8**. In cell **A10**, type **Projected Increase** and then in cell **A12**, type **Year** In cell **A13**, type **Projected Costs** and then in the range **B12:F12**, use the fill handle to enter the years 2016 through 2020. Apply **Bold** to the years. **Copy** the value in cell **F5** to cell **B13**. In cell **B10**, type **6%** which is the projected increase estimated by the City financial analysts. To the range **A10:B10**, apply **Bold** and **Italic**.

7 In cell **C13**, construct a formula to calculate the annual projected street maintenance costs for the year 2017 after the projected increase of 6% is applied. Fill the formula through cell **F13**, and then use **Format Painter** to copy the formatting from cell **B13** to the range **C13:F13**.

8 In cell **A15**, type **Projected Estimates 2016 to 2020** and then use **Format Painter** to copy the format from cell **A8** to cell **A15**. In cells **A17:A19**, type the following row titles:

> **Year**
>
> **6% Increase**
>
> **4% Increase**

9 **Copy** the range **B12:F12**, and then **Paste** the selection to **B17:F17**. Copy the range **B13:F13** and then paste the **Values & Number Formatting** to the range **B18:F18**. Complete the Projected Estimates section of the worksheet by changing the *Projected Increase* in **B10** to **4%** and then copying and pasting the **Values & Number Formatting** to the appropriate range in the worksheet. **Save** your workbook.

10 Select **rows 8:24**, and then **Insert** the same number of blank rows as you selected. **Clear Formatting** from the inserted rows. By using the data in **A4:F5**, insert a **Line with Markers** chart in the worksheet. Move the chart so that its upper left corner is positioned in cell **A9** and visually centered under the data above.

11 Format the **Bounds** of the **Vertical (Value) Axis** so that the **Minimum** is **2000000** and the **Major unit** is at **200000** Format the **Fill** of the **Chart Area** with a **Texture fill** by applying the **Parchment** texture—in the third row, the fifth texture. Format the **Plot Area** with a **Solid fill** by using **White, Background 1**—in the first column, the first color. Format the **Chart Area** with a **Border** by applying a **Solid line** by using **Olive Green, Accent 1, Darker 50%**—in the fifth column, the last color. Change the **Width** of the border to **2**

12 Click cell **A1** to deselect the chart. From the **Page Setup** dialog box, center the worksheet **Horizontally**, and then insert a **Custom Footer** in the **left section** with the file name.

13 Show all the properties, and then as the **Tags**, type **street maintenance costs** As the **Subject**, type your course name and section number. Be sure your name displays as the **Author**. In **Backstage** view, on the left, click **Print** to view the Print Preview. Print or submit electronically as directed. **Save** your workbook. If required by your instructor, print or create an electronic version of your worksheet with formulas displayed by using the instructions in Project 1A, and then close Excel without saving so that you do not save the changes you made to print formulas.

END | You have completed Project 3F

Mastering Excel Project 3G Operations

In the following project, you will edit a workbook for Jennifer Carson, City Finance Manager, that summarizes the operations costs for the Public Works Department. Your completed worksheets will look similar to Figure 3.49.

Apply a combination of 3A and 3B skills:

1 Chart Data with a Pie Chart

2 Format a Pie Chart

3 Edit a Workbook and Update a Chart

4 Use Goal Seek to Perform What-If Analysis

5 Design a Worksheet for What-If Analysis

6 Answer What-If Questions by Changing Values in a Worksheet

7 Chart Data with a Line Chart

PROJECT FILES

For Project 3G, you will need the following file:

e03G_Expenses

You will save your workbook as

Lastname_Firstname_3G_Expenses

PROJECT RESULTS

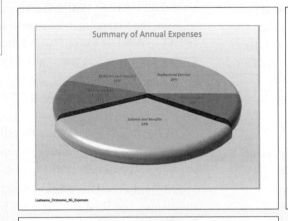

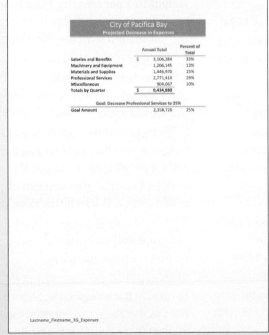

FIGURE 3.49

(Project 3G Operations continues on the next page)

CONTENT-BASED ASSESSMENTS

1 Start Excel. From your student data files, open **e03G_Expenses**. **Save** the file in your **Excel Chapter 3** folder as **Lastname_Firstname_3G_Expenses**

2 In the **Expenses** worksheet, calculate row totals for each expense item in the range **F5:F9**. Format the range **F6:F9** by applying the cell style **Comma [0]**. Calculate column totals for each quarter and for the Annual Total in the range **B10:F10**. In cell **G5**, construct a formula to calculate the **Percent of Total** by dividing the **Annual Total** for **Salaries and Benefits** by the **Annual Total** for all quarters. Use absolute cell references as necessary, format the result in **Percent Style**, and then **Center**. Fill the formula down through cell **G9**.

3 Use a **3-D Pie** chart to chart the **Annual Total** for each item. Move the chart to a **New sheet**; name the sheet **Annual Expenses Chart** As the text for the **Chart Title** element, type **Summary of Annual Expenses** Format the **Chart Title** by using **WordArt Style Fill - Blue, Accent 1, Shadow**—in the first row, the second style and a **Font Size** of **28**.

4 Remove the **Legend** from the chart, and then add **Data Labels** formatted so that only the **Category Name** and **Percentage** display positioned in the **Center**. Format the data labels with **Bold** and **Italic** and a **Font Size** of **12**.

5 Format the **Data Series** by using a **3-D Format** effect. Change the **Top bevel** and **Bottom bevel** to **Circle**. Set the **Top bevel Width** and **Height** to **50 pt** and then set the **Bottom bevel Width** and **Height** to **256 pt** Change the **Material** to the fourth **Standard Effect**—**Metal**.

6 Display the **Series Options**, and then set the **Angle of first slice** to **125** so that the **Salaries and Benefits** slice is in the front of the pie. Select the **Salaries and Benefits** slice, and then explode the slice **10%**. Change the **Fill Color** of the **Salaries and Benefits** slice to a **Solid fill** by using **Green, Accent 6, Lighter 40%**—in the last column, the fourth color.

7 Format the **Chart Area** by applying a **Gradient fill** using the **Preset gradients Light Gradient – Accent 4**. Format the **Border** of the **Chart Area** by adding a **Solid line** border using **Gold, Accent 4** and a **5 pt Width**.

8 Display the **Page Setup** dialog box, and then for this chart sheet, insert a **Custom Footer** in the **left section** with the file name. **Save** your workbook.

9 Display the **Expenses** worksheet, and then by using the Quarter names and the Totals by Quarter, insert a **Line with Markers** chart in the worksheet. Move the chart so that its upper left corner is positioned slightly inside the upper left corner of cell **A12**, and then drag the right sizing handle so that the chart extends slightly inside the right border of **column G**. As the **Chart Title** type **City of Pacifica Bay Annual Expense Summary**

10 Format the **Bounds** of the **Vertical (Value) Axis** so that the **Minimum** is **2100000** and the **Major unit** is at **50000** Format the **Fill** of the **Chart Area** with a **Gradient fill** by applying the preset **Light Gradient - Accent 3**—in the first row, the third gradient. Format the **Plot Area** with a **Solid fill** by using **White, Background 1**—in the first column, the first color. Close any panes on the right, click cell **A1** to deselect the chart, and then **Save** your workbook.

11 Copy the **Annual Total** in cell **F10** and then use **Paste Special** to paste **Values & Number Formatting** in cell **B35**. In cell **C35**, construct a formula to calculate the **Projected Expenses** after the forecasted increase of **3.5%** in cell **B31** is applied. Fill the formula through cell **F35**, and then use **Format Painter** to copy the formatting from cell **B35** to the range **C35:F35**.

12 Change the **Orientation** of this worksheet to **Landscape**, and then use the **Scale to Fit** options to fit the **Height** to **1 page**. In the **Page Setup** dialog box, center this worksheet **Horizontally**, and insert a **Custom Footer** in the **left section** with the file name. **Save** your workbook.

13 Display the **Projected Decrease** worksheet. In cell **C5**, calculate the **Percent of Total** for the first expense, apply **Percent Style**, and then copy the formula down for the remaining expenses.

14 Copy cell **B8**, and then use **Paste Special** to paste the **Values & Number Formatting** to cell **B13**. **Copy** and **Paste** cell **C8** to cell **C13**. With cell **C13** selected, use **Goal Seek** to determine the goal amount of Professional Services expenses in cell **B13** if the value in **C13** is set to **25%**

15 In the **Page Setup** dialog box, center this worksheet **Horizontally**, and insert a **Custom Footer** in the **left section** with the file name.

16 Select all the sheets, and then click the **FILE tab** to display **Backstage** view. Show all the properties, and then as the **Tags**, type **annual expense summary** As the **Subject**, type your course name and section number. Be sure your name displays as the **Author**. On the left, click

(Project 3G Operations continues on the next page)

Print to display the **Print Preview**, and view all three worksheets. Note any necessary changes or corrections. In **Backstage** view, on the left click **Save**, and then print or submit electronically as directed. If required by your instructor, print or create an electronic version of your worksheet with formulas displayed by using the instructions in Project 1A, and then close Excel without saving so that you do not save the changes you made to print formulas.

END | You have completed Project 3G

CONTENT-BASED ASSESSMENTS

Build from Scratch

| GO! Fix It | Project 3H Schools | Online |

| GO! Make It | Project 3I Tax | Online |

| GO! Solve It | Project 3J Staffing | Online |

| GO! Solve It | Project 3K Water Usage | |

Build from Scratch

PROJECT FILES

For Project 3K, you will need the following files:

New blank Excel workbook
e03K_Beach

You will save your workbook as:

Lastname_Firstname_3K_Water_Usage

Pacifica Bay is a growing community and the City Council has requested an analysis of future resource needs. In this project, you will create a worksheet for the Department of Water and Power that illustrates residential water usage over a five-year period. Create a worksheet with the following data:

	2014	2015	2016	2017	2018
Water Use in Acre Feet	62518	65922	71864	76055	82542

Calculate the percent increase for the years 2015 to 2018. Below the Percent Increase, insert a line chart that illustrates the city's water usage from 2014 to 2018. Format the chart and worksheet attractively with a title and subtitle, and apply appropriate formatting. If you choose to format the chart area with a picture, you can use e03K_Beach located with your student files. Include the file name in the footer and enter appropriate document properties. Save the workbook as **Lastname_Firstname_3K_Water_Usage** and submit as directed.

Performance Level

Performance Criteria	Exemplary: You consistently applied the relevant skills	Proficient: You sometimes, but not always, applied the relevant skills	Developing: You rarely or never applied the relevant skills
Create formulas	All formulas are correct and are efficiently constructed.	Formulas are correct but not always constructed in the most efficient manner.	One or more formulas are missing or incorrect or only numbers were entered.
Insert and format a line chart	Line chart created correctly and is attractively formatted.	Line chart was created but the data was incorrect or the chart was not appropriately formatted.	No line chart was created.
Format attractively and appropriately	Formatting is attractive and appropriate.	Adequately formatted but difficult to read or unattractive.	Inadequate or no formatting.

END | You have completed Project 3K

OUTCOMES-BASED ASSESSMENTS

RUBRIC

The following outcomes-based assessments are open-ended assessments. That is, there is no specific correct result; your result will depend on your approach to the information provided. Make Professional Quality your goal. Use the following scoring rubric to guide you in how to approach the problem and then to evaluate how well your approach solves the problem.

The *criteria*—Software Mastery, Content, Format and Layout, and Process—represent the knowledge and skills you have gained that you can apply to solving the problem. The *levels of performance*—Professional Quality, Approaching Professional Quality, or Needs Quality Improvements—help you and your instructor evaluate your result.

	Your completed project is of Professional Quality if you:	Your completed project is Approaching Professional Quality if you:	Your completed project Needs Quality Improvements if you:
1-Software Mastery	Choose and apply the most appropriate skills, tools, and features and identify efficient methods to solve the problem.	Choose and apply some appropriate skills, tools, and features, but not in the most efficient manner.	Choose inappropriate skills, tools, or features, or are inefficient in solving the problem.
2-Content	Construct a solution that is clear and well organized, contains content that is accurate, appropriate to the audience and purpose, and is complete. Provide a solution that contains no errors in spelling, grammar, or style.	Construct a solution in which some components are unclear, poorly organized, inconsistent, or incomplete. Misjudge the needs of the audience. Have some errors in spelling, grammar, or style, but the errors do not detract from comprehension.	Construct a solution that is unclear, incomplete, or poorly organized; contains some inaccurate or inappropriate content; and contains many errors in spelling, grammar, or style. Do not solve the problem.
3-Format & Layout	Format and arrange all elements to communicate information and ideas, clarify function, illustrate relationships, and indicate relative importance.	Apply appropriate format and layout features to some elements, but not others. Overuse features, causing minor distraction.	Apply format and layout that does not communicate information or ideas clearly. Do not use format and layout features to clarify function, illustrate relationships, or indicate relative importance. Use available features excessively, causing distraction.
4-Process	Use an organized approach that integrates planning, development, self-assessment, revision, and reflection.	Demonstrate an organized approach in some areas, but not others; or, use an insufficient process of organization throughout.	Do not use an organized approach to solve the problem.

OUTCOMES-BASED ASSESSMENTS

Apply a combination of the 3A and 3B skills.

Build from
Scratch

GO! Think   Project 3L Employment

PROJECT FILES

For Project 3L, you will need the following file:

New blank Excel workbook

You will save your workbook as:

Lastname_Firstname_3L_Employment

Sandy Ingram, the Director of the Employment Development Department for the city of Pacifica Bay, has requested an analysis of employment sectors in the city. Employment data for the previous two years is listed below:

Job Sector	2015 Employment	2016 Employment
Government	1,795	1,524
Healthcare	2,832	2,952
Retail	2,524	2,480
Food Service	3,961	3,753
Industrial	1,477	1,595
Professional	2,515	2,802

Create a workbook to provide Sandy with the employment information for each sector and the total employment for each year. Insert a column to calculate the percent change from 2015 to 2016. Note that some of the results will be negative numbers. Format the percentages with two decimal places. Insert a pie chart in its own sheet that illustrates the 2016 employment figures, and format the chart attractively. Format the worksheet so that it is professional and easy to read and understand. Insert a footer with the file name and add appropriate document properties. Save the file as **Lastname_Firstname_3L_Employment** and print or submit as directed by your instructor.

END | You have completed Project 3L

Build from
Scratch

GO! Think   Project 3M Population   Online

Build from
Scratch

You and GO!   Project 3N Expense Analysis   Online

Build from
Scratch

GO! Cumulative Group Project   Project 3O Bell Orchid Hotels
Online

Use Financial and Lookup Functions, Define Names, Validate Data, and Audit Worksheets

4

GO! to Work
Video E4

PROJECT **4A**

OUTCOMES
Calculate loan options and create a loan amortization schedule.

OBJECTIVES
1. Use Financial Functions
2. Use Goal Seek
3. Create a Data Table
4. Use Defined Names in a Formula

PROJECT **4B**

OUTCOMES
Automate workbooks to look up information automatically and to validate data. Audit workbook formulas to locate and correct errors.

OBJECTIVES
5. Use Lookup Functions
6. Validate Data
7. Audit Worksheet Formulas
8. Use the Watch Window to Monitor Cell Values

Yuri Arcurs/Fotolia

In This Chapter

In this chapter, you will use Financial functions and What-If Analysis tools to make your worksheets more valuable for analyzing data and making financial decisions. In addition, you will define names and use them in a formula. You will use the Lookup functions to locate information that is needed in a form and create a validation list to ensure that only accurate data is entered. In this chapter, you will also use Excel's auditing features to help you understand the construction of formulas in a worksheet, and locate and correct any errors. For example, by tracing relationships you will be able to test your formulas for accuracy.

The projects in this chapter relate to **Jesse Jewelers**, a Toronto-based retailer of jewelry and accessories for men and women. Jesse sells unique and beautiful items at a great price. Products include necklaces, bracelets, key chains, business cases, jewelry boxes, handmade bags, and personalized items. Founded in 2005 by two college friends, this growing company has several retail locations and an online store. It distributes its products to department and specialty stores throughout the United States and Canada. Jesse Jewelers provides exceptional customer service from a well-trained staff of product experts.

Amortization Schedule and Merchandise Costs

PROJECT ACTIVITIES

In Activities 4.01 through 4.09, you will create a worksheet for Alaina Dubois, International Sales Director for Jesse Jewelers, that details the loan information to purchase furniture and fixtures for a new store in Houston. You will also define names for ranges of cells in a workbook containing quarterly and annual merchandise costs for the new store. Your completed worksheets will look similar to Figure 4.1.

PROJECT FILES

For Project 4A, you will need the following files:

e04A_Merchandise_Costs
e04A_Store_Loan

You will save your workbooks as:

Lastname_Firstname_4A_Merchandise_Costs
Lastname_Firstname_4A_Store_Loan

PROJECT RESULTS

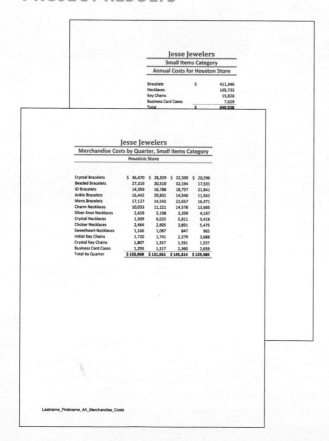

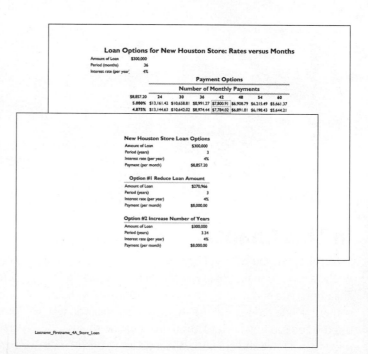

FIGURE 4.1 Project 4A Amortization Schedule and Merchandise Costs

Objective 1 | Use Financial Functions

Video E4-1

Financial functions are prebuilt formulas that make common business calculations such as calculating a loan payment on a vehicle or calculating how much to save each month to buy something. Financial functions commonly involve a period of time such as months or years.

When you borrow money from a bank or other lender, the amount charged to you for your use of the borrowed money is called *interest*. Loans are typically made for a period of years, and the interest that must be paid is a percentage of the loan amount that is still owed. In Excel, this interest percentage is called the *rate*.

The initial amount of the loan is called the *Present value (Pv)*, which is the total amount that a series of future payments is worth now, and is also known as the *principal*. When you borrow money, the loan amount is the present value to the lender. The number of time periods—number of payments—is abbreviated *Nper*. The value at the end of the time periods is the *Future value (Fv)*—the cash balance you want to attain after the last payment is made. The future value is usually zero for loans, because you will have paid off the full amount at the end of the term.

Activity 4.01 | Inserting the PMT Financial Function

In this activity, you will calculate the monthly payments that Jesse Jewelers must make to finance the purchase of the furniture and fixtures for a new store in Houston, the total cost of which is $300,000. You will calculate the monthly payments, including interest, for a three-year loan at an annual interest rate of 4.0%. To stay within Alaina's budget, the monthly payment must be approximately $8,000.

1 Start Excel. From your student files, open **e04A_Store_Loan**. Display the **Save As** dialog box, navigate to the location where you will store your workbooks for this chapter, and then create a new folder named **Excel Chapter 4** Open the folder, and then **Save** the workbook as **Lastname_Firstname_4A_Store_Loan**

2 In the range **A2:B5**, enter the following row titles and data. Recall that you can format the numbers as you type by typing them with their symbols as shown. Compare your screen with Figure 4.2.

Amount of Loan	$300,000
Period (years)	3
Interest Rate (per year)	4%
Payment (per month)	

FIGURE 4.2

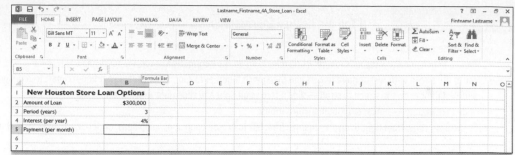

FIGURE 4.2

3 ► Click cell **B5**. On the **FORMULAS tab**, in the **Function Library group**, click **Financial**. In the list, scroll down as necessary, and then click **PMT**.

The Function Arguments dialog box displays. Recall that *arguments* are the values that an Excel function uses to perform calculations or operations.

4 ► If necessary, drag the Function Arguments dialog box to the right side of your screen so you can view columns A:B.

The *PMT function* calculates the payment for a loan based on constant payments and at a constant interest rate.

5 ► With your insertion point positioned in the **Rate** box, type **b4/12** and then compare your screen with Figure 4.3.

Excel will divide the annual interest rate of 4%, which is 0.04 in decimal notation, located in cell B4 by 12 (months), which will result in a *monthly* interest rate.

When borrowing money, the interest rate and number of periods are quoted in years. The payments on a loan, however, are usually made monthly. Therefore, the number of periods, which is stated in years, and the *annual* interest rate, must be changed to a monthly equivalent in order to calculate the monthly payment amount. You can see that calculations like these can be made as part of the argument in a function.

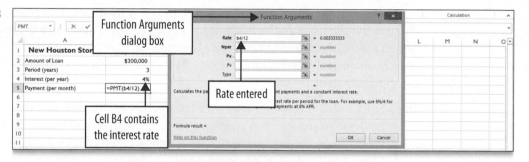

FIGURE 4.3

6 ► Press [Tab] to move the insertion point to the **Nper** box. In the lower portion of the dialog box, notice Excel points out that *Nper is the total number of payments for the loan* (number of periods).

7 ► Type **b3*12** to have Excel convert the number of years in the loan in cell **B3** (3 years) to the total number of months.

Recall that the PMT function calculates a *monthly* payment. Therefore, all values in the function must be expressed in months. To complete the PMT function, you must determine the total number of loan payment periods (months), which is 3 years × 12 months, or 36 months.

8 ► Press [Tab] to move to the **Pv** box, and then type **b2** to indicate the cell that contains the amount of the loan.

Pv represents the present value—the amount of the loan before any payments are made. In this instance, the Pv is $300,000.

9 ▸ In cell **B5** and on the **Formula Bar**, notice that the arguments that comprise the PMT function are separated by commas. Notice also, in the **Function Arguments** dialog box, that the value of each argument displays to the right of the argument box. Compare your screen with Figure 4.4.

FIGURE 4.4

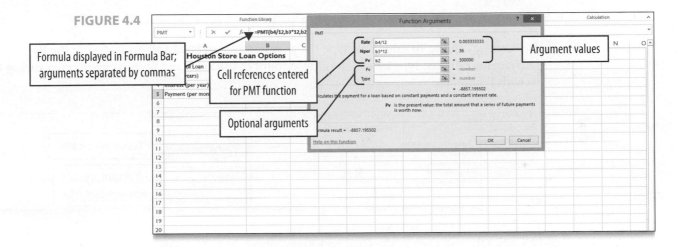

10 ▸ In the lower right corner of the **Function Arguments** dialog box, click **OK**.

The monthly payment amount—($8,857.20)—displays in cell B5. The amount displays in red and in parentheses to show that it is a negative number, a number that will be paid out. This monthly payment of $8,857.20 is over the $8,000 per month that Alaina has budgeted for her payments.

11 ▸ Click in the **Formula Bar**, and then using the arrow keys on the keyboard, position the insertion point between the equal sign and PMT. Type – (minus sign) to insert a minus sign into the formula, and then press Enter.

By placing a minus sign in the formula, the monthly payment amount, $8,857.20, displays in cell B5 as a *positive* number, which is more familiar and simpler to work with.

12 ▸ **Save** 🖫 your workbook.

Objective 2   Use Goal Seek

Video E4-2

What-If Analysis is a process of changing the values in cells to determine how those changes affect the outcome of formulas on the worksheet; for example, you might vary the interest rate to determine the amount of loan payments.

Goal Seek is part of a suite of data tools used for a What-If Analysis. It is a method to find a specific value for a cell by adjusting the value of one other cell. With Goal Seek, you can work backward from the desired outcome to find the number necessary to achieve your goal. If you have a result in mind, you can try different numbers in one of the cells used as an argument in the function until you get close to the result you want.

Activity 4.02 | Using Goal Seek to Produce a Desired Result

Alaina knows that her budget cannot exceed $8,000 per month for the new store loan. The amount of $300,000 is necessary to purchase the furniture and fixtures to open the new store. Now she has two options: borrow less money and reduce the amount or quality of the furniture and fixtures in the store or extend the time to repay the loan. To find out how much she can borrow for three years to stay within the budget or how much to increase the repayment period, you will use the Goal Seek tool.

1 Click cell **B5**. On the **DATA tab**, in the **Data Tools group**, click **What-If Analysis**, and then in the list, click **Goal Seek**. In the **Goal Seek** dialog box, in the **Set cell** box, confirm that *B5* displays.

The cell address in this box is the cell that will display the desired result.

2 Press Tab. In the **To value** box, type the payment goal of **8000** and press Tab. In the **By changing cell** box, type **b2** which is the amount of the loan, and then compare your dialog box with Figure 4.5.

FIGURE 4.5

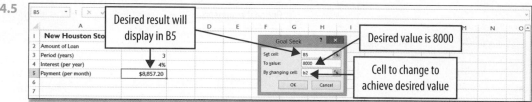

3 Click **OK**, and then in the **Goal Seek Status** dialog box, click **OK**.

Excel's calculations indicate that to achieve a monthly payment of $8,000.00 using a three-year loan, Alaina can borrow only *$270,966*—not $300,000.

4 Click cell **A7**. Type **Option #1 Reduce Loan Amount** and then on the **Formula Bar**, click **Enter** ✓ to keep the cell active. **Merge and Center** ⊞▾ this heading across the range **A7:B7**, on the **HOME tab**, display the **Cell Styles** gallery, and then under **Titles and Headings**, click the **Heading 2** cell style.

5 Select the range **A2:B5**, right-click, and then click **Copy**. Point to cell **A8**, right-click, point to **Paste Special**, and then under **Paste Values**, click the **second** button—**Values & Number Formatting (A)** 📋. Press Esc to cancel the moving border.

ANOTHER WAY   Click cell A8, right-click, and then click Paste Special. In the Paste Special dialog box, under Paste, click the Values and number formats option button, and then click OK.

6 Save 💾 your workbook, and then compare your worksheet with Figure 4.6.

Recall that by using the Paste Special command, you can copy the *value* in a cell, rather than the formula, and the cell formats are retained—cell B5 contains the PMT function formula, and here you need only the value that *results* from that formula.

FIGURE 4.6

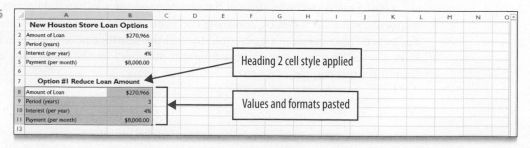

For Alaina's purchase of furniture and fixtures for the new store in Houston, an alternative to borrowing less money—which would mean buying fewer items or items of lesser quality—would be to increase the number of years of payments.

1. In cell **B2**, replace the existing value by typing **300000** and then press Enter to restore the original loan amount. Click cell **B5**. On the **DATA tab**, in the **Data Tools group**, click **What-If Analysis**, and then click **Goal Seek**.

2. In the **Set cell** box, confirm that *B5* displays. Press Tab. In the **To value** box, type **8000** and then press Tab. In the **By changing cell** box, type **b3** which is the number of years for the loan. Compare your screen with Figure 4.7.

FIGURE 4.7

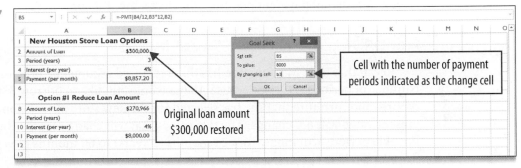

3. Click **OK** two times.

   Excel's calculations indicate that by making payments for 3.3 years—*3.343845511*—the monthly payment is the desired amount of $8,000.00.

4. Click cell **A13**. Type **Option #2 Increase Number of Years** and then press Enter. Right-click over cell **A7**, on the mini toolbar, click **Format Painter**, and then click cell **A13** to copy the format.

5. Select the range **A2:B5**, right-click, and then click **Copy**. Point to cell **A14**, right-click, point to **Paste Special**, and then under **Paste Values**, click the **second** button—**Values & Number Formatting (A)**. Press Esc to cancel the moving border.

BY TOUCH   Press and hold an item to display a shaded square and then release to right-click it.

6. Click cell **B15**, right-click to display the mini toolbar, and then click **Decrease Decimal** until the number of decimal places displayed is two. Click cell **B3**. Type **3** and then press Enter to restore the original value. **Save** your workbook, and then compare your screen with Figure 4.8.

FIGURE 4.8

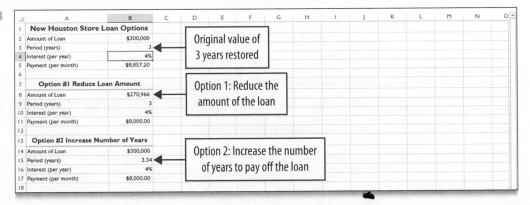

Video E4-3

A *data table* is a range of cells that shows how changing certain values in your formulas affects the results of those formulas. Data tables make it easy to calculate multiple versions in one operation, and then to view and compare the results of all the different variations.

For example, banks may offer loans at different rates for different periods of time, which require different payments. By using a data table, you can calculate the possible values for each argument.

A *one-variable data table* changes the value in only one cell. For example, use a one-variable data table if you want to see how different interest rates affect a monthly payment. A *two-variable data table* changes the values in two cells—for example, if you want to see how different interest rates and different payment periods will affect a monthly payment.

Activity 4.04 | Designing a Two-Variable Data Table

Recall that the PMT function has three required arguments: Present value (Pv), Rate, and Number of periods (Nper). Because Alaina would still like to borrow $300,000 and purchase the fixtures and furniture that she has selected for the new store in Houston, in this data table, the present value will *not* change. The two values that will change are the Rate and Number of periods. Possible periods will range from 24 months (2 years) to 60 months (5 years) and the rate will vary from 5% to 3%.

1   At the lower edge of the worksheet, click the **New sheet** button ⊕. Double-click the **Sheet1** tab, type **Payment Table** and then press Enter.

2   In cell **A1**, type **Loan Options for New Houston Store: Rates versus Months** and then press Enter. **Merge and Center** 🖽▾ this title across the range **A1:J1**, and then apply the **Title** cell style.

3   In the range **A2:B4**, enter the following row titles and data:

Amount of Loan	$300,000
Period (months)	36
Interest rate (per year)	4%

4   Point to the border between **columns A** and **B** and double-click to AutoFit **column A**. In cell **C5**, type **Payment Options** and press Enter, and then **Merge and Center** 🖽▾ this title across the range **C5:I5**. From the **Cell Styles** gallery, under **Titles and Headings**, click the **Heading 1** cell style.

5   In cell **C6**, type **Number of Monthly Payments** and press Enter, and then use the **Format Painter** 🖌 to apply the format of cell **C5** to cell **C6**.

6   In cell **C7**, type **24** and then press Tab. Type **30** and then press Tab. Select the range **C7:D7**, point to the fill handle, and then drag to the right through cell **I7** to fill in a pattern of months from 24 to 60 in increments of six months.

> Recall that the Auto Fill feature will duplicate a pattern of values that you set in the beginning cells.

7   In cell **B8**, type **5.000%** and then press Enter. In cell **B9**, type **4.875%** and then press Enter.

> Excel rounds both values to two decimal places.

8   Select the range **B8:B9**. Point to the fill handle, and then drag down through cell **B24** to fill a pattern of interest rates in decrements of .125 from 5.00% down to 3.00%.

9 Right-click anywhere over the selected range, and then on the mini toolbar, click **Increase Decimal** ⬗. **Save** 🖫 your workbook. Compare your screen with Figure 4.9.

> Row 7 represents the number of monthly payments, and column B represents a range of possible annual interest rates. These two arguments will be used to calculate varying payment arrangements for a loan of $300,000.

FIGURE 4.9

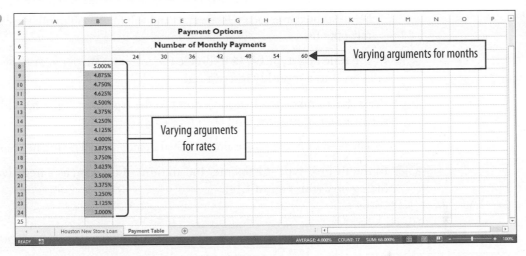

10 In cell **A8**, type **Rates** and then press Enter. Select the range **A8:A24**. On the **HOME tab**, in the **Alignment group**, click **Merge and Center** ⬒▾, click **Align Right** ▤, and then click **Middle Align** ▤. Display the **Cell Styles** gallery, and then under **Data and Model**, click the **Explanatory Text** style. Compare your screen with Figure 4.10.

FIGURE 4.10

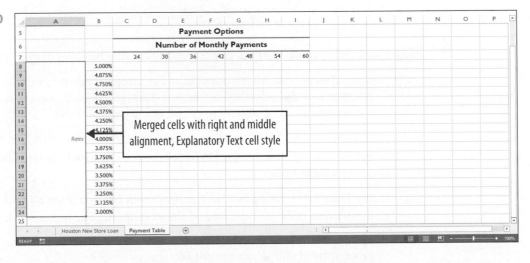

Activity 4.05 | Using a Data Table to Calculate Options

Recall that a data table is a range of cells that shows how changing certain values in your formulas affects the results of those formulas.

In this activity, you will create a table of payments for every combination of payment periods, which are represented by the column titles under *Number of Monthly Payments*, and interest rates, which are represented by the row titles to the right of *Rates*. From the resulting table, Alaina can find a combination of payment periods and interest rates that will enable her to go forward with her plan to borrow $300,000 to purchase the necessary furniture and fixtures for the new store in Houston.

1 Press `Ctrl` + `Home` to view the top of your worksheet. Then, in cell **B7**, type **=** Notice that in the upper left corner of your screen, in the **Name Box**, *PMT* displays indicating the most recently used function. Click in the **Name Box** to open the **Function Arguments** dialog box and select the **PMT** function.

> When creating a data table, you enter the PMT function in the upper left corner of your range of data, so that when the data table is completed, the months in row 7 and the rates in column B will be substituted into each cell's formula and will fill the table with the range of months and interest rate options.

2 In the **Rate** box, type **b4/12** to divide the interest rate per year shown in cell **B4** by 12 and convert it to a monthly interest rate.

3 Press `Tab` to move the insertion point to the **Nper** box. Type **b3** which is the cell that contains the number of months, and then press `Tab`.

> The periods in cell B3 are already stated in months and do not need to be changed.

4 In the **Pv** box, type **-b2** to enter the amount of the loan as a negative number. Compare your dialog box with Figure 4.11.

FIGURE 4.11

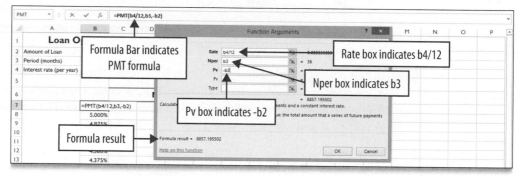

5 Click **OK** to close the **Function Arguments** dialog box and display the result in cell **B7**.

> The payment—*$8,857.20*—is calculated by using the values in cells B2, B3, and B4. This is the same payment that you calculated on the first worksheet. Now it displays as a positive number because you entered the loan amount in cell B2 as a negative number.

6 Select the range **B7:I24**, which encompasses all of the months and all of the rates. With the range **B7:I24** selected, on the **DATA tab**, in the **Data Tools group**, click **What-If Analysis**, and then click **Data Table**.

7 In the **Data Table** dialog box, in the **Row input cell** box, type **b3** and then press `Tab`. In the **Column input cell** box, type **b4** and then compare your screen with Figure 4.12.

> The row of months will be substituted for the value in cell B3, and the column of interest rates will be substituted for the value in cell B4.

FIGURE 4.12

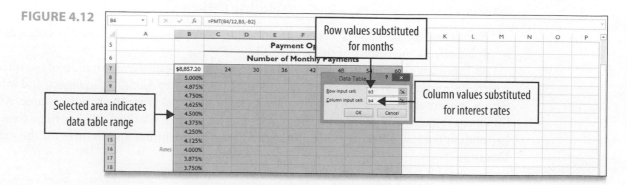

8 Click **OK**. Click cell **F8**, and then examine the formula in the **Formula Bar**. Compare your screen with Figure 4.13.

The table is filled with payment options that use the month and interest rate corresponding to the position in the table. So, if Alaina chooses a combination of 42 months at an interest rate of 5.0%, the monthly payment will be $7,800.91, which is slightly under the monthly payment she wanted. The data table is one of a group of Excel's What-If Analysis tools.

FIGURE 4.13

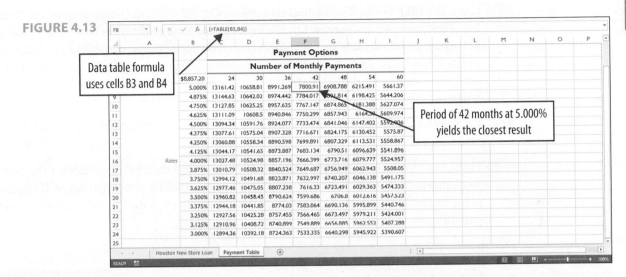

9 Point to cell **B7**, right-click, and then on the mini toolbar, click **Format Painter**. With the pointer, select the range **C8:I24** to apply the same format. AutoFit columns **C:I** to display all values.

10 Select the range **F8:F19**. From the **HOME tab**, display the **Cell Styles** gallery, and then under **Data and Model**, click the **Note** cell style to highlight the desired payment options.

11 Select the range **B8:B24**, hold down Ctrl, and then select the range **C7:I7**. Right-click over the selection, and then on the mini toolbar, click **Bold B** and then click **Center**. Click anywhere to deselect the range, and then compare your worksheet with Figure 4.14.

BY TOUCH   Swipe to select the range B8:B24, hold it, and then select the range C7:I7.

By using a data table of payment options, you can see that Alaina must get a loan for a 42-month period (3.5 years) for any of the interest rates between 5.000% and 3.000% in order to purchase the furniture and fixtures she wants and still keep the monthly payment under $8,000.

FIGURE 4.14

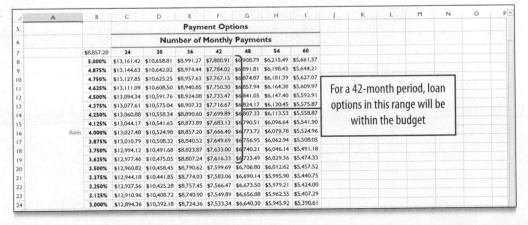

12 ▶ Right-click the **Payment Table sheet tab** and click **Select All Sheets**. With the two sheets grouped, insert a footer in the **left section** that includes the **file name**. Click outside the footer area. On the status bar, click **Normal** ⊞. Press Ctrl + Home to move to the top of the worksheet. Click the **PAGE LAYOUT tab**, in the **Page Setup group**, set the **Orientation** to **Landscape**. Click **Margins**, and then click **Custom Margins**. In the **Page Setup** dialog box, under **Center on page**, select **Horizontally**, and then click **OK**.

13 ▶ Click the **FILE tab** to display **Backstage** view. On the right, at the bottom of the **Properties** list, click **Show All Properties**. On the list of **Properties**, in the **Tags** box, type **amortization schedule, payment table** In the **Subject** box, type your course name and section #. Under **Related People**, be sure that your name displays as the author. If necessary, right-click the author name, click Edit Property, type your name, click outside of the Edit person dialog box, and then click OK.

14 ▶ Click **Print**, examine the **Print Preview**, make any necessary adjustments, and then **Save** 🖫 and Close your workbook.

15 ▶ Hold this workbook until the end of this project, and then print or submit the two worksheets in this workbook electronically as directed by your instructor. If required, print or create an electronic version of your worksheets with formulas displayed using the instructions in Project 1A.

Objective 4   Use Defined Names in a Formula

Video E4-4

A *name*, also referred to as a ***defined name***, is a word or string of characters in Excel that represents a cell, a range of cells, a formula, or a constant value. A defined name that is distinctive and easy to remember typically defines the *purpose* of the selected cells. When creating a formula, the defined name may be used instead of the cell reference.

All names have a ***scope***, which is the location within which the name is recognized without qualification. The scope of a name is usually either to a specific worksheet or to an entire workbook.

Activity 4.06 | Defining a Name

In this activity, you will use three ways to define a name for a cell or group of cells. After defining a name, you can use the name in a formula to refer to the cell or cells. Names make it easier for you and others to understand the meaning of formulas in a worksheet.

1 ▶ From your student files, open the file **e04A_Merchandise_Costs**, and then **Save** the file in your **Excel Chapter 4** folder as **Lastname_Firstname_4A_Merchandise_Costs**

2 ▶ Select the range **B6:E17**. In the lower right corner of the selection, click **Quick Analysis** 🖼. Click **TOTALS**, compare your screen to Figure 4.15, and then click the first **Sum** button to total the columns. Click anywhere to cancel the selection.

Use this technique to sum a group of columns or rows simultaneously.

🔄 **ANOTHER WAY**   Select the range B6:E18, which includes the adjacent empty cells in row 18, and then click AutoSum.

FIGURE 4.15

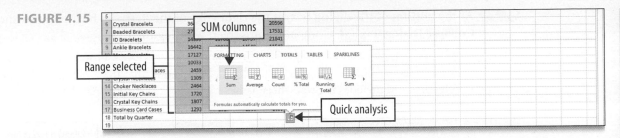

3 Select the range **B6:E6**, hold down Ctrl, and select the range **B18:E18**. From the **Cell Styles** gallery, under **Number Format**, click the **Currency [0]** cell style. Select the range **B7:E17**, display the **Cell Styles** gallery, and then, under **Number Format**, click **Comma [0]**.

You can use these number formats in the Cell Styles gallery in a manner similar to the Accounting Number Format button and the Comma Style button on the ribbon. The advantage to using these styles from the Cell Styles gallery is that you can select the option that formats automatically with zero [0] decimal places.

4 Select the range **B18:E18**, and then from the **Cell Styles** gallery, under **Titles and Headings**, click the **Total** cell style. Press Ctrl + Home to move to the top of the worksheet, and then compare your screen with Figure 4.16.

FIGURE 4.16

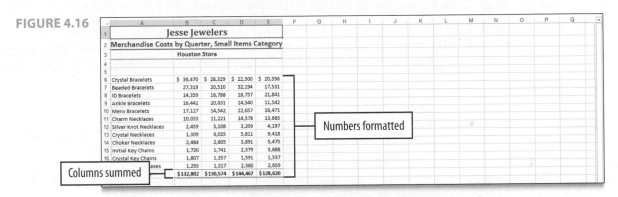

5 Select the range **B6:E9**. On the **FORMULAS tab**, in the **Defined Names group**, click **Define Name**. Compare your screen with Figure 4.17.

The New Name dialog box displays. In the Name box, Excel suggests *Crystal_Bracelets* as the name for this range of cells, which is the text in the first cell adjacent to the selected range. Excel will attempt to suggest a logical name for the selected cells. Notice that Excel replaces the blank space with an underscore, as defined names cannot contain spaces.

FIGURE 4.17

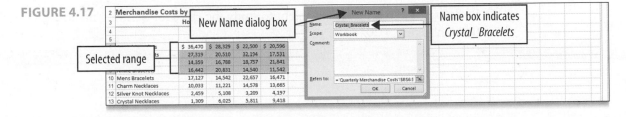

6 With *Crystal_Bracelets* selected, type **Bracelet_Costs** as the name.

Naming cells has no effect on the displayed or underlying values; it simply creates an easy-to-remember name that you can use when creating formulas that refer to this range of cells.

7 At the bottom of the dialog box, at the right edge of the **Refers to** box, point to and click **Collapse Dialog Box**. Compare your screen with Figure 4.18.

> The dialog box collapses (shrinks) so that only the *Refers to* box is visible, and the selected range is surrounded by a moving border. When you define a name, the stored definition is an absolute cell reference and includes the worksheet name.

FIGURE 4.18

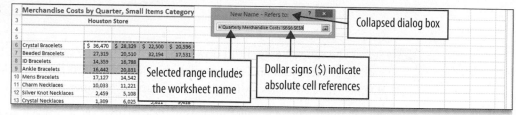

8 If necessary, drag the collapsed dialog box by its title bar to the right of your screen so that it is not blocking the selection. Then, change the range selection by selecting the range **B6:E10**.

> A moving border surrounds the new range. The range, formatted with absolute cell references, displays in the *Refers to* box of the collapsed dialog box. In this manner, it is easy to change the range of cells referred to by the name.

9 Click **Expand Dialog Box** to redisplay the entire **New Name** dialog box, and then click **OK**.

10 Select the range **B11:E14**. In the upper left corner of the Excel window, to the left of the **Formula Bar**, click in the **Name Box**, and notice that the cell reference *B11* moves to the left edge of the box and is highlighted in blue. Type **Necklace_Costs** as shown in Figure 4.19.

FIGURE 4.19

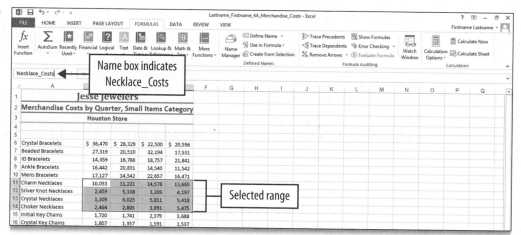

11 Press Enter, and then take a moment to study the rules for defining names, as described in the table in Figure 4.20.

FIGURE 4.20

RULES FOR DEFINING NAMES
The first character of the defined name must be a letter, an underscore (_), or a backslash (\).
After the first character, the remaining characters in the defined name can be letters, numbers, periods, and underscore characters.
Spaces are not valid in a defined name; use a period or the underscore character as a word separator, for example, 1st.Quarter or 1st_Qtr.
The single letter C or R in either uppercase or lowercase cannot be defined as a name, because these letters are used by Excel for selecting a row or column when you enter them in a Name or a Go To text box.
A defined name can be no longer than 255 characters; short, meaningful names are the most useful.
Defined names cannot be the same as a cell reference, for example M$10.
Defined names can contain uppercase and lowercase letters; however, Excel does not distinguish between them. So, for example, if you create the name Sales and then create another name SALES in the same workbook, Excel considers the names to be the same and prompts you for a unique name.

12 Click any cell to cancel the selection. Then, click the **Name Box arrow** and compare your screen with Figure 4.21. If necessary, resize the Name Box by dragging the three vertical dots to the right, to display the full names.

Your two defined names display in alphabetical order.

FIGURE 4.21

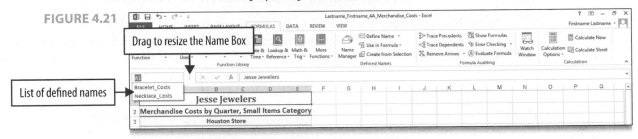

13 From the list, click **Bracelet_Costs** and notice that Excel selects the range of values that comprise the cost of various Bracelet styles.

14 Click the **Name Box arrow** again, and then click **Necklace_Costs** to select the range of values that comprise the Necklace costs.

15 Select the range **B15:E16**. On the **FORMULAS tab**, in the **Defined Names group**, click **Name Manager**, and notice that the two names that you have defined display in a list.

16 In the upper left corner of the **Name Manager** dialog box, click **New**. With *Initial_Key_Chains* selected, type **Key_Chain_Costs** and then click **OK**. Compare your screen with Figure 4.22. **Close** the **Name Manager** dialog box and **Save** 💾 your workbook.

This is another method to define a name—by creating a new name in the Name Manager dialog box. The Name Manager dialog box displays the three range names that you have created, in alphabetical order.

FIGURE 4.22

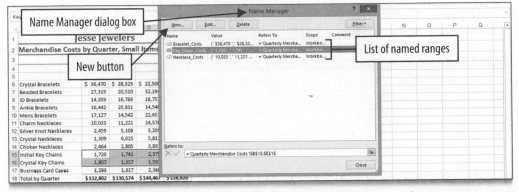

You can insert new data into the range of cells that a name represents. In this activity, you will modify the range named *Necklace_Costs* to include new data.

1 ▶ On the left side of your window, click the **row 15** heading to select the entire row. Right-click over the selected row, and then click **Insert** to insert a new blank row above.

A new row 15 is inserted, and the remaining rows move down one row. Recall that when new rows are inserted in this manner, Excel adjusts formulas accordingly.

2 ▶ Click the **Name Box arrow**, and then click **Key_Chain_Costs**. Notice that Excel highlights the correct range of cells, adjusting for the newly inserted row.

If you insert rows, the defined name adjusts to the new cell addresses to represent the cells that were originally defined. Likewise, if you move the cells, the defined name goes with them to the new location.

3 ▶ In cell **A15**, type **Sweetheart Necklaces** and then press Tab. In cell **B15**, type **1166** and press Tab. In cell **C15**, type **1087** and press Tab. In cell **D15**, type **847** and press Tab. In cell **E15**, type **965** and press Enter.

The cells in the newly inserted row adopt the Currency [0] format from the cells above.

4 ▶ On the **FORMULAS tab**, from the **Defined Names group**, click **Name Manager**.

5 ▶ In the **Name Manager** dialog box, in the **Name** column, click **Necklace_Costs**. At the bottom of the dialog box, click in the **Refers to** box and edit the reference, changing **$E$14** to **$E$15** as shown in Figure 4.23.

This action will include the Sweetheart Necklace values in the named range.

FIGURE 4.23

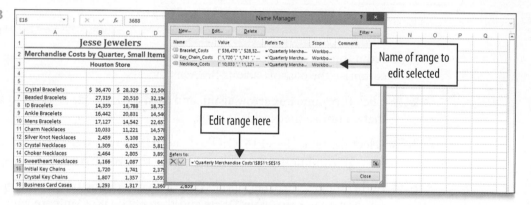

6 ▶ In the **Name Manager** dialog box, click **Close**, and click **Yes** to save the changes you made to the name reference. In the upper left corner of the window, click the **Name Box arrow** and then click the range name **Necklace_Costs**. Notice that the selected range now includes the new row 15. **Save** 🖫 your workbook.

NOTE   **Changing a Defined Name**

If you create a defined name and then decide to change it, you can use the Name Manger to edit the name. Display the Name Manager dialog box, select the defined name, and then at the top of the dialog box, click Edit. If the defined name is used in a formula, the new name is automatically changed in any affected formulas.

You can use the Create from Selection command to use existing row or column titles as the name for a range of cells.

1 Select the range **A18:E18**. On the **FORMULAS tab**, in the **Defined Names group**, click **Create from Selection**. Compare your screen with Figure 4.24.

The Create Names from Selection dialog box displays. A check mark displays in the *Left column* check box, which indicates that Excel will use the value of the cell in the leftmost column of the selection as the range name, unless you specify otherwise.

FIGURE 4.24

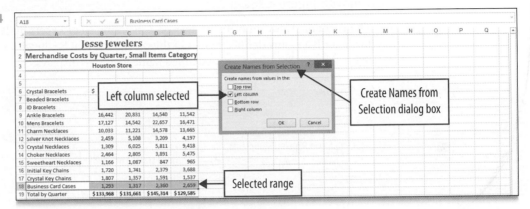

2 In the **Create Names from Selection** dialog box, click **OK**, and then click anywhere to cancel the selection.

3 Click the **Name Box arrow**, and then click the name **Business_Card_Cases**, and notice that in the new range name, Excel inserts the underscore necessary to fill a blank space in the range name. Also notice that the actual range consists of only the numeric values, as shown in Figure 4.25. **Save** your workbook.

This method is convenient for naming a range of cells without having to actually type a name—Excel uses the text of the first cell to the left of the selected range as the range name and then formats the name properly.

FIGURE 4.25

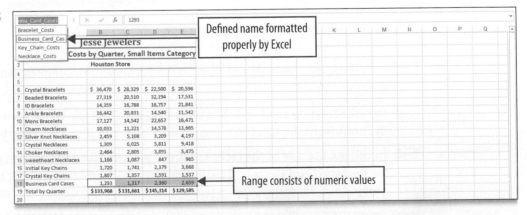

NOTE **Deleting a Defined Name**

If you create a defined name and then decide that you no longer need it, you can delete the name and its accompanying range reference. Display the Name Manager dialog box, select the defined name, and then at the top of the dialog box, click Delete. Deleting a defined name does not modify the cell contents or formatting of the cells. Deleting a defined name does not delete any cells or any values. It deletes only the name that you have applied to a group of cells. However, any formula that contains the range name will display the #NAME? error message, and will have to be adjusted manually.

The advantage to naming a range of cells is that you can use the name in a formula in other parts of your workbook. The defined name provides a logical reference to data. For example, referring to data as Bracelet_Costs is easier to understand than referring to data as B6:E10.

When you use a defined name in a formula, the result is the same as if you typed the cell references.

1 Display the **Annual Merchandise Costs** worksheet.

2 In cell **B5**, type **=sum(B** and then scroll to the bottom of the AutoComplete list; compare your screen with Figure 4.26.

> The Formula AutoComplete list displays containing all of Excel's built-in functions that begin with the letter B and any defined names in this workbook that begin with the letter B. To the left of your defined name *Bracelet_Costs*, a defined name icon ⊞ displays.

FIGURE 4.26

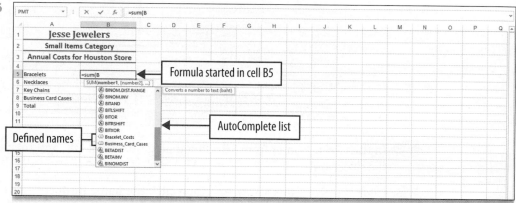

3 Double-click **Bracelet_Costs** and then press Enter.

> Your result is *411346*. Recall that SUM is a function—a formula already built by Excel—that adds all the cells in a selected range. Therefore, Excel sums all the cells in the range you defined as Bracelet_Costs on the first worksheet in the workbook, and then places the result in cell B5 of this worksheet.

🔄 **ANOTHER WAY**   You can simply type the defined name in the formula.

4 In cell **B6**, type **=sum(N** and then on the **Formula AutoComplete** list, double-click **Necklace_Costs** to insert the formula. Press Enter to display the result *105,733*.

5 In cell **B7**, type **=sum(** and then on the **FORMULAS tab**, in the **Defined Names group**, click **Use in Formula**. In the list, click **Key_Chain_Costs**, and then press Enter to display the total *15,820*.

6 In cell **B8**, use any of the techniques you just practiced to sum the cells containing the costs for **Business Card Cases** and to display a result of *7,629*. In cell **B9**, in the **Function Library group**, click **AutoSum** Σ AutoSum ▾ to sum **column B** and display a result of *540,528*.

7 Select the nonadjacent cells **B5** and **B9**, and then on the **HOME tab**, display the **Cell Styles** gallery. Under **Number Format**, click the **Currency [0]** cell style. Select the range **B6:B8**, display the **Cell Styles** gallery, and then under **Number Format**, click **Comma [0]**.

8 Click cell **B9** and under **Titles and Headings**, click the **Total** cell style. Click cell **B5** and then compare your screen with Figure 4.27.

FIGURE 4.27

9 Select both worksheets so that *[Group]* displays in the title bar. With the two worksheets grouped, insert a footer in the **left section** that includes the file name. Return to **Normal** view and make cell **A1** active. **Center** the worksheets **Horizontally** on the page.

10 Click the **FILE tab** to display **Backstage** view. On the right, at the bottom of the **Properties** list, click **Show All Properties**. Under **Related People**, be sure that your name displays as the author. If necessary, right-click the author name, click Edit Property, and then type your name. In the **Subject** box, type your course name and section #, and in the **Tags** box, type **small items category, merchandise costs** Display the grouped worksheets in **Print Preview, Close** the **Print Preview**, and then make any necessary corrections or adjustments. Right-click any of the grouped sheet tabs, and then click **Ungroup Sheets**.

11 **Save** 🖫 your workbook. Print or submit the two worksheets in this workbook electronically as directed by your instructor. If required, print or create an electronic version of your worksheets with formulas displayed using the instructions in Project 1A. **Close** Excel.

END | You have completed Project 4A

PROJECT 4B

Lookup Form and Revenue Report

PROJECT ACTIVITIES

In Activities 4.10 through 4.18, you will assist Mike Connor, the Vice President of Marketing at Jesse Jewelers, by adding lookup functions to a phone order form so that an order taker can complete the form quickly. You will use the Formula Auditing features to review a revenue worksheet and to resolve the errors and you will use the Watch Window to monitor changes in sales worksheets. Your completed workbooks will look similar to Figure 4.28.

PROJECT FILES

For Project 4B, you will need the following files:

e04B_First_Quarter_Sales
e04B_Miami_Revenue
e04B_Phone_Form

You will save your workbooks as:

Lastname_Firstname_4B_First_Quarter_Sales
Lastname_Firstname_4B_Miami_Revenue
Lastname_Firstname_4B_Phone_Form

PROJECT RESULTS

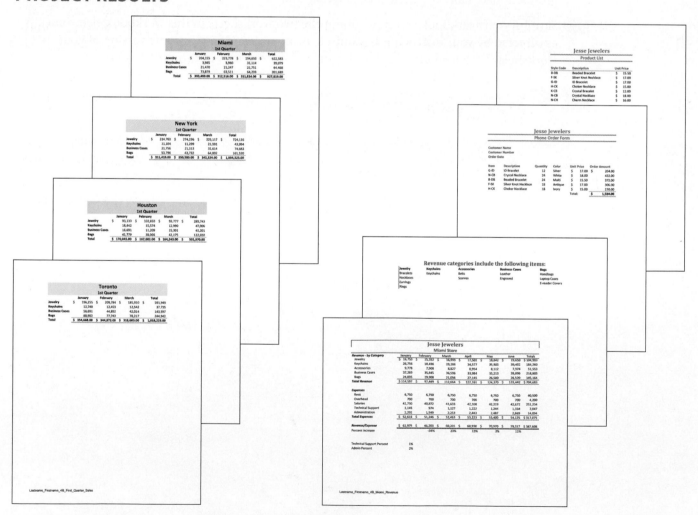

FIGURE 4.28 Project 4B Lookup Form and Revenue Report

Video E4-5

Lookup functions look up a value in a defined range of cells located in another part of the workbook to find a corresponding value. For example, you can define a two-column range of cells containing names and phone numbers. Then, when you type a name in the cell referred to by the lookup formula, Excel fills in the phone number by looking it up in the defined range. In the lookup formula, the defined range is referred to as the ***table array***.

The ***VLOOKUP*** function looks up values in a table array arranged as vertical columns. The function searches the first column of the table array for a corresponding value, and then returns a value from any cell on the same row. The ***HLOOKUP*** function looks up values in a table array arranged in horizontal rows. The function searches the top row of the table array for a corresponding value, and then returns a value from any cell in the same column. The ***LOOKUP*** function looks up values in either a one-row or a one-column range.

There is one requirement for the lookup functions to work properly. The data in the table array, which can be numbers or text, must be sorted in ascending order. For the VLOOKUP function, the values must be sorted on the first column in ascending order. For the HLOOKUP function, the values must be sorted on the first row in ascending order.

Activity 4.10 | Defining a Range of Cells for a Lookup Function

The first step in using a lookup function is to define the range of cells that will serve as the table array. In the Jesse Jewelers Phone Order form, after an Item Number is entered on the form, Mr. Connor wants the description of the item to display automatically in the Description column. To accomplish this, you will define a table array that includes the item number in one column and a description of the item in the second column.

1 Start Excel. From your student files, open the file **e04B_Phone_Form**, and then **Save** the file in your **Excel Chapter 4** folder as **Lastname_Firstname_4B_Phone_Form**

2 With cell **A1** active, display the **Cell Styles** gallery, and then, under **Titles and Headings**, click **Title**. Right-click cell **A1**, and on the mini toolbar, click the **Format Painter** , and then click cell **A2**. Compare your screen with Figure 4.29.

When store managers call Jesse Jewelers headquarters to place an order, the order taker uses this type of worksheet to record the information.

FIGURE 4.29

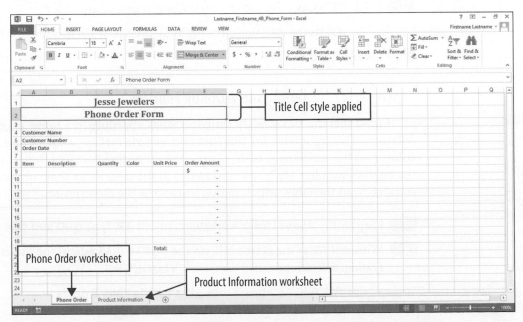

3 ▶ Click the **Product Information sheet tab** to display the second worksheet.

> The Product Information worksheet contains the Style Code, Description, and Unit Price of specific bracelets and necklaces.

4 ▶ On the **Product Information** worksheet, select the range **A4:C11**. On the **DATA tab**, in the **Sort & Filter group**, click **Sort**. If necessary, drag the Sort dialog box to the right side of your screen so you can view columns A:C.

> To use this list to look up information with the Excel VLOOKUP function, you must sort the list in ascending order by Style Code, which is the column that will be used to look up the matching information.

5 ▶ In the **Sort** dialog box, under **Column**, click the **Sort by arrow**. Notice that the selected range is now **A5:C11** and that the column titles in the range **A4:C4** display in the **Sort by** list. Compare your screen with Figure 4.30.

> When the selected range includes a header row that should remain in place while the remaining rows are sorted, Excel usually recognizes those column headings, selects the *My data has headers* check box, and then displays the column headings in the Sort by list.

FIGURE 4.30

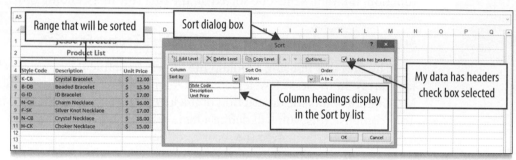

6 ▶ On the **Sort by** list, click **Style Code**, which is the first column heading and the column heading that Excel selects by default.

7 ▶ Under **Sort On**, verify that *Values* displays, and under **Order**, verify that *A to Z* displays.

> *Values* indicates that the sort will be based on the values in the cells of the first column, rather than cell color or some other cell characteristic. *A to Z* indicates that the cell will be sorted in ascending order.

8 ▶ Click **OK** to sort the data by *Style Code* in ascending order.

> Excel sorts the data alphabetically by Style Code; *B-DB* is first in the list and *N-CH* is last.

9 ▶ Save 🖬 your workbook.

Activity 4.11 | Inserting the VLOOKUP Function

Recall that the VLOOKUP function looks up values in a range of cells arranged as vertical columns. The arguments for this function include *lookup_value*—the value to search in the first column of the table array, *table_array*—the range that contains the data, and *col_index_num*—the column number (1, 2, 3, 4, and so on) in the table array that contains the result you want to retrieve from the table, which in this instance is the Description.

1 ▶ Display the **Phone Order** worksheet. In cell **A9**, type **G-ID** and press ⎋Tab⎋.

2 ▶ With cell **B9** as the active cell, on the **FORMULAS tab**, in the **Function Library group**, click **Lookup & Reference**, and then click **VLOOKUP**.

> The Function Arguments dialog box for VLOOKUP displays.

3 With the insertion point in the **Lookup_value** box, click cell **A9** to look up the description of Item G-ID.

4 Click in the **Table_array** box, and then at the bottom of the workbook, click the **Product Information sheet tab**. On the **Product Information** worksheet, select the range **A4:C11**, and then press F4.

This range (table array) includes the value that will be looked up—*G-ID* and the corresponding value to be displayed—*ID Bracelet*. By pressing F4, the absolute cell reference is applied to the table array so that the formula can be copied to the remainder of the column in the Phone Order sheet.

BY TOUCH Tap in the Table_array box, and then at the bottom of the workbook, tap the Product Information sheet tab. On the Product Information sheet, select the range A4:C11, and then edit the reference to $A$4:$C$11 to make it absolute.

5 Click in the **Col_index_num** box and type **2** Compare your screen with Figure 4.31.

The description for the selected item—the value to be looked up—is located in column 2 of the table array.

FIGURE 4.31

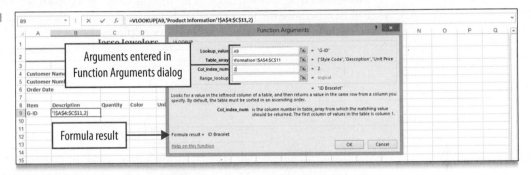

6 Click **OK**.

The description for Item G-ID displays in cell B9.

7 With cell **B9** as the active cell and containing the VLOOKUP formula, point to the fill handle in the lower right corner of the cell, and then drag to fill the VLOOKUP formula down through cell **B18**. Compare your screen with Figure 4.32.

The *#N/A* error notation displays in the cells where you copied the formula. Excel displays this error when a function or formula exists in a cell but has no value available with which to perform a calculation; values have not yet been entered in column A in those rows.

FIGURE 4.32

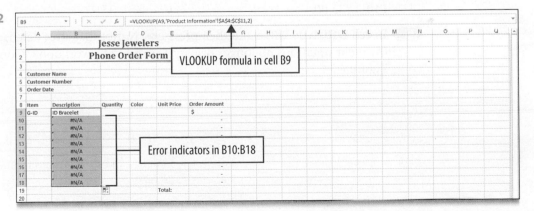

8 Click cell **C9**, type **12** as the quantity ordered and press Tab. In cell **D9**, type **Silver** and press Tab.

9 With cell **E9** as the active cell, on the **FORMULAS tab**, in the **Function Library group**, click **Lookup & Reference**, and then click **VLOOKUP**.

10 With the insertion point in the **Lookup_value** box, click cell **A9** to look up information for Item G-ID. Click in the **Table_array** box, display the **Product Information** sheet, and then select the range **A4:C11**. Press F4 to make the values in the range absolute.

11 In the **Col_index_num** box, type **3** to look up the price in the third column of the range, and then click **OK**.

> The Unit Price for the ID Bracelet—*$17.00*—displays in cell E9.

12 Click cell **F9**, and notice that a formula to calculate the total for the item, Quantity times Unit Price, has already been entered in the worksheet.

> This formula has also been copied to the range F10:F18.

13 Click cell **E9**, and then copy the VLOOKUP formula down through cell **E18**. Compare your screen with Figure 4.33.

> The *#N/A* error notation displays in the cells where you copied the formula, and also in cells F10:F18, because the formulas there have no values yet with which to perform a calculation— values have not yet been entered in column A in those rows.

FIGURE 4.33

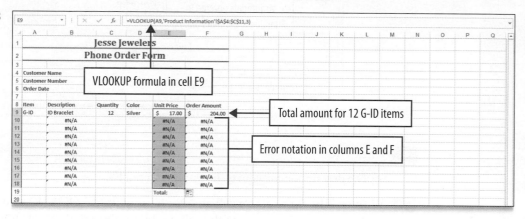

14 Click cell **A10**, type **N-CB** and press Tab two times.

> Excel looks up the product description and the product price in the vertical table array on the Product Information sheet, and then displays the results in cells B10 and E10.

15 In cell **C10**, type **24** and press Tab. Notice that Excel calculates the total for this item in cell **F10**—*432.00*.

16 In cell **D10**, type **White** and then press Enter. Notice that after data is entered in the row, the error notations no longer display. **Save** 💾 your workbook. Compare your screen with Figure 4.34.

FIGURE 4.34

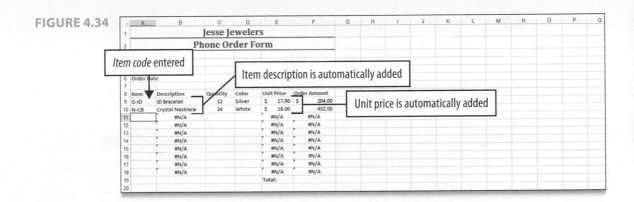

Objective 6 Validate Data

Video E4-6

Another technique to improve accuracy when completing a worksheet is **data validation**—a technique in which you control the type of data or the values that are entered into a cell. This technique improves accuracy because it limits and controls the type of data an individual, such as an order taker, can enter into the form.

One way to control the type of data entered is to create a **validation list**—a list of values that are acceptable for a group of cells. Only values in the list are valid; any value *not* in the list is considered invalid. For example, in the Phone Order sheet, it would be useful if in the Item column, only valid Style Codes could be entered.

Activity 4.12 | Creating a Validation List

A list of valid values must either be on the same worksheet as the destination cell, or if the list is in another worksheet, the cell range must be named. In this activity, you will create a defined name for the Style Codes, and then create a validation list for column A of the Phone Order worksheet.

1 Display the **Product Information** worksheet. Select the range **A4:A11**. On the **FORMULAS tab**, in the **Defined Names group**, click **Create from Selection**.

Recall that by using the Create from Selection command, you can automatically generate a name from the selected cells that uses the text in the top row or the leftmost column of a selection.

2 In the **Create Names from Selection** dialog box, be sure the **Top row** check box is selected, and then click **OK** to use *Style Code* as the range name.

3 In the **Defined Names group**, click **Name Manager**, and then notice that the new defined name is listed with the name *Style_Code*.

Style_Code displays as the defined name for the selected cells. Recall that Excel replaces spaces with an underscore when it creates a range name.

4 **Close** the **Name Manager** dialog box. Display the **Phone Order** sheet, and then select the range **A9:A18**.

Before you set the validation requirement, you must first select the cells that you want to restrict to only valid entries from the list.

5 On the **DATA tab**, in the **Data Tools group**, click **Data Validation**. In the **Data Validation** dialog box, be sure the **Settings tab** is selected.

6 Under **Validation criteria**, click the **Allow arrow**, and then click **List**.

A Source box displays as the third box in the Data Validation dialog box. Here you select or type the source data.

7 Click to position the insertion point in the **Source** box, type **=Style_Code** and then compare your screen with Figure 4.35.

FIGURE 4.35

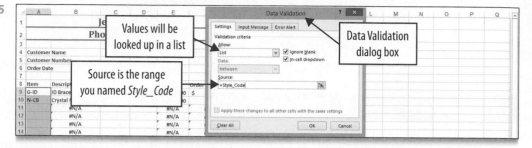

8 Click **OK**. Click cell **A11**, and notice that a list arrow displays at the right edge of the cell.

9 In cell **A11**, click the **list arrow** to display the list, and then compare your screen with Figure 4.36.

FIGURE 4.36

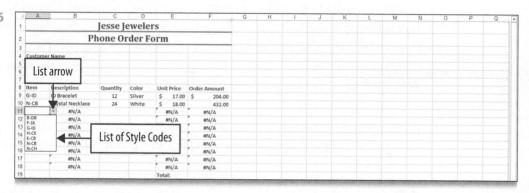

10 From the list, click **B-DB**.

The Style Code is selected from the list and the Item, Description, and Unit Price cells are filled in for row 11.

11 Press Tab two times, type **24** and press Tab, type **Multi** and then press Enter to return to the beginning of the next row. Compare your screen with Figure 4.37.

You can see that when taking orders by phone, it will speed the process if all of the necessary information can be filled in automatically. Furthermore, accuracy will be improved if item codes are restricted to only valid data.

FIGURE 4.37

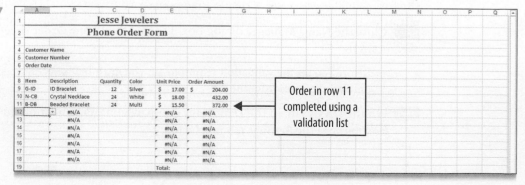

12 With cell **A12** active, click the **list arrow**, and then click **F-SK**. As the **Quantity**, type **18** and as the **Color**, type **Antique** and then press Enter.

13 In cell **A13**, type **G-W** and press Tab.

An error message displays indicating that you entered a value that is not valid; that is, it is not on the validation list you created. If the order taker mistakenly types an invalid value into the cell, this message will display.

Restricting the values that an order taker can enter will greatly improve the accuracy of orders. Also, encouraging order takers to select from the list, rather than typing, will reduce the time it takes to fill in the order form.

14 In the error message, click **Cancel**. Click the **list arrow** again, click **H-CK,** and press Tab two times. As the **Quantity**, type **18** and as the **Color**, type **Ivory** and then press Enter.

15 Select the unused rows **14:18**, right-click over the selection, and then click **Delete**.

16 In cell **F14**, sum the **Order Amount** column, and apply the **Total** cell style.

17 Select both worksheets so that *[Group]* displays in the title bar. With the two worksheets grouped, insert a footer in the **left section** that includes the file name. **Center** the worksheets **Horizontally** on the page. Return to **Normal** view and make cell **A1** active.

18 Click the **FILE tab** to display **Backstage** view. On the right, at the bottom of the **Properties** list, click **Show All Properties**. On the list of **Properties**, in the **Tags** box, type **phone order form** In the **Subject** box, type your course name and section #. Under **Related People**, be sure that your name displays as the author. If necessary, right-click the author name, click Edit Property, type your name, click outside of the Edit person dialog box, and then click OK. Display the grouped worksheets in **Print Preview, Close** the **Print Preview**, and then make any necessary corrections or adjustments.

19 Ungroup the worksheets and then **Save** your workbook. Hold this workbook until the end of this project, and then print or submit the two worksheets in this workbook electronically as directed by your instructor. If required, print or create an electronic version of your worksheets with formulas displayed using the instructions in Project 1A. **Close** this workbook.

More **Knowledge** — **Creating Validation Messages**

In the Data Validation dialog box, you can use the Input Message tab to create a ScreenTip that will display when the cell is selected. The message can be an instruction that tells the user what to do. You can also use the Error Alert tab to create a warning message that displays if invalid data is entered in the cell.

Objective 7 Audit Worksheet Formulas

Video E4-7

Auditing is the process of examining a worksheet for errors in *formulas*. Formulas are equations that perform calculations on values in your worksheet. A formula consists of a sequence of values, cell references, names, functions, or operators in a cell, which together produce a new value. Recall that a formula always begins with an equal sign.

Excel includes a group of *Formula Auditing* features, which consists of tools and commands accessible from the FORMULAS tab that help you to check your worksheet for errors. In complex worksheets, use these Formula Auditing features to show relationships between cells and formulas, to ensure that formulas are logical and correct, and to resolve error messages. Although sometimes it is appropriate to hide the error message, at other times error notations can indicate a problem that should be corrected.

Activity 4.13 | Tracing Precedents

Precedent cells are cells that are referred to by a formula in another cell. The *Trace Precedents command* displays arrows that indicate what cells affect the values of the cell that is selected. By using the Trace Precedents command, you can see the relationships between formulas and cells. As an auditing tool, the process of tracing a formula is a way to ensure that you constructed the formula correctly.

1 From your student files, open the file **e04B_Miami_Revenue,** and then **Save** the file in your **Excel Chapter 4** folder as **Lastname_Firstname_4B_Miami_Revenue** Compare your screen with Figure 4.38.

> The worksheet details the revenue and expenses related to the Miami store over a six-month period. Several error notations are present (#VALUE!, #REF!, #DIV/0!), green triangles display in the top left corners of several cells indicating a potential error, and two columns are too narrow to fit the data which Excel indicates by displaying pound signs—####.

FIGURE 4.38

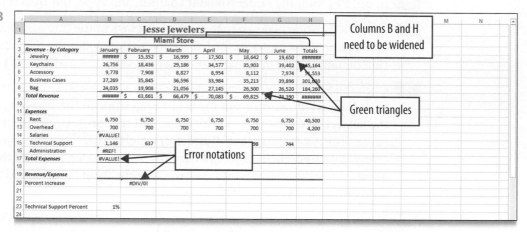

2 Click the **FILE tab,** and then on the left, click **Options.** In the **Excel Options** dialog box, click **Formulas.** Under **Error checking rules,** point to the small information icon after the first Error checking rule to display the ScreenTip. Compare your screen with Figure 4.39.

> Here you can control which error checking rules you want to activate, and you can get information about each of the rules by clicking the small blue information icon at the end of each rule. By default, all but the next to last rule are selected, and it is recommended that you maintain these default settings. This textbook assumes the default settings.

FIGURE 4.39

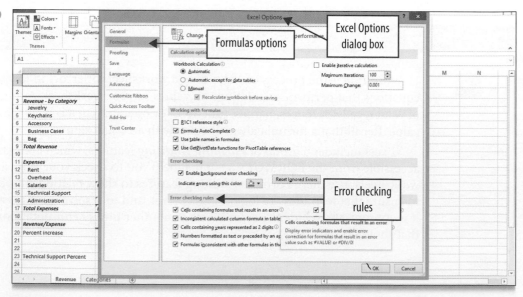

3 In the lower right corner of the dialog box, click **Cancel** to close the dialog box.

4 Take a moment to study the table in Figure 4.40, which details some common error values that might display on your worksheet.

An *error value* is the result of a formula that Excel cannot evaluate correctly.

FIGURE 4.40

MICROSOFT EXCEL ERROR VALUES		
ERROR VALUE	MEANING	POSSIBLE CAUSE
#####	Cannot see data.	The column is not wide enough to display the entire value.
#DIV/0!	Cannot divide by zero.	The divisor in a formula refers to a blank cell or a cell that contains zero.
#NAME?	Does not recognize a name you used in a formula.	A function or a named range may be misspelled or does not exist.
#VALUE!	Cannot use a text field in a formula.	A formula refers to a cell that contains a text value rather than a numeric value or a formula.
#REF!	Cannot locate the reference.	A cell that is referenced in a formula may have been deleted or moved.
#N/A	No value is available.	No information is available for the calculation you want to perform.
#NUM!	Invalid argument in a worksheet function.	An unacceptable argument may have been used in a function. Or, a formula result could be too large or too small.
#NULL!	No common cells.	A space was entered between two ranges in a formula to indicate an intersection, but the ranges have no common cells.

5 On your worksheet, in the **column heading area**, select **column B**, hold down Ctrl, and then select **column H**. Point to the right edge of either of the selected column headings to display the ┿ pointer, and then double-click to apply AutoFit.

AutoFit widens the columns to accommodate the longest values in each column; the ##### errors no longer display.

 BY TOUCH   Tap the column B heading and hold it, then tap column H. With both columns selected double-tap the border to the right edge of either of the selected column headings to apply AutoFit.

6 Click cell **C9**, and then notice the **green triangle** in the top left corner of the cell.

A green triangle in the upper left corner of a cell indicates that the formula in the cell is suspect for some reason. Typically, this is because the formula does not match the formula in the cells next to it, or because it does not include all of the adjacent cells.

7 In cell **C9**, to the left of the cell, point to **Error Checking** ◈ ·, and then read the **ScreenTip** that displays. Compare your screen with Figure 4.41.

The ScreenTip indicates that adjacent cells containing numbers are not included in the formula. It is possible that the formula purposely consists of a group of cells that excludes some of the cells adjacent to it. However, because that is not as common as including *all* of the cells that are adjacent to one another, Excel flags this as a potential error.

FIGURE 4.41

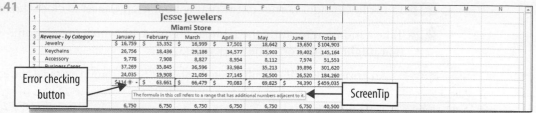

8 On the **FORMULAS tab**, in the **Formula Auditing group**, click **Trace Precedents**. Notice that the range **C6:C8** is bordered in blue and a blue arrow points to cell **C9**.

Recall that precedent cells are cells that are referred to by a formula in another cell. Here, the precedent cells are bordered in blue. A blue arrow, called a *tracer arrow*, displays from C6:C8, pointing to the selected cell C9. A tracer arrow shows the relationship between the active cell and its related cells. Tracer arrows are blue when pointing from a cell that provides data to another cell.

Because this total should include *all* of the revenue categories for February, this is an error in the formula—the formula should include the range C4:C8. By tracing the precedents, you can see that two cells were mistakenly left out of the formula.

9 To the left of cell **C9**, click **Error Checking** to display a list of error checking options. Compare your screen with Figure 4.42.

FIGURE 4.42

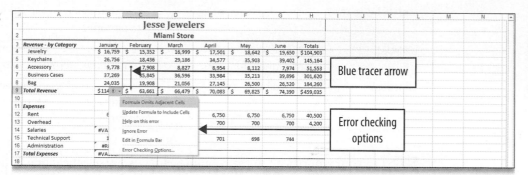

10 In the list, notice that Excel indicates the potential error highlighted in blue—*Formula Omits Adjacent Cells*. Notice also that you can update the formula, seek help with the error, ignore the error, edit the formula in the **Formula Bar**, or display the **Error Checking Options** in the **Excel Options** dialog box. Click **Update Formula to Include Cells**, and then look at the formula in the **Formula Bar**.

As shown in the Formula Bar, the formula is updated to include the range C4:C8; the green triangle no longer displays in the cell.

11 Click cell **D9**, which also displays a green triangle, and then point to **Error Checking** to display the **ScreenTip**.

The same error exists in cell D9—not all adjacent cells in the column were included in the formula. This error also exists in the range E9:G9. You can click in each cell and use the Error Checking button's options list to correct each formula, or, you can use the fill handle to copy the corrected formula in cell C9 to the remaining cells.

12 Click cell **C9,** drag the fill handle to copy the corrected formula to the range **D9:G9** and then notice that all the green triangles are removed from the range.

13 Click cell **H5**, point to **Error Checking**, and read the **ScreenTip**.

The formula in this cell is not the same as the formula in the other cells in this area of the worksheet.

14 On the **FORMULAS tab**, in the **Formula Auditing group**, click **Trace Precedents**. Compare your screen with Figure 4.43.

> A blue border surrounds the range B8:G8, and a blue tracer arrow displays from the cell B8 to cell H5. This indicates that the formula in cell H5 is summing the values in row 8 rather than the values in row 5.

FIGURE 4.43

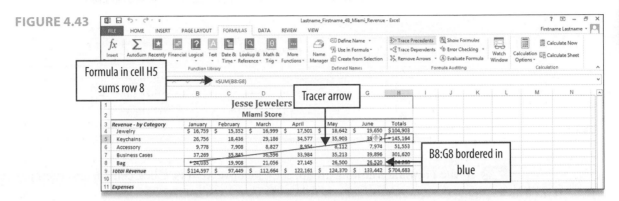

15 To the left of cell **H5**, click **Error Checking** ◈▾ to display the list of error checking options, notice the explanation *Inconsistent Formula*, examine the formula in the **Formula Bar**, and then click **Copy Formula from Above**. If necessary, AutoFit column H to display the values correctly.

16 Look at the **Formula Bar** to verify that the formula is summing the numbers in **row 5**—the range **B5:G5**. With cell **H5** still selected, from the **HOME tab**, display the **Cell Styles** gallery, and then, under **Number Format**, click the **Comma [0]** number format.

> The blue tracer arrow no longer displays, the formula sums row 5, and the proper number format is applied.

17 Click cell **H4**. On the **FORMULAS tab**, in the **Formula Auditing group**, click **Trace Precedents**. Notice the tracer arrow indicates that the appropriate cells are included in the formula, as shown in Figure 4.44.

FIGURE 4.44

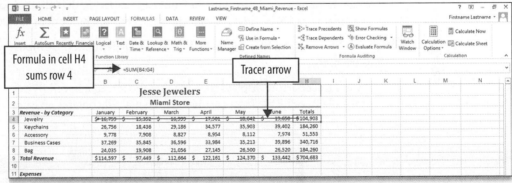

18 Click cell **H5**, click **Trace Precedents**, notice the **tracer arrow**, and then click cell **H6**. Click **Trace Precedents**, notice the tracer arrow, and verify that the correct cells are included in the formula.

19 ▶ Click cell **H7**, click **Trace Precedents**, and then click cell **H8**. Click **Trace Precedents**. Compare your screen with Figure 4.45.

> Cells H7 and H8 display blue tracer arrows that are inconsistent with the other formulas in this column. However, green triangle indicators do not display in either of these cells. When auditing a worksheet, you cannot rely on the error notations and triangle indicators alone. To ensure the accuracy of a worksheet, you should use the tracer arrows to verify that all of the formulas are logical and correct.

FIGURE 4.45

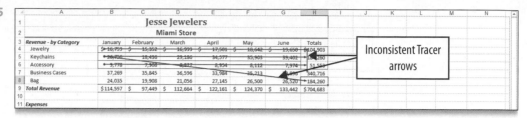

20 ▶ In the **Formula Auditing group**, click **Remove Arrows**. Click cell **H6** and then use the fill handle to copy the correct formula down to cells **H7:H8**.

21 ▶ Save 🖫 your workbook.

Activity 4.14 | Tracing Dependents

Dependent cells are cells that contain formulas that refer to other cells—they depend on the values of other cells to display a result. The *Trace Dependents command* displays arrows that indicate what cells are affected by the value of the currently selected cell.

1 ▶ Click cell **B14**, which displays the error *#VALUE!*. To the left of the cell, point to **Error Checking** ◈ ▾ and read the ScreenTip.

> This formula contains a reference to a cell that is the wrong data type—a cell that does not contain a number.

2 ▶ In the **Formula Auditing group**, click **Trace Precedents**.

> A blue tracer arrow indicates that cell B3 is included in the formula. Because cell B3 contains text—*January*—and not a number, no mathematical calculation is possible. The salaries should be calculated as 5% of *Total Revenue*, plus the constant amount of $36,000.

3 ▶ In the **Formula Auditing group**, click **Trace Dependents**. Compare your screen with Figure 4.46.

> A red tracer arrow displays showing that the formula in cell B17 depends on the result of the formula in cell B14. Tracer arrows are red if a cell contains an error value, such as #VALUE!.

FIGURE 4.46

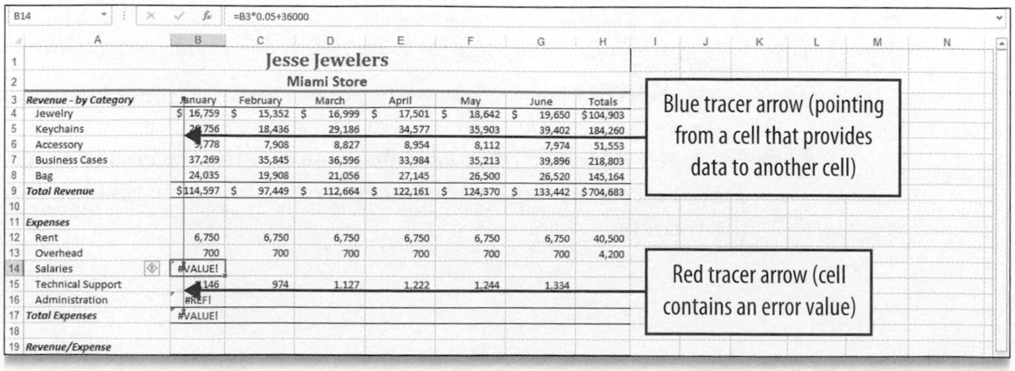

4 Click **Error Checking** ⬦ ▾ and then click **Show Calculation Steps**.

The Evaluate Formula dialog box opens and indicates the formula as =*"January"**0.05+36000. January is not a number, nor is it a range name that refers to a group of numbers; so, it cannot be used in a mathematical formula. At the bottom of the dialog box, Excel indicates that the next evaluation will result in an error.

5 At the bottom of the dialog box, click **Evaluate**.

The formula in the Evaluation box indicates *#Value!+36000*. You can use this box to evaluate each step of the formula. With complex formulas, this can be helpful in examining each piece of a formula to see where the error has occurred.

6 **Close** the **Evaluate Formula** dialog box. With cell **B14** still the active cell, click in the **Formula Bar** and edit the formula to change cell **B3** to **B9**, and then press Enter. If necessary, AutoFit column B.

The error is removed and the result—41,730—displays in cell B14.

7 Click cell **B14**. Drag the fill handle to copy the corrected formula in cell **B14** across the row to cells **C14:G14**.

8 Click cell **B9**. In the **Formula Auditing group**, click **Trace Dependents**. Compare your screen with Figure 4.47.

Each cell where an arrowhead displays indicates a dependent relationship.

FIGURE 4.47

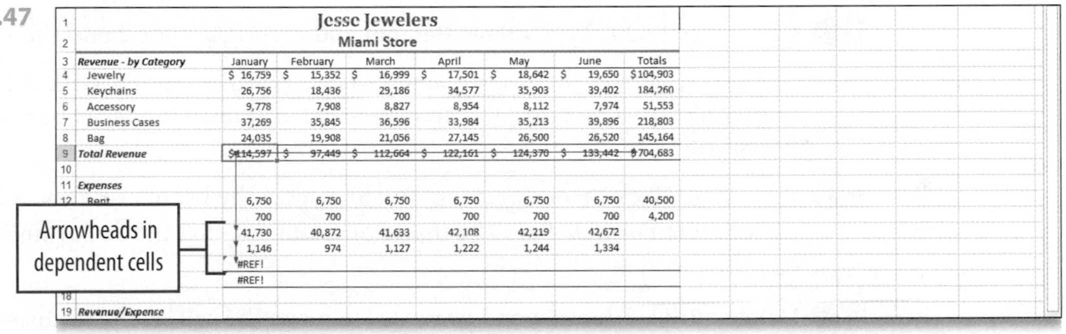

9 In the **Formula Auditing group**, click **Remove Arrows**. **Save** 💾 your workbook.

Activity 4.15 | Tracing Formula Errors

Another tool you can use to help locate and resolve an error is the ***Trace Error command***. Use this command to trace a selected error value such as #VALUE!, #REF!, #NAME?, or #DIV/0!.

1 Click cell **B16**, point to **Error Checking** ⬦ ▾ and read the **ScreenTip**.

The error message indicates that a cell that was referenced in the formula has been moved or deleted, or the function is causing an invalid reference error. In other words, Excel does not know where to look to get the value that should be used in the formula.

2 In the **Formula Auditing group**, click the **Error Checking arrow** to display a list, and then compare your screen with Figure 4.48.

FIGURE 4.48

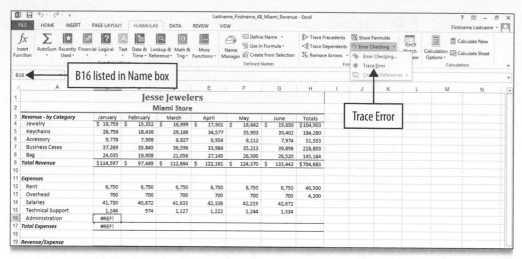

3 In the list, click **Trace Error**.

A precedent arrow is drawn from cell B9 to B16.

4 In the **Formula Auditing group**, click the **Error Checking arrow** again, and then click **Trace Error** again.

An arrow is drawn between cells B9 and B4 and the range B4:B8 is bordered in blue. The blue border indicates that this range is used in the formula in cell B9, which sums the values.

5 Click in cell **A24**. Type **Admin Percent** and press Tab, type **2** and then press Enter.

The percent used to calculate administrative expenses was moved or deleted from the worksheet causing the #REF! error. You must re-enter the value so that it can be referenced in the formula in cell B16.

6 Click **B16**. Click **Error Checking** ⬦ ▾ to display the list of error checking options, and then click **Edit in Formula Bar**. The insertion point displays in the **Formula Bar** so that you can edit the formula.

7 Delete **#REF!**. Type **b24** and press F4 to make the cell reference absolute, and then press Enter.

The error notation in cell B16 is replaced with 2,292. The corrected formula needs to be copied across row 16, and it needs to use an absolute reference. That way, the 2% Admin Percent will be applied for each month.

8 Click cell **B16** and then drag the fill handle to copy the formula to the right into cells **C16:G16**.

9 Save 🖫 your workbook, press Ctrl + Home, and then compare your screen with Figure 4.49.

FIGURE 4.49

	A	B	C	D	E	F	G	H	I	J	K	L	M	N
1			Jesse Jewelers											
2			Miami Store											
3	Revenue - by Category	January	February	March	April	May	June	Totals						
4	Jewelry	$ 16,759	$ 15,352	$ 16,999	$ 17,501	$ 18,642	$ 19,650	$104,903						
5	Keychains	26,756	18,436	29,186	34,577	35,903	39,402	184,260						
6	Accessory	9,778	7,908	8,827	8,954	8,112	7,974	51,553						
7	Business Cases	37,269	35,845	36,596	33,984	35,213	39,896	218,803						
8	Bag	24,035	19,908	21,056	27,145	26,500	26,520	145,164						
9	Total Revenue	$114,597	$ 97,449	$ 112,664	$ 122,161	$ 124,370	$ 133,442	$704,683						
10														
11	Expenses													
12	Rent	6,750	6,750	6,750	6,750	6,750	6,750	40,500						
13	Overhead	700	700	700	700	700	700	4,200						
14	Salaries	41,730	40,872	41,633	42,108	42,219	42,672							
15	Technical Support	1,146	974	1,127	1,222	1,244	1,334							
16	Administration	2,292	1,949	2,253	2,443	2,487	2,669							
17	Total Expenses	$ 52,618												
18														
19	Revenue/Expense													
20	Percent increase		#DIV/0!											
21														
22														
23	Technical Support Percent	1%												
24	Admin Percent	2%												
25														

Activity 4.16 | Using Error Checking

The **Error Checking command** checks for common errors that occur in formulas. The behavior is similar to checking for spelling; that is, the command uses a set of rules to check for errors in formulas. The command opens the Error Checking dialog box, which provides an explanation about the error and enables you to move from one error to the next. Therefore, you can review all of the errors on a worksheet.

1 Be sure that cell **A1** is the active cell. In the **Formula Auditing group**, click the **Error Checking arrow**, and then click **Error Checking**.

> The Error Checking dialog box displays, and indicates the first error—in cell C20. Here the error notation *#DIV/0!* displays. The Error Checking dialog provides an explanation of this error—a formula or function is trying to divide by zero or by an empty cell.

2 In the **Error Checking** dialog box, click **Show Calculation Steps**.

> The Evaluate Formula dialog box displays, and in the Evaluation box, *0/0* displays.

3 In the **Evaluate Formula** dialog box, click **Evaluate**.

> The Evaluation box displays the error *#DIV/0!* And the Evaluate button changes to Restart.

4 Click **Restart**.

> The formula *(C19-B19)/C19* displays; the first reference to C19 is underlined. The underline indicates that this is the part of the formula that is being evaluated. Each time you click the Evaluate button, it moves to the next cell reference or value in the formula.

5 In the **Evaluate Formula** dialog box, click **Step In**. Compare your screen with Figure 4.50.

> A second box displays, which normally displays the value in the referenced cell. In this instance, the cell that is referenced is empty, as indicated in the message in the lower part of the dialog box. In a complex formula, this dialog box can help you examine and understand each part of the formula and identify exactly where the error is located.

FIGURE 4.50

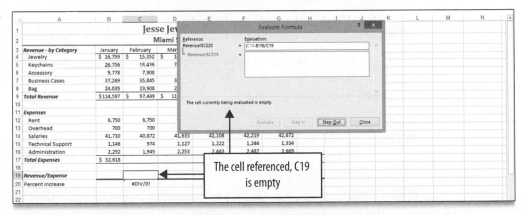

6 Click **Step Out**.

> The cell evaluation box closes and the underline moves to the next cell in the formula—B19—which you can visually verify is empty by looking at the worksheet. To remove this error, you must complete the remainder of the worksheet.

7 Close the **Evaluate Formula** dialog box. In the **Error Checking** dialog box, click **Next**.

> A message box displays stating that the error checking is complete for the entire sheet.

8 Click **OK**.

> Both the message box and the Error Checking dialog box close.

9 ▶ Click cell **H13** and then use the fill handle to copy this formula down to cells **H14:H16**. Click cell **B17** and use the fill handle to copy this formula to the right into cells **C17:H17**. AutoFit any columns, if necessary, to display all of the data.

The formulas in the rows and columns are completed.

10 ▶ Click cell **B19** and type **=b9-b17** Press (Enter), and then copy the formula to the right into cells **C19:H19**.

The revenue/expense for each month is calculated. Notice that the *#DIV/0!* error in cell C20 is removed, but the formatting of the cell needs to be changed from dollars to percent.

11 ▶ Click cell **C20**, and on the **HOME tab**, in the **Number group**, click **Percent Style** %. Copy the formula to the right into cells **D20:G20**.

This formula calculates the percent change in revenue versus expenses, month to month.

12 ▶ Press (Ctrl) + (Home), **Save** 💾 your workbook. Compare your screen with Figure 4.51.

FIGURE 4.51

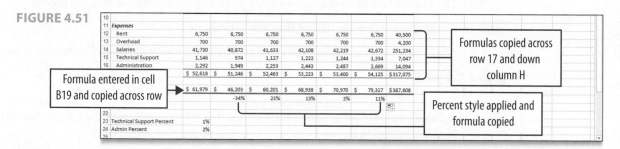

More Knowledge

One common error in Excel worksheets is a **circular reference**, in which a formula directly or indirectly refers to itself. The result is an **iterative calculation**, where Excel recalculates the formula over and over. To prevent this, Excel flags the formula as an error and does not perform the calculation. If you need to, you can enable iterative calculations and specify the maximum number of iterations Excel performs in the Excel Options dialog box.

Activity 4.17 | Circling Invalid Data

If you use validation lists in a worksheet, you can apply data validation and instruct Excel to circle invalid data. In this manner you can verify that valid values—values from the list—have been entered on the worksheet.

1 ▶ Click the **Categories sheet tab**.

This worksheet lists the merchandise types included in each category; only merchandise types from these categories are valid.

2 ▶ Click the **Name Box arrow**, and then click **Items**, which is the only range name that displays in the list box. Compare your screen with Figure 4.52.

The named range in row 2 is highlighted.

FIGURE 4.52

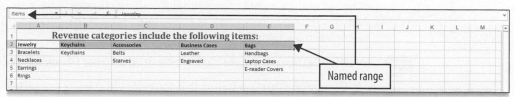

3 ▶ Display the **Revenue** worksheet. On the **DATA tab**, in the **Data Tools group**, click the **Data Validation arrow**, and then click **Circle Invalid Data**. Compare your screen with Figure 4.53.

Red circles display around Accessory and Bag.

FIGURE 4.53

	Jesse Jewelers							
	Miami Store							
Revenue - by Category	January	February	March	April	May	June	Totals
Jewelry	$ 16,759	$ 15,352	$ 16,999	$ 17,501	$ 18,642	$ 19,650	$104,903
Keychains	26,756				35,903	39,402	184,260
Accessory	5,778	*Cells with invalid data circled*			8,112	7,974	51,553
Business Cases	37,269				35,213	39,896	218,803
Bag	4,895				26,500	26,520	145,164
Total Revenue	$114,597	$			$ 124,370	$ 133,442	$704,683
Expenses							

4 ▶ Click cell **A6** and click the arrow that displays at the right side of the cell.

The validation list displays.

5 ▶ In the list, click **Accessories**.

The item is corrected but the red circle is not removed.

6 ▶ Click cell **A8**, click the arrow, and then click **Bags**.

7 ▶ In the **Data Tools group**, click the **Data Validation arrow**, and then click **Clear Validation Circles** to remove the circles.

8 ▶ In the **Data Tools group**, click the **Data Validation arrow**, and then click **Circle Invalid Data**.

No circles are applied, which confirms that the data is now valid against the validation list.

9 ▶ **Save** 🖫 your workbook.

10 ▶ Select both worksheets so that *[Group]* displays in the title bar. With the two worksheets grouped, insert a footer in the **left section** that includes the file name. **Center** the worksheets **Horizontally** on the page and set the **Orientation** to **Landscape**. On the status bar, click **Normal** ▦. Press Ctrl + Home.

11 ▶ Click the **FILE tab** to display **Backstage** view. On the right, at the bottom of the **Properties** list, click **Show All Properties**. On the list of **Properties**, in the **Tags** box, type **Miami revenue** In the **Subject** box, type your course name and section #. Under **Related People**, be sure that your name displays as the author. If necessary, right-click the author name, click Edit Property, type your name, click outside of the Edit person dialog box, and then click OK. Display the grouped worksheets in **Print Preview**, **Close** the print preview, and then make any necessary corrections or adjustments.

12 ▶ Ungroup the worksheets, **Save** 🖫 and **Close** your workbook.

13 ▶ Hold this workbook until the end of this project, and then print or submit the two worksheets in this workbook electronically as directed by your instructor. If required, print or create an electronic version of your worksheets with formulas displayed using the instructions in Project 1A.

Objective 8 ▶ Use the Watch Window to Monitor Cell Values

Video E4-8

You can monitor cells in one part of a workbook while working on another part of the workbook using the *Watch Window*—a window that displays the results of specified cells. You can monitor cells on other worksheets and see the results as soon as formulas are calculated or changes are made that affect the outcome of the watched cells. This feature is also useful on large worksheets for which the total rows and columns are not visible on the screen with the details.

Activity 4.18 | Using the Watch Window to Monitor Changes

Mike Connor's assistant is preparing the 1st Quarter sales worksheets using the Watch Window for sales totals for the four largest retail stores.

1 From your student files, open the file **e04B_First_Quarter_Sales** and then **Save** the file in your **Excel Chapter 4** folder as **Lastname_Firstname_4B_First_Quarter_Sales**

2 On the **Toronto** worksheet, click cell **E8**. On the **FORMULAS tab**, in the **Formula Auditing group**, click **Watch Window**.

> The Watch Window displays on your screen. As you create totals for the columns and rows on each worksheet in this activity, you will be able to use the Watch Window to view the results for all the worksheets at once.

3 In the upper left corner of the **Watch Window**, click **Add Watch**. Drag the window below your data, and then compare your screen with Figure 4.54.

> The Add Watch dialog box displays the address for the selected cell—Toronto!$E$8

FIGURE 4.54

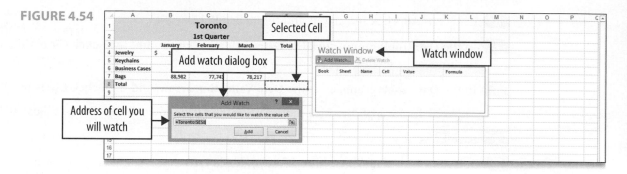

4 In the **Add Watch** dialog box, click **Add**.

> Because there is no value or formula in the cell at this time, the Name, Value, and Formula columns are empty.

5 Display the **Houston** worksheet and then click cell **E8**. In the **Watch Window**, click **Add Watch**, and then in the **Add Watch** dialog box, click **Add**. Compare your screen with Figure 4.55.

> A second cell is added to the Watch Window.

FIGURE 4.55

6 Following the same procedure, add cell **E8** from the **New York** sheet and from the **Miami** sheet to the **Watch Window**. Adjust the size of the **Watch Window** columns as necessary to view all four sheets. Compare your screen with Figure 4.56, and verify cell **E8** is listed for each of the four worksheets.

FIGURE 4.56

7 ▶ With the **Miami** worksheet active, hold down `Shift`, and then click the **Toronto sheet tab**.

The four store worksheets are selected and *[Group]* displays in the title bar.

8 ▶ In the **Miami** worksheet, select the range **B4:E8**.

This includes the data and the empty row and column immediately adjacent to the data. Because the sheets are grouped, this action is taking place on all four worksheets.

9 ▶ On the **FORMULAS tab**, in the **Function Library group**, click **AutoSum**. Compare your screen with Figure 4.57.

The totals for the rows and columns in this worksheet, as well as in the other three worksheets, are calculated. The results display immediately in the Watch Window, indicating that calculations took place on all four sheets simultaneously.

FIGURE 4.57

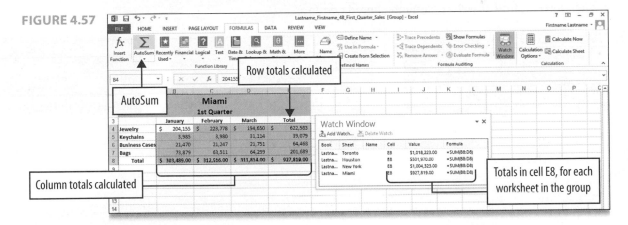

10 ▶ Close ☒ the **Watch Window**.

11 ▶ With the four worksheets grouped, insert a footer in the **left section** that includes the file name. **Center** the sheets **Horizontally**. On the status bar, click **Normal** ▦. Press `Ctrl` + `Home` to move to the top of the worksheet.

12 ▶ Click the **FILE tab** to display **Backstage** view. On the right, at the bottom of the **Properties** list, click **Show All Properties**. On the list of **Properties**, in the **Tags** box, type **first quarter sales** In the **Subject** box, type your course name and section #. Under **Related People**, be sure that your name displays as the author. If necessary, right-click the author name, click Edit Property, type your name, click outside of the Edit person dialog box, and then click OK. Display the grouped worksheets in **Print Preview**, and then view your worksheets. **Close** the print preview, and then make any necessary corrections or adjustments.

13 ▶ Right-click any sheet tab and click **Ungroup Sheets**. **Save** 🖫 and **Close** your workbook and **Exit** Excel. Print or submit the four worksheets in this workbook electronically as directed by your instructor. If required, print your worksheets with formulas displayed using the instructions in Project 1A.

END | You have completed Project 4B

END OF CHAPTER

SUMMARY

The PMT function is used to calculate the payment for a loan. The PMT function has three required arguments: Rate (interest), Nper (number of payments), and Pv (present value), and two optional arguments.

Two of Excel's What-If Analysis tools are Goal Seek—used to find a specific value for a cell by adjusting the value of another cell; and Data Tables—which display the results of different inputs into a formula.

A defined name can represent a cell, range of cells, formula, or constant value and can be used in a formula. A Lookup function looks up data located in another part of a workbook to find a corresponding value.

Data validation is used to control the type of data or the values that are entered into a cell. Formula auditing improves the accuracy of data entry and checks a worksheet for various types of errors.

GO! LEARN IT ONLINE

Review the concepts and key terms in this chapter by completing these online challenges, which you can find at **www.pearsonhighered.com/go**.

Matching and Multiple Choice:
Answer matching and multiple choice questions to test what you learned in this chapter. MyITLab®

Crossword Puzzle:
Spell out the words that match the numbered clues, and put them in the puzzle squares.

Flipboard:
Flip through the definitions of the key terms in this chapter and match them with the correct term.

END OF CHAPTER

REVIEW AND ASSESSMENT GUIDE FOR EXCEL CHAPTER 4

Your instructor may assign one or more of these projects to help you review the chapter and assess your mastery and understanding of the chapter.

	Review and Assessment Guide for Excel Chapter 4		
Project	**Apply Skills from These Chapter Objectives**	**Project Type**	**Project Location**
4C	Objectives 1–4 from Project 4A	**4C Skills Review** A guided review of the skills from Project 4A.	On the following pages
4D	Objectives 5–8 from Project 4B	**4D Skills Review** A guided review of the skills from Project 4B.	On the following pages
4E	Objectives 1–4 from Project 4A	**4E Mastery (Grader Project)** A demonstration of your mastery of the skills in Project 4A with extensive decision making.	In MyITLab and on the following pages
4F	Objectives 5–8 from Project 4B	**4F Mastery (Grader Project)** A demonstration of your mastery of the skills in Project 4B with extensive decision making.	In MyITLab and on the following pages
4G	Combination of Objectives from Projects 4A and 4B	**4G Mastery (Grader Project)** A demonstration of your mastery of the skills in Projects 4A and 4B with extensive decision making.	In MyITLab and on the following pages
4H	Combination of Objectives from Projects 4A and 4B	**4H GO! Fix It** A demonstration of your mastery of the skills in Projects 4A and 4B by creating a correct result from a document that contains errors you must find.	Online
4I	Combination of Objectives from Projects 4A and 4B	**4I GO! Make It** A demonstration of your mastery of the skills in Projects 4A and 4B by creating a result from a supplied picture.	Online
4J	Combination of Objectives from Projects 4A and 4B	**4J GO! Solve It** A demonstration of your mastery of the skills in Projects 4A and 4B, your decision making skills, and your critical thinking skills. A task-specific rubric helps you self-assess your result.	Online
4K	Combination of Objectives from Projects 4A and 4B	**4K GO! Solve It** A demonstration of your mastery of the skills in Projects 4A and 4B, your decision making skills, and your critical thinking skills. A task-specific rubric helps you self-assess your result.	On the following pages
4L	Combination of Objectives from Projects 4A and 4B	**4L GO! Think** A demonstration of your understanding of the Chapter concepts applied in a manner that you would outside of college. An analytic rubric helps you and your instructor grade the quality of your work by comparing it to the work an expert in the discipline would create.	On the following pages
4M	Combination of Objectives from Projects 4A and 4B	**4M GO! Think** A demonstration of your understanding of the Chapter concepts applied in a manner that you would outside of college. An analytic rubric helps you and your instructor grade the quality of your work by comparing it to the work an expert in the discipline would create.	Online
4N	Combination of Objectives from Projects 4A and 4B	**4N You and GO!** A demonstration of your understanding of the Chapter concepts applied in a manner that you would in a personal situation. An analytic rubric helps you and your instructor grade the quality of your work.	Online

GLOSSARY

GLOSSARY OF CHAPTER KEY TERMS

Arguments The values that an Excel function uses to perform calculations or operations.

Auditing The process of examining a worksheet for errors in formulas.

Circular reference An Excel error that occurs when a formula directly or indirectly refers to itself.

Data table A range of cells that shows how changing certain values in your formulas affect the results of those formulas and that makes it easy to calculate multiple versions in one operation.

Data validation A technique by which you can control the type of data or the values that are entered into a cell by limiting the acceptable values to a defined list.

Defined name A word or string of characters in Excel that represents a cell, a range of cells, a formula, or a constant value; also referred to as simply a *name*.

Dependent cells Cells that contain formulas that refer to other cells.

Error Checking command A command that checks for common errors that occur in formulas.

Error value The result of a formula that Excel cannot evaluate correctly.

Financial functions Pre-built formulas that perform common business calculations such as calculating a loan payment on a vehicle or calculating how much to save each month to buy something; financial functions commonly involve a period of time such as months or years.

Formula An equation that performs mathematical calculations on values in a worksheet.

Formula Auditing Tools and commands accessible from the FORMULAS tab that help you check your worksheet for errors.

Future value (Fv) The value at the end of the time periods in an Excel function; the cash balance you want to attain after the last payment is made—usually zero for loans.

Goal Seek One of Excel's What-If Analysis tools that provides a method to find a specific value for a cell by adjusting the value of one other cell—find the right input when you know the result you want.

HLOOKUP An Excel function that looks up values that are displayed horizontally in a row.

Interest The amount charged for the use of borrowed money.

Iterative calculation When Excel recalculates a formula over and over because of a circular reference.

LOOKUP An Excel function that looks up values in either a one-row or one-column range.

Lookup functions A group of Excel functions that look up a value in a defined range of cells located in another part of the workbook to find a corresponding value.

Name A word or string of characters in Excel that represents a cell, a range of cells, a formula, or a constant value; also referred to as *a defined name*.

Nper The abbreviation for *number of time periods* in various Excel functions.

One-variable data table A data table that changes the value in only one cell.

PMT function An Excel function that calculates the payment for a loan based on constant payments and a constant interest rate.

Precedent cells Cells that are referred to by a formula in another cell.

Present value (Pv) The total amount that a series of future payments is worth now; also known as the *principal*.

Principal The total amount that a series of future payments is worth now; also known as the *Present value (Pv)*.

Rate In the Excel PMT function, the term used to indicate the interest rate for a loan.

Scope The location within which a defined name is recognized without qualification—usually either to a specific worksheet or to the entire workbook.

Table array A defined range of cells, arranged in a column or a row, used in a VLOOKUP or HLOOKUP function.

Trace Dependents command A command that displays arrows that indicate what cells are affected by the value of the currently selected cell.

Trace Error command A tool that helps locate and resolve an error by tracing the selected error value.

Trace Precedents command A command that displays arrows to indicate what cells affect the value of the cell that is selected.

Tracer arrow An indicator that shows the relationship between the active cell and its related cell.

Two-variable data table A data table that changes the values in two cells.

Type argument An optional argument in the PMT function that assumes that the payment will be made at the end of each time period.

Validation list A list of values that are acceptable for a group of cells; only values in the list are valid and any value *not* in the list is considered invalid.

VLOOOKUP An Excel function that looks up values that are displayed vertically in a column.

Watch Window A window that displays the results of specified cells.

What-If Analysis The process of changing the values in cells to see how those changes affect the outcome of formulas in a worksheet.

CHAPTER REVIEW

Skills Review   Project 4C Auto Loan

Apply 4A skills from these Objectives:

1 Use Financial Functions
2 Use Goal Seek
3 Create a Data Table
4 Use Defined Names in a Formula

In the following Skills Review, you will create a worksheet for Patricia Murphy, U.S. Sales Director, which details loan information for purchasing seven automobiles for Jesse Jewelers sales representatives. The monthly payment for the seven automobiles cannot exceed $3,500. You will also help Ms. Murphy calculate quarterly Store Supply costs using Defined Names. Your completed two worksheets will look similar to Figure 4.58.

PROJECT FILES

For Project 4C, you will need the following files:

e04C_Auto_Loan
e04C_Store_Supplies

You will save your workbooks as:

Lastname_Firstname_4C_Auto_Loan
Lastname_Firstname_4C_Store_Supplies

PROJECT RESULTS

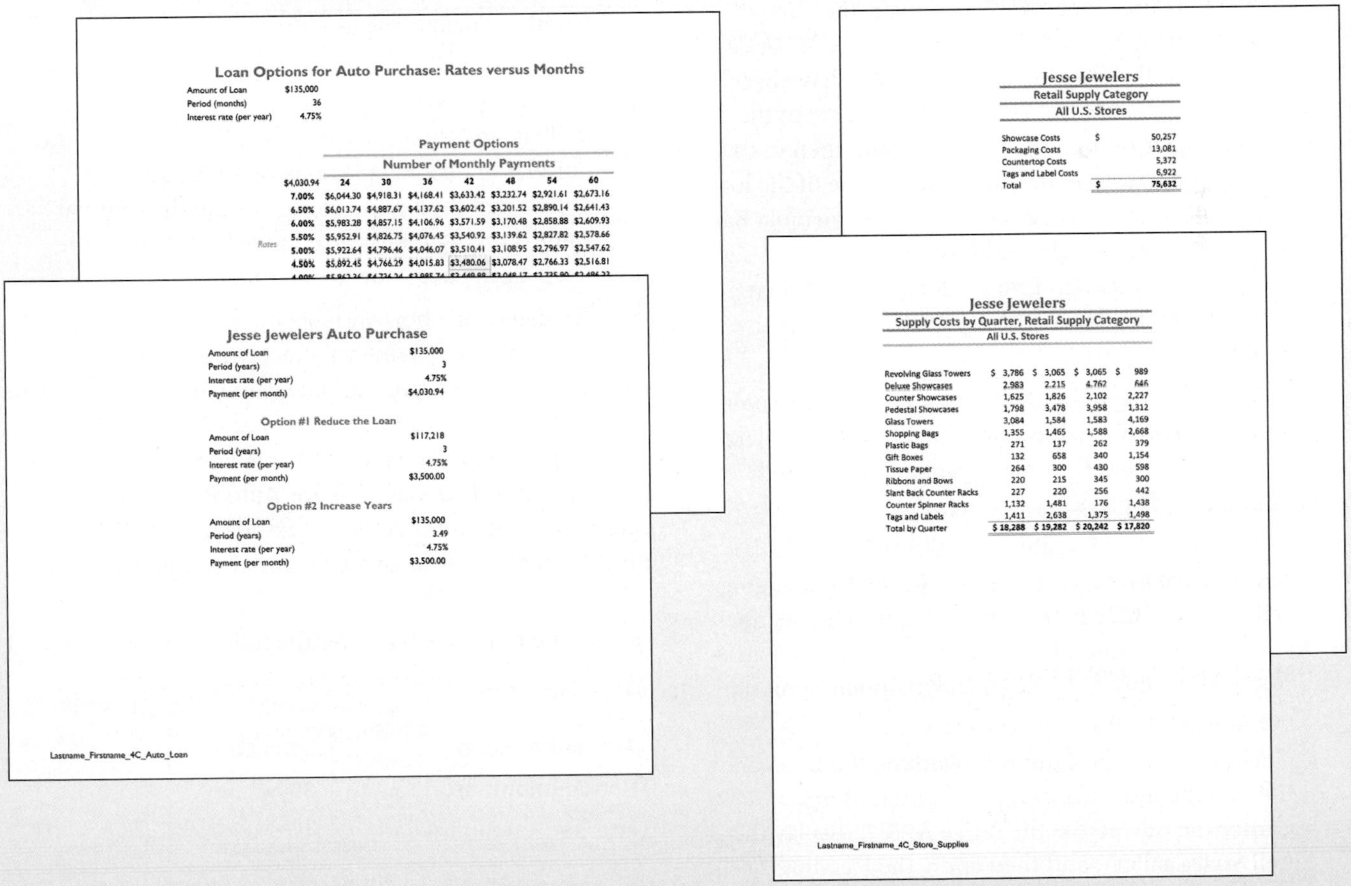

Loan Options for Auto Purchase: Rates versus Months

Amount of Loan	$135,000
Period (months)	36
Interest rate (per year)	4.75%

Payment Options

Number of Monthly Payments

$4,030.94	24	30	36	42	48	54	60
7.00%	$6,044.30	$4,918.31	$4,168.41	$3,633.42	$3,232.74	$2,921.61	$2,673.16
6.50%	$6,013.74	$4,887.67	$4,137.62	$3,602.42	$3,201.52	$2,890.14	$2,641.43
6.00%	$5,983.28	$4,857.15	$4,106.96	$3,571.59	$3,170.48	$2,858.88	$2,609.93
5.50%	$5,952.91	$4,826.75	$4,076.45	$3,540.92	$3,139.62	$2,827.82	$2,578.66
5.00%	$5,922.64	$4,796.46	$4,046.07	$3,510.41	$3,108.95	$2,796.97	$2,547.62
4.50%	$5,892.45	$4,766.29	$4,015.83	$3,480.06	$3,078.47	$2,766.33	$2,516.81

Rates

Jesse Jewelers Auto Purchase

Amount of Loan	$135,000
Period (years)	3
Interest rate (per year)	4.75%
Payment (per month)	$4,030.94

Option #1 Reduce the Loan

Amount of Loan	$117,218
Period (years)	3
Interest rate (per year)	4.75%
Payment (per month)	$3,500.00

Option #2 Increase Years

Amount of Loan	$135,000
Period (years)	3.49
Interest rate (per year)	4.75%
Payment (per month)	$3,500.00

Lastname_Firstname_4C_Auto_Loan

Jesse Jewelers
Retail Supply Category
All U.S. Stores

Showcase Costs	$	50,257
Packaging Costs		13,081
Countertop Costs		5,372
Tags and Label Costs		6,922
Total	$	75,632

Jesse Jewelers
Supply Costs by Quarter, Retail Supply Category
All U.S. Stores

Revolving Glass Towers	$ 3,786	$ 3,065	$ 3,065	$ 989
Deluxe Showcases	2,983	2,215	4,762	646
Counter Showcases	1,625	1,826	2,102	2,227
Pedestal Showcases	1,798	3,478	3,958	1,312
Glass Towers	3,084	1,584	1,583	4,169
Shopping Bags	1,355	1,465	1,588	2,668
Plastic Bags	271	137	262	379
Gift Boxes	132	658	340	1,154
Tissue Paper	264	300	430	598
Ribbons and Bows	220	215	245	300
Slant Back Counter Racks	227	220	256	442
Counter Spinner Racks	1,132	1,481	176	1,438
Tags and Labels	1,411	2,638	1,375	1,498
Total by Quarter	$ 18,288	$ 19,282	$ 20,242	$ 17,820

Lastname_Firstname_4C_Store_Supplies

FIGURE 4.58

(Project 4C Auto Loan continues on the next page)

CHAPTER REVIEW

1 Start Excel. From your student files, open the file e04C_Auto_Loan, and then **Save** the file in your **Excel Chapter 4** folder as **Lastname_Firstname_4C_Auto_Loan**

a. In the range **A2:B5**, enter the following row titles and data.

Amount of Loan	$135,000
Period (years)	3
Interest Rate (per year)	4.75%
Payment (per month)	

b. Click cell **B5**. On the **FORMULAS tab**, in the **Function Library group**, click **Financial**, and then scroll down and click **PMT**. Drag the **Function Arguments** dialog box to the right side of your screen so you can view **columns A:B**.

c. In the **Rate** box, type **b4/12** to convert the annual interest rate to a monthly interest rate. Press [Tab], and then in the **Nper** box, type **b3*12** to have Excel convert the number of years in the loan (3) to the total number of months. Press [Tab], and then in the **Pv** box, type **b2** to enter the present value of the loan. Click **OK** to create the function. In the **Formula Bar**, between the equal sign and PMT, type **–** (minus sign) to insert a minus sign into the formula, and then press [Enter] to display the loan payment as a positive number.

2 Click cell **B5**. On the **DATA tab**, in the **Data Tools group**, click **What-If Analysis**, and then in the list, click **Goal Seek**. In the **Goal Seek** dialog box, in the **Set cell** box, confirm that **B5** displays.

a. Press [Tab]. In the **To value** box, type the payment goal of **3500** and then press [Tab]. In the **By changing cell** box, type **b2** which is the amount of the loan. Click **OK** two times. For three years at 4.75%, Lauren can borrow only $117,218 if she maintains a monthly payment of $3,500.

b. Click cell **A7**. Type **Option #1 Reduce the Loan** and then on the **Formula Bar**, press **Enter**. **Merge and Center** the title across the range **A7:B7**, display the **Cell Styles** gallery, and then apply the **Heading 2** cell style.

c. Select the range **A2:B5**, right-click, and then click **Copy**. Point to cell **A8**, right-click, point to **Paste**

Special, and then under **Paste Values**, click the second button—**Values & Number Formatting (A)**. Press [Esc] to cancel the moving border.

d. In cell **B2**, type **135000** and then press [Enter] to restore the original loan amount. Click cell **B5**. On the **DATA tab**, in the **Data Tools group**, click **What-If Analysis**, and then click **Goal Seek**.

e. In the **Set cell** box, confirm that **B5** displays. Press [Tab]. In the **To value** box, type **3500** and then press [Tab]. In the **By changing cell** box, type **b3** which is the number of years for the loan. Click **OK** two times.

f. Click **A13**. Type **Option #2 Increase Years** and then press [Enter]. Use the **Format Painter** to copy the format from cell **A7** to cell **A13**. Select the range **A2:B5**, right-click, and then click **Copy**. Point to cell **A14**, right-click, point to **Paste Special**, and then under **Paste Values**, click the second button—**Values & Number Formatting (A)**. Press [Esc] to cancel the moving border.

g. Point to cell **B15**, right-click to display the mini toolbar, and then click **Decrease Decimal** until the number of decimal places is two. Click cell **B3**. Type **3** and then press [Enter] to restore the original value. Press [Ctrl] + [Home] to move to the top of the worksheet. **Save** your workbook.

3 To determine how variable interest rates and a varying number of payments affect the payment amount, Lauren will set up a two-variable data table. Click the **New sheet** button to create a new worksheet. Double-click the **Sheet1 tab**, rename it **Payment Table** and then press [Enter]. In cell **A1**, type **Loan Options for Auto Purchase: Rates versus Months** and then press [Enter]. **Merge and Center** this title across the range **A1:I1**, and then apply the **Title** cell style.

a. In the range **A2:B4**, enter the following row titles and data.

Amount of Loan	$135,000
Period (months)	36
Interest Rate (per year)	4.75%

b. Change the width of **column A** to 20.Click cell **C8**. Type **24** and then press [Tab]. Type **30** and then press [Tab]. Select the range **C8:D8**. Drag the fill handle to

(Project 4C Auto Loan continues on the next page)

the right through cell **I8** to fill a pattern of months from 24 to 60 in increments of six months.

c. In cell **B9**, type **7.0%** and press [Enter]. Type **6.5%** and press [Enter]. Select the range **B9:B10**, and then drag the fill handle down through cell **B16** to fill a pattern of interest rates in increments of .5% from 7.00% down to 3.50%. If necessary, adjust to display two decimal places.

d. Click cell **C6**. Type **Payment Options** and then press [Enter]. **Merge and Center** this title across the range **C6:I6**. Apply the **Heading 1** cell style. Click cell **C7**. Type **Number of Monthly Payments** and then use the **Format Painter** to apply the format of cell **C6** to cell **C7**.

e. Click cell **A9**, type **Rates** and then press [Enter]. Select the range **A9:A16**. On the **HOME tab**, in the **Alignment group**, click **Merge and Center**, click **Align Right**, and then click **Middle Align**. Apply the **Explanatory Text** cell style.

f. Click cell **B8**. On the **FORMULAS tab**, in the **Function Library group**, click **Financial**, and then click **PMT**. In the **Rate** box, type **b4/12** to divide the interest rate per year by 12 to convert it to a monthly interest rate. Press [Tab], and then in the **Nper** box, type **b3** and press [Tab]. In the **Pv** box, type **-b2** and then click **OK**.

g. Select the range **B8:I16**. On the **DATA tab**, in the **Data Tools group**, click **What-If Analysis**, and then in the list, click **Data Table**. In the **Data Table** dialog box, in the **Row input cell** box, type **b3** and then press [Tab]. In the **Column input cell** box, type **b4** In the **Data Table** dialog box, click **OK** to create the data table. Click in any cell outside of the table to deselect.

h. Use the **Format Painter** to copy the format from cell **B8** to the range **C9:I16**.

i. Select the range **F14:F16** and apply the **Note** cell style to highlight the desired payment option. Select the nonadjacent ranges **C8:I8** and **B9:B16**, apply **Bold** and **Center**. On the **PAGE LAYOUT tab**, set the **Orientation** for this worksheet to **Landscape**.

j. Group both worksheets. Click the **INSERT tab**, insert a footer, and then in the left section, click **File Name**. Click in a cell just above the footer to exit the **Footer area** and view your file name. From the **PAGE LAYOUT tab**, display the **Page Setup** dialog

box, and on the **Margins tab**, select the **Horizontally** check box. Click **OK**, and then on the status bar, click **Normal**. AutoFit **columns C:I**. Press [Ctrl] + [Home] to move to the top of the worksheet.

k. Click the **FILE tab** to display **Backstage** view. On the right, at the bottom of the **Properties** list, click **Show All Properties**. On the list of **Properties**, in the **Tags** box, type **amortization schedule, payment table** In the **Subject** box, type your course name and section #. Under **Related People**, be sure that your name displays as the author. If necessary, right-click the author name, click Edit Property, type your name, click outside of the Edit person dialog box, and then click OK. Return to **Normal** view and make cell **A1** active. Display each worksheet in **Print Preview**, and then make any necessary corrections or adjustments. **Close** the **Print Preview**.

l. Ungroup the worksheets, **Save** and **Close** your workbook but leave Excel open. Print or submit the two worksheets in this workbook electronically as directed by your instructor. If required, print or create an electronic version of your worksheets with formulas displayed using the instructions in Project 1A.

4 Open the file **e04C_Store_Supplies**, and then **Save** the file in your **Excel Chapter 4** folder as **Lastname_Firstname_4C_Store_Supplies**

a. Select the range **B6:E18**, which includes the empty cells in **row 18**, and then click **AutoSum**. Click anywhere to cancel the selection. Select the range **B6:E6**, hold down [Ctrl] and select the range **B18:E18**, and then from the **Cell Styles** gallery, under **Number Format**, apply the **Currency [0]** cell style. Select the range **B7:E17**, display the **Cell Styles** gallery, and then under **Number Format**, click **Comma [0]**. Select the range **B18:E18**, and then apply the **Total** cell style.

b. Select the range **B6:E9**. On the **FORMULAS tab**, in the **Defined Names group**, click **Define Name**. With *Revolving_Glass_Towers* selected, type **Showcase_ Costs** as the name. At the bottom of the dialog box, at the right edge of the **Refers to** box, point to and click **Collapse Dialog Box**. Change the range by selecting the range **B6:E10**.

c. Click **Expand Dialog Box** to redisplay the **New Name** dialog box, and then click **OK**. Select the

(Project 4C Auto Loan continues on the next page)

range **B11:E14**. In the upper left corner of the Excel window, to the left of the **Formula Bar**, click in the **Name Box**. Type **Wrapping_Costs** and press Enter.

d. Select the range **B15:E16**. On the **FORMULAS tab**, in the **Defined Names group**, click **Name Manager**. In the upper left corner of the **Name Manager** dialog box, click **New**. With *Slant_Back_Counter_Racks* selected, type **Countertop_Costs** and then click **OK**. **Close** the **Name Manager** dialog box and **Save** your workbook.

e. On the left side of your window, in the **row heading area**, point to the **row 15** heading and right-click to select the entire row and display a shortcut menu. Click **Insert** to insert a new blank row above. Click cell **A15**, type **Ribbons and Bows** and then press Tab. In cell **B15**, type **220** and press Tab. In cell **C15**, type **215** and press Tab. In cell **D15**, type **345** and press Tab. In cell **E15**, type **300** and press Enter.

f. On the **FORMULAS tab**, from the **Defined Names group**, display the **Name Manager** dialog box. In the **Name Manager** dialog box, in the **Name** column, click **Wrapping_Costs**. At the bottom of the dialog box, click in the **Refers to** box and edit the reference, changing $E$14 to $E$15 to include the new row in the range. **Close** the **Name Manager** dialog box, and click **Yes** to save the changes you made to the name reference.

g. On the **FORMULAS tab**, from the **Defined Names group**, display the **Name Manager** dialog box. Click **Wrapping_Costs**, and then click **Edit**. In the **Edit Name** dialog box, with *Wrapping_Costs* selected, type **Packaging_Costs** Click **OK**, and then **Close** the **Name Manager** dialog box. In the upper left corner of the window, click the **Name Box arrow** and notice the modified range name, Packaging_Costs. Click any cell to close the list, and then **Save** your workbook.

h. Select the range **A18:E18**. On the **FORMULAS tab**, in the **Defined Names group**, click **Create from Selection**. In the **Create Names from Selection** dialog box, click **OK**, and then click anywhere to cancel the selection. Click the **Name Box arrow**, and then click the name **Tags_and_Labels**. Notice that in the new range name, Excel inserted the underscore necessary to fill a blank space in the range name.

5 Display the **Annual Supply Costs** worksheet.

a. In cell **B5**, type **=sum(S** Continue typing **Showcase_ Costs** and then press Enter. Your result is 50257. In cell **B6**, type **=sum(P** and then on the **Formula AutoComplete list**, double-click **Packaging_Costs** to insert the formula. Press Enter to display the result 13081.

b. In cell **B7**, type **=sum(** and then on the **FORMULAS tab**, in the **Defined Names group**, click **Use in Formula**. In the list, click **Countertop_Costs** and then press Enter to display the total 5372.

c. In cell **B8**, use any of the techniques you just practiced to sum the cells containing the costs for **Tags and Labels Costs** and to display a result of 6922. Click cell **B9**, hold down Alt and press = to insert the SUM function, and then press Enter to display a total of *75632*.

d. Select the nonadjacent cells **B5** and **B9**, and then from the **HOME tab**, display the **Cell Styles** gallery. Under **Number Format**, click the **Currency [0]** cell style. To the range **B6:B8**, apply the **Comma [0]** cell style. Click cell **B9** and apply the **Total** cell style.

e. Select both worksheets so that [*Group*] displays in the title bar. With the two worksheets grouped, insert a footer in the left section that includes the file name. **Center** the worksheets **Horizontally** on the page.

f. Click the **FILE tab** to display **Backstage** view. On the right, at the bottom of the **Properties** list, click **Show All Properties**. On the list of **Properties**, in the **Tags** box, type **retail supply category, supply costs** In the **Subject** box, type your course name and section #. Under **Related People**, be sure that your name displays as the author. If necessary, right-click the author name, click Edit Property, type your name, click outside of the Edit person dialog box, and then click OK. Return to **Normal** view and make cell **A1** active, display the grouped worksheets in **Print Preview**, **Close** the **Print Preview**, and then make any necessary corrections or adjustments. Right-click any of the grouped sheet tabs, and then click **Ungroup Sheets**.

g. **Save** your workbook. Print or submit the two worksheets in both workbooks electronically as directed by your instructor. If required, print or create an electronic version of your worksheets with formulas displayed using the instructions in Project 1A. **Close** Excel.

END | You have completed Project 4C

CHAPTER REVIEW

Apply 4B skills from these Objectives:

5 Use Lookup Functions

6 Validate Data

7 Audit Worksheet Formulas

8 Use the Watch Window to Monitor Cell Values

Skills Review | **Project 4D Quarterly Cost Report and Lookup Form**

In the following Skills Review, you will assist Mike Connor, the Vice President of Marketing at Jesse Jewelers by adding lookup functions to a Packing Slip form so that an order taker can complete the form quickly. You will use the Formula Auditing tools to review a revenue worksheet for the Houston store and you will use the Watch Window to edit the store's utility cost worksheets. Your completed workbooks will look similar to Figure 4.59.

PROJECT FILES

For Project 4D, you will need the following files:

e04D_Houston Revenue

e04D_Packing_Slip

e04D_Utilities

You will save your workbooks as:

Lastname_Firstname_4D_Houston Revenue

Lastname_Firstname_4D_Packing_Slip

Lastname_Firstname_4D_Utilities

PROJECT RESULTS

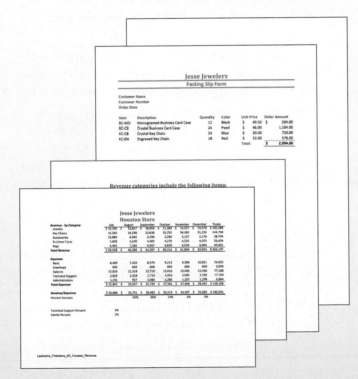

FIGURE 4.59

(Project 4D Quarterly Cost Report and Lookup Form continues on the next page)

CHAPTER REVIEW

1 From your student files, open the file **e04D_Packing_Slip**, and then **Save** the file in your **Excel Chapter 4** folder as **Lastname_Firstname_4D_Packing_Slip**

a. Display the **Product Information** worksheet. Select the range **A4:C11**. On the **DATA tab**, in the **Sort & Filter group**, click **Sort**. If necessary, drag the Sort dialog box to the right side of your screen so you can view columns A:C.

b. In the **Sort** dialog box, under **Column**, click the **Sort by arrow**. Notice that the selected range is now **A5:C11** and that the column titles in the range **A4:C4** display in the **Sort by** list. In the **Sort by** list, click **Style Code**. Under **Sort On**, verify that Values displays, and under **Order**, verify that A to Z displays. Click **OK** to sort the data by Style Code in ascending order. **Save** your workbook.

c. Display the **Packing Slip** worksheet. In cell **A9**, type **BC-MO** and press Tab. With cell **B9** as the active cell, on the **FORMULAS tab**, in the **Function Library group**, click **Lookup & Reference**, and then click **VLOOKUP**.

d. With the insertion point in the **Lookup_value** box, click cell **A9** to look up the description of Item BC-MO. Click in the **Table_array** box, and then at the bottom of the workbook, click the **Product Information sheet tab**. On the **Product Information** sheet, select the range **A4:C11**, and then press F4. Click in the **Col_index_num** box, type **2** and then click **OK**.

e. With cell **B9** as the active cell and containing the VLOOKUP formula, point to the fill handle in the lower right corner of the cell, and then drag to fill the VLOOKUP formula down through cell **B18**.

f. Click cell **C9**, type **12** as the quantity ordered, and then press Tab. In cell **D9**, type **Black** and press Tab. With cell **E9** as the active cell, on the **FORMULAS tab**, in the **Function Library group**, click **Lookup & Reference**, and then click **VLOOKUP**.

g. With the insertion point in the **Lookup_value** box, click cell **A9** to look up information for Item BC-MO. Click in the **Table_array** box, display the **Product Information** sheet, and then select the range **A4:C11**. Press F4 to make the values in the range absolute.

h. In the **Col_index_num** box, type **3** to look up the price in the third column of the range, and then

click **OK**. The Unit Price for the Monogrammed Business Card Case displays in cell **E9**. Click cell **F9**, and notice that a formula to calculate the total for the item, Quantity times Unit Price, has already been entered in the worksheet.

i. Click cell **E9**, and then copy the VLOOKUP formula down through cell **E18**.

j. Click cell **A10**, type **BC-CB** and press Tab two times. In cell **C10**, type **24** and press Tab. Notice that Excel calculates the total for this item in cell **F10**—1,104.00. In cell **D10**, type **Pearl** and then press Enter. **Save** your workbook.

2 Display the **Product Information** sheet. Select the range **A4:A11**. On the **FORMULAS** tab, in the **Defined Names** group, click **Create from Selection**.

a. In the **Create Names from Selection** dialog box, be sure only the **Top row** check box is selected, and then click **OK**.

b. Display the **Packing Slip** worksheet, and then select the range **A9:A18**. On the **DATA tab**, in the **Data Tools group**, click **Data Validation**. In the **Data Validation** dialog box, be sure the **Settings tab** is selected.

c. Under **Validation criteria**, click the **Allow arrow**, and then click **List**. Click to position the insertion point in the **Source** box, type **=Style_Code** and then click **OK**.

d. Click cell **A11**, and notice that a list arrow displays at the right edge of the cell. In cell **A11**, click the list arrow to display the list. In the list, click **KC-CB**. Press Tab two times, type **24** and press Tab, type **Blue** and then press Enter to return to the beginning of the next row.

e. With cell **A12** active, click the **list arrow**, and then click **KC-EN**. As the **Quantity**, type **18** and as the **Color**, type **Red** and press Enter. In cell **A13**, type **B-W** and press Tab. An error message displays indicating that you entered a value that is not valid; that is, it is not on the validation list you created. In the error message, click **Cancel** and then **Save** your workbook.

f. Select the unused **rows 13:18**, right-click over the selected rows, and then click **Delete**. In cell **F13**, **Sum** the order amounts and then apply the **Total** cell style.

3 Select both worksheets so that [*Group*] displays in the title bar. With the two worksheets grouped, insert

(Project 4D Quarterly Cost Report and Lookup Form continues on the next page)

CHAPTER REVIEW

a footer in the left section that includes the file name. **Center** the worksheets **Horizontally** on the page.

a. Click the **FILE tab** to display **Backstage** view. On the right, at the bottom of the **Properties** list, click **Show All Properties**. On the list of **Properties**, in the **Tags** box, type **luggage, bag, order form** In the **Subject** box, type your course name and section #. Under **Related People**, be sure that your name displays as the author. If necessary, right-click the author name, click Edit Property, type your name, click outside of the Edit person dialog box, and then click OK.

b. Return to **Normal** view and make cell **A1** active, display the grouped worksheets in **Print Preview**, **Close** the **Print Preview**, and then make any necessary corrections or adjustments. Ungroup the worksheets, **Save** and **Close** your workbook.

c. Print or submit the two worksheets in this workbook electronically as directed by your instructor. If required, print or create an electronic version of your worksheets with formulas displayed using the instructions in Activity 1.16 in Project 1A.

4 From your student files, open the file **e04D_Houston Revenue**. In your **Excel Chapter 4** folder, **Save** the file as **Lastname_Firstname_4D_Houston Revenue**

a. In the **column heading area**, select **column B**, hold down Ctrl, and then select **column H**. Point to the *right* edge of either of the selected column headings to display the pointer, and then double-click to AutoFit the columns.

b. Click cell **C9**. On the **FORMULAS tab**, in the **Formula Auditing group**, click **Trace Precedents**. To the left of the cell, click **Error Checking**, and then click **Update Formula to Include Cells**. Drag the fill handle to copy the corrected formula in cell **C9** to the range **D9:G9**.

c. Click cell **H5**, and then point to the **Error Checking** button to read the ScreenTip. On the **FORMULAS tab**, in the **Formula Auditing group**, click **Trace Precedents**. To the left of cell **H5**, click **Error Checking** to display the list of error checking options, click **Copy Formula from Above**, and then look at the **Formula Bar** to verify that the formula is summing the numbers in **row 5**. With cell **H5** still selected, from the **HOME tab**, display the **Cell Styles** gallery, and then click the **Comma [0]** number format.

d. Click cell **H6**, on the **FORMULAS tab**, click **Trace Precedents**, and then verify that the row is correctly summed. Click cell **H7**, click **Trace Precedents**. Notice that the formula is not correct. Click cell **H8**, click **Trace Precedents**; notice that the formula is not correct. In the **Formula Auditing group**, click **Remove Arrows**. Click cell **H6**, and then use the fill handle to copy the correct formula down to cells **H7:H8**.

5 Click cell **B14**, which displays the error *#VALUE!*. To the left of the cell, point to **Error Checking** and read the ScreenTip. In the **Formula Auditing group**, click **Trace Precedents**.

a. Click **Error Checking**, and then, click **Show Calculation Steps**. Notice that the formula is multiplying by a text value.

b. **Close** the **Evaluate Formula** dialog box. With cell **B14** still the active cell, click in the **Formula Bar**, and then edit the formula to change the reference to cell **B3** to **B9** and press Enter. Click cell **B14**, and then drag the fill handle to copy the corrected formula across the row to cells **C14:G14**.

6 Click cell **B16**, point to **Error Checking**, and read the ScreenTip. In the **Formula Auditing group**, click the **Error Checking arrow** to display a list. Click **Trace Error**. In the **Formula Auditing group**, click the **Error Checking arrow**, and then click **Trace Error** again to view the precedent cells. Click in cell **A24**. Type **Admin Percent** and press Tab, and then type **2** to fill in the missing data.

a. Click **B16**. Remove the arrows. Click **Error Checking** to display the list of error checking options, and then click **Edit in Formula Bar**. Delete *#REF!*. Type **b24** and press F4 to make the cell reference absolute. Press Enter. Click cell **B16**, and then use the fill handle to copy the formula to the right into cells **C16:G16**.

7 Click cell **A1**. In the Formula Auditing group, click the **Error Checking arrow**, and then click **Error Checking**—cell **C20** is selected. In the **Error Checking** dialog box, click **Show Calculation Steps**; notice that the divisor is an empty cell. In the **Evaluate Formula** dialog box, click **Evaluate**. Click **Restart**.

a. In the **Evaluate Formula** dialog box, click **Step In** to examine the formula. Click **Step Out**. Close the **Evaluate Formula** dialog box.

(Project 4D Quarterly Cost Report and Lookup Form continues on the next page)

CHAPTER REVIEW

b. In the **Error Checking** dialog box, click **Next**. Click **OK**. Click cell **H13**, and then use the fill handle to copy this formula down to cells **H14:H16**. Click cell **B17** and drag the fill handle to copy this formula to the right into cells **C17:H17**.

c. Click cell **B19** and type **=b9-b17** Press Enter, and then copy the formula to the right into cells **C19:H19**. Click cell **C20**, and then on the **HOME tab**, in the **Number group**, click **Percent Style**. Copy the formula to the right into cells **D20:G20**.

8 Display the **Categories** worksheet. To the left of the **Formula Bar**, click the **Name Box** arrow, and then click **Items**—the only range name in the worksheet. Examine the selected range.

a. Redisplay the **Revenue** worksheet. On the **DATA tab**, in the **Data Tools group**, click the **Data Validation arrow**, and then click **Circle Invalid Data**.

b. Click cell **A8**, and then click the arrow at the right side of the cell. From the list, click **Bags**. In the **Data Tools group**, click the **Data Validation arrow**, and then click **Clear Validation Circles**.

c. Select both worksheets so that *[Group]* displays in the title bar. With the two worksheets grouped, insert a footer in the **left section** that includes the file name. **Center** the worksheets **Horizontally**. Set the **Orientation** to **Landscape**. On the status bar, click **Normal**. Press Ctrl + Home.

d. Click the **FILE tab** to display **Backstage** view. On the right, at the bottom of the **Properties** list, click **Show All Properties**. On the list of **Properties**, in the **Tags** box, type **Houston revenue** In the **Subject** box, type your course name and section #. Under **Related People**, be sure that your name displays as the author. If necessary, right-click the author name, click Edit Property, type your name, click outside of the Edit person dialog box, and then click OK.

e. Display the grouped worksheets in **Print Preview**, close the print preview, and then make any necessary corrections or adjustments. Ungroup the worksheets, **Save** and **Close** your workbook. Print or submit the two worksheets in this workbook electronically as directed by your instructor. If required, print or create an electronic version of your worksheets with formulas displayed using the instructions in Project 1A.

9 From your student files, open the file **e04D_Utilities**, and then **Save** the file in your **Excel Chapter 4** folder as **Lastname_Firstname_4D_Utilities** Display the **Toronto** worksheet, and then click cell **E8**. On the **FORMULAS tab**, in the **Formula Auditing group**, click **Watch Window**. In the upper left corner of the **Watch Window**, click **Add Watch**. In the **Add Watch** dialog box, click **Add**.

a. Display the **Houston** worksheet, and using the same technique, add cell **E8** from the **Houston** worksheet. Repeat this for the **New York** worksheet and for the **Miami** worksheet. Adjust the size of the **Watch Window** and columns as necessary to view all four sheets, and verify that cell **E8** is listed for each of the four worksheets.

b. With the **Miami** worksheet active, hold down Shift and click the **Toronto sheet tab** to select all four worksheets. In the **Miami** worksheet, select the range **B4:E8**. On the **FORMULAS tab**, in the **Function Library group**, click **AutoSum**. **Close** the **Watch Window**. Select the range **E5:E7**, and then apply **Comma Style** with zero decimal places.

c. With the four worksheets grouped, insert a footer in the **left section** that includes the file name. **Center** the sheets **Horizontally**. On the status bar, click **Normal**. Press Ctrl + Home to move to the top of the worksheet.

d. Click the **FILE tab** to display **Backstage** view. On the right, at the bottom of the **Properties** list, click **Show All Properties**. On the list of **Properties**, in the **Tags** box, type **Utilities** In the **Subject** box, type your course name and section #. Under **Related People**, be sure that your name displays as the author. If necessary, right-click the author name, click Edit Property, type your name, click outside of the Edit person dialog box, and then click OK.

e. Display the grouped worksheets in **Print Preview**. Redisplay the worksheets. Make any necessary corrections or adjustments. Right-click any of the grouped sheet tabs, and then click **Ungroup Sheets**. **Save** your workbook. Print or submit the four worksheets in this workbook electronically as directed by your instructor. If required, print or create an electronic version of your worksheets with formulas displayed using the instructions in Project 1A. **Close** Excel.

END | You have completed Project 4D

Apply 4A skills from these Objectives:

1 Use Financial Functions
2 Use Goal Seek
3 Create a Data Table
4 Use Defined Names in a Formula

In the following Mastering Excel project, you will create a worksheet for Jacques Celestine, President of Jesse Jewelers, which analyzes loan options for a condo in Toronto that the company is considering purchasing. Jacques wants to provide a lodging facility for company visitors, but would like to keep the monthly loan payment below $6,250. You will also define names for ranges of cells in a workbook containing quarterly Advertising costs. The worksheets of your workbooks will look similar to Figure 4.60.

PROJECT FILES

For Project 4E, you will need the following files:

e04E_Advertising_Costs
e04E_Condo_Loan

You will save your workbooks as:

Lastname_Firstname_4E_Advertising_Costs
Lastname_Firstname_4E_Condo_Loan

PROJECT RESULTS

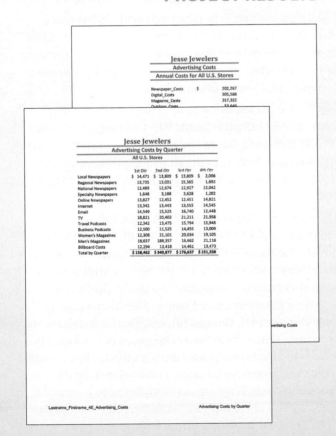

FIGURE 4.60

(Project 4E Condo Loan and Quarterly Cost Report continues on the next page)

CONTENT-BASED ASSESSMENTS

1 Start Excel. From your student files, locate and **open e04E_Condo_Loan. Save** the file in your **Excel Chapter 4** folder as **Lastname_Firstname_4E_Condo_Loan** In cell **B5**, insert the **PMT** function using the data from the range **B2:B5**—be sure to divide the interest rate by 12, multiply the years by 12, and display the payment as a positive number. The result, $6,598.44, is larger than the payment of $6,250.

2 Use **Goal Seek** to change the amount of the loan so that the payment is under $6,250. Then, in **A7**, type **Option #1 Reduce the Loan** and then **Copy** the format from cell **A1** to cell **A7**. **Copy** the range **A2:B5**, and then **Paste** the **Values & Number Formatting (A)** to cell **A8**. In cell **B2**, type **615000** to restore the original loan amount.

3 Use **Goal Seek** to change the period of the loan so that the payment does not exceed $6,250. In **A13**, type **Option #2 Increase Years** Format the cell the same as cell **A7**. **Copy** the range **A2:B5**, and then **Paste** the **Values & Number Formatting (A)** to cell **A14**. Display the value in **B15** with two decimal places, and then in cell **B3**, type **10** to restore the original value. Insert a footer with the **File Name** in the left section, and then **Center** the worksheet **Horizontally** on the page.

4 **Save** and return to **Normal** view. Set up a two-variable data table. Rename the **Sheet2 tab** to **Condo Payment Table** In the range **A2:B4**, enter the following row titles and data.

Amount of Loan	$615,000
Period (months)	120
Interest Rate (per year)	5.25%

5 In cell **C8**, type **60**—the number of months in a five-year loan. In **D8**, type **120**—the number of months in a 10-year loan. Fill the series through cell **H8**; apply **Bold** and **Center**.

6 Beginning in cell **B9**, enter varying interest rates in decrements of .5% beginning with **7.5%** and ending with **4.0%** Format all the interest rates with two decimal places, and then **Bold** and **Center** the range **B8:B16**. In cell **B8**, enter a **PMT** function using the information in cells **B2:B4**. Be sure that you convert the interest rate to a monthly rate and that the result displays as a positive number.

7 Create a **Data Table** in the range **B8:H16** using the information in cells **B2:B4** in which the **Row input cell**

is the **Period** and the **Column input cell** is the **Interest rate. Copy** the format from **B8** to the results in the data table. Format cell **D16** with the **Note** cell style as payment option that is close to but less than $6,250 per month. Change the **Orientation** to **Landscape**. Insert a footer with the **File Name** in the left section, and **Center** the worksheet **Horizontally** on the page. Return to **Normal** view and move to cell **A1**.

8 Click the **FILE tab** to display **Backstage** view. On the right, at the bottom of the **Properties** list, click **Show All Properties**. On the list of **Properties**, in the **Tags** box, type **condo, payment table** In the **Subject** box, type your course name and section #. Under **Related People**, be sure that your name displays as the author. If necessary, right-click the author name, click Edit Property, type your name, click outside of the Edit person dialog box, and then click OK.

Print Preview, make any necessary corrections or adjustments, ungroup the worksheets, and **Save** and **Close** your workbook. Print or submit electronically as directed.

9 From your student files, open **e04E_Advertising_Costs. Save** it in your **Excel Chapter 4** folder as **Lastname_Firstname_4E_Advertising_Costs** Display the **Advertising Costs by Quarter** worksheet, and then apply appropriate **Currency [0]**, **Comma [0]**, and **Total** cell styles.

10 Name the following ranges: **B6:E10 Newspaper_Costs**; **B10:E14 Digital_Costs**; **B15:E16 Magazine_Costs**; **B17:E17 Billboard_Costs** Insert a new **row 15**. In cell **A15**, type **Business Podcasts** In cell **B15**, type **12500** In cell **C15**, type **11525** In cell **D15**, type **14455** In cell **E15**, type **13009**.

11 Display **Name Manager**, click **Digital_Costs**, and then change cell **E14** to **E15**. Select the **Billboard_Costs**, and **Edit** the name to **Outdoor_Costs**. Display the **Annual Advertising Costs** sheet. In cell **B5**, type **=sum(N** and sum Newspaper costs using its defined name in the formula. Do this for the other named ranges. Sum all the costs. Apply **Currency [0]**, **Comma [0]**, and **Total** cell styles to the appropriate cells. Group the worksheets, insert a footer that includes the file name. **Center** the worksheets **Horizontally** on the page. Document properties should include the tags **advertising costs** Ungroup the worksheets, **Save** your file and then print or submit your worksheet electronically as directed by your instructor. **Close** Excel.

END | You have completed Project 4E

CONTENT-BASED ASSESSMENTS

Apply 4B skills from these Objectives:

5 Use Lookup Functions
6 Validate Data
7 Audit Worksheet Formulas
8 Use the Watch Window to Monitor

In the following Mastering Excel project, you will assist Mike Connor, the Vice President of Marketing at Jesse Jewelers, by adding lookup functions to an Advertising Order form so that an order taker can complete the form quickly. You will also use the Formula Auditing features and visual inspection to find and correct several types of errors. Your completed workbooks will look similar to Figure 4.61.

PROJECT FILES

For Project 4F, you will need the following files:

e04F_Advertising_Form
e04F_New_York_Revenue

You will save your workbooks as:

Lastname_Firstname_4F_Advertising_Form
Lastname_Firstname_4F_New_York_Revenue

PROJECT RESULTS

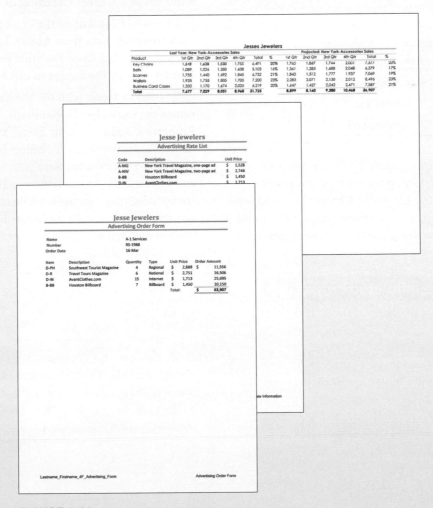

FIGURE 4.61

(Project 4F Lookup Form and Sales Revenue continues on the next page)

1 Open **e04F_Advertising_Form**. **Save** the file in your **Excel Chapter 4** folder as **Lastname_Firstname_4F_Advertising_Form** Display the **Advertising Rate Information** sheet, select the range **A4:C11**, and **Sort** by **Code**. Name the range **A4:A11** using **Create from Selection**. Display the **Advertising Order Form** sheet; in the range **A9:A18** create a **data validation list** using the defined name *Code*.

2 Click cell **A9**, click the **list arrow**, click **D-PH**. With cell **B9** as the active cell, insert a **VLOOKUP** function that will look up the **Description** from the **Advertising Rate Information** sheet using the **Item** number.

3 With cell **B9** as the active cell, fill the VLOOKUP formula through cell **B18**. In cell **C9**, type **4** and in cell **D9**, type **Regional** With cell **E9** as the active cell, insert a **VLOOKUP** function to look up Unit Price. **Copy** the VLOOKUP formula through cell **E18**. Add the following orders:

Item	Quantity	Type
D-R	6	National
D-IN	15	Internet
B-BB	7	Billboard

4 Delete unused rows, sum the **Order Amount**, and apply **Total** cell style. Group the worksheets, insert a footer that includes the file name. **Center** the worksheets **Horizontally** on the page. Document properties should include the tags **advertising costs** and **form** Ungroup the worksheets, **Save** and **Close** your workbook but leave Excel open.

5 Open the file **e04F_New_York_Revenue**, and then **Save** the file in your **Excel Chapter 4** folder as **Lastname_Firstname_4F_New_York_Revenue**

6 Click cell **I5**, which displays a green triangle indicating a potential error, and then on the **FORMULAS tab**, click **Trace Precedents**. Click **Error Checking**, and then click **Edit in Formula Bar**. Change *$B$14* to **$B$15** so that the formula is using the Growth Assumption for *Belts*, not for Key Chains.

7 On the **FORMULAS tab**, in the **Formula Auditing group**, click **Error Checking** to begin checking for errors from this point in the worksheet. In cell **M6**, the flagged error, notice the formula is trying to divide by cell **L10**, which is empty. Click **Edit in Formula Bar**, change **10** to **9** and then in the **Error Checking** dialog box, click **Resume**.

8 In cell **F7**, examine the error information, and then click **Copy Formula from Above**. Examine the error in cell **J8**, and then click **Copy Formula from Left**. Use **Format Painter** to copy the format in cell **M5** to cell **M6**.

9 Insert a footer with the file name in the **left section**, **center** the worksheet **Horizontally**. Display the **Document Properties**, add your name as the **Author**, type your course name and section # in the **Subject** box, and as the **Tags**, type **New York revenue** **Save** your workbook. Display and examine the **Print Preview**, make any necessary corrections, ungroup the worksheets, **Save**, and then print or submit electronically as directed by your instructor. If you are directed to do so, print the formulas. **Close** Excel.

END | You have completed Project 4F

CONTENT-BASED ASSESSMENTS

Mastering Excel | Project 4G Warehouse Loan and Staff Lookup Form

Apply 4A and 4B skills from these Objectives:

1 Use Financial Functions
2 Use Goal Seek
3 Create a Data Table
4 Use Defined Names in a Formula
5 Use Lookup Functions
6 Validate Data
7 Audit Worksheet Formulas
8 Use the Watch Window to Monitor Cell Values

In the following Mastering Excel project, you will create a worksheet for Jacques Celestine, President of Jesse Jewelers, which analyzes loan options for a warehouse that the company is considering purchasing. Jacques wants to establish an additional storage facility in the United States, but would like to keep the monthly loan payment below $10,000. You will also assist Mike Connor, the Vice President of Marketing at Jesse Jewelers by adding lookup functions to a Staff Planning Form so that a manager can complete the form quickly. You will also use Formula Auditing to check a workbook for errors. Your completed workbooks will look similar to Figure 4.62.

PROJECT FILES

For Project 4G, you will need the following files:

e04G_Online_Bracelet_Revenue
e04G_Staff_Form
e04G_Warehouse_Loan

You will save your workbooks as:

Lastname_Firstname_4G_Online_Bracelet_Revenue
Lastname_Firstname_4G_Staff_Form
Lastname_Firstname_4G_Warehouse_Loan

PROJECT RESULTS

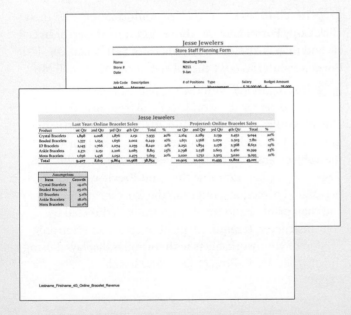

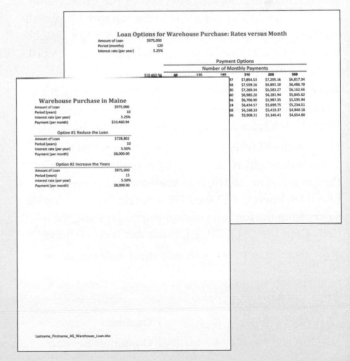

FIGURE 4.62

(Project 4G Warehouse Loan and Staff Lookup Form continues on the next page)

CONTENT-BASED ASSESSMENTS

1 In your student files, locate and **open** the file **e04G_Warehouse_Loan**, and **Save** it in your **Excel Chapter 4** folder as **Lastname_Firstname_4G_Warehouse_Loan** Display the **Warehouse Payment Table** sheet. In cell **B9**, enter rates in decrements of .5% beginning with **7.5%** and ending with **4%** in cell **B16**. Format rates with two decimal places.

2 In cell **B8**, enter a **PMT** function using the information in cells **B2:B4**. Create a **Data Table** in the range **B8:H16** using the information in cells **B2:B4** in which the **Row input cell** is the **Period** and the **Column input cell** is the **Interest rate**. Apply the format from **B8** to the results in the data table. Select the payment option closest to $10,000 per month and format the option with the **Note** cell style.

3 Insert a footer that includes the file name, and document properties that include your firstname and lastname as the **Author**, your course name and section # as the **Subject**, and the tags **warehouse loan** Change the **Orientation** to **Landscape**, center **Horizontally**, and return to **Normal** view. **Print Preview**, **Save**, and then print or submit electronically as directed. **Close** this workbook.

4 Open the file **e04G_Staff_Form**, and **Save** it in your **Excel Chapter 4** folder as **Lastname_Firstname_4G_Staff_Form** On the **Job Information** sheet, select the range **A4:C11**, and then **Sort** the selection by **Job Code**. Name the range **A4:A11** by the name in the top row. Display the **Staffing Plan** sheet, and select the range **A9:A18**. Display the **Data Validation** dialog box, and validate from a **List** using the **Source =Job_Code**

5 Click cell **A9**, and then click **M-MG**. Click cell **B9**, and insert a **VLOOKUP** function that looks up the **Description** from the **Job Information** worksheet using the **Job Code**.

6 With cell **B9** as the active cell, fill the VLOOKUP formula through cell **B18**. In cell **C9**, type **1** as the # of **Positions** and in cell **D9**, type **Management** as the **Type**. In cell **E9**, insert the **VLOOKUP** function that looks up the **Salary** from the **Job Information** worksheet using the **Job Code Copy** the VLOOKUP formula down into cell **E18**.

7 Beginning in cell **A10**, add these staff positions:

8 Delete any unused rows between the last item and the Total row. Sum the **Budget Amount** column and apply the **Total** cell style. Group the worksheets, insert a footer in the left section with the file name, **center** the worksheets **Horizontally**, and change the **Orientation** to **Landscape**. Update the document properties with your name and course name and section #, and add the **Tags planning, staff Print Preview**, ungroup the worksheets, **Save**, and then submit it as directed. **Close** this workbook.

9 From your student files, open **e04G_Online_Bracelet_Revenue**, and then **Save** the file in your **Excel Chapter 4** folder as **Lastname_Firstname_4G_Online_Bracelet_Revenue**

10 Click cell **I5**, and then on the **FORMULAS tab**, click **Trace Precedents**. Click **Error Checking**, and then click **Edit in Formula Bar**. Change *$B$14* to **$B$15** so that the formula is using the Growth Assumption for *Beaded Bracelets*, not for *Crystal Bracelets*.

11 On the **FORMULAS tab**, in the **Formula Auditing group**, click **Error Checking**. In cell **M6**, notice the formula is trying to divide by cell **L10**, which is empty. Click **Edit in Formula Bar**, change **10** to **9** and then in the **Error Checking** dialog box, click **Resume**.

12 In cell **F7**, examine the error information, and then click **Copy Formula from Above**. Examine the error in cell **J8**, and then click **Copy Formula from Left**. Click **OK**. Use **Format Painter** to copy the format in cell **M5** to cell **M6**.

13 Insert a footer with the file name in the **left section** and **center** the worksheet **Horizontally**. To the **Document Properties**, add your firstname and lastname as the **Author**, add your course name and section # as the **Subject**, and add **online bracelet revenue** as the **Tags**. Display and examine the **Print Preview**, make any necessary corrections, ungroup the worksheets, **Save**, and then print or submit electronically as directed by your instructor. If required, print or create an electronic version of your worksheets with formulas displayed using the instructions in Project 1A. **Close** Excel.

Item	# of Positions	Type
C-CASH	3	Cashier
C-CSA	1	Customer Service
M-AMG	3	Management

END | You have completed Project 4G

CONTENT-BASED ASSESSMENTS

Apply a combination of the 4A and 4B skills.

| GO! Fix It | Project 4H Bag Costs by Quarter | Online |

| GO! Make It | Project 4I Arizona Store Loan | Online |

| GO! Solve It | Project 4J Store Furnishings | Online |

| GO! Solve It | Project 4K Order Form |

PROJECT FILES

For Project 4K, you will need the following file:

e04K_Order_Form

You will save your workbook as:

Lastname_Firstname_4K_Order_Form

Open the file **e04K_Order_Form** and save it as **Lastname_Firstname_4K_Order_Form**
Prepare the Product Information worksheet for a VLOOKUP function by sorting the items by Style Code, and then create a named range for the Style Code information. On the Order Form worksheet, using the named range, set data validation for the Item column. Insert the VLOOKUP function in column B and column E, referencing the appropriate data in the Product Information worksheet. Then enter the data below.

Item	Description	Quantity	Color
C-S		12	White
C-T		15	Natural
M-MC		25	Assorted
M-CF		50	Green

Delete the unused row. Construct formulas to total the order, and then apply appropriate financial formatting. On both sheets, include your file name in the footer, add appropriate properties, and then submit them as directed.

CONTENT-BASED ASSESSMENTS

Performance Level

Performance Criteria		Exemplary	Proficient	Developing
	Use Lookup Functions	The VLOOKUP function correctly looks up data on the Validation List.	The VLOOKUP function looks up some but not all data on the Validation List.	The VLOOKUP function does not look up any of the correct information.
	Validate Data	The Validation List is sorted correctly and used on the order form.	The Validation List was sorted, but not used on the order form.	The Validation List is not sorted and not used on the order form.
	Calculate and Format the Order Amount	The Order Amount and financial information is properly calculated and formatted.	Some, but not all, of the Order Amount and financial information is properly calculated and formatted.	Incorrect formulas and/or incorrect financial formatting were applied in most of the cells.

END | You have completed Project 4K

OUTCOMES-BASED ASSESSMENTS

RUBRIC

The following outcomes-based assessments are open-ended assessments. That is, there is no specific correct result; your result will depend on your approach to the information provided. Make Professional Quality your goal. Use the following scoring rubric to guide you in how to approach the problem and then to evaluate how well your approach solves the problem.

The criteria—Software Mastery, Content, Format and Layout, and Process—represent the knowledge and skills you have gained that you can apply to solving the problem. The levels of performance—Professional Quality, Approaching Professional Quality, or Needs Quality Improvements—help you and your instructor evaluate your result.

	Your completed project is of Professional Quality if you:	Your completed project is Approaching Professional Quality if you:	Your completed project Needs Quality Improvements if you:
1-Software Mastery	Choose and apply the most appropriate skills, tools, and features and identify efficient methods to solve the problem.	Choose and apply some appropriate skills, tools, and features, but not in the most efficient manner.	Choose inappropriate skills, tools, or features, or are inefficient in solving the problem.
2-Content	Construct a solution that is clear and well organized, contains content that is accurate, appropriate to the audience and purpose, and is complete. Provide a solution that contains no errors in spelling, grammar, or style.	Construct a solution in which some components are unclear, poorly organized, inconsistent, or incomplete. Misjudge the needs of the audience. Have some errors in spelling, grammar, or style, but the errors do not detract from comprehension.	Construct a solution that is unclear, incomplete, or poorly organized; contains some inaccurate or inappropriate content; and contains many errors in spelling, grammar, or style. Do not solve the problem.
3-Format & Layout	Format and arrange all elements to communicate information and ideas, clarify function, illustrate relationships, and indicate relative importance.	Apply appropriate format and layout features to some elements, but not others. Overuse features, causing minor distraction.	Apply format and layout that does not communicate information or ideas clearly. Do not use format and layout features to clarify function, illustrate relationships, or indicate relative importance. Use available features excessively, causing distraction.
4-Process	Use an organized approach that integrates planning, development, self-assessment, revision, and reflection.	Demonstrate an organized approach in some areas, but not others; or, use an insufficient process of organization throughout.	Do not use an organized approach to solve the problem.

OUTCOMES-BASED ASSESSMENTS

GO! Think	Project 4L Key Chains

PROJECT FILES

For Project 4L, you will need the following file:

e04L_Key_Chains

You will save your workbook as:

Lastname_Firstname_4L_Key_Chains

From your student files, open the file **e04L_Key_Chains**, and then save it in your chapter folder as **Lastname_Firstname_4L_Key_Chains** So that order takers do not have to type the Style Code, Description, and Unit Price in the Order Form worksheet, use the information on the Product Information sheet to create a validation list for the Item and then insert a VLOOKUP function in the Description and Unit Price columns. Then create an order for two of the Plush Animal Key Chains (K-S) and two of the Classic Key Chains (M-TF). Delete unused rows, create appropriate totals, apply financial formatting, and then save and submit it as directed.

END | You have completed Project 4L

Build from Scratch

GO! Think	Project 4M Delivery Van Purchase	Online

Build from Scratch

You and GO!	Project 4N Vehicle Loan	Online

Build from Scratch

Managing Large Workbooks and Using Advanced Sorting and Filtering

GO! to Work
Video E5

5

PROJECT 5A

OUTCOMES
Manage large workbooks, create attractive workbooks, and save workbooks to share with others.

OBJECTIVES

1. Navigate and Manage Large Worksheets
2. Enhance Worksheets with Themes and Styles
3. Format a Worksheet to Share with Others
4. Save Excel Data in Other File Formats

PROJECT 5B

OUTCOMES
Analyze information in a database format using advanced sort, filter, subtotaling, and outlining.

OBJECTIVES

5. Use Advanced Sort Techniques
6. Use Custom and Advanced Filters
7. Subtotal, Outline, and Group a List of Data

Stephen Coburn/Fotolia

In This Chapter

In this chapter, you will navigate within a large worksheet, insert a hyperlink in a worksheet, and save a worksheet as a webpage or other file formats that you can share with others. You will practice applying and modifying themes, styles, lines, and borders to enhance the format of your worksheets. You will use Excel's advanced table features and database capabilities to organize data in a useful manner. You will use advanced sorting, sorting on multiple columns, and custom filtering to compare subsets of data. You will also limit data to display records that meet one or more specific conditions, add subtotals, and outline data.

The projects in this chapter relate to **Laurel College**. The college offers this diverse geographic area in Pennsylvania a wide range of academic and career programs, including associate degrees, certificate programs, and noncredit continuing education courses. Over 2,100 faculty and staff make student success a top priority. The college makes positive contributions to the community through cultural and athletic programs and partnerships with businesses and nonprofit organizations. The college also provides industry-specific training programs for local businesses through its Economic Development Center.

Large Worksheet for a Class Schedule

PROJECT ACTIVITIES

In Activities 5.01 through 5.13, you will assist Michael Schaeffler, Vice President, Instruction, in formatting and navigating a large worksheet that lists the class schedule for the Business Office Systems and Computer Information Systems departments at Laurel College. You will also save Excel data in other file formats. The worksheets in your completed workbooks will look similar to Figure 5.1.

PROJECT FILES

For Project 5A, you will need the following files:

e05A_Class_Schedule
e05A_Faculty_Contacts
e05A_Fall_Classes
e05A_Teaching_Requests

You will save your workbooks as:

Lastname_Firstname_5A_Class_Schedule
Lastname_Firstname_5A_Faculty_Contacts
Lastname_Firstname_5A_Fall_PDF
Lastname_Firstname_5A_Fall_XPS
Lastname_Firstname_5A_Schedule_CVS
Lastname_Firstname_5A_Schedule_Webpage

PROJECT RESULTS

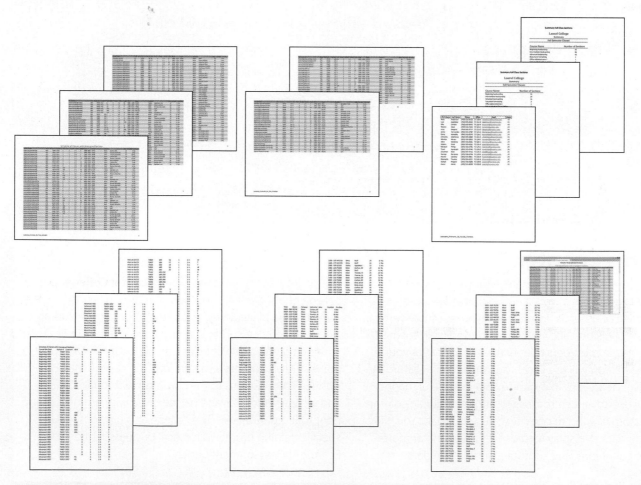

FIGURE 5.1 Project 5A Large Worksheet for a Class Schedule

Objective 1   Navigate and Manage Large Worksheets

Video E5-1

Because you cannot view all the columns and rows of a large worksheet on your screen at one time, Excel provides features that help you control the screen display and navigate the worksheet so you can locate information quickly. For example, you can hide columns or use the *Freeze Panes* command, which sets the column and row titles so that they remain on the screen while you scroll. The locked rows and columns become separate *panes*—portions of a worksheet window bounded by and separated from other portions by vertical or horizontal lines.

You can also use the *Find* command to find and select specific text, formatting, or a type of information within the workbook quickly.

Activity 5.01 | Using the Go To Special Command

Use the *Go To Special* command to move to cells that have special characteristics, for example, to cells that are blank or to cells that contain constants, as opposed to formulas.

1 ▶ Start Excel. From your student files, open **e05A_Class_Schedule**. In your storage location, create a new folder named **Excel Chapter 5** and then press F12 and **Save** the file as **Lastname_Firstname_5A_Class_Schedule**

This worksheet lists the computer courses that are available for the upcoming semester in three college departments.

2 ▶ On the **HOME tab,** in the **Editing group,** click **Find & Select,** and then click **Go To Special.** Compare your screen with Figure 5.2.

In the Go To Special dialog box, you can click an option button to move to cells that contain the special options listed.

FIGURE 5.2

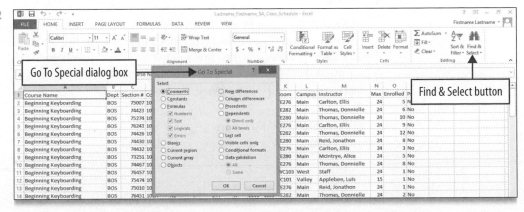

ANOTHER WAY   Press Ctrl + G, and then in the lower left corner of the dialog box, click the Special button.

3 In the first column, click **Blanks**, and then click **OK**.

All blank cells in the active area of the worksheet are located and selected, and the first blank cell—J124—is active. The active area is the area of the worksheet that contains data or has contained data—it does not include any empty cells that have not been used in this worksheet. Cell J124 is missing the time for a Linux/UNIX class held on Tuesday.

4 Point to cell **J124** and right-click. On the mini toolbar, click the **Fill Color arrow** 🎨▾ and then under **Standard Colors**, click the fourth color—**Yellow**—to highlight the blank cells.

This missing information must be researched before a time can be entered, and the yellow fill color will help locate this cell later, when the correct time for the class is determined.

5 Scroll down and locate the other two cells identified as blank—**J148** and **J160**— **Save** your workbook and compare your screen with Figure 5.3.

When you initiated the Go To Special command for Blank cells, Excel located and selected *all* blank cells in the active area. As a result, the formatting you applied to the first blank cell, yellow fill, was applied to all the selected cells.

FIGURE 5.3

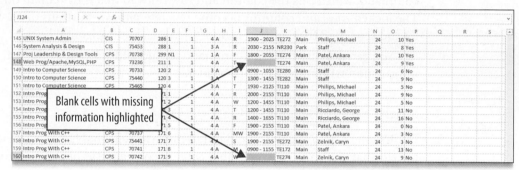

Activity 5.02 | Hiding Columns

In a large worksheet, you can hide columns that are not necessary for the immediate task, and then unhide them later. You can also hide columns or rows to control the data that will print or to remove confidential information from view—hidden data does not print. For example, to create a summary report, you can hide the columns between the row titles and the totals column, and the hidden columns would not display on the printed worksheet, resulting in a summary report.

1 Press ⌃Ctrl + Home. From the column heading area, select **columns E:H**.

2 Right-click over the selected columns, and then click **Hide**. Compare your screen with Figure 5.4.

Columns E, F, G, and H are hidden from view—the column headings skip from D to I. A dark line between columns D and I indicates that columns from this location are hidden from view. After you click in another cell, this line will not be visible; however, the column letters provide a visual indication that some columns are hidden from view.

FIGURE 5.4

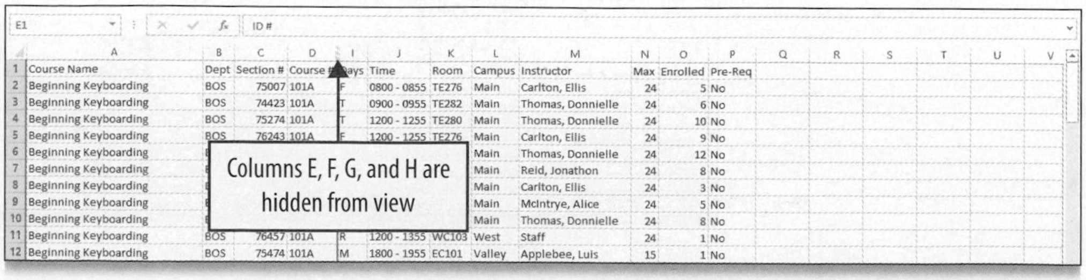

ANOTHER WAY   On the HOME tab, in the Cells group, click the Format button. Under Visibility, point to Hide & Unhide, and
                   then click Hide Columns.

BY TOUCH   Drag to select the columns, tap and hold over the selected columns, and then click Hide.

3 Notice that the line between the **column D heading** and the **column I heading** is slightly wider,
indicating hidden columns. Press Ctrl + Home, and then **Save** your workbook.

Activity 5.03 | Using the Go To Command

Use the *Go To* command to move to a specific cell or range of cells in a large worksheet.

1 On the **HOME tab**, in the **Editing group**, click **Find & Select**, and then click **Go To**. In the
Go To dialog box, with the insertion point blinking in the **Reference** box, type **m172** and then
click **OK**.

2 With cell **M172** active, on the **FORMULAS tab**, in the **Functions Library group**, click **More
Functions**, point to **Statistical**, scroll down the list, and then click **COUNTIF**. As the **Range**,
type **m2:m170** and as the **Criteria**, type **Staff** Click **OK**. Compare your screen with Figure 5.5.

Your result is 47, indicating that 47 courses still indicate *Staff* and need an instructor assigned.

FIGURE 5.5

160	Intro Prog With C++	CPS	70742	171	W		TE274	Main	Zelnik, Caryn	24	9 No
161	Intro Prog With C++	CPS	75458	171	R	0900 - 1255	TI112	Main	Zelnik, Caryn	24	6 No
162	Intro To Visual Basic	CPS	76875	185	T	1500 - 1655	TI130	Main	Zelnik, Caryn	24	9 No
163	Intro To Visual Basic	CPS	76807	185	MW	1500 - 1655	TI110	Main	Staff	24	5 No
164	Intro To Visual Basic	CPS	76822	185	MW	1730 - 1925	TI110	Main	Staff	24	9 No
165	Intro To Visual Basic	CPS	76823	185	MW	1730 - 1925	TI110	Main	Philips, Michael	24	5 No
166	Intro To Visual Basic	CPS	76824	185	T	1900 - 2155	TI112	Main	Philips, Michael	24	11 No
167	Intro to Oracle SQL & PL/SQL	CPS	76825	271	T	1900 - 2155	TE176	Main	Staff	24	16 No
168	Intro to Oracle SQL & PL/SQL	CPS	76826	271	W	1730 - 1855	TI102	Main	Staff	24	0 No
169	Intro to Oracle SQL & PL/SQL	CPS	76827	271	M	1230 - 1525	TI130	Main	Staff	24	3 No
170	Intro to Oracle Developer	CPS	76828	272	F	1730 - 2025	TI102	Main	Staff	24	3 No
171											
172										47	

Formula result is 47

3 In cell **J172**, type **Unassigned classes** and press Enter.

4 Press Ctrl + Home, and then **Save** your workbook.

Activity 5.04 | Arranging Multiple Workbooks and Splitting Worksheets

If you need to refer to information in one workbook while you have another workbook open,
you can arrange the window to display sheets from more than one workbook—instead of jumping
back and forth between the two workbooks from the taskbar. This is accomplished by using the
Arrange All command, which tiles all open Excel windows on the screen. Additionally, you can
view separate parts of the *same* worksheet on your screen by using the *Split* command, which
splits the window into multiple resizable panes to view distant parts of your worksheet at once.

1 Press Ctrl + F12 to display the **Open** dialog box, and then from your student files, open the
file **e05A_Teaching_Requests**.

The e05A_Teaching_Requests file opens, and your Lastname_Firstname_5A_Class_Schedule
file is no longer visible on your screen. This worksheet contains a list of instructors who submitted
requests for classes they would like to teach. You do not need to save this file; it is for reference only.

2 On the **VIEW tab**, in the **Window group**, click **Switch Windows**, and, click your
Lastname_Firstname_5A_Class_Schedule file to make it the active worksheet.

3 On the **VIEW tab**, in the **Window group**, click **Arrange All**. Click **Horizontal** and then compare
your screen with Figure 5.6.

Here, in the Arrange Windows dialog box, you can control how two or more worksheets from
multiple open workbooks are arranged on the screen.

FIGURE 5.6

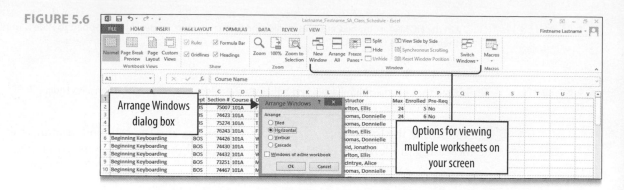

Arrange Windows dialog box

Options for viewing multiple worksheets on your screen

---

4 ▶ Click **OK**. Compare your screen with Figure 5.7.

The screen is split horizontally, and the e05A_Teaching_Requests worksheet displays below your Lastname_Firstname_5A_Class_Schedule worksheet. The active window title bar displays the file name in a darker shade of gray, and the row and column headings are shaded to indicate active cells. When multiple worksheets are open on the screen, only one is active at a time. To activate a worksheet, click anywhere on the worksheet or click the worksheet's title bar.

FIGURE 5.7

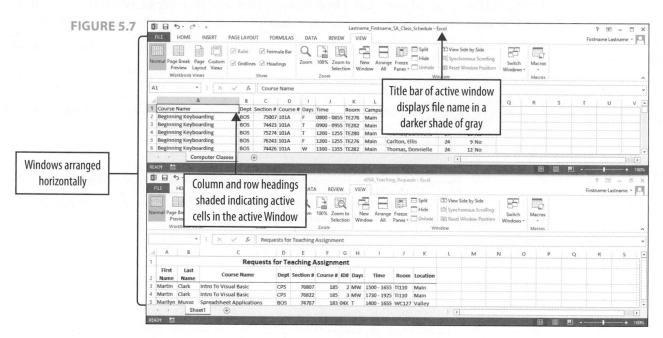

Windows arranged horizontally

Title bar of active window displays file name in a darker shade of gray

Column and row headings shaded indicating active cells in the active Window

---

5 ▶ Press Ctrl + End to move to cell **P172**, which is now the end of the active area of the worksheet.

6 ▶ Click cell **A172**. On the **VIEW tab**, in the **Window group**, click **Split** to split this upper window horizontally at row 172. Compare your screen with Figure 5.8.

A light gray horizontal bar displays at the top of row 172, and two sets of vertical scroll bars display in the Lastname_Firstname_5A_Class_Schedule worksheet—one in each of the two worksheet panes displayed in this window. You can drag the horizontal bar up slightly to make the lower pane easier to see.

FIGURE 5.8

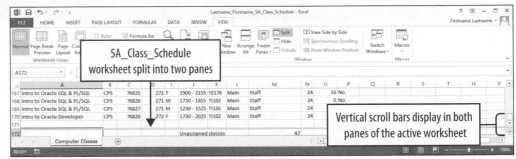

5A_Class_Schedule worksheet split into two panes

Vertical scroll bars display in both panes of the active worksheet

7 Above the **split bar**, click in any cell in **column C**. Press Ctrl + F to display the **Find tab** of the **Find and Replace** dialog box.

Column C lists the Section # for each class. This is a unique number that identifies each class.

 BY TOUCH   On the HOME tab, in the Editing group, tap Find.

8 Drag the title bar of the dialog box into the upper right area of your screen. Then, in the lower half of your screen, look at the first request in the **e05A_Teaching_Requests** worksheet, which is from *Martin Clark* to teach *Intro to Visual Basic Section # 76807*. In the **Find what** box, type **76807** so that you can locate the course in the **Lastname_Firstname_5A_Class_Schedule** worksheet.

9 Click **Find Next**, be sure that you can see the **Name Box**, and then compare your screen with Figure 5.9.

Section # 76807 is located and selected in cell C163 of the Class Schedule worksheet.

FIGURE 5.9

Name Box visible, indicates cell C163

Find and Replace dialog box

10 In your **Lastname_Firstname_5A_Class_Schedule** worksheet, click in cell **M163**, type **Clark, Martin** to delete *Staff* and assign the class to Mr. Clark. Press Enter.

The class is assigned to Mr. Clark, and the number of unassigned classes, which you can view below the split bar, goes down by one, to 46. Use the Split command when you need to see two distant parts of the same worksheet simultaneously.

11 In the **e05A_Teaching_Requests** worksheet, look at **row 4** and notice that the next request, also from Mr. Clark, is to teach *Section # 76822*.

This class is listed in the next row of your Lastname_Firstname_5A_Class_Schedule worksheet—row 164.

12 In cell **M164**, type **Clark, Martin** and press Enter. Notice below the split bar that the number of unassigned classes in cell **M172** goes down to *45*.

13 In the **Find and Replace** dialog box, in the **Find what** box, type **74787** which is the next requested Section #, and then click **Find Next**.

Section # 74787 in cell C66 is selected. Marilyn Musso has requested to teach this class.

14 Click cell **M66**, type **Musso, Marilyn** and press Enter; notice that the unassigned number is now *44*.

15 In the **e05A_teaching_Requests** worksheet in the lower pane, scroll down to view the remaining teaching requests. Click the title bar of your **Lastname_Firstname_5A_Class_Schedule** worksheet to make it active. In the **Find and Replace** dialog box, in the **Find what** box, type **75451** which is the next requested Section #, and then click **Find Next**.

Section # 75451 in cell C78 is selected. Marilyn Musso has requested to teach this class also.

16 In cell **M78**, type **Musso, Marilyn** and press Enter; *43* classes remain unassigned.

17 Continue to use the **Find and Replace** dialog box to locate the remaining two **Section #s** listed in the **e05A_Teaching_Requests** worksheet, and enter the appropriate instructor name for each class in **column M** of your **Lastname_Firstname_5A_Class_Schedule** worksheet.

18 In the **Find and Replace** dialog box, click **Close**. In cell **M172**, notice that *41* classes remain unassigned.

19 Click any cell in the **e05A_Teaching_Requests** worksheet to make it the active sheet. Compare your screen with Figure 5.10.

FIGURE 5.10

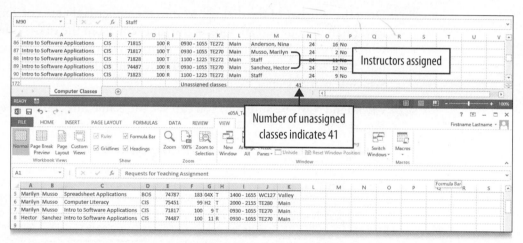

20 Click **Close** ⊠ to close the **e05A_Teaching_Requests** workbook. Then, on the title bar of your **Lastname_Firstname_5A_Class_Schedule** workbook, click **Maximize** ▣ to restore the size of the worksheet to its full size.

21 On the **VIEW tab**, in the **Window group**, click **Split** to remove the split.

22 Press Ctrl + Home. From the **column heading area**, select **columns D:I**—recall that columns E:H are still hidden. Right-click over the selected area, and then click **Unhide**.

To redisplay hidden columns, first select the columns on either side of the hidden columns—columns D and I in this instance.

23 Press Ctrl + Home, and then **Save** 🖫 your workbook.

Objective 2 Enhance Worksheets with Themes and Styles

Video E5-2

Worksheets used to be uninteresting grids of columns and rows viewed primarily on paper by accountants and managers. Now individuals may commonly use worksheets to communicate information both within an organization and to the public. A worksheet might be seen by individuals in an email, in a PowerPoint presentation, or in public blogs and publications. Accordingly, you will want to use some creative elements when preparing your worksheets.

A *theme* is a predesigned set of colors, fonts, lines, and fill effects that look good together and that can be applied to your entire Office 2013 file or to specific items. A theme combines two sets of fonts—one for text and one for headings. In the default Office theme, Calibri Light is the font for headings and Calibri is the font for body text.

In Excel, the applied theme has a set of complimentary *cell styles*—a defined set of formatting characteristics, such as fonts, font sizes, number formats, cell borders, and cell shading. The applied theme also has a set of complimentary table styles for data that you format as a table.

You can create your own themes, cells styles, and table styles.

Activity 5.05 | Changing and Customizing a Workbook Theme

1 Point to the **row 1 heading** to display the ⇥ pointer, right-click, and then click **Insert** to insert a new blank row. In cell **A1**, type **Schedule of Classes with Unassigned Sections** and press Enter. On the **HOME tab**, **Merge & Center** this title across the range **A1:P1**, and then apply the **Title** cell style.

2 On the **PAGE LAYOUT tab**, in the **Themes group**, click **Themes**. Compare your screen with Figure 5.11.

> The gallery of predesigned themes that come with Microsoft Office displays. Office—the default theme—is selected.

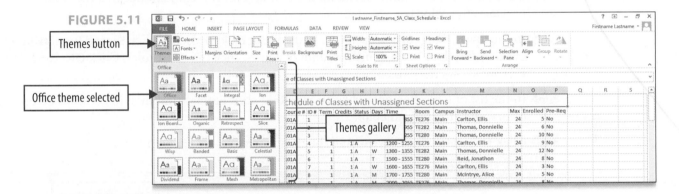

FIGURE 5.11
Themes button
Office theme selected
Themes gallery

3 Point to several of the themes and notice how Live Preview displays the colors and fonts associated with each theme. Then, click the **Ion** theme.

4 In the **Themes group**, point to **Fonts** and read the **ScreenTip**.

> The font associated with the Ion theme for both headings and body text is Century Gothic, but you can customize a theme by mixing the Colors, Fonts, and Effects from any of the supplied themes.

5 Click **Fonts**. If necessary, scroll to the top and click **Office**. Save 🔲 your workbook.

Activity 5.06 | Creating and Applying a Custom Table Style

Excel comes with many predefined table styles, but if none of these meets your needs, you can create and apply a custom table style of your own design. Custom table styles that you create are stored only in the current workbook, so they are not available in other workbooks.

1 On the **HOME tab**, in the **Styles group**, click **Format as Table**. At the bottom, click **New Table Style**.

2 In the **New Table Style** dialog box, in the **Name** box, replace the existing text by typing **Class Schedule**

3 In the list under **Table Element**, click **First Row Stripe**, and then compare your screen with Figure 5.12.

> Here you can select one or more elements of the table, and then customize the format for each element.

FIGURE 5.12

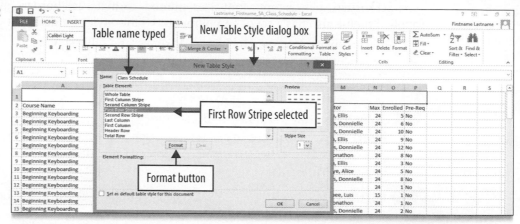

4 Below the list of table elements, click **Format**. In the **Format Cells** dialog box, click the **Fill tab**. In the fourth column of colors, click the second color, and notice that the **Sample** area previews the color you selected.

5 In the lower right corner, click **OK**. In the list of table elements, click **Second Row Stripe**, click **Format**, and then in the fourth column of colors, click the third color. Click **OK**. Notice the **Preview** shows the two colors.

6 In the list of table elements, click **Header Row**, click **Format**, and then in the third column of colors, click the second color.

7 Click **OK**, notice the **Preview**, and then compare your screen with Figure 5.13.

FIGURE 5.13

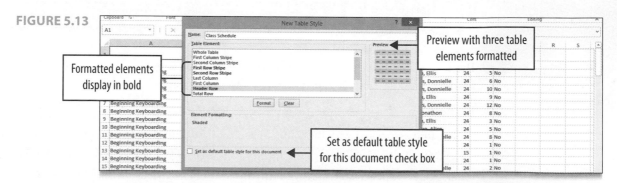

8 In the lower left corner of the dialog box, click to select the check box **Set as default table style for this document**. Click **OK**.

> You must select this check box to make your table style available in the gallery of table styles.

9 Select the range **A2:P171**—do *not* include row 1 in your selection—and then in the **Styles group**, click **Format as Table**. At the top of the gallery, under **Custom**, point to your custom table style to display the **ScreenTip** *Class Schedule*. Compare your screen with Figure 5.14.

FIGURE 5.14

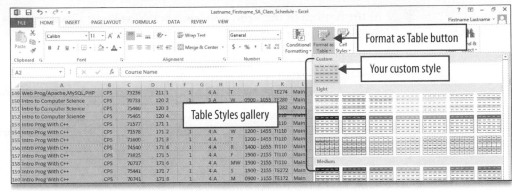

10 ▶ Click your **Class Schedule** table style, and then in the **Format As Table** dialog box, click **OK**. Then, because you do not need to filter the table, in the **Tools group**, click **Convert to Range**, and then click **Yes**.

> If you do not want to work with your data in a table by filtering and sorting, you can convert the table to a normal range to keep the table style formatting that you applied.

11 ▶ Press Ctrl + Home to deselect and move to cell **A1**, and then **Save** 🖫 your workbook.

Objective 3 Format a Worksheet to Share with Others

Video E5-3

You can share a worksheet with others by printing and distributing paper copies, sending it electronically as an Excel file or some other file format, or posting it to the web or to a shared workspace. Regardless of how you distribute the information, a large worksheet will be easier for others to view if you insert appropriate page breaks and repeat column or row titles at the top of each page.

You can also add a *hyperlink* to a worksheet, which, when clicked, takes you to another location in the worksheet, to another file, or to a webpage on the Internet or on your organization's intranet.

Activity 5.07 | Previewing and Modifying Page Breaks

Before you print or electronically distribute a large worksheet, preview it to see where the pages will break across the columns and rows. You can move the page breaks to a column or row that groups the data logically, and you can change the orientation between portrait and landscape if you want to display more rows on the page (portrait) or more columns on the page (landscape). You can also apply *scaling* to the data to force the worksheet into a selected number of pages. Scaling reduces the horizontal and vertical size of the printed data by a percentage or by the number of pages that you specify.

1 ▶ From the column heading area, select **columns A:P**, in the **Cells group**, click **Format**, and then click **AutoFit Column Width**.

🔄 **ANOTHER WAY**   After selecting the columns, in the column heading area, point to any of the column borders and double-click.

2 ▶ Click cell **A1**, and then press Ctrl + F2 to view the **Print Preview**. Notice that as currently formatted, the worksheet will print on eight pages.

3 At the bottom of the **Print Preview**, click **Next Page** ▶ seven times to view the eight pages required to print this worksheet.

As you view each page, notice that pages 5 through 8 display the Time, Room, Campus, Instructor, Max, Enrolled, and Pre-Req columns that relate to the first four pages of the printout. You can see that the printed worksheet will be easier to read if all the information related to a class is on the same page.

4 Return to the worksheet. Click the **VIEW tab**, and then in the **Workbook Views group**, click **Page Break Preview**. Compare your screen with Figure 5.15.

The Page Break Preview window displays blue dashed lines to show where the page breaks are in the current page layout for this worksheet.

FIGURE 5.15

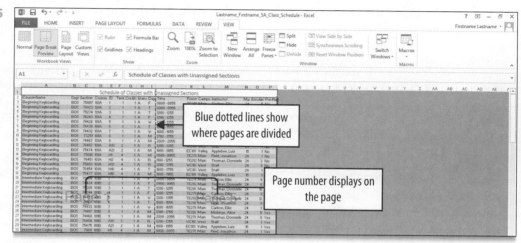

N O T E   **Welcome to Page Break Preview**

The Welcome to Page Break Preview dialog box may display with a message informing you that page breaks can be adjusted by clicking and dragging the breaks with your mouse. If this box displays, click OK to close it.

---

5 Scroll down to view the other pages and see where the page breaks are indicated. Then, in the **Workbook Views group**, click **Normal** to redisplay the worksheet in Normal view.

Dashed lines display at the page break locations on the worksheet.

6 On the **PAGE LAYOUT tab**, in the **Page Setup group**, set the **Orientation** to **Landscape**. Then, in the **Scale to Fit group**, click the **Width arrow**, and then click **1 page**.

In the Scale to Fit group, there are two ways to override the default printout size. In the Scale box, you can specify a scaling factor from between 10% and 400%. Or, you can use the Width and Height arrows to fit the printout to a specified number of pages. To return to a full-size printout after scaling, in the Scale box, type 100 as the percentage.

ANOTHER WAY   On the PAGE LAYOUT tab, in the Page Setup group, click the Dialog Box Launcher to display the Page Setup dialog box.

7 From the **INSERT tab**, insert a footer that includes the file name in the **left section** and the **Page Number** in the **right section**.

It is good practice to insert any headers or footers *before* making the final page break decisions on your worksheet.

8 Click any cell above the footer to exit the footer area. Press Ctrl + F2 to display the **Print Preview**, and at the bottom, notice that the worksheet is now a total of four pages.

> By applying the scaling, each complete row of data will fit on one page.

9 Return to the worksheet, click the **VIEW tab**, and in the **Workbook Views group**, click **Page Break Preview**. Scroll to view the page break between **Page 2** and **Page 3**.

10 If necessary, scroll left to view column A. Point to the horizontal page break line between **Page 2** and **Page 3**. When the vertical resize pointer ⬍ displays, drag the line up between **row 77** and **row 78**; this will break the pages between the BOS courses and the CIS courses. Compare your screen with Figure 5.16.

FIGURE 5.16

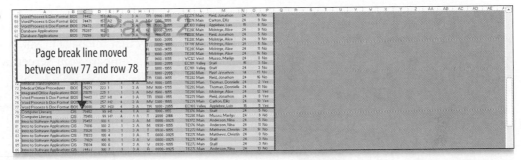

11 Scroll down to view the page break line between **Page 4** and **Page 5**. Drag the line up to break the page between **row 147** and **row 148**, which is the end of the CIS section.

12 Display the **Print Preview**. At the bottom of the window, click **Next Page** ▶ four times to scroll through the five pages that will print.

> With the new page breaks that you have inserted, the pages will break when a new Department begins.

ALERT! **Page Breaks Differ**

The default printer and screen resolution on your computer may cause the page breaks to differ from those in this text.

---

13 Return ⊖ to the worksheet. On the **VIEW tab**, in the **Workbook Views group**, click **Normal** to redisplay the worksheet in Normal view. Press Ctrl + Home, and then click **Save** 🖫.

Activity 5.08 | Repeating Column or Row Titles

When your worksheet layout spans multiple pages, you will typically want to repeat the column titles on each page. If your worksheet is wider than one page, you will also want to repeat the row titles on each page.

1 Display the **Print Preview** scroll through the pages, and notice that the column titles display only on the first page. Return ⊖ to the worksheet.

> Repeating the column titles on each page will make it easier to understand and read the information on the pages.

2 On the **PAGE LAYOUT tab**, in the **Page Setup group**, click **Print Titles** to display the **Sheet tab** of the **Page Setup** dialog box.

> Here you can select rows to repeat at the top of each page and columns to repeat at the left of each page.

3 Under **Print titles**, click in the **Rows to repeat at top** box, and then from the **row heading area**, select **row 2**. Compare your screen with Figure 5.17.

> A moving border surrounds row 2, and the mouse pointer displays as a black select row arrow. The absolute reference $2:$2 displays in the Rows to repeat at top box.

FIGURE 5.17

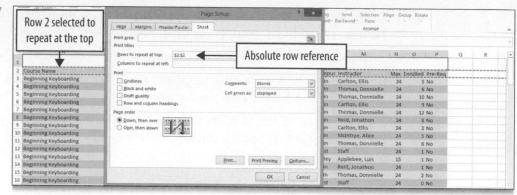

Row 2 selected to repeat at the top

Absolute row reference

4 Click **OK**. Display the **Print Preview**, scroll through the pages and notice that the column titles display at the top of each page. Verify that the page breaks are still located between each department. Display **Page 2**, and then compare your screen with Figure 5.18. **Save** your worksheet.

FIGURE 5.18

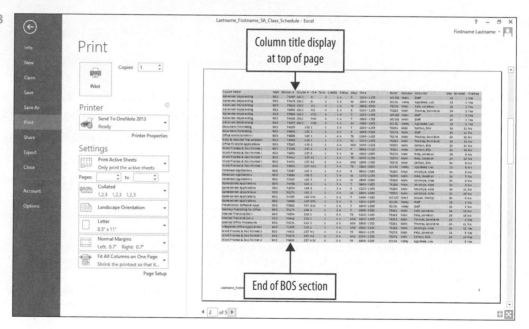

Column title display at top of page

End of BOS section

NOTE | **To Print a Multi-Sheet Workbook**

To print all the pages in a multi-page workbook, either group the sheets, or under Settings, select Print Entire Workbook.

Activity 5.09 | **Inserting a Hyperlink in a Worksheet**

When a hyperlink is colored and underlined text that you can click to go to a file, a location in a file, a webpage on the Internet, or a webpage on your organization's intranet. Hyperlinks can be attached to text or to graphics. In this activity, you will add a hyperlink that will open a file containing the contact information for instructors.

1 Click cell **M2**. On the **INSERT tab**, in the **Links group**, click **Hyperlink** to display the **Insert Hyperlink** dialog box.

2 Under **Link to**, if necessary, click **Existing File or Web Page**. Click the **Look in arrow**, navigate to your student files, and then select the file **e05A_Faculty_Contacts**, which contains faculty contact information.

3 In the upper right corner of the **Insert Hyperlink** dialog box, click **ScreenTip**.

4 In the **Set Hyperlink ScreenTip** dialog box, in the **ScreenTip text** box, type **Click here for contact information** Compare your dialog box with Figure 5.19.

When you point to the hyperlink on the worksheet, this is the text of the ScreenTip that will display.

FIGURE 5.19

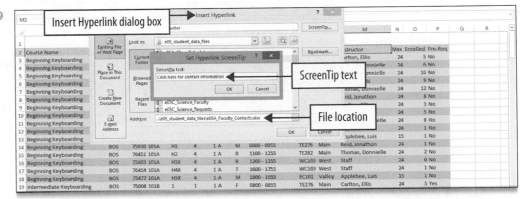

5 Click **OK** in the **Set Hyperlink ScreenTip** dialog box, and then click **OK** in the **Insert Hyperlink** dialog box.

In the Ion theme, the color for a hyperlink is light blue.

6 Point to the **Instructor hyperlink** and read the **ScreenTip** that displays. Compare your screen with Figure 5.20.

When you point to the hyperlink, the Link Select pointer 🖑 displays and the ScreenTip text displays.

FIGURE 5.20

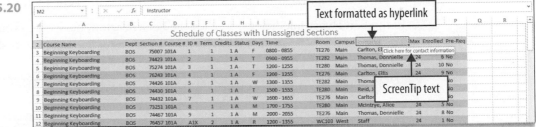

7 Click the **Instructor hyperlink**.

The e05A_Faculty_Contacts file opens in a new window and displays the contact information.

8 Click **Close** ⊠ to close the **e05A_Faculty_Contacts** file and redisplay your **Lastname_Firstname_5A_Class_Schedule** worksheet.

9 On the **PAGE LAYOUT** tab, in the **Themes group**, click the **Colors arrow**. At the bottom of the page, click **Customize Colors**. At the bottom of the dialog box, locate the colors for **Hyperlink** and **Followed Hyperlink**. Compare your screen with Figure 5.21.

Each color scheme uses a set of colors for a hyperlink and for a hyperlink that has been clicked (followed) one time. Now that you have followed your inserted hyperlink one time, the text displays in the Followed Hyperlink color. Here you can also change the colors for any of the colors associated with a theme.

FIGURE 5.21

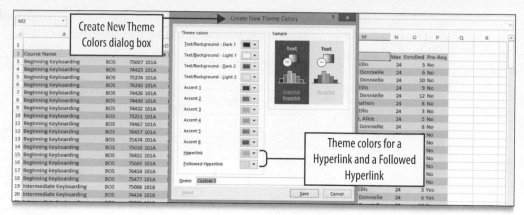

10 In the lower corner of the dialog box, click **Cancel**, and then **Save** 🖫 your workbook.

Activity 5.10 | Modifying a Hyperlink

If the file to which the hyperlink refers is moved or renamed, or a webpage to which a hyperlink refers gets a new address, the hyperlink must be modified to reflect the change.

1 In cell **M2**, click the **Instructor hyperlink** to open the **e05A_Faculty_Contacts** workbook.

2 Save this file in your **Excel Chapter 5** folder as **Lastname_Firstname_5A_Faculty_Contacts**

3 Insert a footer in the **left section** with the file name, return to **Normal** view, click **Save** 🖫, and then click **Close** ⊠ to close your **Lastname_Firstname_5A_Faculty_Contacts** file and redisplay your **Lastname_Firstname_5A_Class_Schedule** file.

4 Right-click cell **M2**—the Instructor hyperlink—and then click **Edit Hyperlink**.

5 In the **Edit Hyperlink** dialog box, click the **Look in arrow**, navigate to your **Excel Chapter 5** folder, and then select your **Lastname_Firstname_5A_Faculty_Contacts** file, as shown in Figure 5.22.

FIGURE 5.22

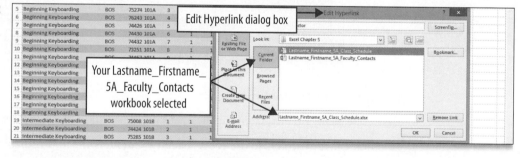

6 Click **OK**. In cell **M2**, click the hyperlinked text—**Instructor**.

Verify that your Lastname_Firstname_5A_Faculty_Contacts file opens, and your hyperlink is now up to date.

7 Click **Close** ⊠ to close **Lastname_Firstname_5A_Faculty_Contacts**.

8 Click the **FILE tab** to display **Backstage** view. On the right, at the bottom of the **Properties** list, click **Show All Properties**. On the list of **Properties**, in the **Tags** box, type **class schedule** In the **Subject** box, type your course name and section #. Under **Related People**, be sure that your name displays as the author. If necessary, right-click the author name, click Edit Property, type your name, click outside of the Edit person dialog box, and then click OK.

9 Click **Save**, leave the **Lastname_Firstname_5A_Class_Schedule** workbook open.

By default, Excel 2013 files are saved in the Excel Workbook file format with the *.xlsx file name extension*, which is a set of characters that helps your Windows operating system understand what kind of information is in a file and what program should open it.

Using the Save As command, you can choose to save an Excel file in another file format from the Save as type list. Some frequently used file formats are: Excel 97-2003 Workbook, Excel Template, Single File Web Page, Web Page, Excel Macro-Enabled Workbook, Text (Tab Delimited), and CSV (Comma Delimited).

For the purpose of posting Excel data to a website or transferring data to other applications, you can save your Excel file in a variety of other file formats. For example, saving an Excel worksheet as a *tab delimited text file* separates the cells of each row with tab characters. Saving an Excel worksheet as a *CSV (comma separated values) file* separates the cells of each row with commas. This type of file is also referred to as a *comma delimited file*. Text formats are commonly used to import data into a database program.

You can also save an Excel file in an electronic format that is easy to read for the viewer of the workbook. Such files are not easily modified and are considered to be an electronic printed version of the worksheet.

You can also add a hyperlink to a worksheet, which, when clicked, takes you to another location in the worksheet, to another file, or to a webpage on the Internet or on your organization's intranet.

Activity 5.11 | Viewing and Saving a Workbook as a Web Page

Before you save a worksheet as a webpage, it is a good idea to view it as a webpage to see how it will display. When saving a multiple-page workbook as a webpage, all of the worksheets are available and can be accessed. You can also save a single worksheet as a webpage. Excel changes the contents of the worksheet into *HTML (Hypertext Markup Language)*, which is a language web browsers can interpret, when you save a worksheet as a webpage. In this activity, you will save and publish a worksheet as a webpage.

1 Be sure your **Lastname_Firstname_5A_Class_Schedule** workbook is open and displayed on your screen. Press F12 to display the **Save As** dialog box, navigate to your **Excel Chapter 5** folder, in the lower portion of the dialog box, click the **Save as type arrow**, and then click **Web Page**.

Your Excel files no longer display in the dialog box, because only files with the type Web Page are visible. The file type changes to Web Page and additional web-based options display below.

2 In the lower portion of the dialog box, click **Change Title**.

The text that you type here will become the title when the file displays as a webpage.

3 In the **Enter Text** dialog box, in the **Page title** box, using your own name, type **Computer Courses Lastname Firstname** Compare your screen with Figure 5.23.

FIGURE 5.23

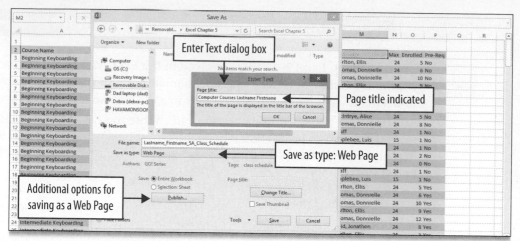

4 In the **Enter Text** dialog box, click **OK**, and notice that in the **Page title** box, your typed text displays.

5 In the **Save As** dialog box, click **Publish**.

6 In the **Publish as Web Page** dialog box, click the **Choose arrow**, notice the objects that can be published as a webpage, and then click **Items on Computer Classes**—recall that the worksheet name is *Computer Classes*. In the lower left corner, click to select (place a check mark in) the **Open published web page in browser** check box. Compare your screen with Figure 5.24.

> Under Item to publish, you can choose which elements to include. You can select the entire workbook, a specific worksheet in the workbook, a range of cells, or previously published items that you are modifying. The *Open published web page in browser* selection ensures that the Internet browser software, for example Internet Explorer, will automatically start and display the page.

FIGURE 5.24

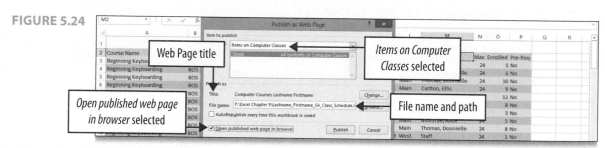

7 Click **Browse** to display the **Publish As** dialog box.

8 If necessary, navigate to your **Excel Chapter 5** folder. In the **File name** box, type **Lastname_Firstname_5A_Schedule_Webpage** Compare your screen with Figure 5.25.

FIGURE 5.25

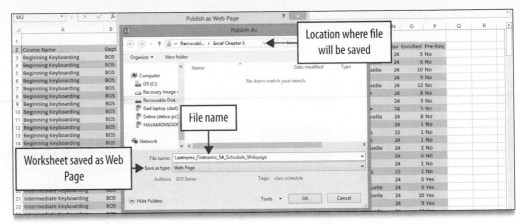

9 ▶ Click **OK**, and then on the **Publish as Web Page** dialog box, click **Publish**. Compare your screen with Figure 5.26.

> The webpage is saved in your selected folder, and the Class Schedule file opens in your default Internet browser. The browser title bar displays the text you typed in the Enter Text dialog box.

FIGURE 5.26

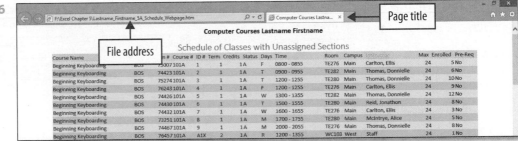

10 ▶ If you are instructed to print your webpage on paper, consult the instructions to print from your specific browser software.

> Your printed results will vary depending on which browser software you are using. Do not be concerned about the printout; webpages are intended for viewing, not printing.

11 ▶ On the browser title bar, click **Close** [X].

Activity 5.12 | Saving Excel Data in CSV File Format

You can save an Excel worksheet as a CSV file, which saves the contents of the cells by placing commas between them and an end-of-paragraph mark at the end of each row.

1 ▶ With your **Lastname_Firstname_5A_Class_Schedule** workbook open, display the **Save As** dialog box, click the **Save as type arrow**, and then click **CSV (Comma delimited)**. Be sure you save the file in your **Excel Chapter 5** folder. In the **File name** box, using your own name, type **Lastname_Firstname_5A_Schedule_CSV** Compare your screen with Figure 5.27.

> Your Excel files no longer display, because only CSV files are displayed.

FIGURE 5.27

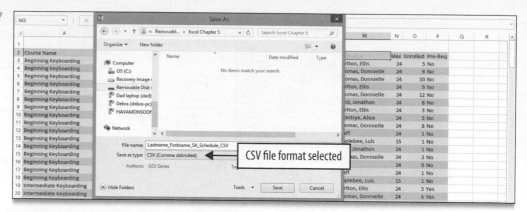

CSV file format selected

2 ▶ Click **Save**. Compare your screen with Figure 5.28.

A dialog box displays to inform you that some features of the file may not be compatible with the CSV format. Features such as merged cells and formatting are lost. You can save the file and leave out incompatible features by clicking Yes, preserve the file in an Excel format by clicking No, or see what might be lost by clicking Help.

FIGURE 5.28

Three options displayed

3 ▶ Click **Yes** to keep the CSV format.

The file is saved in the new format. The new file name displays in the title bar. If file extensions—the three letters that identify the type of files—are displayed on your computer, you will also see .csv after the file name.

4 ▶ **Close** ❌ your **Lastname_Firstname_5A_Schedule_CSV** file. Click **Save** to save changes, and then click **Yes** to acknowledge the warning message.

Activity 5.13 | Saving Excel Data as a PDF or XPS File

You can create portable documents to share across applications and platforms with accurate visual representations. To publish a document and ensure that the appearance of the document is the same no matter what computer it is displayed on, save the document in *PDF (Portable Document Format)* or *XPS (XML Paper Specification)* format. PDF is a widely used format developed by Adobe Systems. XPS is a format developed by Microsoft. Both formats let you create a representation of *electronic paper* that displays your data on the screen as it would look when printed. Use one of these formats if you want someone to be able to view a document but not change it. In this activity, you will create PDF and XPS portable documents.

1 ▶ In Excel, from your student files, open the file **e05A_Fall_Classes**. Display the footer area, click in the **left section**, and then type **Lastname_Firstname_5A_Fall_PDF** Click in a cell just above the footer to exit the Footer. In the lower right corner of your screen, on the status bar, click **Normal** ⊞ to return to **Normal** view.

2 ▶ Press (F12) to display the **Save As** dialog box and navigate to your **Excel Chapter 5** folder. Click the **Save as type arrow**, and then click **PDF**.

 **ANOTHER WAY**   From Backstage view, click Export, and then click Create PDF/XPS document to open the Publish as PDF or XPS dialog box.

3 In the lower right section of the dialog box, if necessary, select the **Open file after publishing** check box. As the file name, type **Lastname_Firstname_5A_Fall_PDF** and then click **Save**.

> The file is saved in PDF format, and then opens as a PDF document using the default PDF program on your computer.

4 **Close** ⊠ the **Lastname_Firstname_5A_Fall_PDF** document.

5 With the **e05A_Fall_Classes** file open, edit the footer in the left section and type **Lastname_ Firstname_5A_Fall_XPS** Click in a cell just above the footer to exit the Footer. In the lower right corner of your screen, on the status bar, click **Normal** ⊞ to return to **Normal** view.

6 Press F12 to display the **Save As** dialog box, navigate to your **Excel Chapter 5** folder, and then in the **File name** box, type **Lastname_Firstname_5A_Fall_XPS**

7 At the bottom of the **Save As** dialog box, click the **Save as type arrow**, and then click **XPS Document**. In the lower right section of the **Save As** dialog box, if necessary, select the **Open file after publishing** check box, and then compare your screen with Figure 5.29.

FIGURE 5.29

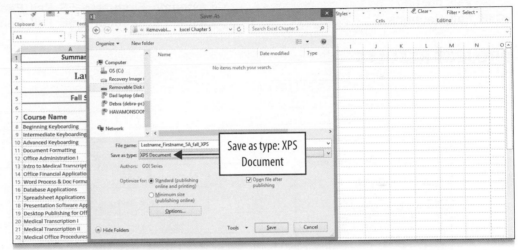

> Save as type: XPS Document

8 Click **Save**.

> The file is saved in XPS format, and then opens as an XPS document in the XPS Viewer window.

ALERT! **XPS Viewer**

If the Open with dialog box opens, choose XPS viewer and then click OK to open the file.

---

9 **Close** ⊠ the **XPS Viewer** window. **Close** the **e05A_Fall_Classes** file. **Don't Save** when the message displays—you do not need to save this file.

10 Submit your six files from this project as directed by your instructor, and then **Close** Excel.

More Knowledge **Converting a Tab Delimited Text File to a Word Table**

By choosing Text File as the file type, you can save an Excel worksheet as a text file, which saves the contents of the cells by placing a tab character, rather than commas, between the cells and an end-of-paragraph mark at the end of each row. This type of file can be readily exchanged with various database programs, in which it is referred to as a tab delimited text file. A text file can be converted from tab delimited text to a Word table. Word has a *Convert Text to Table* command that can easily convert a tabbed file into a table. A table displays in a row and column format, like an Excel spreadsheet.

END | You have completed Project 5A

Sorted, Filtered, and Outlined Database

MyITLab®
Project 5B Training

PROJECT ACTIVITIES

In Activities 5.14 through 5.21 you will use advanced table features to provide Dr. Kesia Toomer, the Dean of the Computer and Business Systems Division, information about the Fall course sections and assigned faculty in the Division. Your completed worksheets will look similar to Figure 5.30.

PROJECT FILES

For Project 5B, you will need the following files:

e05B_Fall_Advising
e05B_Fall_Faculty
e05B_Fall_Sections

You will save your workbooks as:

Lastname_Firstname_5B_Fall_Advising
Lastname_Firstname_5B_Fall_Faculty
Lastname_Firstname_5B_Fall_Sections

PROJECT RESULTS

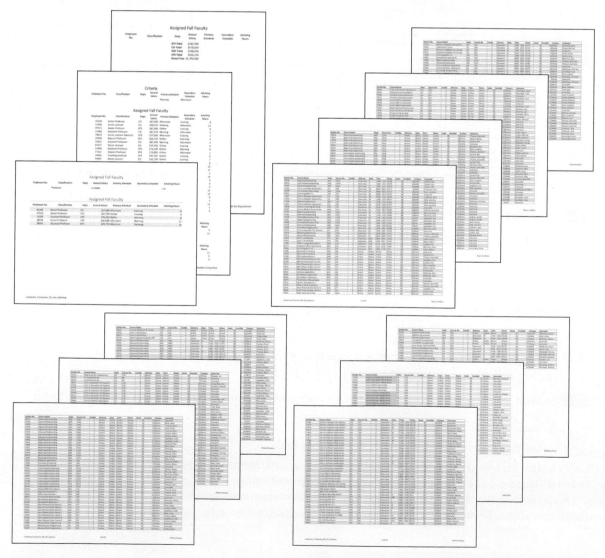

FIGURE 5.30 Project 5B Advising

Video E5-5

Sort means to organize data in a particular order; for example, alphabetizing a list of names. An *ascending* sort refers to text that is sorted alphabetically from A to Z, numbers sorted from lowest to highest, or dates and times sorted from earliest to latest. A *descending* sort refers to text that is sorted alphabetically from Z to A, numbers sorted from highest to lowest, or dates and times sorted from latest to earliest.

Sorting helps you to visualize your data. By sorting in various ways, you can find the data that you want, and then use your data to make good decisions. You can sort data in one column or in multiple columns. Most sort operations are column sorts, but you can also sort by rows.

Activity 5.14 | Sorting on Multiple Columns

To sort data based on several criteria at once, use the *Sort dialog box*, which enables you to sort by more than one column or row. For example, Dean Toomer wants to know, by department, how each course is delivered—either online or in a campus classroom. She also wants to examine the data to determine if there are any conflicts in room assignments. In this activity, you will convert the data into an Excel table, and then use the Sort dialog box to arrange the data to see the information the Dean needs.

1 Start Excel. From your student files, open **e05B_Fall_Sections,** and then **Save** the file in your **Excel Chapter 5** folder as **Lastname_Firstname_5B_Fall_Sections**

2 Be sure that the first worksheet, **Room Conflicts**, is the active sheet. In the **Name Box**, type **a1:m170** and press [Enter] to select this range. On the **INSERT tab**, in the **Tables group**, click **Table**. In the **Create Table** dialog box, be sure that the **My table has headers** check box is selected, and then click **OK**.

 **ANOTHER WAY**   With cell A1 active, on the INSERT tab, in the Tables group, click Table, and Excel will select all the contiguous data as the range.

3 On the **DESIGN tab**, in the **Table Styles group**, click **More** ▾, and then under **Light**, click **Table Style Light 16**. Click any cell to deselect the table, and then compare your screen with Figure 5.31.

A table of data like this one forms a *database*—an organized collection of facts related to a specific topic. In this table, the topic relates to the Fall course sections for this division of the college.

Each table row forms a *record*—all of the categories of data pertaining to one person, place, thing, event, or idea. In this table, each course section is a record. Each table column forms a *field*—a single piece of information that is stored in every record, such as a name or course number.

When information is arranged as records in rows and fields in columns, then you can *query*—ask a question of—the data. A query restricts records through the use of criteria conditions that will display records that will answer a question about the data.

FIGURE 5.31

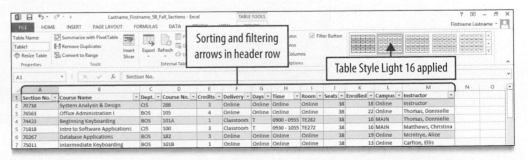

4 ▷ On the **DATA tab**, in the **Sort & Filter group**, click **Sort**.

In the Sort dialog box, you can sort on up to 64 columns (levels) of data.

N O T E	**Defining Data as a Table Prior to Sort Operations Is Optional**

Defining your range of data as an Excel table is not required to perform sort operations. Doing so, however, is convenient if you plan to perform sorts on all of the data, because any sort commands will be performed on the entire table. Defining the data as a table also freezes the column titles automatically, so they will not move out of view as you scroll down a worksheet that contains many rows. If you want to sort only part of a list of data, do not convert the data to a table. Instead, select the range, and then click the Sort button.

---

5 ▷ In the **Sort** dialog box, under **Column**, click the **Sort by arrow**. Notice that the list displays in the order of the field names—the column titles. In the list, click **Dept**.

6 ▷ Under **Sort On**, click the **arrow**, and then click **Values**. Under **Order**, click the **arrow**, and then click **A to Z**. Compare your screen with Figure 5.32.

The default Sort On option *Values* indicates that the sort will be based on the values in the cells of the Sort by column—the Dept. column. The default sort Order *A to Z* indicates that the values in the column will be sorted in ascending alphabetical order.

FIGURE 5.32

7 ▷ In the upper left corner of the **Sort** dialog box, click **Add Level**. In the second level row, click the **Then by arrow**, and then click **Course No**. Be sure that **Sort On** indicates *Values* and **Order** indicates *Smallest to Largest*.

When you initiate the sort operation, these numeric values will be sorted from the smallest number to the largest.

8 ▷ Click **Add Level** again. In the new row, under **Column**, click the **Then by arrow**, and then click **Section No**. Sort on the default options **Values**, from **Smallest to Largest**. Compare your screen with Figure 5.33.

FIGURE 5.33

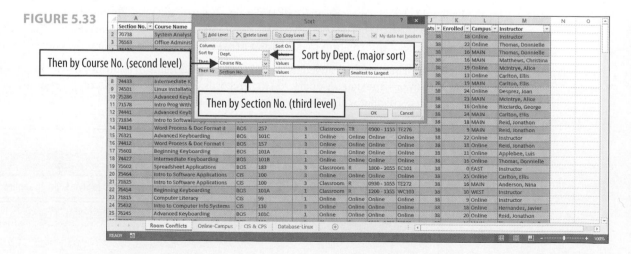

9 Click **OK**. Scroll down until **row 139** is at the top of the worksheet, take a moment to examine the arrangement of the data, and then compare your screen with Figure 5.34.

The first sort level, sometimes referred to as the *major sort*, is by the Dept. field in alphabetic order, so after the BOS department, the CIS department sections are listed, then the CNT department sections, then the CPS department sections, and so on.

The second sort level is by the Course No. field in ascending order, so within each department, the courses are sorted in ascending order by course number.

The third sort level is by the Section No. field in ascending order, so within each Course No. the section numbers display in ascending order.

FIGURE 5.34

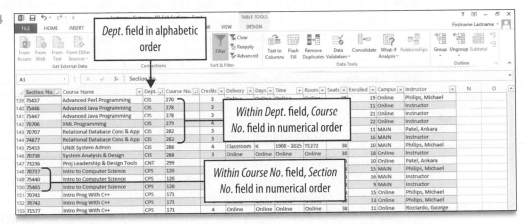

10 From the row heading area, select **rows 148:150**, and then notice that all three sections of the course *CPS 120 Intro to Computer Science* are offered in a campus classroom.

By studying the information in this arrangement, Dean Toomer can consider adding an additional section of this course in an online delivery.

11 Click any cell to deselect. On the **DATA tab**, in the **Sort & Filter group**, click **Sort** to redisplay the **Sort** dialog box.

12 Under **Column**, in the first row, click the **Sort by arrow**, and then click **Days**, change the second sort level to **Time**, and change the third sort level to **Room**. For each sort level, sort on **Values** in **A to Z** order. Compare your screen with Figure 5.35.

FIGURE 5.35

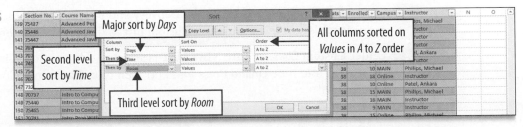

🔄 **ANOTHER WAY**   Click any row in the dialog box, click Delete Level, and then add new levels.

13 Click **OK**, and then scroll to view the top of the worksheet.

Because the days are sorted alphabetically, F (for Friday) is listed first, and then the times for the Friday classes are sorted in ascending order. Within the Friday group, the classes are further sorted from the earliest to the latest. Within each time period, the data is further sorted by room.

14 Examine the sorted data. Notice that the first three classes listed are on *Friday*, at *12:00*, in room *TE276*, with *Ellis Carlton* as the instructor.

These are all keyboarding classes, and the instructor teaches the three levels of keyboarding at the same time, so this is not a room conflict.

15 Scroll down to row 24. Notice in **rows 24:25** that two *Intro to Visual Basic* classes are scheduled on *MW* from 8:00 to 9:25 in room *TE110* with two different instructors listed. Press Ctrl + Home to move to the top of the worksheet.

This is a conflict of room assignment that will need to be resolved. Sorting data can help you identify such problems.

16 On the **PAGE LAYOUT tab**, in the **Page Setup group**, click **Print Titles**. On the **Sheet tab** of the **Page Setup** dialog box, click in the **Rows to repeat at top** box, point to the **row 1** heading to display the pointer, and click to select **row 1** so that the column titles will print on each sheet. In the dialog box, click **OK**.

17 Save your workbook.

Activity 5.15 | Sorting by Using a Custom List

You can use a ***custom list*** to sort in an order that you define. Excel includes a day-of-the-week and month-of-the-year custom list, so that you can sort chronologically by the days of the week or by the months of the year from January to December.

Optionally, you can create your own custom list by typing the values you want to sort by, in the order you want to sort them, from top to bottom; for example, *Fast, Medium, Slow*. A custom list that you define must be based on a value—text, number, date, or time.

In this activity, you will provide Dean Toomer with a list showing all the Fall sections sorted first by Delivery, with all online courses listed first. Within each delivery type—Online and Classroom—the data will be further sorted by Dept. and then by Course Name.

1 In the **sheet tab area**, click **Online-Campus** to display the *second* worksheet in the workbook.

2 In the **Name Box**, type **a1:m170** and press Enter to select the range. Click **Quick Analysis**, click **TABLES**, and then click **Table**. On the **DESIGN tab**, in the **Table Styles group**, click **More**, and then click **Table Style Light 17**. On the **DATA tab**, in the **Sort & Filter group**, click **Sort** to display the **Sort** dialog box.

3 Set the first (major) level to sort by **Delivery** and to sort on **Values**. Then, click the **Order arrow** for this sort level, and click **Custom List** to display the **Custom Lists** dialog box.

4 Under **Custom Lists**, be sure **NEW LIST** is selected. Then, under **List entries**, click in the empty box and type **Online** Press Enter, and then type **Classroom** Compare your screen with Figure 5.36.

FIGURE 5.36

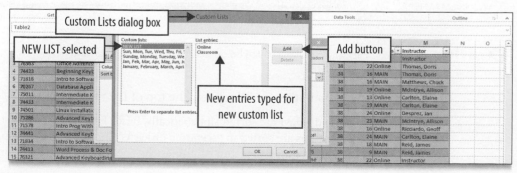

5 In the **Custom Lists** dialog box, click **Add**. On the left, under **Custom lists**, verify **Online, Classroom** is selected, and then click **OK** to redisplay the **Sort** dialog box.

6 In the **Sort** dialog box, click **Add Level**, and then as the second level sort, click the **Sort by** arrow, and then click **Dept**. Click **Add Level** again, and as the third level sort, select **Course Name**. Compare your screen with Figure 5.37.

FIGURE 5.37

7 Click **OK** and then click any cell to deselect the table. Scroll down the worksheet, and notice that all of the online courses are listed first, and then scroll down to display **row 76**. Notice the **Classroom** sections begin in **row 92**. Compare your screen with Figure 5.38.

Within each grouping, Online and Classroom, the sections are further sorted alphabetically by *Dept.* and then by *Course Name.*

FIGURE 5.38

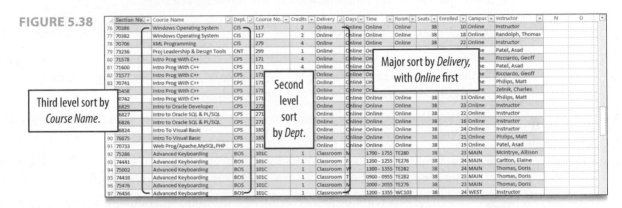

8 Press Ctrl + Home to move to cell **A1**. On the **PAGE LAYOUT tab**, in the **Page Setup group**, click **Print Titles**. On the **Sheet tab** of the **Page Setup** dialog box, click in the **Rows to repeat at top** box, point to the **row 1** heading to display the pointer, and click to select **row 1**, and then click **OK**. Save 🖫 your workbook.

More Knowledge   **A Custom List Remains Available for All Workbooks in Excel**

When you create a custom list, the list remains available for all workbooks that you use in Excel. To delete a custom list, display Excel Options, on the left click Advanced, under General, click the Edit Custom Lists button, select the custom list, and then click the Delete button to permanently delete the custom list. Click OK to confirm the deletion. Click OK two more times to close both dialog boxes.

Video E5-6

Filtering displays only the rows that meet the *criteria*—conditions that you specify to limit which records are included in the results—and hides the rows that do not meet your criteria.

When you format a range of data as a table, or select a range and click the Filter command, Excel displays filter arrows in the column headings, from which you can display the *AutoFilter menu* for a column—a drop-down menu from which you can filter a column by a list of values, by a format, or by criteria.

Use a *custom filter* to apply complex criteria to a single column. Use an *advanced filter* to specify three or more criteria for a particular column, to apply complex criteria to two or more columns, or to specify computed criteria. You can also use an advanced filter for extracting—copying the selected rows to another part of the worksheet, instead of displaying the filtered list.

Activity 5.16 | Filtering by Format and Value Using AutoFilter

There are three types of filters that you can create with AutoFilter. You can filter by one or more values, for example *CIS* for the CIS department. You can filter by a format, such as cell color. Or, you can filter by criteria; for example, course sections that are greater than two credits, which would display courses that have three or more credits. Each of these filter types is mutually exclusive for the column; that is, you can use only one at a time.

1 Click the **CIS & CPS sheet tab** to display the *third* worksheet in the workbook.

2 Be sure that cell **A1** is the active cell, and then on the **INSERT tab**, in the **Tables group**, click **Table**. In the **Create Table** dialog box, be sure that the data indicates the range *$A$1:$M$170* and the *My table has headers* checkbox is selected.

> The Table command causes Excel to suggest a table range based on the contiguous cells surrounding the active cell.

3 Click **OK** to accept the selection as the table range. On the **DESIGN tab**, in the **Table Styles group**, click **More**, and then click **Table Style Light 19.** Click cell **A1** to deselect the table.

4 Click the **DATA tab**. In the **Sort & Filter group**, notice that **Filter** is active—it displays green. In **row 1**, notice the **filter arrows** in each column title.

> When you format a range of data as an Excel table, filter arrows are automatically added in the header row of the table. A filter arrow, when clicked, displays the AutoFilter menu. On the ribbon, the active Filter button indicates that the data is formatted to use filters.

5 In **column B**, notice that some courses are formatted with a yellow fill color, which indicates courses that have been designated as introductory courses recommended for high school seniors who want to take a college class.

6 In cell **B1**, click the **Course Name filter arrow**. On the **AutoFilter** menu, below **Filter by Color**, click the **yellow block**.

> Only courses with a yellow fill color in column B display; the status bar indicates that 79 of the 169 records display.

7 Point to the filter arrow in cell **B1**, and notice the **ScreenTip** *Course Name: Equals a Yellow cell color*. Notice also that a small funnel displays to the right of the arrow. Compare your screen with Figure 5.39.

> The funnel indicates that a filter is applied, and the ScreenTip indicates how the records are filtered.

FIGURE 5.39

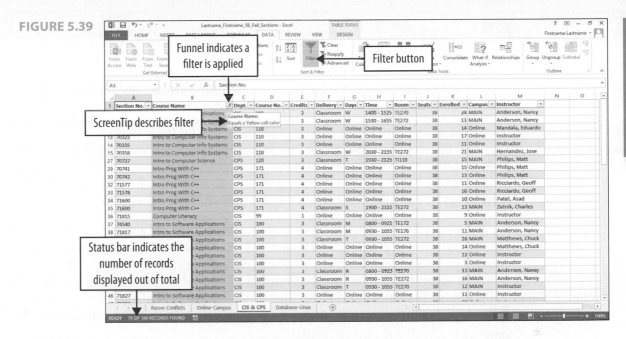

8 ▶ In cell **B1**, click the **Course Name filter arrow** ☐, and then click **Clear Filter from "Course Name"**. Then, in cell **B1**, point to the **Course Name filter arrow**, and notice that *(Showing All)* displays.

> The funnel no longer displays. The status bar no longer indicates that a filter is active. A filter arrow without a funnel means that filtering is enabled but not applied; if you point to the arrow, the ScreenTip will display (Showing All).

9 ▶ Click cell **I5**, which contains the value *TE280*. Right-click over the selected cell, point to **Filter**, and then click **Filter by Selected Cell's Value**. Notice that only the courses that meet in Room TE280 display; all the other records are hidden.

> Excel filters the records by the selected value—TE280—and indicates in the status bar that 10 of the 169 records are displayed. This is a quick way to filter a set of records.

10 ▶ On the **DATA tab**, in the **Sort & Filter group**, click **Clear** ☒ to clear all of the filters.

> Use this command to clear all filters from a group of records. This command also clears any sorts that were applied.

11 ▶ In cell **C1**, click the **Dept. filter arrow** ☐. Click the **(Select All)** check box to clear all the check boxes, and then select the **CIS** and **CPS** check boxes. Click **OK**.

> The records are filtered so that only course sections in the CIS and CPS departments display. The status bar indicates that 93 of 169 records are found; that is, 93 course sections are either in the CIS or CPS departments.

12 ▶ In cell **E1**, click the **Credits filter arrow** ☐, click the **(Select All)** check box to clear all the check boxes, and then select the **3** check box. Click **OK**.

> The status bar indicates that 61 of 169 records are found. That is, of the sections in either the CIS or CPS departments, 61 are three-credit courses. You can see that filtering actions are *additive*—each additional filter that you apply is based on the current filter, which further reduces the number of records displayed.

13 In cell **F1**, click the **Delivery filter arrow** ⏷, and then using the technique you just practiced, filter the list further by **Online**.

> The status bar indicates 30 of 169 records found. That is, 30 course sections are either in the CIS or CPS departments and three-credit courses are offered online. The filter drop-down lists make it easy to apply filters that provide quick views of your data. For best results, be sure the data in the filtered column has the same data type; for example, in a column, be sure all the values are numbers or text.

14 Save 🖫 your workbook.

Activity 5.17 | Filtering by Custom Criteria Using AutoFilter

By using a custom filter, you can apply complex criteria to a single column. For example, you can use comparison criteria to compare two values by using the **comparison operators** such as Equals (=), Greater Than (>), or Less Than (<) singly or in combinations. When you compare two values by using these operators, your result is a logical value that is either true or false.

1 Click **Database-Linux sheet tab** to display the *fourth* worksheet in the workbook.

2 Be sure that cell **A1** is the active cell, and then on the **INSERT tab**, in the **Tables group**, click **Table**. In the **Create Table** dialog box, be sure that the data indicates the range *$A$1:$M$170* and the *My table has headers checkbox* is selected. Click **OK**, and then apply **Table Style Light 21**. Click any cell to deselect.

3 In cell **K1**, click the **Enrolled filter arrow** ⏷, point to **Number Filters**, and then click **Less Than Or Equal To**. On the **Custom AutoFilter** dialog box in the first box, be sure that *is less than or equal to* displays, and then in the second box type **12** Compare your screen with Figure 5.40.

> In the Custom AutoFilter dialog box, you can create a **compound filter**—a filter that uses more than one condition—and one that uses comparison operators.

FIGURE 5.40

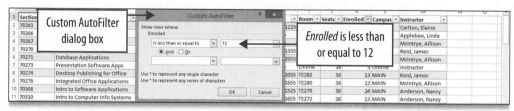

🔄 **ANOTHER WAY**   Click Custom Filter, click the first arrow in the first row, and then click is less than or equal to.

4 Click **OK** to display 49 records.

> This filter answers the question, *Which course sections have 12 or fewer students enrolled?*

5 On the **DATA tab**, in the **Sort & Filter group**, click **Clear** 🗙 to clear all filters.

6 In cell **B1**, click the **Course Name filter arrow** ⏷, point to **Text Filters**, and then click **Contains**.

7 In the **Custom AutoFilter** dialog box, under **Course Name**, in the first box, be sure that *contains* displays. In the box to the right, type **database**

8 Between the two rows of boxes, select **Or**. For the second filter, in the first box, click the arrow, scroll down as necessary, and then click **contains**. In the second box, type **linux** and then compare your screen with Figure 5.41.

> For the *Or comparison operator*, only one of the two comparison criteria that you specify must be true. By applying this filter, only courses that contain the words *database* or *linux* will display.

> For the *And comparison operator*, each and every one of the comparison criteria that you specify must be true.

FIGURE 5.41

9 Click **OK** to display 14 records. **Save** 💾 your workbook.

> This filter answers the question, Which course sections relate to either databases or the Linux operating system?

Activity 5.18 | Inserting the Sheet Name and Page Numbers in a Footer

You have practiced inserting the file name into the footer of a worksheet. In this activity, you will add the sheet name to the footer.

1 Point to the **Database-Linux sheet tab**, right-click, and then click **Select All Sheets**. With the sheets grouped, insert a footer in the left section that includes the file name.

2 In the footer area, click in the **center section** of the footer, and then on the **DESIGN tab**, in the **Header & Footer Elements group**, click **Page Number**. Press Spacebar one time, type **of** and press Spacebar again, and then click **Number of Pages**.

3 In the footer area, click in the **right section** of the footer, and then on the **DESIGN tab**, in the **Header & Footer Elements group**, click **Sheet Name**. Click a cell outside of the footer and compare your screen with Figure 5.42.

FIGURE 5.42

4 On the **PAGE LAYOUT tab**, set the **Orientation** to **Landscape**, and set the **Width** to **1 page**. On the status bar, click **Normal** ▦. Press Ctrl + Home to move to cell **A1**.

5 Click the **FILE tab**, and then in the lower right portion of the screen, click **Show all properties**. In the **Tags** box, type **sort, filter, sections** and in the **Subject** box type your course name and section #. In the **Author** box, replace the existing text with your first and last name. Display **Print Preview**.

> Ten pages display in Print Preview. The four worksheets in the workbook result in 10 pages—the first worksheet has four pages (blue), the second worksheet has four pages (pink), the third worksheet has one page (gold), and the fourth worksheet has one page (green).

6 Redisplay the workbook, and then make any necessary corrections or adjustments. Right-click any of the grouped sheet tabs, and then click **Ungroup Sheets**.

7 **Save** 🖫 your workbook. Hold this workbook until the end of this project, and then print or submit the four worksheets—10 total pages—in this workbook electronically as directed by your instructor. There are no formulas in these worksheets. **Close** this workbook, but leave Excel open.

Activity 5.19 | Filtering by Using Advanced Criteria

Use an advanced filter when the data you want to filter requires complex criteria; for example, to specify three or more criteria for a particular column, to apply complex criteria to two or more columns, or to specify computed criteria. When you use the Advanced Filter command, the Advanced dialog box displays, rather than the AutoFilter menu, and you type the criteria on the worksheet above the range you want to filter.

In this activity, you will create an advanced filter to determine which faculty members whose classification includes Professor and that have an annual salary of $70,000 or more, have 8 or more hours of assigned advising hours.

1 From your student files, open **e05B_Fall_Advising** and then **Save** the file in your **Excel Chapter 5** folder as **Lastname_Firstname_5B_Fall_Advising**

2 Select the range **A6:G7**, right-click, and then click **Copy**.

> The first step in filtering by using advanced criteria is to create a *criteria range*—an area on your worksheet where you define the criteria for the filter. The criteria range indicates how the displayed records are filtered.

> Typically, the criteria range is placed *above* the data. The criteria range must have a row for the column headings and at least one row for the criteria—you will need additional rows if you have multiple criteria for a column. You can also add a title row. Separate the criteria range from the data by a blank row.

3 Point to cell **A1**, right-click, under **Paste Options**, click the first button, **Paste (P)** 📋, and then press Esc to cancel the moving border. Click cell **A1**, type **Criteria** and then press Enter.

4 Select **rows 1:2**, on the **HOME tab**, in the **Cells group**, click **Format**, and then click **AutoFit Row Height**. Compare your screen with Figure 5.43.

> By copying the title and field names, you also copy the formatting that has been applied.

FIGURE 5.43

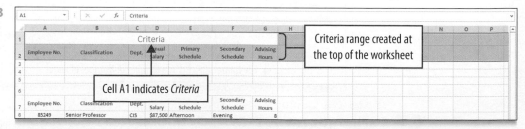

5 Select the range **A2:G3**—the column names and the blank row in the Criteria range. Click in the **Name Box**, type **Criteria** and then press Enter. Compare your screen with Figure 5.44.

> By naming the range Criteria, which is a predefined name recognized by Excel, the reference to this range will automatically display as the Criteria range in the Advanced Filter dialog box. This defined criteria range includes the field names and one empty row, where the limiting criteria will be placed. It does not include the title Criteria.

FIGURE 5.44

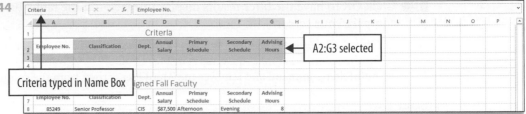

6 Select the range **A7:G34**, on the **INSERT tab**, in the **Tables group**, click **Table**. In the **Create Table** dialog box, be sure that *My table has headers checkbox* is selected. Click **OK**, and then apply **Table Style Light 5**. Click anywhere in the table to deselect.

7 On the **FORMULAS tab**, in the **Defined Names** group, click **Name Manager**, and then compare your screen with Figure 5.45.

By defining the range as a table, Excel automatically assigns a name to the range. It is not required to format the range as a table. You can select the range and name it Table or Database; however, doing so enables you to use the Table Tools, such as formatting and inserting a Total row into the filtered data.

The defined table range will automatically display as the List range in the Advanced Filter dialog box.

FIGURE 5.45

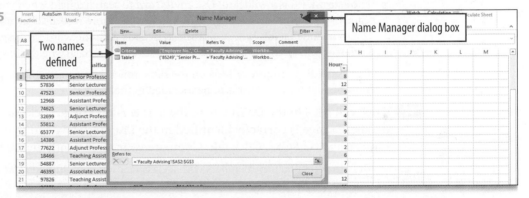

8 **Close** the **Name Manager** dialog box.

9 Scroll to view the top of the worksheet, click cell **D3**, type **>=70000** and then press [Enter].

This action creates a criteria using a comparison operator to look for salary values that are greater than or equal to $70,000. Do not include a comma when you type this value, because the comma is a cell format, not part of the value.

10 Click cell **A7**. On the **DATA tab**, in the **Sort & Filter group**, click **Advanced**.

11 In the **Advanced Filter** dialog box, locate the **List range**, and verify the range indicates **$A$7:$G$34**, which is your Excel table. Be sure the **Criteria range** is identified as cells **$A$2:$G$3**. Compare your screen with Figure 5.46.

Here you define the database area—the List range—and the Criteria range where the results will display. Both ranges use an absolute reference. Under Action, you can choose to display the results in the table—in-place—or copy the results to another location.

FIGURE 5.46

12 ▶ Click **OK** to have the filter results display in-place—in the table. Press Ctrl + Home and compare your screen with Figure 5.47.

Only the records for faculty members whose salary is $70,000 or more display. The row numbers for the records that meet the criteria display in blue. The Advanced command disables the AutoFilter command and removes the AutoFilter arrows from the column headings.

FIGURE 5.47

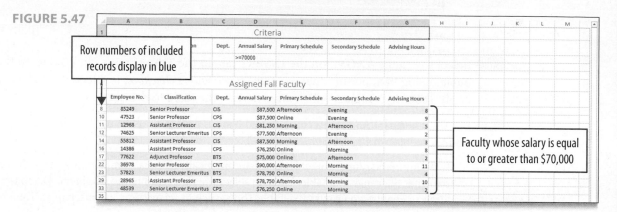

13 ▶ Click cell **B3**, type ***Professor** and then press Enter.

The asterisk (*) is a wildcard. Use a ***wildcard*** to search a field when you are uncertain of the exact value or you want to widen the search to include more records. The use of a wildcard enables you to include faculty whose classification ends with the word *Professor*. It directs Excel to find Professor and anything before it. The criterion in the Salary field still applies.

The use of two or more criteria on the same row is known as ***compound criteria***—all conditions must be met for the records to be included in the results.

14 ▶ Click cell **A7**. On the **DATA tab**, in the **Sort & Filter group**, click **Advanced**. Verify that the database range is correctly identified in the **List range** box and that the **Criteria range** still indicates *$A$2:$G$3*. Click **OK**. Compare your screen with Figure 5.48.

Only the eight faculty members with a classification containing *Professor* and a salary of $70,000 or more display.

FIGURE 5.48

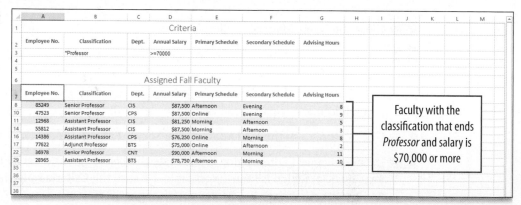

15 ▶ Using the techniques you just practiced, filter the data further by adding an additional criteria—faculty who are assigned 8 hours or more of advising. Compare your result with Figure 5.49.

Five faculty members meet all three of the criteria in the Criteria range.

FIGURE 5.49

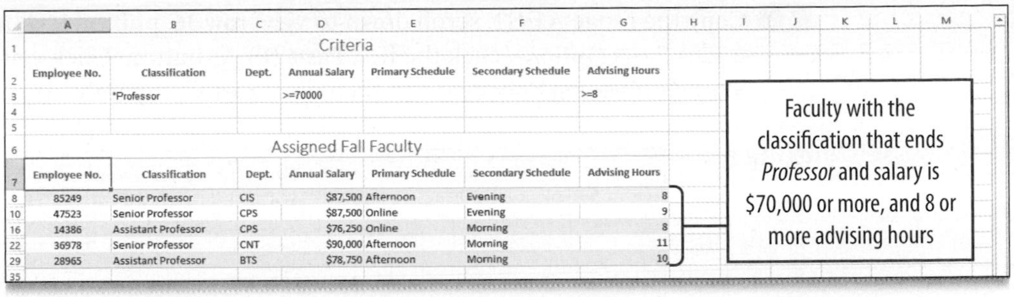

Faculty with the classification that ends *Professor* and salary is $70,000 or more, and 8 or more advising hours

16 ▶ Insert a footer in the **left section** that includes the file name, click outside the footer area, and then on the **PAGE LAYOUT tab**, set the **Orientation** to **Landscape**. On the status bar, click **Normal** ⊞. Press Ctrl + Home to move to cell **A1**.

17 ▶ Click the **FILE tab**, and then in the lower right portion of the screen, click **Show all properties**. In the **Tags** box, type **advanced filter, advising** and in the **Subject** box type your course name and section #. In the **Author** box, replace the existing text with your first and last name.

18 ▶ Display the **Print Preview**. Near the bottom of the window, click **Page Setup** to display the **Page Setup** dialog box. Click the **Margins tab**, center the worksheet horizontally, and then click **OK**. Redisplay the worksheet and make any necessary corrections or adjustments.

19 ▶ **Save** 🖫 your workbook. Hold this workbook until the end of this project, and then print or submit electronically as directed; there are no formulas in this worksheet. **Close** this workbook, but leave Excel open.

More Knowledge | **Using Wildcards**

A wildcard can help you locate information when you are uncertain how the information might be displayed in your records. The placement of the asterisk in relationship to the known value determines the result. If it is placed first, the variable will be in the beginning of the string of characters. For example, in a list of names if you used *son as the criteria, it will look for any name that ends in son. The results might display Peterson, Michelson, and Samuelson. If the asterisk is at the end of the known value in the criteria, then the variable will be at the end. You can also include the asterisk wildcard at the beginning and at the end of a known value. You can also use an asterisk wildcard in the middle, so searching for m*t will result in both mat and moist.

A question mark (?) can also be used as part of your search criteria. Each question mark used in the criteria represents a single position or character that is unknown in a group of specified values. Searching for m?n would find, for example, *min*, *men*, and *man*; whereas searching for m??d would find, for example, *mind*, *mend*, *mold*.

Activity 5.20 | Extracting Filtered Rows

You can copy the results of a filter to another area of your worksheet instead of displaying a filtered list as you did in the previous activity. The location to which you copy the records is the *Extract area*, and is commonly placed below the table of data. Using this technique you can *extract*—pull out—multiple sets of data for comparison purposes.

In this activity, you will extract data to compare how many faculty have a Morning-Evening schedule and how many have a Morning-Afternoon schedule.

1 ▶ From your student files, open **e05B_Fall_Faculty**. Display the **Save As** dialog box, navigate to your **Excel Chapter 5** folder, and then save the workbook as **Lastname_Firstname_5B_Fall_Faculty**

2 ▶ Verify that the first worksheet, **Schedule Comparison**, is the active sheet. **Copy** the range **A6:G7**, **Paste** it in cell **A1**, and then change the title in cell **A1** to **Criteria**

3 ▶ Select the range **A2:G3**, and then in the **Name Box**, type **Criteria** and then press Enter to name this range.

4 ▶ **Copy** the range **A1:G2**, scroll down to view **row 36**, point to cell **A36**, right-click, and then under **Paste Options**, click the first **Paste (P)** 📋 button. Click cell **A36**, change the title to **Morning-Evening Schedule** and then press Enter. Compare your screen with Figure 5.50.

FIGURE 5.50

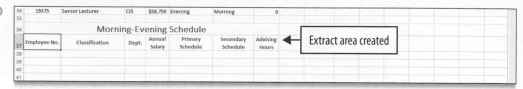

Extract area created

5 ▶ Select the range **A37:G37** and then in the **Name Box**, name this range **Extract**

This action defines the Extract area so that the range will display automatically in the Copy to box of the Advanced Filter dialog box. Excel recognizes *Extract* as the location in which to place the results of an advanced filter.

6 ▶ Select the range **A7:G34** and then in the **Name Box**, name this range **Database**

Excel recognizes the name Criteria as a criteria range, the name Database as the range to be filtered, and the name Extract for the area where you want to paste the result.

7 ▶ At the top of your worksheet, in cell **E3**, type **Morning** In cell **F3**, type **Evening** and then press Enter.

When applied, the filter will display only those records where the Primary Schedule is Morning and the Secondary Schedule is Evening.

8 ▶ On the **DATA tab**, in the **Sort & Filter group**, click **Advanced**.

9 ▶ Under **Action**, click **Copy to another location**. Verify that in the **Copy to** box, the absolute reference to the Extract area—*$A$37:$G$37*—displays. Compare your screen with Figure 5.51.

FIGURE 5.51

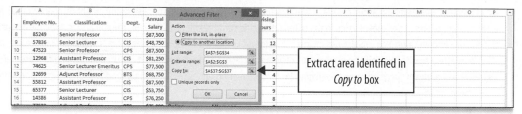

Extract area identified in *Copy to* box

10 ▶ Click **OK**, and then scroll to view the lower portion of your worksheet. Compare your screen with Figure 5.52.

Two records meet the criteria and are copied to the Extract area on your worksheet. When you use an Extract area in this manner, instead of reformatting the table to display the qualifying records, Excel places a copy of the qualifying records in the Extract area.

FIGURE 5.52

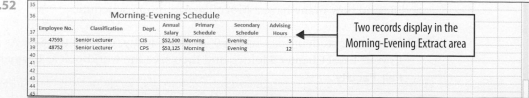

Two records display in the Morning-Evening Extract area

11 ▶ **Copy** the range **A36:G37**, and then **Paste** it in cell **A41**. In cell **A41**, change the word *Evening* to **Afternoon**

12 At the top of your worksheet, in cell **F3**, change the criteria to **Afternoon** Display the **Advanced Filter** dialog box, and then click **Copy to another location**.

13 In the **Copy to** box, click the **Collapse Dialog** button, scroll down as necessary, and then select the range **A42:G42**. Click the **Expand Dialog** button, and then click **OK**. Scroll to view the lower portion of the worksheet, and then compare your screen with Figure 5.53.

Three records meet the criteria and are copied to the Extract area on your worksheet.

FIGURE 5.53

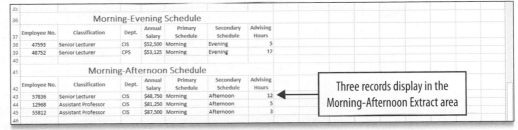

Three records display in the Morning-Afternoon Extract area

14 Save and then leave this workbook open for the next activity.

Objective 7   Subtotal, Outline, and Group a List of Data

Video E5-7

You can group and summarize a *list*—a series of rows that contains related data—by adding subtotals. The first step in adding subtotals is to sort the data by the field for which you want to create a subtotal.

Activity 5.21 | Subtotaling, Outlining, and Grouping a List of Data

In this activity, you will assist Dean Toomer in summarizing the faculty salaries by department.

1 In your **Lastname_Firstname_5B_Fall_Faculty** workbook, click the **Salaries by Department sheet tab.**

2 Select the range **A2:G29**. On the **DATA tab**, in the **Sort & Filter group**, click **Sort**. In the **Sort** dialog box, click the **Sort by arrow**, and then click **Dept**. Click **Add Level**, click the **Then by arrow**, and then click **Annual Salary**. Compare your **Sort** dialog box with Figure 5.54.

FIGURE 5.54

Sort dialog box

Sort by *Dept.* and then *Annual Salary*

3 Click **OK**. With the range still selected, on the **DATA tab**, in the **Outline group**, click **Subtotal**.

The *Subtotal command* totals several rows of related data together by automatically inserting subtotals and totals for the selected cells.

4 In the **Subtotal** dialog box, in the **At each change in** box, click the arrow to display the list, and then click **Dept**. In the **Use function** box, display the list and, if necessary, click **Sum**. In the **Add subtotal to** list, select the **Annual Salary** check box, and then scroll the list and *deselect* any other check boxes that are selected. Compare your screen with Figure 5.55.

These actions direct Excel to create a group for each change in value in the Dept. field. Excel will then use the Sum function to add a subtotal in the Annual Salary field. The check boxes at the bottom of the dialog box indicate how the subtotals will display.

FIGURE 5.55

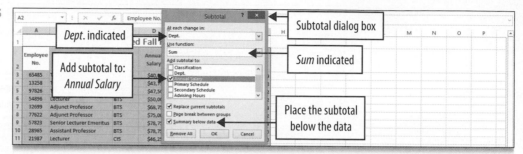

5 Click **OK**, press Ctrl + Home, scroll to view the lower portion of the data, **AutoFit column C**, and then compare your screen with Figure 5.56.

At the end of each Dept. group, inserted rows containing the subtotals for the salaries within each department display.

FIGURE 5.56

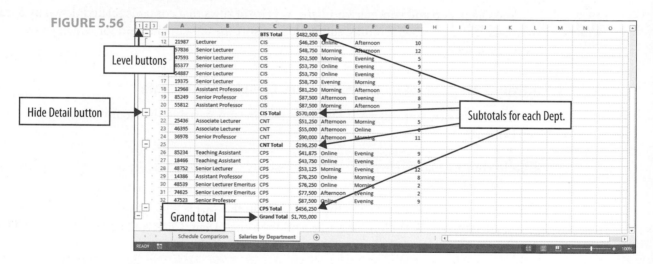

6 Along the left edge of your workbook, locate the outline.

When you add subtotals, Excel defines groups based on the rows used to calculate a subtotal. The groupings form an outline of your worksheet based on the criteria you indicated in the Subtotal dialog box, and the outline displays along the left side of your worksheet.

The outline bar along the left side of the worksheet enables you to show and hide levels of detail with a single mouse click. For example, you can show details with the totals, which is the default view. Or, you can show only the summary totals or only the grand total.

There are three types of controls in the outline. Hide Detail (−) collapses a group of cells, Show Detail (+) expands a collapsed group of cells, and the level buttons (1, 2, 3) can hide all levels of detail below the number clicked.

7 To the left of **row 25**, click **Hide Detail** (−) to collapse the detail for the **CNT** department.

Detail data refers to the subtotaled rows that are totaled and summarized. Detail data is typically adjacent to and either above or to the left of the summary data.

8 Select **rows 13:17**, and then on the **DATA tab**, in the **Outline group**, click **Group**. Compare your screen with Figure 5.57.

A fourth group is created and a bar spans the group.

FIGURE 5.57

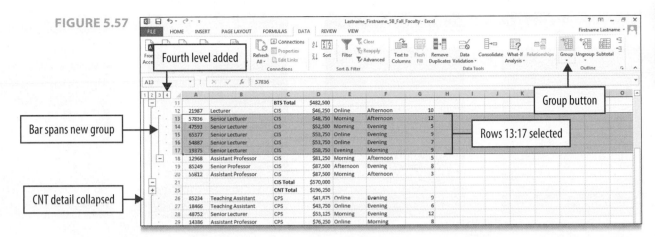

9 To the left of **row 18**, click **Hide Detail** (–) for the new group, and notice that the group is collapsed and a break in the row numbers indicates that some rows are hidden from view.

Hiding the detail data in this manner does not change the subtotal for the CIS group—it remains $570,000.

10 At the top of the outline area, click the **Level 2** button to hide all Level 3 and 4 details and display only the Level 2 summary information and the Level 1 Grand Total. Press [Ctrl] + [Home] and compare your screen with Figure 5.58.

FIGURE 5.58

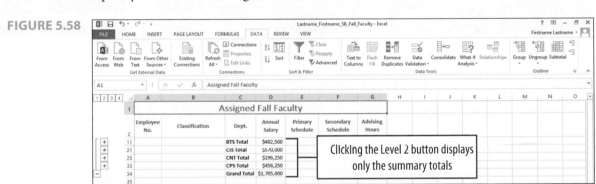

11 Group the two worksheets. Insert a footer that includes the file name in the **left section**, and in the **right section**, insert the **Sheet Name**. Click any cell to exit the footer area, and then on the status bar, click **Normal**. Press [Ctrl] + [Home] to move to cell **A1**. On the **PAGE LAYOUT tab**, set the **Width** to **1 page** and set the **Height** to **1 page**.

12 Click the **FILE tab** to display **Backstage** view. On the right, at the bottom of the **Properties** list, click **Show All Properties**. On the list of **Properties**, in the **Tags** box, type **faculty, schedule, salaries** In the **Subject** box, type your course name and section #. Under **Related People**, be sure that your name displays as the author. If necessary, right-click the author name, click Edit Property, type your name, click outside of the Edit person dialog box, and then click OK.

13 Display the **Print Preview**, redisplay the workbook, and then make any necessary corrections or adjustments. Ungroup the worksheets, and then **Save** 🖫 your workbook. Along with your other two workbooks from this project, print or submit electronically as directed. **Close** Excel.

END | You have completed Project 5B

END OF CHAPTER

SUMMARY

You can navigate a large worksheet using the Freeze Panes, Go To, and Find commands. Control the screen display by hiding rows and columns and work with multiple workbooks using the Arrange All command.

A theme is a set of formatting characteristics, such as fonts, number formats, borders, and shading. Insert page breaks, repeat column or row titles, and use Landscape orientation for worksheets with many columns.

By default, Excel files are saved in the Excel Workbook file format with the .xlsx file name extension. Excel data can also be saved in other file formats such as HTML, CSV, PDF, and XPS.

Sorting organizes data in a particular order. Filtering displays only the rows that meet specific criteria. Sorting and filtering along with subtotaling, outlining, and grouping are used for data analysis.

GO! LEARN IT ONLINE

Review the concepts and key terms in this chapter by completing these online challenges, which you can find at **www.pearsonhighered.com/go**.

Matching and Multiple Choice: Answer matching and multiple choice questions to test what you learned in this chapter. MyITLab®

Crossword Puzzle: Spell out the words that match the numbered clues and put them in the puzzle squares.

Flipboard: Flip through the definitions of the key terms in this chapter and match them with the correct term.

END OF CHAPTER

REVIEW AND ASSESSMENT GUIDE FOR EXCEL CHAPTER 5

Your instructor may assign one or more of these projects to help you review the chapter and assess your mastery and understanding of the chapter.

Project	Apply Skills from These Chapter Objectives	Project Type	Project Location
5C	Objectives 1–4 from Project 5A	**5C Skills Review** A guided review of the skills from Project 5A.	On the following pages
5D	Objectives 5–7 from Project 5B	**5D Skills Review** A guided review of the skills from Project 5B.	On the following pages
5E	Objectives 1–4 from Project 5A	**5E Mastery (Grader Project)** A demonstration of your mastery of the skills in Project 5A with extensive decision making.	In MyITLab and on the following pages
5F	Objectives 5–7 from Project 5B	**5F Mastery (Grader Project)** A demonstration of your mastery of the skills in Project 5B with extensive decision making.	In MyITLab and on the following pages
5G	Combination of Objectives from Projects 5A and 5B	**5G Mastery (Grader Project)** A demonstration of your mastery of the skills in Projects 5A and 5B with extensive decision making.	In MyITLab and on the following pages
5H	Combination of Objectives from Projects 5A and 5B	**5H GO! Fix It** A demonstration of your mastery of the skills in Projects 5A and 5B by creating a correct result from a document that contains errors you must find.	Online
5I	Combination of Objectives from Projects 5A and 5B	**5I GO! Make It** A demonstration of your mastery of the skills in Projects 5A and 5B by creating a result from a supplied picture.	Online
5J	Combination of Objectives from Projects 5A and 5B	**5J GO! Solve It** A demonstration of your mastery of the skills in Projects 5A and 5B, your decision-making skills, and your critical thinking skills. A task-specific rubric helps you self-assess your result.	Online
5K	Combination of Objectives from Projects 5A and 5B	**5K GO! Solve It** A demonstration of your mastery of the skills in Projects 5A and 5B, your decision-making skills, and your critical thinking skills. A task-specific rubric helps you self-assess your result.	On the following pages
5L	Combination of Objectives from Projects 5A and 5B	**5L GO! Think** A demonstration of your understanding of the chapter concepts applied in a manner that you would outside of college. An analytic rubric helps you and your instructor grade the quality of your work by comparing it to the work an expert in the discipline would create.	On the following pages
5M	Combination of Objectives from Projects 5A and 5B	**5M GO! Think** A demonstration of your understanding of the chapter concepts applied in a manner that you would outside of college. An analytic rubric helps you and your instructor grade the quality of your work by comparing it to the work an expert in the discipline would create.	Online
5N	Combination of Objectives from Projects 5A and 5B	**5N You and GO!** A demonstration of your understanding of the chapter concepts applied in a manner that you would in a personal situation. An analytic rubric helps you and your instructor grade the quality of your work.	Online

GLOSSARY

GLOSSARY OF CHAPTER KEY TERMS

Additive The term that describes the behavior of a filter when each additional filter that you apply is based on the current filter, and that further reduces the number of records displayed.

Advanced Filter A filter that can specify three or more criteria for a particular column, apply complex criteria to two or more columns, or specify computed criteria.

And comparison operator The comparison operator that requires each and every one of the comparison criteria to be true.

Arrange All The command that tiles all open program windows on the screen.

Ascending The term that refers to the arrangement of text that is sorted alphabetically from A to Z, numbers sorted from lowest to highest, or dates and times sorted from earliest to latest.

AutoFilter menu A drop-down menu from which you can filter a column by a list of values, by a format, or by criteria.

Cell style A defined set of formatting characteristics, such as font, font size, font color, cell borders, and cell shading.

Comma delimited file A file type that saves the contents of the cells by placing commas between them and an end-of-paragraph mark at the end of each row; also referred to as a CSV (comma separated values) file.

Comparison operators Symbols that evaluate each value to determine if it is the same (=), greater than (>), less than (<), or in between a range of values as specified by the criteria.

Compound criteria The use of two or more criteria on the same row—all conditions must be met for the records to be included in the results.

Compound filter A filter that uses more than one condition—and one that uses comparison operators.

Criteria Conditions that you specify in a logical function or filter.

Criteria range An area on your worksheet where you define the criteria for the filter, and that indicates how the displayed records are filtered.

CSV (comma separated values) file A file type in which the cells in each

row are separated by commas and an end-of-paragraph mark at the end of each row; also referred to as a comma delimited file.

Custom Filter A filter with which you can apply complex criteria to a single column.

Custom list A sort order that you can define.

Database An organized collection of facts related to a specific topic.

Descending The term that refers to the arrangement of text that is sorted alphabetically from Z to A, numbers sorted from highest to lowest, or dates and times sorted from latest to earliest.

Detail data The subtotaled rows that are totaled and summarized; typically adjacent to and either above or to the left of the summary data.

Extract The process of pulling out multiple sets of data for comparison purposes.

Extract area The location to which you copy records when extracting filtered rows.

Field A specific type of data such as name, employee number, or social security number that is stored in columns.

Filtering A process in which only the rows that meet the criteria display; rows that do not meet the criteria are hidden.

Find A command that finds and selects specific text or formatting.

Freeze Panes A command that enables you to select one or more rows or columns and freeze (lock) them into place so that they remain on the screen while you scroll; the locked rows and columns become separate panes.

Go To A command that moves to a specific cell or range of cells that you specify.

Go To Special A command that moves to cells that have special characteristics, for example, to cells that are blank or to cells that contain constants, as opposed to formulas.

HTML (Hypertext Markup Language) A language web browsers can interpret.

Hyperlink Text or graphics that, when clicked, take you to another location

in the worksheet, to another file, or to a webpage on the Internet or on your organization's intranet.

List A series of rows that contains related data that you can group by adding subtotals.

Major sort A term sometimes used to refer to the first sort level in the Sort dialog box.

Or comparison operator The comparison operator that requires only one of the two comparison criteria that you specify to be true.

Pane A portion of a worksheet window bounded by and separated from other portions by vertical and horizontal bars.

PDF (Portable Document Format) A file format developed by Adobe Systems that creates a representation of electronic paper that displays your data on the screen as it would look when printed, but that cannot be easily changed.

Query A process of restricting records through the use of criteria conditions that will display records that will answer a question about the data.

Record All the categories of data pertaining to one person, place, thing, event, or idea.

Scaling The group of commands by which you can reduce the horizontal and vertical size of the printed data by a percentage or by the number of pages that you specify.

Sort The process of arranging data in a specific order.

Sort dialog box A dialog box in which you can sort data based on several criteria at once, and that enables a sort by more than one column or row.

Split The command that enables you to view separate parts of the same worksheet on your screen; splits the window into multiple resizable panes to view distant parts of the worksheet at one time.

Subtotal command The command that totals several rows of related data together by automatically inserting subtotals and totals for the selected cells.

Tab delimited text file A file type in which cells are separated by tabs; this type of file can be readily exchanged with various database programs.

Theme A predesigned set of colors, fonts, lines, and fill effects that look good together and that can be applied to your entire document or to specific items.

Wildcard A character, for example the asterisk or question mark, used to search a field when you are uncertain of the exact value or when you want to widen the search to include more records.

.xlsx file name extension The default file format used by Excel 2013 to save an Excel workbook.

XPS (XML Paper Specification) A file type, developed by Microsoft, which creates a representation of electronic paper that displays your data on the screen as it would look when printed.

CHAPTER REVIEW

Apply 5A skills from these Objectives:

1 Navigate and Manage Large Worksheets
2 Enhance Worksheets with Themes and Styles
3 Format a Worksheet to Share with Others
4 Save Excel Data in Other File Formats

In the following Skills Review, you will assist Susanne Black, Program Chair for Science, in formatting and navigating a large worksheet that lists the class schedule for the Science departments at Laurel College. You will also save Excel data in other file formats. Your completed workbooks will look similar to Figure 5.59.

PROJECT FILES

For Project 5C, you will need the following files:

e05C_Science_Faculty
e05C_Science_Requests
e05C_Science_Schedule

You will save your workbooks as:

Lastname_Firstname_5C_Science_CSV
Lastname_Firstname_5C_Science_Faculty
Lastname_Firstname_5C_Science_Schedule
Lastname_Firstname_5C_Science_Webpage

PROJECT RESULTS

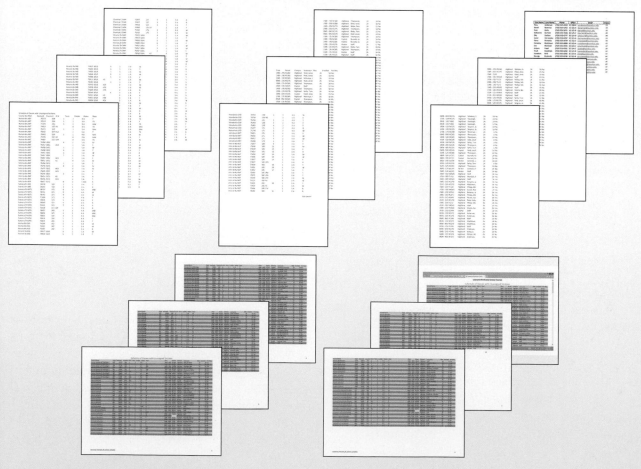

FIGURE 5.59

(Project 5C Science Schedule continues on the next page)

CHAPTER REVIEW

1 Start Excel. From your student files, open the file **e05C_Science_Schedule**. Display the **Save As** dialog box, navigate to your **Excel Chapter 5** folder, and then **Save** the workbook as **Lastname_Firstname_5C_Science_Schedule**

a. On the **HOME tab**, in the **Editing group**, click **Find & Select**, and then click **Go To Special**. In the first column, click **Blanks**, and then click **OK** to select all blank cells in the worksheet's active area. Point to the selected cell **K31** and right-click. On the mini toolbar, click the **Fill Color button arrow**, and then under **Standard Colors**, click the fourth color—**Yellow**—to fill all the selected blank cells. These cells still require Room assignments.

b. Press [Ctrl] + [Home]. From the column heading area, select **columns E:H**. Right-click over the selected area, and then click **Hide**.

c. On the **HOME tab**, in the **Editing group**, click **Find & Select**, and then click **Go To**. In the **Go To** dialog box, in the **Reference** box, type **m172** and then click **OK**. With cell **M172** active, on the **FORMULAS tab**, in the **Function Library** group, click **More Functions**, point to **Statistical**, and then click **COUNTIF**. As the **Range**, type **m2:m170** and as the **Criteria**, type **Staff** Click **OK**. Your result is *27*, indicating that 27 courses still indicate *Staff* and need an instructor assigned. In cell **I172**, type **Still need instructor assigned** and press [Enter]. Press [Ctrl] + [Home] and click **Save**.

2 From your student files, open **e05C_Science_Requests**. On the **VIEW tab**, in the **Window group**, click **Switch Windows**, and then at the bottom of the list, click your **Lastname_Firstname_5C_Science_Schedule** file to make it the active worksheet. On the **VIEW** tab, in the **Window group**, click **Arrange All**. Click **Horizontal**, and then click **OK**. If necessary, click the title bar of your Lastname_Firstname_5C_Science_Schedule worksheet to make it the active worksheet. Press [Ctrl] + [End] to move to cell **P172**.

a. Click cell **A172**. In the **Window group**, click **Split**. Above the split bar, click any cell in **column C**. Press [Ctrl] + [F] to display the **Find and Replace** dialog box. Locate the first request in the **e05C_Science_Requests** worksheet, which is from *Eric Marshall* to teach *Survey of Astronomy Section # 76822*. In the

Find what box, type **76822** so that you can locate the course in the worksheet.

b. Click **Find Next**. Drag the title bar of the dialog box into the upper right area of your screen so that you can see the **Name Box**, which indicates *C38*. In your **Lastname_Firstname_5C_Science_Schedule** worksheet, click in cell **M38**, type **Marshall, Eric** to delete *Staff* and assign the class to Mr. Marshall. Press [Enter].

c. Continue to use the **Find and Replace** dialog box to locate the remaining three **Section #s** listed in the **e05C_Science_Requests** worksheet, and enter the appropriate instructor name for each class in **column M** of your **Lastname_Firstname_5C_Science_Schedule** worksheet. **Close** the **Find and Replace** dialog box. In cell **M172**, notice that *23* classes remain unassigned.

d. Click any cell in the **e05C_Science_Requests** worksheet, and then on this worksheet's title bar, click **Close**. Then, on the title bar of your **Lastname_Firstname_5C_Science_Schedule** worksheet, click **Maximize** to restore the size of the worksheet to its full size. On the **VIEW tab**, in the **Window group**, click **Split** to remove the split.

e. From the **column heading area**, select **columns D:I**. Right-click over the selected area, and then click **Unhide**. Press [Ctrl] + [Home], and then **Save** your workbook.

3 Point to the **row 1 heading**, right-click, and then click **Insert**. In cell A1, type **Schedule of Classes with Unassigned Sections** Merge & Center this title across the range **A1:P1**, and then apply the **Title** cell style.

a. On the **PAGE LAYOUT tab**, in the **Themes group**, click **Themes**, and then, click the **Slice** theme. In the **Themes group**, click **Fonts**. Scroll to the top and then click the **Office** fonts.

b. On the **HOME tab**, in the **Styles group**, click **Format as Table**. At the bottom, click **New Table Style**. In the **New Table Style** dialog box, in the **Name** box, replace the existing text by typing **Science Schedule** In the list under **Table Element**, click **First Row Stripe**, and then click **Format**. In the **Format Cells** dialog box, click the **Fill tab**. In the fifth column of colors, click the second color. In the lower right corner, click **OK**.

(Project 5C Science Schedule continues on the next page)

CHAPTER REVIEW

c. In the list of table elements, click **Second Row Stripe**, click **Format**, and then in the third column of colors, click the sixth color. Click **OK**. In the list of table elements, click **Header Row**, click **Format**, and then in the seventh column, click the fourth color. Click **OK**, in the lower left corner of the dialog box, click to select the check box **Set as default table style for this document**, and then click **OK**.

d. Select the range **A2:P171**, and then in the **Styles group**, click **Format as Table**. At the top of the gallery, under **Custom**, locate and then click your custom **Science Schedule** table style. In the **Format As Table** dialog box, click **OK**. Then, because you do not need to filter the table, in the **Tools group**, click **Convert to Range**, and then click **Yes**. Press Ctrl + Home to deselect and move to cell **A1**. Click **Save**.

4 Select **columns A:P**, in the **Cells group**, click **Format**, and then click **AutoFit Column Width**. On the **PAGE LAYOUT tab**, in the **Page Setup group**, set the **Orientation** to **Landscape**. Then, in the **Scale to Fit group**, click the **Width arrow**, and then click **1 page.**

a. From the **INSERT tab**, insert a footer in the **left section** that includes the file name. Click in the right section, and then in the **Header & Footer Elements group**, click **Page Number**. Click in a cell just above the footer to exit the footer area.

b. On the **VIEW tab**, in the **Workbook Views group**, click **Page Break Preview**, and close the dialog box if necessary. Point to the horizontal page break line between **Page 1** and **Page 2**, and then drag the line up between **row 42** and **row 43**. Position the break between **Page 2** and **Page 3** between **row 74** and **row 75**. Position the break between **Page 3** and **Page 4** between **row 116** and **row 117**. Position the break between **Page 4** and **Page 5** between **row 152** and **row 153.**

c. On the **VIEW tab**, in the **Workbook Views group**, click **Normal** to redisplay the worksheet in **Normal** view, and then press Ctrl + Home.

d. Display the **Print Preview**, scroll through the pages, and notice that the column titles display only on the first page. Redisplay the worksheet. Click the **PAGE LAYOUT tab**, in the **Page Setup group**, click **Print Titles** to display the **Sheet tab** of the **Page Setup** dialog box.

e. Under **Print titles**, click in the **Rows to repeat at top** box, and then in the worksheet, select **row 2**. Click **OK**. Click **Save.**

5 From **Backstage** view, display the **Open** dialog box, and then from your student files, open the file **e05C_Science_Faculty**. Display the **Save As** dialog box, navigate to your **Excel Chapter 5** folder, and then **Save** the file as **Lastname_Firstname_5C_Science_Faculty** Insert a footer in the **left section** with the file name, click outside the footer area, press Ctrl + Home and return to **Normal** view. Click **Save**, and then **Close** this workbook to redisplay your **Lastname_Firstname_5C_Science_Schedule** workbook.

a. Click cell **M2**. On the **INSERT tab**, in the **Links group**, click **Hyperlink**. Under **Link to**, click **Existing File or Web Page**. Click the **Look in arrow**, navigate to your **Excel Chapter 5** folder, and then select your **Lastname_Firstname_5C_Science_Faculty** workbook. Click **OK.**

b. Point to cell **M2** to display the 🖑 pointer, and then click to confirm that the link opens the workbook containing the contact information. **Close** the workbook with the faculty contacts.

c. Point to cell **M2**, right-click, and then click **Edit Hyperlink**. In the upper right corner of the **Insert Hyperlink** dialog box, click **ScreenTip**. In the **ScreenTip text** box, type **Click here for contact information** Click **OK** two times. Point to cell **M2** and confirm that your **ScreenTip** displays.

d. Display the **document properties** and under **Related People**, be sure that your name displays as the author. If necessary, right-click the author name, click Edit Property, and then type your name. In the **Subject** box, type your course name and section number, and in the **Tags** box, type **science schedule** Click **Save**. Leave the workbook open.

6 Press F12 to display the **Save As** dialog box and navigate to your **Chapter 5** folder. In the lower portion, click the **Save as type arrow**, and then click **Web Page.**

a. Click **Change Title**. In the **Enter Text** dialog box, in the **Page title** box, using your own name, type **Lastname Firstname Science Courses** Click **OK**, and notice that in the **Page title** box, your typed text displays. In the **Save As** dialog box, click **Publish.**

(Project 5C Science Schedule continues on the next page)

CHAPTER REVIEW

b. In the **Publish as Web Page** dialog box, click the **Choose arrow**, and then click **Items on Science Classes**—recall that the worksheet name is *Science Classes*. In the lower left corner, if necessary, click to select (place a check mark in) the **Open published web page in browser** check box.

c. Click **Browse** to display the **Publish As** dialog box. If necessary, navigate to your **Excel Chapter 5** folder. In the **File name** box, type **Lastname_Firstname_5C_Science_Webpage** Click **OK**, and then in the **Publish as Web Page** dialog box, click **Publish**.

d. If you are instructed to print your webpage on paper, consult the instructions to print from your specific browser software. On the browser title bar, click **Close**. Leave your **Lastname_Firstname_5C_Science_Schedule** workbook open for the next step.

e. Display the **Save As** dialog box, be sure you are saving in your **Excel Chapter 5** folder, set the **Save as type** to **CSV (Comma delimited)**, and as the **File name**, type **Lastname_Firstname_5C_Science_CSV** Click **Save**, and then click **Yes**.

f. **Close** your **Lastname_Firstname_5C_Science_CSV** file, click **Save**, and then click **Yes**. **Close** Excel. As directed by your instructor, submit the four files that comprise the results of this project.

END | You have completed Project 5C

CHAPTER REVIEW

Skills Review Project 5D Spring Sections

In the following Skills Review, you will use advanced table features to provide Dr. Marshall Eaton, the Dean of the Arts Division, information about the Spring course sections and assigned faculty in the Division. Your completed worksheets will look similar to Figure 5.60.

PROJECT FILES

For Project 5D, you will need the following files:

e05D_Spring_Faculty
e05D_Spring_Sections

You will save your workbooks as:

Lastname_Firstname_5D_Spring_Faculty
Lastname_Firstname_5D_Spring_Sections

PROJECT RESULTS

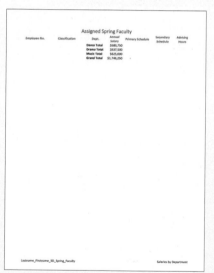
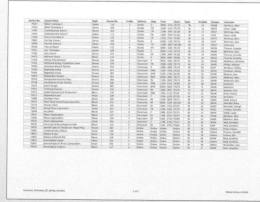
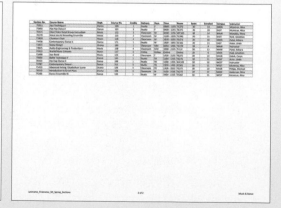

FIGURE 5.60

(Project 5D Spring Sections continues on the next page)

CHAPTER REVIEW

1 Start Excel. From your student files, open the file e05D_Spring_Sections, and then **Save** the file in your **Excel Chapter 5** folder as **Lastname_Firstname_5D_Spring_Sections** Be sure the first worksheet, **Online-Campus-Studio** displays.

a. On the **DATA tab**, in the **Sort & Filter group**, click **Sort**. In the **Sort** dialog box, under **Column**, click the **Sort by arrow**, and then click **Delivery**. Under **Sort On**, click the **arrow**, and then click **Values**. Under **Order**, click the **Order arrow** for this sort level, and then click **Custom List**. In the dialog box, under **Custom lists**, be sure **NEW LIST** is selected. Then, under **List entries**, click in the empty box and type **Studio** Press Enter, type **Classroom** Press Enter, and then type **Online**

b. In the **Custom Lists** dialog box, click **Add**, and then click **OK**. If necessary, in the Sort dialog box, click the Order arrow, and then click your Studio, Classroom, Online custom list so that it displays in the Order box. Click **Add Level**, and then as the second level sort, click **Dept**. Click **Add Level** again, and as the third level sort, click **Course Name**. Click **OK**.

2 Click the **Music & Dance sheet tab** to display the *second* worksheet. In cell **C1**, click the **Dept. filter arrow**. Click the **(Select All)** check box to clear all the check boxes, and then select the **Drama** and the **Music** check boxes. Click **OK**.

a. In cell **E1**, click the **Credits filter arrow**, and then filter the list further by selecting **3**. In cell **F1**, click the **Delivery filter arrow**, and filter the list further by **Online**. The status bar information reveals that *4 of the 39 course sections* that are either in the Music or Drama departments are three-credit courses offered online.

b. On the **DATA tab**, in the **Sort & Filter group**, Clear all filters. In cell **K1**, click the **Enrolled filter arrow**, point to **Number Filters**, and then click **Less Than Or Equal To**. In the first box, be sure that *is less than or equal to* displays, and then in the second box type **15** Click **OK** to display *16 records*.

c. Right-click over either of the two sheet tabs, and then click **Select All Sheets**. With the sheets grouped, insert a footer in the **left section** that includes the file name. Click in the **center section**

of the footer, and then on the **DESIGN tab**, in the **Header & Footer Elements group**, click **Page Number**. Press Spacebar one time, type **of** and press Spacebar again, and then click **Number of Pages**. Click in the **right section** of the footer, and then on the **DESIGN tab**, in the **Header & Footer Elements group**, click **Sheet Name**.

d. Click a cell outside of the footer, and then on the **PAGE LAYOUT tab**, set the **Orientation** to **Landscape**, and set the **Width** to **1 page**. Click **Normal**, and then move to cell **A1**.

e. Display the **document properties** and under **Related People**, be sure that your name displays as the author. If necessary, right-click the author name, click Edit Property, and then type your name. In the **Subject** box, type your course name and section #, and in the **Tags** box, type **sort, filter, sections** Display **Print Preview**. Make any necessary corrections or adjustments.

f. Ungroup the worksheets and **Save** your workbook. Hold this workbook until the end of this project, and then print or submit the two worksheets in this workbook electronically as directed by your instructor. **Close** this workbook, but leave Excel open.

3 From your student files, open e05D_Spring_Faculty. Display the **Save As** dialog box, navigate to your **Excel Chapter 5** folder, and then **Save** the workbook as **Lastname_Firstname_5D_Spring_Faculty** Be sure the **Schedule Comparison** worksheet is active. **Copy** the range **A6:G7**, **Paste** it in cell **A1**, and then change the title in cell **A1** to **Criteria**

a. Select the range **A2:G3**, and then in the **Name Box**, name this range **Criteria** Copy the range **A1:G2**, scroll down to view **row 34**, point to cell **A34**, right-click, and then click **Paste**. Click cell **A34**, and then change the title to **Morning-Evening Schedule** and then press Enter. Select the range **A35:G35** and then in the **Name Box**, name this range **Extract** Select the range **A7:G32** and then in the **Name Box**, name this range **Database**

b. At the top of your worksheet, in cell **E3**, type **Morning** and in cell **F3**, type **Evening** On the **DATA tab**, in the **Sort & Filter group**, click **Advanced**. Under **Action**, click **Copy to another location**. Verify that in the **Copy to** box—*$A$35:$G$35*—displays.

(Project 5D Spring Sections continues on the next page)

CHAPTER REVIEW

Click **OK**, and then scroll to view the lower portion of your worksheet. Two records meet the criteria.

c. Copy the range **A34:G35**, and then **Paste** it in cell **A39**. In cell **A39**, change the word *Evening* to **Afternoon** In cell **F3**, change the criteria to **Afternoon** Display the **Advanced Filter** dialog box, and then click **Copy to another location**.

d. In the **Copy to** box, click the **Collapse Dialog** button, and then select the range **A40:G40**. Click the **Expand Dialog** button and then click **OK**. *Three* records meet the criteria and are copied to the Extract area on your worksheet. **Save** the workbook.

4 Display the **Salaries by Department** worksheet. Select the range **A2:G30**. On the **DATA tab**, in the **Sort & Filter group**, click **Sort**. In the **Sort** dialog box, sort by the **Dept.** column, and then by the **Annual Salary** column. Click **OK**.

a. With the range still selected, on the **DATA tab**, in the **Outline group**, click **Subtotal**. In the **Subtotal** dialog box, in the **At each change in** box, display the list, and then click **Dept**. In the **Use function** box, display the list and click **Sum**. In the **Add subtotal to** list, select the **Annual Salary** check box, and then deselect any other check boxes. Click **OK**.

b. Click any cell to deselect, and then along the left edge of your workbook, locate the outline. To the left of **row 29**, click the **Hide Detail** button to collapse the detail for the **Music** department.

c. Select **rows 17:19**, and then on the **DATA tab**, in the **Outline group**, click **Group**. To the left of **row 20**, click the **Hide Detail** button. At the top of the outline area, click the **Level 2** button to hide all Level 3 and 4 details, and display only the Level 2 summary information, and the Level 1 Grand Total.

d. Group the two worksheets. Insert a footer in the **left section** that includes the file name, and in the **right section**, insert the **Sheet Name**. Click any cell to exit the footer area. On the **PAGE LAYOUT Tab**, set the **Width** to **1 page** and set the **Height** to **1 page**—this will scale each worksheet to fit on a single page. Click **Normal** and then move to cell **A1**.

e. Display the **document properties** and under **Related People**, be sure that your name displays as the author. If necessary, right-click the author name, click Edit Property, and then type your name. In the **Subject** box, type your course name and section #, and in the **Tags** box, type **faculty, schedule, salaries** Display the **Print Preview**. Make any necessary corrections or adjustments.

f. Ungroup the worksheets and **Save** your workbook, and then close it. Along with your other workbook from this project, print or submit electronically as directed. If required, print or create an electronic version of your worksheets with formulas displayed, using the instructions in Project 1A. **Close** Excel.

END | You have completed Project 5D

CONTENT-BASED ASSESSMENTS

Mastering Excel   Project 5E Sports Schedule

Apply 5A skills from these Objectives:

1 Navigate and Manage Large Worksheets

2 Enhance Worksheets with Themes and Styles

3 Format a Worksheet to Share with Others

4 Save Excel Data in Other File Formats

In the following Mastering Excel project, you will assist Damian Howard, Athletic Director at Laurel College, in formatting and navigating a large worksheet that lists the sports events schedule for spring sports. You will also save Excel data in other file formats. Your completed workbooks will look similar to Figure 5.61.

PROJECT FILES

For Project 5E, you will need the following files:

e05E_Sports_Coaches
e05E_Referee_Requests
e05E_Sports_Schedule

You will save your workbooks as:

Lastname_Firstname_5E_Sports_Coaches
Lastname_Firstname_5E_Sports_PDF
Lastname_Firstname_5E_Sports_Schedule
Lastname_Firstname_5E_Sports_Webpage

PROJECT RESULTS

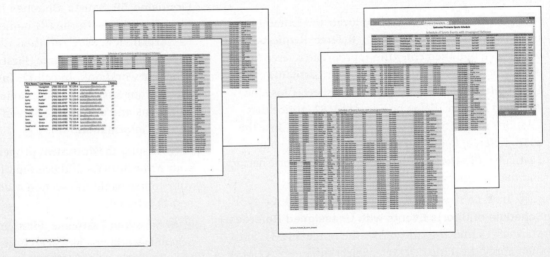

FIGURE 5.61

(Project 5E Sports Schedule continues on the next page)

CONTENT-BASED ASSESSMENTS

1 Start Excel. Open the file **e05E_Sports_Schedule** and **Save** it in your **Excel Chapter 5** folder as **Lastname_ Firstname_5E_Sports_Schedule** Go to cell **M82**, and then insert the **COUNTIF** function. Set the **Range** as **m2:m80** and the **Criteria** as **Staff** resulting in *23* sporting events that still require a Referee assignment. In cell **K82**, type **Events with Unassigned Referees** and press Ctrl + Home. Open the file **e05E_Referee_ Requests**. Switch windows, and then click your **Lastname_Firstname_5E_Sports_Schedule** workbook. **Arrange All** so the files are **Horizontal** with your **Lastname_Firstname_5E_Sports_Schedule** as the active worksheet in the top window.

2 Go to cell **A82**, **Split** the window horizontally, and then click in any cell above the split in **column C**. Display the **Find and Replace** dialog box. Locate the first request in the **e05E_Referee_Requests** worksheet. Use **Find** to locate **76243** and then type **Danny Litowitz** in the appropriate cell to assign him as the *Referee*.

3 Use the **Find** command to locate the remaining three **Event #s** listed in the **e05E_Referee_Requests** worksheet, and then enter the appropriate referee for each sports event in **column M** of your **Lastname_ Firstname_5E_Sports_Schedule** worksheet. **Close** the **Find and Replace** dialog box. In cell **M82**, notice that *19* sports events still need a referee assigned. **Close** the **e05E_Referee_Requests** workbook. **Maximize** your **Lastname_Firstname_5E_Sports_Schedule** worksheet, and then remove the **Split**.

4 Insert a new blank row at row 1. In cell **A1**, type **Schedule of Sports Events with Unassigned Referees Merge & Center** the title across the range **A1:M1**, and then apply the **Title** cell style. Select the range **A2:M81** and **Format as Table**, and then create a **New Table Style** named **Sports Schedule** Format the **First Row Stripe** from the **Fill tab** and in the fifth column of colors, click the second color. For the **Second Row Stripe**, in the fifth column of colors, click the third color. For the **Header Row**, in the fourth column of colors click the

fourth color. Select the check box **Set as default table style for this document**. Apply the **Custom** table style, *Sports Schedule* to the table. Convert the table to a Range. Press Ctrl + Home to deselect the table and move to cell **A1**.

5 AutoFit columns A:M. Set the **Orientation** to **Landscape**, set the **Width** to **1 page**, and **Center** the worksheets **Horizontally**. Insert a footer in the **left section** that includes the file name, and in the **right section**, insert a page number. Apply **Page Break Preview**, and then drag the line to break **Page 1** after **row 49**— to end the page with *TENNIS* and begin **Page 2** with *TRACK*. Return to **Normal** view. Set **Print Titles** to repeat **row 2** at the top of each page. Display **Print Preview** and examine the pages. Redisplay the workbook, make any necessary adjustments, and then **Save**. Leave this workbook open.

6 Open the file **e05E_Sports_Coaches** and **Save** it in your **Excel Chapter 5** folder as **Lastname_ Firstname_5E_Sports_Coaches** Insert a footer in the **left section** with the file name, and then return to **Normal** view. **Save** and then **Close** this workbook to redisplay your **Lastname_Firstname_5E_Sports_ Schedule** workbook. In cell **J2**, **Insert** a **Hyperlink** to link to your **Lastname_Firstname_5E_Sports_Coaches** workbook and display the **ScreenTip Click here for contact information**

7 Display the **document properties** and be sure that your name displays as the author. In the **Subject** box, type your course name and section #, and in the **Tags** box, type **sports schedule**

8 **Save** your **Lastname_Firstname_5E_Sports_ Schedule** workbook as a **Web Page** with the name **Lastname_Firstname_5E_Sports_Webpage** Change the **Page title** to **Lastname Firstname Sports Schedule** and then **Publish**. If you are instructed to print your webpage on paper, consult the instructions to print from your specific browser software. **Close** your browser. Leave your **Lastname_Firstname_5E_Sports_Schedule** workbook open.

(Project 5E Sports Schedule continues on the next page)

CONTENT-BASED ASSESSMENTS

9 Display the **Save As** dialog box and save your **Lastname_Firstname_5E_Sports_Schedule** workbook as a **PDF**, with the name **Lastname_Firstname_5E_Sports_PDF Close** all files. As directed by your instructor, print or submit electronically the four files that comprise the results of this project—two Excel files, a PDF file, and an HTML file.

END | You have completed Project 5E

Apply 5B skills from these Objectives:

5 Use Advanced Sort Techniques

6 Use Custom and Advanced Filters

7 Subtotal, Outline, and Group a List of Data

In the following Mastering Excel project, you will edit a worksheet for Michael Schaeffler, Vice President of Instruction, with data that has been sorted, filtered, and grouped that analyzes vocational programs at Laurel College. The worksheets of your workbook will look similar to Figure 5.62.

PROJECT FILES

For Project 5F, you will need the following file:

e05F_Vocational_Programs

You will save your workbook as:

Lastname_Firstname_5F_Vocational_Programs

PROJECT RESULTS

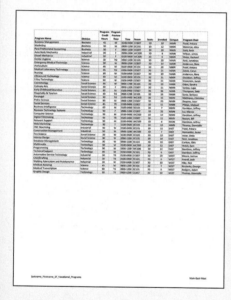

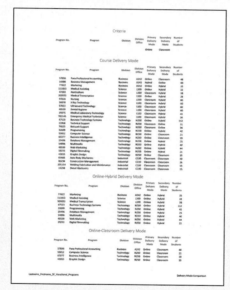

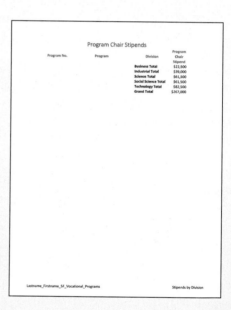

FIGURE 5.62

(Project 5F Vocational Programs continues on the next page)

CONTENT-BASED ASSESSMENTS

1 Start Excel. **Open** the file **e05F_Vocational_Programs**. **Save** the file in your **Excel Chapter 5** folder as **Lastname_Firstname_5F_Vocational_Programs** Display the *first* worksheet, **Main-East-West**. Select the range **A1:J40**, insert a table. Apply **Table Style Light 16**. Click anywhere to deselect, on the **DATA tab**, from the **Sort & Filter group**, display the **Sort** dialog box.

For the first sort level, sort by **Campus**, sort on **Values**, and then under **Order**, create a **Custom List: Main**, **East**, **West** Add a second level, sort by **Division** in alphabetical order on **Values**. Add a third level, sort by **Program Name** in alphabetical order on **Values**.

2 Convert the data to a range. Display the *second* worksheet, **Delivery Mode Comparison**. **Copy** the range **A6:G7**. **Paste** it in cell **A1**, and then change the title in cell **A1** to **Criteria** In the **Name Box**, name the range **A2:G3 Criteria**

Copy the range **A1:G2**, and **Paste** it into cell **A36**. Change the title in cell **A36** to **Online-Hybrid Delivery Mode** Select the range **A37:G37** and then in the **Name Box**, name this range **Extract** Select the range **A7:G34** and then in the **Name Box**, name this range **Database**

3 At the top of your worksheet, in cell **E3**, type **Online** and in cell **F3**, type **Hybrid** On the **DATA tab**, in the **Sort & Filter group**, click **Advanced**. Under **Action**, click **Copy to another location**. Verify that in the **Copy to** box, the absolute reference to the Extract area—$A$37:$G$37—displays. **Copy** the range **A36:G37**, and then **Paste** it in cell **A48**. In cell **A48** change the

word *Hybrid* to **Classroom** In cell **F3**, change the criteria to **Classroom**

Display the **Advanced Filter** dialog box, and then click **Copy to another location**. In the **Copy to** box, change the range to **A49:G49**.

4 Display the *third* worksheet—**Stipends by Division**. Select the range **A2:D41**. Display the **Sort** dialog box, **Sort** first by the **Division**, then by the **Program Chair Stipend**. **Subtotal** at each change in **Division**, select the **Sum** function, add the subtotal to the **Program Chair Stipend**. **Group** the data so each **Division** is collapsed and a break in the row numbers indicates that some rows are hidden from view. **AutoFit columns C:D** to display the **Grand Total**.

5 Select all three worksheets. Insert a footer in the **left section** that includes the file name, and in the **right section**, insert the **Sheet Name**. Return to **Normal** view, and move to cell **A1**. Set the **Width** to **1 page** and set the **Height** to **1 page**, and **Center** the worksheets **Horizontally**.

6 Display the **document properties** and be sure that your name displays as the author. In the **Subject** box, type your course name and section number, and in the **Tags** box, type **vocational programs** Examine the **Print Preview**, make any necessary corrections or adjustments, and then **Save** your workbook. Print or submit your workbook electronically as directed. If required, print or create an electronic version of your worksheets with formulas displayed, using the instructions in Project 1A. **Close** all files and **Close** Excel.

END | You have completed Project 5F

Apply 5A and 5B skills from these Objectives:

1 Navigate and Manage Large Worksheets

2 Enhance Worksheets with Themes and Styles

3 Format a Worksheet to Share with Others

4 Save Excel Data in Other File Formats

5 Use Advanced Sort Techniques

6 Use Custom and Advanced Filters

7 Subtotal, Outline, and Group a List of Data

In the following Mastering Excel project, you will create a worksheet for Sandy Chase, Assistant Director of Athletics, with data that has been sorted, filtered, and grouped and that analyzes sports programs. Assistant Director Chase will use this information to make decisions for these sports programs for the upcoming academic year. The worksheets of your workbook will look similar to Figure 5.63.

PROJECT FILES

For Project 5G, you will need the following files:

e05G_Coach_Information
e05G_Sports_Programs

You will save your workbooks as:

Lastname_Firstname_5G_Coach_Information
Lastname_Firstname_5G_Sports_Programs

PROJECT RESULTS

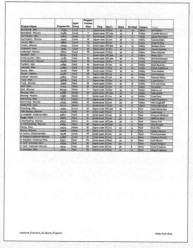

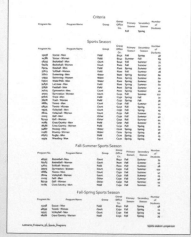

FIGURE 5.63

(Project 5G Sports Programs continues on the next page)

CONTENT-BASED ASSESSMENTS

1 Start Excel. From your student files, locate and open **e05G_Sports_Programs. Save** the file in your **Excel Chapter 5** folder as **Lastname_Firstname_5G_Sports_Programs** Display the **Valley-Park-West** worksheet. Select the range **A1:J40**, insert a table, and then apply **Table Style Light 17**. In the **Sort** dialog box, **Sort** by **Campus**, sort on **Values**, and then click **Custom List**. With **NEW LIST** selected, under **List entries**, create entries for **Valley** and **Park** and **West**

As the second level, sort the **Sport Group** column alphabetically on **Values**. As the third level, sort the **Program Name** column alphabetically on **Values**. Convert the table to a range.

2 Display the **Sports Season Comparison** worksheet. Copy the range **A6:G7**, **Paste** it in cell **A1**, and then change the title in cell **A1** to **Criteria** Select the range **A2:G3**, and then in the **Name Box**, name this range **Criteria**

Copy the range **A1:G2**, and then **Paste** the copied range in cell **A36**. Change the title in cell **A36** to **Fall-Summer Sports Season** Name the range **A37:G37 Extract** and then name the range **A7:G34 Database**

3 At the top of your worksheet, in cell **E3**, type **Fall** and in cell **F3**, type **Summer** On the **DATA tab**, in the **Sort & Filter group**, click **Advanced**. Under **Action**, click **Copy to another location**. Verify that in the **Copy to** box, the absolute reference to the Extract area—**$A$37:$G$37**—displays.

4 Scroll to view the lower portion of your worksheet. Copy the range **A36:G37**, and then **Paste** it in cell **A48**. In cell **A48**, change the word *Summer* to **Spring** In cell **F3**, change the criteria to **Spring**

Display the **Advanced Filter** dialog box, and then click **Copy to another location**. In the **Copy to** box, change the range **A49:G49**.

5 Display the **Stipends by Group** worksheet. Select the range **A2:D41**. **Sort** by **Group**, then by the **Coach**

Stipend. **Subtotal** at each change in **Group**, select the **Sum** function, select the **Add subtotal to** the **Coach Stipend**. Display the **Level 2** summary information, and the **Level 1** Grand Total. **AutoFit** columns as necessary.

6 Select all three worksheets. Insert a footer in the **left section** that includes the file name, and in the **right section**, insert the **Sheet Name**.

Return to **Normal** view, and then move to cell **A1**. Change the theme to **Slice**, and then change the **Fonts** to **Corbel**. Set the **Width** to **1 page** and set the **Height** to **1 page**, and **Center** the worksheets **Horizontally**. Display the **document properties** and be sure that your name displays as the author. In the **Subject** box, type your course name and section #, and in the **Tags** box, type **sports programs, campus, sports season, stipends** Display the worksheet in **Print Preview**, make any necessary corrections or adjustments.

7 Open the file **e05G_Coach_Information** and **Save** it in your **Excel Chapter 5** folder as **Lastname_Firstname_5G_Coach_Information** Insert a footer in the **left section** with the file name, and then return to **Normal** view. **Save** and then **Close** this workbook to redisplay your **Lastname_Firstname_5G_Sports_Programs** workbook.

8 On the **Valley-Park-West** worksheet, in cell **J1**, **Insert** a **Hyperlink** to link to your **Lastname_Firstname_5G_Coach_Information** workbook and the **ScreenTip text** box displays, type **Click here for contact information** Change the **Hyperlink Font Color** in cell **J1** to **Orange, Accent 5, Darker 25%**.

9 Save your **Lastname_Firstname_5G_Sports_Programs** workbook as an **XPS Document** with the **File name Lastname_Firstname_5G_Sports_XPS** As directed by your instructor, print or submit electronically the three files that comprise the results of this project—two Excel files and one XPS file. **Close** all files and **Close** Excel.

END | You have completed Project 5G

(Project 5G Sports Programs continues on the next page)

CONTENT-BASED ASSESSMENTS

GO! Fix It	Project 5H Programs	Online

GO! Make It	Project 5I Arts Faculty	Online

GO! Solve It	Project 5J Organizations	Online

GO! Solve It	Project 5K Dept Tutors	

Apply a combination of the 5A and 5B skills.

PROJECT FILES

For Project 5K, you will need the following file:

e05K_Dept_Tutors

You will save your workbook as:

Lastname_Firstname_5K_Dept_Tutors

Open the file e05K_Dept_Tutors and save it in your Excel Chapter 5 folder as **Lastname_Firstname_5K_Dept_Tutors**

The Director of the Tutoring Center wants to know which tutors who are classified as grad student tutors are available in the afternoons from the CNT and CPS departments. By using the table feature and filtering, filter the data to present the information requested. Include the file name in the footer, add appropriate properties, and then save your workbook. Submit as directed.

Performance Level

Performance Criteria	Exemplary	Proficient	Developing
Convert Data to a Table	The data is properly converted to a table.	Only part of the data is in the form of a table.	The data is not properly converted to a table.
Filter on Multiple Columns	The Filter Function is properly applied using supplied criteria.	The Filter Function is properly applied to some but not all supplied criteria.	The Filter Function is not properly applied and did not meet the supplied criteria.

END | You have completed Project 5K

OUTCOMES-BASED ASSESSMENTS

RUBRIC

The following outcomes-based assessments are *open-ended assessments*. That is, there is no specific correct result; your result will depend on your approach to the information provided. Make *Professional Quality* your goal. Use the following scoring rubric to guide you in *how* to approach the problem and then to evaluate *how well* your approach solves the problem.

The *criteria*—Software Mastery, Content, Format and Layout, and Process—represent the knowledge and skills you have gained that you can apply to solving the problem. The *levels of performance*—Professional Quality, Approaching Professional Quality, or Needs Quality Improvements—help you and your instructor evaluate your result.

	Your completed project is of Professional Quality if you:	Your completed project is Approaching Professional Quality if you:	Your completed project Needs Quality Improvements if you:
1-Software Mastery	Choose and apply the most appropriate skills, tools, and features and identify efficient methods to solve the problem.	Choose and apply some appropriate skills, tools, and features, but not in the most efficient manner.	Choose inappropriate skills, tools, or features, or are inefficient in solving the problem.
2-Content	Construct a solution that is clear and well organized, contains content that is accurate, appropriate to the audience and purpose, and is complete. Provide a solution that contains no errors in spelling, grammar, or style.	Construct a solution in which some components are unclear, poorly organized, inconsistent, or incomplete. Misjudge the needs of the audience. Have some errors in spelling, grammar, or style, but the errors do not detract from comprehension.	Construct a solution that is unclear, incomplete, or poorly organized; contains some inaccurate or inappropriate content; and contains many errors in spelling, grammar, or style. Do not solve the problem.
3-Format & Layout	Format and arrange all elements to communicate information and ideas, clarify function, illustrate relationships, and indicate relative importance.	Apply appropriate format and layout features to some elements, but not others. Overuse features, causing minor distraction.	Apply format and layout that does not communicate information or ideas clearly. Do not use format and layout features to clarify function, illustrate relationships, or indicate relative importance. Use available features excessively, causing distraction.
4-Process	Use an organized approach that integrates planning, development, self-assessment, revision, and reflection.	Demonstrate an organized approach in some areas, but not others; or, use an insufficient process of organization throughout.	Do not use an organized approach to solve the problem.

OUTCOMES-BASED ASSESSMENTS

GO! Think	Project 5L Summer Sections

PROJECT FILES

For Project 5L, you will need the following file:

e05L_Summer_Sections

You will save your workbook as:

Lastname_Firstname_5L_Summer_Sections

From your student files, open the file e05L_Summer_Sections, and then save it in your Excel Chapter 5 folder as **Lastname_Firstname_5L_Summer_Sections** Select the entire range and insert a table with headers. Create a custom table style, name it **Summer Sections** and then apply it to the table. Create a custom sort, and then custom sort the Campus information in Online, Valley, Park, West order. Include the file name in the footer, add appropriate properties, include **summer sections** as Tags, set orientation to landscape and width to 1 page, save the file as a PDF, and then submit as directed.

END | You have completed Project 5L

Build from Scratch

GO! Think	Project 5M Social Science	Online

Build from Scratch

You and GO!	Project 5N Personal Expenses	Online

Creating Charts, Diagrams, and Templates

EXCEL 2013

GO! to Work
Video E6

PROJECT 6A

OUTCOMES
Create column charts, line charts, process diagrams, and organization charts.

PROJECT 6B

OUTCOMES
Create and use an Excel template and protect worksheets to ensure consistency in formulas and data.

OBJECTIVES

1. Create and Format Sparklines and a Column Chart
2. Create and Format a Line Chart
3. Create and Modify a SmartArt Graphic
4. Create and Modify an Organization Chart

OBJECTIVES

5. Create an Excel Template
6. Protect a Worksheet
7. Create a Worksheet Based on a Template

auremar/Fotolia

In This Chapter

In this chapter, you will create charts and diagrams to communicate data visually. Charts make a set of numbers easier to understand by displaying data in a graphical format. Excel's SmartArt illustrations make diagrams, like an organizational chart or process cycle, easy to comprehend.

In this chapter, you will also work with templates. Templates have built-in formulas for performing calculations and are used for standardization and protection of data. You will use predefined templates that can be used for financial reports such as an expense report or purchase order, and you will create a template for an order form.

The Dallas – Ft. Worth Job Fair is a nonprofit organization that brings together employers and job seekers in the Dallas – Ft. Worth metropolitan area. Each year the organization holds a number of targeted job fairs and the annual Dallas – Ft. Worth fair draws over 900 employers in more than 75 industries and registers more than 30,000 candidates. Candidate registration is free; employers pay a nominal fee to display and present at the fairs. Candidate resumes and employer postings are managed by a state-of-the-art database system, allowing participants quick and accurate access to job data and candidate qualifications.

Attendance Charts and Diagrams

PROJECT ACTIVITIES

In Activities 6.01 through 6.17, you will create and format column and line charts for the Dallas – Ft. Worth Job Fair that display attendance patterns at the fairs over a five-year period. You will also create a process diagram and an organization chart. Your completed worksheets will look similar to Figure 6.1.

PROJECT FILES

For Project 6A, you will need the following file:

e06A_Attendance

You will save your workbook as:

Lastname_Firstname_6A_Attendance

PROJECT RESULTS

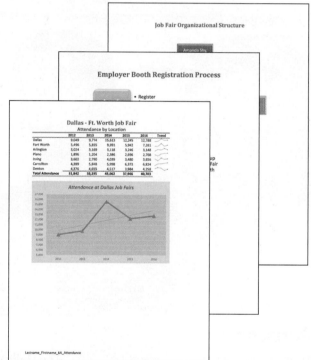

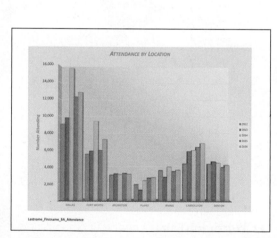

FIGURE 6.1 Project 6A Attendance Charts and Diagrams

Objective 1   Create and Format Sparklines and a Column Chart

Video E6-1

Recall that **sparklines** are tiny charts that fit within a cell and give a visual trend summary alongside your data. Also recall that a **column chart**, which presents data graphically in vertical columns, is useful to make comparisons among related data.

Activity 6.01   Creating and Formatting Sparklines

To create sparklines, first select the data you want to plot—represent graphically—and then select the range of cells alongside each row of data where you want to display the sparklines.

1 ▶ Start Excel. From your student files, open the file **e06A_Attendance**. Press F12 to display the **Save As** dialog box, navigate to the location where you will store your workbooks for this chapter, and then create a new folder named **Excel Chapter 6** Open your folder, and then **Save** the workbook as **Lastname_Firstname_6A_Attendance**

This data shows the number of applicants who have attended job fairs held over a five-year period at various locations in the greater Dallas - Ft. Worth area.

2 ▶ Select the range **B4:F10**. Click **Quick Analysis** [icon], and then click **SPARKLINES**. Compare your screen with Figure 6.2.

⟳ ANOTHER WAY   On the INSERT tab, in the Sparklines group, click Line.

FIGURE 6.2

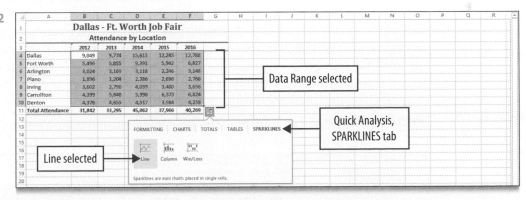

3 ▶ On the **SPARKLINES** tab, click **Line**. Compare your screen with Figure 6.3.

Sparklines display alongside each row of data and provide a quick visual trend summary for each city's job fair attendance. The sparklines provide a quick indication that for each location, attendance has had an overall upward trend over the five-year period.

FIGURE 6.3

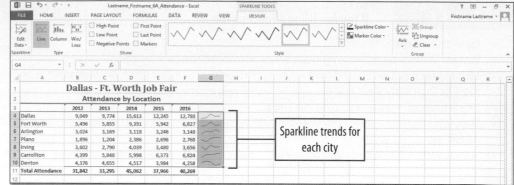

4 ▷ On the **DESIGN tab**, in the **Show group**, select the **High Point** check box and the **Last Point** check box.

   By adding the High Point and Last Point markers, you further emphasize the visual story that sparklines depict.

5 ▷ On the **DESIGN tab**, in the **Style group**, click **More** ⬇, and then in the third row, click the first style—**Sparkline Style Accent 1, (no dark or light)**.

6 ▷ In cell **G3**, type **Trend** and press Enter. Press Ctrl + Home, **Save** 🖫 your workbook, and then compare your screen with Figure 6.4.

   Use styles in this manner to further enhance your sparklines.

FIGURE 6.4

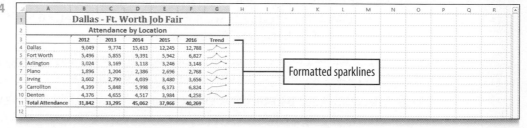

Activity 6.02 | Creating a Column Chart

A chart is a graphic representation of data. When you create a chart, first decide whether you are going to plot the values representing totals or the values representing details—you cannot plot both in the same chart. Excel's ***Recommended Charts*** feature can help you make this decision by previewing suggested charts based upon patterns in your data. In this activity, you will select the details—the number of attendees at each location each year. To help the reader understand the chart, you will also select the *labels* for the data—the column and row headings that describe the values. Here, the labels are the location names and the years.

1 ▷ Take a moment to study the data elements shown in Figure 6.5.

FIGURE 6.5

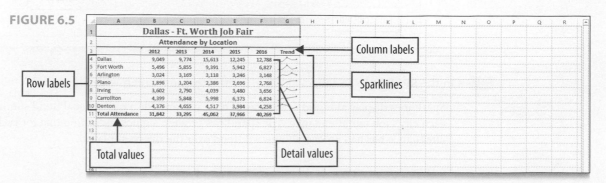

2 Select the range **A3:F10**. On the **INSERT tab**, in the **Charts group**, click **Recommended Charts**. Compare your screen with Figure 6.6.

Excel recommends several charts based upon your data. The Clustered Column chart is displayed in the preview window.

FIGURE 6.6

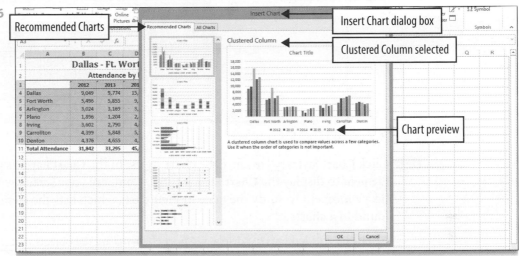

ANOTHER WAY   Click Quick Analysis, click CHARTS, and then click More Charts to open the Insert Chart dialog box.

3 In the **Insert Chart** dialog box, with the **Clustered Column** chart selected, click **OK**.

4 On the **DESIGN tab**, in the **Location group**, click **Move Chart**.

The Move Chart dialog box displays. You can accept the default to display the chart as an object within the worksheet, which is an ***embedded chart***. Or, you can place the chart on a separate sheet, called a ***chart sheet***, in which the chart fills the entire page. A chart sheet is useful when you want to view a chart separately from the worksheet data.

5 In the Move Chart dialog box, click **New sheet**. In the **New sheet** box, type **Attendance Chart** and then click **OK**.

6 On the **DESIGN tab**, in the **Type group**, click **Change Chart Type**. In the **Change Chart Type** dialog box, on the **All Charts** tab, if necessary, click **Column** on the left, and then click the fourth chart icon—**3-D Clustered column**. Click **OK**.

In this manner you can change the chart type.

7 In the upper right corner of the chart, click **Chart Styles**. Click **Style 3**. Compare your screen with Figure 6.7.

ANOTHER WAY   On the DESIGN tab, in the Chart Styles group, click More, and then click Style 3.

FIGURE 6.7

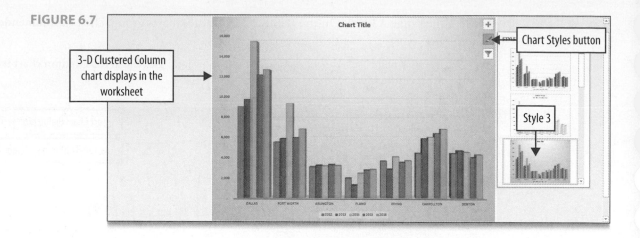

Chart Styles button

3-D Clustered Column chart displays in the worksheet

Style 3

8 Click **Chart Styles** to close the chart styles. In the **Chart Layouts group**, click **Add Chart Element** to display the **Chart Elements** list. Compare your screen with Figure 6.8, and then take a moment to study the table in Figure 6.9, which lists the elements that are typically found in a chart.

The Chart Elements list displays. *Chart elements* are the objects that make up a chart. From the Chart Elements list, you can select a chart element to format it.

FIGURE 6.8

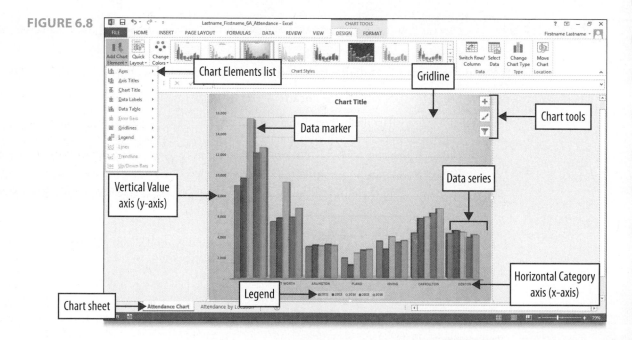

Chart Elements list

Gridline

Data marker

Chart tools

Vertical Value axis (y-axis)

Data series

Legend

Horizontal Category axis (x-axis)

Chart sheet

FIGURE 6.9

OBJECT	DESCRIPTION
Axis	A line that serves as a frame of reference for measurement and that borders the chart plot area.
Category labels	The labels that display along the bottom of the chart to identify the category of data.
Chart area	The entire chart and all its elements.
Data labels	Labels that display the value, percentage, and/or category of each particular data point and can contain one or more of the choices listed—Series name, Category name, Value, or Percentage.
Data marker	A column, bar, area, dot, pie slice, or other symbol in a chart that represents a single data point.
Data points	The numeric values of the selected worksheet.
Data series	A group of related data points that are plotted in a chart.
Gridlines	Lines in the plot area that aid the eye in determining the plotted values.
Horizontal Category axis (x-axis)	The axis that displays along the bottom of the chart to identify the category of data. Excel uses the row titles as the category names.
Legend	A key that identifies patterns or colors that are assigned to the categories in the chart.
Major unit value	The value that determines the spacing between tick marks and between the gridlines in the plot area.
Plot area	The area bounded by the axes, including all the data series.
Tick mark labels	Identifying information for a tick mark generated from the cells on the worksheet used to create the chart.
Tick marks	The short lines that display on an axis at regular intervals.
Vertical Value axis (y-axis)	The axis that displays along the left side of the chart to identify the numerical scale on which the charted data is based.
Walls and floor	The areas surrounding a 3-D chart that give dimension and boundaries to the chart. Two walls and one floor display within the plot area.

MICROSOFT EXCEL CHART ELEMENTS

9 If necessary, click the **Add Chart Elements arrow**. In the **Chart Elements** list, point to **Legend**, and then click **Right**.

The legend is easier to see on the right side of the chart.

BY TOUCH   In the upper right corner of the chart, tap the Chart Elements button, tap Legend, and then tap Right.

10 In the **Chart Area**, click the **Chart Title** to select it. In the **Formula Bar**, type **Attendance** as the chart title, and then press Enter to display the text in the chart.

11 Click the tallest column displayed for the Dallas category. Compare your screen with Figure 6.10.

All the columns representing the Series *2014* are selected—selection handles display at the corners of each column in the series—and a ScreenTip displays the value for the column you are pointing to. Recall that a data series is a group of related data—in this case, the attendees to all the job fairs that were held in 2014. Also notice that the Formula Bar displays the address for the selected data series.

FIGURE 6.10

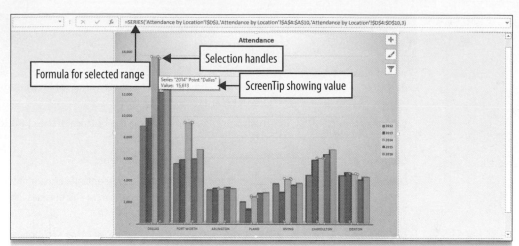

12 ▶ Locate the **Plano** category, and then click the shortest column in that group.

    The selected series changes to those columns that represent the attendees at the job fairs in 2013. The Formula Bar and Chart Elements box change and a new ScreenTip displays.

13 ▶ Click outside the chart area to deselect the series.

More **Knowledge**   **Sizing Handles and Selection Handles**

Sizing handles and selection handles look the same, and the terms are often used interchangeably. If a two-headed resize arrow—⬍, ↔, ⤡, ⤢—displays when you point to boxes surrounding an object, it is a sizing handle; otherwise, it is a selection handle. Some objects in a chart cannot be resized, such as the category axis or the value axis, but they can be selected and then reformatted.

Activity 6.03 | Changing the Display of Chart Data

    As you create a chart, you make choices about the data to include, the chart type, chart titles, and location. You can change the chart type, change the way the data displays, add or change titles, select different colors, and modify the background, scale, and chart location.

    In the column chart you created, the attendance numbers are displayed along the value axis—the vertical axis—and the locations for each job fair are displayed along the category axis—the horizontal axis. The cells you select for a chart include the row and column labels from your worksheet. In a column or line chart, Excel selects whichever has more items—either the rows or the columns—and uses those labels to plot the data series, in this case, the locations.

    After plotting the data series, Excel uses the remaining labels—in this example, the years identified in the row headings—to create the data series labels on the legend. The legend is the key that defines the colors used in the chart; here it identifies the data series for the years. A different color is used for each year in the data series. The chart, as currently displayed, compares the change in attendance year to year grouped by category location. You can change the chart to display the years on the category axis and the locations as the data series identified in the legend.

1 ▶ In the **Dallas** category, click the fourth column.

    All columns with the same color are selected. The ScreenTip displays *Series "2015" Point "Dallas" Value: 12,245.*

2 ▶ Point to each of the other purple columns that are selected and notice that the ScreenTip that displays identifies each purple column as being in the *Series "2015."*

3 ▶ On the **DESIGN tab**, in **the Data group**, click **Switch Row/Column**, and then compare your screen with Figure 6.11.

    The chart changes to display the locations as the data series. The locations are the row headings in the worksheet and are now identified in the legend. The years display as the category labels.

FIGURE 6.11

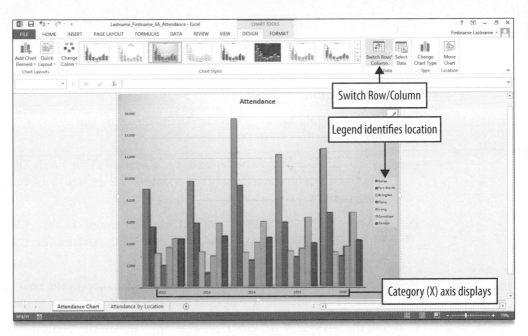

4 Click one of the purple columns. Point to each purple column and read the ScreenTip.

The ScreenTips for the purple columns now identify this as the Plano series.

5 On the **DESIGN tab**, in the **Data group**, click **Switch Row/Column** again, and then **Save** 🖫 your workbook.

The chart changes back to the more useful arrangement with the years identified in the legend and the locations displayed as the category labels.

More Knowledge | **Changing the Data in a Chart**

After you have created a chart, you can adjust the range of data that is displayed in the chart or add an additional data series. To do so, on the DESIGN tab, in the Data group, click Select Data. Edit the source address displayed in the Chart data range box, or drag the data in the worksheet to adjust the range as needed.

Activity 6.04 | Editing and Formatting the Chart Title

The data displayed in the chart focuses on the attendance by location. It is good practice to create a chart title to reflect your charted data.

1 Click the **Chart Title**—*Attendance*—to select it, and then click to position the mouse pointer to the right of *Attendance*.

To edit a title, click once to select the chart object, and then click a second time to position the insertion point in the title and change to editing mode.

2 Press [Spacebar] one time, and then type **by Location**

3 Point to the **Chart Title**—*Attendance by Location*—right-click the border of the chart title, and then click **Font** to display the **Font** dialog box.

4 Set the **Font style** to **Bold Italic** and change the **Font Size** to **20**. Click the **Font color arrow**, and then under **Theme Colors**, in the first column, click the last color—**White, Background 1, Darker 50%**. Apply the **Small Caps** effect. Click **OK**, and then **Save** 🖫 your workbook.

Use the Font dialog box in this manner to apply multiple formats to a chart title.

Activity 6.05 | Adding, Formatting, and Aligning Axis Titles

You can add a title to display with both the value axis and the category axis.

1 On the **DESIGN tab**, in the **Chart Layouts group**, click **Add Chart Element**, click **Axis Titles**, and then click **Primary Vertical**.

2 In the **Formula Bar**, type **Number Attending** as the **Vertical Axis Title**, and then press Enter to display the title text in the chart.

3 On the left side of the chart, point to the **Vertical (Value) Axis Title** you just added, select the text, and then on the mini toolbar, change the **Font Size** to **14** and the **Font Color** to **White, Background 1, Darker 50%**.

4 On the **FORMAT tab**, in the **Current Selection group**, click the **Chart Elements arrow**, click **Horizontal (Category) Axis**, and then at the bottom of the chart, notice that the **Category axis** is selected.

5 Point to the selected axis, right-click, click **Font**, and in the **Font dialog box**, click the **Font style arrow**, click **Bold**, and change the **Font Color** to **White, Background 1, Darker 50%**. Click **OK**.

6 On the left side of the chart, point to any value in the **Vertical (Value) Axis**, and then right-click to select the axis. Click the **HOME tab**, and then in the **Font group**, change the **Font Size** to **12**.

7 Save your workbook, and then compare your screen with Figure 6.12.

FIGURE 6.12

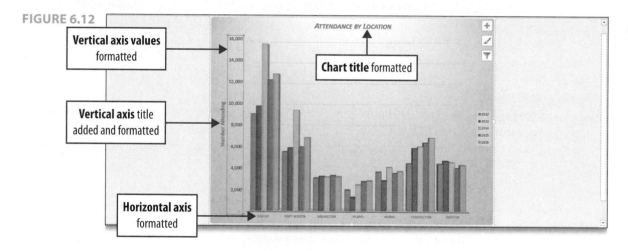

Activity 6.06 | Editing Source Data

One of the characteristics of an Excel chart is that it reflects changes made to the underlying data.

1 In the **Fort Worth** column cluster, point to the last column—**2016**. Notice that the *Value* for this column is *6,827*.

2 Display the **Attendance by Location** worksheet, and then in cell **F5**, type **7261** and press Enter.

3 Redisplay the **Attendance Chart** worksheet, Save your workbook, and then point to the **Fort Worth** column for 2016. Compare your screen with Figure 6.13.

FIGURE 6.13

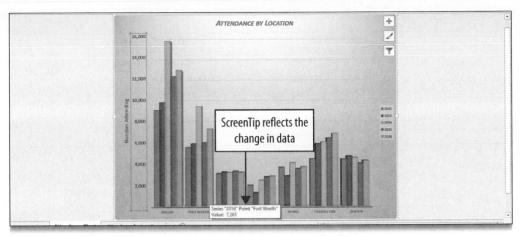

Activity 6.07 | Formatting the Chart Floor and Chart Walls

If your chart style includes shaded walls and a floor, you can format these elements.

1 On the **FORMAT tab**, in the **Current Selection group**, click the **Chart Elements arrow**, and then click **Back Wall**. Then in the same group, click **Format Selection**.

2 In the **Format Wall** pane, if necessary, click ▷ to expand **FILL**, click **Solid fill**, and then click the **Fill Color arrow**. Under **Theme Colors**, in the fourth column, click the fourth color—**Dark Blue, Text 2, Lighter 40%**—and then drag the slider to set the **Transparency** to **75%**.

3 Click the arrow to the right of **WALL OPTIONS** to display the **Chart Elements** list. Select **Side Wall**, and then apply the same fill, but with a **Transparency** of **60%**.

4 From the **Chart Elements** list, select the **Floor**, and then apply a **Solid fill** using the last Theme color in the first column—**White, Background 1, Darker 50%** with **0% Transparency**.

5 From the **Chart Elements** list, select the **Chart Area**, and then apply a **Solid fill** using **Olive Green, Accent 3, Lighter 60%**—in the seventh column, the third color. **Close** ✖ the **Format Chart Area** pane, click **Save** 🖫, and then compare your screen with Figure 6.14.

FIGURE 6.14

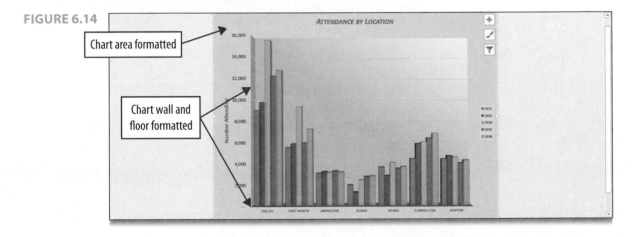

Video E6-2

Line charts show trends over time. A line chart can consist of one line, such as the price of a single company's stock over time, or it can display more than one line to show a comparison of related numbers over time. For example, charts tracking stock or mutual fund performance often display the price of the mutual fund on one line and an industry standard for that particular type of fund on a different line.

Activity 6.08 | Creating a Line Chart

In this activity, you will create a line chart showing the change in attendance at the Dallas – Ft. Worth Job Fair over a five-year period.

1 Display the **Attendance by Location** worksheet.

2 Select the range **A3:F4**, and then, on the **INSERT tab**, in the **Charts group**, click **Insert Line Chart** ⑂▾. In the second row, click the first chart type—**Line with Markers**. Compare your screen with Figure 6.15.

> Cell A3 must be included in the selection, despite being empty, because the same number of cells must be in each selected row. Excel identifies the first row as a category because of the empty first cell.

FIGURE 6.15

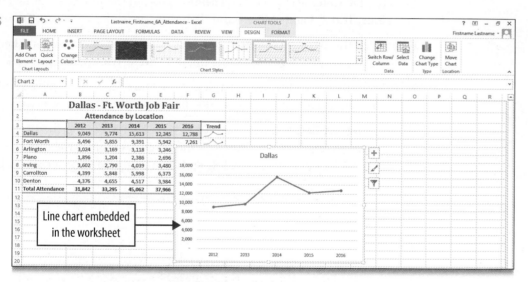

3 Point to the chart border to display the 🔖 pointer, and then drag the upper left corner of the chart inside the upper left corner of cell **A13**.

4 Scroll down as necessary to view **row 30**. Point to the lower right corner of the chart to display the ⤢ pointer, and then drag the lower right corner of the chart inside the lower right corner of cell **G29**. Click anywhere outside the chart to deselect. **Save** 🖫 your workbook. Compare your screen with Figure 6.16.

> When you use the corner sizing handles to resize an object, the proportional dimensions—the relative height and width—are retained.

FIGURE 6.16

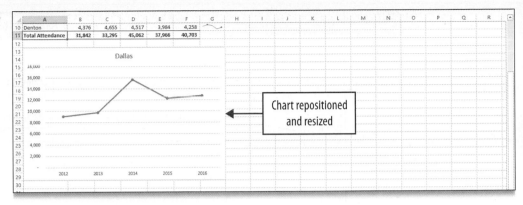

Chart repositioned and resized

Activity 6.09 | Changing a Chart Title

When you select the chart type, the resulting chart might contain elements that you want to delete or change. For example, the chart title can be more specific.

1 Click the **Chart Title**—*Dallas*. In the **Formula Bar**, type **Attendance at Dallas Job Fairs** as the chart title, and then press Enter to display the title text in the chart.

2 Point to the **Chart Title**, right-click, and then click **Font**. Change the **Font Size** to **16** and the **Font Style** to **Bold Italic**. Click **OK**. Click outside of the chart to deselect it, **Save** 🖫 your workbook, and then compare your chart with Figure 6.17.

The size of the title increases, and the plot area decreases slightly.

FIGURE 6.17

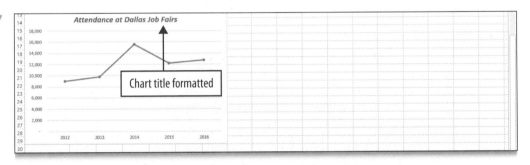

Chart title formatted

Activity 6.10 | Changing the Values on the Value Axis

You can change the values on the value axis to increase or decrease the variation among the numbers displayed. The *scale* is the range of numbers in the data series; the scale controls the minimum, maximum, and incremental values on the value axis. In the line chart, the attendance figures for Dallas are all higher than 7,000, but the scale begins at zero, so the line occupies only the upper area of the chart. Adjust the scale as necessary to make your charts meaningful to the reader.

1 On the left side of the line chart, point to any number, and then when the ScreenTip displays *Vertical (Value) Axis*, right-click, and then click **Format Axis**.

2 In the **Format Axis** pane, if necessary, click ▷ to expand **AXIS OPTIONS**. Under **Bounds**, in the **Minimum** box, type **5000** Under **Units**, change the **Major unit** to **1000** and then press Enter. Compare your screen with Figure 6.18.

Here you can change the beginning and ending numbers displayed on the chart and also change the unit by which the major gridlines display. Excel formats the values with one decimal.

FIGURE 6.18

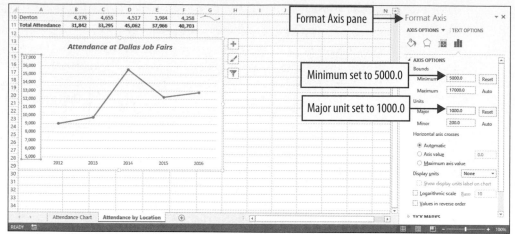

3 In the upper right corner of the **Format Axis** pane, click **Close** ☒. Click **Save** 🖫, and then compare your screen with Figure 6.19.

> The Value Axis begins at 5000 with major gridlines at intervals of 1000. This will emphasize the change in attendance over the five years by starting the chart at a higher number and decreasing the interval for gridlines.

FIGURE 6.19

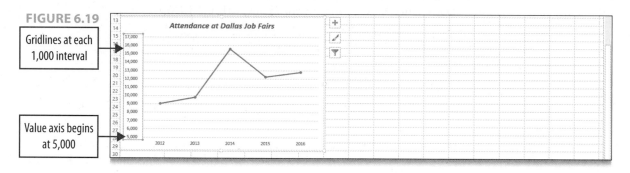

Activity 6.11 | Formatting the Plot Area and the Data Series

1 Right-click anywhere within the lined **Plot Area**, and then click **Format Plot Area**.

> The Format Plot Area pane displays. Here you can change the border of the plot area or the background color.

2 In the **Format Plot Area** pane, if necessary, click ▷ to expand **FILL**. Click **Solid fill**. Click the **Fill Color arrow**, and then under **Theme Colors**, in the first column, click the fourth color—**White, Background 1, Darker 25%**.

3 Point to the blue chart line, right-click, and then click **Format Data Series**.

> In the Format Data Series pane, you can change the data markers—the indicators for a data point value, which on the line chart is represented by a diamond shape. You can also change the line connecting the data markers.

4 In the **Format Data Series** pane, click **Fill & Line** 🖎. Under **LINE**, click **Solid line**. Use the spin box arrows to set the **Width** to **4 pt**.

5 Under the **Fill & Line** icon, click **MARKER**. Click ▷ to expand **MARKER OPTIONS**. Click **Built-in**, click the **Type arrow**, and then click the **triangle**—the third symbol in the list. Set the **Size** of the **Marker Type** to **12**

6 Under **FILL**, click **Solid fill**, and then click the **Fill Color arrow**. Under **Theme Colors**, in the first column, click the last color—**White, Background 1, Darker 50%**.

7 Under **Border**, click **No line**, and **Close** ✖ the **Format Data Series** pane.

8 On the **FORMAT tab**, in the **Current Selection** group, click the **Chart Elements arrow**, and then click **Chart Area**. In the same group, click **Format Selection** to display the **Format Chart Area** pane, and then apply a **Solid fill** using **White, Background 1, Darker 15%**—in the first column, the third color. **Close** ✖ the **Format Data Series** pane.

9 Click in any cell outside of the chart, **Save** 🖫 your workbook, and then compare your screen with Figure 6.20.

FIGURE 6.20

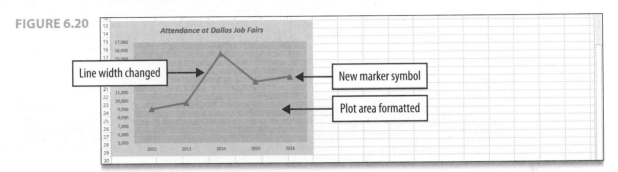

Activity 6.12 | Inserting a Trendline

A *trendline* is a graphic representation of trends in a data series, such as a line sloping upward to represent increased sales over a period of months. A trendline is always associated with a data series, but it does not represent the data of that data series. Rather, a trendline depicts trends in the existing data.

1 Click slightly inside the chart border to select the entire chart. Next to the chart, click **Chart Elements** ➕, click **Trendline**, and then click **Linear**. **Save** 🖫 your workbook, and then compare your screen with Figure 6.21.

> A linear trendline displays in the chart. The chart shows a significant increase in attendance for 2014, a drop in attendance in 2015, but the trendline indicates an overall increasing trend in attendance over the past five years.

FIGURE 6.21

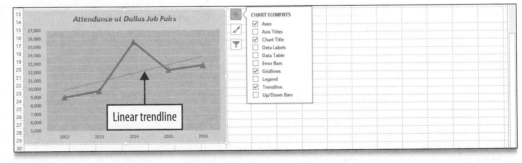

Objective 3   Create and Modify a SmartArt Graphic

Video E6-3

A *SmartArt graphic* is a visual representation of your information and ideas. You can create SmartArt graphics by choosing from among many different layouts to communicate complex messages and relationships easily and effectively.

Unlike charts, a SmartArt graphic does not depend on any underlying data in a worksheet; rather, it is a graphical tool that depicts ideas or associations. In the following activities, you will create a process diagram to illustrate how to register for an employer booth at the job fair.

Activity 6.13 | Creating a Process SmartArt Graphic

In this activity, you will use a Process SmartArt graphic, which shows steps in a process or timeline.

1 Click **New sheet** ⊕. Double-click the **Sheet1 tab**, and rename the sheet tab **Process Chart** In cell **A1** type **Employer Booth Registration Process** and then press Enter.

2 Merge and center the text you just typed across **A1:H1**, apply the **Title** cell style, and then change the **Font Size** to **22**.

3 On the **INSERT tab**, in the **Illustrations group**, click **SmartArt**.

4 On the left, notice the types of SmartArt graphics that are available, and then take a moment to examine the table in Figure 6.22.

FIGURE 6.22

SMARTART	
USE THIS SMARTART TYPE:	**TO DO THIS:**
List	Show non-sequential information
Process	Show steps in a process or timeline
Cycle	Show a continual process
Hierarchy	Create an organization chart or show a decision tree
Relationship	Illustrate connections
Matrix	Show how parts relate to a whole
Pyramid	Use a series of pictures to show relationships
Picture	Display pictures in a diagram

5 On the left, click **Process**, and then in the first row, click the third option—**Step Down Process**. Click **OK**.

6 With your insertion point blinking in the first bullet of the **Text Pane**, type **Apply**

The text *Apply* displays in the Text Pane and in the first box in the diagram. Use the ***Text Pane***, which displays to the left of the graphic, to input and organize the text in your graphic. The Text Pane is populated with placeholder text that you replace with your information. If you prefer, close the Text Pane and type directly into the graphic.

7 In the **Text Pane**, click the next bullet, which is indented, and then type **Register for Booth** Compare your screen with Figure 6.23.

FIGURE 6.23

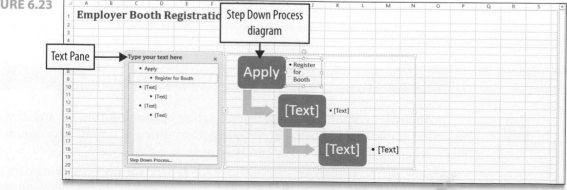

8 In the **Text Pane**, click the next bullet, and then type **Prepare** Under *Prepare* click the indented bullet and type **Booth Number Assigned**

9 Click the next bullet and type **Attend** Click the next bullet, and then type **Set up Job Fair Booth** Compare your diagram with Figure 6.24.

The Text Pane entries display on the left in the Text Pane, and the process diagram with entries displays on the right in the process diagram.

FIGURE 6.24

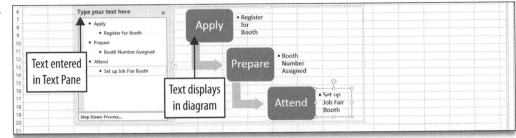

10 **Close** the **Text Pane**, and then **Save** your workbook.

Activity 6.14 | **Modifying the Diagram Style**

Excel offers preformatted SmartArt styles that can be applied to a diagram.

1 With the SmartArt still selected, on the **DESIGN tab**, in the **SmartArt Styles group**, click **More**. Under **3-D**, click the first style—**Polished**.

2 In the **SmartArt Styles group**, click **Change Colors**, and then under **Colorful**, click the third option—**Colorful Range – Accent Colors 3 to 4**.

3 By using the pointer, drag the upper left corner of the graphic border inside the upper left corner of cell **A4**. Point to the lower right corner of the graphic's border to display the pointer, and then drag to resize the graphic and position the lower right corner inside the lower right corner of cell **H22**. **Save** your workbook, and then compare your screen with Figure 6.25.

FIGURE 6.25

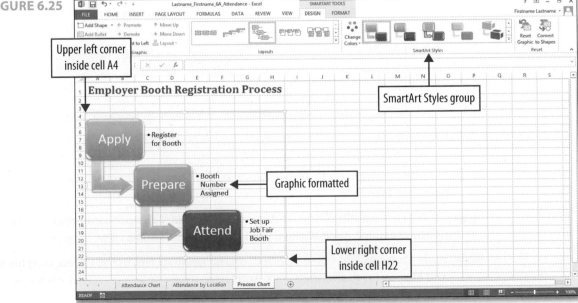

Video E6-4

An ***organization chart*** depicts reporting relationships within an organization.

Activity 6.15 | Creating and Modifying a SmartArt Organization Chart

In this activity, you will create an organizational chart that shows the reporting relationship among the Job Fair Director, Employer Relations Manager, Job Applicant Program Manager, Tech Support Supervisor, and Help Desk Technician.

1 Click **New sheet** ⊕. Double-click the **Sheet2 tab** and rename it **Organization Chart** In cell **A1**, type **Job Fair Organizational Structure** and then merge and center this title across the range **A1:H1**. Apply the **Title** cell style.

2 On the **INSERT tab**, in the **Illustrations group**, click **SmartArt** 🖼. On the left, click **Hierarchy**, and then in the first row, click the first graphic—**Organization Chart**. Click **OK**. If the Text Pane displays, close it.

N O T E   **Displaying the Text Pane**

Typing in the Text Pane is optional. If you have closed the Text Pane and want to reopen it, select the graphic, click the DESIGN tab, and then in the Create Graphic group, click Text Pane. Alternatively, click the arrow on left border of SmartArt graphic to display the Text Pane.

---

3 In the graphic, with the first [**Text**] box selected, type **Amanda Shy, Job Fair Director**

4 In the box below the *Job Fair Director*, click on the *edge* of the box to display a solid line border—if a dashed border displays, click the edge of the box again. With the box bordered with a solid line, press Delete. Compare your screen with Figure 6.26.

Three shapes comprise the second level of the organization chart.

FIGURE 6.26

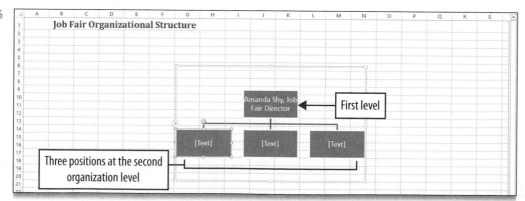

5 In leftmost shape on the second level of the organization chart, type **Linda Wong, Employer Relations Manager**

6 Click in the middle shape, and type **Miriam Ruiz, Job Applicant Program Manager** In the rightmost shape, type **Michael Gold, Tech Support Supervisor**

7 With *Michael Gold* shape selected, on the **DESIGN tab**, in the **Create Graphic group**, click the **Add Shape arrow**, and then click **Add Shape Below**.

A new shape displays below the Tech Support Supervisor shape.

8 Type **Ivan Soklov, Help Desk Technician**

9 In the **SmartArt Styles group**, click **More**, and then under **3-D**, click the first style—**Polished**. Click **Change Colors**, and then under **Colorful**, click the fifth color arrangement—**Colorful Range – Accent Colors 5 to 6**. Click **Save** and then compare your screen with Figure 6.27.

FIGURE 6.27

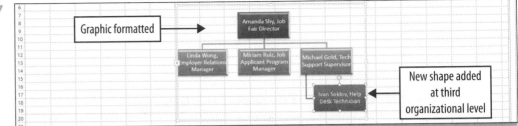

Graphic formatted

New shape added at third organizational level

Activity 6.16 | Adding Effects to a SmartArt Graphic

In this activity, you will change the formatting and layout of the graphic.

1 With the *Ivan Soklov* shape selected, on the **FORMAT tab**, in the **Shape Styles group**, click the **Shape Fill arrow**, and then under **Theme Colors**, in the seventh column, click the fifth color—Olive **Green, Accent 3, Darker 25%**.

2 Click the edge of the *Ivan Soklov* shape so that it is surrounded by a solid line and sizing handles and the polished shape displays. Hold down [Ctrl], and click each of the other shapes until all five are selected.

3 With all five shapes selected, on the **FORMAT tab** in the **Shape Styles group**, click the **Shape Effects arrow**, point to **Bevel**, and then under **Bevel**, in the third row, click the second bevel shape—**Riblet**.

4 By using the pointer, drag the upper left corner of the graphic inside the upper left corner of cell **A4**. By using the pointer, drag the lower right corner of the chart inside the lower right corner of cell **H20**.

5 In the shape for *Amanda Shy*, click to position the insertion point after the comma, hold down [Shift], and then press [Enter] to insert a line break. Press [Delete] to delete the extra space. Use the same technique in the remaining shapes to move the job title to the second line.

6 Click cell **A1**, and then **Save** your workbook. Compare your screen with Figure 6.28.

FIGURE 6.28

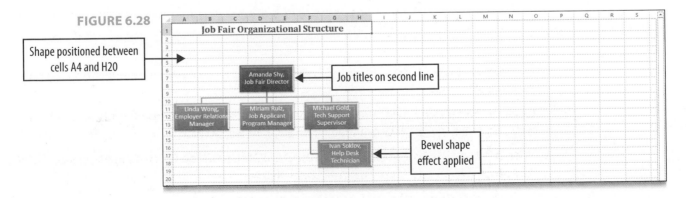

Shape positioned between cells A4 and H20

Job titles on second line

Bevel shape effect applied

1 Display the **Attendance Chart** worksheet. On the **INSERT tab**, in the **Text group**, click **Header & Footer**, and then in the **Page Setup** dialog box, click **Custom Footer**.

2 With the insertion point in the **left section**, in the small toolbar in the center of the dialog box, click **Insert File Name** 📄, and then click **OK** two times.

3 Click the **Attendance by Location sheet tab**, hold down Ctrl, and then click the **Process Chart sheet tab** and the **Organization Chart sheet tab** to select the remaining three worksheets and group them.

4 With the three sheets grouped, insert a footer in the **left section** that includes the file name. Click outside the footer area, and then on the **PAGE LAYOUT tab**, click **Margins**, click **Custom Margins**, and then center the sheets horizontally. Click **OK**. Press Ctrl + Home and return to **Normal** 🔲 view.

5 Click the **FILE tab** to display **Backstage** view. On the right, at the bottom of the **Properties** list, click **Show All Properties**. On the list of **Properties**, in the **Tags** box, type **attendance statistics, organization charts** In the **Subject** box, type your course name and section #. Under **Related People**, be sure that your name displays as the author. If necessary, right-click the author name, click **Edit Property**, type your name, click outside of the Edit person dialog box, and then click OK.

6 Click **Print** and examine the **Print Preview**, make any necessary adjustments, and then **Save** 💾 your workbook. Right-click any of the grouped sheet tabs, and then click **Ungroup Sheets**.

7 Print or submit your workbook electronically as directed by your instructor. **Close** Excel.

END | You have completed Project 6A

PROJECT ACTIVITIES

In Activities 6.18 through 6.25, you will create, format, and edit a booth registration order form template for use by Job Fair staff to ensure that totals for items ordered are calculated accurately. You will also protect the template. Your completed worksheets will look similar to Figure 6.29.

PROJECT FILES

Build from Scratch

For Project 6B, you will need the following files:

e06B_Logo
New blank Excel workbook

You will save your workbooks as:

Lastname_Firstname_6B_Booth_Order
Lastname_Firstname_6B_Order_Template
Lastname_Firstname_6B_Topaz_Order

PROJECT RESULTS

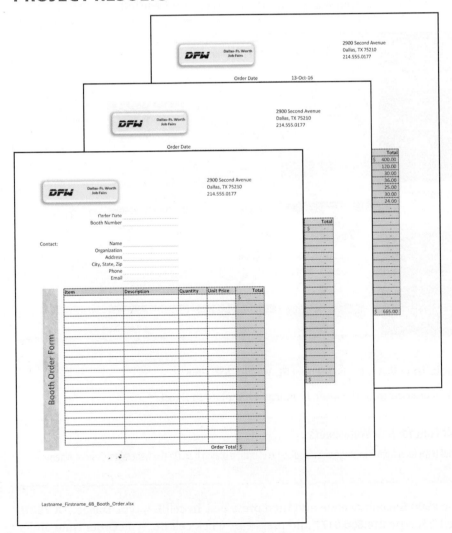

FIGURE 6.29 Project 6B Order Form Template

Video E6-5

A *template* is a workbook that you create and use as the basis for other similar workbooks. Excel also has predesigned templates that include, among others, financial forms to record expenses, time worked, balance sheet items, and other common financial reports.

Standardization and protection are the two main reasons for creating templates for commonly used forms in an organization. *Standardization* means that all forms created within the organization will have a uniform appearance; the data will always be organized in the same manner. *Protection* means that individuals entering data cannot change areas of the worksheet that are protected, and therefore cannot alter important formulas and formats built in to the template.

Activity 6.18 | Entering Template Text

To create a template, start with a blank worksheet; enter the text, formatting, and formulas needed for the specific worksheet purpose, and then save the file as a template. Saving a workbook as a template adds the extension *.xltx* to the file name. In this activity, you will start a workbook for the purpose of creating a purchase order template.

1 ▸ Start Excel. Scroll through the various templates and compare your screen with Figure 6.30.

From the *Search online templates box*, you can find and download many different predesigned templates from Microsoft's Office.com site. Microsoft updates this list frequently.

FIGURE 6.30

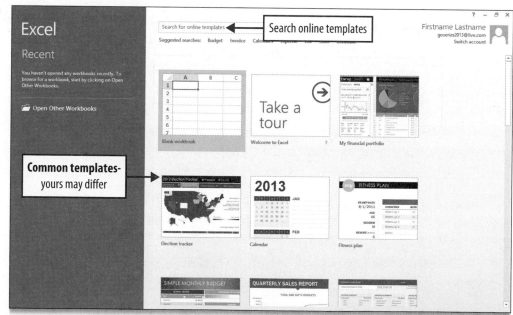

2 ▸ Click **Blank workbook**. In cell **A1**, type **Dallas - Ft. Worth Job Fair**

A blank workbook is created from the built-in Normal template in Excel.

More Knowledge   **Setting the Default Font for New Worksheets**

To change the default body font used in the Excel Normal template, from Backstage view display Excel Option dialog box. On the General tab, under When creating new workbooks, change the default font.

---

3 ▸ Click in cell **E1**, type **2900 Second Avenue** and then press ⏎Enter. In cell **E2**, type **Dallas, TX 75210** and press ⏎Enter. In cell **E3**, type **214.555.0177** and press ⏎Enter. Click cell **B6**, type **Order Date** and press ⏎Enter. In cell **B7**, type **Booth Number** and press ⏎Enter.

4 Click cell **B10**. Type **Name** and press Enter. In cell **B11**, type **Organization** and press Enter. In cell **B12**, type **Address** and press Enter. In cell **B13**, type **City, State, Zip** and press Enter. In cell **B14**, type **Phone** and press Enter. In cell **B15**, type **Email** and press Enter. Click cell **A10**. Type **Contact:** and press Enter.

These labels will comprise the form headings.

5 Click cell **B17**. Type **Item** and press Tab to move to cell **C17**. Continuing across **row 17**, in cell **C17**, type **Description** and press Tab, in cell **D17**, type **Quantity** and press Tab, in cell **E17**, type **Unit Price** and press Tab, and in cell **F17**, type **Total** and press Enter. Select the range **B17:F17**, and then in the **Font** group, click **Bold** B.

The column headings are added to the order form.

6 Save 🖫 the file in your **Excel Chapter 6** folder as **Lastname_Firstname_6B_Booth_Order** Compare your screen with Figure 6.31, and then make any necessary corrections.

Until the format and design of the order form is complete, you will save your work as a normal workbook.

FIGURE 6.31

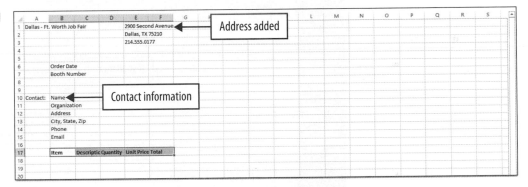

Activity 6.19 | Formatting a Template

One of the goals in designing a template is to make it easy for others to complete. It should be obvious to the person completing the form what information is necessary and where to place the information.

1 Select **column B**. On the **HOME tab**, in the **Cells group**, click **Format**, and then click **Column Width**. In the **Column Width** dialog box, type **21.5** and then click **OK**. In the same manner, widen **column C** to **20.0** Select **columns D:F** and widen to **10.0**

2 Select the range **B6:B15**, and on the **HOME tab**, in the **Alignment group**, click **Align Right** ≣.

3 Click cell **F17**, and then in the **Alignment group**, click **Align Right** ≣.

4 Select the range **C6:C7**. In the **Alignment group**, click the **Dialog Box Launcher** ⬚. In the **Format Cells** dialog box, click the **Border tab**. Under **Line**, in the **Style** list, click the second line in the first column—**the dotted line**.

5 Click the **Color arrow**, and then under **Theme Colors**, in the sixth column, click the third color—**Orange, Accent 2, Lighter 60%**. Under **Border**, click **Middle Border** ⬚, and **Bottom Border** ⬚. Click **OK**.

6 With the range **C6:C7** still selected, in the **Alignment group**, click **Align Right** ≣. Then, with the range still selected, right-click, and on the mini toolbar, click the **Format Painter**, and then select the range **C10:C15** to copy the format.

Inserting borders on cells in a template creates lines as a place to record information when the form is filled out. This provides a good visual cue to the person filling out the form as to where information should be placed.

7 Select the range **B17:F40**. Right-click the selected area and click **Format Cells**. In the **Format Cells** dialog box, if necessary, click the **Border tab**. Under **Presets**, click **Outline** ⊞ and **Inside** ⊞, and then click **OK**.

> This action applies a grid of columns and rows, which is helpful to those individuals completing the form.

8 Select the range **B17:F17**, hold down [Ctrl] and select the nonadjacent range **F18:F40**. In the **Font group**, click the **Fill Color arrow** ⬧ ▾, and then under **Theme Colors**, in the last column, click the third color—**Green, Accent 6, Lighter 60%**. Press [Ctrl] + [Home].

> The fill color is applied to the column headings and to the Total column that will contain the formulas for the template.

9 Press [Ctrl] + [F2] to view the **Print Preview**, and then compare your screen with Figure 6.32.

FIGURE 6.32

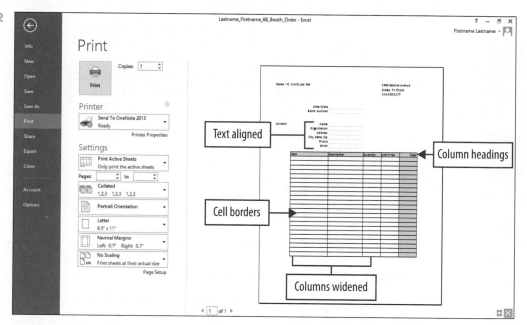

10 Click **Save** to save and return to your workbook.

> A dotted line on the worksheet indicates where the first page would end if the worksheet were printed as it is currently set up. As you develop your template, use the Print Preview to check your progress.

Activity 6.20 | Entering Template Formulas

After the text is entered and formatted in your template, add formulas to the cells where you want the result of the calculations to display. In this activity, you will create a formula in the Total column to determine the dollar value for the quantity of each item ordered, and then create another formula to sum the Total column.

1 In cell **F18**, type **=d18*e18** and click **Enter** ✓.

> A value of 0 displays in cell F18. However, when the person entering information into the worksheet types the Quantity in cell D18 and the Unit Price in cell E18, the formula will multiply the two values to calculate a total for the item.

2 Use the fill handle to copy the formula in cell **F18** down through cell **F39**.

3 Click cell **F40**. On the **HOME tab**, in the **Editing group**, click **AutoSum** Σ AutoSum ▾. Be sure the range displays as *F18:F39*, and then press [Enter].

4 ▶ Select the range **E18:E39**. On the **HOME tab**, in the **Number group**, click **Comma Style** ⟨ ⟩.

The Comma Style is applied. When values are typed into the form, they will display with two decimals and commas in the appropriate locations.

5 ▶ Click cell **F18**, hold down ⟨Ctrl⟩, and then click cell **F40**. In the **Number group**, click **Accounting Number Format** ⟨$ ⟩. Select the range **F19:F39**, and then click **Comma Style** ⟨ ⟩.

Formats are applied to the Total column, and the zero in each cell displays as a hyphen.

6 ▶ Select the range **D40:E40**. In the **Alignment group**, click **Merge and Center**. Type **Order Total** and click **Enter** ⟨✓⟩. In the **Alignment group**, click **Align Right** ⟨≡⟩. In the **Font** group, click **Bold** ⟨B⟩.

A label is added and formatted to identify the total for the entire order.

7 ▶ Select the range **B40:C40**, right-click, and then click **Format Cells**. In the **Format Cells** dialog box, if necessary, click the **Border tab**, and then in the **Border preview** area, click **Left Border**, **Middle Border** ⟨⊞⟩, and **Bottom Border** ⟨⊡⟩ to *remove* these borders from the preview—be sure the right and top lines remain in the preview area. Compare your dialog box with Figure 6.33.

FIGURE 6.33

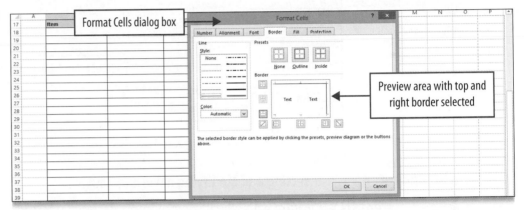

8 ▶ Click **OK**. Press ⟨Ctrl⟩ + ⟨F2⟩ to view the **Print Preview**. Compare your screen with Figure 6.34.

FIGURE 6.34

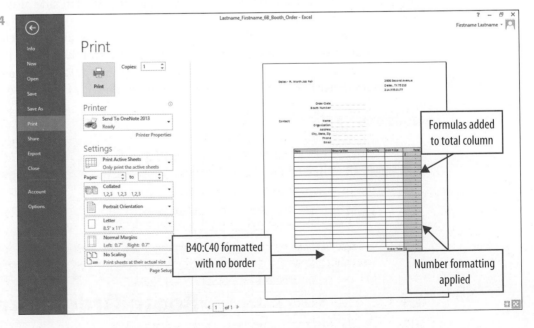

9 ▶ In the **Backstage** view, click **Save** to save and return to your workbook.

Activity 6.21 | Inserting and Modifying an Image

In the following activity, you will add a logo image to the form.

1 Click cell **A1** and press Delete to remove the company name. On the **INSERT tab**, in the **Illustrations group**, click **Pictures**.

2 In the **Insert Picture** dialog box, navigate to your student files, and then insert the file **e06B_Logo**.

The Dallas – Ft. Worth Job Fair logo displays in the upper left corner of the worksheet. The Picture Tools contextual tab displays when the object is selected.

3 With the image selected, on the **FORMAT tab**, in the **Picture Styles group**, click **More** ⏷, and then, in the third row, click the last style—**Bevel Rectangle**.

4 In the **Picture Styles group**, click the **Picture Effects arrow**, point to **Glow**, and then under **Glow Variations**, in second row, click the last effect—**Green, 8 pt. glow, Accent color 6**. Point to the image to display the ⬚ pointer, and then drag the image down and to the right slightly, as shown in Figure 6.35. **Save** 💾 your workbook.

FIGURE 6.35

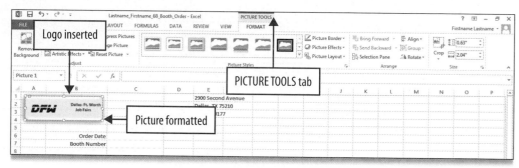

Activity 6.22 | Inserting and Modifying a WordArt Image

WordArt is a feature with which you can insert decorative text in your document, for example to create a stylized image for a heading or logo. Because WordArt is a graphical object, it can be moved and resized. In addition, you can change its shape and color. In this activity, you will create and modify a vertical WordArt heading and place it at the left side of the order form grid.

1 Scroll so that **row 16** is at the top of the Excel window, and then, click cell **A17**. On the **INSERT tab**, in the **Text group**, click **WordArt** ◢▾, and then in the third row, click the first WordArt—**Fill – Black, Text 1, Outline – Background 1, Hard Shadow – Background 1**. Type **Booth Order Form** and then compare your screen with Figure 6.36.

FIGURE 6.36

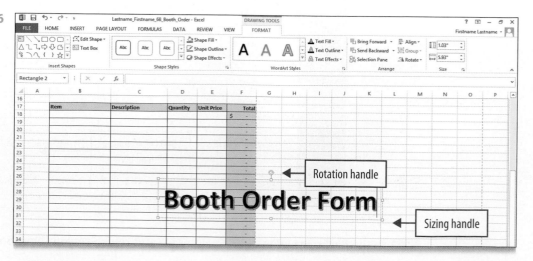

2 ❯ Select the text you just typed, and then from the mini toolbar, change the **Font Size** to **20**.

The WordArt image floats on your screen. Sizing handles display around the outside of the WordArt, and a ***rotation handle*** displays on the top side of the image. Use the rotation handle to rotate an image to any angle.

3 ❯ Point to the **rotation handle** until the 🔄 pointer displays, drag to the left until the WordArt is vertical, as shown in Figure 6.37, and then release the mouse button.

You can use the rotation handle to revolve the image 360 degrees.

FIGURE 6.37

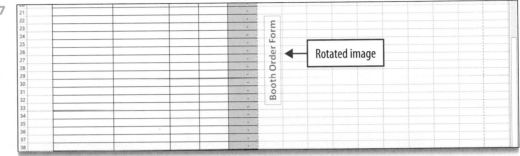

4 ❯ Point to the edge of the **WordArt** image to display the ⛶ pointer. Drag the WordArt image to **column A** and align the top of the image with the top of cell **A17**—centered in the column.

5 ❯ At the lower edge of the WordArt image, point to the center resize handle and drag down so the end of the image aligns at the lower edge of cell **A39**.

6 ❯ With the WordArt image still selected, on the **FORMAT tab**, in the **Shape Styles group**, click the **Shape Fill arrow**, point to **Texture**, and then in the fourth row, click the last texture— **Stationery**. Compare your screen with Figure 6.38.

The WordArt text box fills with Stationery texture and color.

FIGURE 6.38

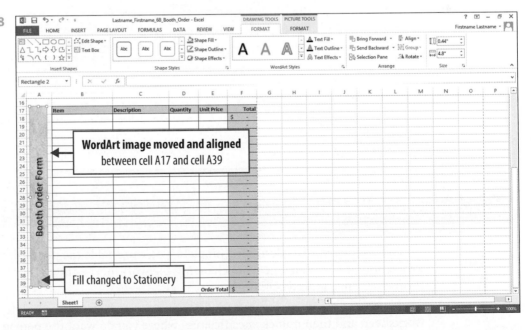

7 ❯ In the **left section**, insert a footer that includes the file name. Click any cell outside the footer to deselect. On the status bar, click **Normal** ⊞. Press Ctrl + Home to move to the top of the worksheet. **Save** 💾 your workbook.

Activity 6.23 | Saving a File as a Template

After you complete the formatting and design of a worksheet that you would like to use over and over again, save it as a template file. When saved as a template file, the *.xltx* file extension is added to the file name instead of *.xlsx*.

If a template is saved in the Templates folder on the hard drive of your computer, or the network location where the Excel software resides, the template will be available to other people who have access to the same system from the New tab in Backstage view.

Regardless of where the template file is saved, when the template is opened, a new *copy* of the workbook opens, preserving the original template for future use.

Instead of the Custom Office Templates folder, which might be restricted in a college lab, you will save the template in your **Excel Chapter 6** folder.

1 Press F12 to display the **Save As** dialog box, and then click the **Save as type arrow**. On the list, click **Excel Template**.

2 Navigate to your **Excel Chapter 6** folder.

3 In the **File name** box, change the **File name** to **Lastname_Firstname_6B_Order_Template** and then click **Save**.

A copy of the template is saved with your other files.

4 **Close** the file and **Close** Excel.

5 From the **Windows Taskbar**, click **File Explorer**. Navigate to your **Excel Chapter 6** folder, and then notice that the *Lastname_Firstname_6B_Order_Template* **Type** is listed as *Microsoft Excel Template*. Compare your screen with Figure 6.39. **Close** ⎡ **X** ⎤ the **File Explorer** window.

FIGURE 6.39

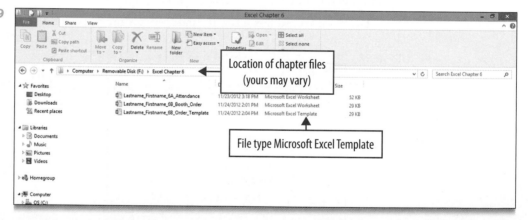

Location of chapter files (yours may vary)

File type Microsoft Excel Template

Objective 6   Protect a Worksheet

Video E6-6

When the template design is complete, you can enable the protection of the worksheet. Protection prevents anyone from changing the worksheet—they cannot insert, modify, delete, or format data in a locked cell.

For purposes of creating a form that you want someone to complete, you can protect the worksheet, and then unlock specific areas where you do want the person completing the form to enter data.

By default, all cells in Excel are *locked*—data cannot be typed into them. However, the locked feature is disabled until you protect the worksheet. After protection is enabled, the locked cells cannot be changed. Of course, you will want to designate some cells to be *unlocked*, so that individuals completing your form can type in their data into those cells.

The basic process is to determine the cells that you will allow people to change or unlock, and then protect the entire worksheet. Then, only the cells that you designated as unlocked will be available to any person using the worksheet. You may add an optional *password* to prevent someone from disabling the worksheet protection. The password can be any combination of numbers, letters, or symbols up to 15 characters long. The password should be shared only with people who have permission to change the template.

Activity 6.24 | Protecting a Worksheet

1 Start Excel. From your **Excel Chapter 6** folder, open your template file **Lastname_Firstname_ 6B_Order_Template**. Select the range **C6:C7**, hold down Ctrl, select the nonadjacent ranges **C10:C15** and **B18:E39**.

> The selected cells are the ones that you want individuals placing booth orders to be able to fill in— they should *not* be locked when protection is applied.

ALERT! **Opening a Template**

If you double-click the template from File Explorer, you will create a new document based on the template, but you will not open the template itself.

---

2 With the three ranges selected, on the **HOME tab**, in the **Cells group**, click **Format**, and then click **Format Cells**. In the **Format Cells** dialog box, click the **Protection tab**.

3 Click to *clear* the check mark from the **Locked** check box, and then compare your screen with Figure 6.40.

> Recall that all cells are locked by default, but the locking feature is enabled only when protection is applied. Therefore, you must *unlock* the cells you want to have available for use in this manner *before* you protect the worksheet.

FIGURE 6.40

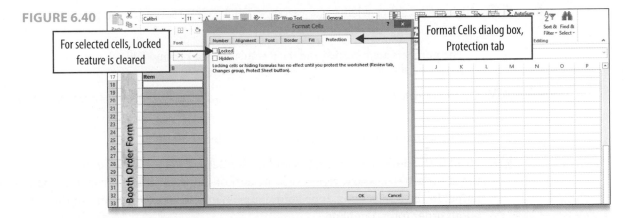

4 Click **OK** to close the **Format Cells** dialog box.

5 In the **Cells group**, click **Format**, and then under **Protection**, click **Protect Sheet**.

> The Protect Sheet dialog box displays. Under *Allow all users of this worksheet to*, the *Select locked cells* and *Select unlocked cells* check boxes are selected by default. The *Select locked cells* option allows the user to click the locked cells and *view* the formulas, but because the cells are locked, they cannot *change* the content or format of the locked cells. If you deselect this option, the user cannot view or even click in a locked cell.

> For the remaining check boxes, you can see that, because they are not selected, users are restricted from performing all other actions on the worksheet.

6 Leave the first two check boxes selected. At the top of the dialog box, be sure the **Protect worksheet and contents of locked cells** check box is selected. In the **Password to unprotect sheet** box type **goseries** Compare your screen with Figure 6.41.

> The password does not display—rather bullets display as placeholders for each letter or character that is typed. Passwords are case sensitive; therefore, *GOSeries* is different from *goseries*.

FIGURE 6.41

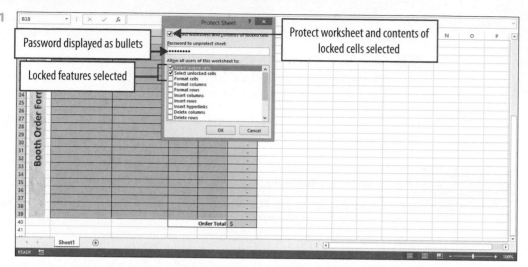

7 Click **OK**. In the **Confirm Password** dialog box, type **goseries** to confirm the password, and then click **OK** to close both dialog boxes.

8 Click in any cell in the **Total** column, type **123** and observe what happens.

> The number is not entered; instead a message informs you that the cell you are trying to change is protected and therefore, read-only.

9 Click **OK** to acknowledge the message. Click cell **D18**, type **2** and press [Tab], type **150** and press [Enter].

> The numbers are recorded and the formulas in cell F18 and F40 calculate and display the results—$300.00.

10 On the **Quick Access Toolbar**, click **Undo** ⤺ two times to remove the two numbers that you typed, and then click **Save** 🖫.

> You have tested your template, and it is protected and saved.

11 Display the **document properties** and under **Related People**, be sure that your name displays as the author. If necessary, right-click the author name, click Edit Property, and then type your name. In the **Subject** box, type your course name and section #, and in the **Tags** box, type **booth order form, template**

12 Display the **Print Preview**, redisplay the workbook, and then make any necessary corrections or adjustments.

13 Save 🖫 your workbook, and then print or submit electronically as directed by your instructor. If required, print or create an electronic version of your worksheet with formulas displayed. **Close** the workbook, but leave Excel open.

More **Knowledge**   **Modifying a Template**

If you need to make changes to a template after it is protected, you must first remove the protection.

Video E6-7

After the template is protected, it is ready for use. If the template is stored in the Templates folder, anyone using the system or network on which it is stored can open it from the New tab in Backstage view. When opened from this location, Excel opens a new copy of the template as a workbook. Then the user can enter information in the unlocked cells and save it as a new file. Templates can be provided to coworkers by storing them on a company intranet, or they can be made available to customers through a website.

Activity 6.25 | Creating a Worksheet Based on a Template

1 ▶ From **Backstage** view, open your **Lastname_Firstname_6B_Order_Template** file.

2 ▶ Press F12 to display the **Save As** dialog box, and then set the **Save as type box** to **Excel Workbook**—the first choice at the top of the list. Navigate to your **Excel Chapter 6** folder, and then in the File name box, type **Lastname_Firstname_6B_Topaz_Order** Compare your screen with Figure 6.42.

FIGURE 6.42

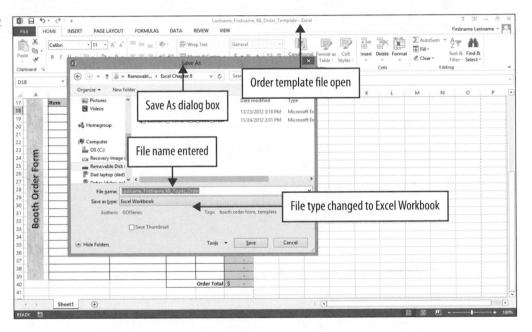

N O T E   Creating a Workbook from a Template in the My Templates Folder in Backstage View

When you are able to open a template from the Templates folder in Backstage view, a new copy of the template opens as a workbook, not as a template, and displays a 1 at the end of the file name in the title bar. The 1 indicates a new workbook. If you are able to work from the Templates folder, the Save operation will automatically set the file type to Excel Workbook.

---

3 ▶ Click **Save**. Click cell **C6**, type **October 13, 2016** and press Enter, and notice that Excel applies the default date format. As the booth number, type **A-3421** and then press Tab to move to cell **C10**.

4 Starting in cell **C10**, enter the company information as follows:

Name	Peter Marsden
Company	Topaz Business, Inc.
Address	6553 Riverside Drive
City, State, Postal code	Ft. Worth, TX 76111
Phone	214.555.0230
Email	pmarsden@topaz.net

5 In cell **B18**, type **Booth space** and press (Tab), type **10 feet by 10 feet** and press (Tab), type **1** and press (Tab), type **400.00** and then press (Tab).

6 Complete the order by entering the following items, pressing (Tab) to move from cell to cell. When you are finished, scroll to display **row 16** at the top of your screen, and then compare your screen with Figure 6.43.

ITEM	DESCRIPTION	QUANTITY	UNIT PRICE
Flooring	Carpet squares	20	6
Table	6 feet, skirted	1	30
Chairs	Guest chair	3	12
Projector screen	Standard	1	25
Sign	Standard	2	15
Curtain	Back wall	2	12

FIGURE 6.43

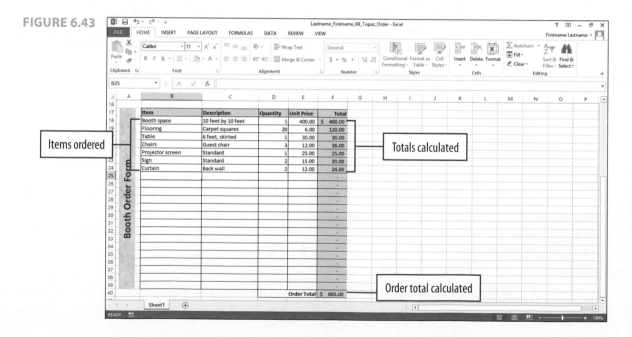

7 Display the **document properties**. Be sure your name displays in the **Author** box and your course name and section # displays in the **Subject** box. Change the **Tags** box to **Topaz booth order**

8 Display the **Print Preview**, be sure the file name displays in the **left section** of the footer. Redisplay the workbook. Make any necessary corrections or adjustments.

9 **Save** 🖫 your workbook, and then print or submit electronically as directed by your instructor. If required, print or create an electronic version of your worksheet with formulas displayed. **Close** Excel.

END | You have completed Project 6B

END OF CHAPTER

SUMMARY

Excel's Recommended Charts feature displays suggested charts based upon your data and helps you to decide the best chart type to use. You can easily modify, create, and format various chart elements.

Excel includes many different chart types, including column and line charts. A column chart shows a comparison among related numbers and a line chart displays a trend over time.

A SmartArt graphic is a visual representation of your information and ideas. SmartArt diagrams are not linked to the underlying worksheet data but float on top of the worksheet like other images.

Templates have built-in formulas and are used for standardization and protection of data. You created a template using text, formatting, formulas, locked and unlocked cells, and password protection.

GO! LEARN IT ONLINE

Review the concepts and key terms in this chapter by completing these online challenges, which you can find at **www.pearsonhighered.com/go.**

Matching and Multiple Choice: Answer matching and multiple choice questions to test what you learned in this chapter. MyITLab®

Crossword Puzzle: Spell out the words that match the numbered clues, and put them in the puzzle squares.

Flipboard: Flip through the definitions of the key terms in this chapter and match them with the correct term.

END OF CHAPTER

REVIEW AND ASSESSMENT GUIDE FOR EXCEL CHAPTER 6

Your instructor may assign one or more of these projects to help you review the chapter and assess your mastery and understanding of the chapter.

		Review and Assessment Guide for Excel Chapter 6	
Project	**Apply Skills from These Chapter Objectives**	**Project Type**	**Project Location**
6C	Objectives 1–4 from Project 6A	**6C Skills Review** A guided review of the skills from Project 6A.	On the following pages
6D	Objectives 5–7 from Project 6B	**6D Skills Review** A guided review of the skills from Project 6B.	On the following pages
6E	Objectives 1–4 from Project 6A	**6E Mastery (Grader Project)** A demonstration of your mastery of the skills in Project 6A with extensive decision making.	In MyITLab and on the following pages
6F	Objectives 5–7 from Project 6B	**6F Mastery (Grader Project)** A demonstration of your mastery of the skills in Project 6B with extensive decision making.	In MyITLab and on the following pages
6G	Combination of Objectives from Projects 6A and 6B	**6G Mastery (Grader Project)** A demonstration of your mastery of the skills in Projects 6A and 6B with extensive decision making.	In MyITLab and on the following pages
6H	Combination of Objectives from Projects 6A and 6B	**6H GO! Fix It** A demonstration of your mastery of the skills in Projects 6A and 6B by creating a correct result from a document that contains errors you must find.	Online
6I	Combination of Objectives from Projects 6A and 6B	**6I GO! Make It** A demonstration of your mastery of the skills in Projects 6A and 6B by creating a result from a supplied picture.	Online
6J	Combination of Objectives from Projects 6A and 6B	**6J GO! Solve It** A demonstration of your mastery of the skills in Projects 6A and 6B, your decision-making skills, and your critical thinking skills. A task-specific rubric helps you self-assess your result.	Online
6K	Combination of Objectives from Projects 6A and 6B	**6K GO! Solve It** A demonstration of your mastery of the skills in Projects 6A and 6B, your decision-making skills, and your critical thinking skills. A task-specific rubric helps you self-assess your result.	On the following pages
6L	Combination of Objectives from Projects 6A and 6B	**6L GO! Think** A demonstration of your understanding of the chapter concepts applied in a manner that you would outside of college. An analytic rubric helps you and your instructor grade the quality of your work by comparing it to the work an expert in the discipline would create.	On the following pages
6M	Combination of Objectives from Projects 6A and 6B	**6M GO! Think** A demonstration of your understanding of the chapter concepts applied in a manner that you would outside of college. An analytic rubric helps you and your instructor grade the quality of your work by comparing it to the work an expert in the discipline would create.	Online
6N	Combination of Objectives from Projects 6A and 6B	**6N You and GO!** A demonstration of your understanding of the chapter concepts applied in a manner that you would in a personal situation. An analytic rubric helps you and your instructor grade the quality of your work.	Online

GLOSSARY

GLOSSARY OF CHAPTER KEY TERMS

Axis A line that serves as a frame of reference for measurement and that borders the chart plot area.

Category labels The labels that display along the bottom of a chart to identify the categories of data.

Chart area The entire chart and all of its elements.

Chart elements Objects that make up a chart.

Chart sheet A workbook sheet that contains only a chart.

Column chart A chart in which the data is arranged in columns and that is useful for showing data changes over a period of time or for illustrating comparisons among items.

Cycle A category of SmartArt graphics that illustrates a continual process.

Data labels Labels that display the value, percentage, and/or category of each particular data point and can contain one or more of the choices listed— Series name, Category name, Value, or Percentage.

Data marker A column, bar, area, dot, pie slice, or other symbol in a chart that represents a single data point; related data points form a data series.

Data point A value that originates in a worksheet cell and that is represented in a chart by a data marker.

Data series Related data points represented by data markers; each data series has a unique color or pattern represented in the chart legend.

Embedded chart A chart that is inserted into the same worksheet that contains the data used to create the chart.

Gridlines Lines in the plot area that aid the eye in determining the plotted values.

Hierarchy A category of SmartArt graphics used to create an organization chart or show a decision tree.

Horizontal Category axis (x-axis) The area along the bottom of a chart that identifies the categories of data; also referred to as the x-axis.

Labels Column and row headings that describe the values and help the reader understand the chart.

Legend A chart element that identifies the patterns or colors that are assigned to the categories in the chart.

Line charts A chart type that is useful to display trends over time; time displays along the bottom axis and the data point values are connected with a line.

List A category of SmartArt graphics used to show non-sequential information.

Locked [cells] In a protected worksheet, data cannot be inserted, modified, deleted, or formatted in these cells.

Major unit value A number that determines the spacing between tick marks and between the gridlines in the plot area.

Matrix A category of SmartArt graphics used to show how parts relate to a whole.

Organization chart A type of graphic that is useful to depict reporting relationships within an organization.

Password An optional element of a template added to prevent someone from disabling a worksheet's protection.

Picture A category of SmartArt graphics that is used to display pictures in a diagram.

Plot area The area bounded by the axes of a chart, including all the data series.

Process A category of SmartArt graphics that is used to show steps in a process or timeline.

Protection This prevents anyone from altering the formulas or changing other template components.

Pyramid A category of SmartArt graphics that uses a series of pictures to show relationships.

Recommended Charts An Excel feature that helps you choose a chart type by previewing suggested charts based upon patterns in your data.

Relationship A category of SmartArt graphics that is used to illustrate connections.

Rotation handle A circle that displays on the top side of a selected object used to rotate the object up to 360 degrees.

Scale The range of numbers in the data series that controls the minimum, maximum, and incremental values on the value axis.

SmartArt graphic A visual representation of information and ideas.

Sparklines Tiny charts that fit within a cell and give a visual trend summary alongside data.

Standardization All forms created within the organization will have a uniform appearance; the data will always be organized in the same manner.

Template A special workbook which may include formatting, formulas, and other elements, that is used as a pattern for creating other workbooks.

Text Pane The pane that displays to the left of the graphic, is populated with placeholder text, and is used to build a graphic by entering and editing text.

Tick mark labels Identifying information for a tick mark generated from the cells on the worksheet used to create the chart.

Tick marks The short lines that display on an axis at regular intervals.

Trendline A graphic representation of trends in a data series, such as a line sloping upward to represent increased sales over a period of months.

Unlocked [cells] Cells in a protected worksheet that may be filled in.

Vertical Value axis (y-axis) A numerical scale on the left side of a chart that shows the range of numbers for the data points; also referred to as the y-axis.

Walls and floor The areas surrounding a 3-D chart that give dimension and boundaries to the chart.

WordArt A feature with which you can insert decorative text in your document.

CHAPTER REVIEW

Skills Review | Project 6C Employer Attendance

Apply 6A skills from these Objectives:

1 Create and Format Sparklines and a Column Chart
2 Create and Format a Line Chart
3 Create and Modify a SmartArt Graphic
4 Create and Modify an Organization Chart

In the following Skills Review, you will assist Linda Wong, Employer Relations Manager, in displaying the employer participation for the Dallas – Ft. Worth Job Fair in charts and diagrams. Your completed workbook will look similar to Figure 6.44.

PROJECT FILES

For Project 6C, you will need the following file:

e06C_Employer_Participation

You will save your workbook as:

Lastname_Firstname_6C_Employer_Participation

PROJECT RESULTS

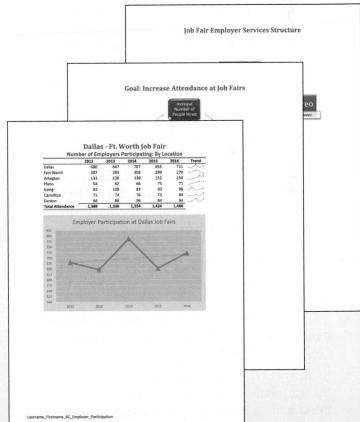

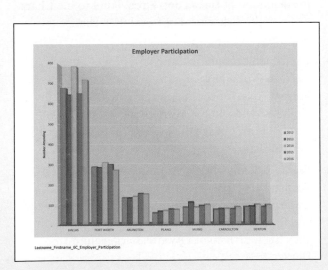

FIGURE 6.44

(Project 6C Employer Attendance continues on the next page)

1 Start Excel. From your student files, open **e06C_Employer_Participation**. **Save** the file in your **Excel Chapter 6** folder as **Lastname_Firstname_6C_Employer_Participation**

a. Select the range **B4:F10**. Click **Quick Analysis**, click **SPARKLINES**, and then click **Line**. On the **DESIGN tab**, in the **Show group**, select the **High Point** check box and the **Last Point** check box. On the **DESIGN tab**, in the **Style group**, click **More**, and then in the third row, click the first style—**Sparkline Style Accent 1, (no dark or light)**. In cell **G3**, type **Trend**

b. Select the range **A3:F10**. On the **INSERT tab**, in the **Charts group**, click **Recommended Charts**. With the **Clustered Column** chart selected, click **OK**. On the **DESIGN tab**, in the **Location group**, click **Move Chart**. Click **New sheet**, name the new sheet **Participation Chart** and then click **OK**.

c. On the **DESIGN tab**, in the **Type group**, click **Change Chart Type**. In the **Change Chart Type** dialog box, click the **All Charts** tab. Click **Column** on the left, and then click the fourth chart—**3-D Clustered Column**, and then click **OK**.

d. In the upper right corner of the chart, click **Chart Styles**. Scroll down and click **Style 3**. On the **DESIGN tab**, in the **Chart Layouts group**, click **Add Chart Element**. In the **Chart Elements** list, point to **Legend**, and then click **Right**. Click **Add Chart Element**, click **Axis Titles**, and then click **Primary Vertical**. In the **Formula Bar**, type **Number Attending** and then press [Enter].

e. Click **Chart Title**, in the **Formula Bar**, type **Employer Participation** as the chart title, and then press [Enter]. **Save** your workbook.

f. In the **Fort Worth** column cluster, point to the last column—**2016**. Notice that the Value for this column is 306. Display the **Participation by Location** worksheet, and then in cell **F5**, type **270** and press [Enter]. Display the **Participation Chart** worksheet and verify the value for the column has changed.

g. On the **FORMAT tab**, in the **Current Selection group**, click the **Chart Elements arrow**, and then click **Back Wall**. Then in the same group, click **Format Selection**. In the **Format Wall** pane, click **Fill**, click **Solid fill**, and then click the **Fill Color arrow**. Under

Theme Colors, in the fourth column, click the fourth color—**Dark Blue, Text 2, Lighter 40%**—and then set the **Transparency** to **75%**.

h. In the **Format** pane, click the arrow to the right of **WALL OPTIONS** to display the **Chart Elements** list. Select **Side Wall**, and then apply the same fill, but with a **Transparency** of **60%**. To the **Floor**, apply a **Solid fill** using the last color in the first column—**White, Background 1, Darker 50%** with **0% Transparency**. To the **Chart Area**, apply a **Solid fill** using **Tan, Background 2, Darker 10%**—in the third column, the second color. **Close** the **Format** pane.

2 Display the **Participation by Location** worksheet. Select the range **A3:F4**, and then on the **INSERT tab**, in the **Charts group**, click **Insert Line Chart**. In the second row, click the first chart type—**Line with Markers**. Drag the upper left corner of the chart inside the upper left corner of cell **A13**. Drag the lower right corner of the chart inside the lower right corner of cell **G29**.

a. In the embedded chart, click the **Chart Title** Dallas, in the **Formula bar** type **Employer Participation at Dallas Job Fairs**. Point to the **Chart Title**, right-click, click **Font**, and then change the font size to **16**.

b. On the left side of the line chart, point to the **Vertical (Value) axis**, right-click, and then click **Format Axis**. If necessary, expand AXIS OPTIONS. Under **Bounds**, in the **Minimum** box, type **500** Under **Units**, change the **Major unit** to **25 Close** the **Format** pane.

c. Right-click anywhere within the **Plot Area**, click **Format Plot Area**, and if necessary, expand FILL. Under **Fill**, click **Solid fill**, click the **Fill Color arrow**, and then under **Theme Colors**, in the first column, click the fourth color—**White, Background 1, Darker 25%**.

d. Point to the chart line, right-click, and then click **Format Data Series**. Under **SERIES OPTIONS**, click **Fill & Line**. Under **Line**, click **Solid line**. Use the spin box arrows to set the **Width** to **4 pt**. Under the **Fill & Line** icon, click **MARKER**. Expand **MARKER OPTIONS**. Click **Built-in**, click the **Type arrow**, and then click the **triangle**—the third symbol in the list. Set the **Size** of the **Marker Type** to **14**

(Project 6C Employer Attendance continues on the next page)

e. Under **FILL**, click **Solid fill**, and then click the **Fill Color arrow**. Under **Theme Colors**, in the first column, click the sixth color—**White, Background 1, Darker 50%**.

f. Under **BORDER**, click **No line**. Using any of the techniques you have practiced to select a chart element, select the **Chart Area** and apply a **Solid fill** using **White, Background 1, Darker 15%**—in the first column, the third color. **Close** the **Format pane**. Click in any cell outside of the chart.

g. Click slightly inside the chart border to select the entire chart. On the **DESIGN tab**, in the **Charts Layouts group**, click **Add Chart Element**, point to **Trendline**, and then click **Linear**. **Save** your workbook.

3 ▸ Click **New sheet**, and then rename the sheet **Process Chart** In cell **A1**, type **Goal: Increase Attendance at Job Fairs** and then press Enter. Merge and center the text across the range **A1:H1** and apply the **Title** cell style. On the **INSERT tab**, in the **Illustrations group**, click **SmartArt**. On the left, click **Cycle**, and then in the first row, click the third option—**Block Cycle**. Click **OK**.

a. On the **DESIGN tab**, in the **Create Graphic group**, if necessary, click **Text Pane**. As the first bullet, type **Increase Number of People Hired** Click the next bullet, and then type **Attract More Attendees** As the third bullet, type **Attract More Employers** As the fourth bullet, type **Reduce Costs** As the last bullet, type **Increase Profits Close** the **Text Pane**.

b. Click the edge of the graphic to select it. On the **DESIGN tab**, in the **SmartArt Styles group**, click **More**. Under **3-D**, click the first style—**Polished**. Click **Change Colors**, and then under **Colorful**, click the first option—**Colorful – Accent Colors**. Drag the upper left corner of the graphic into the left corner of cell **A3**. Drag the lower right corner inside the lower right corner of cell **H20**. Click cell **A1**, and then click **Save**.

4 ▸ Click **New sheet**, and rename the sheet tab **Organization Chart** In cell **A1**, type **Job Fair Employer Services Structure** and then merge and center this title across the range **A1:H1**. Apply the **Title** cell style. On the **INSERT tab**, in the **Illustrations group**, click **SmartArt**. On the left, click **Hierarchy**, and then in the first row,

click the third graphic—**Name and Title Organization Chart**. Click **OK**.

a. If the **Text Pane** displays, close it. In the graphic, click in the first [**Text**] box, and then type **Holly Lance** Click the edge of the small white box below Holly Lance to select it and type **Employer Manager** In the [**Text**] box below Employer Manager, click on the edge of the box to display a solid line border—if a dashed border displays, click the edge of the box again. With the box bordered with a solid line, press Delete.

b. On the second level, click in the leftmost shape, and then using the technique you just practiced, type **Jack Nix** and **Operations Manager** In the next shape, type **MJ Marks** and **Marketing Specialist** In the rightmost shape, type **Mary Treo** and **Finance Analyst** Hold down Ctrl, and then click the edge of each of the smaller title boxes to select all four. Then, on the **HOME tab**, in the **Font group**, change the font size to **8**, and click **Center**.

c. Drag the upper left corner of the graphic into cell **A3** and the lower right corner into cell **H20**. On the **DESIGN tab**, in the **SmartArt Styles group**, apply **Intense Effect style**. Change the colors to **Colorful – Accent Colors**.

d. Display the **Participation Chart** sheet. On the **INSERT tab**, click **Header & Footer**, and then click **Custom Footer**. With the insertion point in the **left section**, from the small toolbar in the dialog box, click **Insert File Name**. Click **OK** two times.

e. Display the **Participation by Location** sheet. Hold down Ctrl and select the remaining two worksheets to group the three sheets. Insert a footer with the file name in the **left section**. Click outside the footer area to deselect. On the **PAGE LAYOUT tab**, click **Margins**, click **Custom Margins**, and then center the sheets horizontally. Click **OK**. Return to **Normal** view and press Ctrl + Home to move to cell **A1**.

f. Right-click any of the grouped sheet tabs and click **Ungroup Sheets**. Click the **FILE tab** to display **Backstage** view. On the right, at the bottom of the **Properties** list, click **Show All Properties**. On the list of **Properties**, in the **Tags** box, type **employer**

(Project 6C Employer Attendance continues on the next page)

CHAPTER REVIEW

participation, organization chart In the **Subject** box, type your course name and section #. Under **Related People**, be sure that your name displays as the author. If necessary, right-click the author name, click Edit Property, type your name, click outside of the Edit person dialog box, and then click OK.

g. Click **Save**. Display and examine the **Print Preview**, make any necessary corrections, **Save**, and then print or submit electronically as directed by your instructor. If you are directed to do so, print the formulas on the Participation by Location worksheet. **Close** Excel.

END | You have completed Project 6C

CHAPTER REVIEW

Apply 6B skills from these Objectives:

5 Create an Excel Template
6 Protect a Worksheet
7 Create a Worksheet Based on a Template

In the following Skills Review, you will assist Job Fair Director, Amanda Shay, in creating a template for a Purchase Order, and then a Purchase Order for items with a logo and name imprint of the Dallas – Ft. Worth Job Fair. Your completed worksheets will look similar to Figure 6.45.

Build from Scratch

PROJECT FILES

For Project 6D, you will need the following files:

E06D_Logo
New blank Excel workbook

You will save your workbooks as:

Lastname_Firstname_6D_Hancock_PO
Lastname_Firstname_6D_PO_Template
Lastname_Firstname_6D_Purchase_Order

PROJECT RESULTS

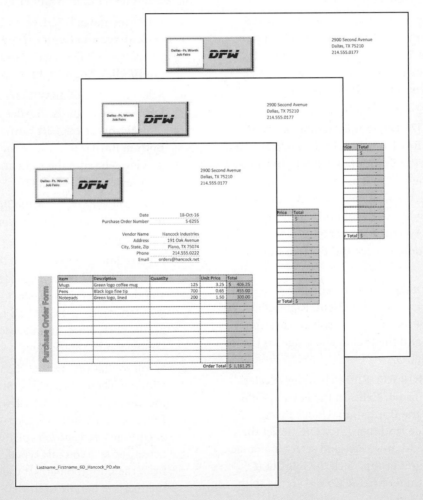

FIGURE 6.45

(Project 6D Purchase Order continues on the next page)

CHAPTER REVIEW

1 Start Excel and display a new blank workbook. **Save** the file in your **Excel Chapter 6** folder as **Lastname_ Firstname_6D_Purchase_Order** Beginning in cell **E1**, type **2900 Second Avenue** and press Enter. In cell **E2**, type **Dallas, TX 75210** and in cell **E3**, type **214.555.0177** and press Enter.

a. Click cell **C8**, type **Date** and press Enter. In cell **C9**, type **Purchase Order Number** Click cell **C11**. Type **Vendor Name** and press Enter. In cell **C12**, type **Address** In cell **C13**, type **City, State, Zip** In cell **C14**, type **Phone** In cell **C15**, type **Email**

b. Click cell **B18**. Type **Item** and press Tab to move to cell **C18**. Continuing across **row 18**, in cell **C18**, type **Description** and press Tab, in cell **D18**, type **Quantity** and press Tab, in cell **E18**, type **Unit Price** and press Tab, and in cell **F18**, type **Total** and press Enter. Select the range **B18:F18** and apply **Bold**.

c. Widen **column B** to **100 pixels, column C** to **165 pixels** and **column D** to **145 pixels**. Select **columns E:F** and widen to **75 pixels**. Select the range **C8:C9**, hold down Ctrl and select the nonadjacent range **C11:C15**, and then on the **HOME tab**, in the **Alignment group**, click **Align Right**.

d. Select the range **D8:D9**. In the **Alignment group**, click the **Dialog Box Launcher**. In the **Format Cells** dialog box, click the **Border tab**. Under **Line**, in the **Style** list, click the first line in the first column—a dotted line. Click the **Color arrow**, and then under **Theme Colors**, in the sixth column, click the sixth color—**Orange, Accent 2, Darker 50%**. Under **Border**, click **Middle Border** and **Bottom Border**. Click **OK**.

e. With the range **D8:D9** still selected, in the **Alignment group**, click **Align Right**. Right-click over the selected range, on the mini toolbar, click the **Format Painter**, and then select the range **D11:D15** to copy the format.

f. Select the range **B18:F32**. Right-click the selected range and click **Format Cells**. In the **Format Cells** dialog box, click the **Border tab**. Under **Presets**, click **Outline** and **Inside**, and then click **OK**. Select the range **B18:F18**, hold down Ctrl and select the range **F19:F32**. In the **Font group**, click the **Fill Color arrow**, and then under **Theme Colors**, in the sixth

column, click the third color—**Orange, Accent 2, Lighter 60%**.

g. Press Ctrl + Home. Press Ctrl + F2 to examine the **Print Preview**. Click **Save** to save and return to your workbook.

2 To construct a formula to multiply the Quantity times the Unit Price, in cell **F19**, type **=d19*e19** and click **Enter**. Use the fill handle to copy the formula in cell **F19** down through cell **F31**. Click cell **F32**. On the **HOME tab**, in the **Editing group**, click **AutoSum**. Be sure the range displays as **F19:F31**, and then press Enter. Select the range **E19:E31**. In the **Number group**, click **Comma Style**. Click cell **F19**, hold down Ctrl, and then click cell **F32**. In the **Number group**, click **Accounting Number Format**. Select the range **F20:F31**, and then click **Comma Style**. Select the range **D19:D31**, and then in the **Styles group**, click **Cell Styles**, and then under **Number Format**, click **Comma [0]**.

a. Select the range **D32:E32**. In the **Alignment group**, click **Merge and Center**. Type **Order Total** and press Enter. Click cell **D32** again, and then in the **Alignment group**, click **Align Right**. Apply **Bold**.

b. Select the range **B32:C32**, right-click, and then click **Format Cells**. On the **Border tab**, in the **Border** preview area, click **Left Border, Middle Border**, and **Bottom Border** to remove these borders from the preview—be sure the right and top lines remain in the preview area. Click **OK**.

c. Press Ctrl + F2 to view the **Print Preview**. Click **Save** to save and return to your workbook.

d. Click cell **A1**. On the **INSERT tab**, in the **Illustrations group**, click **Pictures**. In the **Insert Picture** dialog box, navigate to your student files, and then insert the file **e06D_Logo**. With the image selected, click the **FORMAT tab**, in the **Picture Styles group**, click **More**, and then locate and click the **Simple Frame, Black**. **Save** your workbook.

e. Scroll so that **row 16** is at the top of the Excel window. Then, click cell **A18**. On the **INSERT tab**, in the **Text group**, click **WordArt**, and then in the first row, click the third WordArt—**Fill – Orange, Accent 2, Outline – Accent 2**. Type **Purchase Order Form** Select the text you just typed, right-click, and then from the mini toolbar, set the **Font Size** to **20**. Drag the rotation handle to the left until the WordArt is

(Project 6D Purchase Order continues on the next page)

CHAPTER REVIEW

vertical. Then, drag the WordArt image to **column A** and align the top of the image with the top of cell **A18**—centered in the column. At the lower edge of the WordArt image, point to the center resize handle and drag down so the end of the image aligns at the lower edge of cell **A32**.

f. With the WordArt still selected, on the **FORMAT tab**, in the **Shape Styles group**, click the **Shape Fill arrow**, click **Texture**, and then in the fourth row, click the second texture—**Recycled Paper**. Click to deselect the WordArt, and then press Ctrl + Home. Insert a footer in the **left section** that includes the file name. Click any cell outside the footer to deselect. On the status bar, click **Normal**. Press Ctrl + Home to move to the top of the worksheet. From **Backstage** view, display the **document properties**, type your firstname and lastname as the **Author**, your course name and section # as the **Subject**, and **purchase order** as the **Tags**, and then **Save** your workbook.

g. Press F12 to display the **Save As** dialog box, and then click the **Save as type arrow**. On the list, click **Excel Template**. Navigate to your **Excel Chapter 6** folder. In the **File name** box, change the **File name** to **Lastname_Firstname_6D_PO_Template** and then click **Save**.

3 ▸ Select the range **D8:D9**, hold down Ctrl, select the range **D11:D15** and the range **B19:E31**. With the three ranges selected, on the **HOME tab**, in the **Cells group**, click **Format**, and then click **Format Cells**. In the **Format Cells** dialog box, click the **Protection tab**. Click to clear the check mark from the **Locked** check box. Click **OK**.

a. In the **Cells group**, click **Format**, and then under **Protection**, click **Protect Sheet**. Under **Allow all users of this worksheet to:** leave the first two check boxes selected. At the top of the dialog box, be sure the **Protect worksheet and contents of locked cells** check box is selected. In the **Password to unprotect sheet** box, type **goseries** Click **OK**. In the displayed **Confirm Password** dialog box, type **goseries** to confirm the password, and then click **OK** to close both dialog boxes. Click **Save**.

b. Display the **document properties**. The **Author** and **Subject** boxes contain your previous information. As the **Tags**, type **purchase order form, template**

c. Check the **Print Preview**, and then **Save** your template.

4 ▸ To create a purchase order from your template, display the **Save As** dialog box, and then set the **Save as type** box to **Excel Workbook**—the first choice at the top of the list. Navigate to your **Excel Chapter 6** folder, and then in the **File name** box, type **Lastname_Firstname_6D_Hancock_PO** Click **Save**.

a. Click cell **D8**, type **October 18, 2016** and press Enter—Excel applies the default date format. As the Purchase Order Number, type **S-6255** and then press Enter two times to move to cell **D11**. Beginning in cell **D11**, enter the vendor information as follows:

Vendor Name:	**Hancock Industries**
Address	**191 Oak Avenue**
City, State, ZIP	**Plano, TX 75074**
Phone	**214.555.0222**
Email	**orders@hancock.net**

b. Click cell **B19**, and then complete the order by entering the items as shown in the following table, pressing Tab to move from cell to cell.

Item	Description	Quantity	Unit Price
Mugs	**Green logo coffee mug**	**125**	**3.25**
Pens	**Black logo fine tip**	**700**	**0.65**
Notepads	**Green logo, lined**	**200**	**1.50**

c. Display the **document properties**. Be sure your name displays in the **Author** box and your course name and section # displays in the **Subject** box. Change the **Tags** to **Hancock, promotional items** Check the **Print Preview** to be sure the file name updated and displays in the **left section** of the footer.

d. **Save** your workbook. As directed by your instructor, print or submit electronically the three workbooks you created in this project. If required to do so, print or create an electronic version of your worksheets that contain formulas. **Close** Excel.

MyITLab® grader

Apply 6A skills from these Objectives:

1 Create and Format Sparklines and a Column Chart

2 Create and Format a Line Chart

3 Create and Modify a SmartArt Graphic

4 Create and Modify an Organization Chart

In the following project, you will assist Linda Wong, Employer Relations Manager, in tracking the number of people who get hired by an employer at each fair. You will create and modify a chart to display the number of people hired at the fairs in the past five years, create a diagram of the communities served, and create an organizational chart for staff at the Job Fair. Your completed worksheets will look similar to Figure 6.46.

PROJECT FILES

For Project 6E, you will need the following file:

e06E_Hires

You will save your workbook as:

Lastname_Firstname_6E_Hires

PROJECT RESULTS

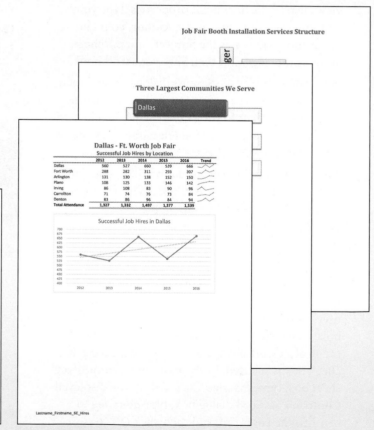

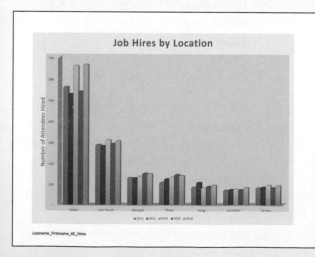

FIGURE 6.46

(Project 6E Hires continues on the next page)

CONTENT-BASED ASSESSMENTS

1 Start Excel. From your student files, open **e06E_Hires** and **Save** the file in your **Excel Chapter 6** folder as **Lastname_Firstname_6E_Hires** Using the data in the range **A4:F10**, insert **Sparklines** using the **Line** format. Place the sparklines in the range adjacent to the **2016** column, show the **High Point** and **Last Point**, and then apply Sparkline **Style Accent 4, Darker 25%**. Type **Trend** in the cell above the sparklines.

2 Using the data for the years and for each location (not the totals), create a **3-D Clustered Column** chart on a separate chart sheet named **Hires by Location Chart** Apply **Style 11**, and change the **Chart Title** to **Job Hires by Location** Set the title's font size to **28**. Format the **Chart Area** with a solid fill using **Olive Green, Accent 3, Lighter 80%**. Format the **Plot Area** with a solid fill two shades darker—**Olive Green, Accent 3, Lighter 40%**. Format the floor and the side wall with a solid fill color using **Aqua, Accent 5, Darker 50%** and **60%** transparency. Add a title to the vertical axis with the text **Number of Attendees Hired** and change the font size to **16**.

3 On the **Job Hires by Location** worksheet, using the data for Dallas, insert a **Line with Markers** line chart. Position the chart between cells **A13** and **G26**. Change the chart title to **Successful Job Hires in Dallas** and set the title's font size to **16**. Format the **Vertical (Value) Axis** so that the **Minimum** value is **400** and the **Major unit** is **25** Add a **Linear Trendline**. Format the **Line Color** of the trendline with **Orange, Accent 6** and set the **Line Style** to a width of **2 pt**.

4 Insert a new sheet and name it **List Chart** In cell **A1**, type **Three Largest Communities We Serve** Merge and center this title across the range **A1:G1** and apply the **Title** cell style. Insert a **SmartArt** graphic using the **Vertical Box List**. In the three boxes, type, in order, **Dallas** and

Fort Worth and **Carrollton** Position the graphic between cells **A3** and **G16**. Apply the **Inset** style and change the colors to **Colorful Range – Accent Colors 4 to 5**. Click cell **A1**.

5 Insert a new sheet and name it **Organization Chart** In cell **A1**, type **Job Fair Booth Installation Services Structure** Merge and center this title across the range **A1:H1** and apply the **Title** cell style. Insert a **SmartArt** graphic using **Horizontal Multi-Level Hierarchy**. In the vertical box, type **Booth Manager** and in the three remaining boxes, type **Safety Inspectors** and **Electricians** and **Carpenters** Position the graphic between cells **A4** and **H16**. Apply the **Subtle Effect** style and change the colors to **Colorful Range – Accent Colors 4 to 5**. Click cell **A1** to deselect.

6 Display the **Hires by Location Chart** sheet. On the **INSERT tab**, click **Header & Footer**, click **Custom Footer** and then insert the File name in the **left section**.

7 Display the **Job Hires by Location** sheet. Hold down **Ctrl** and select the remaining two worksheets to group the three sheets. Insert a footer with the file name in the **left section**. Return to **Normal** view and move to cell **A1**. On the **PAGE LAYOUT tab**, click **Margins**, click **Custom Margins**, and then center the sheets horizontally.

8 Ungroup the worksheets. Display the **document properties**, type your firstname and lastname as the author, type your course name and section # in the **Subject** box, and as the **Tags**, type **hires by location** and **Save**. Display and examine the **Print Preview**, make any necessary corrections, **Save**, and then print or submit electronically as directed by your instructor. If you are directed to do so, print the formulas on the Job Hires by Location worksheet. **Close** Excel.

END | You have completed Project 6E

In the following Mastering Excel project, you will create a budget template for the Dallas location of the Dallas - Ft. Worth Job Fair. You will also create a worksheet based on the budget template for review by Milton Hyken, Dallas Job Fair Director. Your completed worksheets will look similar to Figure 6.47.

Apply 6B skills from these Objectives:

5 Create an Excel Template

6 Protect a Worksheet

7 Create a Worksheet Based on a Template

Build from Scratch

PROJECT FILES

For Project 6F, you will need the following files:

New blank Excel workbook

e06F_Logo

You will save your workbooks as:

Lastname_Firstname_6F_Budget_Template
Lastname_Firstname_6F_Dallas_Budget

PROJECT RESULTS

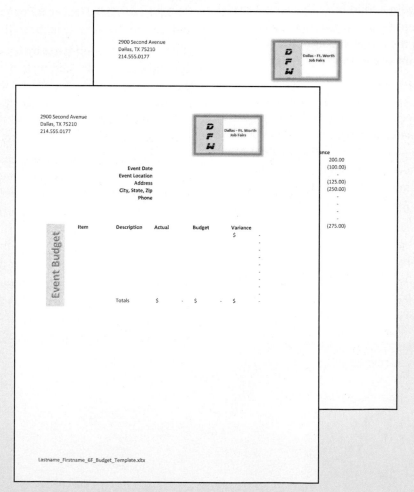

FIGURE 6.47

(Project 6F Event Budget continues on the next page)

CONTENT-BASED ASSESSMENTS

1 Start Excel and display a new blank workbook. In cell **A1**, type **2900 Second Avenue** In cell **A2**, type **Dallas, TX 75210** In cell **A3**, type **214.555.0177**

In cell **C8**, type **Event Date** In cell **C9**, type **Event Location** In cell **C10**, type **Address** In cell **C11**, type **City, State, Zip** In cell **C12**, type **Phone**

In cell **B16**, type **Item** and press Tab. In cell **C16**, type **Description** In cell **D16**, type **Actual** In cell **E16**, type **Budget** In cell **F16**, type **Variance** Click cell **C26** and type **Totals**

2 To the ranges **C8:C12** and **B16:F16**, apply **Bold**. To the range **C8:C12**, apply **Align Right**. To the range **D8:D12**, apply **Align Left**. Widen columns **A:F** to **95 pixels**.

To construct a formula to compute the Variance (Variance = Actual – Budget) for each budget item, in cell **F17**, type **=d17-e17** and copy the formula through cell **F25**. In the range **D26:F26**, insert appropriate formulas to sum these columns. To the range **D18:F25**, apply **Comma Style**. To the ranges **D17:F17** and **D26:F26**, apply **Accounting Number Format**.

3 In cell **E1**, insert the picture **e06F_Logo**. Click cell **A16**, insert a **WordArt** using **Fill – Blue, Accent 1, Outline – Background 1, Hard Shadow – Accent 1**—in the third row, the third WordArt. As the text, type **Event Budget** and set the **Font Size** to **24**. Rotate the WordArt vertically, and align it between cells **A16** and **A26**. In the **Shape Styles group**, click the **Shape Fill arrow**, click **Texture**, and then click **Blue tissue paper**.

4 Select the ranges **D8:D12** and **B17:E25**. Remove the **Locked** formatting from the selected cells, and then protect the worksheet. Be sure the check box at the top and the first two check boxes in the list are selected, and as the password type **goseries**

Insert a footer in the **left section** with the file name. Add your name, course information, and the **Tags budget template** to the **document properties**, and then check the **Print Preview**. **Save** your workbook as an **Excel Template** in your **Excel Chapter 6** folder as **Lastname_Firstname_6F_Budget_Template**

5 To create a new budget report using the template as your model, display the **Save As** dialog box again, and then **Save** the template as an **Excel Workbook** in your **Excel Chapter 6** folder as **Lastname_Firstname_6F_Dallas_Budget** Enter the following data:

Event Date	**October 22, 2016**
Event Location	**Dallas**
Address	**288 Alba Drive**
City, State, ZIP	**Dallas, TX 75210**
Phone	**214.555.6575**

Complete the order by entering the items as shown in the following table.

Item	Description	Actual	Budget
Venue	**Hall rental fee**	**7200**	**7000**
Personnel	**Site staff**	**500**	**600**
Equipment	**Computers**	**400**	**400**
Publicity	**Signage**	**725**	**850**
Speakers	**Speaking fees**	**1750**	**2000**

6 Change the **Tags** to **Dallas event budget** Examine the **Print Preview**. **Save** your workbook. As directed by your instructor, print or submit electronically the two workbooks you created in this project. If required to do so, print or create an electronic version of your worksheets that contain formulas. **Close** Excel.

END | You have completed Project 6F

Mastering Excel Project 6G Internships and Travel Template

Apply 6A and 6B skills from these Objectives:

1 Create and Format Sparklines and a Column Chart
2 Create and Format a Line Chart
3 Create and Modify a SmartArt Graphic
4 Create and Modify an Organization Chart
5 Create an Excel Template
6 Protect a Worksheet
7 Create a Worksheet Based on a Template

In the following project, you will assist Ann Takei, Internship Coordinator, in tracking the number of internships by industry at each job fair and in creating a template to use for travel expenses. Your completed worksheets will look similar to Figure 6.48.

PROJECT FILES

For Project 6G, you will need the following files:

e06G_Internships
e06G_Travel_Expense

You will save your workbooks as:

Lastname_Firstname_6G_Internships
Lastname_Firstname_6G_Jackson_Report
Lastname_Firstname_6G_Travel_Template

PROJECT RESULTS

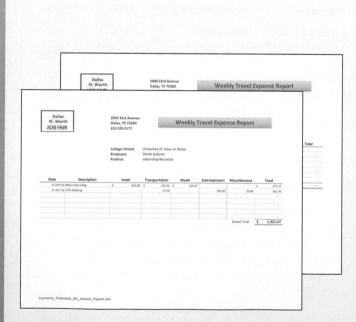

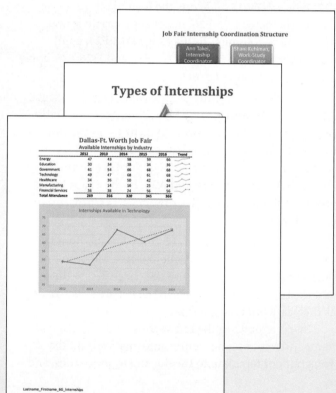

FIGURE 6.48

(Project 6G Internships and Travel Template continues on the next page)

1 Start Excel. From your student files, locate and open **e06G_Internships. Save** the file in your **Excel Chapter 6** folder as **Lastname_Firstname_6G_Internships** Using the range A4:F10, insert **Sparklines** in the **Line** format in the range adjacent to the last year of data. Show the **High Point** and **Last Point** and apply Sparkline **Style Accent 4, (no dark or light)**. In cell G3, type **Trend** and apply the format from cell **F3**.

2 Select the ranges representing the years (including the blank cell A3) and the data for **Technology** internships. Insert a line chart using the **Line with Markers** chart style. Reposition the chart between cells **A13** and **G29**. Change the **Chart Title** to **Internships Available in Technology** Edit the **Vertical (Value) Axis** to set the **Minimum** to **35** and the **Major unit** to **5**

3 Format the **Plot Area** with a solid fill using **Olive Green, Accent 3, Lighter 60%**. Format the **Chart Area** with a solid fill using **Olive Green, Accent 3, Lighter 40%**. Insert a **Linear Trendline** and change the width of the line to **2.5 pt.**

4 Insert a new sheet and name it **List Chart** In cell A1, type **Types of Internships** Merge and center the text across the range A1:H1, apply the **Title** cell style, and then set the **Font Size** to **36**. Insert a **SmartArt** graphic using the **Pyramid List**. Position the graphic between cells **A3** and **H19**. In the top text box, type **Paid** In the second text box, type **Work-Study** and in the last box, type **Unpaid** Apply the **Inset** style and change the colors to **Colored Fill – Accent 1.**

5 Insert a new sheet and name it **Organization Chart** In cell A1, type **Job Fair Internship Coordination Structure** and then merge and center this title across the range A1:I1. Apply the **Title** cell style. Insert a **SmartArt** graphic using the **Hierarchy List**. Position the graphic between cells A3 and I17. On the left, create a list with the following names and titles: **Ann Takei, Internship Coordinator** and **Dennis Maslin, Specialist** and **Cory**

Finley, Specialist On the right, create a list with the following names and titles: **Shani Kuhlman, Work-Study Coordinator** and **Anand Singh, Specialist** and **Vanessa Lopez, Specialist** Apply the **Inset** style and **Gradient Range – Accent 1**.

6 Group the three sheets, insert a footer with the file name in the **left section**, and then center the sheets horizontally. Display the **document properties**. Add your name, your course name and section #, and the **Tags internship organization** Examine the **Print Preview**, ungroup the worksheets, **Save** and **Close** this workbook, but leave Excel open.

7 From your student files, open the file **e06G_Travel_Expense**. Display the **Save As** dialog box, and then **Save** the workbook as an **Excel Template** in your **Excel Chapter 6** folder with the name **Lastname_Firstname_6G_Travel_Template** In the range H15:H21, create formulas to sum the data in each row—do not include the Date or Description columns. In cell **H22**, create a formula to create a grand total of expenses. Apply appropriate financial formatting to all the cells that will contain expenses, including the **Total** cell style in cell H22—refer to Figure 6.48.

8 Select the nonadjacent ranges D8:D10 and A15:G21. Remove the **Locked** formatting from the selected cells and protect the worksheet. Be sure the top check box and the first two check boxes in the list are selected. As the password, type **goseries** Add your name, course information, and the **Tags travel template** to the **document properties**. Insert a footer with the file name in the **left section**. Click **Save**.

9 To use the template for an employee's report, **Save** it as an **Excel Workbook** in your **Excel Chapter 6** folder with the file name **Lastname_Firstname_6G_Jackson_Report** As the College Visited, type **University of Texas at Dallas** As the Employee, type **Derek Jackson** and as the Position, type **Internship Recruiter** Use the data in Table 1 to complete the report:

TABLE 1

Date	Description	Hotel	Transport	Meals	Entertainment	Misc.
11-Oct-16	Dallas Recruiting	325	225.50	123.67		
12-Oct-16	UTD Meeting		37.50		595	19

(Project 6G Internships and Travel Template continues on the next page)

CONTENT-BASED ASSESSMENTS

10 Change the **Tags** to **UTD meeting** Examine the **Print Preview**; notice the file name is updated and displays in the **left section** of the footer. **Save** your workbook.

11 As directed by your instructor, print or submit electronically the two workbooks you created in this project. If required to do so, print or create an electronic version of your worksheets that contain formulas. **Close** Excel.

END | You have completed Project 6G

CONTENT-BASED ASSESSMENTS

Apply a combination of the 6A and 6B skills.		

GO! Fix It	Project 6H Operations Chart	**Online**
GO! Make It	Project 6I Advertisers	**Online**
GO! Solve It	Project 6J Sponsors	**Online**
GO! Solve It	Project 6K Time Card	

PROJECT FILES

For Project 6K, you will need the following file:

e06K_Time_Card

You will save your workbook as:

Lastname_Firstname_6K_Time_Template

Open the file **e06K_Time_Card** and save it as a template in your **Excel Chapter 6** file with the name **Lastname_Firstname_6K_Time_Template** Insert formulas to calculate daily pay (Regular Hours X Rate Per Hour) using an absolute cell reference, to total the hours for the week, and a formula to calculate the total pay. Apply appropriate number and financial formatting. Reposition the WordArt above the Time Card chart. Unlock the cells in which an individual would enter variable data, and then protect the sheet with the password **goseries** Insert the file name in the footer, add appropriate information to the document properties including the **Tags time card, payroll** and submit as directed by your instructor.

(Project 6K Time Card continues on the next page)

CONTENT-BASED ASSESSMENTS

Performance Level

Performance Criteria		Exemplary	Proficient	Developing
	Place WordArt Object and Apply Financial Formatting	Appropriate formulas, cell formatting, and WordArt placement are applied.	Appropriate formulas, cell formatting, and WordArt placement are partially applied.	Appropriate formulas, cell formatting, and WordArt placement are not applied.
	Lock Formulas	Formula cells are locked and variable data cells are unlocked.	Only one of the formula cells or variable data cells has the locked or unlocked feature applied appropriately.	Formula cells are unlocked and variable data cells are locked.
	Protect Worksheet	The worksheet is protected with the password goseries.	The worksheet is protected but not with the password goseries.	The worksheet is not protected with the password goseries.

END | You have completed Project 6K

OUTCOMES-BASED ASSESSMENTS

RUBRIC

The following outcomes-based assessments are open-ended assessments. That is, there is no specific correct result; your result will depend on your approach to the information provided. Make Professional Quality your goal. Use the following scoring rubric to guide you in how to approach the problem and then to evaluate how well your approach solves the problem.

The *criteria*—Software Mastery, Content, Format and Layout, and Process—represent the knowledge and skills you have gained that you can apply to solving the problem. The *levels of performance*—Professional Quality, Approaching Professional Quality, or Needs Quality Improvements—help you and your instructor evaluate your result.

	Your completed project is of Professional Quality if you:	Your completed project is Approaching Professional Quality if you:	Your completed project Needs Quality Improvements if you:
1-Software Mastery	Choose and apply the most appropriate skills, tools, and features and identify efficient methods to solve the problem.	Choose and apply some appropriate skills, tools, and features, but not in the most efficient manner.	Choose inappropriate skills, tools, or features, or are inefficient in solving the problem.
2-Content	Construct a solution that is clear and well organized, contains content that is accurate, appropriate to the audience and purpose, and is complete. Provide a solution that contains no errors in spelling, grammar, or style.	Construct a solution in which some components are unclear, poorly organized, inconsistent, or incomplete. Misjudge the needs of the audience. Have some errors in spelling, grammar, or style, but the errors do not detract from comprehension.	Construct a solution that is unclear, incomplete, or poorly organized; contains some inaccurate or inappropriate content; and contains many errors in spelling, grammar, or style. Do not solve the problem.
3-Format & Layout	Format and arrange all elements to communicate information and ideas, clarify function, illustrate relationships, and indicate relative importance.	Apply appropriate format and layout features to some elements, but not others. Overuse features, causing minor distraction.	Apply format and layout that does not communicate information or ideas clearly. Do not use format and layout features to clarify function, illustrate relationships, or indicate relative importance. Use available features excessively, causing distraction.
4-Process	Use an organized approach that integrates planning, development, self-assessment, revision, and reflection.	Demonstrate an organized approach in some areas, but not others; or, use an insufficient process of organization throughout.	Do not use an organized approach to solve the problem.

OUTCOMES-BASED ASSESSMENTS

> **GO! Think**   Project 6L Tech Industry

PROJECT FILES

For Project 6L, you will need the following file:

e06L_Tech_Industry

You will save your workbook as:

Lastname_Firstname_6L_Tech_Industry

From your student files, open the file **e06L_Tech_Industry**, and then save it in your **Excel Chapter 6** folder as **Lastname_Firstname_6L_Tech_Industry** Format the data attractively, add appropriate formulas, add sparklines, and insert a line chart in the sheet that tracks the data for the Irving location. Create a 3-D chart on a separate page based on the data in the worksheet, and format it attractively. Change the Fort Worth 2016 data point from 84 to 96. Insert the file name in the footer on each page, format each sheet for printing, add appropriate information to the document properties including the **Tags technology employers** and submit as directed by your instructor.

> **END | You have completed Project 6L**

> **GO! Think**   Project 6M Location List   **Online**

Build from Scratch

> **You and GO!**   Project 6N Job Finding   **Online**

Creating PivotTable and PivotChart Reports and Using BI Tools in Excel

GO! to Work
Video E7

PROJECT 7A

OUTCOMES
Query large amounts of data, subtotal and aggregate numeric data, and filter and group data to analyze for relationships and trends.

OBJECTIVES

1. Create a PivotTable Report
2. Use Slicers and Search Filters
3. Modify a PivotTable Report
4. Create a PivotChart Report

PROJECT 7B

OUTCOMES
Use the Excel Business Analysis Tools: Data Model, PowerPivot, and Power View, to analyze data from multiple sources.

OBJECTIVES

5. Create a Data Model Using PowerPivot
6. Create a PivotTable Using PowerPivot
7. Create a Dashboard Using Power View

quasarphotos/Fotolia

In This Chapter

In this chapter, you will use Excel's Business Intelligence (BI) tools to create a PivotTable and a PivotChart report, and use Power View to organize and display data. Organizations gather large amounts of data, but the data is not useful until it is organized in a manner that reveals patterns or trends. You will subtotal, aggregate, and summarize data. You will extract information from data by organizing the data into groups from which trends, comparisons, patterns, and relationships can be determined, and you will create different views of the data so that more than one pattern or trend can be observed.

The projects in this chapter relate to **Golden Grove**, a growing city located between Los Angeles and San Diego. Just 10 years ago the population was under 100,000; today it has grown to almost 300,000. Community leaders have always focused on quality and economic development in decisions on housing, open space, education, and infrastructure, and encourage best environmental practices, making the city a model for other communities its size around the United States. The city provides many recreational and cultural opportunities with a large park system, thriving arts, and a friendly business atmosphere.

PivotTable and PivotChart

PROJECT ACTIVITIES

In Activities 7.01 through 7.13, you will create a PivotTable report and a PivotChart report that summarize calls handled at Fire Department stations and Police Department precincts during the first quarter of the year for the City of Golden Grove. Your completed worksheets will look similar to Figure 7.1.

PROJECT FILES

For Project 7A, you will need the following file:

e07A_Fire_Police

You will save your workbook as:

Lastname_Firstname_7A_Fire_Police

PROJECT RESULTS

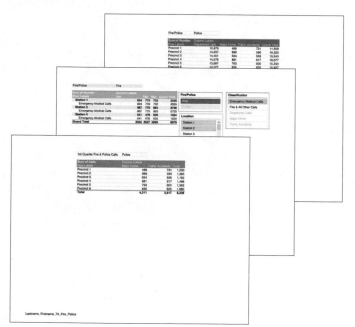

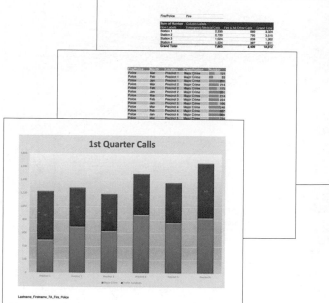

FIGURE 7.1 Project 7A PivotTable and PivotChart

Objective 1   Create a PivotTable Report

Video E7-1

A long list of numerical data is not useful until it is organized in a way that is meaningful to the reader. To combine and compare large amounts of data, use Excel's PivotTable report—also called simply a *PivotTable*—which is an interactive Excel report that summarizes and analyzes large amounts of data.

Using a PivotTable report, you can show the same data in a table in more than one arrangement. For example, you can manipulate the rows and columns of the table to view or summarize the data from different perspectives. In this manner, you pivot—turn—the information around to get varying views of the data. A PivotTable report is especially useful when you want to analyze related totals, such as when you have a long list of numbers to sum and you want to compare several facts about each total. The *source data* for a PivotTable must be formatted in columns and rows, and can be located in an Excel worksheet or an external source.

Activity 7.01   Creating a PivotTable Report

The data you use to create your PivotTable report should be in the format of a list—a series of rows that contains related data—with column titles in the first row. Subsequent rows should contain data appropriate to its column title, and there should be no blank rows. Excel will use your column titles as the *field names*—the categories of data. The data in each column should be of the same type.

Michael Thomas, Director of Public Safety, prepares quarterly reports about Fire Department and Police Department calls. He tracks the total number of calls at each location grouped by the classifications used by the Fire Department and the Police Department.

To prepare for each City Council meeting, Mr. Thomas needs to know the average number of calls handled by each location during the quarter. He also needs a separate report regarding the number of major crimes reported by each Police Department precinct. Finally, he needs to know which Fire Department station had the lowest number of emergency medical calls during the quarter, in the event the City Council votes to close or combine facilities.

1 Start Excel. From your student files, open the file **e07A_Fire_Police**. Display the **Save As** dialog box, navigate to the location where you will store your workbooks for this chapter, and then create a new folder named **Excel Chapter 7** Open your new folder, and then **Save** the workbook as **Lastname_Firstname_7A_Fire_Police**

2 Take a moment to scroll through the worksheet and examine the data.

Recall that a PivotTable report combines and compares large amounts of data. This worksheet displays three months of calls. There are two classifications for Fire Department calls and three classifications for Police Department calls.

To place the information in proper locations on the PivotTable report, think about the questions Mr. Thomas wants to answer. For his internal tracking report, he needs to know the total number of calls handled at each Fire Department station or Police Department precinct during the first quarter—grouped according to the classifications used by the Fire Department and the Police Department.

3 Click cell **A2**. On the **INSERT tab**, in the **Tables group**, click **Recommended PivotTables**. Compare your screen with Figure 7.2.

> The Recommended PivotTables dialog box displays and a moving border surrounds the range of data—this is referred to as the source data. A cell in your data must be active before you create a PivotTable; in this manner you identify the source of your data.

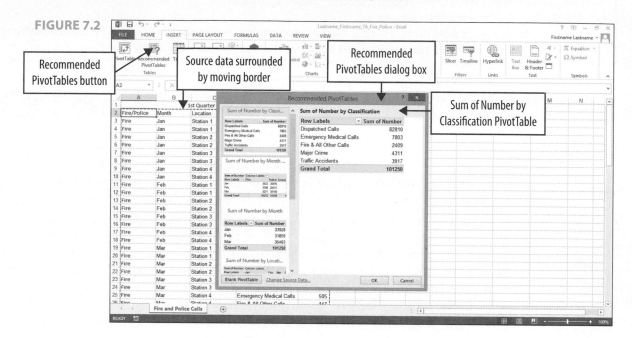

FIGURE 7.2

4 In the **Recommended PivotTables** dialog box, scroll down, point to each preview to display a ScreenTip, and then click the fifth PivotTable—**Sum of Number by Location** (+). Compare your screen with Figure 7.3.

> Excel suggests PivotTables based upon the organization of your data.

BY TOUCH Select the range A2:E80 and tap Quick Analysis. Tap the TABLES tab and point to each PivotTable example to view a preview of the selection, then tap the table you wish to create.

FIGURE 7.3

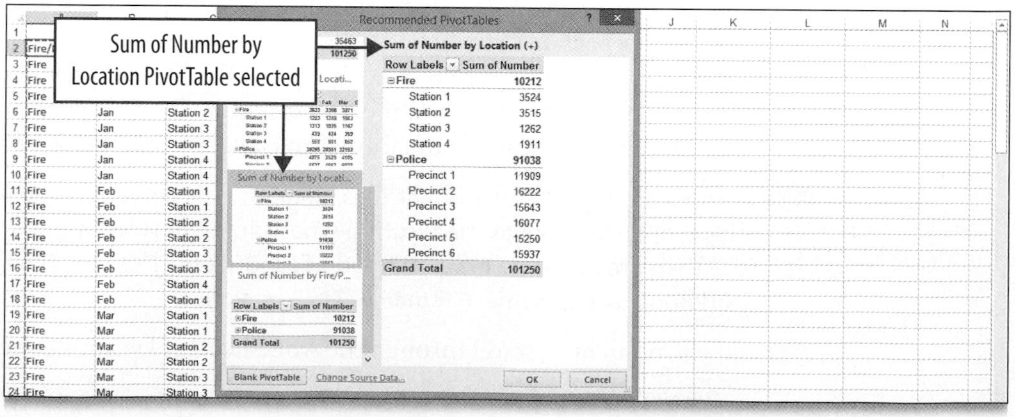

5 ▸ Click **OK**.

Excel adds a new sheet—Sheet1—to the workbook. On the left side of the new worksheet, Excel generates a PivotTable report.

On the right side of the window, Excel displays the PivotTable Fields pane. The upper portion, referred to as the field section, lists the field names—the column titles from your source data. Use the field section to add fields to and remove fields from the PivotTable. The lower portion, referred to as the layout section, displays four areas where you can build the PivotTable by rearranging and repositioning fields. On the ribbon, the PIVOTTABLE TOOLS adds two tabs—ANALYZE and DESIGN.

> **More Knowledge**
>
> If your source data is already formatted as an Excel table, you can create a PivotTable easily. Select a single cell within the source data, and then on the DESIGN tab, in the Tools group, click Summarize with PivotTable

6 ▸ **Save** 🖫 your workbook, and then take a moment to study Figure 7.4 and the table in Figure 7.5.

FIGURE 7.4

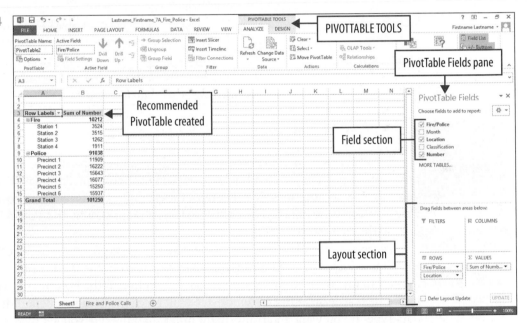

> **ALERT!**   **If the PivotTable Fields Pane Does Not Display**
>
> If the PivotTable Fields pane is not visible, click any cell in the PivotTable report to display it. If you accidently close the PivotTable Fields pane, you can redisplay it by clicking any cell in the PivotTable report to display the PivotTable Tools tabs on the ribbon. On the ANALYZE tab, in the Show group, click Field List.

FIGURE 7.5

PIVOTTABLE SCREEN ELEMENTS	
SCREEN ELEMENT	**DESCRIPTION**
PivotTable Fields pane	A window that lists, at the top, all of the fields—column titles—from the source data for use in the PivotTable report and at the bottom, an area in which you can arrange the fields in the PivotTable.
FILTERS area	An area to position fields by which you want to filter the PivotTable report, enabling you to display a subset of data in the PivotTable report.
COLUMNS area	An area to position fields that you want to display as columns in the PivotTable report. Field names placed here become column titles, and the data is grouped in columns by these titles.
ROWS area	An area to position fields that you want to display as rows in the PivotTable report. Field names placed here become row titles, and the data is grouped by these row titles.
VALUES area	An area to position fields that contain data that is summarized in a PivotTable report or PivotChart report. The data placed here is usually numeric or financial in nature and the data is summarized—summed. You can also perform other basic calculations such as finding the average, the minimum, or the maximum.
Layout section	The lower portion of the PivotTable Fields pane containing the four areas for layout; use this area to rearrange and reposition fields in the PivotTable.
Field section	The upper portion of the PivotTable Fields pane containing the fields—column titles—from your source data; use this area to add fields to and remove fields from the PivotTable.

Activity 7.02 | Adding Fields to a PivotTable Report

Recall that a PivotTable report can combine and compare large amounts of data for the purpose of analyzing related totals. By viewing the combined information in different ways, you can answer questions. Mr. Thomas, for example, wants to know how many calls of every classification were handled by each Fire Department station and Police Department precinct during the first quarter.

There are several ways to place the data from your list into the PivotTable report. From the PivotTable Fields pane, you can drag field names from the field section at the top and then drop them into one of the four areas in the layout section at the bottom. Or, you can select a field name in the field section at the top, and Excel will place the field in a default location based on the field's data type. If you want an arrangement other than the one you get by default, you can move fields from one location to another by simply dragging them between the various areas in the layout section.

1 On the right side of the worksheet, in the **PivotTable Fields** pane, in the **field section**, notice that **Fire/Police** check box is selected, and Excel has placed the field in the **ROWS area** of the **layout section**.

> By default, non-numeric fields are added to the ROWS area and numeric fields are added to the VALUES area, but you can move fields as desired.

2 In the **layout section**, in the **ROWS area**, point to **Fire/Police**, hold down the left mouse button, and then drag the field name upward into the **FILTERS area**.

> Mr. Thomas wants to use the PivotTable report to analyze the call data by Department—either Fire Department calls or Police Department calls. To do so, filter the report based on the Fire/Police field by moving this field to the FILTERS area. The Report Filter filters the entire report based on this field.

> As you drag, a small blue icon attaches to the mouse pointer to indicate you are moving a field. *Fire/Police* displays in the FILTERS area. On the left, the Fire/Police field is added at the top of the PivotTable report.

🔄 **ANOTHER WAY**   In the ROWS area, click the Fire/Police arrow, and then click Move to Report Filter.

3 In the **PivotTable Fields** pane, in the **field section**, verify the **Location** field check box is selected.

> In the layout section, the Location field displays in the ROWS area. The Location names—Precincts and Stations—display as rows in the PivotTable report. There are six Police Department precincts and four Fire Department stations. Recall that by default, non-numeric fields are added to the ROWS area.

4 In the **PivotTable Fields** pane, in the **field section**, select the **Classification** field check box. Right-click cell **A4**, point to **Expand/Collapse**, and then click **Expand Entire Field**. Compare your screen with Figure 7.6.

> In the layout section, the Classification field displays as the second field in the ROWS area. The Classification names are added as indented row headings under each Police Department precinct location and under each Fire Department station location. In this manner, a row that is lower in position in the ROWS area is nested within the row immediately above it. Notice that, under each precinct location, only the call classifications related to the Police Department display. Likewise, as you scroll down, under station locations, only the call classifications related to the Fire Department display.

FIGURE 7.6

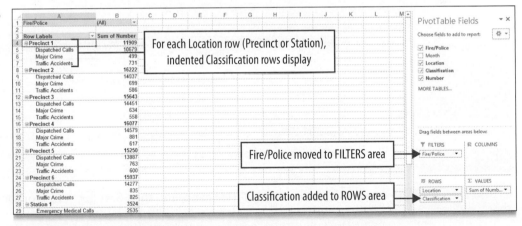

5 In the **PivotTable Fields** pane, from the **field section**, drag the **Month** field down to the **COLUMNS area**. Verify that **Sum of Number** displays in the **VALUES area**. Compare your screen with Figure 7.7.

> Use any of these techniques to place fields in the layout section. The arrangement of fields in the layout section reflects the arrangement of the data in the PivotTable report.

> The PivotTable report is complete; the result is a group of related totals. The long list of figures from the Fire and Police Calls worksheet is summarized, and you can make comparisons among the data. *Sum of Number* displays in cell A3, which refers to the field name *Number*—the number of calls for each call classification has been summed.

FIGURE 7.7

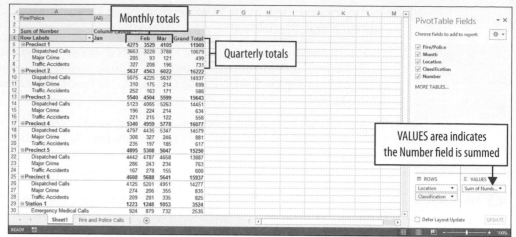

6 Click cell **B5**, point to the selected cell, and then notice the ScreenTip that displays.

Now that the data is organized and the number of calls calculated, you can view and compare various facts about the data. For example, you can see that in January, in Precinct 1, there were a total of 4275 calls, compared with 3529 calls in February. This summary information was not available in the original worksheet. By summarizing and pivoting (turning) data in various ways, you can see different information. Additionally, ScreenTips describe the cell contents.

7 On the **DESIGN tab**, in the **PivotTable Styles group**, click **More**, and then under **Medium**, in the second row, click the fourth style—**Pivot Style Medium 11**. Compare your screen with Figure 7.8.

FIGURE 7.8

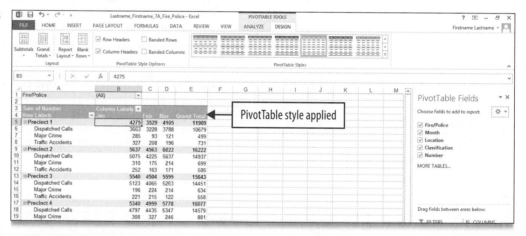

8 **Close** the **PivotTable Fields** pane, and then **Save** your workbook.

Objective 2   Use Slicers and Search Filters

Video E7-2

You can *filter*—limit the display of data to only specific information—a PivotTable by using a search filter or by using slicers. *Slicers* are easy-to-use filtering controls with buttons that enable you drill down through large amounts of data. Slicers display as movable floating objects on your worksheet in the same manner as charts and shapes and make it easy to see what filters are currently applied.

Activity 7.03 | Using Slicer to Filter a PivotTable

Limiting the data displayed enables you to focus on parts of the data without the distraction of data you do not need to see. Mr. Thomas wants to limit the data to only the Fire Department information and then determine which Fire Department station had the lowest number of emergency medical calls. Then he wants to hide that station and look at the numbers for the remaining stations.

1 ▸ On the **ANALYZE tab**, in the **Filter group**, click **Insert Slicer**. Compare your screen with Figure 7.9.

The Insert Slicers dialog box displays all the field names from your PivotTable report.

FIGURE 7.9

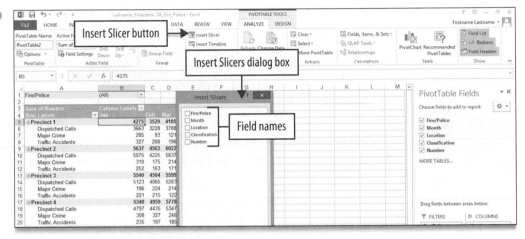

2 ▸ Select the **Fire/Police** check box, and then click **OK**. Compare your screen with Figure 7.10.

The Fire/Police slicer displays.

FIGURE 7.10

3 ▸ Point to the upper border of the **Fire/Police** slicer to display the 🔘 pointer, and then drag the slicer up to align with the top of the PivotTable and to the right so that it is not blocking your view of the PivotTable.

4 ▸ Point to the lower sizing handle on the **Fire/Police** slicer list until the ⬍ pointer displays, and then drag upward to shorten the length of the slicer to just below **Police**. Compare your screen with Figure 7.11.

A slicer includes a **slicer header** that indicates the category of the slicer items, ***filtering buttons*** to select the item by which to filter, and a Clear Filter button. When a filtering button is selected, the item is included in the filter. ***Clear Filter*** removes a filter. You can move a slicer to another location on the worksheet, and resize it as needed.

FIGURE 7.11

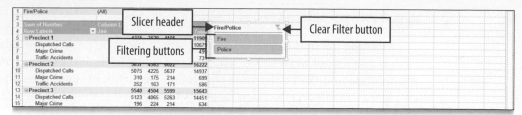

5 On the **OPTIONS tab**, in the **Slicer Styles group**, click **More** ▼, and then under **Dark**, click the second slicer style—**Slicer Style Dark 2**. Compare your screen with Figure 7.12.

You can apply various styles to slicers to make them easier to differentiate or to match the PivotTable report.

FIGURE 7.12

6 In the PivotTable report, notice that the Police Department precincts display first. Then, on the **Fire/Police slicer**, click the **Fire** filtering button, move your pointer out of the slicer, and then compare your screen with Figure 7.13.

The records for the Police Department precincts are hidden and only the Fire Department station items display. Recall that filtering displays only the data that you want to see. A filtering button that is not selected—displays in gray—indicates that the item is *not* included in the filtered list. By looking at this slicer, you can see that only Fire items are included. Because slicers indicate the current filtering state, it is easy to see exactly what is shown in the PivotTable report—and also to see what is *not* shown.

FIGURE 7.13

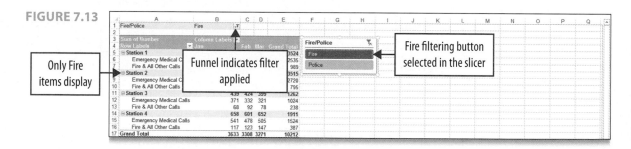

7 Click any cell in the PivotTable. On the **ANALYZE tab**, in the **Filter group**, click **Insert Slicer**. In the **Insert Slicers** dialog box, select the **Classification** check box, and then click **OK**.

8 Drag the **Classification** slicer to the right of the **Fire/Police** slicer, and then resize the field list to remove the blank area below **Traffic Accidents**. Notice that call classifications associated with the Police Department—Dispatched Calls, Major Crime, and Traffic Accidents—are dimmed.

Because the PivotTable is currently filtered by Fire, no filters related to Police are available.

9 Display the **Slicer Styles** gallery, and then apply **Slicer Style Light 4**. If necessary, widen the slicer to view the entire name of each filtering button, click cell **A1** to select the PivotTable, and then compare your screen with Figure 7.14.

FIGURE 7.14

Classification slicer added

Filter buttons related to Police calls unavailable

10 On the **Classification slicer**, click the **Emergency Medical Calls** filtering button, and then compare your screen with Figure 7.15.

The data is further filtered by the call classification *Emergency Medical Calls*; that is, only Fire Department station items with *Emergency Medical Calls* as the call classification displays in the PivotTable report. Now, at a glance, Mr. Thomas can see which Fire Department station had the lowest number of emergency medical calls. Mr. Thomas may want to investigate this further to find the reason for the low number and to determine if the number is up or down from previous quarters.

FIGURE 7.15

Emergency Medical Calls filter applied

11 With cell **A1** active, on the **ANALYZE tab**, in the **Filter group**, click **Insert Slicer**. In the **Insert Slicers** dialog box, select the **Location** check box, and then click **OK**.

12 Drag the **Location slicer** below the **Fire/Police slicer**, and notice that the **Precinct** filtering buttons are dimmed.

Because the PivotTable is already filtered by Fire Department stations, and no Police Department precincts display in the PivotTable, the Precinct filtering buttons are dimmed—unavailable—for filtering in the current arrangement.

13 Shorten the **Location slicer** to display only the Stations, and then from the **Slicer Styles** gallery, apply **Slicer Style Light 6**. Click cell **A1**, and then compare your screen with Figure 7.16.

For each field of data in the PivotTable, you can display a slicer to enable ways to slice—display a thin piece of—the data in meaningful ways.

FIGURE 7.16

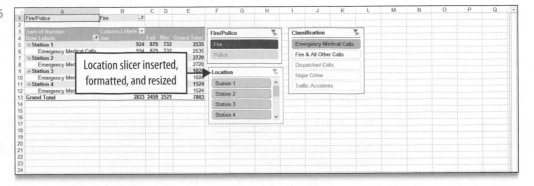

Location slicer inserted, formatted, and resized

14 To display all the stations *except* Station 3, hold down Ctrl, and then in the **Location slicer**, click the **Station 3** filtering button. Release Ctrl, move the pointer away from the PivotTable, and then compare your screen with Figure 7.17.

Use the Ctrl key in this manner to select all the filtering buttons *except* the one that you click. In the Location slicer, Stations 1, 2, and 4 are selected and Station 3 is not. In the PivotTable report, the Station 3 data is hidden, and only the data for Stations 1, 2, and 4 displays.

The number of Emergency Medical Calls for the remaining Fire Department stations range from a low of 478 in February at Station 4 to a high of 987 in January at Station 2. The Grand Total recalculates to reflect only the three stations currently displayed.

FIGURE 7.17

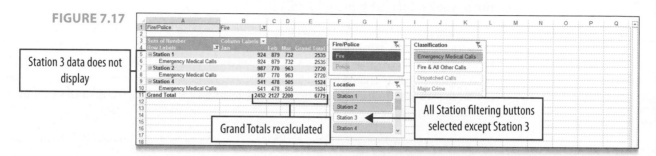

15 In the sheet tab area at the lower left of your screen, point to the **Sheet1 sheet tab**, right-click, and then, click **Move or Copy**. In the **Move or Copy** dialog box, at the lower left, select the **Create a copy** check box. Compare your screen with Figure 7.18.

FIGURE 7.18

16 Click **OK**. Right-click the **Sheet 1 (2) sheet tab**, click **Rename**, and then type **Slicers** Press Enter.

The sheet is copied and renamed. In this worksheet, your instructor will be able to verify that you have filtered the worksheet using slicers and the slicers are formatted.

17 Save 🖫 your workbook.

Activity 7.04 | Clearing Filters and Filtering by Using the Search Box

Using the search filter is another way to filter data in a PivotTable report and find relevant information easily.

1 At the bottom of the Excel window, click the **Sheet1 sheet tab** to display this worksheet.

2 In the **Sheet1** worksheet, in the **Location slicer**, click **Clear Filter** 🕅.

This action clears all the filters within a slicer; therefore, the data for all four Fire Department stations displays.

3 In the **Classification slicer**, click the **Fire & All Other Calls** filtering button, and then compare your screen with Figure 7.19.

> Clicking a filtering button cancels the selection of another filtering button, unless you hold down the Ctrl key to include multiple filters. By examining this data, Mr. Thomas can see that Station 3 also has the lowest number of *Fire & All Other Calls*. Mr. Thomas will need to investigate further to determine why Station 3 has the lowest number of calls in both classifications and whether this represents a trend.

FIGURE 7.19

Fire & All Other Calls filter applied

4 In the **Classification slicer**, click **Clear Filter**. In the **Fire/Police** slicer, click **Clear Filter**.

> No filters are applied and data from both the Police Department and the Fire Department displays.

5 Point to the **Fire/Police slicer header** and right-click. Click **Remove "Fire/Police"**. By using the same technique, remove the **Location slicer** and the **Classification slicer**.

6 Click cell **A1** to select the PivotTable, and then on the **ANALYZE tab**, in the **Show group**, click **Field List** to display the **PivotTable Fields** pane. In the **field section**, point to **Location**, and then on the right, click the **Location arrow**. Click in the **Search** box, type **Station 3** and then click **OK**. Compare your screen with Figure 7.20.

> The filter is applied and only Station 3 data displays.

FIGURE 7.20

Only Station 3 displays

Filter by Location

7 With cell **A1** still active, on the **ANALYZE tab**, in the **Actions group**, click **Clear**, and then click **Clear Filters**.

> You can also clear filters by using this command.

8 **Save** your workbook.

Objective 3 | Modify a PivotTable Report

Video E7-3

You have seen how, after you have added fields to the PivotTable report, you can pivot (turn) the information in various ways; for example, by removing or rearranging the fields. With different views of your data, you can answer different questions. You can display a field as a column rather than a row. You can display parts of the data on separate pages; for example, by creating separate pages for the Fire Department calls and Police Department calls. After data is displayed in a useful way, you can format it using any methods you have practiced.

In the Fire/Police PivotTable report, a large amount of detail information displays. Although totals display for both the rows and the columns for each location and for each classification, it is still difficult for a reader to make comparisons across precincts and stations. Mr. Thomas needs to be able to respond to questions from City Council members representing different sections of the city. He must know the average number of service calls by department, by classification, and by precinct or station. For the City Council meeting, he does not need to see the monthly detail. In this activity, you will remove and rearrange fields to produce arrangements of this data that will be useful for answering questions at the City Council meeting.

1 In the **layout section** of the **PivotTable Fields** pane, from the **COLUMNS area**, drag the **Month** field name upward into the white **field section**—a black X attaches to the pointer as you drag—and then release the mouse button. Compare your screen with Figure 7.21.

The X indicates that the field is being removed from the PivotTable report. When you release the mouse button, the details for each month no longer display in the PivotTable report; only the quarterly totals for the various call classifications at each location display. In PivotTable Fields pane, *Month* is no longer selected or bold.

↻ ANOTHER WAY Click the Month arrow, and then click Remove Field.

FIGURE 7.21

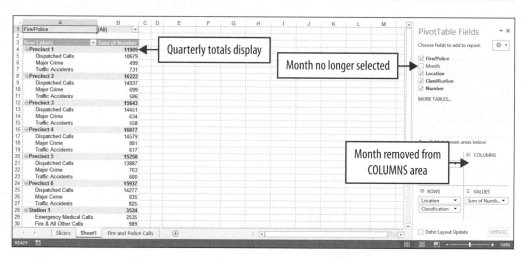

Quarterly totals display

Month no longer selected

Month removed from COLUMNS area

2 In the **layout section** of the **PivotTable Fields** pane, from the **ROWS area**, drag the **Classification** field into the **COLUMNS area**. Compare your screen with Figure 7.22.

By moving *Classification* from the ROWS area to the COLUMNS area, the various classifications become column titles instead of row titles. The classifications are arranged alphabetically across columns B:F. Now the police-related calls—Dispatched Calls, Major Crime, and Traffic Accidents—display as separate classifications.

FIGURE 7.22

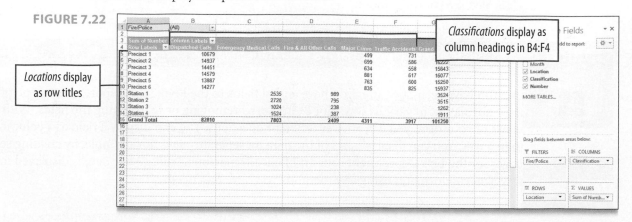

Classifications display as column headings in B4:F4

Locations display as row titles

3 **Close** ☒ the **PivotTable Fields** pane. Click cell **B4**—the column title *Dispatched Calls*. Right-click, point to **Move**, and then click **Move "Dispatched Calls" Down**.

The Dispatched Calls column moves one column to the right.

4 Click cell **C4**, and then use the same technique to move the **Dispatched Calls** column to the right one column again. **Save** 🖫 your workbook, and then compare your screen with Figure 7.23.

By placing the three police-related call classifications adjacent to one another, you have a clearer view of the activity by location.

FIGURE 7.23

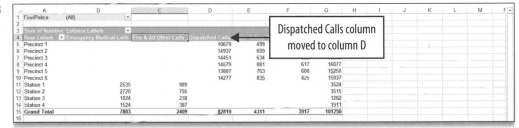

Activity 7.06 | Displaying PivotTable Report Details in a New Worksheet

From the PivotTable report, you can display details for a particular category of information in a separate worksheet. Mr. Thomas needs a separate report showing major crimes reported each month by precinct.

1 Click cell **E15**—the total for the *Major Crime* classification—and then point to the selected cell to view the ScreenTip.

To display the Major Crime field as a separate report, first select the total. Recall that the ScreenTips provide details about the cell's contents.

2 Right-click cell **E15**, and then click **Show Details**.

A new sheet—*Sheet3*—is added to your workbook, and the records for the Major Crime calls display in a table, along with the other fields from the Excel source data. Notice that the *Month* field is included, even though that field is not used in the PivotTable report.

🔄 **ANOTHER WAY**   Double-click a total to display the data on a new worksheet.

3 On **Sheet3**, with the table selected, in the lower right corner, click **Quick Analysis** 📧, and then click **Data Bars**.

Conditional formatting is applied to the data in column E.

4 Rename the **Sheet3** tab **Major Crimes** Click cell **A1** to deselect the data, and then **Save** 🖫 your workbook. Compare your screen with Figure 7.24.

FIGURE 7.24

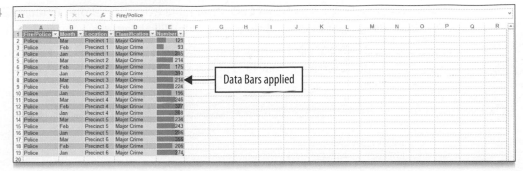

Activity 7.07 | Displaying PivotTable Data on Separate Pages

Recall that Mr. Thomas wanted to analyze the call data by Department—Police Department and Fire Department. To do so, you moved the Fire/Police field to the FILTERS area and filtered the entire report on this field.

Adding a field to the FILTERS area is optional; however, if the report is filtered in this manner, you can display multiple pages for your PivotTable data. For example, you can display the Fire Department calls on one page and the Police Department calls on another page. Doing so will make it easier to answer questions about the calls handled by each Department.

1 Click the **Sheet1 tab**, and then rename it **Combined Calls PivotTable**

2 Click cell **A1** to select the PivotTable report. On the **ANALYZE tab**, in the **PivotTable group**, click the **Options arrow**. Click **Show Report Filter Pages**. Click **OK**.

Because the Fire/Police field was placed in the FILTERS area, this action adds two new sheets to the workbook, one labeled *Fire* and another labeled *Police*.

3 Click the **Police sheet tab**.

The data for the Police Department calls displays on a separate sheet. The data remains in the form of a PivotTable—you can move fields from a row position to a column position and vice versa.

4 Click the **Fire sheet tab**. **Save** 🖫 your workbook, and then compare your screen with Figure 7.25.

The data for the Fire calls displays on a separate sheet.

FIGURE 7.25

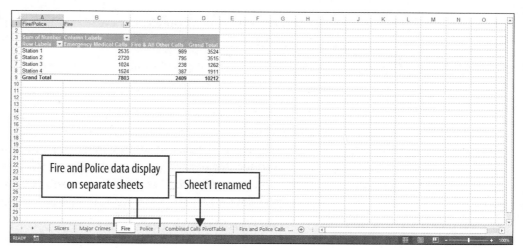

Activity 7.08 | Changing Calculations in a PivotTable Report

A PivotTable report combines and compares large amounts of data so that you can analyze related totals. The default calculation in a PivotTable report is to *sum* the numeric data. You can modify the calculation to display an average, minimum, maximum, or some other calculation. Here, Mr. Thomas needs to report the *average* number of calls for the first quarter.

1 Display the **Combined Calls PivotTable** worksheet. Point to any cell containing numerical data, right-click, and then click **Value Field Settings**.

The Value Field Settings dialog box displays. In the Custom Name box, *Sum of Number* displays; in the Summarize value field by list, *Sum* is selected.

🔁 **ANOTHER WAY**   On the ANALYZE tab, in the Active Field group, click Field Settings.

2 Under **Summarize value field by**, click **Average**. Compare your screen with Figure 7.26.

The Custom Name box displays *Average of Number*.

FIGURE 7.26

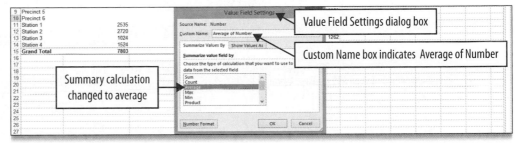

Value Field Settings dialog box

Custom Name box indicates Average of Number

Summary calculation changed to average

3 Click **OK**.

An average for the three months is calculated and displays with six decimal places in the data cells. Cell A3 indicates *Average of Number*.

4 Right-click any numeric value, and then on the shortcut menu, click **Value Field Settings**. In the lower left corner of the dialog box, click **Number Format**.

The Format Cells dialog box displays, with only the Number tab included.

5 Under **Category**, click **Number**. Change the **Decimal places** box to **0**. Select the **Use 1000 Separator** (,) check box. Click **OK** two times to close both dialog boxes. Click cell **A1**, and then compare your screen with Figure 7.27.

The average figures display as whole numbers with the 1000 separator comma appropriately applied.

FIGURE 7.27

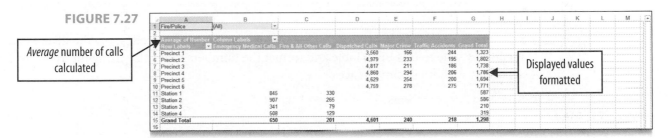

Average number of calls calculated

Displayed values formatted

6 Save 💾 your workbook.

Activity 7.09 | Formatting a PivotTable Report

You can apply a PivotTable Style to the entire PivotTable report and change field names to make them easier to understand. For example, the field name *Average of Number* would be easier to understand as *Average Number of Calls*.

1 In cell **A1**, type **1st Quarter Fire & Police Calls** and then press Enter.

2 Click cell **A3**, type **Average Number of Calls** and then press Enter. AutoFit **column A**.

3 On the **DESIGN tab**, in the **PivotTable Styles group**, click **More** ⬇.

4 Under **Medium**, in the first row, click the sixth style—**Pivot Style Medium 6**. Click cell **G4** and type **Average** and press Enter. Notice that cell **A15** changes to *Average*. Compare your screen with Figure 7.28.

FIGURE 7.28

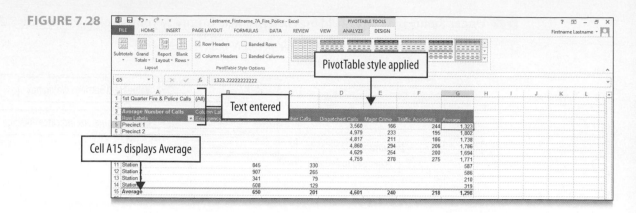

PivotTable style applied

Text entered

Cell A15 displays Average

5 ▸ Display the **Police** worksheet. On the **DESIGN tab**, in the **PivotTable Styles group**, display the **PivotTable Styles** gallery, and then under **Medium**, in the first row apply the second style—**Pivot Style Medium 2**.

6 ▸ Point to any numerical value, right-click, and then click **Value Field Settings**. In the lower left corner, click **Number Format**. Under **Category**, click **Number**. Change the **Decimal places** box to **0**, and then select the **Use 1000 Separator (,)** check box. Click **OK** two times to close both dialog boxes. Click cell **A1**, and then compare your screen with Figure 7.29.

FIGURE 7.29

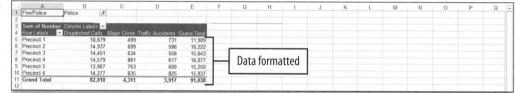

Data formatted

7 ▸ Display the **Fire** worksheet. Using the techniques you just practiced, apply the **Pivot Style Medium 3** style to this PivotTable and format the numbers to display using the 1000 comma separator with no decimal places.

8 ▸ **Save** 🖫 your workbook.

Activity 7.10 Updating PivotTable Report Data

In the previous activities, you created a combined PivotTable report to display the *average* number of calls by classification type for the Police Department precincts and the Fire Department stations. You created a separate PivotTable report for Fire and for Police to show the *total* number of calls for the quarter by Location and Classification. You also created a separate list of the major crimes by precinct. Finally, Station 3 was identified as the fire station with the lowest call numbers; Mr. Thomas plans to gather supporting information to determine if this is a change from previous quarters.

In this activity, you will update some of the data. If you change the underlying data on which the PivotTable report is based, you must also *refresh*—update—the PivotTable to reflect the new data.

1 ▸ On the **Fire** worksheet, in cell **B5**, notice that the total **Emergency Medical Calls** for **Station 1** is *2,535*.

2 ▸ Display the **Combined Calls PivotTable** worksheet, and then click cell **B11**. Notice that the *average* number of **Emergency Medical Calls** for **Station 1** is *845*.

3 ▶ Display the **Fire and Police Calls** worksheet—your original source data. Click cell **E3** and change the number from *924* to **824** Press [Enter], and then click cell **E11** and change the number from *879* to **779** and press [Enter].

The calls for January and February were both mistakenly overstated by 100 calls and are reduced from 924 and 879 to 824 and 779, respectively.

4 ▶ Display the **Combined Calls PivotTable** worksheet. Although you adjusted the underlying data, notice that in cell **B11**, the average number of Emergency Medical Calls for Station 1 has not changed—it still indicates *845*.

5 ▶ On the **ANALYZE tab**, in the **Data group**, click the **Refresh arrow**, and then click **Refresh**. Compare your screen with Figure 7.30.

The average number of Emergency Medical Calls for Station 1 updates to *778*, and the average for this type of call from all stations changes to *634*.

FIGURE 7.30

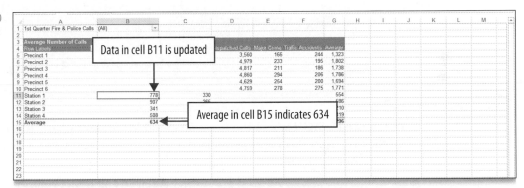

6 ▶ Display the **Fire** worksheet, and then click cell **B5**. Notice that the total number of Emergency Medical Calls for Station 1 has been updated to *2,335*. **Save** 🖫 your workbook.

Objective 4 | Create a PivotChart Report

Video E7-4

A **PivotChart report** is a graphical representation of the data in a PivotTable—referred to as the **associated PivotTable report**. A PivotChart report usually has an associated PivotTable and the two are interactive; that is, if you change the field layout or data in the associated PivotTable report, the changes are immediately reflected in the PivotChart report. A PivotChart report and its associated PivotTable report must be in the same workbook.

Most of the operations you have practiced in standard charts work the same way in a PivotChart. A PivotChart report displays data series, categories, data markers, and axes in the same manner as a standard chart. There are some differences. For example, whereas standard charts are linked directly to a range of worksheet cells, PivotChart reports are based on the data source of the associated PivotTable report.

Activity 7.11 | Creating a PivotChart Report from a PivotTable Report

Mr. Thomas wants to analyze Police calls—specifically the calls related to Major Crime and Traffic Accidents—and he thinks that a chart would be useful to City Council members to convey this information.

1 ▶ Display the **Combined Calls PivotTable** worksheet, and then press [Ctrl] + [Home] to make cell **A1** the active cell and to select the PivotTable.

2 On the **ANALYZE tab**, in the **Tools group**, click **PivotChart**. In the **Insert Chart** dialog box, on the left side, if necessary, click **Column**, and then click **OK** to accept the default chart—**Clustered Column**. Compare your screen with Figure 7.31.

> The PivotChart displays *field buttons*. You can click on any button with an arrow to choose a filter and so change the data that is displayed in the chart. Filters you apply will be reflected in the PivotTable report and vice versa. After your chart is complete, you can hide the field buttons from view. Here, the Classification field items form the legend, and the Location field items form the category axis.

FIGURE 7.31

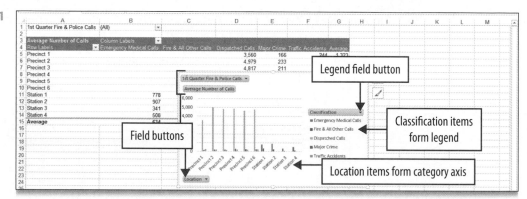

3 On the **DESIGN tab**, in the **Location group**, click **Move Chart**. In the **Move Chart** dialog box, click the **New sheet** option, replace the highlighted text *Chart1* by typing **1st Quarter Chart** and then click **OK**.

4 In the **1st Quarter Chart** sheet, on the **DESIGN tab**, in the **Chart Layouts group**, click **Quick Layout**, and then click the third chart layout—**Layout 3**—which places the legend at the bottom of the chart. In the **Chart Styles group**, click **More** ⬇, and then apply **Style 14**.

5 Click the **Chart Title** and watch the **Formula Bar** as you type **1st Quarter Calls** and press Enter to display the title text in the chart. Compare your screen with Figure 7.32.

FIGURE 7.32

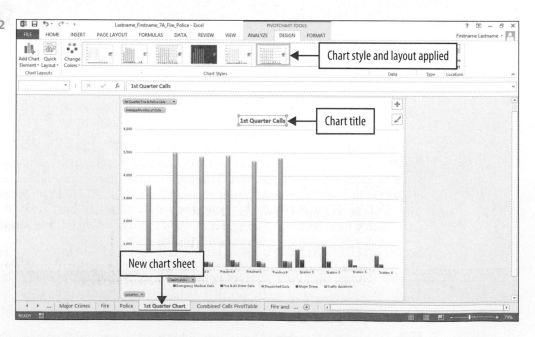

6 On the **INSERT tab**, in the **Text group**, click **Header & Footer**. In the **Page Setup** dialog box, click **Custom Footer**. With the insertion point in the **left section**, from the small toolbar in the dialog box, click **Insert File Name** 🖾. Click **OK** two times. **Save** 🖫 your workbook.

Activity 7.12 | Modifying a PivotChart Report

You can filter and change the values of the data in the PivotChart report by using the gray field buttons that display on the chart. Recall that you can click on any button with an arrow to choose a filter, and that filters you apply will be reflected in the PivotTable report.

For example, most of the calls number in the hundreds, but the Dispatched Calls number in the thousands, resulting in a larger vertical scale. This disparity prevents Mr. Thomas from being able to easily compare the other two call classifications—Major Crime and Traffic Accidents. In this activity, you will filter the data to show only Police calls in the Major Crime and Traffic Accidents classifications. You will also change the summary data back to *total* number of calls rather than the average.

1 In the upper left corner of the chart, click the **Report Filter** field button, which indicates *1st Quarter Fire & Police Calls*. In the lower left corner of the list, select the **Select Multiple Items** check box. Click to clear the **(All)** check box, and select the **Police** check box. Click **OK**, and then compare your screen with Figure 7.33.

Only the Police precinct calls display.

FIGURE 7.33

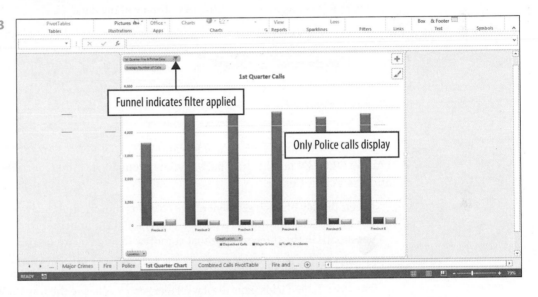

2 At the bottom of the PivotChart, click the **Classification** button above the chart legend. Click to *clear* the check box for **Dispatched Calls**, and then click **OK**.

This action removes the Dispatched Calls classification; only the two remaining call classifications for Police precincts display. The Legend field button displays a funnel icon to indicate that a filter is applied. Because the number of dispatched calls is in the thousands, compared to hundreds for the other call types, removing this classification allows for a clearer comparison of the other call classifications.

3 On the **DESIGN tab**, in the **Type group**, click **Change Chart Type**. In the **Change Chart Type** dialog box, with **Column** selected, click the second chart type—**Stacked Column**—and then click **OK**. Compare your screen with Figure 7.34.

Stacked columns display the two call classifications by location. Within each location, the stacked column shows the amount of activity as part of a whole.

FIGURE 7.34

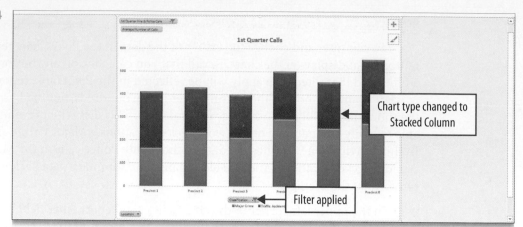

Chart type changed to Stacked Column

Filter applied

4 Display the **Combined Calls PivotTable** worksheet, and then compare your screen with Figure 7.35.

The data is rearranged and only the precinct calls display. The fire station calls do not currently display on the Combined PivotTable sheet. Each time you changed the PivotChart, the underlying PivotTable changed to reflect the new display of the data.

FIGURE 7.35

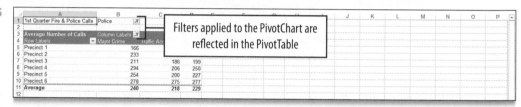

Filters applied to the PivotChart are reflected in the PivotTable

5 Click the **1st Quarter Chart sheet tab** and then click in the chart title to make the chart active. On the **DESIGN tab**, in the **Chart Layouts group**, click **Add Chart Element**, point to **Data Labels**, and then click **Center**.

Labels display on each segment of the columns showing the value for that portion of the column. For the call classification at a particular station, the number represents the *average* number of calls per month in the three months that comprise the first quarter.

6 On the **ANALYZE tab**, in the **Show/Hide group**, click **Field List**.

The PivotTable Fields pane displays. Here you can change the way the data is summarized.

7 In the **PivotChart Fields** pane, in the **VALUES area**, click **Average Number of Calls**, and then click **Value Field Settings**. In the dialog box, click **Sum**, and then click **OK**. On the **chart**, click **Chart Elements** ✛, point to **Data Labels**, click the arrow, and then click **Center**. Click **Chart Elements** ✛ to close the **CHART ELEMENTS** list, and then, compare your screen with Figure 7.36.

The chart changes to display the *total* number of calls rather than the average number of calls.

FIGURE 7.36

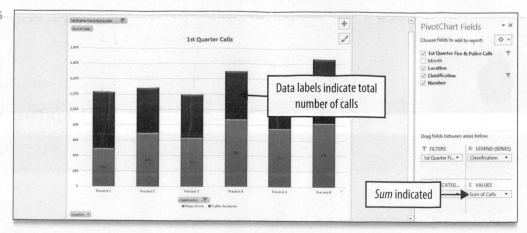

Data labels indicate total number of calls

Sum indicated

8 Display the **Combined Calls PivotTable** worksheet. **Close** ✖ the **PivotTable Fields** pane. In cells **D4** and **A11**, notice that *Average* is still indicated. Click cell **A11** and type **Total** Press Enter.

> *Total* displays in both cells D4 and A11.

9 Redisplay the **1st Quarter Chart** sheet. On the **FORMAT tab**, in the **Current Selection group**, click the **Chart Elements arrow**, click **Chart Area**, and then click **Format Selection**. In the **Format Chart Area** pane, click **FILL**. Click **Solid fill**, click the **Fill Color arrow** 🎨▾, and then in the fifth column, click the second color—**Blue Accent 1, Lighter 80%**.

10 In the **Format Chart Area** pane, click the arrow next to **CHART OPTIONS** to display the **Chart Elements** list, and then click **Plot Area**. Click **Gradient fill**, click the **Preset gradients arrow**, and then in the second column, click the first color—**Light Gradient – Accent 2**. **Close** ✖ the **Format Plot Area** pane. Right-click the **Chart Title**, click **Font**, and then change the font size to **32** and change the font color to the first color in the fourth column—**Dark Blue, Text 2**. Click **OK**.

11 On the **ANALYZE tab**, in the **Show/Hide group**, click **Field Buttons arrow**, and then click **Hide All**. Click an outer edge of the chart to select the entire chart, and then compare your screen with Figure 7.37.

FIGURE 7.37

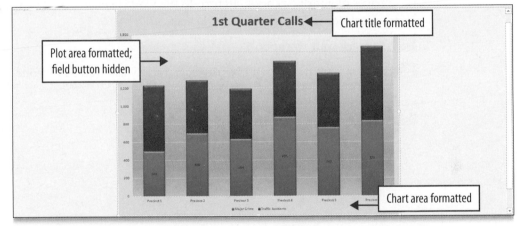

Activity 7.13 | Arranging and Hiding Worksheets in a Multi-sheet Workbook

1 At the bottom of the Excel window, to the left of the sheet tabs, click the **left arrow** twice and make the **Slicers** worksheet active. To the right of the sheet tabs, locate the horizontal scroll bar. At the left end of the scroll bar, point to the three vertical dots to display the ◀▮▶ pointer, and then drag to the right to decrease the width of the scroll bar to display all seven worksheets in this workbook as shown in Figure 7.38.

FIGURE 7.38

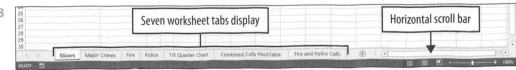

2 Drag the **Combined Calls PivotTable sheet tab** to the left until it is the first worksheet. In the same manner, rearrange the remaining sheet tabs so they are in the following order: Combined Calls PivotTable, Slicers, Major Crimes, Fire, Police, 1st Quarter Chart, Fire and Police Calls. Click the **Fire and Police Calls sheet tab** and then compare your screen with Figure 7.39.

FIGURE 7.39

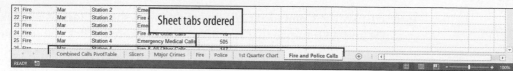

3 ▸ Right-click the **Fire and Police Calls sheet tab** and then click **Hide**.

    In this manner you can hide a worksheet to prevent a user from altering the data.

4 ▸ Point to the **Combined Calls PivotTable sheet tab**, right-click, and then click **Select All Sheets**. Insert a footer in the **left section** that includes the file name. From the **PAGE LAYOUT tab**, center the worksheets horizontally on the page, change the Orientation to **Landscape**, and then in the **Scale to Fit group**, set the **Width** to **1 page**. On the status bar, click **Normal** ⊞. Press Ctrl + Home to move to the top of the worksheet.

5 ▸ Display the **document properties** and under **Related People**, be sure that your name displays as the author. If necessary, right-click the author name, click **Edit Property**, and then type your name. In the **Subject** box, type your course name and section #, and in the **Tags** box, type **fire, police, call activity**

6 ▸ With the sheets still grouped, display the **Print Preview**, and then examine the six visible pages of your workbook. Return to the worksheet and make any necessary corrections or adjustments. Ungroup the worksheets.

7 ▸ **Save** 🖫 your workbook.

8 ▸ Print or submit the workbook electronically as directed by your instructor.

END | You have completed Project 7A

PowerPivot and Power View

PROJECT ACTIVITIES

In Activities 7.14 through 7.21, you will use two of Excel's Business Intelligence tools, PowerPivot and Power View, to create a report and dashboard for the district recreation center. Your completed worksheets will look similar to Figure 7.40.

PROJECT FILES

For Project 7B, you will need the following files:

New blank Excel workbook
e07B_Medical_Supplies

You will save your workbook as:

Lastname_Firstname_7B_First_Aid

PROJECT RESULTS

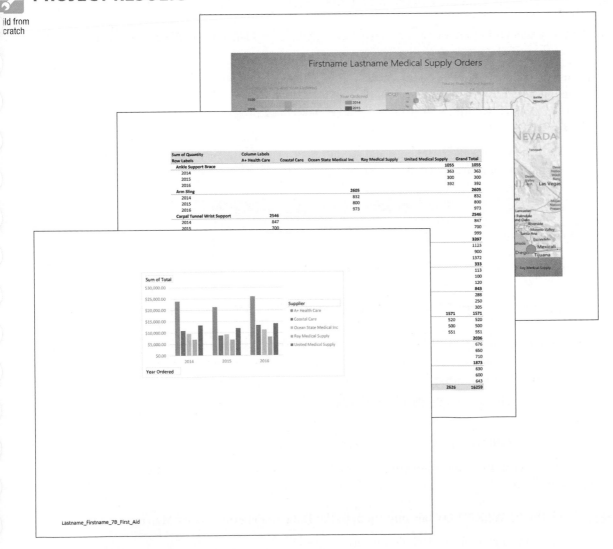

FIGURE 7.40 Project 7B PowerPivot and Power View

Video E7-5

Excel includes several *Business Intelligence tools* that can be used to perform data analysis and create sophisticated charts and reports. The *Data Model* is a method of incorporating data from multiple, related tables into an Excel worksheet. The data can be in an Excel workbook, imported from an Access database, or imported from an external source such as a corporate database, a public data feed, or an analysis service. The related tables can be used to create PivotTables, Pivot Charts, and Power View reports.

Traditional PivotTables use data from a single table. With *PowerPivot*, you can analyze data from multiple sources, work with multiple data tables, and create relationships between tables. A *relationship* is an association between tables that share a common field.

Power View allows you to create and interact with multiple charts, slicers, and other data visualizations in a single sheet.

Activity 7.14 | Enabling the PowerPivot and Power View Add-ins

The PowerPivot and Power View Add-ins are disabled by default. You must enable PowerPivot and Power View from the Excel Options dialog box. In this activity, you will enable PowerPivot and Power View and add the PowerPivot tab to the ribbon.

1 Start Excel and open a new blank workbook. Click the **FILE tab** to display **Backstage** view, and then click **Options**.

2 In the **Excel Options** dialog box, on the left, click **Add-Ins**. At the bottom of the **Excel Options** dialog box, click the **Manage arrow** and click **COM Add-Ins**. Click **Go**. Select the **Microsoft Office PowerPivot for Excel 2013** and **Power View** check boxes. Compare your dialog box with Figure 7.41

Add-ins are optional commands and features that are not immediately available; you must first install and/or activate an add-in to use it.

FIGURE 7.41

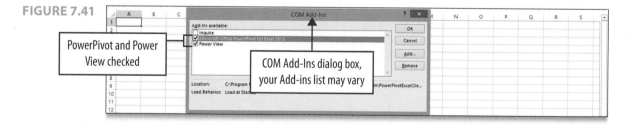

PowerPivot and Power View checked

COM Add-Ins dialog box, your Add-ins list may vary

3 Click **OK**. If the **POWERPIVOT tab** is not displayed on the ribbon, right-click the **VIEW tab** and click **Customize the Ribbon**. On the right, under **Customize Ribbon**, verify **Main Tabs** is selected, select the **Power View** and **PowerPivot** check boxes, and then click **OK**.

The PowerPivot tab is displayed on the ribbon.

Activity 7.15 | Importing Data into the Excel Data Model

In this activity, you will import multiple tables from an Access database into the Data Model using PowerPivot.

1 Click the **POWERPIVOT tab**, and then, in the **Data Model group**, click **Manage**.

The PowerPivot for Excel window opens.

2 Maximize the **PowerPivot** window. In the **Get External Data group**, click **From Database**, and then click **From Access**. Compare your screen with Figure 7.42

FIGURE 7.42

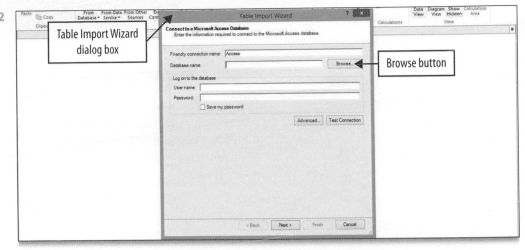

3 In the **Table Import Wizard**, click **Browse**. Navigate to your student files, click **e07B_Medical_Supplies**, and then click **Open**. Click **Next**.

4 Verify *Select from a list of tables and views to choose the data to import* is selected and then click **Next**. Compare your screen with Figure 7.43

FIGURE 7.43

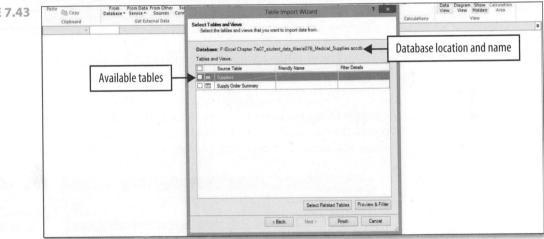

5 Select both tables and then click **Finish** to import the tables into the Excel Data Model. Compare your screen with Figure 7.44.

FIGURE 7.44

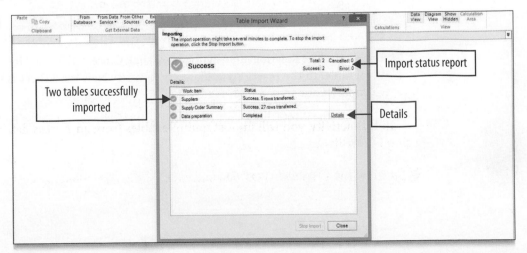

6 Click **Details** to verify a relationship was created between the imported tables. Click **OK**. Click **Close**. Compare your screen with Figure 7.45.

The two tables are imported into the Data Model and display in the PowerPivot window. The data does not display in the Excel workbook. To work with multiple tables in Excel, a relationship must be created between the tables.

FIGURE 7.45

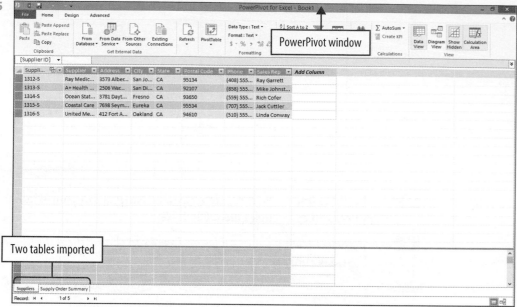

7 In the **PowerPivot** window, with the **Suppliers** table active, click the **Design tab**. In the **Relationships group**, click **Manage Relationships**. Compare your screen with Figure 7.46.

The Manage Relationships dialog box indicates a relationship between the Supplier ID field in the Supply Order Summary table and the Suppliers table. Because the two tables were imported together, the relationship between them was detected and created in the Excel Data Model. You can also manually create, edit, or delete relationships between tables.

FIGURE 7.46

8 In the **Manage Relationships** dialog box, click **Close**. Click the **Home tab**, and then click **PivotTable**. In the **Insert Pivot** dialog box, verify **New Worksheet** is selected and then click **OK**. Compare your screen with Figure 7.47.

Notice the PivotTable is created in the Excel workbook, not in the PowerPivot window.

FIGURE 7.47

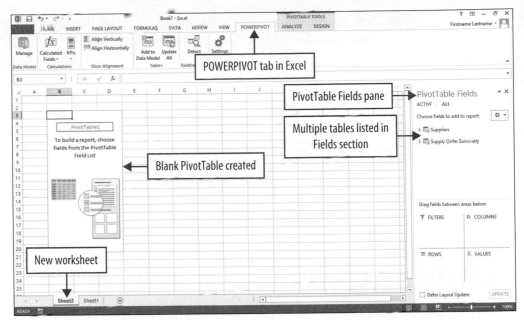

9 ▶ **Save** your file in your **Excel Chapter 7** folder as **Lastname_Firstname_7B_First_Aid**

Objective 6   Create a PivotTable Using PowerPivot

Video E7-6

Activity 7.16 | Creating a PivotTable Using Multiple Tables

The Data Model allows you to use PowerPivot to create PivotTables using the data from multiple, related tables.

1 ▶ In the **PivotTable Fields** pane, notice there are two tabs: **ACTIVE** and **ALL**. With the **ALL tab** active, expand the **Suppliers** table, and then drag the **Supplier** field to the **COLUMNS area**. Collapse the **Suppliers** table, expand the **Supply Order Summary** table, and then drag the **Item** and **Year Ordered** fields to the **ROWS area**. Drag the **Quantity** field to the **VALUES area**. Compare your screen with Figure 7.48.

You have created a PivotTable using data from two related tables.

FIGURE 7.48

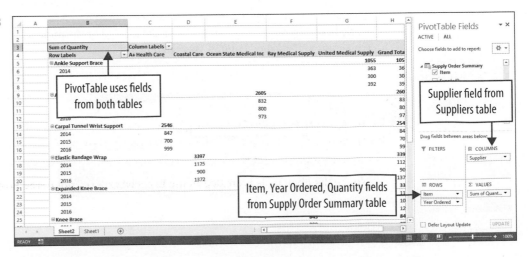

2 ▶ Click cell **B5**. In the lower right corner of the cell, click **Quick Explore** 🔍. Expand **Supply Order Summary** and compare your screen with Figure 7.49.

> *Quick Explore* allows you to drill down through PivotTable data with a single click.

FIGURE 7.49

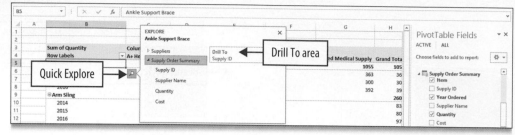

3 ▶ Click **Drill to Supply ID**. With cell **B5** selected, click **Quick Explore** 🔍 and then click **Drill to Item**. Compare your screen with Figure 7.50.

> In this manner you can drill through the data in a PivotTable.

FIGURE 7.50

4 ▶ Click **Undo** ↺ two times. **Save** 💾 your workbook.

Activity 7.17 | Adding a Calculated Field and Creating a PivotChart Using PowerPivot

The imported data does not include a total column, so you will add one in PowerPivot.

1 ▶ On the **Windows taskbar**, click the **PowerPivot** button to switch to the **PowerPivot** window. Click the **Supply Order Summary sheet tab**. Click the **Add Column** header and in the **Formula Bar**, type **=[** and then, double-click [**Quantity**]. Type ***[** and then double-click [**Cost**]. Press Enter. Compare your screen with Figure 7.51.

> The tables in the PowerPivot window do not contain row and column headings like an Excel worksheet, but rather field names like a database. This formula uses the field names *Quantity* and *Cost*. A new calculated column is created in the Data Model that can be used in the PivotTables and other reports.

FIGURE 7.51

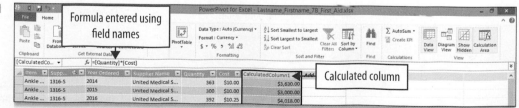

2 ▶ Right-click the **CalculatedColumn1** and click **Rename Column**. Type **Total** and then press Enter.

3 ▶ On the **Home tab**, click the **PivotTable arrow** and then click **PivotChart**. In the **Insert Pivot** dialog box, verify that **New Worksheet** is selected, and then click **OK**.

4 ► In the **PivotChart Fields** pane, expand the **Suppliers** table, and then drag the **Supplier** field to the **LEGEND (SERIES) area**. Collapse the **Suppliers** table, expand the **Supply Order Summary** table, and then drag the **Total** field to the **VALUES area**. Drag the **Year Ordered** field to the **AXIS (CATEGORY) area**. Compare your screen with Figure 7.52. **Save** 🔲 your workbook.

Using PowerPivot, a PivotChart does not have to be associated with a PivotTable.

FIGURE 7.52

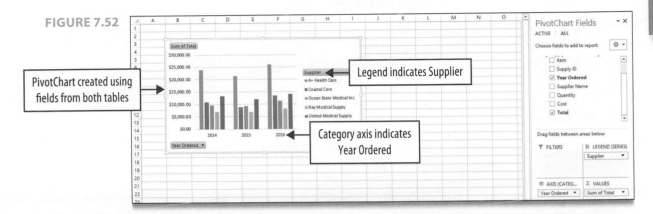

PivotChart created using fields from both tables

Legend indicates Supplier

Category axis indicates Year Ordered

Objective 7 — Create a Dashboard Using Power View

Video E7-7

Power View is a data visualization tool that can be used to create interactive dashboards and reports. Power View can be used with data in worksheet tables or with data in the Data Model. The charts and other objects created on a Power View worksheet are related, and can be cross-filtered. Filtering one object will also filter the other objects on the worksheet. You can create multiple Power View sheets in a workbook.

Activity 7.18 | Create a Power View Worksheet and Column Chart Visualization

In this activity, you will create a Power View worksheet and a Column chart.

1 ► Click the **Sheet1 sheet tab**. Click the **INSERT tab**. In the **Reports group**, click **Power View**. Compare your screen with Figure 7.53.

A new Power View worksheet is created. The Power View canvas displays on the left and the Power View Fields pane displays on the right. The *canvas* is the area of a Power View worksheet that contains data visualizations.

> **NOTE**
>
> The Power View Add-in is installed by default, but must be enabled the first time it is used. You must also have Silverlight installed. If you do not have Silverlight installed, Excel will prompt you to install it at this point.

FIGURE 7.53

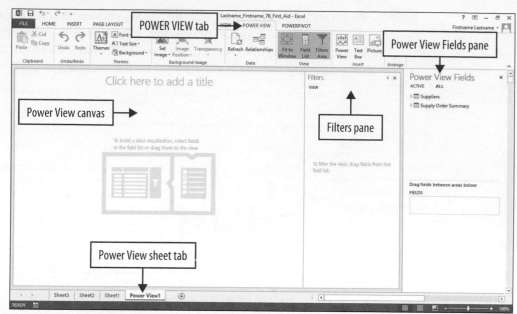

POWER VIEW tab

Power View Fields pane

Power View canvas

Filters pane

Power View sheet tab

2 ▶ At the top of the **Power View** worksheet, click *Click here to add a title*, and then type **Firstname Lastname Medical Supply Orders**

3 ▶ Notice both tables are visible in the **Power View Fields** pane. Expand the **Supply Order Summary** table. Drag the **Item, Quantity,** and **Year Ordered** fields to the **FIELDS area**. Compare your screen with Figure 7.54.

A table is created in the upper left quadrant of the Power View canvas.

🔄 **BY TOUCH**   Tap the check box next to a field to select it.

FIGURE 7.54

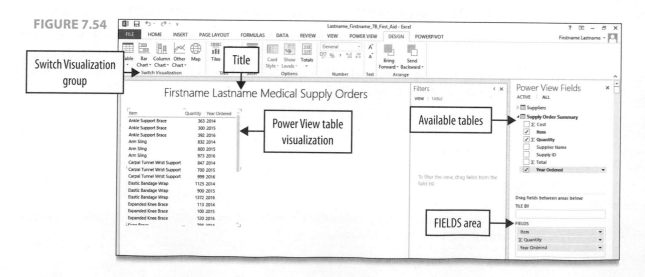

Switch Visualization group

Title

Power View table visualization

Available tables

FIELDS area

4 ▶ On the **DESIGN tab**, in the **Switch Visualization group**, click the **Column Chart arrow** and then click **Stacked Column**. Compare your screen with Figure 7.55. **Save** 💾 your workbook.

The table is changed to a stacked column chart.

FIGURE 7.55

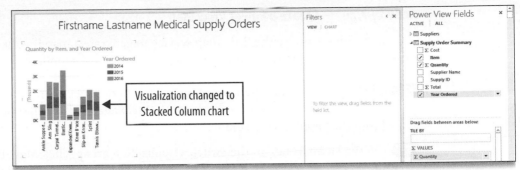

Firstname Lastname Medical Supply Orders

Visualization changed to Stacked Column chart

Activity 7.19 | Create a Power View Pie Chart Visualization

In this activity, you will add a pie chart to the Power View worksheet.

1 Click a blank area of the **Power View** canvas to deselect the column chart. In the **Power View Fields** pane, expand the **Suppliers** table and drag the **Supplier** field to the **FIELDS area**. From the **Supply Order Summary** table drag the **Total** field to the **FIELDS area**. Compare your screen with Figure 7.56.

Recall that the Total field is a calculated field that you created in the Data Model.

FIGURE 7.56

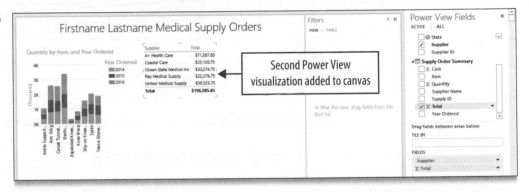

Firstname Lastname Medical Supply Orders

Second Power View visualization added to canvas

2 On the **DESIGN tab**, in the **Switch Visualization group**, click **Other Chart** and then click **Pie**. Point to the lower right edge of the pie chart to display the 🖑 pointer, and then drag the pie chart below the column chart. Point to the lower right corner of the pie chart area to display the 🖘 pointer and drag to resize the pie chart until it is the same width as the column chart and touches the bottom edge of the canvas. Compare your screen with Figure 7.57. **Save** 🖫 your workbook.

FIGURE 7.57

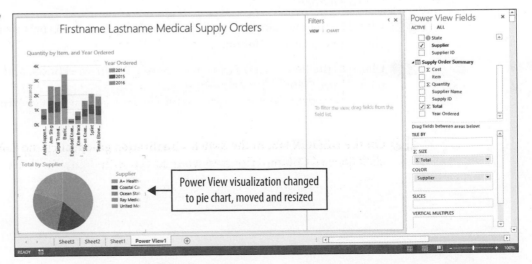

Firstname Lastname Medical Supply Orders

Power View visualization changed to pie chart, moved and resized

Activity 7.20 | Create a Power View Map

Power View can use the Bing map service to generate a map if your data contains location information. In this activity, you will create a map of local suppliers.

1 Click a blank area of the **Power View** canvas to deselect the pie chart. In the **Power View Fields** pane, from the **Suppliers** table, drag the **City**, **State**, and **Supplier** fields to the **FIELDS area**. From the **Supply Order Summary** table drag the **Total** field to the **FIELDS area**.

2 On the **DESIGN tab**, in the **Switch Visualization group**, click **Map**. If necessary, in the **PRIVACY WARNING** bar, click **Enable Content**. Drag the lower right corner of the map to resize it to fill the right side of the canvas. Compare your screen with Figure 7.58. **Save** 🖫 your workbook.

FIGURE 7.58

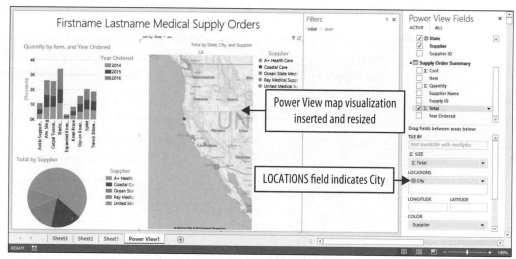

Activity 7.21 | Formatting the Power View Worksheet

A Power View report can be formatted to make it more attractive.

1 Click the canvas to deselect the map. **Close** ✖ the **Filters** pane. On the **POWER VIEW tab**, in the **Themes group**, click **Text Size**, and then click **75%**.

This makes the text smaller so more of the text is visible on the sheet.

2 In the **Themes group**, click **Background**, and then click the first color in the third row—**Light 1 Center Gradient**.

3 Click the map to select it. Click the **LAYOUT tab**, in the **Labels group**, click **Legend**, and then click **Show Legend at Bottom**.

4 **Close** ✖ the **Power View Fields** pane, **Save** 🖫 your workbook, and then compare your screen with Figure 7.59.

FIGURE 7.59

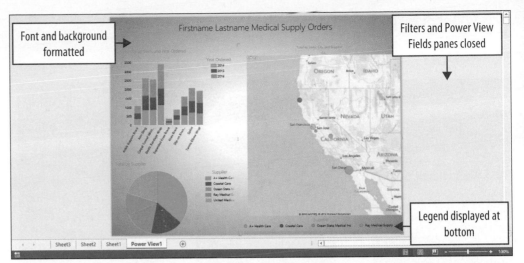

On the pie chart, click the blue slice that represents *A + Health Care*. Notice that the other slices on the pie chart are dimmed. Also notice the effect on the column chart and map. Compare your screen with Figure 7.60.

> The objects on the Power View sheet are related, so highlighting or filtering one object also affects the other objects.

FIGURE 7.60

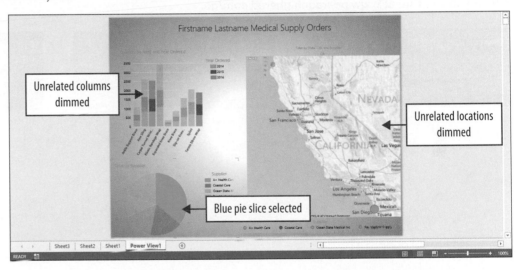

6 Rename **Sheet3 PivotChart** Rename **Sheet2 PivotTable** Delete **Sheet1**. Group the **PivotChart** and **PivotTable** worksheets and insert a footer with the file name in the **left section**. Return to **Normal** view, center horizontally, change the **Orientation** to **Landscape**, and scale the **Width** and **Height** to **1 page**. Press Ctrl + Home to return to cell **A1**.

7 Display the **document properties** and under **Related People**, be sure that your name displays as the author. If necessary, right-click the author name, click **Edit Property**, and then type your name. In the **Subject** box, type your course name and section #, and in the **Tags** box, type **first aid, BI** Return to your worksheet, ungroup the worksheets, and **Save** your workbook.

8 Print or submit the workbook electronically as directed by your instructor. **Close** your workbook and **Close** Excel.

NOTE

A Power View worksheet must be printed separately from the other worksheets.

END | You have completed Project 7B

END OF CHAPTER

SUMMARY

PivotTables and PivotCharts are used to organize and display data. PivotTables are useful for summarizing and analyzing large amounts of data. PivotCharts graphically represent the data in PivotTables.

By manipulating data in PivotTable and PivotChart reports you can present and organize information into groups from which trends, comparisons, patterns, and relationships can be determined.

Business Intelligence tools in Excel, including PowerPivot and Power View, can be used to perform data analysis and create sophisticated charts and reports using data from multiple sources and tables.

Excel uses the Data Model to incorporate data from multiple sources into related tables in Excel. The data can come from an Excel worksheet or external sources such as databases and data feeds.

GO! LEARN IT ONLINE

Review the concepts and key terms in this chapter by completing these online challenges, which you can find at **www.pearsonhighered.com/go**.

Matching and Multiple Choice:
Answer matching and multiple choice questions to test what you learned in this chapter. MyITLab®

Crossword Puzzle:
Spell out the words that match the numbered clues, and put them in the puzzle squares.

Flipboard:
Flip through the definitions of the key terms in this chapter and match them with the correct term.

REVIEW AND ASSESSMENT GUIDE FOR EXCEL CHAPTER 7

Your instructor may assign one or more of these projects to help you review the chapter and assess your mastery and understanding of the chapter.

	Review and Assessment Guide for Excel Chapter 7		
Project	**Apply Skills from These Chapter Objectives**	**Project Type**	**Project Location**
7C	Objectives 1–4 from Project 7A	**7C Skills Review** A guided review of the skills from Project 7A.	On the following pages
7D	Objectives 5–7 from Project 7B	**7D Skills Review** A guided review of the skills from Project 7B.	On the following pages
7E	Objectives 1–4 from Project 7A	**7E Mastery (Grader Project)** A demonstration of your mastery of the skills in Project 7A with extensive decision making.	In MyITLab and on the following pages
7F	Objectives 5–7 from Project 7B	**7F Mastery (Grader Project)** A demonstration of your mastery of the skills in Project 7B with extensive decision making.	In MyITLab and on the following pages
7G	Objectives 1–7 from Projects 7A and 7B	**7G Mastery (Grader Project)** A demonstration of your mastery of the skills in Projects 7A and 7B with extensive decision making.	In MyITLab and on the following pages
7H	Combination of Objectives from Projects 7A and 7B	**7H GO! Fix It** A demonstration of your mastery of the skills in Projects 7A and 7B by creating a correct result from a document that contains errors you must find.	Online
7I	Combination of Objectives from Projects 7A and 7B	**7I GO! Make It** A demonstration of your mastery of the skills in Projects 7A and 7B by creating a result from a supplied picture.	Online
7J	Combination of Objectives from Projects 7A and 7B	**7J GO! Solve It** A demonstration of your mastery of the skills in Projects 7A and 7B, your decision-making skills, and your critical thinking skills. A task-specific rubric helps you self-assess your result.	Online
7K	Combination of Objectives from Projects 7A and 7B	**7K GO! Solve It** A demonstration of your mastery of the skills in Projects 7A and 7B, your decision-making skills, and your critical thinking skills. A task-specific rubric helps you self-assess your result.	On the following pages
7L	Combination of Objectives from Projects 7A and 7B	**7L GO! Think** A demonstration of your understanding of the chapter concepts applied in a manner that you would outside of college. An analytic rubric helps you and your instructor grade the quality of your work by comparing it to the work an expert in the discipline would create.	On the following pages
7M	Combination of Objectives from Projects 7A and 7B	**7M GO! Think** A demonstration of your understanding of the chapter concepts applied in a manner that you would outside of college. An analytic rubric helps you and your instructor grade the quality of your work by comparing it to the work an expert in the discipline would create.	Online
7N	Combination of Objectives from Projects 7A and 7B	**7N You and GO!** A demonstration of your understanding of the chapter concepts applied in a manner that you would in a personal situation. An analytic rubric helps you and your instructor grade the quality of your work.	Online

GLOSSARY

GLOSSARY OF CHAPTER KEY TERMS

Add-in An optional command or feature that is not immediately available; you must first install and/or activate an add-in to use it.

Associated PivotTable report The PivotTable report in a workbook that is graphically represented in a PivotChart.

Business Intelligence tools Tools that can be used to perform data analysis and create sophisticated charts and reports.

Canvas The area of a Power View worksheet that contains data visualizations.

Clear Filter A button that removes a filter.

COLUMNS area An area to position fields that you want to display as columns in the PivotTable report. Field names placed here become column titles, and the data is grouped in columns by these titles.

Data Model A method of incorporating data from multiple, related tables into an Excel worksheet.

Field button A button on a PivotChart with an arrow to choose a filter, and thus change the data that is displayed in the chart.

Field names The column titles from source data that form the categories of data for a PivotTable.

Field section The upper portion of the PivotTable Fields pane containing the fields—column titles—from your source data; use this area to add fields to and remove fields from the PivotTable.

Filter To limit the display of data to only specific information.

FILTER area An area in the lower portion of the PivotTable Fields pane to position fields by which you want to filter the PivotTable report, enabling you to display a subset of data in the PivotTable report.

Filtering button A button on a slicer which you use to select the item by which to filter.

Layout section The lower portion of the PivotTable Fields pane containing the four areas for layout; use this area to rearrange and reposition fields in the PivotTable.

PivotChart report A graphical representation of the data in a PivotTable report.

PivotTable An interactive Excel report that summarizes and analyzes large amounts of data.

PivotTable Fields pane A window that lists, at the top, all of the fields—column titles—from the source data for use in the PivotTable report and at the bottom, an area in which you can arrange the fields in the PivotTable.

Power View An Excel BI tool that allows you to create and interact with multiple charts, slicers, and other data visualizations in a single sheet.

PowerPivot An Excel BI tool that allows you to analyze data from multiple sources, work with multiple data tables, and create relationships between tables.

Quick Explore A tool that allows you to drill down through PivotTable data with a single click.

Refresh The command to update a worksheet to reflect the new data.

Relationship An association between tables that share a common field.

ROWS area An area to position fields that you want to display as rows in the PivotTable report. Field names placed here become row titles, and the data is grouped by these row titles.

Slicer Easy-to-use filtering control with buttons that enable you to drill down through large amounts of data.

Slicer header The top of a slicer that indicates the category of the slicer items.

Source data The data for a PivotTable, formatted in columns and rows, which can be located in an Excel worksheet or an external source.

VALUES area An area to position fields that contain data that is summarized in a PivotTable report or PivotChart report. The data placed here is usually numeric or financial in nature and the data is summarized—summed. You can also perform other basic calculations such as finding the average, the minimum, or the maximum.

CHAPTER REVIEW

Apply 7A skills from these Objectives:

1 Create a PivotTable Report

2 Use Slicers and Search Filters

3 Modify a PivotTable Report

4 Create a PivotChart Report

Skills Review   Project 7C Parks and Pools Calls

In the following Skills Review, you will assist Lindsay Johnson, Director of Parks and Recreation, in preparing a comparative report for phone calls received by the various park and pool facilities in the city. You will create and modify a PivotTable report and PivotChart report. The first six worksheets in your workbook will look similar to Figure 7.61.

PROJECT FILES

For Project 7C, you will need the following file:

e07C_Parks_Pools

You will save your workbook as:

Lastname_Firstname_7C_Parks_Pools

PROJECT RESULTS

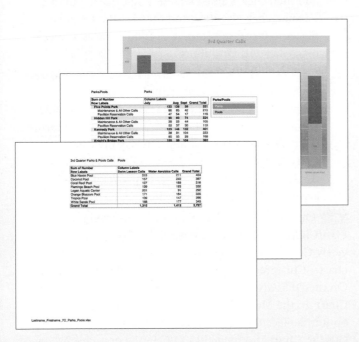

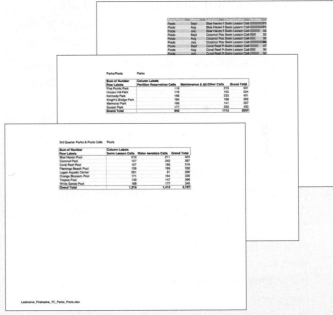

FIGURE 7.61

(Project 7C Parks and Pools Calls continues on the next page)

CHAPTER REVIEW

1 ▶ Start Excel. From your student files, open **e07C_Parks_Pools**. **Save** the file in your **Excel Chapter 7** folder as **Lastname_Firstname_7C_Parks_Pools** Click cell **A2**. On the **INSERT tab**, in the **Tables group**, click **Recommended PivotTables**, and then, in the **Recommended PivotTables** dialog box, click **Sum of Number by Location (+) PivotTable**. Click **OK**.

a. In the **PivotTable Fields** pane, in the **layout section**, verify **Parks/Pools** and **Location** are listed in the **ROWS area**, and **Sum of Number** is listed in the **VALUES area**.

b. Drag the **Parks/Pools** field from the **ROWS area** up to the **FILTERS area**.

c. In the **field section**, select the **Classification** field check box. Right-click cell **A4**, point to **Expand/Collapse**, and then click **Expand Entire Field**.

d. In the **PivotTable Fields** pane, from the **field section**, drag the **Month** field down to the **COLUMNS area**.

e. On the **DESIGN tab**, in the **PivotTable Styles group**, click **More**, and then under **Light**, click **Pivot Style Light 8**.

2 ▶ On the **ANALYZE tab**, in the **Filter group**, click **Insert Slicer**. Select the **Parks/Pools** check box, and then click **OK**. Drag the **Parks/Pools** slicer to the right of the PivotTable. Shorten the slicer to just below **Pools**.

a. On the **OPTIONS tab**, in the **Slicer Styles group**, click **More**, and then under **Dark**, click **Slicer Style Dark 6**. Click cell **A1**. On the **Parks/Pools slicer**, click the **Parks** filtering button. Point to the **Sheet1 sheet tab**, right-click, and then click **Move or Copy**. In the **Move or Copy** dialog box, select the **Create a copy** check box. Click **OK**. Right-click the **Sheet 1 (2) sheet tab**, click **Rename**, and then type **Filtered by Parks**

b. Display the **Sheet1** worksheet. In the **Parks/Pools slicer**, click **Clear Filter**. Point to the **Parks/Pools slicer header**, right-click, and then click **Remove "Parks/Pools"**.

3 ▶ In the **layout section** of the **PivotTable Fields** pane, from the **COLUMNS area**, drag the **Month** field name upward into the white **field section** and then release the mouse button. In the **layout section**, from the **ROWS area**, drag the **Classification** field into the **COLUMNS area**. **Close** the **PivotTable Fields** pane.

a. Click cell **B4**. Right-click, point to **Move**, and then click **Move "Maintenance & All Other Calls" Down**. Point to cell **E19** and right-click; click **Show Details**. In in the lower right corner, click **Quick Analysis**, and then click **Data Bars**. Rename the **Sheet3** tab **Swim Lesson Calls** Click cell **A1**.

b. Click the **Sheet1 tab**, and then rename it **Combined Calls PivotTable** Click cell **A1**. On the **ANALYZE tab**, in the **PivotTable group**, click the **Options arrow**, and then click **Show Report Filter Pages**. In the dialog box, click **OK** to create worksheets for Parks and for Pools.

c. Display the **Combined Calls PivotTable** worksheet. Point to any cell with numerical data, right-click, and then click **Value Field Settings**. Click **Number Format**, click **Number**, and then set the **Decimal places** to **0** and select the **Use 1000 Separator** check box. Click **OK** two times.

d. Click cell **A1**. Type **3rd Quarter Parks & Pools Calls** press Enter, and then apply AutoFit to **column A**. Display the **Parks and Pools Calls** worksheet, which is your source data. Change the value in cell **E3** from 95 to **85** and then press Enter. Display the **Combined Calls PivotTable** worksheet. Click cell **A1**. On the **ANALYZE tab**, in the **Data group**, click the **Refresh arrow**, and then click **Refresh**.

4 ▶ On the **ANALYZE tab**, in the **Tools group**, click **PivotChart**. In the **Insert Chart** dialog box, on the left verify **Column** is selected, on the right, verify the first chart—**Clustered Column** is selected, and then click **OK**. On the **DESIGN tab**, in the **Location group**, click **Move Chart**. In the **Move Chart** dialog box, click the **New sheet** option, replace the highlighted text *Chart1* by typing **3rd Quarter Chart** and then click **OK**. In the new chart sheet, on the **DESIGN tab**, in the **Chart Layouts group**, click **Quick Layout**, and then click **Layout 3**. In the **Chart Styles group**, click **More**, and then apply **Style 13**.

a. Click the **Chart Title** and watch the **Formula Bar** as you type **3rd Quarter Calls** and press Enter. On the **INSERT tab**, in the **Text group**, click **Header & Footer**. In the **Page Setup** dialog box, click **Custom Footer**. With the insertion point in the **left section**, from the small toolbar in the dialog box, click **Insert File Name**, and then click **OK** two times.

(Project 7C Parks and Pools Calls continues on the next page)

b. In the upper left corner of the chart, click **Report Filter**, which indicates *3rd Quarter Parks & Pools Calls*. In the lower left corner of the list, select (place a check mark in) the **Select Multiple Items** check box. Click to clear the **(All)** check box, select the **Pools** check box, and then click **OK**. At the bottom of the PivotChart, click **Legend**, which indicates *Classification*. Click to *clear* the check box for **Pool Party Calls**, and then click **OK**.

c. On the **DESIGN tab**, in the **Type group**, click **Change Chart Type**. In the **Change Chart Type** dialog box, click **Stacked Column**, and then click **OK**. On the **DESIGN tab**, in the **Chart Layouts group**, click **Add Chart Element**, point to **Data Labels**, and then click **Center**.

d. On the **FORMAT tab**, in the **Current Selection group**, click the **Chart Elements arrow**, click **Chart Area**, and then click **Format Selection**. In the **Format Chart Area** pane, click **FILL**. Click **Solid fill**, click the **Fill Color arrow**, and then in the fifth column, click the third color—**Green, Accent 1, Lighter 60%**. Format the **Plot area** with **Gradient fill**. Click the **Preset gradients arrow**, and then in the second column, click the first color—**Light Gradient – Accent 2**. **Close** the **Format Plot Area** pane.

e. On the **ANALYZE tab**, in the **Show/Hide group**, click the **Field Buttons arrow**, and then click **Hide All**.

END | You have completed Project 7C

f. Drag the **Combined Calls PivotTable sheet tab** to the left until it is the first worksheet. Arrange the remaining sheet tabs so they are in the following order: Combined Calls PivotTable, Filtered by Parks, 3rd Quarter Chart, Swim Lesson Calls, Parks, Pools, Parks and Pool Calls. Hide the **Parks and Pool Calls** worksheet.

g. Point to the **Combined Calls PivotTable sheet tab**, right-click, and then click **Select All Sheets**. Insert a footer in the **left section** that includes the file name. From the **PAGE LAYOUT tab**, center the worksheets horizontally on the page, change the **Orientation** to **Landscape**, and then in the **Scale to Fit group**, set the **Width** to **1 page**. On the status bar, click **Normal**. Press Ctrl + Home to move to the top of the worksheet. Display the **document properties** and under **Related People**, be sure that your name displays as the author. If necessary, right-click the author name, click **Edit Property**, and then type your name. In the **Subject** box, type your course name and section #, and in the **Tags** box, type **parks, pools, call activity** With the sheets still grouped, display the **Print Preview**, and then examine the six visible pages of your workbook. If necessary, make any necessary corrections or adjustments and ungroup the worksheets. Submit the workbook electronically as directed by your instructor.

CHAPTER REVIEW

Apply 7B skills from these Objectives:

5 Create a Data Model Using PowerPivot

6 Create a PivotTable Using PowerPivot

7 Create a Dashboard Using Power View

In the following Skills Review, you will assist City Council Office Manager Jake Curley create a Data Model, PivotTable, and PivotChart using PowerPivot. You will also create a Power View worksheet. Your results will look similar to those in Figure 7.62.

PROJECT FILES

For Project 7D, you will need the following files:

New blank workbook
e07D_Office_Supplies

You will save your workbook as:

Lastname_Firstname_7D_Council_Office

Build from Scratch

PROJECT RESULTS

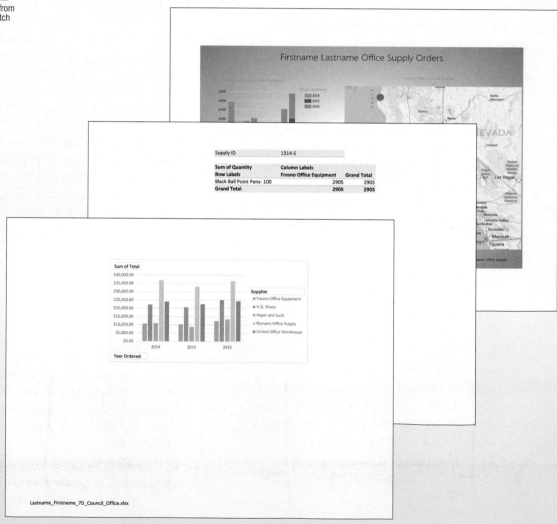

FIGURE 7.62

(Project 7D Office Supplies continues on the next page)

1 Start Excel and display a new blank workbook. If the **POWERPIVOT** tab is not visible, follow the directions in Activity 7.14 to enable it. Click the **POWERPIVOT tab**, and then, in the **Data Model group**, click **Manage**.

a. Maximize the **PowerPivot** window. In the **Get External Data group**, click **From Database**, and then click **From Access**. In the **Table Import Wizard**, click **Browse**. Navigate to your student files and open the file **e07D_Office_Supplies**. Click **Next**. Verify *Select from a list of tables and views to choose the data to import* is selected and then click **Next**. Select both tables and then click **Finish**. Click **Close**.

b. In the **PowerPivot** window, with the **Suppliers** table active, click the **Design tab**. In the **Relationships group**, click **Manage Relationships**. Verify the relationship was created between the two imported tables and then **Close** the **Manage Relationships** dialog box.

c. Click the **Home tab**, and then click **PivotTable**. In the **Insert Pivot** dialog box, verify **New Worksheet** is selected and then click **OK**. **Save** your file in your **Excel Chapter 7** folder as **Lastname_Firstname_7D_Council_Office**

2 In the **PivotTable Fields** pane, with the **ALL tab** active, expand the **Suppliers** table, and then drag the **Supplier** field to the **COLUMNS area**. Expand the **Supply Order Summary** table and drag the **Item** and **Year Ordered** fields to the **ROWS area**. Drag the **Quantity** field to the **VALUES area**.

a. Click cell **B5**. In the lower right corner of the cell, click the **Quick Explore** icon. Expand **Supply Order Summary**. Click **Drill to Supply ID**. With cell **B5** selected, click **Quick Explore** and then click **Drill to Item**.

3 Use the buttons on the **Windows taskbar** to return to the **PowerPivot** window. Click the **Supply Order Summary sheet tab**. Click the **Add Column** header and in the **Formula Bar,** type **=[** Double-click [**Quantity**], type *****[** Double-click [**Cost**], and then press Enter.

a. Right-click the **CalculatedColumn1** and click **Rename Column**. Type **Total** and then press Enter.

b. Click the **PivotTable arrow** and then click **PivotChart**. Verify that **New Worksheet** is selected in the **Insert Pivot** dialog box and then click **OK**.

c. In the **PivotChart Fields** pane, expand the **Suppliers** table, and then drag the **Supplier** field to the **LEGEND (SERIES) area**. Expand the **Supply Order Summary** table and drag the **Total** field to the **VALUES area**. Drag the **Year Ordered** field to the **AXIS (CATEGORY) area**.

4 Click the **Sheet1 sheet tab**. On the **INSERT tab**, in the **Reports group**, click **Power View**. At the top of the **Power View** worksheet, click *Click here to add a title*, and then type **Firstname Lastname Office Supply Orders**

a. In the **Power View Fields** pane, expand the **Supply Order Summary** table. Drag the **Item**, **Quantity**, and **Year Ordered** fields to the **FIELDS area**.

b. On the **DESIGN tab**, in the **Switch Visualization group**, click the **Column Chart arrow** and then click **Stacked Column**.

5 Click a blank area of the **Power View** canvas to deselect the column chart. In the **Power View Fields** pane, expand the **Suppliers** table and drag the **Supplier** field to the **FIELDS area**. From the **Supply Order Summary** table drag the **Total** field to the **FIELDS area**.

a. In the **Switch Visualization group**, click **Other Chart** and then click **Pie**. Point to the lower right edge of the pie chart to display the selection pointer, and then drag the pie chart below the column chart. Point to the lower right corner of the pie chart area to display the diagonal resize pointer and drag to resize the pie chart until it is the same width as the column chart and touches the bottom edge of the canvas.

b. Click a blank area of the **Power View** canvas to deselect the pie chart. In the **Power View Fields** pane, from the **Suppliers** table drag the **City**, **State**, and **Supplier** fields to the **FIELDS area**. From the **Supply Order Summary** table drag the **Total** field to the **FIELDS area**.

c. In the **Switch Visualization group**, click **Map**. If necessary, click **Enable Content**. Drag the lower right corner of the map to resize it to fill the right side of the canvas.

(Project 7D Office Supplies continues on the next page)

CHAPTER REVIEW

6 Click the canvas to deselect the map. **Close** the **Filters** pane. On the **POWER VIEW tab**, in the **Themes group**, click **Text Size**, and then click **75%**.

a. Click **Background**, and then click the first color in the third row—**Light 1 Center Gradient**.

b. Click the map to select it. Click the **LAYOUT tab**, in the **Labels group**, click **Legend**, and then click **Show Legend at Bottom**. **Close** the **Power View Fields** pane and close the **Filters** pane.

7 Rename **Sheet3 PivotChart** Rename **Sheet2 PivotTable** Delete **Sheet1**. Group the **PivotChart** and **PivotTable** worksheets and insert a footer with the file name in the **left section**. Return to **Normal** view, center horizontally, change the **Orientation** to **Landscape**, and scale the **Width** and **Height** to **1 page**. Press Ctrl + Home to return to cell **A1**.

END | You have completed Project 7D

8 Display the **document properties** and under **Related People**, be sure that your name displays as the author. If necessary, right-click the author name, click **Edit Property**, and then type your name. In the **Subject** box, type your course name and section #, and in the **Tags** box, type **office supplies, BI Save** your workbook. Print or submit the workbook electronically as directed by your instructor.

Mastering Excel Project 7E Concessions

In the following Mastering Excel project, you will help Lindsay Johnson, the Director of Parks and Recreation, create and modify a PivotTable report and PivotChart report to analyze revenue from park concessions such as food, boat rentals, and golf fees. Your completed workbooks will look similar to Figure 7.63.

Apply 7A skills from these Objectives:

1 Create a PivotTable Report
2 Use Slicers and Search Filters
3 Modify a PivotTable Report
4 Create a PivotChart Report

PROJECT FILES

For Project 7E, you will need the following file:

e07E_Concessions_Revenue

You will save your workbook as:

Lastname_Firstname_7E_Concessions_Revenue

PROJECT RESULTS

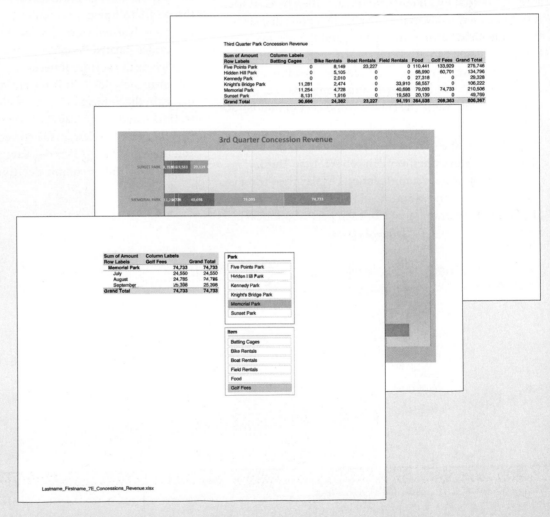

FIGURE 7.63

(Project 7E Concessions continues on the next page)

CONTENT-BASED ASSESSMENTS

1 Start Excel. From your student files, open **e07E_Concessions_Revenue** and **Save** the file in your **Excel Chapter 7** folder as **Lastname_Firstname_7E_Concessions_Revenue**

2 Click cell **A2**. Insert the Recommended PivotTable *Sum of Amount by Park*. Add the **Month** field to the **ROWS area**. Place the **Item** field in the **COLUMNS area**. **Close** the **PivotTable Fields** pane.

3 Insert a slicer for the **Park** field and a slicer for the **Item** field. Resize and move the slicers so that they are to the right of the PivotTable, with the Park slicer above the Item slicer. Apply **Slicer Style Light 4** and **Slicer Style Light 6** to the slicers, respectively.

4 Filter first by **Memorial Park**, and then by **Golf Fees**. Right-click any value in the PivotTable report, display the **Value Field Settings** dialog box, and then format the **Number** category to display zero decimal places and the **1000 Separator**. Move the two slicers to the immediate right of the filtered PivotTable, and then make a copy of this worksheet. Name the copied worksheet **Memorial-3Q Golf Fees**

5 Rename **Sheet1 Concessions Revenue** Clear the filters and remove the slicers. In cell **A1**, type **Third Quarter Park Concession Revenue** Display the **Field List**, and then *remove* the **Month** field from the **ROWS area** to display only the grand totals for each park and for each item. **Close** the **PivotTable Fields** pane.

6 Insert a **PivotChart** using the **Stacked Bar** chart type. Move the chart to a new worksheet named **3rd Quarter Concessions Chart** Apply the **Layout 3** chart layout and **Chart Style 4**. As the **Chart Title**, type **3rd Quarter Concession Revenue** Format the **Plot Area** with the **Gradient** fill **Light Gradient-Accent 6**, the sixth column, first color. Format the **Chart Area** with a solid fill using **Blue, Accent 1, Lighter 60%** in the fifth column, the third color. Hide all of the field buttons on the chart. Insert a custom footer with the file name in the **left section**.

7 Hide the **Park Concessions** worksheet. Select all worksheets. Insert a footer with the file name in the **left section**. Change the **Orientation** to **Landscape**, set the **Width** to **1 page**, and center the sheets horizontally. Return to **Normal** view. Display the **document properties** and under **Related People**, be sure that your name displays as the author. If necessary, right-click the author name, click **Edit Property**, and then type your name. In the **Subject** box, type your course name and section #, and in the **Tags** box, type **concession revenue** Display **Print Preview**, make corrections or adjustments and ungroup the worksheets. **Save** and **Close** the workbook. Print or submit electronically as directed.

END | You have completed Project 7E

CONTENT-BASED ASSESSMENTS

Mastering Excel   Project 7F Vehicle Maintenance

Apply 7B skills from these Objectives:

5 Create a Data Model Using PowerPivot

6 Create a PivotTable Using PowerPivot

7 Create a Dashboard Using Power View

In the following Skills Review, you will assist Caryn Black, the Vehicle Fleet Manager, create a Data Model, PivotTable, and PivotChart using PowerPivot. You will also create a Power View worksheet. Your results will look similar to those in Figure 7.64.

PROJECT FILES

For Project 7F, you will need the following files:

New blank workbook
e07F_Vehicle_Parts

You will save your workbook as:

Lastname_Firstname_7F_Fleet_Maintenance

PROJECT RESULTS

Build from
Scratch

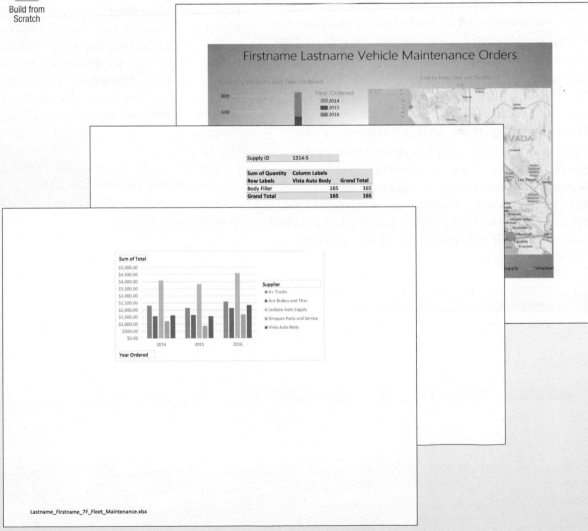

FIGURE 7.64

(Project 7F Vehicle Maintenance continues on the next page)

CONTENT-BASED ASSESSMENTS

1 Start Excel and display a new blank workbook. If the **POWERPIVOT tab** is not visible, follow the directions in Activity 7.14 to enable it. Use **POWERPIVOT tab**, to import the Access database **e07F_Vehicle_Parts** into the **Data Model**. Verify the relationship was created between the two imported tables. Insert a **PivotTable** in a new worksheet. **Save** your file in your **Excel Chapter 7** folder as **Lastname_Firstname_7F_Fleet_Maintenance**

2 Place the **Supplier** field from the **Suppliers** table in the **COLUMNS area**. From the **Supply Order Summary** table, place the **Item** and **Year Ordered** fields in the **ROWS area**, and the **Quantity** field in the **VALUES area**. In cell **B5**, use **Quick Explore** to drill to **Supply ID**, and then drill to **Item**.

3 Return to the **PowerPivot** window. On the **Supply Order Summary** worksheet, add a calculated column that multiplies **[Quantity] * [Cost]**. Rename the column **Total**

4 Insert a **PivotChart** in a new worksheet. Place the **Supplier** field from the **Suppliers** table in the **LEGEND (SERIES) area**. From the **Supply Order Summary** table, place the **Total** field to the **VALUES area**, and place the **Year Ordered** field to the **AXIS (CATEGORY) area**.

5 Click the **Sheet1 sheet tab**. Insert a **Power View** report. Add the title **Firstname Lastname Vehicle Maintenance Orders** From the **Supply Order Summary** table, place the **Item**, **Quantity**, and **Year Ordered** fields in the **FIELDS area**. Change the visualization to a **Stacked Column** chart. Drag to widen the chart until all nine columns are visible.

6 Create a pie chart by placing the **Suppliers** table **Supplier** field, and the **Supply Order Summary** table **Total** field, in the **FIELDS area**. Move and resize the pie chart to fit below the column chart.

7 Insert a Map visualization using the **City**, **State**, and **Supplier** fields from **Suppliers** and the **Total** field from the **Supply Order Summary**. Resize the map to fill the right side of the canvas. Set the legend to display at the bottom.

8 Change the **Power View** worksheet **Text Size** to **75%**. Set the background, to the first color in the third row—**Light 1 Center Gradient**. Close the **Power View Fields** pane and Close the **Filters** pane.

9 Rename **Sheet3 PivotChart** Rename **Sheet2 PivotTable** Delete **Sheet1**. Group the **PivotChart** and **PivotTable** worksheets and insert a footer with the file name in the **left section**. Return to **Normal** view, center horizontally, change the **Orientation** to **Landscape**, and scale the **Width** and **Height** to **1 page**. Press Ctrl + Home to return to cell **A1**. Display the **document properties** and under **Related People**, be sure that your name displays as the author. If necessary, right-click the author name, click **Edit Property**, and then type your name. In the **Subject** box, type your course name and section #, and in the **Tags** box, type **vehicle maintenance, BI Save** your workbook. Print or submit the workbook electronically as directed by your instructor.

> **END | You have completed Project 7F**

CONTENT-BASED ASSESSMENTS

Mastering Excel Project 7G Aquatics Revenue

In the following Mastering Excel project, you will assist Lindsay Johnson, the Director of Pools and Recreation, in creating and modifying a PivotTable report and a PivotChart report to analyze revenuc from the Aquatics Program. Your completed workbooks will look similar to Figure 7.65.

Apply 7A and 7B skills from these Objectives:

1. Create a PivotTable Report
2. Use Slicers and Search Filters
3. Modify a PivotTable Report
4. Create a PivotChart Report
5. Create a Data Model Using PowerPivot
6. Create a PivotTable Using PowerPivot
7. Create a Dashboard Using Power View

PROJECT FILES

For Project 7G, you will need the following files:

e07G_Aquatics_Revenue
e07G_Pool_Supplies

You will save your workbooks as:

Lastname_Firstname_7G_Aquatics_Revenue
Lastname_Firstname_7G_Pool_Orders

PROJECT RESULTS

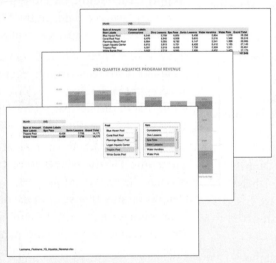

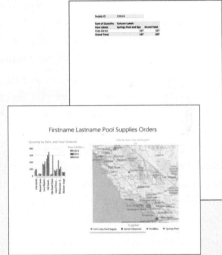

FIGURE 7.65

(Project 7G Aquatics Revenue continues on the next page)

1 From your student files, open the file **e07G_Aquatics_Revenue**. **Save** the file as **Lastname_Firstname_7G_Aquatics_Revenue** in your **Excel Chapter 7** folder.

2 Click cell **A2**, and then insert a **PivotTable**. Use the **Month** field as the **Report Filter**. Use the **Pool** field as the row labels and the **Item** field as the column labels. Place the **Amount** field in the **VALUES area**. **Close** the **PivotTable Fields** pane.

3 Right-click any value in the PivotTable report, display the **Value Field Settings** dialog box, and then format the **Number** category to display zero decimal places and the **1000 Separator**.

4 Insert a slicer for the **Pool** field and for the **Item** field. Apply **Slicer Style Light 4** and **Slicer Style Light 5** to the slicers, respectively.

5 By using the two slicers, filter the data to show, for the **Tropics Pool**, the total revenue for **Spa Fees** and **Swim Lessons**. Resize and move the two slicers to the right of the filtered PivotTable, and then make a copy of this worksheet. Name the copied worksheet **Tropics Pool - 2Q**

6 Rename **Sheet1 2Q Revenue** In each slicer, click the **Clear Filter** button, and then remove the slicers from the worksheet. Insert a **PivotChart** using the **Stacked Column** chart type. Move the chart to a new worksheet named **2Q Revenue Chart** Apply the **Layout 3** chart layout and **Chart Style 9**. As the **Chart Title**, type **2nd Quarter Aquatics Program Revenue** Add centered data labels, and then hide all of the field buttons on the chart. Insert a custom footer with the file name in the **left section**.

7 Hide the worksheet that contains your source data. Display the **2Q Revenue** worksheet, select all the worksheets, and then insert a footer with the file name in the **left section**. Change the **Orientation** to **Landscape**, set the **Width** to **1 page**, and center the sheets horizontally. Display the **document properties** and under **Related People**, be sure that your name displays as the author. If necessary, right-click the author name, click **Edit Property**, and then type your name. In the **Subject** box, type your course name and section #, and in the **Tags** box, type **aquatics program, revenue** Display **Print Preview**, make any corrections or adjustments, ungroup the worksheets, and then **Save** the workbook. Print or submit electronically as directed by your instructor. **Close** this workbook, but leave Excel open.

8 Open a new blank workbook. Use PowerPivot to import the Access database **e07G_Pool_Supplies** into the **Data Model**. Verify the relationship was created between the two imported tables. On the **Supply Order Summary** worksheet, add a calculated column that multiplies **[Quantity] * [Cost]**. Rename the column **Total**

9 Insert a **PivotTable** in a new worksheet. Rename the new sheet **PivotTable** Place the **Supplier** field from the **Suppliers** table in the **COLUMNS area**. From the **Supply Order Summary** table, place the **Item** field in the **ROWS area**, and the **Quantity** field in the **VALUES area**. In cell **B5**, use **Quick Explore** to drill to **Supply ID**, and then drill to **Item**. Insert a footer with the file name in the **left** section.

10 Insert a **Power View** report. Add the title **Firstname Lastname Pool Supplies Orders** From the **Supply Order Summary** table, place the **Item**, **Quantity**, and **Year Ordered** fields in the **FIELDS area**. Change the visualization to a **Clustered Column** chart.

11 Insert a Map visualization using the **City**, **State**, and **Supplier** fields from **Suppliers** and the **Total** field from the **Supply Order Summary**. Resize the map to fill the right side of the canvas. Set the legend to display at the bottom. Close the **Power View Fields** and **Filters** panes.

12 **Save** your file in your **Excel Chapter 7** folder as **Lastname_Firstname_7G_Pool_Orders** Delete **Sheet1**. Display the **document properties** and under **Related People**, be sure that your name displays as the author. If necessary, right-click the author name, click **Edit Property**, and then type your name. In the **Subject** box, type your course name and section #, and in the **Tags** box, type **pool supplies, BI** Save your workbook. Print or submit both workbooks electronically as directed by your instructor.

END | You have completed Project 7G

CONTENT-BASED ASSESSMENTS

Apply a combination of the 7A and 7B skills.

PROJECT FILES

For Project 7K, you will need the following file:

e07K_Park_Expenses

You will save your workbook as:

Lastname_Firstname_7K_Park_Expenses

Open the file e07K_Park_Expenses and save it as **Lastname_Firstname_7K_Park_Expenses** From the source data, create a PivotTable. Use the Month and Park fields as row labels. Use the Expense Item field as a column label. Place the Amount field in the VALUES area. Format the numbers to display zero decimal places and the 1000 separator. Format the PivotTable with an attractive style. Create a PivotChart on a separate sheet using the column chart style, and then use the report filters on the chart to show only the data for June, only the data for Knight's Bridge, Five Points, and Sunset Parks, and only the expenses for Equipment, Grounds & Maintenance, and Utilities. Format the chart attractively. Hide the Park Expenses worksheet. On all sheets, insert the file name in the footer in the left section. Set the orientation to landscape and center horizontally. Add appropriate information to the document properties including the tag **park grounds expenses** and submit as directed by your instructor.

(Project 7K Park Expenses continues on the next page)

CONTENT-BASED ASSESSMENTS

GO! Solve It | Project 7K Park Expenses (continued)

Performance Level

Performance Criteria		Exemplary	Proficient	Developing
	Create a PivotTable Report	The PivotTable Report displays Month and Park as row labels, Expense Item in COLUMNS area, and amount field in the VALUES area.	The PivotTable Report displays some of the items from the field list, but not all according to the directions.	The PivotTable was not created.
	Format a PivotTable Report	The PivotTable is formatted with the numbers displaying zero decimal places, the 1000 separator, and an attractive style.	The PivotTable is formatted with some but not all of the formatting, numbers displaying zero decimal places, the 1000 separator, and some attractive formatting.	The PivotTable was not formatted.
	Create and Format a PivotChart	A PivotChart displays on a separate sheet using the column chart style. The chart is filtered showing the data for June, only for Knight's Bridge, Five Points, and Sunset Parks, and only the expenses for Equipment, Grounds & Maintenance, and Utilities. The chart is formatted attractively.	A PivotChart displays on a separate sheet using the column chart style. The chart is filtered showing some but not all of the data for June, only for Knight's Bridge, Five Points, and Sunset Parks, and only the expenses for Equipment, Grounds & Maintenance, and Utilities. Some of the chart is formatted attractively.	The PivotChart was not created.

END | You have completed Project 7K

OUTCOMES-BASED ASSESSMENTS

RUBRIC

The following outcomes-based assessments are open-ended assessments. That is, there is no specific correct result; your result will depend on your approach to the information provided. Make Professional Quality your goal. Use the following scoring rubric to guide you in how to approach the problem and then to evaluate how well your approach solves the problem.

The *criteria*—Software Mastery, Content, Format and Layout, and Process—represent the knowledge and skills you have gained that you can apply to solving the problem. The *levels of performance*—Professional Quality, Approaching Professional Quality, or Needs Quality Improvements—help you and your instructor evaluate your result.

	Your completed project is of Professional Quality if you:	Your completed project is Approaching Professional Quality if you:	Your completed project Needs Quality Improvements if you:
1-Software Mastery	Choose and apply the most appropriate skills, tools, and features and identify efficient methods to solve the problem.	Choose and apply some appropriate skills, tools, and features, but not in the most efficient manner.	Choose inappropriate skills, tools, or features, or are inefficient in solving the problem.
2-Content	Construct a solution that is clear and well organized, contains content that is accurate, appropriate to the audience and purpose, and is complete. Provide a solution that contains no errors in spelling, grammar, or style.	Construct a solution in which some components are unclear, poorly organized, inconsistent, or incomplete. Misjudge the needs of the audience. Have some errors in spelling, grammar, or style, but the errors do not detract from comprehension.	Construct a solution that is unclear, incomplete, or poorly organized; contains some inaccurate or inappropriate content; and contains many errors in spelling, grammar, or style. Do not solve the problem.
3-Format & Layout	Format and arrange all elements to communicate information and ideas, clarify function, illustrate relationships, and indicate relative importance.	Apply appropriate format and layout features to some elements, but not others. Overuse features, causing minor distraction.	Apply format and layout that does not communicate information or ideas clearly. Do not use format and layout features to clarify function, illustrate relationships, or indicate relative importance. Use available features excessively, causing distraction.
4-Process	Use an organized approach that integrates planning, development, self-assessment, revision, and reflection.	Demonstrate an organized approach in some areas, but not others; or, use an insufficient process of organization throughout.	Do not use an organized approach to solve the problem.

OUTCOMES-BASED ASSESSMENTS

Apply a combination of the 7A and 7B skills.

GO! Think   Project 7L Golf Course Revenue

PROJECT FILES

For Project 7L, you will need the following file:

e07L_Golf_Courses

You will save your workbook as:

Lastname_Firstname_7L_Golf_Courses

Open the file e07L_Golf_Courses, and then save it in your Excel Chapter 7 folder as **Lastname_Firstname_7L_Golf_Courses** From the source data, create a PivotTable and filter the report on Month. Use Course as row label and Item as column label. Sum the amounts. Create an attractive PivotChart report for the 3rd Quarter Revenue. Exclude Logo Shirts and Golf Balls from the PivotChart. Hide the source data worksheet. Insert the file name in the left section of the footer on each page, center horizontally, set the orientation to landscape, add appropriate information to the document properties, including the tags **golf courses revenue** and submit as directed by your instructor.

END | You have completed Project 7L

GO! Think   Project 7M Pool Expenses   **Online**

Build from
Scratch

You and GO!   Project 7N Inventory   **Online**

Using the Data Analysis, Solver, and Scenario Features, and Building Complex Formulas

GO! to Work
Video E8

8

PROJECT 8A

OUTCOMES

Analyze sales data to evaluate business solutions and compare data with a line chart.

OBJECTIVES

1. Calculate a Moving Average
2. Project Income and Expenses
3. Determine a Break-Even Point

PROJECT 8B

OUTCOMES

Use Solver and Scenario Tools, and create complex formulas.

OBJECTIVES

4. Use Solver
5. Create Scenarios
6. Use Logical Functions
7. Create Complex Formulas

Lasse Kristensen/Fotolia

In This Chapter

Organizations forecast future results based on current trends. You will use Excel tools to analyze data, project values, determine the moving average of sales, project sales based on an expected growth rate, and determine a break-even point.

You will use the Solver and Scenario tools to search for solutions to problems. Solver can analyze financial planning problems that involve a quantity that changes over time. By using a scenario, you can look at a set of values and project forward to focus on possible results. Finally, you will create complex formulas to determine which employees meet specific performance criteria.

The projects in this chapter relate to **Brina's Bistro**, which is a chain of 25 casual, full-service restaurants based in Ft. Lauderdale, Florida. The Brina's Bistro owners plan an aggressive expansion program. To expand by 15 additional restaurants in Tennessee, Florida, Georgia, North Carolina, and South Carolina by 2021, the company must attract new investors, develop new menus, and recruit new employees, all while adhering to the company's quality guidelines and maintaining its reputation for excellent service. To succeed, the company plans to build on its past success and maintain its quality elements.

Sales Analysis

PROJECT ACTIVITIES

In Activities 8.01 through 8.06, you will use Excel's data analysis tools to determine the moving average of sales for the first six weeks at the new Brina's Bistro restaurant in Charlotte, North Carolina. Then you will project sales based on an expected growth rate and determine the break-even point for the restaurant. Your completed worksheets will look similar to Figure 8.1.

PROJECT FILES

For Project 8A, you will need the following file:

e08A_Charlotte_Sales

You will save your workbook as:

Lastname_Firstname_8A_Charlotte_Sales

PROJECT RESULTS

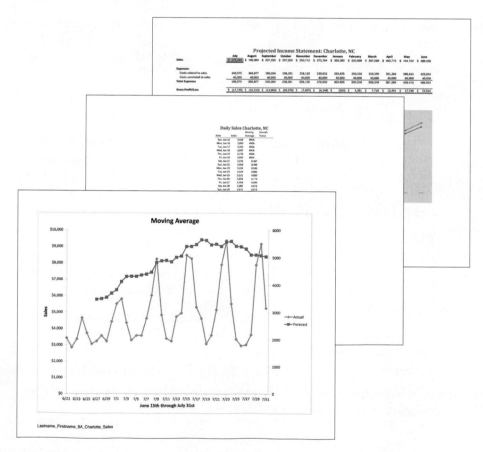

FIGURE 8.1 Project 8A Sales Analysis

- Tap an item to click it.
- Press and hold for a few seconds to right-click; release when the information or commands display.
- Touch the screen with two or more fingers and then pinch together to zoom in or stretch your fingers apart to zoom out.
- Slide your finger on the screen to scroll—slide left to scroll right and slide right to scroll left.
- Slide to rearrange—similar to dragging with a mouse.
- Swipe from edge: from right to display charms; from left to expose open apps, snap apps, or close apps; from top or bottom to show commands or close an app.
- Swipe to select—slide an item a short distance with a quick movement—to select an item and bring up commands, if any.

Objective 1 | Calculate a Moving Average

Video E8-1

Start-up businesses usually operate at a loss while the business grows, with an expectation that at some future point, the business will become profitable. Owners and investors want to know if the business is on track to become profitable and when the point of profitability is likely to occur.

Excel offers Data Analysis tools, which range from basic to very sophisticated, to help you project future results based on past performance. One of the basic tools is a moving average. A *moving average* is a sequence of averages computed from parts of a data series. In a chart, a moving average smoothes the fluctuations in data, showing a pattern or trend more clearly. When you use a moving average, you choose how many preceding intervals to include in the average. A series of averages is calculated by moving—or changing—the range of cells used to calculate each average.

Activity 8.01 | Creating a Custom Number Format

Kelsey Tanner, the Chief Financial Officer of Brina's Bistro, wants to see how sales have grown in the first six weeks at the new restaurant in Charlotte, North Carolina. Because there is a wide variation in sales at restaurants between weekday and weekend sales, Ms. Tanner first needs to add the day of the week to the Charlotte sales report. To accomplish this, you will customize the format applied to the date. You can customize numbers or dates when the available options do not match your needs.

1 Start Excel. From your student files, open the file **e08A_Charlotte_Sales**. Display the **Save As** dialog box, navigate to the location where you will store your workbooks for this chapter, and then create a new folder named **Excel Chapter 8** In your new folder, **Save** the workbook as **Lastname_Firstname_8A_Charlotte_Sales**

2 Select the range A3:AV4. Right-click anywhere over the selection and click **Copy**. Click cell **A5**. Right-click and under **Paste Options**, click **Transpose (T)** 📋. Compare your screen with Figure 8.2.

> If the data in a worksheet is arranged in rows but you want to work with columns instead, you can use this method to *transpose*, or switch, the rows and columns.

FIGURE 8.2

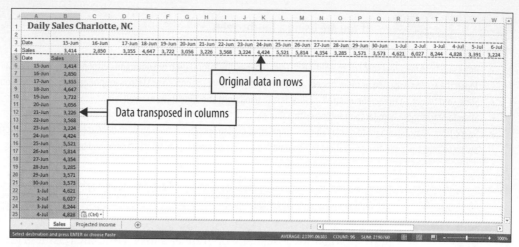

Original data in rows

Data transposed in columns

More Knowledge   The Transpose Function

You can use the TRANSPOSE function to swap rows and columns. TRANSPOSE is an array function. The advantage to using the TRANSPOSE function is that a link is maintained between the original and transposed data.

3 ▶ Delete **rows 2:4**. In cell **C2**, type **Moving Average** In cell **D2**, type **Growth Trend** Select the range **A2:D2** and apply the **Heading 3** cell style. In the **Alignment group**, click **Wrap Text**.

4 ▶ Click cell **A3**. On the **HOME tab**, in the **Number group**, click the **Dialog Box Launcher** 🔲. In the **Format Cells** dialog box, be sure the **Number tab** is selected. Under **Category**, click **Custom**. Examine the table in Figure 8.3 to familiarize yourself with the codes used to create a custom date format.

Custom codes display under Type, and the code for the selected date in cell A3 displays in the Type box. You can use this format as a starting point and then modify it or you can type a new code in the Type box.

FIGURE 8.3

DATE CODES	
TO DISPLAY	**USE THIS CODE**
Months as 1–12	m
Months as 01–12	mm
Months as Jan–Dec	mmm
Months as January–December	mmmm
Months as the first letter of the month	mmmmm
Days as 1–31	d
Days as 01–31	dd
Days as Sun–Sat	ddd
Days as Sunday–Saturday	dddd
Years as 00–99	yy
Years as 1900–9999	yyyy

5 ▶ Select the code in the **Type** box and type **ddd, mmm dd** to replace it. Compare your screen with Figure 8.4.

As you type, you can see the date displayed in the new format in the Sample box. This code creates a date that displays as *Sun, Jun 15*. The comma displays as a comma.

FIGURE 8.4

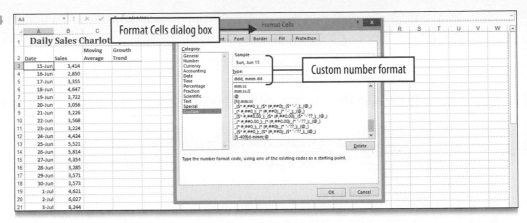

6 ▸ Click **OK**, if necessary, AutoFit column A, and notice the new date format in cell **A3**. Drag the fill handle to copy the new format down through cell **A49**. Click cell **A50** and type **Total** Click cell **B50** and in the **Editing group**, click **AutoSum**. Verify that the range to be summed is **B3:B49** and then press Enter. Apply the **Currency [0]** cell style to cell **B50**. Your total equals *$232,844*. Apply the **Total** cell style to the range **A50:B50**. Press Ctrl + Home, AutoFit **column A**, click **Save** 🖫, and then compare your screen with Figure 8.5.

FIGURE 8.5

Custom date format applied

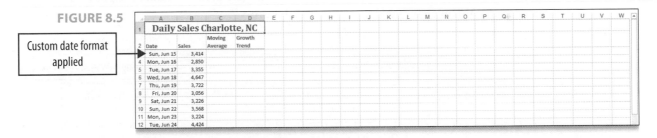

Activity 8.02 | Calculating a Moving Average

Recall that a moving average calculates an average for a group of numbers over a specified interval. The number range that is averaged is constantly changing, dropping off the first number in the range and adding on the most recent number. In this manner, you can see a trend for widely fluctuating numbers. The sales activity for the new Charlotte restaurant has been strong on the weekends and slower during the week. You need to determine if, overall, the sales activity is trending upward or downward. The moving average tool is one of several Data Analysis tools.

1 ▸ Click the **FILE tab** and then click **Options**. In the **Excel Options** dialog box, on the left, click **Add-Ins**. At the bottom of the dialog box, verify that the **Manage** box displays *Excel Add-ins*, and then click **Go**. In the **Add-Ins** dialog box, if necessary, select the **Analysis ToolPak** check box. Compare your screen with Figure 8.6.

Recall that *Add-ins* are optional commands and features that are not immediately available; you must first install and/or activate an add-in to use it.

FIGURE 8.6

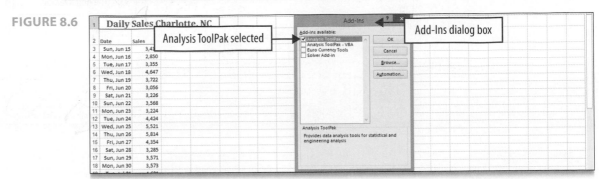

2 Click **OK**, and then click cell **A2** to make it the active cell. On the **DATA tab**, in the **Analysis group**, click **Data Analysis**. Scroll the list as necessary, and then click **Moving Average**. Click **OK**.

The Moving Average dialog box displays. Here you define the input range, the *interval*—the number of cells to include in the average—and the output range.

3 With the insertion point blinking in the **Input Range** box, type **b2:b49** and then click the **Labels in First Row** check box.

The input range consists of the sales figures for the first six weeks, from Jun 15 through Jul 31. The first cell in the range, B2, contains the label *Sales*.

N O T E **Moving Average Using Data in Rows**

When using data that is listed in rows, rather than columns, do not check the Labels in First Row box.

---

4 Click in the **Interval** box, and then type **7**

The moving average will be a weekly (7-day) average of sales. The first average will be from Sun, Jun 15 through Sat, Jun 21. The next average will be from Mon, Jun 16 through Sun, Jun 22. This pattern—dropping the oldest date and adding in the next date—will continue for the entire range.

5 Click in the **Output Range** box, type **c3** and then click the **Chart Output** check box. Compare your **Moving Average** dialog box with Figure 8.7.

FIGURE 8.7

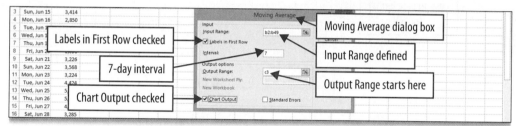

6 Click **OK**. Save 🖫 your workbook, and then compare your screen with Figure 8.8.

The moving averages display in column C and a chart is added to the worksheet. The first six cells in column C display the error code *#N/A* because there were not seven numbers available to use in the average. Green triangles display because the formulas in these cells refer to a range that has additional numbers adjacent. The first average—for Sun, Jun 15 through Sat, Jun 21—is *3,467*.

FIGURE 8.8

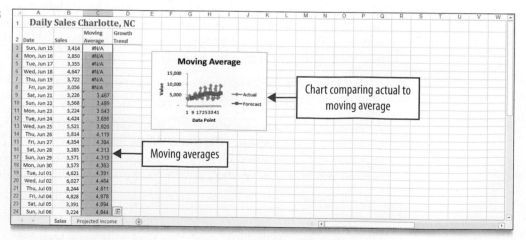

To gain a clearer image of a trend, you can modify the moving average chart. In the moving average chart, the moving average is labeled Forecast. A *forecast* is a prediction of the future, often based on past performances.

1 ▸ Click the outer edge of the chart to select it, and then on the **DESIGN tab**, in the **Location group**, click **Move Chart**.

2 ▸ Click **New sheet**, type **Sales Trend Chart** and then click **OK**.

By displaying this chart on a separate chart sheet, you can more easily see the actual data points—in dark blue—versus the moving average—in red—which is labeled *Forecast*. The horizontal category axis—the X-axis—is titled *Data Point*. This represents the dates for each sales figure. You can see by the red line that, overall, the sales activity for the first six weeks is trending slightly upward.

3 ▸ At the bottom of the chart, point to any of the data points to display the ScreenTip *Horizontal (Category) Axis*, and then click to select the axis. On the **DESIGN tab**, in the **Data group**, click **Select Data**.

In the Select Data Source dialog box, you can change the category axis labels to display the range of dates that correspond to the sales figures. You can also use this method to add or edit the data series used in a chart.

🔄 **ANOTHER WAY**   Right-click the axis, and then click Select Data.

4 ▸ In the **Select Data Source** dialog box, under **Horizontal (Category) Axis Labels**, click **Edit**. Click the **Sales sheet tab** to display the *Sales* worksheet, and then select the range **A9:A49**. Compare your screen with Figure 8.9.

The selected range displays in the dialog box. You can select the range of cells to use as labels for the category axis. Start with cell A9 because that is the first row for which there is a moving average calculation.

FIGURE 8.9

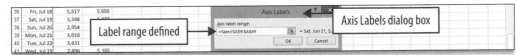

5 ▸ In the **Axis Labels** dialog box, click **OK**. In the **Select Data Source** dialog box, click **OK**.

Dates display along the category axis at the bottom of the chart.

6 ▸ Right-click the **Horizontal (Category) Axis**, and then click **Format Axis**. In the **Format Axis** pane, with **Axis Options** ▼ selected, scroll down and click **Number**, scroll down and click the **Category arrow**, and then click **Date**. Click the **Type arrow**, click the **3/14** format, and then **Close** ☒ the **Format Axis** pane.

This action shortens the date format displayed on the axis.

7 ▸ Click the **Horizontal (Category) Axis Title**—*Data Point*—to select it. On the **Formula Bar**, type **June 15th through July 31st** and then press Enter. Click the **Horizontal Axis Title**, triple-click to select the text, and then on the mini toolbar, change the font size to **12**. Click the **Vertical (Value) Axis Title**—*Value*—to select it. On the **Formula Bar** type **Sales** and then press Enter. Point to the **Vertical Axis Title**, double-click, and then on the mini toolbar, change the font size to **12**.

The Horizontal Axis and Vertical Axis titles are changed and formatted.

8 ▸ Right-click any value on the **Vertical (Value) Axis**, and then click **Format Axis**. In the **Format Axis** pane, click **Number**, scroll down and click the **Category arrow**, and then click **Currency**. If necessary, set **Decimal places** to **0**, and then **Close** ☒ the **Format Axis** pane.

This action changes the values to Currency with 0 decimal places.

9 On the **FORMAT tab**, in the **Current Selection group**, click the **Chart Elements arrow**, and then click **Series "Forecast"**. In the same group, click **Format Selection**. In the **Format Data Series** pane, if necessary, click the **Series Options** icon [▲]. Under **Plot Series on**, click **Secondary Axis**. **Close** the **Format Data Series** pane. **Save** [💾] your workbook, and then compare your chart with Figure 8.10.

Plotting the Forecast series on the secondary axis makes the trend easier to visualize because the scale is adjusted to reflect the smaller differences in the Forecast series values. A *dual-axis chart* is useful when comparing data series that use different scales or different types of measurements.

FIGURE 8.10

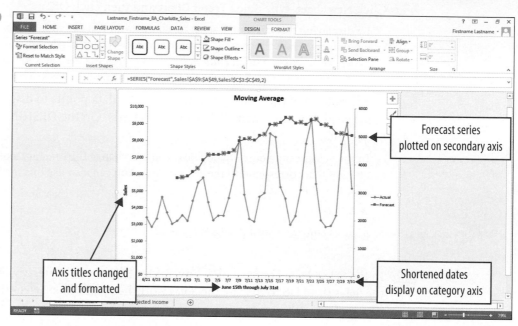

More Knowledge   **Using a Moving Average to Forecast Trends**

It is common to see moving averages used to calculate stock or mutual fund performance, where fluctuations in value may be frequent, but the overall trend is what is important. Moving averages can also be used as a tool to help predict how much inventory will be needed to meet demand. Although this is a forecasting tool, it is important to recognize its limitations. A moving average is based on historical data, and it is not necessarily a good prediction of what will occur in the future. Changes in the economy, competition, or other factors can affect sales dramatically, causing the moving average trend to change.

Activity 8.04 | **Calculating Growth Based on a Moving Average**

You can also use a moving average to calculate the growth rate at different intervals.

1 Display the **Sales** worksheet. Scroll to position **row 21** near the top of your screen. Click cell **D21**, type **=(c21-c14)/c14** and then click **Enter** [✓].

This formula calculates a weekly sales growth percentage from one Saturday to the next, based on the moving average.

2 Point to cell **D21**, right-click, and then on the mini toolbar, click **Percent Style** [%]. Click **Increase Decimal** [⬆] one time to display one decimal place—your result is *16.8%*.

3 With cell **D21** still selected, point to the cell and right-click, and then click **Copy**. Point to cell **D28**, right-click, and then under **Paste Options**, click **Paste (P)** [📋].

The formula is copied to the next date that is a Thursday.

4 Point to cell **D35**, right-click, and then click **Paste (P)** [📋]. Continue in the same manner to paste the formula in cells **D42** and **D49** for the next two Thursday dates. Click **Save** [💾], and then compare your screen with Figure 8.11.

The formula results show that the trend has moved up and down over five weeks of business.

FIGURE 8.11

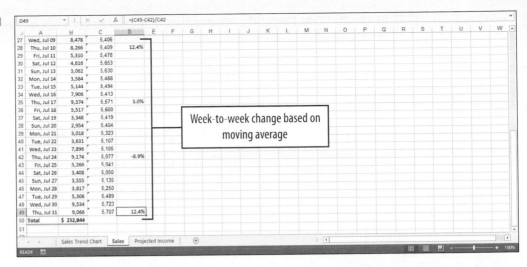

Objective 2   Project Income and Expenses

Video E8-2

Income generally consists of sales for products and services. In a restaurant, this includes the sale of food and beverages. Expenses can be classified into two broad categories: fixed expenses and variable expenses. **Fixed expenses** remain the same each month regardless of the amount of activity. They include items such as rent, utilities, insurance, and general overhead. **Variable expenses** vary depending on the amount of sales. In a restaurant, the cost of the food—otherwise known as cost of goods sold—and wages are the two most common variable expenses. In this activity, you will work with a worksheet that uses these two broad categories of expenses.

Activity 8.05   Projecting Income and Expenses

1 Click cell **A51**, type **July Sales** Click cell **B51**, type **=SUM(B19:B49)** and then press Enter. Display the **Projected Income** worksheet. Click cell **B3**. Type **=** click the **Sales sheet tab**, click cell **B51**, the July sales total, click **Enter** ☑, and then compare your screen with Figure 8.12.

This sheet contains the first portion of an income statement for the Charlotte restaurant. You have referenced the July total from the Sales worksheet. You will use that value to project sales and expenses through June of next year.

FIGURE 8.12

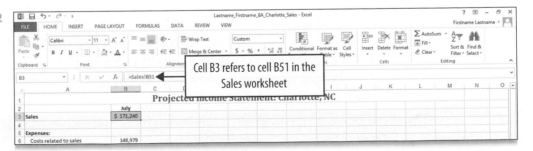

2 Click cell **B2**, and then use the fill handle to fill the months for a year—from July to June—across to **column M**. With the range **B2:M2** selected, apply **Center** ☰.

3 Click cell **C3**, type **=b3*(1+b12)** and then click **Enter** ☑. Apply the **Currency [0]** cell style.

This formula takes the previous month's sales in cell B3 and multiplies it by 110% to determine a growth rate of 10 percent over the previous month—*$188,364*. Cell B12 indicates the Required Sales Growth rate of 10%, and the absolute cell reference is used so this formula can be copied across the row.

4 With cell **C3** as the active cell, use the fill handle to copy the formula and the formatting across to **column M**. Compare your screen with Figure 8.13.

Based on this projection, by June of next year, the Charlotte restaurant should have *$488.568* in monthly sales.

FIGURE 8.13

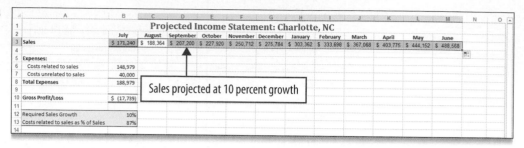

5 Click cell **B6** and examine the formula.

This formula multiplies the sales for July by the value in cell B13—*87%*. It is estimated that variable expenses for the first year will be 87 percent of sales. An absolute reference is used so this formula can be copied across the worksheet.

6 Use the fill handle to copy the formula from cell **B6** across the row to **column M**.

The variable expenses, which are based on sales, are projected for the next year. Variable expenses for June are calculated to be *425,054*.

7 Click cell **B7**. Use the fill handle to copy the value from cell **B7** across the row to **column M**.

These are fixed costs—costs such as rent and insurance that are not directly tied to sales—which total *40,000*.

8 Select the range **C8:M8**, and then on the **HOME tab**, in the **Editing group**, click **AutoSum** Σ AutoSum ▾.

For each month, the total expenses are calculated.

9 Click cell **B10**.

This formula calculates the gross profit or loss for a month—sales minus expenses.

10 Use the fill handle to copy the formula from cell **B10** across to **column M**. **Save** 🖫 your workbook, and then compare your screen with Figure 8.14.

FIGURE 8.14

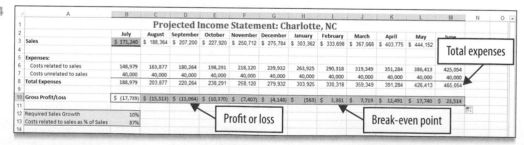

Objective 3   Determine a Break-Even Point

Video E8-3

The goal of a business is to make a profit. However, a new business often operates at a loss for a period of time before becoming profitable. The point at which a company starts to make a profit is known as the *break-even point*. A break-even point can be calculated for a product, a branch office, a division, or an entire company. The Brina's Bistro restaurants use a model for new restaurants that projects 10 percent growth, month-to-month, in the first year, with the expectation that sometime during the first year the restaurant will start to make a profit. Ms. Tanner wants to estimate when the new Charlotte restaurant will become profitable, based on sales for its first full month of business.

Activity 8.06 | **Charting the Break-Even Point with a Line Chart**

You can chart the results of the estimated income statement to create a visual image of the income and expenses and the projected break-even point.

Recall that a line chart displays trends over time. Time is displayed along the bottom axis and the data point values are connected with a line. If you want to compare more than one set of values, each group is connected by a different line. The curves and directions of the lines make trends noticeable to the reader.

1 Be sure that **columns A:M** display on your screen. If necessary, in the lower right corner of your screen, set the Zoom to 80%. Select the range **A2:M3**.

By including the months in row 2 and the labels in column A in the selection, the chart will be properly labeled.

2 On the **INSERT tab**, in the **Charts group**, click **Recommended Charts**. In the **Insert Chart** dialog box, with the **Line chart** selected, click **OK**.

3 On the **DESIGN tab**, in the **Data group**, click **Select Data**. In the **Select Data Source** dialog box, under **Legend Entries (Series)**, click **Add**. With the insertion point in the **Series name** box, click cell **A8**. Press Tab, select the range **B8:M8** and then click **OK**. Verify that the **Chart data range** is *$A2:$M3* and *$A8:$M8*. Compare your screen with Figure 8.15.

By selecting the income totals and the expense totals, you will be able to see where they cross each other on a graph when you chart the break-even point. The Chart data range box displays the selected range—including the sheet name—using absolute references.

FIGURE 8.15

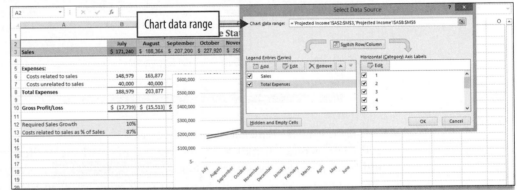

4 Click **OK**. On the **DESIGN tab**, in the **Chart Layouts** group, click **Quick Layout**, and then click **Layout 3**. Click **Chart Title**, and then watch the **Formula Bar** as you type **Expected Break-Even Point** Press Enter.

5 By using the pointer, drag to position the upper left corner of the chart inside the upper left corner of cell **B15**.

6 Scroll to position **row 13** at the top of your screen. Drag the lower right sizing handle of the chart inside the lower right corner of cell **M36**. Compare your chart with the one shown in Figure 8.16.

FIGURE 8.16

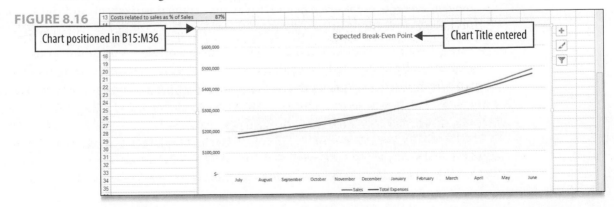

7 On the **DESIGN tab**, apply **Chart Style 12**.

8 On the left side of the chart, right-click the **Vertical (Value) Axis**, and then click **Format Axis**. In the **Format Axis** pane, verify that **Axis Options** is selected. Under **AXIS OPTIONS**, in the **Minimum** box, type **100000** Press Enter. In the same manner, change the **Maximum** value to **500000**

> Because there are no figures less than $100,000, changing the scale in this manner provides more vertical space on the chart and results in a more dramatic slope on the line.

9 Click the **AXIS OPTIONS arrow** and then click **Chart Area**. Click **Fill & Line**. Click **Solid Fill**, and then click the **Fill Color arrow**. Click the second color in the third column, **Tan, Background 2, Darker 10%**. Click the **CHART OPTIONS arrow** and click **Plot Area**. Format the **Plot Area** with the same fill. **Close** the **Format Plot** Area pane. Compare your screen with Figure 8.17.

FIGURE 8.17

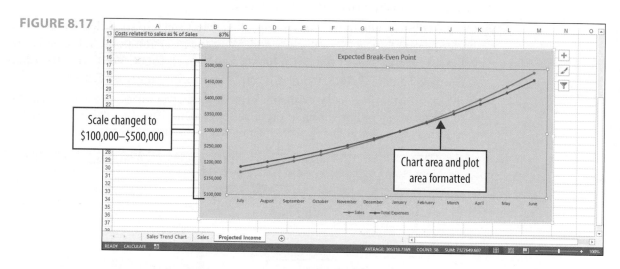

10 Display the **Sales Trend Chart** worksheet, and then insert a custom footer with the file name in the **left section**. Display the **Projected Income** worksheet, click anywhere outside the chart, and then, if necessary, set the **Zoom** back to **100%**. Right-click the **sheet tab**, and then click **Select All Sheets** so that *[Group]* displays in the title bar. Insert a footer in the **left section** that includes the file name. Click the cell above the footer to deselect it.

11 On the **PAGE LAYOUT tab**, set the **Orientation** to **Landscape**, and then in set the **Width** to **1 page** and the **Height** to **1 page**. Center the worksheets horizontally on the page. On the status bar, click **Normal**. Press Ctrl + Home to move to the top of the worksheet.

12 Display the **document properties** and under **Related People**, be sure that your name displays as the author. If necessary, right-click the author name, click **Edit Property**, and then type your name. In the **Subject** box, type your course name and section #, and in the **Tags** box, type **moving average, break-even point** Display the grouped worksheets in **Print Preview**. Make any necessary corrections or adjustments.

13 Save your workbook, and then **Print** the three worksheets or submit your workbook electronically as directed. If required, print or create an electronic version of your worksheets with formulas displayed. **Close** Excel.

END | You have completed Project 8A

PROJECT ACTIVITIES

In Activities 8.07 through 8.17, you will assist Jillian Zachary, manager of the Ft. Lauderdale restaurant, in determining the most efficient work schedule for the server staff. You will also evaluate sales to determine which servers are eligible for Employee of the Week status. Your completed worksheets will look similar to Figure 8.18.

PROJECT FILES

For Project 8B, you will need the following file:
e08B_Staffing_Analysis

You will save your workbook as:
Lastname_Firstname_8B_Staffing_Analysis

PROJECT RESULTS

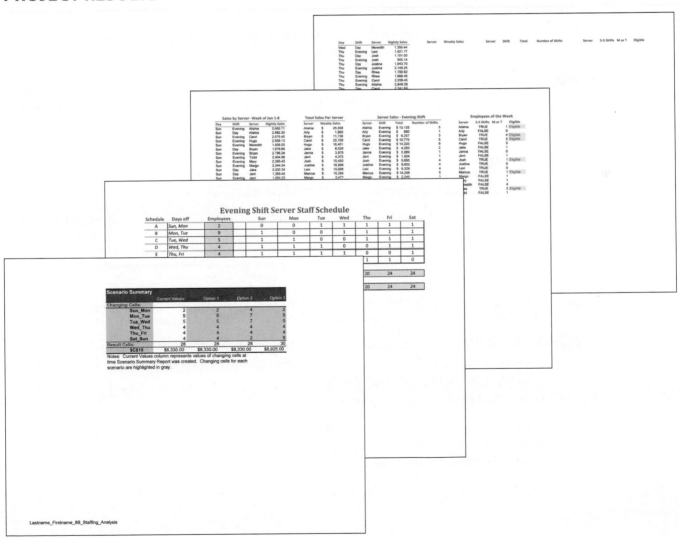

FIGURE 8.18 Project 8B Staffing Analysis

Video E8-4

Solver is an Excel's what-if analysis tool with which you can find an optimal (maximum or minimum) value for a formula in one cell—referred to as the objective cell—subject to constraints, or limits, on the values of other formula cells on a worksheet.

Use Solver when you need to make a decision that involves more than one variable. For example, the manager of the Ft. Lauderdale restaurant needs to determine the number of servers to assign to each evening shift so there are enough servers to handle customer demand, but not too many servers for the work required. Additionally, the schedule must allow each server to have two consecutive days off. Solver can help determine values like these—values that result in minimums, maximums, or specific results.

When you use Solver, the focus is on the *objective cell*—the cell that contains a formula for the results you are trying to determine, such as minimum weekly payroll expense. Your worksheet will have *decision variables*—also referred to as *variable cells*—that are cells in which the values will change to achieve the desired results. Your worksheet will also have *constraint cells*—cells that contain values that limit or restrict the outcome. As an example of a constraint, in determining a work schedule, you cannot schedule more than the total number of employees on the payroll.

Activity 8.07 | Installing Solver

Recall that add-ins are optional commands and features that are not immediately available; you must first install and/or activate an add-in to use it. Solver is an add-in.

1 Start Excel and display a new blank workbook. Click the **DATA tab**, and then at the right end of the **DATA tab**, check to see whether the **Analysis group** and **Solver** display. Compare your screen with Figure 8.19.

FIGURE 8.19

2 If **Solver** displays, Solver has been installed on your computer and you can move to Activity 8.08. If Solver does *not* display, complete the remaining steps in this activity to install it.

3 On the **FILE tab**, click **Options**. In the Excel **Options dialog** box, on the left, click **Add-Ins**, and then at the bottom of the screen, in the **Manage** box, if necessary, select **Excel Add-ins**. Compare your screen with Figure 8.20.

FIGURE 8.20

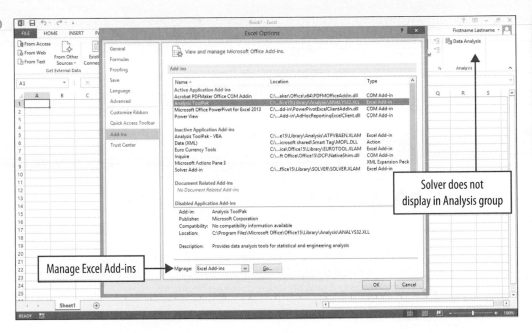

4 Click **Go**.

The Add-Ins dialog box displays.

5 In the **Add-Ins** dialog box, select the **Solver Add-in** check box, and then click **OK**.

The Solver Add-in is installed. On the DATA tab, in the Analysis group, Solver displays.

Activity 8.08 | Understanding a Solver Worksheet

The manager of the Ft. Lauderdale restaurant wants to minimize the weekly payroll expense by scheduling only enough servers to handle established customer activity. She has reviewed customer activity for the past three months and determined how many servers are needed for the evening schedule on each day of the week. For example, more servers are needed on Friday and Saturday evenings than on Tuesday and Wednesday evenings. You will use Solver to determine the number of servers to schedule for each evening shift to meet the demand while minimizing the payroll expense. Before you can solve the problem of minimizing payroll expenses, familiarize yourself with the components of the worksheet.

1 From your student files, open the file **e08B_Staffing_Analysis**. Display the **Save As** dialog box, navigate to your **Excel Chapter 8** folder, and then **Save** the workbook as **Lastname_Firstname_8B_Staffing_Analysis**

2 Examine the range **A2:K8**, and then compare your screen with Figure 8.21.

Six possible schedules are labeled—A through F. Column B lists the two consecutive days off for each schedule. For example, servers who work Schedule B have Monday and Tuesday off. Servers who work Schedule C have Tuesday and Wednesday off.

For each schedule, the cells in columns E through K indicate a 0 for days off and a 1 for days worked. For example, Schedule B indicates 0 under Mon and Tue—the days off—and 1 under Sun, Wed, Thu, Fri, and Sat—the days worked.

FIGURE 8.21

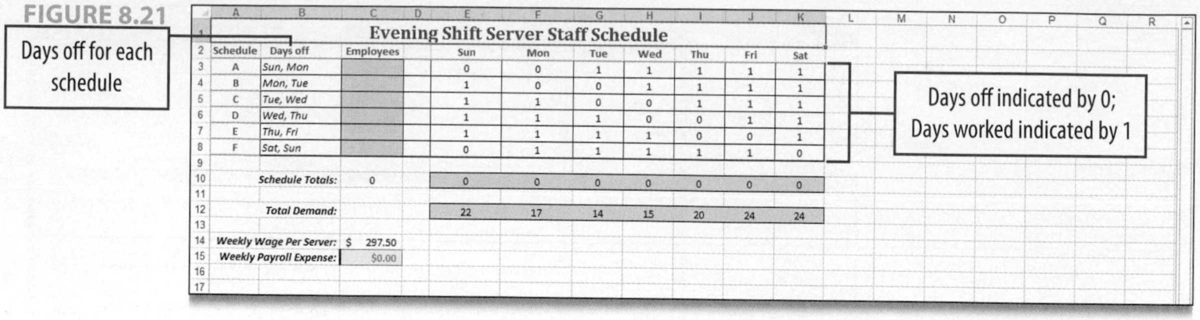

Days off for each schedule

Evening Shift Server Staff Schedule

Schedule	Days off	Employees	Sun	Mon	Tue	Wed	Thu	Fri	Sat
A	Sun, Mon		0	0	1	1	1	1	1
B	Mon, Tue		1	0	0	1	1	1	1
C	Tue, Wed		1	1	0	0	1	1	1
D	Wed, Thu		1	1	1	0	0	1	1
E	Thu, Fri		1	1	1	1	0	0	1
F	Sat, Sun		0	1	1	1	1	1	0
	Schedule Totals:	0	0	0	0	0	0	0	0
	Total Demand:		22	17	14	15	20	24	24
Weekly Wage Per Server:	$ 297.50								
Weekly Payroll Expense:	$0.00								

Days off indicated by 0; Days worked indicated by 1

3 Click cell **C10**, and then look at the **Formula Bar**.

Cell C10 sums the range C3:C8. It represents the number of servers who are assigned to each schedule. It is currently zero because no servers have been assigned to a schedule. The range C3:C8 is shaded in orange. These are the decision variables—the values that will change to achieve the desired results. Here, the desired result is to have only enough staff assigned to meet customer demand and hence minimize payroll expense.

4 Click cell **C14** and examine the formula.

This formula calculates the weekly wage, based on $8.50 per hour, multiplied by seven hours worked each day, multiplied by five days worked per week. The proposed schedule shows all servers working five days each week.

5 Click cell **C15**, which is formatted using the **Calculation cell** style, and examine the formula.

This cell calculates the total weekly payroll expense by multiplying the number of servers scheduled to work—cell C10—by the Weekly Wage Per Server—cell C14. Cell C15 is the objective cell. Recall that the objective cell contains the result that you are trying to achieve. In this instance, you are trying to achieve the minimum payroll expense that must be paid while maintaining enough servers on duty to meet established customer demand.

6 Select the range **E12:K12**.

These cells represent the minimum number of servers required to serve the number of customers expected each day of the week. The cells in this row will be one of the constraints used to determine the minimum weekly payroll expense. Recall that *constraints* are conditions or restrictions that must be met. In this case, the number of servers scheduled must be equal to or greater than the number required for each day.

7 Click cell **E10**.

The formulas in this row multiply the number of people assigned to work each schedule, arriving at a total number available each day of the week.

8 Click cell **C3**, and then click the **Name Box arrow**. Notice that cell **C3** has been named *Sun_Mon*. Compare your screen with Figure 8.22 and take a moment to review each of the cells you will work with in this project.

The cells in the range C3:C8, the decision variables, have been named with their corresponding days off.

FIGURE 8.22

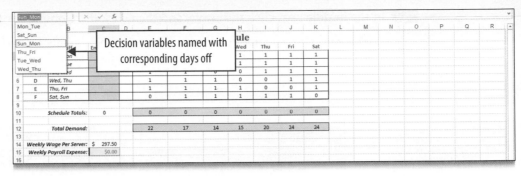

Decision variables named with corresponding days off

6	D	Wed, Thu		1	1	1	0	0	1	1
7	E	Thu, Fri		1	1	1	1	0	0	1
8	F	Sat, Sun		0	1	1	1	1	1	0
9										
10		Schedule Totals:	0	0	0	0	0	0	0	0
11										
12		Total Demand:		22	17	14	15	20	24	24
13										
14		Weekly Wage Per Server:	$ 297.50							
15		Weekly Payroll Expense:	$0.00							
16										

Activity 8.09 | Using Solver

In this activity, you will use Solver to determine the minimum payroll expense; that is, the minimum number of servers who can be on duty and still meet expected customer demand. This process involves identifying the objective cell, the decision variable cells, and the constraint cells.

1 ▶ Click cell **C15**—the objective cell. On the **DATA tab**, in the **Analysis group**, click **Solver**. If necessary, drag the **Solver Parameters** dialog box to the right side of your worksheet. Compare your screen with Figure 8.23.

The Solver Parameters dialog box displays and cell C15 displays as an absolute reference in the Set Objective box.

FIGURE 8.23

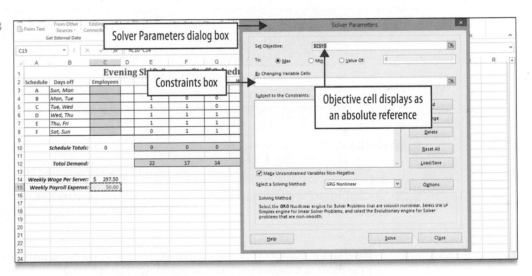

2 ▶ To the right of **To**, click **Min**.

The three option buttons here enable you to use the Solver tool to maximize, minimize, or solve for a specific value.

3 ▶ Click in the **By Changing Variable Cells** box, and then select the range **C3:C8**.

The range displays as an absolute reference. In this cell range, Solver will place the optimum number of servers who must be assigned to each schedule to minimize payroll and meet the constraints that are set.

4 ▶ To the right of the **Subject to the Constraints** area, click **Add**.

In the Add Constraint dialog box, you enter constraints—limitations caused by various circumstances.

5 ▶ With the insertion point blinking in the **Cell Reference** box, select the range **C3:C8**.

6 In the middle box, click the **arrow**, and then click **int**. Compare your screen with Figure 8.24.

This constraint requires that only an *integer*—a whole number—can be used, because you cannot assign part of a person as a server. In the Add Constraint dialog box, in the Constraint box, *integer* displays.

FIGURE 8.24

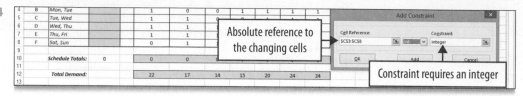

7 Click **OK**.

The Add Constraint dialog box closes and the first constraint is added to the Solver Parameters dialog box.

8 Click **Add**. With the insertion point in the **Cell Reference** box, select the range **C3:C8**. In the middle box, click the **arrow**, and then click **>=**. In the **Constraint** box, type **0** Compare your dialog box with Figure 8.25.

This constraint (limitation) requires that the number of servers assigned to each schedule be a positive number—a negative number of servers cannot be assigned.

FIGURE 8.25

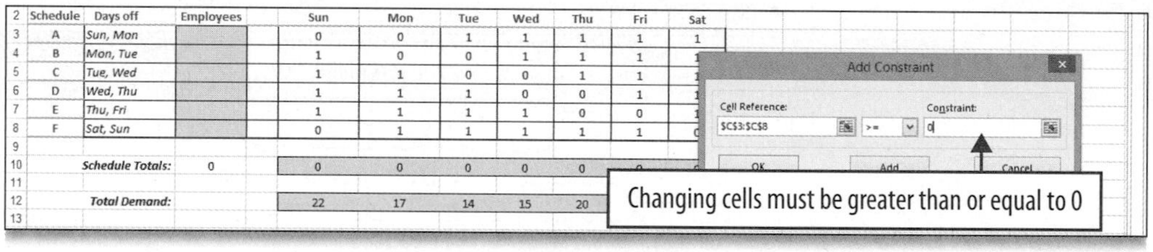

2	Schedule	Days off	Employees	Sun	Mon	Tue	Wed	Thu	Fri	Sat
3	A	Sun, Mon		0	0	1	1	1	1	1
4	B	Mon, Tue		1	0	0	1	1	1	
5	C	Tue, Wed		1	1	0	0	1	1	
6	D	Wed, Thu		1	1	1	0	0	1	
7	E	Thu, Fri		1	1	1	1	0	0	
8	F	Sat, Sun		0	1	1	1	1	1	
9										
10		Schedule Totals:	0	0	0	0	0	0		
11										
12		Total Demand:		22	17	14	15	20		
13										

Changing cells must be greater than or equal to 0

9 Click **OK**.

The second constraint is added to the Solver Parameters dialog box.

10 Click **Add**. In the **Cell Reference** box, select the range **E10:K10**. In the middle box, click the **arrow**, and then click **>=**. In the **Constraint** box, select the range **E12:K12**.

This constraint requires that the number of servers assigned to each shift be greater than or equal to the number of servers required each day to meet the projected demand. For example, on Saturday, the number of servers assigned must be at least 24.

11 Click **OK**. Compare your dialog box with Figure 8.26.

Three constraints display in the Solver Parameters dialog box. First, the number of servers assigned to any given schedule—C3:C8—must be a whole number. Second, the number of servers—C3:C8—assigned to any given schedule must be a positive number equal to or greater than zero. Third, the number of servers—E10:K10—assigned to each day's shift must be equal to or greater than the number of servers needed to meet the established demand in cells E12:K12. With the constraints established, you can solve for (calculate) the minimum payroll expense.

FIGURE 8.26

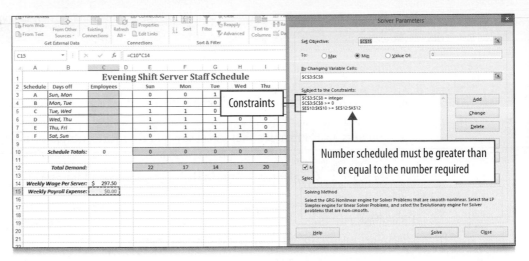

Figure 8.26 callouts: Constraints · Number scheduled must be greater than or equal to the number required

12 At the bottom of the **Solver Parameters** dialog box, click **Solve.** In the **Solver Results** dialog box, with **Keep Solver Solution** selected, click **OK. Save** 🖫 your workbook, and then compare your screen with Figure 8.27.

> The Solver Results dialog box displays. The decision variables—the cell range C3:C8—displays the number of servers who should be assigned to each schedule to meet the demand while minimizing payroll. Cell C15—the objective cell—shows the Weekly Payroll Expense as *$8,330.00*, and the number of servers who will work each schedule displays in cells E10:K10. Thus, to adequately staff the evening shifts and to give servers two consecutive days off requires a total of 28 servers each working 5 days a week and 7 hours each day—cell C10. The minimum payroll expense for 28 servers is $8,330.00—28 servers times $297.50.

FIGURE 8.27

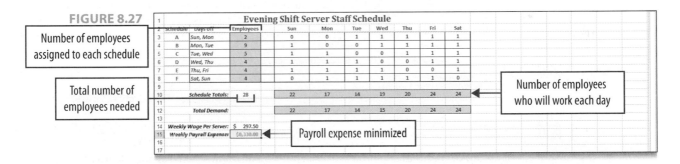

Figure 8.27 callouts: Number of employees assigned to each schedule · Total number of employees needed · Number of employees who will work each day · Payroll expense minimized

13 This is one possible solution. Later, you will consider alternatives with a different distribution of staff over the week.

More Knowledge   **Solver Reports**

The Solver Results dialog box offers three reports—Answer, Sensitivity, and Limits—that can be created to help you understand the results. The Answer Report displays the original and final values for the objective cell and the decision variables. It also shows the impact of the constraints on determining values for the decision variables and whether the result for each cell is binding or nonbinding. It helps you understand where there may be some flexibility in the results if you want to do further analysis or consider other alternatives. The Sensitivity and Limits reports are not meaningful in the current example because of the integer constraints that have been applied.

Video E8-5

The current solution indicates nine servers assigned to *Schedule B, Mon and Tue off*, and only two servers assigned to *Schedule A, Sun and Mon off*. Ms. Zachary wants to see what would happen if she assigned more servers to Schedule A. You can create several possible solutions to a problem and then use Excel's ***Scenario Manager*** what-if analysis tool to compare the alternatives. A ***scenario*** is a set of values that Excel saves and can substitute automatically in your worksheet.

Activity 8.10 | Creating a Scenario Using the Scenario Manager

You can create a scenario from the Solver dialog box, or you can open the Scenario Manager dialog box and create a scenario. Here, you will use the Scenario Manager dialog box to save the existing solution for minimizing the weekly server staff payroll.

1 Select the range **C3:C8**.

These are the decision variable cells defined in Solver that are used to calculate the minimum payroll expense while matching the staffing requirements that are shown in row 12.

2 On the **DATA tab**, in the **Data Tools group**, click **What-If Analysis**, and then click **Scenario Manager**. Compare your screen with Figure 8.28.

The Scenario Manager dialog box displays. It shows that no scenarios have been defined.

FIGURE 8.28

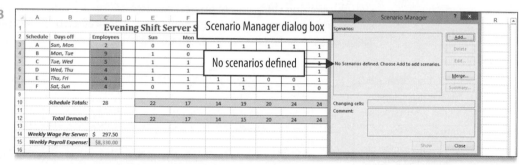

3 In the **Scenario Manager** dialog box, click **Add**.

The Add Scenario dialog box displays. Here you name the scenario and identify the decision variable cells.

4 In the **Scenario Name** box, type **Option 1** Verify that the **Changing cells** box displays *C3:C8*.

You will save the existing solution as your first scenario.

5 Click **OK**. Compare your screen with Figure 8.29.

The Scenario Values dialog box displays and the current value in each of the decision variable cells is listed. You will accept the values that are displayed.

FIGURE 8.29

6 In the **Scenario Values** dialog box, click **OK**.

The Scenario Manager dialog box redisplays, and the first scenario is listed in the Scenarios box as *Option 1*.

7 In the **Scenario Manager** dialog box, click **Close**. Save 🖫 your workbook.

Activity 8.11 | Creating a Scenario Using Solver

You can also create a scenario using the Solver Parameters dialog box. Ms. Zachary wants to add another schedule option that would assign more servers to Schedule A so more people could be off on Sunday, a more traditional day off, and to help balance the numbers of shifts among employees.

1 Click cell **C15**—the objective cell. On the **DATA tab**, in the **Analysis group**, click **Solver**. In the **Solver Parameters** dialog box, verify that the **Set Objective** box displays *$C$15* and the **By Changing Variable Cells** box displays *$C$3:$C$8*.

The values from the first solution display in the Solver Parameters dialog box.

2 To the right of **Subject to the Constraints** box, click **Add**.

3 In the **Add Constraint** dialog box, click the **Cell Reference** box, and then click cell **C3**. In the middle box, click the **arrow**, and then click **=**. In the **Constraint** box, type **4**

This constraint will assign four servers to *Schedule A—Sun and Mon off*.

4 Click **OK**.

A fourth constraint is added to the Solver Parameters dialog box. Recall that because each of the cells in the range C3:C8 were named, the constraint displays as Sun_Mon =4. The range name displays when you summarize the alternatives you are creating.

5 In the lower right corner of the dialog box, click **Solve**. Drag the **Solver Results** dialog box to the right side of the screen and compare your screen with Figure 8.30.

A new solution is found and the Solver Results dialog box displays. The Weekly Payroll Expense remains at $8,330.00, but the servers are more evenly distributed across the schedules, with more servers scheduled on Friday and Saturday when the restaurant is the busiest. This provides a better distribution of staff on the busiest weekend days, while giving more people Sunday off. This shows that there may be more than one acceptable solution to the problem of minimizing the payroll.

FIGURE 8.30

The number of employees assigned to each schedule is changed

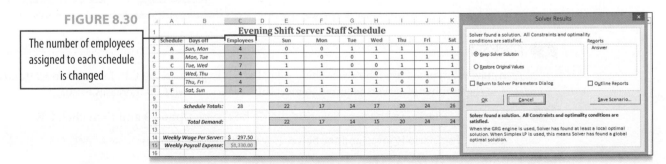

6 Click **Save Scenario** to display the **Save Scenario** dialog box.

7 In the **Scenario Name** box, type **Option 2** and then click **OK**.

A second scenario is saved and the Solver Results dialog box displays.

8 In the **Solver Results** dialog box, click **Restore Original Values**, and then click **OK**. Save 🖫 your workbook.

The dialog box closes and the previous solution is redisplayed on the worksheet.

Activity 8.12 | Creating a Scenario Summary

Ms. Zachary wants to see what would happen if she schedules six servers to have Saturday off. Schedule F includes both Saturday and Sunday off, which would give more employees a traditional weekend off. After the third scenario is created, you will view a summary of the results of all three alternatives.

1 Verify that cell **C15** is still the active cell. On the **DATA tab**, in the **Analysis group**, click **Solver**.

In the Solver Parameters dialog box, all four constraints (from Option 2) display, even though the currently displayed solution—Option 1—does not use the constraint that requires four servers be assigned to schedule A—*Sun_Mon = 4*.

2 In the **Subject to the Constraints** box, select the fourth constraint—**Sun_Mon = 4**—and then click **Delete**.

3 Click **Add**.

4 In the **Add Constraint** dialog box, click in the **Cell Reference** box, and then click cell **C8**. Change the middle box to **=**. In the **Constraint** box, type **6** and then click **OK**. Compare your screen with Figure 8.31.

Four constraints are listed in the Solver Parameters dialog box.

FIGURE 8.31

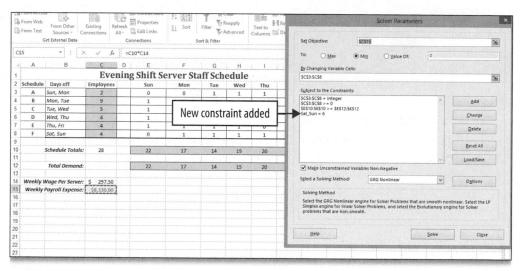

5 Click **Solve**.

A new solution is found; however, the Weekly Payroll Expense in cell C16 increases to *$8,925.00*, and the number of servers required to meet this scenario in cell C10 increases to 30.

6 Click **Save Scenario**. In the **Save Scenario** dialog box, type **Option 3** and then click **OK**.

The third scenario is saved and the Solver Results dialog box displays.

7 Click **Restore Original Values**, and then click **OK**.

The previous solution is restored to the worksheet.

8 On the **DATA tab**, in the **Data Tools group**, click **What-If Analysis**, and then click **Scenario Manager**. Compare your screen with Figure 8.32.

The Scenario Manager dialog box displays the three scenario names that you have created.

FIGURE 8.32

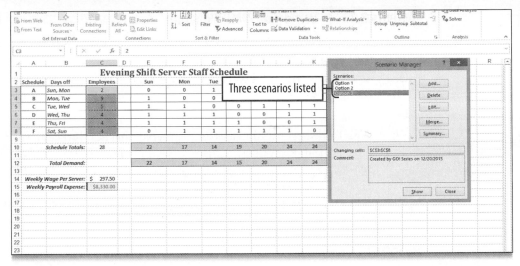

9 ▸ In the **Scenario Manager** dialog box, click **Summary**.

The Scenario Summary dialog box displays. Here you can choose between a Scenario Summary, which displays the data in a table, or a Scenario PivotTable report.

10 ▸ Be sure **Scenario Summary** is selected, and then click **OK**. Compare your screen with Figure 8.33.

Excel inserts a new worksheet in your workbook—the *Scenario Summary* sheet, which compares the three options side-by-side. The results for Option 1 and Option 2 indicate the same amount in the results cell—*$8,330.00*—and Option 3 indicates *$8,925.00* in payroll expenses. The outline pane displays along the top and left side of the worksheet.

FIGURE 8.33

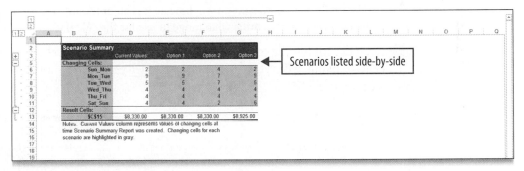

11 ▸ Select the range **D12:G12** and then, on the **HOME tab**, in the **Editing group**, click **AutoSum** ∑ AutoSum ▾ . **Save** 🖫 your workbook.

The total number of servers required for each scenario is added to the Scenario Summary sheet. Options 1 and 2 require 28 servers to fill the schedule and Option 3 requires 30 servers.

Objective 6 Use Logical Functions

Video E8-6

There are a number of *logical functions* that are used to test for specific conditions. The results of a logical test are either TRUE or FALSE. Recall that the SUM function adds values in a specified range of cells. The *SUMIF function* contains a logic test—it will add values in a specified range that meet a certain condition or criteria. The *SUMIFS function* is similar to the SUMIF function, but allows you to specify multiple ranges and multiple criteria to test. The *COUNTIF function* and *COUNTIFS function* work in the same way, counting cells that meet specific criteria in specified ranges. The *syntax*, or arrangement of the arguments in a function, displays in a ScreenTip as you begin to build the function.

Activity 8.13 | Using the SUMIF Function

Ms. Zachary wants to see the total each server has sold over the past week. SUMIF can be used to add values in a range that meet a specific condition or criteria. In this activity you will use SUMIF to calculate the total weekly sales for each server.

1 ▶ Display the **Weekly Sales** worksheet.

This worksheet lists the sales for each server that has worked the day or evening shift the week of January 1–8.

2 ▶ Click cell **G3**, and then type **=sumif(** Compare your screen with Figure 8.34.

The syntax displays for the SUMIF function. It has two required arguments: *range* and *criteria*, and one optional argument: *sum_range*.

FIGURE 8.34

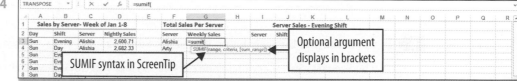

3 ▶ Notice *range* is bold in the ScreenTip that displays. Select the range **C3:C102** and press F4 to make the value absolute. Type **,** (a comma) and notice *criteria* is now bold in the ScreenTip.

4 ▶ Click cell **F3**, and then type **,** (a comma).

5 ▶ Notice *[sum_range]* is now bold. Select the range **D3:D102** and press F4. Type **)** and then, on the **Formula Bar**, click **Enter** ☑.

The brackets around *sum_range* indicate it is an optional argument. If you do not include it, Excel will attempt to determine what range to use for the calculation.

6 ▶ Drag the fill handle to copy the formula down through cell **G19**. Format the range **G3:G19** using cell style **Currency [0]**. **Save** 💾 your workbook and compare your screen with Figure 8.35.

FIGURE 8.35

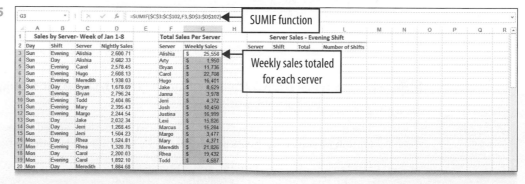

Activity 8.14 | Using the SUMIFS Function

Because each server may work multiple shifts, you can use the SUMIFS function to include a second criteria—Shift—to SUM. In this activity, you will use SUMIFS to calculate sales for each server for the evening shift.

1 ▶ Select the range **F3:F19**, which contains the server names. Right-click over the selection and click **Copy**. Right-click cell **I3** and click **Paste (P)** 📋. Click cell **J3**, and then type **Evening** and then copy the cell down through **I19**.

2 ► Click cell **K3** and type **=sumifs(** Compare your screen with Figure 8.36.

In the SUMIFS function, the *sum_range* argument is specified first, followed by the first *criteria_range1* and *critera1*. Additional *criteria_range* and *criteria* arguments can follow, up to a maximum of 127.

FIGURE 8.36

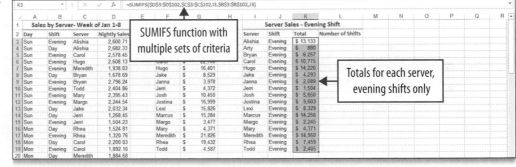

3 ► Select the range **D3:D102** and press F4 to make the value absolute. Type **,** (a comma), select the range **C3:C102**, and press F4. Type **,** (a comma). Click cell **I3**, and then type **,** (a comma).

The optional arguments [criteria_range2, criteria2] display in brackets in the ScreenTip.

4 ► Select the range **B3:B102** and then press F4. Type **,** (a comma) and then click cell **J3**. Type **)** and then click **Enter** ✓.

5 ► Drag the fill-handle to copy the formula down through cell **K19**. Format the range **K3:K19** using cell style **Currency [0]**. Save 🖫 your workbook and compare your screen with Figure 8.37.

In this SUMIFS function, you used the Nightly Sales as the sum_range, the Server as the first criteria, and the Shift as the second criteria.

FIGURE 8.37

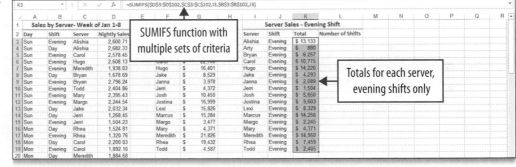

Activity 8.15 | Using the COUNTIFS Function

Ms. Zachary wants to see the number of evening shifts each server has worked over the past week. The COUNTIFS function can be used to count items that meet multiple conditions—in this case, the server and the shift worked.

1 ► Click cell **L3** and type **=countifs(** Compare your screen with Figure 8.38.

The COUNTIFS function has two required arguments: *criteria_range1* and *critera1*. Additional *criteria_range* and *criteria* arguments can follow.

FIGURE 8.38

2 Select the range **C3:C102** and press F4 to make the value absolute. Type **,** (a comma), click cell **I3**, and then type **,** (a comma).

> The optional arguments [criteria_range2, criteria2] display in brackets in the ScreenTip.

3 Select the range **B3:B102** and then press F4. Type **,** (a comma) and then click cell **J3**. Type **)** and then click **Enter** ✓.

4 Drag the fill handle to copy the formula down through cell **L19**. **Save** 🖫 your workbook and compare your screen with Figure 8.39.

> Using the COUNTIFS function, Ms. Zachary is able to see how many evening shifts each server worked this week.

FIGURE 8.39

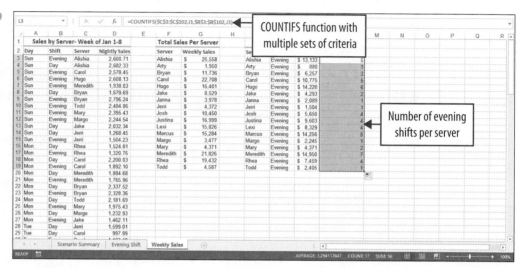

Objective 7   Create Complex Formulas

Video E8-7

The logical functions AND and OR can be used to develop compound logical tests using up to 255 arguments. The **AND function** returns a result of TRUE if *ALL* of the conditions are met. The **OR function** returns a value of TRUE if *ANY* of the conditions are met. The **NOT function** takes only one argument and is used to test one condition. If the condition is true, NOT returns the logical opposite false. If the condition is false, then true is returned.

Activity 8.16 | Building Compound Conditional Tests Using AND

To determine the Employee of the Week, Ms. Zachary needs to determine the server with the best sales that worked at least three shifts but no more than five evening shifts during the week, and worked a least one shift during the slower days Monday and Tuesday. To do this, she needs to use a compound conditional test.

1 Click cell **N1** and type **Employees of the Week** and press Enter. **Merge & Center** the text over the range **N1:Q1** and apply the **Heading 2** cell style. In cell **N2**, type **Server** In cell **O2**, type **3-5 Shifts** In cell **P2**, type **M or T** Copy the server names from **I3:I19** to **N3:N19**.

2 Select the range **A3:A102**, in the **Name Box**, type **DAY** and then press Enter. Select the range **B3:B102**, in the **Name Box**, type **SHIFT** and then press Enter. Select the range **C3:C102**, in the **Name Box**, type **SERVER** and then press Enter.

> By naming the ranges, you have made it easier to construct and understand complex formulas.

3 In cell **O2**, type **=and(** and compare your screen with Figure 8.40.

> The AND function takes the argument *logical1*, followed by optional additional logical tests.

FIGURE 8.40

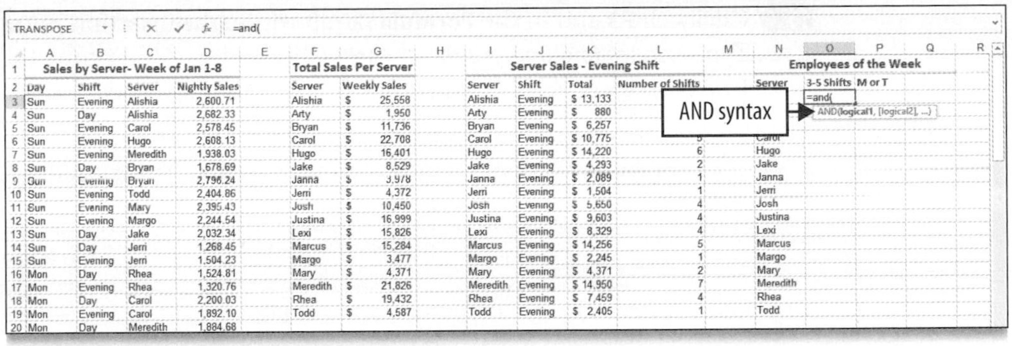

4 ▶ Click cell **L3**, type **>=3,** (include the comma) Click cell **L3**, and type **<=5)** Click **Enter** ✓ and copy the formula down through cell **O19**. Compare your screen with Figure 8.41.

The AND function performs two logical tests *L3>=3* and *L3<=5*. Both of the tests must be true for the function to return TRUE. If either or both tests fail, the function returns the result FALSE.

FIGURE 8.41

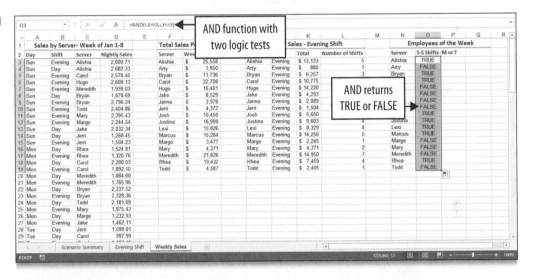

5 ▶ Click cell **P3**, and then type the formula **=countifs(server,n3,day,"Mon")** Click **Enter** ✓ and copy the formula down through cell **P19**. Compare your screen with Figure 8.42.

This formula uses the named ranges SERVER and DAY as the criteria ranges to determine the number of Monday shifts each server has worked.

FIGURE 8.42

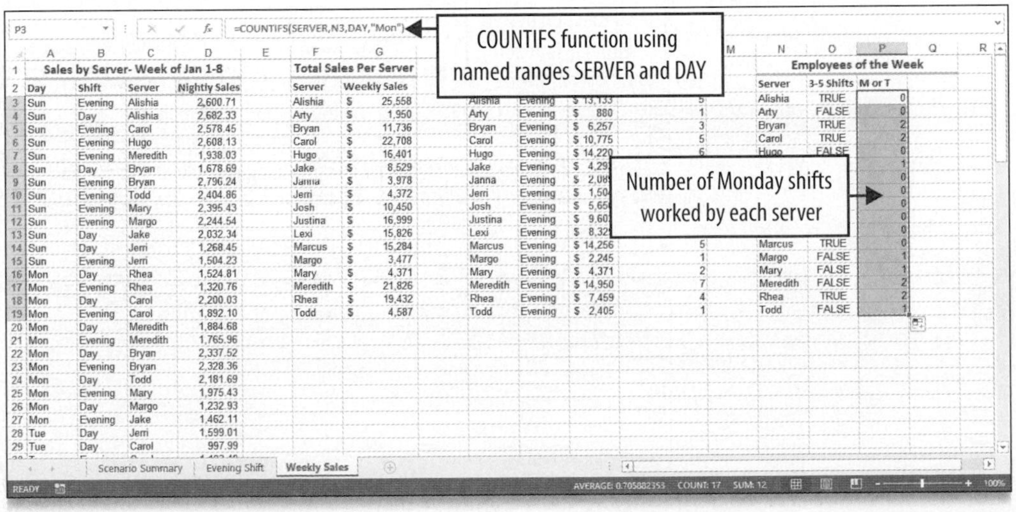

6 ▶ Click cell **P3** and in the **Formula Bar**, position the insertion point at the end of the formula. Type **+countifs(server,n3,day, "Tue")** Click **Enter** ☑ and copy the formula down through cell **P19**. **Save** 🖫 your worksheet and compare your screen with Figure 8.43.

The mathematical operators plus sign (+), minus sign (-), division sign (/), and multiplication sign (*) can be used to build complex formulas. In this case, by adding the results of two functions.

FIGURE 8.43

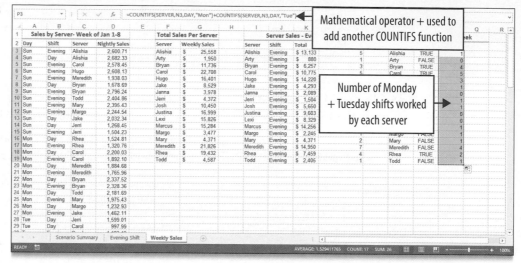

Activity 8.17 │ Using Nested Functions

Complex formulas can be built by nesting functions. A ***nested function*** is contained inside another function. The inner, nested function is evaluated first and the result becomes the argument for the outer function. Recall that the IF function uses a single logic test and returns one value if true and another value if false. In this activity you will use an IF function with a nested AND function to determine which servers are eligible for Employee of the Week status.

1 ▶ Click cell **Q2**, type **Eligible** and then press Enter.

2 ▶ In cell **Q3**, type **=if(and(o3, p3>=1), "Eligible","")** Click **Enter** ☑ and copy the formula down through cell **Q19**. **Save** 🖫 your worksheet and compare your screen with Figure 8.44.

There are six servers that meet both criteria—O3 is true and P3 is greater than or equal to 1—and are listed as *Eligible*. The double quotes make the cell blank rather than displaying the word FALSE if the result is false.

FIGURE 8.44

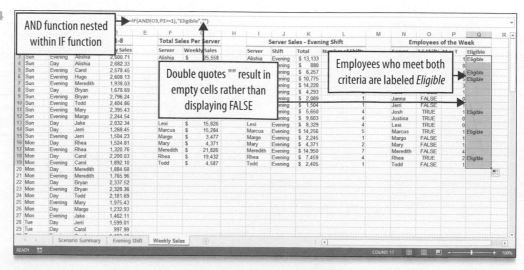

3 ▶ Press Ctrl + Q to open **Quick Analysis** 📊 at the bottom of the selection, and then click **Text Contains**. In the **Text That Contains** dialog box, verify **Format cells that contain the text** displays *Eligible*. Click the **with arrow**, and then click **Green Fill with Dark Green Text**. Compare your screen with Figure 8.45.

This applies conditional formatting to the cells in the selected range that contain text, which makes it easy for Ms. Zachary to see which employees are eligible.

FIGURE 8.45

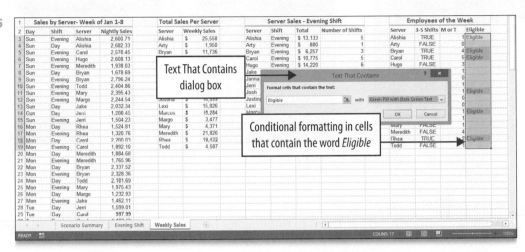

4 ▶ Click **OK**. On the **PAGE LAYOUT tab**, click **Print Titles**. Under **Print Titles**, click in the **Rows to repeat at top** box, and then from the **row heading area**, select **row 2**. Click **OK**.

This worksheet will print on two pages so adding column titles will make it easier to understand the information on the second page.

5 ▶ Select all three worksheets so that *[Group]* displays in the title bar. With the worksheets grouped, set the **Orientation** to **Landscape**. Center the worksheets horizontally on the page and set the **Width** to **1 page**. Insert a footer in the **left section** that includes the file name. On the status bar, click **Normal** ▦ and make cell **A1** active.

6 ▶ Display the **document properties** and if necessary, right-click the author name, click **Edit Property**, and then type your name. In the **Subject** box, type your course name and section #, and in the **Tags** box, type **staff schedule** Display the grouped worksheets in **Print Preview**. If necessary, return to the workbook and make any necessary corrections or adjustments. Ungroup the worksheets and **Save** 💾 your workbook.

7 ▶ **Print** or submit the three worksheets in this workbook electronically as directed by your instructor. If required, print or create an electronic version of your worksheets with formulas. **Close** Excel.

END | You have completed Project 8B

END OF CHAPTER

SUMMARY

A moving average is a sequence of averages computed from parts of a data series. It smoothes the data, showing a pattern or trend. The break-even point is the point at which a company starts to make a profit.

Solver is a what-if analysis tool used to find an optimal value for a formula in one cell—referred to as the objective cell—subject to constraints, on the values of other formula cells in a worksheet.

You can create several possible solutions to a problem and use Scenario Manager to compare the alternatives. A scenario is a set of values that Excel saves and can substitute automatically in your worksheet.

Complex formulas can be built by nesting functions. A nested function is contained inside another function. The inner function is evaluated first and the result becomes the argument for the outer function.

GO! LEARN IT ONLINE

Review the concepts and key terms in this chapter by completing these online challenges, which you can find at **www.pearsonhighered.com/go**.

Matching and Multiple Choice: Answer matching and multiple choice questions to test what you learned in this chapter. MyITLab®

Crossword Puzzle: Spell out the words that match the numbered clues, and put them in the puzzle squares.

Flipboard: Flip through the definitions of the key terms in this chapter and match them with the correct term.

END OF CHAPTER
REVIEW AND ASSESSMENT GUIDE FOR EXCEL CHAPTER 8

Your instructor may assign one or more of these projects to help you review the chapter and assess your mastery and understanding of the chapter.

	Review and Assessment Guide for Excel Chapter 8		
Project	**Apply Skills from These Chapter Objectives**	**Project Type**	**Project Location**
8C	Objectives 1–3 from Project 8A	**8C Skills Review** A guided review of the skills from Project 8A.	On the following pages
8D	Objectives 4–7 from Project 8B	**8D Skills Review** A guided review of the skills from Project 8B.	On the following pages
8E	Objectives 1–3 from Project 8A	**8E Mastery (Grader Project)** A demonstration of your mastery of the skills in Project 8A with extensive decision making.	In MyITLab and on the following pages
8F	Objectives 4–7 from Project 8B	**8F Mastery (Grader Project)** A demonstration of your mastery of the skills in Project 8B with extensive decision making.	In MyITLab and on the following pages
8G	Objectives 1–7 from Projects 8A and 8B	**8G Mastery (Grader Project)** A demonstration of your mastery of the skills in Projects 8A and 8B with extensive decision making.	In MyITLab and on the following pages
8H	Combination of Objectives from Projects 8A and 8B	**8H GO! Fix It** A demonstration of your mastery of the skills in Projects 8A and 8B by creating a correct result from a document that contains errors you must find.	Online
8I	Combination of Objectives from Projects 8A and 8B	**8I GO! Make It** A demonstration of your mastery of the skills in Projects 8A and 8B by creating a result from a supplied picture.	Online
8J	Combination of Objectives from Projects 8A and 8B	**8J GO! Solve It** A demonstration of your mastery of the skills in Projects 8A and 8B, your decision-making skills, and your critical thinking skills. A task-specific rubric helps you self-assess your result.	Online
8K	Combination of Objectives from Projects 8A and 8B	**8K GO! Solve It** A demonstration of your mastery of the skills in Projects 8A and 8B, your decision-making skills, and your critical thinking skills. A task-specific rubric helps you self-assess your result.	On the following pages
8L	Combination of Objectives from Projects 8A and 8B	**8L GO! Think** A demonstration of your understanding of the chapter concepts applied in a manner that you would outside of college. An analytic rubric helps you and your instructor grade the quality of your work by comparing it to the work an expert in the discipline would create.	On the following pages
8M	Combination of Objectives from Projects 8A and 8B	**8M GO! Think** A demonstration of your understanding of the chapter concepts applied in a manner that you would outside of college. An analytic rubric helps you and your instructor grade the quality of your work by comparing it to the work an expert in the discipline would create.	Online
8N	Combination of Objectives from Projects 8A and 8B	**8N You and GO!** A demonstration of your understanding of the chapter concepts applied in a manner that you would in a personal situation. An analytic rubric helps you and your instructor grade the quality of your work.	Online

GLOSSARY

GLOSSARY OF CHAPTER KEY TERMS

Add-in Optional command or feature that is not immediately available; you must first install and/or activate it to use it.

AND function A logical function that can be used to develop compound logical tests using up to 255 arguments. The function returns a result of TRUE if ALL of the conditions are met.

Break-even point The point at which a company starts to make a profit.

Constraint In Solver, a condition or restriction that must be met.

Constraint cell In Solver, a cell that contains a value that limits or restricts the outcome.

COUNTIF function A logical function that counts the cells that meet specific criteria in a specified range.

COUNTIFS function A logical function that counts the cells that meet specific criteria in multiple ranges.

Decision variable In Solver, a cell in which the value will change to achieve the desired results.

Dual-axis chart A chart that has one series plotted on a secondary axis. Useful when comparing data series that use different scales or different types of measurements.

Fixed expense Expense that remains the same each month regardless of the amount of activity.

Forecast A prediction of the future, often based on past performances.

Integer A whole number.

Interval The number of cells to include in the average.

Logical function A function that tests for specific conditions.

Moving average A sequence of averages computed from parts of a data series.

Nested function A function that is contained inside another function. The inner function is evaluated first and the result becomes the argument for the outer function.

NOT function A logical function that takes only one argument and is used to test one condition. If the condition is true, the function returns the logical opposite false. If the condition is false, true is returned.

Objective cell In Solver, a cell that contains a formula for the results you are trying to determine.

OR function A logical function that can be used to develop compound logical tests using up to 255 arguments. The function returns a value of TRUE if ANY of the conditions are met.

Scenario A set of values that Excel saves and can substitute automatically in your worksheet.

Scenario Manager A what-if analysis tool that compares alternatives.

Solver A what-if analysis tool with which you can find an optimal (maximum or minimum) value for a formula in one cell—referred to as the objective cell—subject to constraints, or limits, on the values of other formula cells on a worksheet.

SUMIF function A logical function that contains one logic test—it will add values in a specified range that meet certain conditions or criteria.

SUMIFS function A logical function that will add values in multiple ranges that meet multiple criteria.

Syntax The arrangement of the arguments in a function.

Transpose To switch the data in rows and columns.

Variable cell In Solver, a cell in which the value will change to achieve the desired results.

Variable expense Expense that varies depending on the amount of sales.

CHAPTER REVIEW

Apply 8A skills from these Objectives:

1 Calculate a Moving Average

2 Project Income and Expenses

3 Determine a Break-Even Point

In the following Skills Review, you will create a worksheet for Kelsey Tanner, the Chief Financial Officer of Brina's Bistro, who wants to see how sales have grown in the first six weeks at the new restaurant in Orlando, Florida. Your completed worksheets will look similar to Figure 8.46.

PROJECT FILES

For Project 8C, you will need the following file:

e08C_Orlando_Sales

You will save your workbook as:

Lastname_Firstname_8C_Orlando_Sales

PROJECT RESULTS

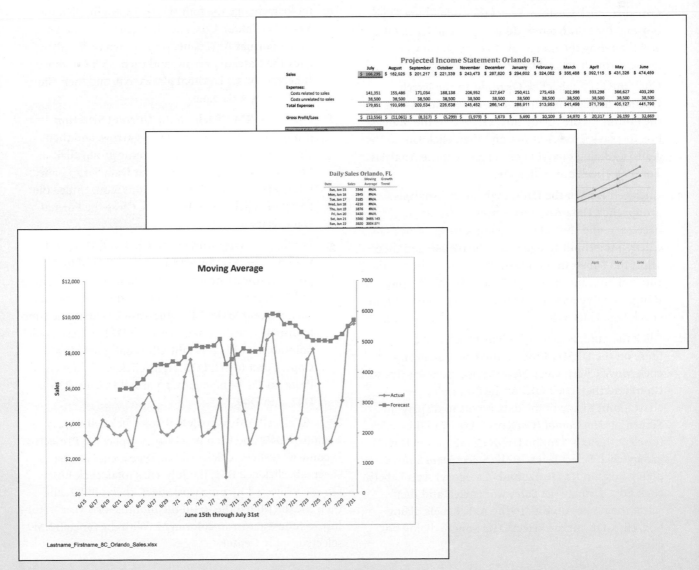

FIGURE 8.46

(Project 8C Orlando Sales continues on the next page)

CHAPTER REVIEW

1 Start Excel. From your student files, open the file **e08C_Orlando_Sales**, and then in your **Excel Chapter 8** folder, **Save** the file as **Lastname_Firstname_8C_Orlando_Sales**

a. Select the range **A3:AV4**. Right-click anywhere over the selection and click **Copy**. Click cell **A5**. Right-click and under **Paste Options**, click **Transpose (T)**. Delete **rows 2:4**. In cell **C2** type **Moving Average** In cell **D2** type **Growth Trend** Select the range **A2:D2** and apply the **Heading 3** cell style and, in the **Alignment group**, click **Wrap Text**. Click cell **A3**. On the **HOME tab**, in the **Number group**, click the **Dialog Box Launcher**. In the **Format Cells** dialog box, be sure the **Number tab** is selected. Under **Category**, click **Custom**. Select the code in the **Type** box and type **ddd, mmm dd** to replace it. Click **OK**, and then drag the fill handle to copy the new format down through cell **A49**. Press Ctrl + Home.

b. Click **the FILE tab**, click **Options**. In the **Excel Options** dialog box, on the left, click **Add-Ins**. At the bottom of the dialog box, verify that the **Manage** box displays *Excel Add-ins*, and then click **Go**. In the **Add-Ins** dialog box, if necessary, select the **Analysis ToolPak** check box. Click **OK**.

c. Click cell **A2**. On the **DATA tab**, in the **Analysis group**, click **Data Analysis**. Scroll the list as necessary, and then click **Moving Average**. Click **OK**. Click in the **Input Range** box, type **b2:b49** and then select the **Labels in First Row** check box. Click in the **Interval** box, and then type **7** Click in the **Output Range** box, type **c3** and then select the **Chart Output** check box. Click **OK**.

d. Click the outer edge of the chart to select it and then, on the **DESIGN tab**, in the **Location group**, click **Move Chart**. Click **New sheet**, type **Sales Trend Chart** and then click **OK**. At the bottom of the chart, point to any of the data points to display the ScreenTip *Horizontal (Category) Axis*, and then click to select the axis. On the **DESIGN tab**, in the **Data group**, click **Select Data**. In the **Select Data Source** dialog box, under **Horizontal (Category) Axis Labels**, click **Edit**. Display the **Sales** worksheet, and then select the range **A3:A49**. In the **Axis Labels** dialog box, click **OK**. In the **Select Data Source** dialog box, click **OK**.

e. Right-click the **Horizontal (Category)Axis**, and then click **Format Axis**. In the **Format Axis** pane, with **Axis Options** selected, scroll down and click **Number**, click the **Category arrow** and then click **Date**. Click the **Type arrow**, click the **3/14 format**, and then **Close** the **Format Axis** pane. Click the **Horizontal (Category)Axis Title** to select it. On the **Formula Bar** type **June 15th through July 31st** and then press Enter. Point to the **Horizontal (Category) Axis Title**, triple-click, and then on the mini toolbar, change the font size to **12**. Click the **Vertical (Value) Axis Title** to select it. On the **Formula Bar** type **Sales** and then press Enter. Point to the **Vertical (Value) Axis Title**, double-click, and then on the mini toolbar, change the font size to **12**. Right-click the **Vertical (Value) Axis**, and then click **Format Axis**. In the **Format Axis** pane, scroll down to **Number**, click the **Category arrow**, and then click **Currency**. If necessary, set **Decimal places** to **0**, and then **Close** the **Format Axis** pane.

f. On the **FORMAT tab**, in the **Current Selection group**, click the **Chart Elements arrow**, and then click **Series "Forecast"**. In the same group click **Format Selection**. In the **Format Data Series** pane, if necessary, click the **Series Options** icon. Under **Plot Series on**, click **Secondary Axis**. **Close** the **Format Data Series** pane.

g. Display the **Sales** worksheet. Click cell **D21**, and then type **=(c21-c14)/c14** Press Enter. Scroll to position **row 21** near the top of your screen. Point to cell **D21**, right-click, and then on the mini toolbar, click **Percent Style**. Click **Increase Decimal** one time to display one decimal. With cell **D21** still selected, point to the cell and right-click, and then click **Copy**. Point to cell **D28**, right-click, and then click **Paste**. In the same manner, paste it in cells **D35**, **D42**, and **D49**.

2 Click cell **A51**, type **July Sales** Click cell **B51**, type **=sum(b19:b49)** and then press Enter. Display the **Projected Income** worksheet. Click cell **B3**. Type **=** click the **Sales sheet tab**, click cell **B51**, the July sales total, click **Enter**. On the **Projected Income** worksheet, click cell **B2**, and then use the fill handle to fill the months for a year—from July to June—across to **column M**. With the range **B2:M2** selected, apply **Center**.

(Project 8C Orlando Sales continues on the next page)

a. Click cell **B3**; in the **Formula Bar**, notice the cell reference. Click cell **C3**, type **=b3*(1+b12)** and then click Enter. Apply the **Currency [0]** cell style. Use the fill handle to copy the formula in cell **C3** across the row to cell **M3**.

b. Click cell **B6** and examine the formula. Use the fill handle to copy the formula from cell **B6** across the row to cell **M6**. **Copy** the value in cell **B7** across the row to cell **M7**. Select the range **C8:M8**, and then on the **HOME tab**, in the **Editing group**, click **AutoSum**. **Copy** the formula in cell **B10** across the row to cell **M10**.

3 In the lower right corner of your screen, if necessary, set the **Zoom** to **80%** so that **columns A:M** display on your screen. Select the range **A2:M3**. On the **INSERT tab**, in the **Charts group**, click **Recommended Charts**. In the **Insert Chart** dialog box, with the **Line chart** selected, click **OK**.

a. On the **DESIGN tab**, in the **Data group**, click **Select Data**. In the **Select Data Source** dialog box, under **Legend Entries (Series)**, click **Add**. With the insertion point in the **Series name** box, click cell **A8**. Press [Tab], select the range **B8:M8** and then click **OK**. Verify that the **Chart data range** is *$A2:$M3* and *$A8:$M8*. Click **OK**. Click **Chart Title**, and then type **Expected Break-Even Point** Press [Enter].

b. Drag to position the upper left corner of the chart inside the upper left corner of cell **B15**. Scroll to position **row 13** near the top of your screen. Drag the lower right corner of the chart inside the lower right corner of cell **M36**.

c. On the **DESIGN tab**, apply **Chart Style 12**. On the left side of the chart, right-click the **Value (Value) Axis**, and then click **Format Axis**. In the **Format Axis** pane verify that **Axis Options** is selected. Under **AXIS OPTIONS**, in the **Minimum** box, type

150000 Press [Enter]. In the same manner, change the **Maximum** value to **500000**

d. Format both the **Plot Area** and the **Chart Area** with a **Solid fill** using the color **Light Yellow, Background 2**. **Close** the **Format Chart Area** pane.

e. Display the **Sales Trend Chart** worksheet. On this chart sheet, insert a custom footer with the file name in the **left section**.

4 Display the **Projected Income** worksheet, click anywhere outside the chart, and then, if necessary, set the **Zoom** back to **100%**. Right-click the **sheet tab**, and then click **Select All Sheets** so that *[Group]* displays in the title bar. With the worksheets grouped, insert a footer in the **left section** that includes the file name. Click the cell above the footer to deselect it.

a. On the **PAGE LAYOUT tab**, set the **Orientation** to **Landscape**, and then, set the **Width** to **1 page**, and the **Height** to **1 page**. Center the worksheets horizontally on the page. On the status bar, click **Normal**. Press [Ctrl] + [Home] to move to the top of the worksheet.

b. Display the **document properties** and under **Related People**, be sure that your name displays as the author. If necessary, right-click the author name, click **Edit Property**, and then type your name. In the **Subject** box, type your course name and section #, and in the **Tags** box, type **Orlando, break-even** Display the grouped worksheets in **Print Preview**; if necessary, return to the workbook and make any necessary corrections or adjustments. Ungroup the worksheets.

c. **Save** your workbook, and then **Print** the three worksheets or submit your workbook electronically as directed. If required, print or create an electronic version of your worksheets with formulas displayed. **Close** Excel.

END | You have completed Project 8C

CHAPTER REVIEW

Apply 8B skills from these Objectives:

4 Use Solver

5 Create Scenarios

6 Use Logical Functions

7 Create Complex Formulas

In the following Skills Review, you will assist Stephanie Wheaton, manager of the Charlotte restaurant, in determining the most efficient work schedule for the evening server staff. Your completed worksheets will look similar to Figure 8.47.

PROJECT FILES

Build from Scratch

For Project 8D, you will need the following file:

e08D_Charlotte_Staffing

You will save your workbook as:

Lastname_Firstname_8D_Charlotte_Staffing

PROJECT RESULTS

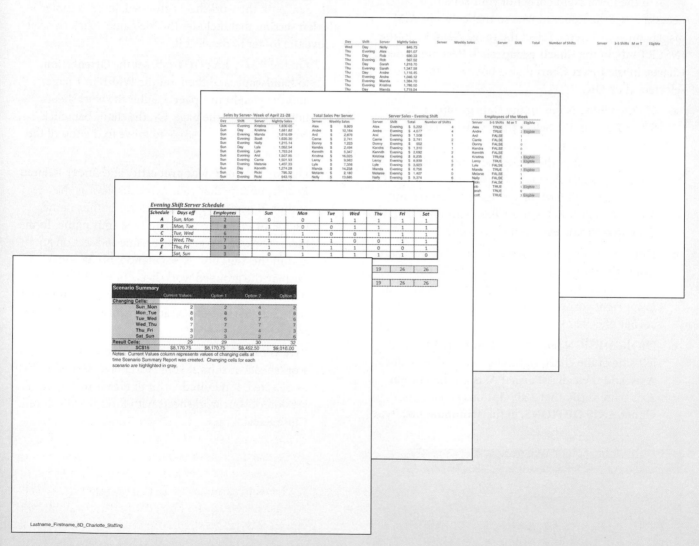

FIGURE 8.47

(Project 8D Charlotte Staffing continues on the next page)

1 Start Excel. Click the **DATA tab**, and then at the right end of the **DATA tab**, check to see if the **Analysis group** and **Solver** display. If **Solver** displays, Solver is installed; move to Step a. If Solver does *not* display, on the **FILE tab**, click **Options**. On the left, click **Add-Ins**, and then at the bottom of the screen, in the **Manage** box, if necessary, select **Excel Add-ins**. Click **Go**. Select the **Solver Add-in** check box, and then click **OK**.

a. From your student files, open the file **e08D_Charlotte_Staffing**. Display the **Save As** dialog box, navigate to your **Excel Chapter 8 folder**, and then **Save** the workbook as **Lastname_Firstname_8D_Charlotte_Staffing**

b. Examine the formulas in cells **C10**, **C14**, and **C15**. Click cell **C3**, and then click the **Name Box arrow**; notice that cell **C3** is named *Sun_Mon* and the other schedules also have been named.

c. Click cell **C15**—the objective cell. On the **DATA tab**, in the **Analysis group**, click **Solver**.

d. To the right of **To**, click **Min**. Click in the **By Changing Variable Cells** box, and then select the range **C3:C8**. To the right of the **Subject to the Constraints** area, click **Add** to add the first constraint. With the insertion point blinking in the **Cell Reference** box, select the range **C3:C8**. In the middle box, click the **arrow,** and then click **int**. Click **OK**—the result must be a whole number.

e. Click **Add** to add the second constraint. With the insertion point in the **Cell Reference** box, select the range **C3:C8**. In the middle box, click the **arrow,** and then click **>=**. In the **Constraint** box, type **0** Click **OK**.

f. Click **Add** to add the third constraint. In the **Cell Reference** box, select the range **E10:K10**. In the middle box, click the **arrow,** and then click **>=**. In the **Constraint** box, select the range **E12:K12**. Click **OK**; the result must be equal to or greater than the demand for each day. At the bottom of the **Solver Parameters** dialog box, click **Solve**. With **Keep Solver Solution** selected, click **OK**. Cell **C15** indicates *$8,170.75*.

2 Select the range **C3:C8**. On the **DATA tab**, in the **Data Tools group**, click **What-If Analysis**, and then click **Scenario Manager**. In the **Scenario Manager** dialog box, click **Add**. In the **Scenario Name** box, type **Option 1** Verify

that the **Changing cells** box displays *C3:C8*. Click **OK**. In the **Scenario Values** dialog box, click **OK**. In the **Scenario Manager** dialog box, click **Close**.

a. Click cell **C15**—the objective cell. On the **DATA tab**, in the **Analysis group**, click **Solver**. In the **Solver Parameters** dialog box, verify that the **Set Objective** box displays *$C$15* and the **By Changing Variable Cells** box displays *$C$3:$C$8*.

b. To the right of **Subject to the Constraints** box, click **Add** to add an additional constraint. In the **Add Constraint** dialog box, click the **Cell Reference** box, and then click cell **C3**. In the middle box, click the **arrow,** and then click **=**. In the **Constraint** box, type **4** Click **OK**; this constraint will raise the number of employees who have Sunday and Monday off to 4.

c. In the lower right corner of the dialog box, click **Solve**. Click **Save Scenario** to display the **Save Scenario** dialog box. In the **Scenario Name** box, type **Option 2** and then click **OK**. In the **Solver Results** dialog box, click **Restore Original Values**, and then click **OK**.

d. Verify that cell **C15** is still the active cell. On the **DATA tab**, in the **Analysis group**, click **Solver**. In the **Subject to the Constraints** box, select the fourth constraint—*Sun_Mon = 4*—and then click **Delete** to delete this constraint.

e. Click **Add**. In the **Add Constraint** dialog box, click in the **Cell Reference** box, and then select cell **C8**. Change the middle box to **=**. In the **Constraint** box, type **6** and then click **OK**; this constraint will raise the number of employees who have Saturday and Sunday off to 6.

f. Click **Solve**. Click **Save Scenario**. In the **Save Scenario** dialog box, type **Option 3** and then click **OK**. Click **Restore Original Values**, and then click **OK**.

g. On the **DATA tab**, in the **Data Tools group**, click **What-If Analysis**, and then click **Scenario Manager**. In the **Scenario Manager** dialog box, click **Summary**. Be sure **Scenario Summary** is selected, and then click **OK** to summarize the three options on a new worksheet. Select the range **D12:G12** and then, on the **HOME tab**, in the **Editing group**, click **AutoSum**.

3 Display the **Weekly Sales** worksheet. Click cell **G3**, and then type **=sumif(** Select the range **C3:C102** and

(Project 8D Charlotte Staffing continues on the next page)

CHAPTER REVIEW

press F4 to make the value absolute. Type , (a comma). Click cell **F3**, and then type , (a comma). Select the range **D3:D102** and press F4. Type) and then, on the **Formula Bar**, click **Enter**.

  a. Drag the fill handle to copy the formula down through cell **G19**. Format the range **G3:G19** using cell style **Currency [0]**.

  b. Select the range **F3:F19**. Right-click over the selection and click **Copy**. Right-click cell **I3** and click **Paste (P)**. Click cell **J3**, and then type **Evening** and then copy the cell down through **I19**.

  c. Click cell **K3** and type **=sumifs(** Select the range **D3:D102** and press F4 to make the value absolute. Type , (a comma), select the range **C3:C102**, and press F4. Type , (a comma). Click cell **I3**, and then type , (a comma). Select the range **B3:B102** and then press F4. Type , (a comma) and then click cell **J3**. Type) and then click **Enter**. Drag the fill handle to copy the formula down through cell **K19**. Format the range **K3:K19** using cell style **Currency [0]**.

  d. Click cell **L3** and type **=countifs(** Select the range **C3:C102** and press F4 to make the value absolute. Type , (a comma), click cell **I3**, and then type , (a comma). Select the range **B3:B102**, and then press F4. Type , (a comma) and then click cell **J3**. Type) and then click **Enter**. Drag the fill handle to copy the formula down through cell **L19**.

4 Click cell **N1** and type **Employees of the Week** and press Enter. **Merge & Center** the text over cells **N1:Q1** and apply the **Heading 2** cell style. In cell **N2** type **Server** In cell **O2** type **3-5 Shifts** In cell **P3** type **M or T** Copy the server names from **I3:I19** to **N3:N19**.

  a. Select the range **A3:A102**, in the **Name Box**, type **DAY** and then press Enter. Select the range **B3:B102**, in the **Name Box**, type **SHIFT** and then press Enter. Select the range **C3:C102**, in the **Name Box**, type **SERVER** and then press Enter.

  b. In cell **O3**, type **=and(** Click cell **L3**, type **>=3**, (include the comma). Click cell **L3** and type **<=5)** Click **Enter** and copy the formula down through cell **O19**.

  c. Click cell **P3**, and then type the formula **=countifs(server,n3,day,"Mon")** Click **Enter** and copy the formula down through cell **P19**. Click cell **P3** and in the **Formula Bar**, position the insertion point at the end of the formula. Type **+countifs(server,n3,day,"Tue")** Click **Enter** and copy the formula down through cell **P19**.

  d. Click cell **Q2**, type **Eligible** and then press Enter. In cell **Q3**, type **=if(and(o3, p3>=1),"Eligible","")** Click **Enter** and copy the formula down through cell **Q19**.

  e. Press Ctrl + Q to open **Quick Analysis** at the bottom of the selection, and then click **Text Contains**. In the **Text That Contains** dialog box, in the **Format cells that contain the text** box type **Eligible** Click the **with** arrow, and then click **Green Fill with Dark Green Text**. Click **OK**. On the **PAGE LAYOUT tab**, click **Print Titles**. Under **Print Titles**, click in the **Rows to repeat at top** box, and then from the **row heading area**, select **row 2**. Click **OK**.

5 Select all worksheets so that *[Group]* displays in the title bar. With the worksheets grouped, insert a footer in the **left section** that includes the file name. On the status bar, click **Normal**. Press Ctrl + Home.

  a. Set the **Orientation** to **Landscape**. Center the worksheets horizontally on the page and set the **Width** to **1 page**. Display the document properties and under **Related People**, be sure that your name displays as the author. If necessary, right-click the author name, click **Edit Property,** and then type your name. In the **Subject** box, type your course name and section #, and in the **Tags** box, **Charlotte, server schedule**

  b. Display the grouped worksheets in **Print Preview**. If necessary, return to the workbook and make any necessary corrections or adjustments. **Save** your workbook. **Print** or submit the two worksheets in this workbook electronically as directed by your instructor. If required, print or create an electronic version of your worksheets with formulas displayed. **Close** Excel.

END | You have completed Project 8D

Mastering Excel Project 8E Seafood Inventory

Apply 8A skills from these Objectives:

1 Calculate a Moving Average

2 Project Income and Expenses

3 Determine a Break-Even Point

In this Mastering Excel project, you will create a worksheet for Joe Flores, manager of the Dallas region, who wants to analyze the fluctuation in the quantity of shrimp that is used at the four Dallas restaurants. In this project, you will use the moving average tool to help identify the variation in shrimp usage in recipes over a four-week period. Your completed worksheets will look similar to Figure 8.48.

PROJECT FILES

For Project 8E, you will need the following file:

e08E_Seafood_Inventory

You will save your workbook as:

Lastname_Firstname_8E_Seafood_Inventory

PROJECT RESULTS

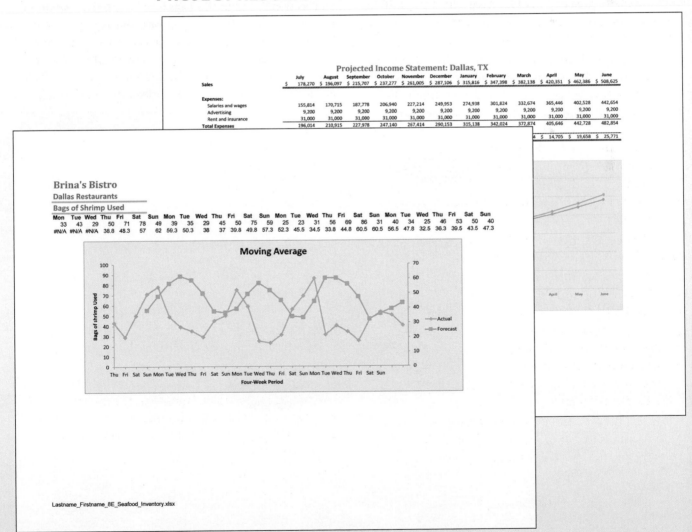

FIGURE 8.48

(Project 8E Seafood Inventory continues on the next page)

CONTENT-BASED ASSESSMENTS

1 Start Excel. From your student files, open the file **e08E_Seafood Inventory**, and then **Save** it in your **Excel Chapter 8** folder as **Lastname_Firstname_8E_Seafood_ Inventory** Be sure that the **Analysis ToolPak** is enabled.

2 On the **Moving Average** worksheet, insert a **Moving Average a5:ab5** as the **Input Range**, **4** as the **Interval**, and **a6** as the **Output Range**. Select the **Chart Output** check boxes. Do not select the Labels in First Row check box. Position the chart between cells **C8** and **Z29**. Edit the **Vertical (value) Axis Title** to **Bags of Shrimp Used** Edit the **Horizontal (Category) Axis Title** to **Four-Week Period**

3 Edit the **Horizontal (Category) Axis Labels** using the range **A4:AB4**.

4 Plot the **Forecast series on a secondary axis.** Format both the **Chart Area** and the **Plot Area** with a **Solid fill** using the color **Green, Accent 4, Lighter 80%**. Format the range **D6:AB6** with **0** decimal places.

5 Display the **Projected Income** worksheet. Click cell **C3**, type **=b3*(1+b13)** and **Copy** the formula across to cell **M3**. **Copy** the formula in cell **B9** across to cell **M9**. Select the range **A2:M3**, and then insert a **Line chart.**

Add the range **A9:M9** to the Line chart as a second series. Change the **Chart Title** to **Expected Break-Even Point**

6 Position the chart between cell **B15** and cell **M36**. Apply **Chart Style 12**. Format both the **Plot Area** and the **Chart Area** with a **Solid fill** using the color **Gold, Accent 1, Lighter 80%**.

7 Deselect the chart. Select all the sheets and insert a footer in the **left section** that includes the file name. Set the **Orientation** to **Landscape**, and set the **Width** to **1 page**. Center the worksheets horizontally. Click **Normal** and make cell **A1** active.

8 Display the **document properties** and, if necessary, edit the **Author** box, to display your firstname and your lastname. In the **Subject** box, type your course name and section #, and in the **Tags** box, type **Dallas, seafood inventory** Display the grouped worksheets in the **Print Preview**, make any necessary corrections, ungroup the worksheets, and **Save** your workbook. **Print** or submit your workbook electronically. If required, print or create an electronic version of your worksheets with formulas displayed.

END | You have completed Project 8E

Apply 8B skills from these Objectives:

4 Use Solver

5 Create Scenarios

6 Use Logical Functions

7 Create Complex Formulas

In this Mastering Excel project, you will assist Jillian Zachary, manager of the Ft. Lauderdale East restaurant, by using Solver to create several scenarios for how much of each of the three seafood ingredients—scallops, shrimp, and fish—to include in the chowder at the new seasonal prices to maintain a profit margin of 35 percent on a serving of chowder at the current wholesale seafood costs. Your completed worksheet will look similar to Figure 8.49.

PROJECT FILES

For Project 8F, you will need the following file:

e08F_Seafood_Chowder

You will save your workbook as:

Lastname_Firstname_8F_Seafood_Chowder

PROJECT RESULTS

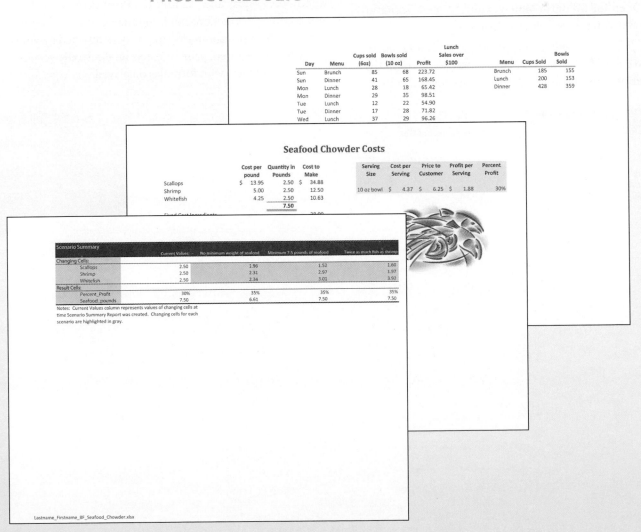

FIGURE 8.49

(Project 8F Seafood Chowder continues on the next page)

CONTENT-BASED ASSESSMENTS

1 Start Excel. From your student files, open the file **e08F_Seafood_Chowder**, and then **Save** the file in your **Excel Chapter 8** folder as **Lastname_Firstname_8F_ Seafood_Chowder** Be sure that **Solver** is installed.

2 With the **Seafood Chowder Costs** worksheet active, open **Solver**. Set the objective cell **$J$5** to the value of **35%** and set the variable cells to the range **C4:C6**. **Save** the scenario as **No minimum weight of seafood** and then restore the original values.

3 Open **Solver**. Add a constraint where cell **C7 >= 7.5** Click **Solve**. **Save** the scenario as **Minimum 7.5 pounds of seafood** and restore the original values.

4 Add a constraint where cell **C6 = c5*2** Click **Solve**. **Save** the scenario as **Twice as much fish as shrimp** Restore the original values.

5 Open the **Scenario Manager** and create a Scenario Summary using the result cells **J5** and **C7**.

6 Click the **Weekly Sales** worksheet. In cell **I2**, enter a **SUMIF** function that uses Named Ranges to count the number of cups of soup sold for each menu and copy the formula down through cell **I4**. In cells **J2:J4**, enter a **SUMIF** function to count the number of bowls of soup sold for each shift.

7 In the range **F2:F15**, enter an **IF** function with a nested **AND** function to test for lunch profits of at least $100. The function should return the word **BEST**, formatted with a red border for those days that meet both conditions, and leave the cells blank for days that do not.

8 Select **All Sheets** and insert a footer with the file name in the **left section**, center the worksheets horizontally, set the **Orientation** to **Landscape**, and then set the **Width** to **1 page**. Return to **Normal** view and make cell **A1** active. Display the **document properties**, add your name as the author, type your course name and section # in the **Subject** box, and as the **Tags**, type **seafood chowder, recipe costs Save** your workbook. Display and examine the **Print Preview**, make any necessary corrections, ungroup the worksheets, **Save**, and then **Print** or submit electronically as directed by your instructor. If required, print or create an electronic version of your worksheets with formulas displayed.

END | You have completed Project 8F

Mastering Excel   Project 8G Income Model

Apply 8A and 8B skills from these Objectives:

1 Calculate a Moving Average

2 Project Income and Expenses

3 Determine a Break-Even Point

4 Use Solver

5 Create Scenarios

6 Use Logical Functions

7 Create Complex Formulas

In this Mastering Excel project, you will assist Kelsey Tanner, CFO of Brina's Bistro, and use a worksheet model and use Solver to create several scenarios that would result in breaking even six months after opening. In this model for projecting the income, a new restaurant is expected to break even eight months after opening. Management wants to examine the assumptions and see what changes are needed to shorten the time it takes to break even. Month 0 is the first month of operation and it assumes that a new restaurant will gross $156,250 in sales in the opening month. The costs related to sales are assumed to be 87 percent; fixed costs are $40,000; and the anticipated growth rate in the first year, month-to-month, is 10 percent. The worksheet extends these assumptions out to month 11, which is the end of the first year of operation. Your completed worksheets will look similar to Figure 8.50.

PROJECT FILES

For Project 8G, you will need the following file:

e08G_Income_Model

You will save your workbook as:

Lastname_Firstname_8G_Income_Model

PROJECT RESULTS

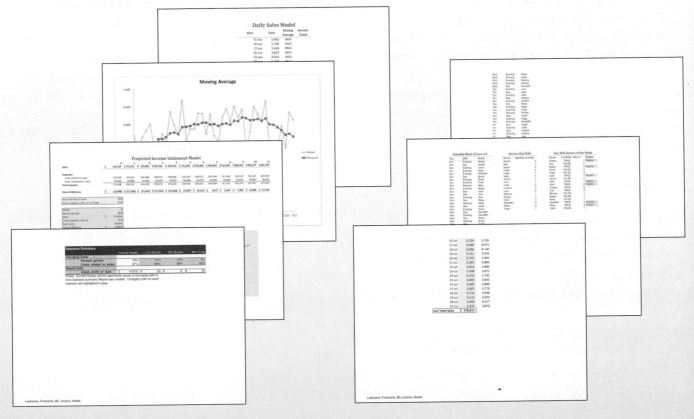

FIGURE 8.50

(Project 8G Income Model continues on the next page)

CONTENT-BASED ASSESSMENTS

1 From your student files, open **e08G_Income_Model**. **Save** the file as **Lastname_Firstname_8G_Income_Model** in your **Excel Chapter 8** folder. Take a moment to examine the **Projected Income** worksheet.

2 Change cell **B15** to **6** Notice in the green shaded area that *Sales* changes to *$276,806* and the *Gross Profit/Loss* changes to *($4,015)*. Note that these match the figures under Month 6 in cells **H3** and **H10**, respectively. Management wants to create several scenarios that would result in breaking even six months after opening.

3 Open **Solver**. Set the **objective cell** to *$B$20* to a **Value of 0** and set the **Variable Cells** to *$B$16,$B$18* to change both the growth rate (in cell **B16**) and the costs related to sales percent (in cell **B18**).

4 Click **Solve**. **Save** this scenario as **11% Growth** and restore the original values.

5 Display the **Solver Parameters** dialog box again. Add a constraint that requires **Percent growth** to be less than or equal to **10% Solve** and then **Save** this scenario as **10% Growth** Restore the original values.

6 Open the **Solver Parameters** dialog box. Delete the existing constraint. Add a constraint for the **Costs related to sales** to equal **85% Solve** and then **Save** the scenario as **85% Costs** Restore the original values.

7 Open the **Scenario Manager**. Create a **Scenario Summary** worksheet with a summary of the scenarios.

8 Display the **Projected Income** worksheet. Select the range **A2:M3**, insert a **Line chart**, and then, add the range **A8:M8** to the chart as a second series. Change the **Chart Title** to **Expected Break-Even Point** Position the chart between cell **B22** and cell **L40**. Format both the **Plot Area** and the **Chart Area** with a **Solid fill** using the color **Olive Green, Accent 4, Lighter 80%**. Add a **Horizontal (Category) Axis Title** with the text **Month Number**

9 Display the **Sales** worksheet. Create a **Moving Average**. As the **Input Range**, type **b2:b49** as the **Interval**

type **7** and as the **Output Range** type **c3** Select the **Labels in First Row** and **Chart Output** check boxes. Move the chart to a new sheet named **Sales Trend Chart**

10 Edit the **Horizontal (Category) Axis Labels** to display the range **A9:A49**. Format the **Horizontal (Category) Axis** using the **3/14 Date** format.

11 On the **Horizontal (Category) Axis**, change *Data Point* to **Date** On the **Vertical (Value) Axis**, set the *Minimum* to **3500** On this chart sheet, insert a custom footer with the file name in the **left section**.

12 Click the **Schedules sheet tab**. In the range **F3:F19**, enter a **COUNTIFS** function to count the number of day shifts each server is scheduled to work. In the range **I3:I19**, enter an **AND** function to determine which servers are scheduled for 2-5 day shifts. In the range **J3:J19**, enter a **COUNTIFS** function to calculate the number of Monday and Tuesday shifts each server is scheduled to work.

13 In the range **K3:K19**, enter an **IF** function with a nested **AND** function to determine which employees are scheduled for 2-5 day shifts, including a Monday or Tuesday. The function should return the word **Eligible** if true, and leave the cell blank if false.

14 Select all the sheets. Insert a footer with the file name in the **left section**, center the worksheets horizontally, and then set the **Orientation** to **Landscape** and the **Width** to **1 page** and **Height** to **2 pages**. Return to **Normal** view and make cell **A1** active. To the **document properties**, add your firstname and lastname as the **Author**, add your course name and section # as the **Subject**, and add **income, sales model** as the **Tags**. **Save** your workbook. Display and examine the **Print Preview**, make any necessary corrections, ungroup the worksheets, **Save**, and then **Print** or submit electronically as directed by your instructor. If required, print or create an electronic version of your worksheets with formulas displayed.

END | You have completed Project 8G

CONTENT-BASED ASSESSMENTS

GO! Fix It	Project 8H Maintenance Expenses	Online

GO! Make It	Project 8I Oyster Usage	Online

GO! Solve It	Project 8J Tampa Income	Online

GO! Solve It	Project 8K Oceana Salad	

PROJECT FILES

For Project 8K, you will need the following file:

e08K_Ahi_Salad

You will save your workbook as:

Lastname_Firstname_8K_Ahi_Salad

Open the file e08K_Ahi_Salad and save it as **Lastname_Firstname_8K_Ahi_Salad** Be sure that Solver is installed. Create three scenarios and a summary. Set the objective cell to J5, value of 60%. Solve for **No minimum weight of vegetables** by changing variable cells to the range C4:C6. Solve for **Minimum 5 pounds of vegetables** by using the constraints cell C5, >=, and 5. Solve for **Twice as many vegetables as greens** by using the constraints cell C5, =, C6*2. Create a Scenario Summary. On all sheets, insert the file name in the footer in the left section. Set the Orientation to Landscape, Width to 1 page, and center horizontally. Add appropriate information to the document properties including the tag **Ahi salad** and submit as directed by your instructor.

(Project 8K Oceana Salad continues on the next page)

CONTENT-BASED ASSESSMENTS

Performance Level

	Exemplary	Proficient	Developing
Use Solver to Create Scenarios	Three scenarios were created using Solver based on the instructions.	Two scenarios were created using Solver based on the instructions.	None or one scenario was created using Solver based on the instructions.
Create a Scenario Summary	A Scenario Summary listing three scenarios was created.	A Scenario Summary listing two scenarios was created.	A Scenario Summary was not created.

Performance Criteria (vertical label on left)

END | You have completed Project 8K

OUTCOMES-BASED ASSESSMENTS

RUBRIC

The following outcomes-based assessments are open-ended assessments. That is, there is no specific correct result; your result will depend on your approach to the information provided. Make Professional Quality your goal. Use the following scoring rubric to guide you in how to approach the problem and then to evaluate how well your approach solves the problem.

The *criteria*—Software Mastery, Content, Format and Layout, and Process—represent the knowledge and skills you have gained that you can apply to solving the problem. The *levels of performance*—Professional Quality, Approaching Professional Quality, or Needs Quality Improvements—help you and your instructor evaluate your result.

	Your completed project is of Professional Quality if you:	Your completed project is Approaching Professional Quality if you:	Your completed project Needs Quality Improvements if you:
1-Software Mastery	Choose and apply the most appropriate skills, tools, and features and identify efficient methods to solve the problem.	Choose and apply some appropriate skills, tools, and features, but not in the most efficient manner.	Choose inappropriate skills, tools, or features, or are inefficient in solving the problem.
2-Content	Construct a solution that is clear and well organized, contains content that is accurate, appropriate to the audience and purpose, and is complete. Provide a solution that contains no errors in spelling, grammar, or style.	Construct a solution in which some components are unclear, poorly organized, inconsistent, or incomplete. Misjudge the needs of the audience. Have some errors in spelling, grammar, or style, but the errors do not detract from comprehension.	Construct a solution that is unclear, incomplete, or poorly organized; contains some inaccurate or inappropriate content; and contains many errors in spelling, grammar, or style. Do not solve the problem.
3-Format & Layout	Format and arrange all elements to communicate information and ideas, clarify function, illustrate relationships, and indicate relative importance.	Apply appropriate format and layout features to some elements, but not others. Overuse features, causing minor distraction.	Apply format and layout that does not communicate information or ideas clearly. Do not use format and layout features to clarify function, illustrate relationships, or indicate relative importance. Use available features excessively, causing distraction.
4-Process	Use an organized approach that integrates planning, development, self-assessment, revision, and reflection.	Demonstrate an organized approach in some areas, but not others; or, use an insufficient process of organization throughout.	Do not use an organized approach to solve the problem.

OUTCOMES-BASED ASSESSMENTS

GO! Think   Project 8L Seasonings Inventory

PROJECT FILES

For Project 8L, you will need the following file:

e08L_Seasonings_Inventory

You will save your workbook as:

Lastname_Firstname_8L_Seasonings_Inventory

Open the file e08L_Seasonings_Inventory, and then save it in your chapter folder as **Lastname_Firstname_8L_Seasonings_Inventory** From the source data, create a Moving Average chart to help identify the variation in seafood seasoning used over a four-week period using a seven-day interval. Begin the output range in cell A6. Move the chart to a new sheet. Format the chart attractively. Insert the file name in the left section of the footer on each page, center horizontally, set the Orientation to Landscape, add appropriate information to the document properties, including the tag **seasonings inventory** and submit as directed by your instructor.

END | You have completed Project 8L

GO! Think   Project 8M PT Staff   Online

Build from
Scratch

You and GO!   Project 8N Entertainment   Online

Using Macros and Visual Basic for Applications

GO! to Work
Video E9

PROJECT 9A

OUTCOMES
Record a macro to automate complex and repetitive tasks.

OBJECTIVES
1. Record a Macro
2. Assign a Macro to a Button on the Quick Access Toolbar
3. Modify a Macro

PROJECT 9B

OUTCOMES
Ensure accuracy and automate instructions using VBA commands and ActiveX Controls.

OBJECTIVES
4. Write a VBA Procedure to Use an ActiveX Control
5. Restore Initial Settings

FotolEdhar/Fotolia

In This Chapter

In this chapter, you will automate Excel worksheets to make it easier and faster to perform complex or repetitive tasks. Because individuals who do the same type of work each day may use a specific sequence of Excel commands repeatedly, Excel enables you to record a sequence of commands in a macro and then activate the sequence with a single button or keystroke. A button can be attached to the macro and placed on the worksheet or ribbon. You can also program Excel to perform tasks that are not represented by existing commands or to validate data against complex criteria that requires more than a simple comparison.

The projects in this chapter relate to **Westland Plains Human Resources Consulting**. WPHR provides its customers with services such as Employee Benefits Administration, Recruitment Services, Payroll Processing, Computer Technology Training, Employee Assistance Programs, and Corporate Health and Wellness Programs. Customers are typically small and mid-size companies who, for cost savings and efficiency, use an outside source for such services. Westland has a staff of 35 full-time employees throughout the region. Westfield's knowledgeable consultants help companies remain compliant with federal and state laws and regulations.

PROJECT ACTIVITIES

In Activities 9.01 through 9.07, you will set a macro security level, remove file protection, record a macro, and assign a macro to the Quick Access Toolbar. You will test and modify a macro to fill in employee information for a Travel Expense Report, and protect the worksheet. Your completed project will look similar to Figure 9.1.

PROJECT FILES

For Project 9A, you will need the following file:

e09A_Travel_Macro

You will save your workbook as:

Lastname_Firstname_9A_Travel_Macro

PROJECT RESULTS

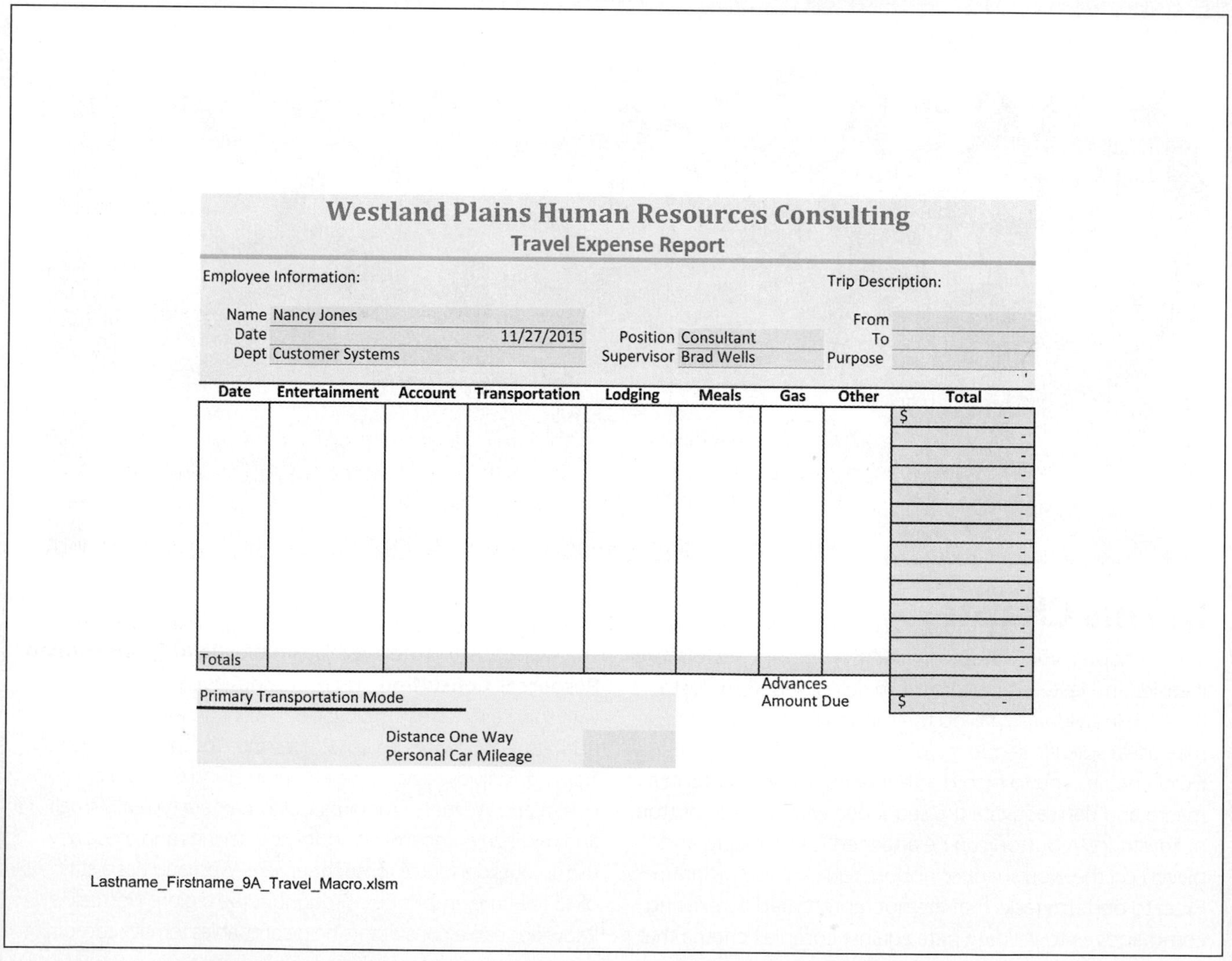

Westland Plains Human Resources Consulting
Travel Expense Report

Employee Information: Trip Description:

Name	Nancy Jones		From	
Date		11/27/2015	Position	Consultant	To	
Dept	Customer Systems		Supervisor	Brad Wells	Purpose	

Date	Entertainment	Account	Transportation	Lodging	Meals	Gas	Other	Total
								$ -
								-
								-
								-
								-
								-
								-
								-
								-
Totals								-

Primary Transportation Mode

Advances
Amount Due $ -

Distance One Way
Personal Car Mileage

Lastname_Firstname_9A_Travel_Macro.xlsm

FIGURE 9.1 Project 9A Travel Expenses

<table>
<tr><td>N O T E</td><td>If You Are Using a Touchscreen</td></tr>
</table>

- Tap an item to click it.
- Press and hold for a few seconds to right-click; release when the information or commands display.
- Touch the screen with two or more fingers and then pinch together to zoom in or stretch your fingers apart to zoom out.
- Slide your finger on the screen to scroll—slide left to scroll right and slide right to scroll left.
- Slide to rearrange—similar to dragging with a mouse.
- Swipe from edge: from right to display charms; from left to expose open apps, snap apps, or close apps; from top or bottom to show commands or close an app.
- Swipe to select—slide an item a short distance with a quick movement—to select an item and bring up commands, if any.

Objective 1   Record a Macro

Video E9-1

A **macro** is an action or a set of actions with which you can automate tasks by grouping a series of commands into a single command. You can perform the command with a single mouse click, a keyboard shortcut, or when a workbook opens.

For example, you could record a macro that automatically enters employee names in the first column, alphabetizes the names, and then applies a fill color to the cells containing the names. When you have a sequence of actions that you perform frequently, record the actions as a macro to automate the task.

Macros are recorded in the **Visual Basic for Applications** programming language—also referred to as **VBA**—which is the language used to write computer programs within the Microsoft Windows environment.

To work with macros, you must:

- Add the DEVELOPER tab to the ribbon, which displays the commands you will need to work with macros.
- Select a macro security setting to enable macros when using Excel.
- Save the workbook that includes macros as an Excel Macro-Enabled Workbook file type.

Activity 9.01   Adding the Developer Tab to the Ribbon

The macro commands are located on the DEVELOPER tab, which, by default, does not display in Excel. You must enable the DEVELOPER tab from the Excel Options dialog box. In this activity, you will add the DEVELOPER tab to the ribbon.

1 Start Excel and open a new blank workbook. Click the **FILE** tab to display **Backstage** view, and then click **Options**.

2 In the **Excel Options** dialog box, on the left, click **Customize Ribbon**. On the right, under **Customize Ribbon:** verify **Main Tabs** is selected, select the **Developer** check box, and then compare your screen with Figure 9.2.

FIGURE 9.2

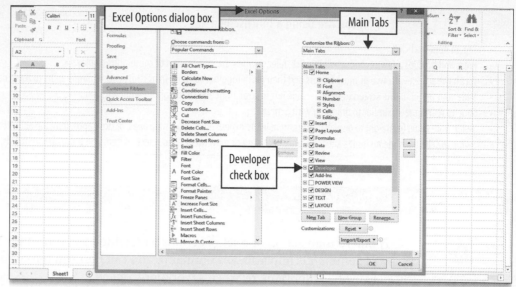

3 In the lower right corner, click **OK**. On the ribbon, click the **DEVELOPER tab**, and then compare your screen with Figure 9.3.

> The *DEVELOPER tab* displays on the ribbon. The *Code group* contains the commands you will need to work with macros.

FIGURE 9.3

Activity 9.02 | Changing the Macro Security Settings in Excel

Opening an Excel workbook that has a macro attached to it might cause a message to display, indicating that macros are disabled. To enable the macro in the workbook, you must set the security level on your computer to allow the option of enabling the macros. The security concern regarding macros is because macros might contain viruses. Because a macro is a computer program, programming code that erases or damages files can be inserted by the person creating the macro. This unauthorized code is called a ***macro virus***. In this activity, you will change the security setting so that you can choose to enable macros when you open a workbook that contains a macro.

Excel provides safeguards that help protect against viruses that can be transmitted by macros. If you share macros with others, you can certify them with a digital signature so that other users can verify that they are from a trustworthy source. A ***digital signature*** is an electronic, encryption-based, secure stamp of authentication on a macro or document. The digital signature confirms that the macro or document originated from the signer and has not been altered. If a file has been digitally signed, a certificate that identifies the source displays; then you can decide whether this is a trusted source before you activate the macros.

1 ▶ On the **DEVELOPER tab**, in the **Code group**, click **Macro Security**. Compare your screen with Figure 9.4, and then take a moment to study the table in Figure 9.5.

The Trust Center dialog box displays. On the left, Macro Settings is selected. The Macro Settings enable you to decide, each time you open a workbook, how or whether to run the macros that are contained in the workbook. The table in Figure 9.5 summarizes how macro virus protection works under each setting. Regardless of which option you choose, any installed antivirus software that works with your Microsoft Office software will scan the workbook for known viruses before it is opened. In an organization, you may not be permitted to change these settings without permission from your System Administrator. Any macro setting changes that you make in Excel in the Macro Settings category apply only to Excel and do not affect any other Office program.

FIGURE 9.4

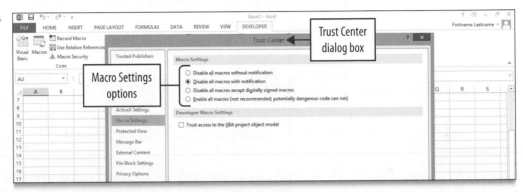

FIGURE 9.5

MACRO SETTINGS AND THEIR EFFECTS	
MACRO SETTING	**DESCRIPTION**
Disable all macros without notification	This setting disables all macros and security alerts unless the Excel document is in a trusted location.
Disable all macros with notification	This setting is enabled by default. You are alerted if macros are present in the workbook. This setting enables you to choose each time you open a workbook whether or not to run the macros that are contained in the workbook.
Disable all macros except digitally signed macros	This setting enables macros from trusted publishers to run; otherwise, this setting is the same as the disable all macros with notification setting.
Enable all macros (not recommended; potentially dangerous code can run)	Use this setting when you want to enable all macros to run on a temporary basis. It is not recommended as a permanent setting because it makes your computer vulnerable to potential malicious code.

2 ▶ Under **Macro Settings**, verify that the default option—**Disable all macros with notification**—is selected, and then click **OK**.

By choosing this option, you decide each time you open a workbook whether or not to run the macros that are contained in the workbook. Consequently, when you attempt to open a workbook that contains a macro, Excel prompts you with a Security Warning. By selecting the security level *Disable all macros with notification*, you have the option of enabling macros on a file-by-file basis. Doing so allows you to use macros if the file is from a trusted source. This security level causes a Security Warning to display, indicating that macros have been disabled, and gives you the option to enable or disable macros.

N O T E   **Message Bar Security Warnings**

When you open a macro-enabled workbook, a Security Warning may display advising you that macros in the file have been disabled.
If you get an information message that indicates you cannot open the workbook, you will want to confirm that your computer will display the Message Bar.
To set the Message Bar to display, do the following: On the left side of the Excel Options dialog box, click Trust Center. Under Microsoft Excel Trust Center, at the right, click Trust Center Settings. On the left side of the Trust Center dialog box, click Message Bar and at the right, confirm that Show the Message Bar in all applications when active content has been blocked is selected. Click OK two times to close both dialog boxes.

Project 9A: Travel Expenses | Excel **511**

3 From your student files, open the file **e09A_Travel_Macro**. Display the **Save As** dialog box, navigate to the location where you will save your projects for this chapter, and then create a new folder for **Excel Chapter 9**

4 Click the **Save as type arrow**, and then click **Excel Macro-Enabled Workbook**. In the **File name** box, type **Lastname_Firstname_9A_Travel_Macro** and then compare your screen with Figure 9.6.

Selecting *Excel Macro-Enabled Workbook* saves the Excel file in the XML-based format, allowing macros to be saved to the workbook.

FIGURE 9.6

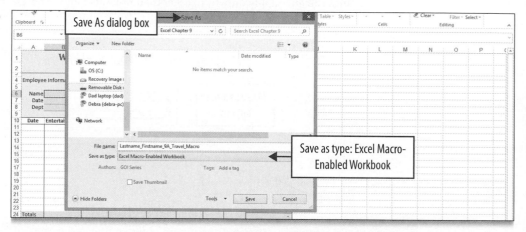

5 Click **Save**. Insert a footer in the **left section** that includes the file name. Return to **Normal** view and scroll to view the top of the worksheet. Display the **document properties** and under **Related People**, be sure that your name displays as the author. If necessary, right-click the author name, click Edit Property, and then type your name. In the **Subject** box, type your course name and section #, and in the **Tags** box, type **travel expense form, macro**

6 Save ⊞ your workbook.

Activity 9.03 | Unprotecting a Workbook

This workbook is a form that employees of Westland Plains Human Resources Consulting use to report travel expenses. A *form* is a worksheet or Excel object that contains fields and controls that enable a user to easily enter or edit data. The worksheet is protected so that employees can fill in their travel expense information only in the unlocked cells. A worksheet must be *unprotected* to record a macro.

1 On the **REVIEW tab**, in the **Changes group**, click **Protect Workbook**.

2 In the **Unprotect Workbook** dialog box, type **goseries** which is the password applied to this form, and then click **OK**.

Activity 9.04 | Recording a Macro

The macro recorder records all the steps (keystrokes and mouse clicks) that you require to complete the actions you want your macro to perform—*except* for navigation on the ribbon, which is not included in the recorded steps. When you record a macro, assign it a name so that you can refer to the macro name later. In this activity, you will record a macro that will fill in employee information for a specific employee on a Travel Expense form.

1 ▸ Click the **DEVELOPER tab**, and then, in the **Code group**, click **Record Macro**.

The Record Macro dialog box displays. Here, you name the macro, assign a shortcut key, and start the recording. The *Record Macro* command records your actions in VBA.

⟳ **ANOTHER WAY**   On the VIEW tab, in the Macros group, click the Macros button arrow, and then click Record Macro.

2 ▸ In the **Macro name** box, delete the existing text, and then type **Employee_Info**

The first character of the macro name must be a letter. Following characters can be letters, numbers, or underscore characters. Spaces are not permitted in a macro name; an underscore character works well as a word separator. Do not use a macro name that could be a cell reference—you will get an error message that the macro name is not valid.

3 ▸ In the **Shortcut key** box, type **r**

You can create a shortcut key to execute the macro, in this instance *Ctrl + r*. If you do not specify a shortcut key at the time you create the macro, you can add it later. Shortcut keys are case sensitive.

> **N O T E**   **Assigning Shortcut Keys to a Macro**
>
> The Excel program uses shortcut keys for common commands, such as Ctrl + S for saving a file or Ctrl + P for printing a file. When you assign a shortcut key to a macro, it takes precedence over the shortcut keys that are built into Excel. For this reason, use caution when you assign a shortcut key so that you do not override an existing shortcut. To see a list of Excel shortcut keys, in the Excel Help files, in the Search window box, type *keyboard shortcuts*, and then examine the topic *Keyboard shortcuts in Excel*.

4 ▸ Click the **Store macro in arrow** to see the available options.

You can store a macro in *This Workbook*—the default setting—in *New Workbook*, or in a *Personal Macro Workbook*. The *New Workbook* option opens a new workbook and adds the macro to that workbook. The *Personal Macro Workbook* is a workbook where you can store macros that you want to be able to use in other workbooks.

5 ▸ Be sure **This Workbook** is selected, and then click the **Store macro in arrow** to close the list. Click in the **Description** box. Type **Fills in the Employee Information section** Compare your screen with Figure 9.7.

FIGURE 9.7

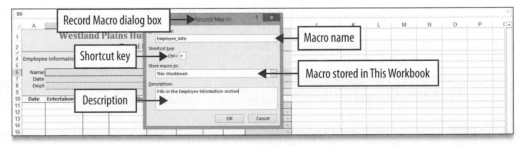

6 ▸ Click **OK**, and in the status bar in the lower left corner of your screen, notice the white square button indicating that a macro is recording.

The macro recorder is turned on. From this point forward, every action you take will be recorded as part of the macro. Be assured that the amount of time you take between actions is not being recorded, so there is no need to rush. If you make an error, take the appropriate steps to correct it; the corrective steps will simply become part of the macro, and you can edit the mistakes out of the macro later.

7 Click cell **B6**, type **Nancy Jones** and then press Enter. With cell **B7** active, hold down Ctrl and press ; (semicolon), which will insert the current date. Press Enter.

8 With cell **B8** active, type **Customer Systems** In cell **F7**, type **Consultant** and then press Enter. In cell **F8**, type **Brad Wells** and then click cell **A11**, so that when the macro completes, the first cell in the data area is active to begin filling in the travel information.

9 On the **DEVELOPER tab**, in the **Code group**, click **Stop Recording**. Compare your screen with Figure 9.8.

> The macro stops recording and cell A11 is selected. The Stop Recording button returns to a Record Macro button on the ribbon. In the status bar, if you point to the button to the right of *Ready*, the ScreenTip indicates *No macros are currently recording. Click to begin recording a new macro.*

FIGURE 9.8

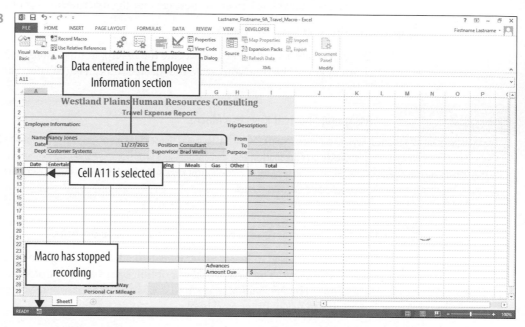

10 Delete the text you just typed in the five cells—**B6**, **B7**, **B8**, **F7**, **F8**. Then, to test that your macro will fill in the employee information and the date, run the macro by pressing the shortcut key Ctrl + R.

> The shortcut key activates the macro, the employee information is filled in, and cell A11 is selected.

11 Save 🖫 your workbook.

Objective 2   Assign a Macro to a Button on the Quick Access Toolbar

Video E9-2

You have practiced activating a macro with a keyboard shortcut, but another option is to activate a macro by clicking a button on the Quick Access Toolbar. To do so, you must create a new toolbar button. Then, when you use the workbook, you can click the button on the Quick Access Toolbar to activate the macro.

Activity 9.05   Adding a Button to the Quick Access Toolbar

In the following activity, you will add a button to the Quick Access Toolbar. Buttons that you add to the Quick Access Toolbar become a permanent part of the toolbar to which it was added unless you specifically remove it or reset the Quick Access Toolbar.

1 Click the **FILE tab**, click **Options** to display the **Excel Options** dialog box, and then on the left, click **Quick Access Toolbar**.

2 Click the **Choose commands from arrow**, and then click **Macros**. Compare your screen with Figure 9.9.

Under <Separator>, your Employee_Info macro and a default icon display.

FIGURE 9.9

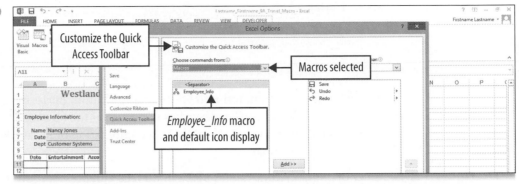

3 Click your **Employee_Info** macro, and then in the center of the dialog box click **Add**. Compare your screen with Figure 9.10.

The Employee_Info macro displays on the right in the panel that contains buttons that currently display on the Quick Access Toolbar.

FIGURE 9.10

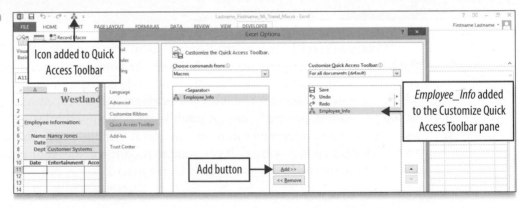

4 With your **Employee_Info** command selected on the right, click **Modify**. Compare your screen with Figure 9.11.

The Modify Button dialog box displays. The first symbol is selected and at the bottom of the dialog box, Display name indicates *Employee_Info*.

FIGURE 9.11

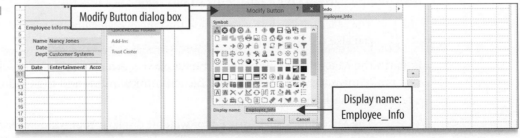

5 Under **Symbol**, in the fourth row, click the last icon—the **Smiley Face**—and then click **OK** two times. **Save** 🖫 your workbook, and then compare your screen with Figure 9.12.

The Smiley Face icon displays on the Quick Access Toolbar.

FIGURE 9.12

The Smiley Face icon displays on the Quick Access Toolbar

Activity 9.06 | Testing the Macro Button

After you add the button, test it to verify that the button performs as you intended. When you point to the button, the ScreenTip describes the name of the button. The action that causes your macro to run is called an *event* and might be a combination of keystrokes or the click of a button on the Quick Access Toolbar.

1 Select the nonadjacent ranges **B6:B8** and **F7:F8** and press Del so that these cells are empty again.

2 On the **Quick Access Toolbar**, click your new **Employee_Info** button—the Smiley Face.

The employee information is filled in, and cell A11 is selected.

Objective 3 | Modify a Macro

Video E9-3

When you record a macro, the Record Macro command stores the macro in a module using the VBA programming language. A *module* is the programming code written in VBA when you record a new macro, the place where the VBA code is stored. A module consists of *procedures*, which is a unit of computer code that performs an action. Procedures are commonly referred to as *sub procedures*, or simply *subs*. A module can contain several sub procedures. VBA is used to write computer programs within the Microsoft Windows environment. As your actions are recorded, VBA code is created. If you want to modify the way your macro performs, you can modify the actual code that was created by the macro.

Activity 9.07 | Changing the Visual Basic Code

You can view and edit the module containing the Visual Basic code in the *Visual Basic Editor* window. In this activity, you will open the module that was created for the *Employee_Info* macro, examine the VBA code, and then modify the code to add the action of centering the worksheet both horizontally and vertically.

1 On the **DEVELOPER tab,** in the **Code group**, click **Macros**.

The Macro dialog box displays and the *Employee_Info* macro is listed. From this dialog box, you can also run the macro.

2 In the Macro dialog box, with the **Employee_Info** macro selected, click **Edit**. If necessary, maximize the Microsoft Visual Basic Editor window and the Code window. Compare your screen with Figure 9.13.

The Microsoft Visual Basic Editor window displays. Your window may be configured differently than the one shown in Figure 9.13. This window has several panes that can be displayed, and some of the available panes may be opened or closed.

FIGURE 9.13

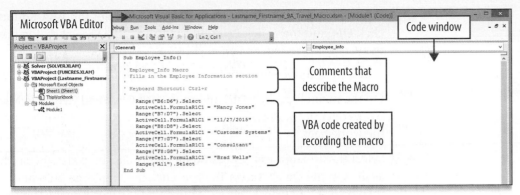

3 ▶ In the **Code window** on the right, locate the green and black lines of text that comprise the comments and code for the Employee_Info macro.

The first section, displayed in green and in lines preceded by an apostrophe ('), consists of comments that describe the macro. These comments do not affect the function of the macro. Here, the comments include the data you entered when you created the macro—the macro name and description and the shortcut key that was assigned.

The VBA code that follows, in black type, includes the instructions to select the cell ranges and enter data. *Sub* indicates the beginning of the sub procedure. *End Sub* indicates the end of the sub procedure.

4 ▶ At the end of the *last* line of code—*Range("A11"). Select*—click to place the insertion point after *Select*, and then press Enter.

In this manner, you can insert a blank line to type new code.

5 ▶ On the new, empty line type **With ActiveSheet.PageSetup** and then press Enter.

The word *With* notes the beginning of a **VBA construct**—an instruction that enables the macro to perform multiple operations on a single object.

6 ▶ Press Tab to indent and type **.CenterHorizontally = True** Press Enter and type **.CenterVertically = True** and then press Enter.

The two centering commands are indented to make it easier to read the code. Verify that you typed the period preceding each line of code. The period identifies the command that follows. Instructions that have a beginning and ending statement, such as *With* and *End With* should be indented at the same level. You can indent code by using the Tab key. After you have indented to a certain level, when you press Enter the text will continue to wrap to that same level of indentation. To decrease the level of indentation, press Shift + Tab, which will move the indentation toward the left margin.

7 ▶ Press Shift + Tab, and then type **End With** Compare your screen with Figure 9.14.

FIGURE 9.14

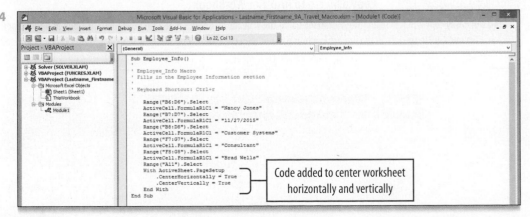

8 If you are directed to print your code, at the top of the **VBA Editor** window, on the menu bar, click **File**, and then click **Print**. In the **Print - VBAProject** dialog box, under **Print What**, verify that **Code** is selected, and then click **OK**.

A copy of your code will print to the default printer on your computer.

9 On the menu bar, click **File**, and then click **Close and Return to Microsoft Excel**. Press Ctrl + F2 to open **Print Preview.** Verify the worksheet is not centered on the page, and return ⊙ to the worksheet.

10 Select the nonadjacent ranges **B6:B8** and **F7:F8** and press Del so that these cells are empty again. On the **Quick Access Toolbar**, click the **Employee_Info** button that you created, and then display the **Print Preview**. Notice that the worksheet is centered both horizontally and vertically. Compare your screen with Figure 9.15.

FIGURE 9.15

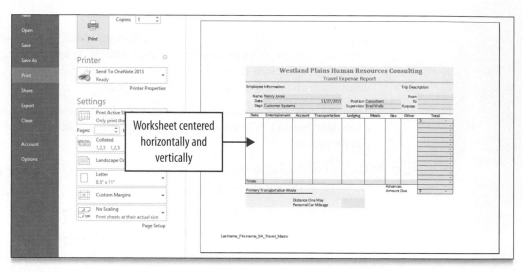

11 **Save** your workbook, and then print or submit it electronically as directed. **Close** Excel.

More **Knowledge**   **Copy a Macro to Another Workbook**

You can easily copy a macro to another workbook using the VBA Editor. Be sure that both Excel files are open, and then open the VBA Editor for the macro that you wish to copy. On the left, in the Project Explorer pane of the editor, both worksheets will be listed. Simply drag the selected module to the destination worksheet.

END | You have completed Project 9A

VBA Procedure

PROJECT ACTIVITIES

In Activities 9.08 through 9.13, you will assist Edward Salisbury, Controller at Westland Plains Human Resources Consulting, by writing a set of commands in the VBA programming language using ActiveX Control buttons to automate the travel policy guidelines for expense reports. Your completed workbook will look similar to Figure 9.16.

PROJECT FILES

For Project 9B, you will need the following file:
e09B_Travel_VBA

You will save your workbook as:
Lastname_Firstname_9B_Travel_VBA

PROJECT RESULTS

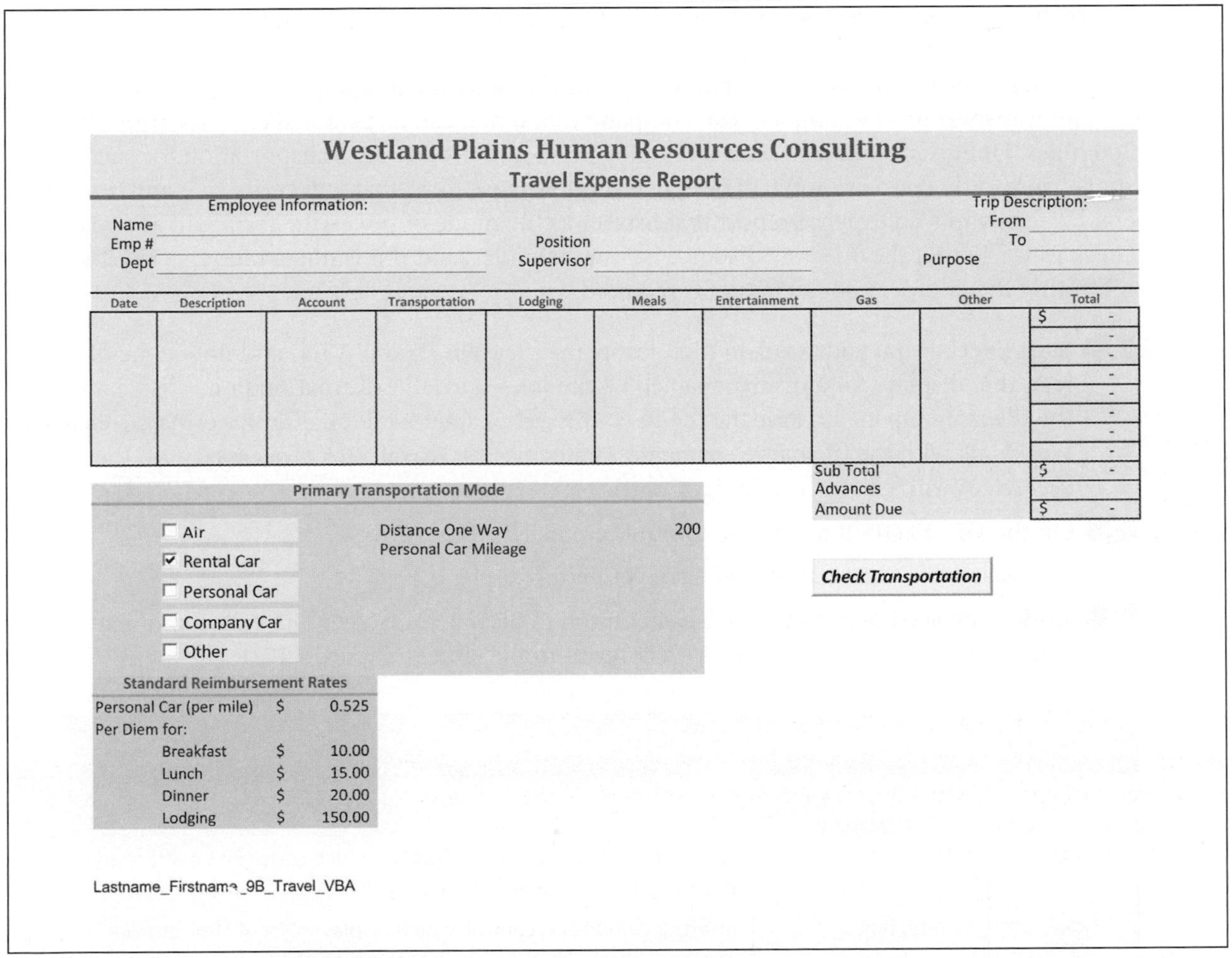

FIGURE 9.16 Project 9B VBA Procedure

Video E9-4

Within VBA, you can write a procedure that will insert an ActiveX control into your worksheet. A procedure is a named sequence of statements in a computer program that performs a task. An *ActiveX control* is a graphic object, such as a check box or a button that can be placed on a worksheet or form to display or enter data, to perform an action, or to make the form easier to read. When the person filling in the form clicks the ActiveX control, VBA code runs that automates a task or offers options.

A *Form control* is a simpler object that does not require VBA code (therefore it works in other versions of Excel that do not support ActiveX). You can assign a macro directly to a Form control without using the VBA Editor. Unlike ActiveX controls, you can put a Form control on a chart sheet. A Form control is formatted by right-clicking to open a Format dialog box, which has fewer formatting options than the ActiveX Properties pane. ActiveX controls are more flexible and customizable than Form controls.

Activity 9.08 | Inserting ActiveX Controls

ActiveX controls are especially useful for forms that individuals complete online, because you can control different events that occur when the control is used. In the following activity, you will insert check boxes. A *check box* is a type of ActiveX control that the person filling in the form can select to indicate a choice.

Westland Plains Human Resources Consulting has a policy that requires employees to use ground transportation—company car, company van, rental car, or personal car—for trips under 200 miles. Unless absolutely necessary, employees should not use air transportation for such short trips. In this project, you will design a travel expense form that will verify that any time an employee submits an expense report that lists air as the mode of travel, the form will automatically check to verify that the one-way distance is over 200 miles, and if it is not, a message will display indicating that a supervisor signature is required.

1 Start Excel. From your student files, locate the file **e09B_Travel_VBA**, and notice the file icon that displays for a macro-enabled workbook—a small exclamation point displays on the file icon. Open and **Save** the file in your **Excel Chapter 9** folder as an **Excel Macro-Enabled Workbook** with the file name **Lastname_Firstname_9B_Travel_VBA** If necessary, on the **Security Warning bar**, click **Enable Content**.

2 On the **DEVELOPER tab**, in the **Controls group**, click **Insert**.

A gallery of Form Controls and ActiveX Controls displays.

3 Under **ActiveX Controls**, point to each button to display the ScreenTip. Take a moment to study the description of the ActiveX controls in the table in Figure 9.17.

FIGURE 9.17

ACTIVEX CONTROLS		
BUTTON	**SCREENTIP**	**DESCRIPTION**
▫	Command Button	Inserts a command button control to which code can be attached, initiating an action when clicked.
🗔	Combo Box	Inserts a combo box control, which displays a list of choices from another source; the user can either select a choice from the list or type his or her own entry in the box.
☑	Check Box	Inserts a check box control that can be turned on (selected) or turned off (cleared).
🖻	Image	Inserts an image control to embed a picture.

ACTIVEX CONTROLS		
BUTTON	**SCREENTIP**	**DESCRIPTION**
A	Label	Inserts a text label to provide information about a control.
	List Box	Inserts a list box control, which displays a list of choices.
	More Controls	Displays a list of additional controls.
	Option Button	Inserts an option button control to indicate an on/off choice.
	Scroll Bar	Inserts a scroll bar control, which scrolls through a range of values.
	Spin Button	Inserts a spin button control, which displays a range of numbers from which the user can increase or decrease a value.
abl	Text Box	Inserts a text box control in which the user can type text.
	Toggle Button	Inserts a toggle button control, which remains pressed in when clicked, and then releases when clicked again.

4 Under **ActiveX Controls**, click **Check Box** ☑ and notice that the mouse pointer changes to the ☐ shape.

5 Point to the upper left corner of cell **B20** and drag to insert a check box object that is approximately the height of the cell and the width of columns **B:C**. Compare your screen with Figure 9.18. The size and placement need not be exact—you will adjust the size and placement later. If you are not satisfied with your result, click **Undo** and begin again, or use the sizing handles to adjust the size.

The object name—*CheckBox1*—displays in the check box and also displays in the Name Box. An EMBED formula displays on the Formula Bar.

The formula defines the object as an embedded object and includes the name of the object source. Recall that to **embed** means to insert something created in one program into another program. ActiveX controls are not part of Excel but may be added to it. This provides other software vendors and individuals the opportunity to write ActiveX controls to handle a wide variety of desired actions. The More Controls button at the end of the ActiveX Controls gallery lists many additional ActiveX controls, and there are more available for download from the Internet.

FIGURE 9.18

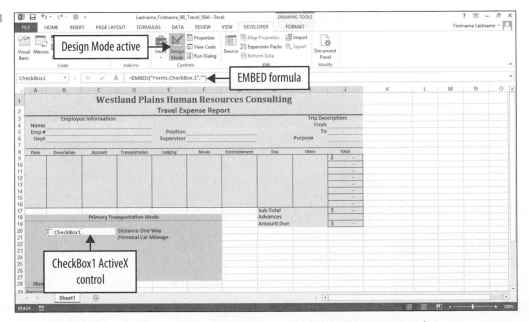

6 Repeat this process to add four more check boxes of the same approximate size under **CheckBox1**. Verify that the boxes do not overlap—leave a slight space between each box. Try to keep the check boxes within the tan shaded area, but the exact size and placement need not be precise—you will adjust them later. Use any technique for moving and sizing objects that you have practiced, and then compare your screen with Figure 9.19.

ActiveX controls are not attached to cells—rather, they float on the worksheet like inserted Shapes or SmartArt. When you are adding ActiveX controls to your worksheet, you are working in *Design Mode*. This mode or view enables you to work with the controls. When you want to return to the worksheet, click Design Mode to toggle it off. In the worksheet, you could use the Go To command to go to the cell where an ActiveX control sits and select the cell, but not the ActiveX control that floats on top of the cell.

FIGURE 9.19

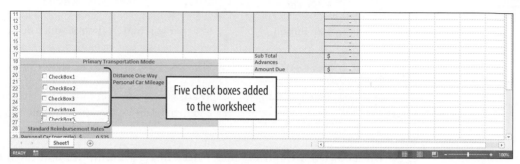

7 Click **CheckBox1**, and then on the **DEVELOPER tab**, in the **Controls group**, notice that **Design Mode** is active.

When you add controls, the Design Mode is activated. Use the Design Mode button to move in and out of Design Mode.

8 With **CheckBox1** selected, hold down Ctrl, and click on each of the remaining check boxes so that all five check boxes are selected.

9 On the **PAGE LAYOUT tab**, in the **Arrange group**, click **Align**, and then click **Align Left** to align the check boxes on the left. **Save** 🖫 your workbook.

Activity 9.09 | Changing the Properties of an ActiveX Control

Each ActiveX control has a set of *properties*—characteristics—that you can change. This is similar to formatting a shape by changing its color, font, or some other property. There are many properties associated with ActiveX controls, and the properties vary depending on the type of control. In this activity, you will change the name of each of the five check boxes, change the caption that displays in each check box, and change the height and width of each check box.

1 Click the **DEVELOPER tab**. In the **Controls group**, verify that **Design Mode** is active.

2 Click another area of the worksheet to deselect the group of check boxes, and then click **CheckBox1** to select the check box. In the **Controls group**, click **Properties**. Drag the **Properties** pane near the upper right of your screen, and then expand and widen its lower edge so that you can see the entire list of properties, as shown in Figure 9.20.

The properties are organized in alphabetical order on the *Alphabetic* tab. On the *Categorized* tab, the same properties are listed, but they are organized by logical groups. You can click the arrow at the top of the dialog box to display a list from which you can select the object whose properties you want to modify.

ALERT!   **Properties Pane Problems**

If your Properties pane does not display the properties for CheckBox1, you may have inserted a Form control, rather than an ActiveX control. Delete your check boxes and re-create them being sure to choose the ActiveX control from the Controls Gallery.

FIGURE 9.20

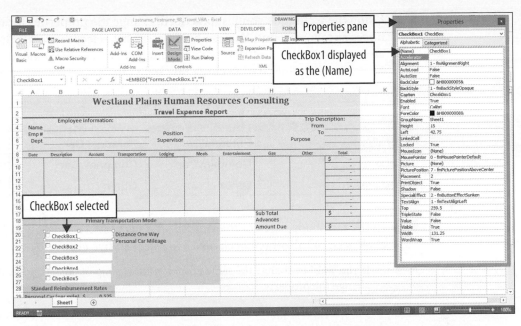

3 At the top of the **Alphabetic** list, in the first column, click **(Name)**, and then type **Air** Notice that your typing displays in the column to the right. Press Enter, and notice that *Air* displays in the **Name Box**.

> Use the (Name) field when you need to refer to an object in a program. The naming convention is the same for naming cells in Excel; that is, the name cannot include spaces or punctuation marks.

4 In the first column, click the **Caption** property, type **Air** and then press Enter.

> The text in the check box changes to *Air*.

5 Under **Alphabetic**, click **Height** and type **15.75** Click **Width** and type **84.75** and then press Enter. Compare your screen with Figure 9.21.

> The check box resizes to a height of 15.75 pixels and a width of 84.75 pixels.

FIGURE 9.21

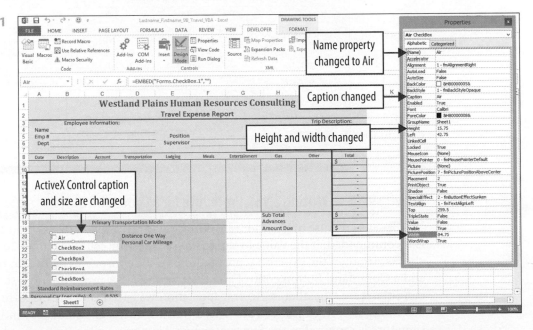

6 Click **CheckBox2** to select the check box, and notice that the **Properties** pane displays the properties for *CheckBox2*.

7 In the **Properties** pane, click **(Name)**, type without any spaces **RentalCar** and then press Enter. Click the **Caption** property, and then type, *with* a space, **Rental Car** Click **Height** and type **15.75** Click **Width** and type **84.75** and press Enter.

8 Using the technique you just practiced, change the properties for the remaining three check boxes as follows. Hint: You can hold down Ctrl, select the remaining check boxes, and then change the Height and Width properties in all three simultaneously. You must change the Name and Caption of each check box individually.

ACTIVEX CONTROL	NAME	CAPTION	HEIGHT	WIDTH
CheckBox3	**PersonalCar**	**Personal Car**	**15.75**	**84.75**
CheckBox4	**CompanyCar**	**Company Car**	**15.75**	**84.75**
CheckBox5	**Other**	**Other**	**15.75**	**84.75**

9 In the tan shaded area of the worksheet, select the **Air** check box, hold down Ctrl, and then click each of the other check boxes to select all five check boxes.

If you want to change the same property for a group of objects, you can select all of them and then change the property.

10 In the **Properties** pane, click **BackColor**, click the **BackColor arrow**, click the **System tab**, scroll down and click **Button Light Shadow**.

11 **Close** the **Properties** pane. On the **PAGE LAYOUT tab**, in the **Arrange group**, click **Align**, and then click **Distribute Vertically**. Drag the group of check boxes as necessary to adjust the position of the group of cells so that they are contained within the tan shaded area. Click cell **A1** to deselect the group of check boxes. **Save** 💾 your workbook. Compare your screen with Figure 9.22.

The space between each of the check boxes is equal.

FIGURE 9.22

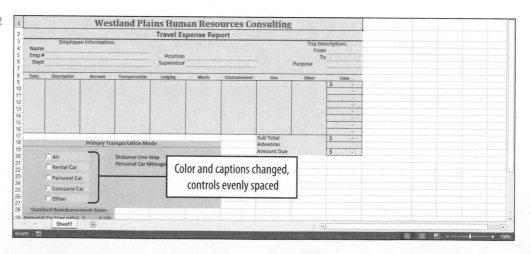

Activity 9.10 | Writing a VBA Procedure for a Command Button

Because the use of ground transportation for trips that are less than 200 miles one way is recommended, if the value in the *Distance One Way* cell is less than 200 and the employee checks *Air*, then the expense report requires a supervisor's signature. In this activity, you will add a Command Button control and then write a VBA procedure to test whether both of these conditions are true; that is, *Air* transportation was used, and the distance one way was less than 200 miles. If both conditions are true, a warning message will display indicating that a supervisor's signature is required in the Supervisor box. First, you will write a procedure that tests whether the *Air* check box is selected, and then you will modify the procedure that will test whether the distance one way is less than 200 miles.

1 Click cell **H22** to identify the location where you will place a Command Button. On the **DEVELOPER tab**, in the **Controls group**, click **Insert**, and then under **ActiveX Controls**, click the **Command Button** ![icon]. Point to upper left corner of cell **H22**, and then click one time to insert a Command Button. Compare your screen with Figure 9.23.

The Command Button is added and a portion of the text *CommandButton1* displays as the caption on the button. By selecting cell H22, you have a visual cue as to where to place the Command Button. Recall, however, that ActiveX objects are not actually attached to a cell—the cell address is only a guide to direct you to the location where the control will be placed.

FIGURE 9.23

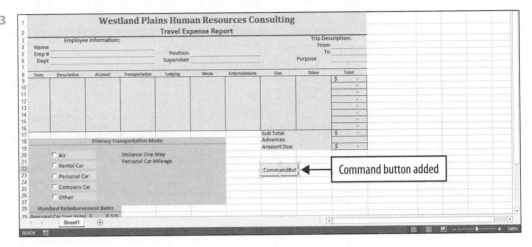

2 In the **Controls group**, click **Properties**. In the **Properties** pane, click **(Name)**, and then type **CheckTransportation** Click the **Caption** property, and then type **Check Transportation** Click **AutoSize**, click the **AutoSize arrow**, and then click **True**.

The button is resized to accommodate the new caption.

3 In the **Properties** pane, click **Font**, and then click **Font build** ![icon] to display the **Font** dialog box. Under **Font style**, click **Bold Italic**, and then click **OK**. Compare your screen with Figure 9.24.

FIGURE 9.24

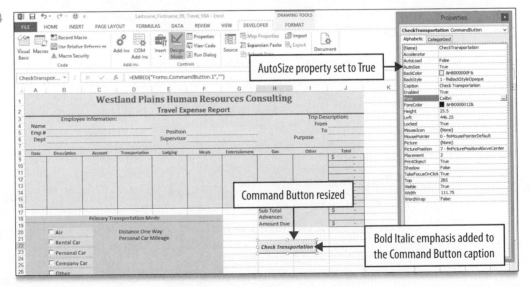

4 **Close** ⊠ the **Properties** pane. Be sure the **Check Transportation** control is selected. On the **DEVELOPER tab**, in the **Controls group**, click **View Code**. At the top of the **Code window**, click the **Object arrow**, and then on the list, click **CheckTransportation**. Compare your screen with Figure 9.25.

The Microsoft Visual Basic Code window displays and *CheckTransportation* displays in the Object box at the top of the window. This is the name of the selected ActiveX control. The beginning of this VBA procedure is indicated by *Private Sub CheckTransportation_Click()*. *Private* indicates that this procedure can be used only in this workbook. *End Sub* indicates the end of the procedure. The event that will activate the Check Transportation Command Button is one click of the button.

FIGURE 9.25

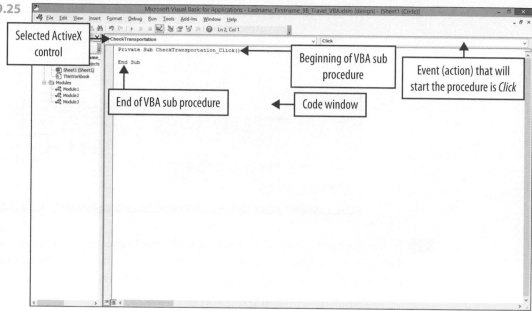

🔄 **ANOTHER WAY**   In Design Mode, right-click the Command Button, and then click View Code, or in Design Mode, double-click the Command Button.

🔄 **ANOTHER WAY**   You can open the VBA Editor by pressing Alt + F11.

5 Click to the left of *Private Sub CheckTransportation_Click()* to place the insertion point there, and then press Enter to insert a blank line. Press ↑ to move to the blank line, and then type the following comments spaced as shown. Enter your first name and last name as the author. At the end of each line, press Enter, and as necessary, press Tab to provide indents and alignment as shown in Figure 9.26.

' Check Transportation Button Procedure Author: Firstname Lastname

' Date Created: November 28, 2015

' Function: When clicked, the Check Transportation button checks if the value in

'   cell F20 is less than 200 and if the Air check box is selected. If these two

'   conditions are true, a message box will display to require a supervisor's

'   signature. Otherwise a message box will display indicating that the

'   transportation mode is OK.

6 Press Enter, and compare your screen with Figure 9.26.

Comments display in green and are preceded by an apostrophe ('). When writing a VBA procedure, it is recommended that you document the procedure with comments to indicate the purpose of the procedure, the author, and the date created. Comments do not affect the running of the procedure.

FIGURE 9.26

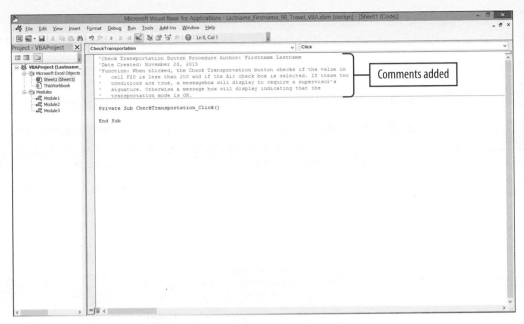

7 Click to position the insertion point on the blank line under *Private Sub CheckTransportation_Click()*. Press Enter, and then press Tab. Type the lines of VBA code spaced as shown below. Use the Tab key to indent the middle three lines and Shift + Tab to reduce the indent by one tab for the last line. As you type, a prompt box will display to assist you with the VBA syntax. Ignore the prompts and type the code as shown. When you are finished, compare your screen with Figure 9.27.

If Air = True Then

    TitleBarText = "Air"

    MessageText = "To use air transportation, miles one way should equal 200 or more."

    MsgBox MessageText, , TitleBarText

End If

The VBA code that you typed defined each component of the message box and then used a line to identify the parts that were used.

FIGURE 9.27

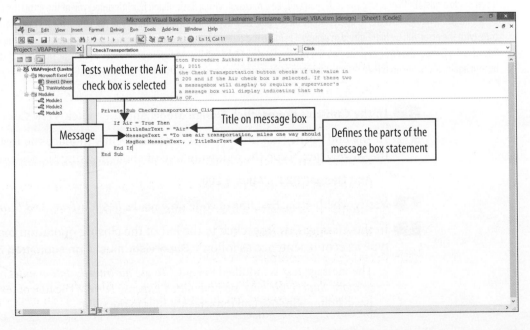

There are several techniques you can use when writing VBA code. The code to create the message box could also be written as: MsgBox "To travel by air, miles one way should be 200 or more.", , "Air"MsgBox

8 ▶ On the menu bar, click **File**, and then click **Close and Return to Microsoft Excel**.

9 ▶ In the **Controls group**, click **Design Mode** to exit Design Mode.

10 ▶ In the tan shaded section, select the **Air** check box, and then click the **Check Transportation** Command Button. If an error message displays, see the Alert box that follows for instructions on how to resolve the error. Compare your screen with Figure 9.28.

A check mark displays in the Air check box, and the Air message box displays.

FIGURE 9.28

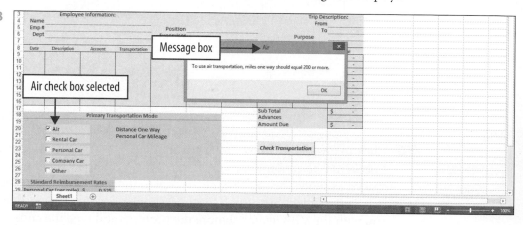

11 ▶ In the **Air** message box, click **OK**. **Save** 🖫 your workbook.

Activity 9.11 | Modifying a VBA Procedure

You can modify a VBA procedure in the same manner that you modified the VBA code that was created when you used a macro. In this activity, you will add a second condition—the distance one way must be 200 miles or more—and a message regarding the supervisor signature. To do this, you will use an If, Then, Else statement.

ALERT! **If an Error Message Displays**

If you made a mistake in entering the code, you will see a Microsoft Visual Basic dialog box informing you of the error. The message varies depending on the error that you have made. If this happens, in the dialog box, click Debug. This action returns you to the Microsoft Visual Basic Editor window, and the line of code with the error will be highlighted in yellow. Examine the code and compare it with the instructions. Look for a typing error, a missing dot, or a missing line of code. Correct the error, and then on the File menu, click Close and Return to Microsoft Excel. In the message box, click OK to stop the debugger. Test the button again. If you are unable to resolve the error, seek assistance from your instructor or lab assistant.

---

1 ▶ In the **Controls group**, click **Design Mode**, and then click **View Code**.

2 ▶ At the end of the first line of the If statement, click to place the insertion point to the *left* of the word *Then*. Type the following line of code, pressing Spacebar one time at the end:

    And Range("F20").Value < 200

3 ▶ Verify whether the first line of code now reads: *If Air = True And Range("F20").Value < 200 Then*

4 ▶ In the *MessageText* line, click to the left of the closing quotation mark, press Spacebar, and then type a second sentence as follows: **Supervisor must sign submitted Expense Form.**

The message text is modified to read: *"To use air transportation miles one way should equal 200 or more. Supervisor must sign submitted Expense Form."* The line of text extends across the Visual Basic Editor window, and the screen scrolls to the right.

5 ▶ Scroll to the left. At the end of the *MsgBox* line, place the insertion point after *TitleBarText* and press [Enter], and then press [Shift] + [Tab]. Type the following code spaced as shown below:

Else

   TitleBarText = "Travel Method Checked"

   MessageText = "Travel method OK."

   MsgBox MessageText, , TitleBarText

This code will cause a second message box to display if the Air check box is selected and the mileage is 200 miles or more. This message box will also display if the Air check box is not selected. Compare your VBA code with Figure 9.29.

FIGURE 9.29

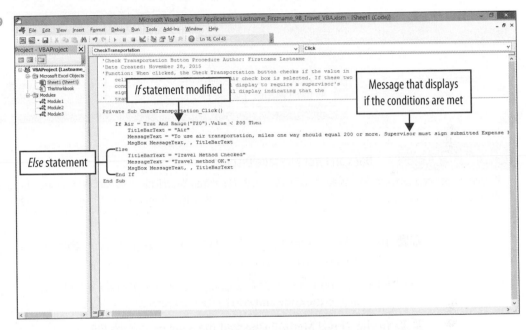

6 ▶ If your instructor requires you to print your VBA code, follow the directions in Activity 9.07. Click **File**, and then click **Close and Return to Microsoft Excel**. On the **DEVELOPER tab**, in the **Controls group**, click **Design Mode** to exit Design Mode. **Save** 🖫 your workbook.

Activity 9.12 | Testing the VBA Procedure and the ActiveX Control

After you create a VBA procedure, you should test it to verify that it works as you intended.

1 ▶ Be sure the **Air** check box is still selected—it displays a check mark. Be sure **Design Mode** is not selected. In cell **F20**, type **150** and then press [Enter]. Click the **Check Transportation** button. Compare your screen with Figure 9.30.

The first message box displays and informs you that a supervisor's signature is required.

FIGURE 9.30

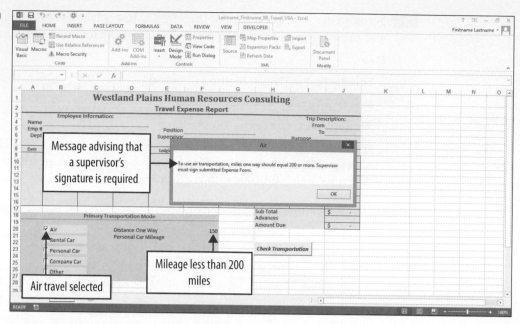

ALERT!   Does an Error Message Display?

If an error message displays, in the message box, click Debug to return to the Visual Basic Editor window and correct the error that is highlighted in yellow. After correcting the highlighted error, on the File menu, click Close and Return to Microsoft Excel. Repeat Step 1 to continue.

2 In the **Air** message box, click **OK**. Click cell **F20**, type **200** and then press [Enter]. Click the **Check Transportation** button.

> The second message box displays indicating *Travel method OK*. If you get the first message box, return to the code and correct the cell reference to F20.

3 In the **Travel Method Checked** message box, click **OK**.

> You have tested both conditions for using air transportation—when the miles are 200 or more, and when the miles are less than 200. You also need to test the Command Button when other modes of transportation are used.

4 Clear the check mark from the **Air** check box. Select the **Rental Car** check box, and then click the **Check Transportation** Command Button.

> The second message box displays indicating *Travel method OK*.

5 Click **OK** to acknowledge the message.

6 Insert a footer in the **left section** that includes the file name. Return to **Normal** view, and then press [Ctrl] + [Home] to move to the top of the worksheet. Click the **FILE tab**, and then in the lower right portion of the screen, click **Show all properties**. In the **Tags** box, type **expense report, VBA** and in the **Subject** box type your course name and section #. In the **Author** box, replace the existing text with your first and last name. Display the worksheet in **Print Preview**, return to the workbook and make any necessary corrections or adjustments.

7 Click the **REVIEW tab**. In the **Changes group**, click **Protect Workbook**. In the **Protect Structure and Windows** dialog box, verify **Structure** is selected and then type **goseries** in the **Password** box. Compare your screen with Figure 9.31.

FIGURE 9.31

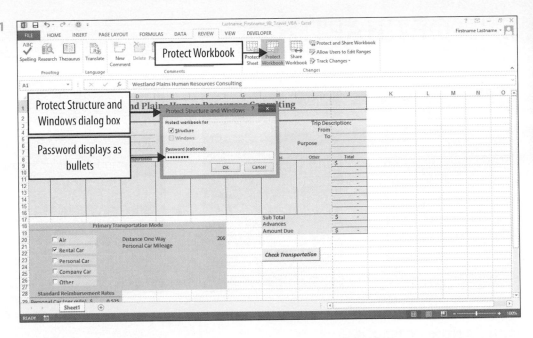

8 ▶ Click **OK**. In the **Confirm Password** dialog box, type **goseries** and click **OK**.

10 ▶ **Save** 🖫 and submit as directed by your instructor. **Close** the workbook but leave Excel open for the next activity.

Objective 5 Restore Initial Settings

Video E9-5

When you use a computer in a public location such as a college computer lab, or when you use someone else's computer, it is proper computer etiquette to return it to the condition in which you found it. In this chapter, you created a macro and then placed a button on the Quick Access Toolbar.

Activity 9.13 │ Removing the Quick Access Toolbar Button, Macro, and the Developer Tab

1 ▶ Right-click the **Smiley Face** icon on the **Quick Access Toolbar,** and then click **Remove from Quick Access Toolbar.**

The Employee_Info button is removed from the Quick Access Toolbar.

2 ▶ On the **DEVELOPER tab**, in the **Code group**, click **Macros**.

3 ▶ Verify that the **Macro** dialog box is empty. If the **Employee_Info** macro you created is displayed, select the macro name, and then click **Delete**.

The Employee_Info macro is part of the workbook Lastname_Firstname_9A_Travel_Macro and Lastname_Firstname_9B_Travel_VBA and will not be deleted from those files. Because the workbooks are closed, the macro name should not display in this list of macros. If you accidentally saved the macro in another place and it displays in this list, it should now be deleted.

4 ▶ Click **Cancel**.

5 ▶ Right-click the **DEVELOPER tab**, and then click **Customize the Ribbon**. In the right pane, click **Developer** to de-select it, and then click **OK** to remove the **DEVELOPER tab**. **Close** Excel.

END | You have completed Project 9B

END OF CHAPTER

SUMMARY

You can automate an Excel worksheet to perform complex tasks faster and to perform repetitive actions using macros and the programming language called Visual Basic for Applications (VBA).

In the Visual Basic Editor window, comments that describe the macro are displayed in green and in lines preceded by an apostrophe ('). The VBA code that follows displays in black type.

A set of instructions that accomplishes a specific task is called a sub procedure, or simply sub. In the VBA code, Sub indicates the beginning of the sub procedure and End Sub indicates the end.

An ActiveX control is a graphic object, such as a check box or button, that can be placed on a worksheet or form. When the ActiveX control is clicked, a macro or code runs that automates a task or offers options.

GO! LEARN IT ONLINE

Review the concepts and key terms in this chapter by completing these online challenges, which you can find at **www.pearsonhighered.com/go.**

Matching and Multiple Choice:
Answer matching and multiple choice questions to test what you learned in this chapter. MyITLab®

Crossword Puzzle:
Spell out the words that match the numbered clues, and put them in the puzzle squares.

Flipboard:
Flip through the definitions of the key terms in this chapter and match them with the correct term.

Your instructor may assign one or more of these projects to help you review the chapter and assess your mastery and understanding of the chapter.

	Review and Assessment Guide for Excel Chapter 9		
Project	**Apply Skills from These Chapter Objectives**	**Project Type**	**Project Location**
9C	Objectives 1–3 from Project 9A	**9C Skills Review** A guided review of the skills from Project 9A.	On the following pages
9D	Objectives 4–5 from Project 9B	**9D Skills Review** A guided review of the skills from Project 9B.	On the following pages
9E	Objectives 1–3 from Project 9A	**9E Mastery (Grader Project)** A demonstration of your mastery of the skills in Project 9A with extensive decision making.	In MyITLab and on the following pages
9F	Objectives 4–5 from Project 9B	**9F Mastery (Grader Project)** A demonstration of your mastery of the skills in Project 9B with extensive decision making.	In MyITLab and on the following pages
9G	Objectives 1–5 from Projects 9A and 9B	**9G Mastery (Grader Project)** A demonstration of your mastery of the skills in Projects 9A and 9B with extensive decision making.	In MyITLab and on the following pages
9H	Combination of Objectives from Projects 9A and 9B	**9H GO! Fix It** A demonstration of your mastery of the skills in Projects 9A and 9B by creating a correct result from a document that contains errors you must find.	Online
9I	Combination of Objectives from Projects 9A and 9B	**9I GO! Make It** A demonstration of your mastery of the skills in Projects 9A and 9B by creating a result from a supplied picture.	Online
9J	Combination of Objectives from Projects 9A and 9B	**9J GO! Solve It** A demonstration of your mastery of the skills in Projects 9A and 9B, your decision-making skills, and your critical thinking skills. A task-specific rubric helps you self-assess your result.	Online
9K	Combination of Objectives from Projects 9A and 9B	**9K GO! Solve It** A demonstration of your mastery of the skills in Projects 9A and 9B, your decision-making skills, and your critical thinking skills. A task-specific rubric helps you self-assess your result.	On the following pages
9L	Combination of Objectives from Projects 9A and 9B	**9L GO! Think** A demonstration of your understanding of the chapter concepts applied in a manner that you would outside of college. An analytic rubric helps you and your instructor grade the quality of your work by comparing it to the work an expert in the discipline would create.	On the following pages
9M	Combination of Objectives from Projects 9A and 9B	**9M GO! Think** A demonstration of your understanding of the chapter concepts applied in a manner that you would outside of college. An analytic rubric helps you and your instructor grade the quality of your work by comparing it to the work an expert in the discipline would create.	Online
9N	Combination of Objectives from Projects 9A and 9B	**9N You and GO!** A demonstration of your understanding of the chapter concepts applied in a manner that you would in a personal situation. An analytic rubric helps you and your instructor grade the quality of your work.	Online

GLOSSARY

ActiveX control Graphic object, such as a check box or button, that you place on a form to display or enter data, perform an action, or make the form easier to read. When the person filling in the form clicks the ActiveX control, VBA code runs that automates a task or offers options.

Check box A type of ActiveX control that the person filling in the form can select to indicate a choice.

Design Mode An Excel mode or view in which you can work with ActiveX controls.

Digital signature An electronic, encryption-based, secure stamp of authentication on a macro or document.

Embed The action of inserting something created in one program into another program.

Event The action that causes a program or macro to run, such as clicking a button or a command or pressing a combination of keys.

Form An Excel worksheet or object that contains fields and controls that enable a user to easily enter or edit data.

Form control A graphic object that does not require VBA code. A Form control is compatible with versions of Excel that do not support ActiveX.

Macro An action or a set of actions with which you can automate tasks by grouping a series of commands into a single command.

Macro virus Unauthorized programming code in a macro that erases or damages files.

Module The programming code written in VBA when you record a new macro; the place where the VBA code is stored.

Procedure A named sequence of statements in a computer program that performs an action.

Property Characteristic of an object that can be changed; details about a file that help identify it, such as the author, date created, and file name.

Record Macro A command that records your actions in Visual Basic for Applications (VBA).

Sub Short for a sub procedure.

Sub procedure A unit of computer code that performs an action.

VBA The abbreviation for the Visual Basic for Applications programming language.

VBA construct An instruction that enables a macro to perform multiple operations on a single object.

Visual Basic Editor The window in which you can view and edit Visual Basic code.

Visual Basic for Applications The programming language used to write computer programs in the Microsoft Windows environment.

CHAPTER REVIEW

Skills Review   Project 9C Summary Reports

In the following Skills Review, you will assist Matt Gallagher, Training Director, in creating a macro that will make it easier for staff members to include the required information in their training department expense reports. You will assign the macro to a button on the Quick Access Toolbar, and then modify the macro by changing the Visual Basic Code. Your completed worksheet will look similar to Figure 9.32.

PROJECT FILES

For Project 9C, you will need the following file:

e09C_Training_Macro

You will save your workbook as:

Lastname_Firstname_9C_Training_Macro

PROJECT RESULTS

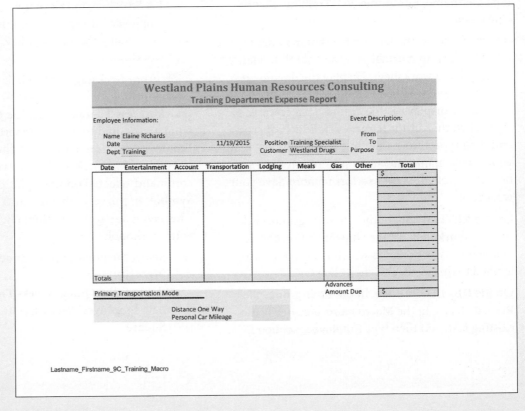

FIGURE 9.32

(Project 9C Summary Reports continues on the next page)

CHAPTER REVIEW

1 ▶ Start Excel and display a new blank workbook. If the **DEVELOPER tab** is not visible, click **FILE** to display **Backstage** view. Click **Options**. In the **Excel Options** dialog box, on the left, click **Customize Ribbon**. Under **Customize Ribbon**, verify **Main Tabs** is selected, select the **Developer** check box, and then click **OK**.

a. On the **DEVELOPER tab**, in the **Code group**, click **Macro Security**. Under **Macro Settings**, verify that **Disable all macros with notification** is selected, and then click **OK**. From your student files, open the file **e09C_Training_Macro**. Display the **Save As** dialog box, navigate to your **Excel Chapter 9** folder, click the **Save as type arrow**, and then click **Excel Macro-Enabled Workbook**. In the **File name** box, type **Lastname_Firstname_9C_Training_Macro** Click **Save**.

b. Insert a footer in the **left section** that includes the file name. Return to **Normal** view and scroll to view the top of the worksheet. Display the **document properties** and under **Related People**, be sure that your name displays as the author. If necessary, right-click the author name, click Edit Property, and then type your name. In the **Subject** box, type your course name and section #, and in the **Tags** box, type **training expense form macro** **Save** your workbook.

c. On the **REVIEW tab**, in the **Changes group**, click **Protect Workbook**. In the **Unprotect Workbook** dialog box, type **goseries** which is the password applied to this form, and then click **OK**.

d. On the **DEVELOPER tab**, in the **Code group**, click **Record Macro**. In the **Macro name** box, delete the existing text, and then type **Employee_section** In the **Shortcut key** box, type **t** Click the **Store macro in arrow**, then click **This Workbook**. Click in the **Description** box. Type **Fills in the Employee section** Click **OK**.

e. Click cell **B6**, type **Elaine Richards** and then press Enter. With cell **B7** active, hold down Ctrl and press ; (semicolon), which will insert the current date. Press Enter. With cell **B8** active, type **Training** Click in cell **F7** and type **Training Specialist** and then press Enter. In cell **F8**, type **Westland Drugs** and then click cell **A11**, so that when the macro completes, the first cell in the data area is active to begin filling in the travel information. On the **DEVELOPER tab**, in the **Code group**, click **Stop Recording**. Delete the text you just typed in the five cells—**B6, B7, B8, F7, F8**. Then, to test that your macro will fill in the employee information and the date, run the macro by pressing the shortcut key Ctrl + T. **Save** your workbook.

2 ▶ From **Backstage** view, click **Options** to display the **Excel Options** dialog box, and then on the left, click **Quick Access Toolbar**. Click the **Choose commands from arrow**, and then click **Macros**. Click your **Employee_Section** macro, and then, in the center of the dialog box, click **Add**. With your **Employee_Section** command selected on the right, click **Modify**. Under **Symbol**, in the seventh row, click the seventh icon—the **Checkered Square**—and then click **OK** two times. **Save** your workbook.

a. Select the nonadjacent ranges **B6:B8** and **F7:F8** and press Del so that these cells are empty again, and then on the **Quick Access Toolbar**, click your new **Employee_Section** button—the Checkered Square.

(Project 9C Summary Reports continues on the next page)

CHAPTER REVIEW

3 On the **DEVELOPER tab,** in the **Code group,** click **Macros.** Be sure the **Employee_Section** macro is selected, and then click **Edit.** In the **Code window,** locate the green and black lines of text that comprise the comments and code for the Employee_Section macro. At the end of the *last* line of code—*Range("A11"). Select*—click to place the insertion point after *Select*, and then press [Enter].

a. On the new, empty line, type **With ActiveSheet. PageSetup** and then press [Enter]. Press [Tab] to indent and type **.CenterHorizontally = True** Press [Enter] and type **.CenterVertically = True** and then press [Enter]. Press [Shift] + [Tab], and then type **End With**

b. On the menu bar, click **File,** and then click **Close and Return to Microsoft Excel.** Delete the text in **B6:B8, F7:F8,** click cell **B6,** and then on the **Quick Access Toolbar,** click the **Employee_Section** button that you created, so that the macro is re-run and includes the centering you added to the macro. Display and check the **Print Preview.** Return to the worksheet.

c. Right-click the **Checkered Square** icon on the **Quick Access Toolbar,** and then click **Remove from Quick Access Toolbar.** If you are directed to remove the **DEVELOPER tab,** follow the directions in Activity 9.13.

d. **Save** your workbook, and then print or submit electronically as directed. If required, print your VBA code using the instructions in Activity 9.07. **Close** Excel.

END | You have completed Project 9C

CHAPTER REVIEW

Apply 9B skills from these Objectives:

4 Write a VBA Procedure to Use an ActiveX Control

5 Restore Initial Settings

Skills Review Project 9D Recruitment Report

In the following Skills Review, you will assist Matt Gallagher, Training Director at Westland Plains Human Resources Consulting, by writing a set of commands in the VBA programming language, using ActiveX Control buttons to automate the Recruitment Department policy guidelines for expense reports. Your completed workbook will look similar to Figure 9.33.

PROJECT FILES

For Project 9D, you will need the following file:

e09D_Recruitment_VBA

You will save your workbook as:

Lastname_Firstname_9D_Recruitment_VBA

PROJECT RESULTS

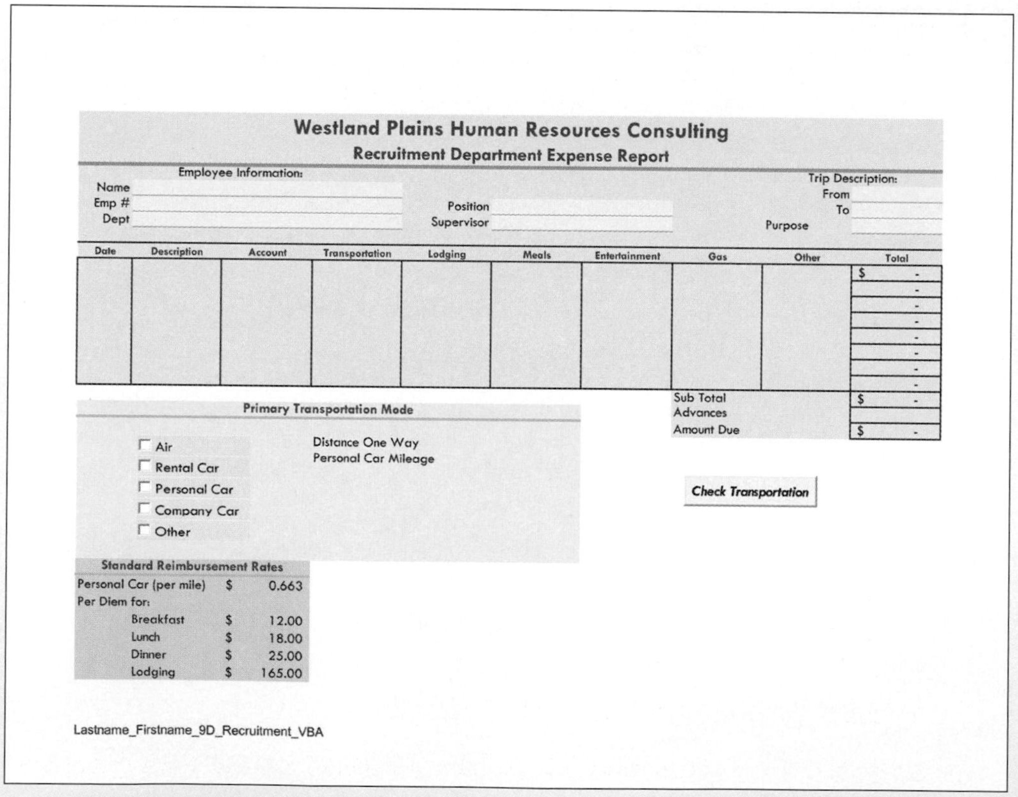

FIGURE 9.33

(Project 9D Recruitment Report continues on the next page)

1 Start Excel. From your student files, locate and open the file **e09D_Recruitment_VBA**, and then **Save** the file in your **Excel Chapter 9** folder as an **Excel Macro-Enabled Workbook** with the file name **Lastname_Firstname_9D_Recruitment_VBA** If necessary, on the **Security Warning bar**, click **Enable Content**.

a. On the **DEVELOPER tab**, in the **Controls group**, click **Insert**. Under **ActiveX Controls**, click **Check Box**. Point to the upper left corner of cell **B20** and drag to insert a check box object that is approximately the height of the cell and the width of columns **B:C**. Repeat this process to add four more check boxes of the same approximate size under **CheckBox1**.

b. Click **CheckBox1**, and then on the **DEVELOPER tab**, in the **Controls group**, notice that **Design Mode** is active. With **CheckBox1** selected, hold down Ctrl and click on each of the remaining check boxes so that all five check boxes are selected. On the **PAGE LAYOUT tab**, in the **Arrange group**, click **Align**, and then click **Align Left** to align the check boxes on the left.

2 Click the **DEVELOPER tab**. In the **Controls group**, verify that **Design Mode** is active. Click another area of the worksheet to deselect the group of check boxes, and then click **CheckBox1** to select the check box. In the **Controls group**, click **Properties**. Drag the **Properties** pane near the upper right of your screen, and then expand its lower edge so that you can see the entire list of properties.

a. At the top of the **Alphabetic** list, in the first column, click **(Name)**, and then type **Air** Press Enter, and notice that *Air* displays in the **Name Box**. In the first column, click the **Caption** property, type **Air** and then press Enter. Click **Height** and type **15.75** click **Width** and type **84.75** and then press Enter. Click **CheckBox2** to select it. In the **Properties** pane, click **(Name)**, type without any spaces **RentalCar** and then press Enter. Click the **Caption** property, and then type, *with* a space, **Rental Car** Click **Height** and type **15.75** Click **Width** and type **84.75** and press Enter. Using the technique you just practiced, change the properties for the remaining three check boxes as shown in the table.

	Name	Caption	Height	Width
CheckBox3	PersonalCar	Personal Car	15.75	84.75
CheckBox4	CompanyCar	Company Car	15.75	84.75
CheckBox5	Other	Other	15.75	84.75

b. In the yellow shaded area of the worksheet, select the **Air** check box, hold down Ctrl, and then click each of the other check boxes to select all five check boxes. In the **Properties** pane, click **BackColor**, click the **BackColor arrow**, click the **System tab**, scroll down and click **Button Light Shadow**. **Close** the **Properties** pane. On the **PAGE LAYOUT tab**, in the **Arrange group**, click **Align**, and then click **Distribute Vertically**. Drag the group of check boxes as necessary to adjust the position of the group so that they are contained within the yellow shaded area. Click cell **A1** to deselect the group of check boxes. Click **Save**.

(Project 9D Recruitment Report continues on the next page)

3 Click cell **H22** to identify the location where you will place a Command Button. On the **DEVELOPER tab**, in the **Controls group**, click **Insert**, and then under **ActiveX Controls**, click the **Command Button**. Point to the upper left corner of cell **H22**, and then click one time to insert the button.

a. In the **Controls group**, click **Properties**. In the **Properties** pane, click (**Name**), and then type **CheckTransportation** Click the **Caption** property, and then type **Check Transportation** Click **AutoSize**, click the **AutoSize arrow**, and then click **True**. In the **Properties** pane, click **Font**, and then click **Font build** to display the **Font** dialog box. Under **Font style**, click **Bold Italic**, and then click **OK**. **Close** the **Properties** pane.

b. Be sure the **Check Transportation** control is selected. On the **DEVELOPER tab**, in the **Controls group**, click **View Code**. Click the **Object arrow**, and then on the list, click **CheckTransportation**.

c. Click to the left of *Private Sub CheckTransportation_Click()* to place the insertion point there, and then press Enter to insert a blank line. Press the up arrow to move to the blank line, and then type the following comments spaced as shown. Use your own name as the author. At the end of each line, press Enter, and as necessary, press Tab to provide indents and alignment.

' Check Transportation Button Procedure Author: Firstname Lastname

' Date Created: February 18, 2016

' Function: When clicked, the Check Transportation button checks if the value in

' cell F20 is less than 200 and if the Air check box is selected. If these two

' conditions are true, a message box will display to require a supervisor's

' signature. Otherwise a message box will display indicating that the

' transportation mode is OK.

d. Press Enter. Click to position the insertion point on the blank line under *Private Sub CheckTransportation_Click()*. Press Tab. Type the lines of VBA code spaced as shown. Use the Tab key to indent the middle three lines and Shift + Tab to reduce the indent by one tab for the last line. As you type, a prompt box will display to assist you with the VBA syntax. Ignore the prompts and type the code as shown.

If Air = True Then

    TitleBarText = "Air"

    MessageText = "To use air transportation, miles one way should equal 200 or more."

    MsgBox MessageText, , TitleBarText

End If

e. On the menu bar, click **File**, and then click **Close and Return to Microsoft Excel**. In the **Controls group**, click **Design Mode** to exit Design Mode. In the yellow shaded section, select the **Air** check box, and then click the **Check Transportation** command button. Click **OK** to acknowledge the message.

(Project 9D Recruitment Report continues on the next page)

4 In the **Controls group**, click **Design Mode**, and then click **View Code**. At the end of the first line of the IF statement, click to place the insertion point to the left of the word *Then*. Type the following line of code, pressing Spacebar at the end:

And Range("F20").Value < 200

a. Verify whether the first line of code now reads: *If Air = True And Range("F20").Value < 200 Then* In the *MessageText* line, click to the left of the closing quotation mark, press Spacebar, and then type a second sentence as follows:

Supervisor must sign this Expense Form.

b. Scroll to the left. At the end of the *MsgBox* line of code, place the insertion point after TitleBarText and press Enter. Then press Shift + Tab. Type the following code spaced as shown:

Else

   TitleBarText = "Travel Method Checked"

   MessageText = "Travel method OK."

   MsgBox MessageText, , TitleBarText

c. On the menu bar, click **File**, and then click **Close and Return to Microsoft Excel**. In the **Controls group**, click **Design Mode** to return to the active worksheet. Be sure the **Air** check box is still selected—it displays a check mark. In cell **F20**, type **150** and then press Enter. Click the **Check Transportation** button. In the **Air** message box, click **OK**. Click cell **F20**, type **200** and then press Enter. Click the **Check Transportation** button.

d. In the **Travel Method Checked** message box, click **OK**. Clear the check mark from the **Air** check box. Select the **Rental Car** check box, and then click the **Check Transportation** Command Button. Click **OK** to acknowledge the message.

e. Insert a footer in the **left section** that includes the file name. On the status bar, click **Normal**, and then press Ctrl + Home to move to the top of the worksheet. Click the **FILE tab**, and then in the lower right portion of the screen, click **Show all properties**. In the Tags box, type **recruitment department expense report, VBA** and in the **Subject** box type your course name and section #. In the **Author** box, replace the existing text with your first and last name. Display the worksheet in **Print Preview**, and then make any necessary corrections or adjustments.

f. Click the **REVIEW tab**. In the **Changes group**, click **Protect Workbook**. In the **Protect Structure and Windows** dialog box, verify **Structure** is selected and then type **goseries** in the **Password** box. **Save** your workbook, and then submit it as directed by your instructor. If required, print your VBA code using the instructions in Activity 9.07 in Project 9A. **Close** the workbook.

g. If you are directed to remove the **DEVELOPER tab**, follow the directions in Activity 9.13. **Close** Excel.

END | You have completed Project 9D

(Project 9D Recruitment Report continues on the next page)

CONTENT-BASED ASSESSMENTS

Mastering Excel   Project 9E Operations Report

Apply 9A skills from these Objectives:

1 Record a Macro
2 Assign a Macro to a Button on the Quick Access Toolbar
3 Modify a Macro

In the following Mastering Excel project, you will assist Bill Roman, Project Director, in creating a macro that will assign an operations department heading required on all reports. You will modify the macro by changing the Visual Basic Code. Your completed worksheet will look similar to Figure 9.34.

PROJECT FILES

For Project 9E, you will need the following file:

e09E_Operations_Macro

You will save your workbook as:

Lastname_Firstname_9E_Operations_Macro

PROJECT RESULTS

WPHRC Operations Department
Quarterly Operations Report

	January	February	March	Totals
Supplies	$ 3,210	$ 2,056	$ 3,773	$ 9,039
Salaries	15,823	14,335	16,300	46,458
Overhead	6,250	6,250	6,250	18,750
Equipment	-	-	1,875	1,875
Meals	331	230	200	761
Other	335	630	275	1,240
Totals	$ 25,949	$ 23,501	$ 28,673	$ 78,123

Lastname_Firstname_9E_Operations_Macro.xlsm

FIGURE 9.34

(Project 9E Operations Report continues on the next page)

CONTENT-BASED ASSESSMENTS

1 Start Excel. Verify the **DEVELOPER tab** is enabled and that the **Macro Settings** are set to **Disable all macros with notification**. From your student files, open the file **e09E_Operations_Macro**. Display the **Save As** dialog box, navigate to your **Excel Chapter 9** folder, set the **Save as type** to **Excel Macro-Enabled Workbook**, and as the file name, type **Lastname_Firstname_9E_Operations_Macro**

2 Insert a footer in the **left section** that includes the file name. Display the **document properties**, type your firstname and lastname as the author, type your course name and section # in the **Subject** box, and as the **Tags, operations department header, macro** Save your workbook.

3 Click cell **A1**. Record a Macro. Name the macro **Operations_Header** Use Ctrl + O as the shortcut key, store the macro in this workbook, and as the description, type **Fills in Operations report heading**

4 Insert two blank rows at the top of the worksheet. Click cell **A1**, and then type **WPHRC Operations Department** Merge and Center the text you just typed across the range **A1:E1**, and then apply the **Title** cell style. In cell **A2**, type **Quarterly Report** and then merge and center the text you just typed across the range **A2:E2**, and then apply the **Heading 1** cell style. **Center** the worksheet

horizontally, click cell **A1**, and then stop recording the macro. Delete **rows 1:2**, click cell **A1**, and then test the macro by pressing Ctrl + O.

5 On the **DEVELOPER tab**, in the **Code group**, click **Macros**. Verify that the **Operations_Header** macro is selected, and then click **Edit**. Scroll down and locate the first instance of *End With*, and then in the fourth line following End With, edit *"Quarterly Report"* to indicate **"Quarterly Operations Report"** If required by your instructor, print the code.

6 Click **File**, and then click **Close and Return to Microsoft Excel**. Delete **rows 1:2**, click cell **A1**, and then use the keyboard shortcut to re-run the macro to test that *Quarterly Operations Report* displays as the subtitle of the report.

7 Display the worksheet in **Print Preview**. If necessary, return to the workbook and make any necessary corrections or adjustments. **Save** your workbook. Print the worksheet or submit your workbook electronically as directed. If required, print your VBA code using the instructions in Activity 9.07.

8 If you are directed to remove the **DEVELOPER tab**, follow the directions in Activity 9.13. **Close** Excel.

END | You have completed Project 9E

(Project 9E Operations Report continues on the next page)

CONTENT-BASED ASSESSMENTS

Apply 9B skills from these Objectives:

4 Write a VBA Procedure to Use an ActiveX Control

5 Restore Initial Settings

In the following Mastering Excel project, you will assist Matt Gallagher, Training Director, by adding ActiveX controls to an evaluation form to gather feedback about training seminars. You will write VBA code to create input boxes that the respondent will use to enter information about the seminar. Your completed worksheet will look similar to Figure 9.35.

PROJECT FILES

For Project 9F, you will need the following file:

e09F_Evaluation_VBA

You will save your workbook as:

Lastname_Firstname_9F_Evaluation_VBA

PROJECT RESULTS

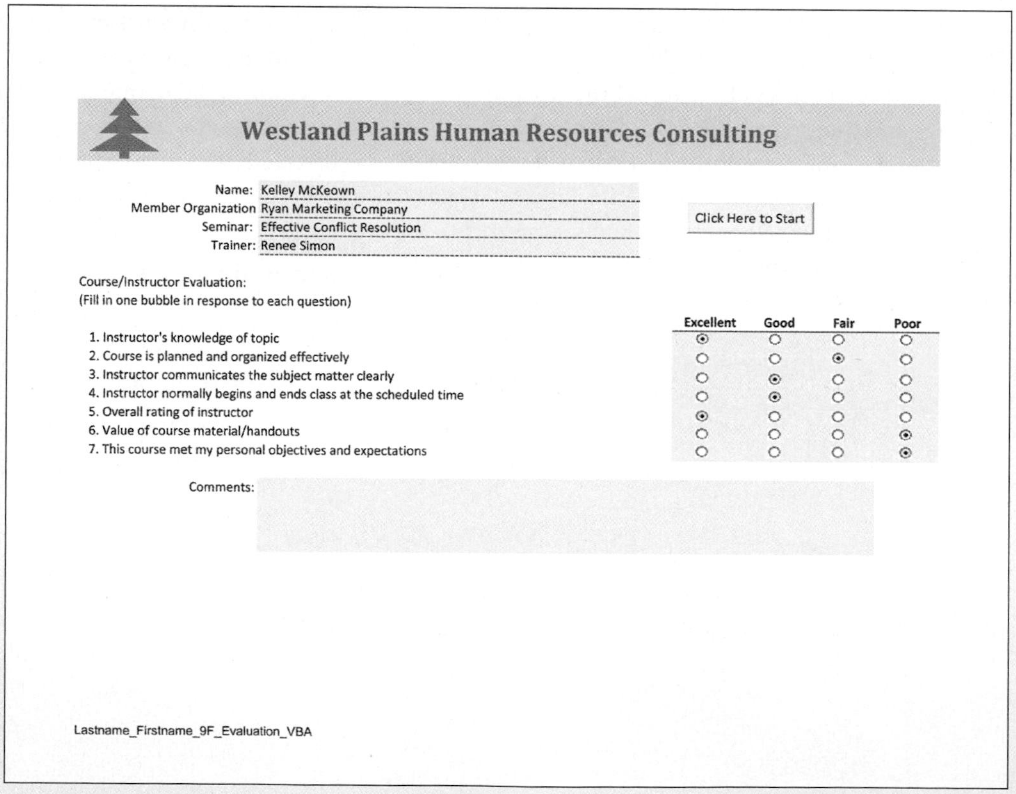

Westland Plains Human Resources Consulting

Name: Kelley McKeown
Member Organization Ryan Marketing Company
Seminar: Effective Conflict Resolution
Trainer: Renee Simon

Click Here to Start

Course/Instructor Evaluation:
(Fill in one bubble in response to each question)

	Excellent	Good	Fair	Poor
1. Instructor's knowledge of topic	●	○	○	○
2. Course is planned and organized effectively	○	○	●	○
3. Instructor communicates the subject matter clearly	○	●	○	○
4. Instructor normally begins and ends class at the scheduled time	○	●	○	○
5. Overall rating of instructor	●	○	○	○
6. Value of course material/handouts	○	○	○	●
7. This course met my personal objectives and expectations	○	○	○	●

Comments:

Lastname_Firstname_9F_Evaluation_VBA

FIGURE 9.35

(Project 9F Evaluation Form continues on the next page)

1 Start Excel. From your student files, locate the file **e09F_Evaluation_VBA**. **Save** the file in your **Excel Chapter 9** folder as an **Excel Macro-Enabled Workbook** with the file name **Lastname Firstname_9F_Evaluation_VBA** If necessary, on the **Security Warning bar**, click **Enable Content**.

2 Display the **ActiveX Controls** gallery. Click the **Option Button** control, and then click cell **G20**. Open the **Properties** pane, click **(Name)** and type **Q7E** Click the **Caption** property, and then delete the caption, **OptionButton1**. Click **GroupName**, and then type **Question7** Change the **Height** property to **9.75** Change the **Left** property to **465** Change **Top** to **279** and **Width** to **9.75** Click the **SpecialEffect arrow**, and then click **0 – fmButtonEffectFlat**.

3 Using the same technique, add three more option buttons in **row 20** and set the following properties using the table below.

4 From the **ActiveX Controls** gallery, click the **Command Button** control, and then click cell **G7** to add the ActiveX control to the worksheet. In the **Properties** pane, click **Name** and type **Start** Click **Caption**, and then type **Click Here to Start** Change **AutoSize** to *True*. **Close** the **Properties** pane.

5 On the **DEVELOPER tab**, in the **Controls group**, click **View Code**. Click the **Object arrow**, scroll down and then click **Start**. In the **Code window**, click to the left of *Private Sub Start_Click()* and press ⏎. Press the up arrow to move to the empty line, and then type the following comments to document the VBA code you will write. Use your own name, and press ⭾ to align or leave extra space.

' Start Button Procedure Author: Firstname Lastname

' Date Created: February 23, 2016

' Function: When clicked, the Start button will display four input

' boxes requesting the user to enter his or her name,

' organization, seminar title, and the name of the trainer.

6 Press ⏎. Click in the empty line following *Private Sub Start_Click()*, press ⭾, and then type the following VBA code:

Range("B6").Value = InputBox("Enter your name", "Name")

Range("B7").Value = InputBox("Enter the name of your organization", "Organization")

Range("B8").Value = InputBox("Enter the seminar title", "Seminar")

Range("B9").Value = InputBox("Enter the trainer's name", "Trainer")

Location/ Property	Name	Caption	GroupName	Height	Left	Top	Width	SpecialEffect
Cell H20	Q7G	Delete caption	Question7	9.75	519.75	279	9.75	0 fmButtonEffectFlat
Cell I20	Q7F	Delete caption	Question7	9.75	567	279	9.75	0 fmButtonEffectFlat
Cell J20	Q7P	Delete caption	Question7	9.75	618	279	9.75	0 fmButtonEffectFlat

(Return to Step 4)

(Project 9F Evaluation Form continues on the next page)

Mastering Excel | Project 9F Evaluation Form (continued)

7 Close the VBA Editor and return to Microsoft Excel. Exit Design Mode.

8 Click your new command button to test it, and type the following in each of the input boxes that display; click **OK** to close each box:

Name

Kelley McKeown

Organization

Ryan Marketing Company

Seminar

Effective Conflict Resolution

Trainer

Renee Simon

9 Click an option button, for example *Excellent*, for each of the seven questions. Now, test to see what happens when you change your mind and select a different rating for one of the questions—verify the original button is cleared, and only the new button is selected.

10 Insert a footer in the **left section** that includes the file name. Display the **document properties**, type your firstname and lastname as the author, type your course name and section # in the **Subject** box, and as the **Tags**, **evaluation report, VBA** Display the worksheet in **Print Preview**, and then make any necessary corrections or adjustments. **Save** your workbook, and then submit as directed by your instructor. If required, print your VBA code using the instructions in Activity 9.07. **Close** the workbook.

11 If you are directed to remove the **DEVELOPER tab**, follow the directions in Activity 9.13. **Close** Excel.

END | You have completed Project 9F

Apply 9A and 9B skills from these Objectives:

1 Record a Macro

2 Assign a Macro to a Button on the Quick Access Toolbar

3 Modify a Macro

4 Write a VBA Procedure to Use an ActiveX Control

5 Restore Initial Settings

In this project, you will assist Matt Gallagher, Training Director, by creating a macro to print name tags. Two different styles of attendee name tags are used by Westland Plains Human Resources Consulting for its training seminars. You will examine the code generated by the macro and use it as a model for creating an ActiveX control—a Command Button—and writing the necessary VBA code to print a name tag with a graphic. Your completed worksheet will look similar to Figure 9.36.

PROJECT FILES

For Project 9G, you will need the following file:

e09G_Name_Tags

You will save your workbook as:

Lastname_Firstname_9G_Name_Tags

PROJECT RESULTS

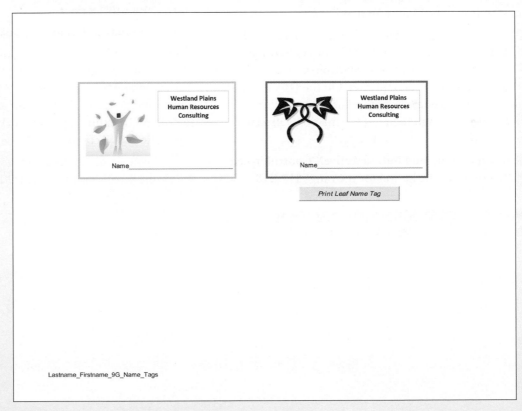

FIGURE 9.36

(Project 9G Name Tags continues on the next page)

1 Start Excel. Be sure the **DEVELOPER tab** is enabled and that the **Macro Settings** are set to **Disable all macros with notification**. From your student files, open the file **e09G_Name_Tags**. **Enable Content. Save** the file in your **Excel Chapter 9** folder as an **Excel Macro-Enabled Workbook** with the name **Lastname_Firstname_9G_Name_Tags**

2 Insert a footer in the **left section** that includes the file name. Display the **document properties**, type your firstname and lastname as the author, type your course name and section # in the **Subject** box, and as the **Tags**, **name tags**

3 Verify that cell **A1** is the active cell. On the **DEVELOPER tab**, in the **Code group**, click **Record Macro**. Name the macro **TreeNameTag** and assign **n** as the **Shortcut key**. Store the macro in this workbook, and as the description, type **Macro for name tags**

4 Select the range **B4:F15**. Click the **FILE tab**, and then click **Print**. In the **Print Preview**, under **Settings**, click the first arrow, click **Print Selection,** and then click **Print** to print to the default printer. On the **DEVELOPER tab**, in the **Code group**, click **Stop Recording**. Click cell **A1** to deselect, and then test the macro by pressing Ctrl + N.

5 Insert a **Command Button ActiveX Control** in cell **I17**. Drag to resize the button for the range **I17:K18**.

6 With the button selected, display the **Properties** pane. As the **(Name)**,type **LeafNameTag** and as the **Caption** type **Print Leaf Name Tag** Change the **Height** to **23.25** and the **Width** to **150** Set the **BackColor** to **Button Light Shadow**, and change the **Font style** to **Bold Italic**. **Close** the **Properties** pane.

7 On the **DEVELOPER tab**, in the **Controls group**, click **View Code**. Click the **Object arrow**, and then click **LeafNameTag**. In the **Code** window, type the following comments above the *Private Sub LeafNameTag_Click ()* line:

' LeafNameTag Command Button

' Prints Leaf Name Tag

8 In the **Code** window, click at the beginning of the blank line below *Private Sub LeafNameTag_Click ()*, press Tab, and then type the following VBA code:

Range("H4:L15").Select

Selection.PrintOut Copies:=1, Collate:=True

9 Close and return to Microsoft Excel. Exit Design **Mode**. Test the button by clicking the **Print Leaf Name Tag command button**. Click cell **A1** to deselect. **Save** your workbook, and then submit as directed by your instructor. If required, print your VBA code using the instructions in Activity 9.07. **Close** the workbook.

10 If you are directed to remove the **DEVELOPER tab**, follow the directions in Activity 9.13. **Close** Excel.

END | You have completed Project 9G

Apply a combination of the **9A** and **9B** skills.

GO! Fix It	Project 9H Finance Report	Online
GO! Make It	Project 9I Timecard	Online
GO! Solve It	Project 9J Filename Macro	Online
GO! Solve It	Project 9K Book Evaluation	

PROJECT FILES

For Project 9K, you will need the following file:

e09K_Book_VBA

You will save your workbook as:

Lastname_Firstname_9K_Book_VBA

Open the file e09K_Book_VBA and save it as an Excel Macro-Enabled Workbook **Lastname_Firstname_9K_Book_VBA** In the following Mastering Excel project, you will assist Matt Gallagher, Training Director, by adding an ActiveX control Command Button to an evaluation form to gather feedback from the consultants about a new book that will be used at customer seminars. In cell H7, add an ActiveX control Command Button to the worksheet. In the properties, change the name to **Start** caption to **Click Here to Start** and AutoSize to *True*. Add the following comments to the VBA code:

```
' Start Button Procedure      Author: Firstname Lastname
' Date Created: March 16, 2016
' Function: When clicked, the Start button will display four input
' boxes requesting the user to enter his or her name,
' position, department, and email.
Add the following VBA code:
Range("B6").Value = InputBox("Enter your name", "Name")
Range("B7").Value = InputBox("Enter the name of your position", "Position")
Range("B8").Value = InputBox("Enter the name of your department", "Department")
Range("B9").Value = InputBox("Enter your email", "Email")
```

Add appropriate name and course information to the document properties including the tags **book evaluation, VBA** and then submit as directed by your instructor.

(Project 9K Book Evaluation continues on the next page)

CONTENT-BASED ASSESSMENTS

Performance Level

Performance Criteria		Exemplary	Proficient	Developing
	Insert an ActiveX Control Command Button and Change Properties	An ActiveX Control Command Button was inserted. Name, caption, and AutoSize properties were assigned.	An ActiveX Control Command Button was inserted but name, caption, and AutoSize properties were not correctly assigned.	An ActiveX Control Command Button was not inserted.
	Write a VBA Procedure for a Command Button	A VBA Procedure for a Start Command Button was correctly written.	A VBA Procedure for a Start Command Button was only partially written.	A VBA Procedure for a Start Command Button was not written.

END | You have completed Project 9K

OUTCOMES-BASED ASSESSMENTS

RUBRIC

The following outcomes-based assessments are open-ended assessments. That is, there is no specific correct result; your result will depend on your approach to the information provided. Make Professional Quality your goal. Use the following scoring rubric to guide you in how to approach the problem and then to evaluate how well your approach solves the problem.

The *criteria*—Software Mastery, Content, Format and Layout, and Process—represent the knowledge and skills you have gained that you can apply to solving the problem. The *levels of performance*—Professional Quality, Approaching Professional Quality, or Needs Quality Improvements—help you and your instructor evaluate your result.

	Your completed project is of Professional Quality if you:	Your completed project is Approaching Professional Quality if you:	Your completed project Needs Quality Improvements if you:
1-Software Mastery	Choose and apply the most appropriate skills, tools, and features and identify efficient methods to solve the problem.	Choose and apply some appropriate skills, tools, and features, but not in the most efficient manner.	Choose inappropriate skills, tools, or features, or are inefficient in solving the problem.
2-Content	Construct a solution that is clear and well organized, contains content that is accurate, appropriate to the audience and purpose, and is complete. Provide a solution that contains no errors in spelling, grammar, or style.	Construct a solution in which some components are unclear, poorly organized, inconsistent, or incomplete. Misjudge the needs of the audience. Have some errors in spelling, grammar, or style, but the errors do not detract from comprehension.	Construct a solution that is unclear, incomplete, or poorly organized; contains some inaccurate or inappropriate content; and contains many errors in spelling, grammar, or style. Do not solve the problem.
3-Format & Layout	Format and arrange all elements to communicate information and ideas, clarify function, illustrate relationships, and indicate relative importance.	Apply appropriate format and layout features to some elements, but not others. Overuse features, causing minor distraction.	Apply format and layout that does not communicate information or ideas clearly. Do not use format and layout features to clarify function, illustrate relationships, or indicate relative importance. Use available features excessively, causing distraction.
4-Process	Use an organized approach that integrates planning, development, self-assessment, revision, and reflection.	Demonstrate an organized approach in some areas, but not others; or, use an insufficient process of organization throughout.	Do not use an organized approach to solve the problem.

OUTCOMES-BASED ASSESSMENTS

GO! Think — Project 9L Accounting Department

PROJECT FILES

For Project 9L, you will need the following file:

e09L_Accounting_Macro

You will save your workbook as:

Lastname_Firstname_9L_Accounting_Macro

Open the file e09L_Accounting_Macro, and then save it in your chapter folder as **Lastname_Firstname_9L_Accounting_Macro**

Record a macro with the shortcut key Ctrl + r, that will insert a header that is required on all reports—Westland Plains Human Resources Consulting in the left section and Accounting Department in the right section. Edit the macro to change the left header to WPHR Consulting. Insert a new worksheet, type a title in cell A1, and test your macro.

Insert the file name in the left section of the footer, add appropriate information to the document properties including the tags **accounting, macro** and submit as directed by your instructor.

END | You have completed Project 9L

GO! Think — Project 9M Sign In Sheet — **Online**

Build from
Scratch

You and GO! — Project 9N Personal Footer — **Online**

External Data, Database Functions, and Side-by-Side Tables

GO! to Work
Video E10

OBJECTIVES

1. Get External Data into Excel
2. Cleanup and Manage Data
3. Create a Query and Use the Query Wizard to Sort and Filter
4. Use Database Functions

OBJECTIVES

5. Insert a Second Table into a Worksheet
6. Apply Conditional Formatting to Side-by-Side Tables
7. Insert a Screenshot
8. Create Custom Headers and Footers

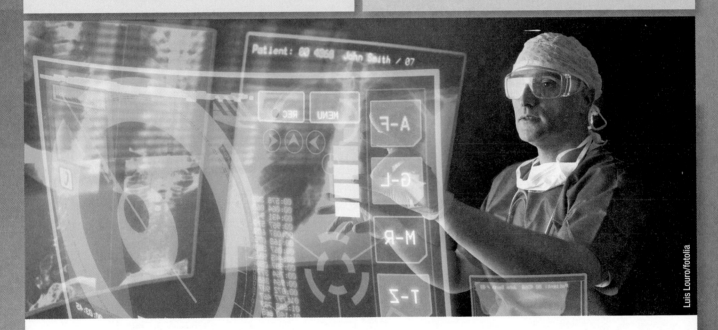

Luis Louro/fotolia

In This Chapter

In this chapter, you will use Excel's database capabilities to organize data. You will import and manage data from other sources and query data in the database. You will also limit data to display records that meet one or more specific conditions. You will add subtotals, and you will group and outline data. You will use database functions to summarize information and analyze data. You will insert a second table into a worksheet and sort data in side-by-side tables, apply conditional formatting to data using icon sets, and insert a screenshot into a worksheet. Finally, you will create custom headers and footers.

The projects in this chapter relate to **Sunshine Health System**, which is the premier patient care and research institution serving the metropolitan area of Miami, Florida. Because of its outstanding reputation in the medical community and around the world, Sunshine Health System is able to attract top physicians, scientists, and researchers in all fields of medicine and achieve a level of funding that allows it to build and operate state-of-the-art facilities and provide the newest, innovative treatment options. Individuals throughout the area travel to Sunshine Health System for world-class diagnosis and care.

Medical Center Information

PROJECT ACTIVITIES

In Activities 10.01 through 10.12, you will import data about medical center nurses, doctors, patients, and supplies into Excel, and query the database to locate information. Your completed worksheet will look similar to Figure 10.1.

PROJECT FILES

For Project 10A, you will need the following files:

e10A_Contacts (Access Database)
e10A_Health_Seminars (HTML Document)
e10A_Medical_Center (Excel Workbook)
e10A_Nurse_Information (Access Database)
e10A_Orthopedic_Supplies (XML Document)
e10A_Physician_Information (Text Document)

You will save your workbook as:

Lastname_Firstname_10A_Medical_Center

PROJECT RESULTS

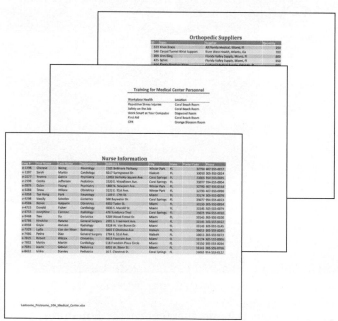
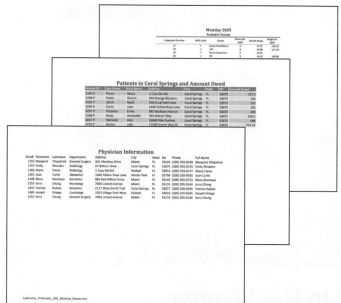

FIGURE 10.1 Project 10A Medical Center Information

> **NOTE**   **If You Are Using a Touchscreen**
>
> - Tap an item to click it.
> - Press and hold for a few seconds to right-click; release when the information or commands display.
> - Touch the screen with two or more fingers and then pinch together to zoom in or stretch your fingers apart to zoom out.
> - Slide your finger on the screen to scroll—slide left to scroll right and slide right to scroll left.
> - Slide to rearrange—similar to dragging with a mouse.
> - Swipe from edge: from right to display charms; from left to expose open apps, snap apps, or close apps; from top or bottom to show commands or close an app.
> - Swipe to select—slide an item a short distance with a quick movement—to select an item and bring up commands, if any.

Objective 1   Get External Data into Excel

Video E10-1

You have used many of Excel's powerful tools for analyzing data, but what if the data you want to analyze is not in Excel? You can get data that resides outside of Excel into Excel by using the commands located on the DATA tab in the **Get External Data** group. This group of commands enables you to bring data from an Access database, from the Web, from a text file, from an XML file, and from other sources such as a database on a SharePoint or SQL server, or an external data feed, into Excel without repeatedly copying the data. Then, you can apply Excel's data analysis tools to the data. You can also establish links, or **data connections**, to the external data so that you can automatically update your Excel workbook from the original data whenever the original data source gets new information.

> **NOTE**   **To Maintain Connections to External Data**
>
> To connect to external data when you open a workbook, you must enable data connections by using the Trust Center bar or by putting the workbook in a trusted location.

Activity 10.01 | Importing Data into Excel from an Access Database

Data in an Access database is organized in a format of horizontal rows and vertical columns—just like an Excel worksheet. Each horizontal row stores all of the data about one database item and is referred to as a **record**. Each vertical column stores information that describes the record and is referred to as a **field**. Data stored in a format of rows and columns is referred to as a **table**. In this activity, you will import data into Excel from an Access database.

1 Start Excel. Locate the student files that accompany this textbook, open the file **e10A_Medical_Center**. Navigate to the location where you are storing your files for this chapter, create a new folder named **Excel Chapter 10** and then **Save** the file as **Lastname_Firstname_10A_Medical_Center**

2 Click the **FILE tab** and then click **Options** to display the **Excel Options** dialog box. On the left, click **Trust Center**, on the right, click **Trust Center Settings**, and then in the **Trust Center** dialog box, on the left, click **External Content**. Verify the default selections *Prompt user about Data Connections* and *Prompt user on automatic update for Workbook links* are selected, and then click **OK**. In the **Excel Options** dialog box, click **OK**.

Here you can make decisions about enabling connections. By default, both settings are set to *Prompt user*, and it is recommended that you maintain these default settings. This textbook assumes the default settings.

3 At the bottom of the Excel window, in the row of sheet tabs, locate the horizontal scroll bar. At the left end of the scroll bar, point to the three vertical dots to display the ⊪ pointer, and then drag to the right to decrease the width of the scroll bar to display all six worksheets in this workbook as shown in Figure 10.2.

FIGURE 10.2

4 On the **Nurse Information** worksheet click in cell **A2**. On the **DATA tab**, in the **Get External Data group**, click **From Access**.

5 In the **Select Data Source** dialog box, locate the student files that accompany this textbook, click the Access file **e10A_Nurse_Information**, and then in the lower right corner of the dialog box, click **Open**.

The Import Data dialog box displays. The option buttons that are selected indicate that the information will be imported as a table and into the existing worksheet in cell A2—the active cell. *Microsoft Access* is a database program used to manage database files. In this manner, you can import data from Access or from other database programs.

6 In the **Import Data** dialog box, be sure that **Table** is selected, and then click **OK**. Compare your screen with Figure 10.3.

Excel imports the table of nurse information. Beside each column title, an arrow displays for easy sorting and filtering. The field names display in row 2 and the records display in rows 3 to 22. On the TABLE TOOLS DESIGN tab, the External Table Data group includes commands to *Unlink* and *Refresh* the data from the external table. If you unlink the table, then your Excel data will not be updated when the external data is changed.

FIGURE 10.3

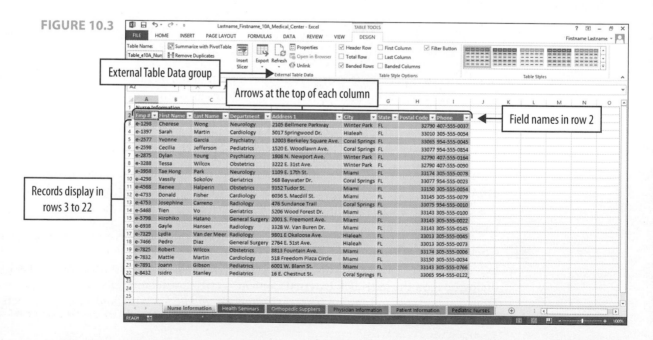

7 **Merge & Center** the text in cell **A1** across the range **A1:I1**, and then apply the **Title** cell style.

8 **Save** 🖫 your workbook.

In this activity, you will import data into Excel from a webpage.

1 Make the next worksheet—**Health Seminars**—the active sheet.

2 Press Ctrl + F12 to display the **Open** dialog box. Navigate to your student files, right-click the HTML document **e10A_Health_Seminars**, and then, point to **Open with**. Compare your screen with Figure 10.4.

FIGURE 10.4

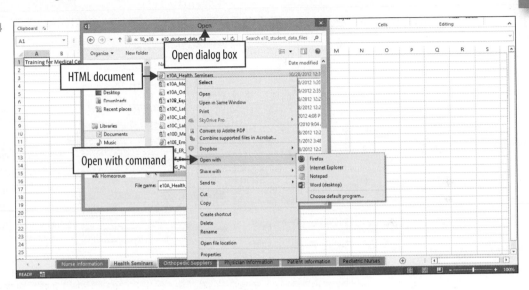

3 Click **Internet Explorer** (or your preferred browser). Compare your screen with Figure 10.5.

The Internet browser opens and displays a Sunshine Health System webpage containing two tables of data with health seminar titles and locations.

FIGURE 10.5

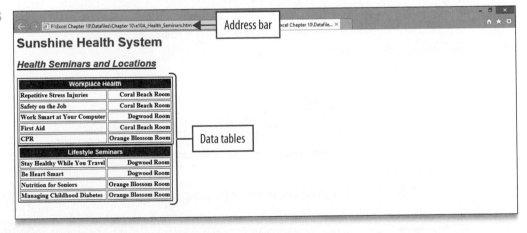

4 On the browser window, point to the **address bar** and right-click, click **Copy**, and then **Close** ☒ the browser window.

5 **Close** ☒ the **Open** dialog box. Click in cell **A3**. On the **DATA tab**, in the **Get External Data group**, click **From Web**.

The New Web Query dialog box displays the home page set on your computer.

ALERT! **Does a Security Information Box Display?**

If your home page contains secure data, click Yes to display the webpage information.

---

6 In the **New Web Query** dialog box, point to the **address bar** and right-click, click **Paste**, and then at the end of **address bar**, click **Go**. As necessary, drag the title bar of the **New Web Query** dialog box to the upper portion of your screen, and then in the lower right corner of the dialog box, drag the 🔁 pointer as necessary to resize the dialog box and display the two tables on the webpage. Compare your screen with Figure 10.6.

Yellow arrows mark the beginning of each table in the webpage. You import tables by selecting the yellow arrow.

FIGURE 10.6

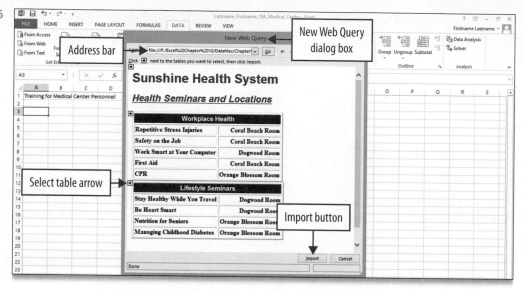

7 On the left side of the **Workplace Health** table, click the **yellow arrow** to select the table. In the lower right corner of the dialog box, click **Import**, and then in the **Import Data** dialog box, verify that **Existing worksheet** and cell **$A$3** are selected. Click **OK**, and then compare your screen with Figure 10.7.

The Workplace Health table data is imported and displays on the Health Seminars worksheet.

FIGURE 10.7

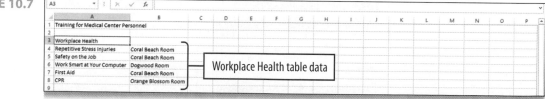

8 In cell **B3**, type **Location** and then press Enter. Select the range **A3:B3**, and then apply the **Heading 3** cell style.

9 **Merge & Center** the title in cell **A1** across the range **A1:B1**, and then apply the **Heading 1** cell style.

10 Save 💾 your workbook.

In this activity, you will import data into Excel from an XML file. **Extensible Markup Language (XML)** is a language that structures data in text files so that it can be read by other systems, regardless of the hardware platform or operating system. Such portability is why XML has become a popular technology for exchanging data.

1 ▶ Display the next worksheet—**Orthopedic Suppliers**.

2 ▶ Click in cell **A2**. On the **DATA tab**, in the **Get External Data group**, click **From Other Sources**, and then click **From XML Data Import**.

3 ▶ In the **Select Data Source** dialog box, navigate to your student files, and then click the XML file **e10A_Orthopedic_Supplies**. At the bottom of the dialog box, notice that the file type is *XML Files*.

The Orthopedic Supplies file contains supplier information for orthopedic supplies at the Medical Center. In this manner, you can import data from an XML file.

4 ▶ With the **e10A_Orthopedic_Supplies** file selected, click **Open**.

A Microsoft Excel information message displays. The specified XML source does not refer to a schema. A *schema* is an XML file that contains the rules for what can and cannot reside in an XML data file. Schemas are not required in XML, but they can be useful in ensuring that any data inserted into an XML document follows predefined rules for both content and structure.

5 ▶ Click **OK** to display the **Import Data** dialog box. Notice that the data will be imported as an XML table into the existing worksheet in cell **$A$2**—the active cell.

6 ▶ Click **OK**, and then compare your screen with Figure 10.8.

The table of orthopedic suppliers is imported as an Excel table with filter arrows in the column titles. The field names display in row 2 and the records display in rows 3 to 10.

FIGURE 10.8

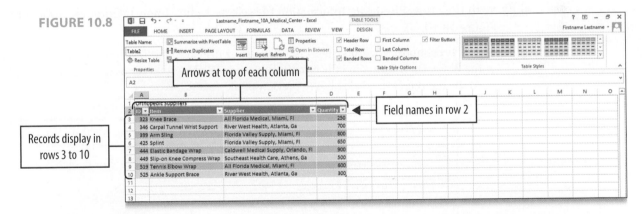

7 ▶ **Merge & Center** the title in cell **A1** across the range **A1:D1**, and then apply the **Title** cell style.

8 ▶ On the **DATA tab**, in the **Connections group**, click **Connections** to open the **Workbook Connections** dialog box. Click **e10A_Orthopedic_Supplies** and then, in the lower pane, click **Click here to see where the selected connections are used**. Compare your screen with Figure 10.9. **Close** ⊠ the **Workbook Connections** dialog box and **Save** 🖫 your workbook.

The Workbook Connections dialog box can be used to view and modify external data connections used in a workbook.

FIGURE 10.9

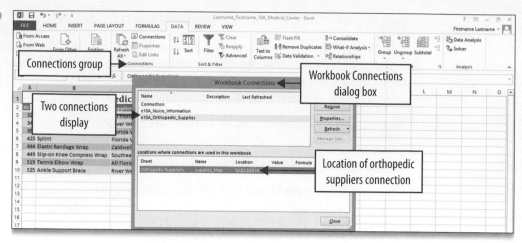

Activity 10.04 | Importing Data into Excel from a Text File

In this activity, you will import information into Excel from a text file.

1 Make the next worksheet—**Physician Information**—active.

2 Click in cell **A8**. On the **DATA tab**, in the **Get External Data group**, click **From Text**.

The Import Text File dialog box displays.

3 In the **Import Text File** dialog box, navigate to your student files, select the text file **e10A_Physician_Information**, and then at the bottom of the dialog box, notice that *Text Files* displays as the file type.

The Physician Information file contains contact information for doctors at the Medical Center. In this manner, you can import data from a text file.

4 With the **e10A_Physician_Information** file selected, click **Import**. Compare your screen with Figure 10.10.

The Text Import Wizard – Step 1 of 3 dialog box displays. The Text Import Wizard determines that the Physician Information file is ***delimited***—separated by commas or tabs—and selects Delimited. At the bottom of the dialog box, a preview of the data displays.

FIGURE 10.10

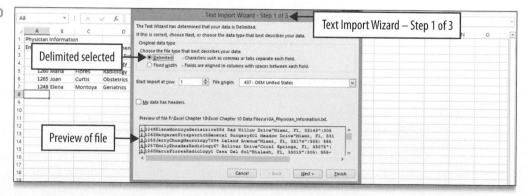

5 Click **Next**, and then compare your screen with Figure 10.11.

The Text Import Wizard – Step 2 of 3 dialog box displays. Here you can set the delimiters your data contains. Under Delimiters, the Tab check box is selected. At the bottom of the dialog box, the Data preview displays.

FIGURE 10.11

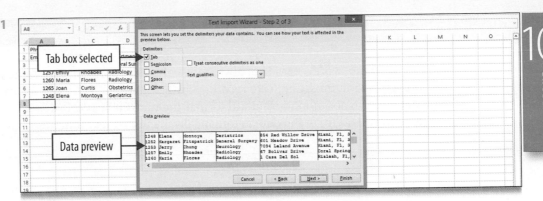

6 ▷ Click **Next**, and then compare your screen with Figure 10.12.

The Text Import Wizard – Step 3 of 3 dialog box displays. Here you can select each column and see the data format. Under Column data format, General is selected. At the bottom of the dialog box, the Data preview displays.

FIGURE 10.12

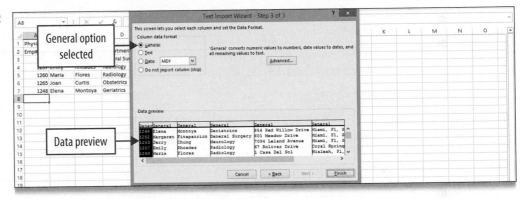

7 ▷ Click **Finish**.

The Import Data dialog box displays, indicating that the table will be imported into the existing worksheet in cell $A$8—the active cell. This will append the data to the existing data in rows 1:7.

8 ▷ Click **OK**, and then compare your screen with Figure 10.13. Notice there are several duplicate records in this data. **Save** 🔲 your workbook.

FIGURE 10.13

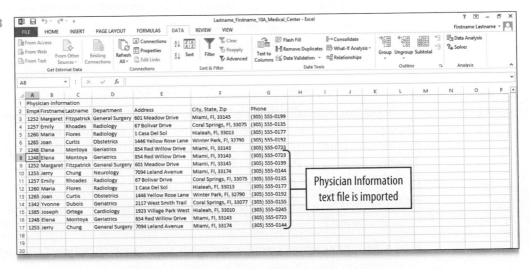

Video E10-2

Data in a worksheet is not always formatted in a way you can use it. The data may be in the wrong columns, duplicate records may be imported, and even the case of the letters may be incorrect. In addition to standard formatting tools such as cell styles, Excel includes several tools to help you clean up the data automatically, including text functions and ribbon commands.

Activity 10.05 | Removing Duplicates

In a worksheet with many records, it can be difficult to locate duplicate records by eye. In the following activity, you will remove duplicate records from the Physician Information worksheet automatically.

1 With the **Physician Information** worksheet active, on the **DATA tab**, in the **Data Tools group**, click **Remove Dsuplicates**.

The Remove Duplicates dialog box includes a list of the columns available in the data.

2 Click **Unselect All**, verify that the *My data has headers* check box is selected, select the *Emp#* and *Department* check boxes, and then click **OK**. Compare your screen with Figure 10.14.

This assures that an employee will only appear once for each department. Six duplicate records were found and deleted. In this manner you can clean up duplicate data automatically.

FIGURE 10.14

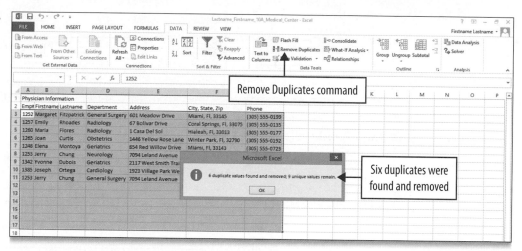

Remove Duplicates command

Six duplicates were found and removed

3 Click **OK** and **Save** your workbook.

Activity 10.06 | Using Flash Fill to Expand Data

Excel can be used to format text data. For example, to make sorting and filtering easier, you can separate data into separate fields using Flash Fill. *Flash Fill* is an Excel feature that predicts how to alter data based upon the pattern you enter into the cell at the beginning of the column. The data must be in the adjacent column to use Flash Fill. In the following activity, you will use Flash Fill to clean up imported data.

1 On the **Physician Information** worksheet, notice the city, state, and zip are all in the same field in **column F**.

2 Click the **column G** header, right-click, and then click **Insert** to insert a new column. Use the same method to insert two additional columns.

Three new columns are added between the *City, State, Zip*, and *Phone Number* fields.

3 ▸ Click cell **G2**, type **City** and then press ⎀Tab⎀. In cell **H2**, type **State** and press ⎀Tab⎀, in cell **I2**, type **Zip** and then press ⎀Enter⎀.

4 ▸ In cell **G3**, type **Miami** and press ⎀Enter⎀. In cell **G4**, type **Co** and compare your screen with Figure 10.15.

Based upon your entries in cell G3 and G4, Flash Fill suggests entries for the remaining cells in the column.

FIGURE 10.15

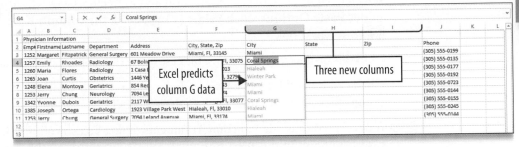

5 ▸ Press ⎀Enter⎀. Click cell **H3** and type **Fl** Use the **fill handle** to copy the text down through **H11**. **Save** 🖫 your workbook.

Excel's Flash Fill feature automatically completes column G using the pattern. Because all employees live in Florida, you can simply drag to fill column H.

Activity 10.07 | Using Text Functions

Text functions can be used to combine or separate data, change case, and apply formatting to a string of characters. The text function *RIGHT* will return the specified number of characters from the end (right) of a string of characters. The similar *LEFT* function returns the specified number of characters from the beginning (left) of a string, and the *MID* function extracts a series of characters from a text string given the location of the beginning character.

The *CONCATENATE* text function can be used to join up to 255 strings of characters. The *TRIM* function is used to remove extra blank spaces from a string. This is especially useful for removing leading blank spaces, which are difficult to see by eye, but can cause problems with sorting and filtering. The *UPPER* and *LOWER* functions will change the case of the characters in a string, making all characters uppercase or lowercase, and the *PROPER* function will capitalize the first letter of each word. In the following activity, you will use several text functions to clean up imported data.

1 ▸ Click cell **I3**. On the **FORMULAS tab**, in the **Function Library group**, click **Text**, and then click **RIGHT**.

2 ▸ If necessary, drag the **Function Arguments** dialog box down so **row 3** is visible. With the insertion point in the **Text** box, click cell **F3**. Press ⎀Tab⎀, and then, in the **Num_chars** box, type **5** Compare your dialog box with Figure 10.16.

FIGURE 10.16

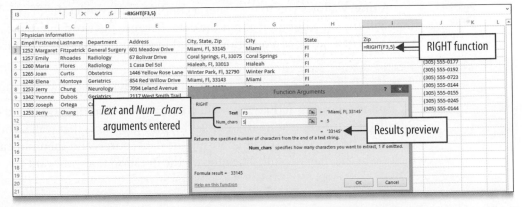

3 Click **OK**. Drag the **fill handle** to copy the function down through cell **I11**.

The text function RIGHT displays the last five characters of the text in column F.

4 Click cell **K3**, in the **Function Library**, click **Text**, scroll down as necessary and then click **UPPER**. With the insertion point in the **Text** box, click cell **H3** and then click **OK**.

5 Drag the **fill handle** to copy the function down through cell **K11**. With the range **K3:K11** selected, right-click over the selection and then click **Copy**. Right-click over cell **H3** and, under **Paste Options**, click **Values (V)** . Click the **column K** heading and press [Delete]. **Save** your workbook.

In this manner you can change the case of the state abbreviations to all uppercase.

6 Click cell **K2** and type **Full Name** Click cell **K3**, on the **FORMULAS tab**, in the **Function Library group**, click **Text**, and then click **CONCATENATE**.

7 If necessary, drag the **Function Arguments** dialog box so **columns B:C** are visible. With the insertion point in the **Text1** box, click cell **B3**. Press [Tab], in the **Text2** box type " and press [Spacebar] and then type " Press [Tab] and in the **Text3** box, click **C3**. Compare your dialog box with Figure 10.17.

FIGURE 10.17

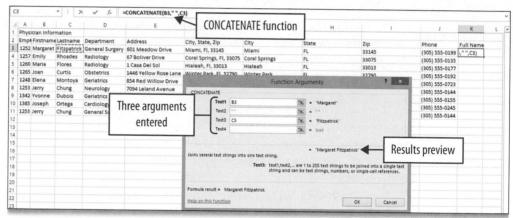

8 Click **OK**. Use the **fill handle** to copy the function down through cell **K11**.

The CONCATENATE function combined the text entered in the argument boxes into a single cell.

9 Click cell **A1**. **Merge & Center** the text across the range **A1:K1** and apply the **Title** cell style. **AutoFit columns A:K**. Click the **column F** heading, right-click, click **Hide**, and then **Save** your workbook.

Objective 3 | Create a Query and Use the Query Wizard to Sort and Filter

Video E10-3

A **query** allows you to use criteria conditions to restrict the display of records to those records that will answer a question about the data. Because the word *query* means *to ask a question*, you can think of a query as a question formed in a manner that Excel can interpret.

Activity 10.08 | Creating a Query to Filter and Sort Data by Using the Query Wizard

In the following activity, you will create a query and then filter and sort data using a wizard. Recall a **wizard** is a feature in Microsoft Office programs that walks you step by step through a process. The process involves choosing the data source, and then indicating the fields you want to include in the query result. The query—the question that you want to ask—is *What is the name,* *complete mailing address, and Patient ID of every patient in the database who lives in Coral Springs zip code 33075, and how much do they owe?*

1 Display the next worksheet—**Patient Information**.

2 Click in cell **A2**. On the **DATA tab**, in the **Get External Data group**, click **From Other Sources**. Click **From Microsoft Query**.

3 In the **Choose Data Source** dialog box, verify that the **Databases tab** is active and, at the bottom, be sure the **Use the Query Wizard to create/edit queries** check box is selected. Then, click **MS Access Database***. Compare your screen with Figure 10.18.

FIGURE 10.18

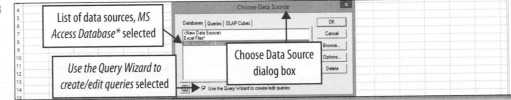

4 Click **OK** to display the **Select Database** dialog box.

5 Under **Directories**, be sure the folder containing your student files is selected—if necessary, scroll down to view and select the folder. Under **Database Name**, click **e10A_Contacts.accdb**. Compare your screen with Figure 10.19.

Connecting to data source displays with red dots moving between the icons.

FIGURE 10.19

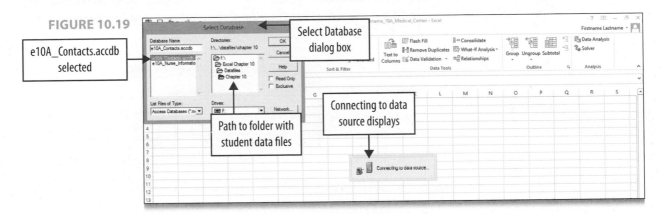

6 Click **OK**, and then compare your screen with Figure 10.20.

The Query Wizard – Choose Columns dialog box displays. Here you choose what columns of data you want to include in your query.

FIGURE 10.20

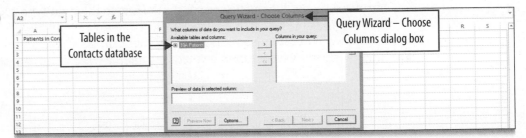

7 Under **Available tables and columns**, to the left of **10A Patients**, click **Expand** ⊞ to expand the table and view the column names.

The column names display. To create a query, first choose the data source—the table from which you will select the data you want. To find the name and complete mailing address of every patient and how much he or she owes, you will need the 10A Patients table.

8 Under **Available tables and columns**, click **Patient ID**, and then click **Add Field** ⟩ to move the field to the **Columns in your query** list on the right. Using the same technique, add the **Last Name** field to the list. Compare your screen with Figure 10.21.

Recall that you choose the fields that you want to include in your resulting query.

🔄 **ANOTHER WAY** Alternatively, double-click the field name to move it to the Columns in your query list.

FIGURE 10.21

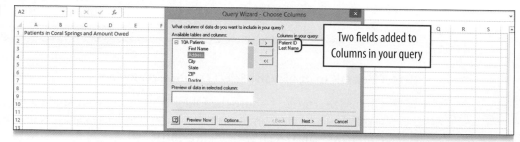

9 Double-click the **First Name** field to add it to your query. Using either **Add Field** ⟩ or by double-clicking, add the following fields to the **Columns in your query** list: **Address**, **City**, **State**, **ZIP**, **Amount Owed**. Compare your screen with Figure 10.22.

FIGURE 10.22

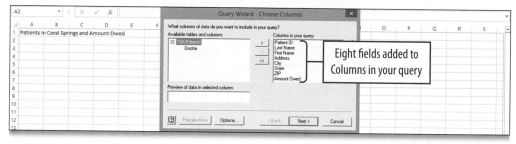

10 In the lower right corner, click **Next**.

The Query Wizard – Filter Data dialog box displays. Here you filter the data to specify which *rows* to include in your query.

11 Under **Column to filter**, click **ZIP**. Under **Only include rows where**, click in the **ZIP box** to display a list, and then click **equals**. In the box to the right type **33075** Compare your screen with Figure 10.23.

FIGURE 10.23

12 Click **Next**. In the **Query Wizard – Sort Order** dialog box, under **Sort by**, click the **arrow**, and then click **Amount Owed**. Verify that **Ascending** is selected. Compare your screen with Figure 10.24.

In the Query Wizard – Sort Order dialog box, you specify how you want your data sorted—in this instance, in Ascending order by Amount Owed.

FIGURE 10.24

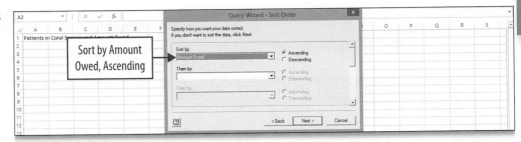

13 In the lower right corner, click **Next**. Compare your screen with Figure 10.25.

The Query Wizard – Finish dialog box displays. Here you specify what you would like to do next with the query information.

FIGURE 10.25

14 Be sure **Return Data to Microsoft Excel** is selected, and then click **Finish**.

15 In the **Import Data** dialog box, verify that **Table** is selected, that **Existing worksheet** is selected, and that cell **$A$2** is indicated. Click **OK**.

16 In cell **A1**, **Merge & Center** the title across the range **A1:H1**, and then apply the **Title** cell style. Compare your screen with Figure 10.26.

Excel runs the query—performs the actions indicated in your query design—by searching the table of records included in the query, finding the records that match the criteria, and then importing and displaying the records on the Patient Information worksheet so that you can see the results. In this manner, a query pulls out and displays from the table only the information that you requested.

FIGURE 10.26

17 Save 💾 your workbook.

Activity 10.09 | Converting a Table into a Range

In this activity, you will convert a table of imported data into a range.

1 In your **Patient Information** worksheet, click any cell in the table data.

2 Click the **DESIGN tab**, and then in the **Tools group**, click **Convert to Range**.

A Microsoft Excel information box displays indicating that this will permanently remove the query definition from the sheet and convert the table to a normal range.

3 Click **OK**, and then **Save** 🔲 your workbook.

Objective 4 | Use Database Functions

Video E10-4

In Excel, you can not only track and manage financial and numerical data, but you can also create simple databases. A *database* is a collection of data related to a particular topic or purpose. *Data* refers to facts about people, events, things, or ideas. Data that is organized in a useful manner is referred to as *information*. An example of information at the Sunshine Health System is the list of nurses who work in various departments or who work various shifts.

Recall that a *function* is a predefined formula that performs calculations by using specific values, called *arguments*. Database functions are identified by the letter *D*—each function starts with a D, for example, DSUM, DAVERAGE, and DCOUNT. The initial letter *D* identifies to Excel that a database range will be used in the formula, rather than a single column or row of numbers.

Activity 10.10 | Using the DAVERAGE Database Function

The *syntax*—arrangement of arguments in a function—for the majority of database functions is: DFunction Name(database, field, criteria), where *database* identifies the range of cells where the data is displayed, *field* is the field name to be considered, and *criteria* is the range of cells where the search criteria has been defined. The criteria is defined in a separate area on the worksheet. In this activity, you will use the DAVERAGE function to determine the average hourly wage for LPNs (Licensed Practical Nurses) in the pediatric wing of the hospital. The **DAVERAGE function** determines an average in a database that is limited by criteria set for one or more cells.

1 In your workbook, display the next worksheet—**Pediatric Nurses**.

This worksheet lists the Employee Number, Shift Code, Status, Hours per Shift, Hourly Wage, and Wage per Shift for pediatric nurses who work on Mondays. The Wage per Shift field contains a formula that multiplies the Hours per Shift in column D times the Hourly Wage in column E. The number in the Shift Code field is a code for the shift. Not all nurses work on Mondays; so, some rows indicate 0 hours per shift.

The Shift Codes represent the following hours:

Shift	Code
Day (6a–2p)	1
Evening (7p–3a)	2
Afternoon (12p–8p)	3
Night (10p–6a)	4
Day 12-hr (6a–6p)	5
Night 12-hr (6p–6a)	6

2 Scroll down to display **row 28**. In cell **A28**, type **Average Hourly Wage for LPNs** and press Enter. **AutoFit column A**.

Average Hourly Wage for LPNs will form the label for the function you will enter.

3 Scroll up, point to cell **C3**, right-click, and then click **Copy**. Scroll down, point to cell **C28**, right-click, and then click **Paste (P)** 📋.

Cell C28 will form the first cell in the criteria range for the DAVERAGE function, which must consist of at least two vertical cells. The top cell is the field name that is to be searched, and the cell immediately below it is the criteria used in the function search.

4 In cell **C29**, type **LPN** and press Tab.

The value—LPN—is the search criteria.

5 Click cell **B28**, and then to the left of the **Formula Bar**, click **Insert Function** 𝑓𝑥.

You can use the Insert Function dialog box to locate any function in Excel.

🔄 **ANOTHER WAY**   On the FORMULAS tab, in the Function Library group, click Insert Function.

6 In the **Insert Function** dialog box, click the **Or select a category arrow**, and then click **Database**. In the **Select a function** box, click **DAVERAGE**, and then click **OK**. Compare your screen with Figure 10.27.

The Function Arguments dialog box for DAVERAGE displays. Recall that *arguments* are the values that an Excel function uses to perform calculations or operations.

FIGURE 10.27

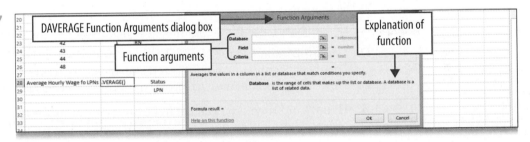

7 In the **Database** box, click **Collapse Dialog Box** 📩, and then select the range **A3:F26**. In the collapsed dialog box, click **Expand Dialog Box** 📩.

This action defines the database range in the first argument box.

8 In the **Field** box, type **Hourly Wage** and press Tab.

This action identifies the field or column in the database that you want to average; the insertion point moves to the Criteria box. Excel adds quotation marks around the Field name, which identifies it as a string of characters to use in the search.

9 With the insertion point in the **Criteria** box, select the range **C28:C29**—the criteria range that was previously defined. Compare your screen with Figure 10.28.

The two cells in the criteria range will limit the DAVERAGE calculation to only those records where *Status* is equal to *LPN*—RNs and Nurse Supervisors will not be included.

FIGURE 10.28

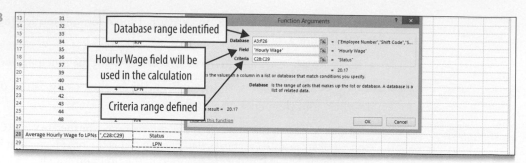

10> Click **OK**. Right-click cell **B28**, and then on the mini toolbar, apply **Accounting Number Format** $ ▾.

The result, *$20.17*, displays in cell B28. This is the average hourly wage for LPNs who work in the pediatric wing of the hospital on Mondays.

11> Save 🖫 your workbook.

Activity 10.11 | Using the DSUM Database Function

The **DSUM function** will sum a column of values in a database that is limited by criteria set for one or more cells. In this activity, you will sum the *Wage per Shift* for RNs who work in the Pediatric wing on Mondays.

1> In cell **A31**, type **Wage per Shift for RNs** and press [Tab].

2> Select and then copy the range **C3:D3**. Point to cell **C31** and right-click, and then click **Paste (P)** 📋.

3> In cell **C32**, type **RN** and press [Tab]. In cell **D32**, type **>0** and then press [Enter].

The *Status* will be limited to RN, and the *Hours Worked* will be limited to those RNs who worked a number of hours greater than zero. This is a **compound criteria**—use of two or more criteria on the same row—all conditions must be met for the records to be included in the results.

4> Click cell **B31**, and then type **=dsum(** to begin the formula for the DSUM function. Compare your screen with Figure 10.29.

Recall that you can type the function arguments directly into the cell instead of using the *Function Argument* dialog box. A ScreenTip displays the parts of the argument that must be included, which guides you through the process of entering all of the arguments necessary for this function.

FIGURE 10.29

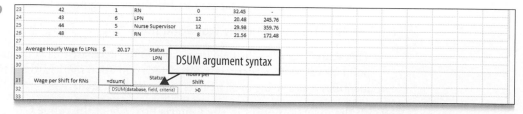

5> Notice that in the function ScreenTip, *database* displays in bold, indicating that you must select a range that is the database. Select the range **A3:F26**, and then type **,** (a comma). Compare your screen with Figure 10.30.

The database range is defined, and the *field* argument displays in bold.

FIGURE 10.30

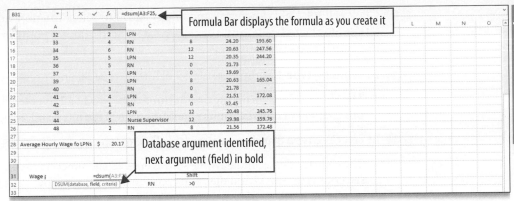

	A	B	C		D	E
14	32	2	LPN			
15	33	4	RN	8	24.20	193.60
16	34	6	RN	12	20.63	247.56
17	35	5	LPN	12	20.35	244.20
18	36	5	RN	0	21.73	-
19	37	1	LPN	0	19.69	-
20	39	1	LPN	8	20.63	165.04
21	40	3	RN	0	21.78	-
22	41	4	LPN	8	21.51	172.08
23	42	1	RN	0	32.45	-
24	43	6	LPN	12	20.48	245.76
25	44	5	Nurse Supervisor	12	29.98	359.76
26	48	2	RN	8	21.56	172.48

Formula Bar displays the formula as you create it

Database argument identified, next argument (field) in bold

6 Notice that in the function ScreenTip, *field* displays in bold, indicating that you must type the name of the field. Being sure to include the comma, type **"Wage per Shift"** to enter the second part of the argument; you can look at the Formula Bar to see your typing and correct as necessary.

The field that you want to sum is the *Wage per Shift* field, so the field name is entered as the second argument. The quotation marks define this as a string of characters; it must match the field name exactly. The comma separates this argument from the next argument.

7 As indicated by *criteria* in the ScreenTip, type the criteria as **c31:d32** and then press Enter.

After you type the criteria range, Excel automatically adds a closing parenthesis. The final result of the formula—1455.72—displays in cell B31. The total cost to pay all the RNs who work in the Pediatric wing on Mondays is $1,455.72.

8 Right-click cell **B31** and apply the **Accounting Number Format** $ ▾.

9 With cell **B31** active, click in the Formula Bar and examine the parts of the DSUM function. Compare your screen with Figure 10.31.

FIGURE 10.31

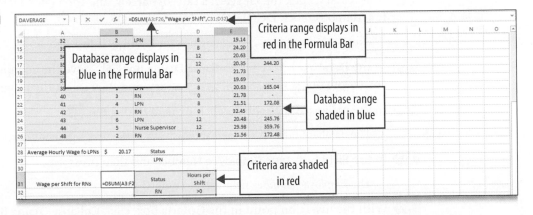

Criteria range displays in red in the Formula Bar

Database range displays in blue in the Formula Bar

Database range shaded in blue

Criteria area shaded in red

10 Save 💾 your workbook.

Activity 10.12 | Using DCOUNT

The **DCOUNT function** counts the number of occurrences of a specified condition in a database.

In this activity, you will count the number of nurses who work the day shift.

1 In cell **A34**, type **Count Day Shift (Code 1, 3, 5)** and press Tab.

This forms the label for the function. Three shifts include daytime hours—Shift Codes 1, 3, and 5—so include all three in the criteria range.

2 Click cell **B3**, hold down Ctrl and click cell **D3** to select the non-adjacent cells. Right-click either of selected cells, and then click **Copy**. Scroll down, point to cell **C34**, right-click, and then click **Paste (P)** .

3 In cell **C35**, type **1** and press Tab. In cell **D35**, type **>0** and press Enter.

The Shift Code value for the first daytime shift, which is *1*, is entered. To meet the conditions of this compound criteria, a nurse must be assigned to Shift 1 and work greater than zero hours.

4 In cell **C36**, type **3** and press Tab. In cell **D36**, type **>0** and press Enter.

The code for the second daytime shift is entered and functions as an *OR* criteria. Excel evaluates the criteria in row 35 and then will consider the criteria in row 36. If a record meets either condition, it will be included in the calculation.

5 In cell **C37**, type **5** and press Tab. In cell **D37**, type **>0** and press Enter. Compare your screen with Figure 10.32.

The code for the third daytime shift—*5*—also functions as an *OR* criteria. Consequently, the calculation will count the number of nurses who worked more than zero hours in one of the three day shifts, whether it is Shift Code 1, 3, or 5.

FIGURE 10.32

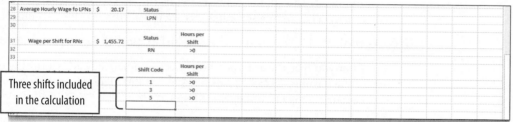

6 Click cell **B34**. To the left of the **Formula Bar**, click **Insert Function** *fx*.

7 If necessary, click the **Or select a category arrow**, and then click **Database**. In the **Select a function** box, click **DCOUNT**, and then click **OK**.

The Function Arguments dialog box for DCOUNT displays.

8 In the **Database** box, click **Collapse Dialog Box**. Move the collapsed box to the upper right corner of your screen. Scroll as necessary, and then select the range **A3:F26**.

9 In the collapsed dialog box, click **Expand Dialog Box**.

The database range is defined and displays in the first argument box.

10 In the **Field** box, type **Employee Number** and then press Tab.

The *Employee Number* field will be counted.

11 With the insertion point in the **Criteria** box, click **Collapse Dialog Box**, scroll as necessary, and then select the range **C34:D37**—the criteria area that was previously defined. In the collapsed dialog box, click **Expand Dialog Box**. Compare your **Function Arguments** dialog box with Figure 10.33.

FIGURE 10.33

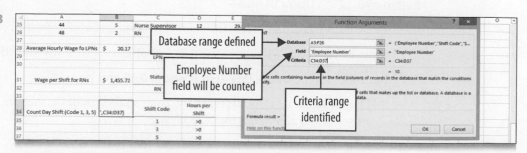

12 Click **OK**. **Save** 🔲 your workbook.

> The result, *10*, displays in cell B34. This is the total number of nurses assigned to work the day shift in the pediatric wing of the hospital on Mondays.

13 Group the worksheets. Insert a footer in the **left section** with the **File Name**, click above the footer area to deselect, and then return to **Normal** view. Make cell **A1** the active cell. Set the **Width** to **1 page** and the **Height** to **1 page**. Display the **document properties** and under **Related People**, if necessary, right-click the author name, click **Edit Property**, and then type your name. In the **Subject** box, type your course name and section number, and in the **Tags** box, type **medical center information** Display **Print Preview**, return to your worksheet and make any necessary corrections.

14 Ungroup the worksheets, **Save** 🔲 your workbook. Print or submit your workbook electronically. If required, print or create an electronic version of your worksheets with formulas displayed. **Close** the workbook and **Close** Excel.

END | You have completed Project 10A

PROJECT ACTIVITIES

In Activities 10.13 through 10.17, you will edit a worksheet for Pat Shepard, Vice President of Operations, detailing the current inventory of two office equipment types—Office Equipment Nursing Station and Office Equipment Administrative. Your completed worksheet will look similar to Figure 10.34.

PROJECT FILES

For Project 10B, you will need the following files:

e10B_Equipment_Inventory
e10B_Logo

You will save your workbook as:

Lastname_Firstname_10B_Equipment_
Inventory

PROJECT RESULTS

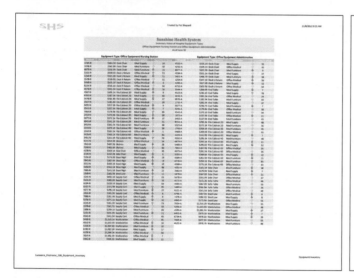

FIGURE 10.34 Project 10B Office Equipment Inventory

Video E10-5

In Excel, you can insert a table beside another table in the *same* worksheet, and then work with the data in each table separately. This enables you to view and compare similar sets of data.

Activity 10.13 | Inserting a Second Table into a Worksheet

1 Start Excel. From your student files, open the file **e10B_Equipment_Inventory**. In your **Excel Chapter 10** folder, **Save** the file as **Lastname_Firstname_10B_Equipment_Inventory**

2 On the **Equipment Inventory** worksheet, select the range **A7:E62**, and then on the **INSERT tab**, in the **Tables group**, click **Table**. In the **Create Table** dialog box, verify that =$A$7:$E$62 displays as the data range and that the **My table has headers** check box is selected. Click **OK**.

The Office Equipment Nursing Station data converts to a table, a table style is applied, and the headings display filter arrows.

3 Click the **Administrative sheet tab**, select the range **A1:E52**, right-click over the selection, and then, click **Copy**.

🔄 BY TOUCH   Press and hold to display the right-click menu.

4 Display the **Equipment Inventory** worksheet, scroll up as necessary, point to cell **F6** and right-click, and then, under **Paste Options**, click **Paste (P)** 📋. Click any cell to deselect. Compare your screen with Figure 10.35.

The data regarding Office Equipment Administrative is added to the right of the Office Equipment Nursing Station table.

FIGURE 10.35

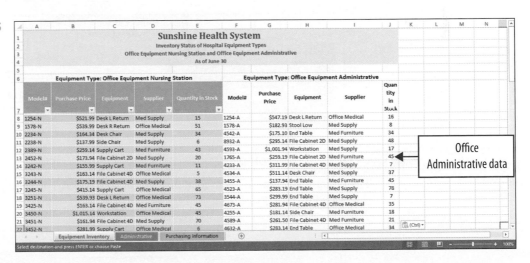

5 Select the range **F7:J57**. In the lower right corner of the selection, click **Quick Analysis** 📊, click **TABLES**, and then click **Table**.

Side-by-side tables do *not* have to contain the same number of rows or columns.

6 On the **DESIGN tab**, in the **Table Styles group**, click **More** ⮟, and then in the gallery, under **Medium**, click **Table Style Medium 13**. Press Ctrl + Home to move to cell **A1** to deselect. Compare your screen with Figure 10.36.

The data for Office Equipment Administrative is converted to a table, a style is applied, and the headings display filter arrows.

FIGURE 10.36

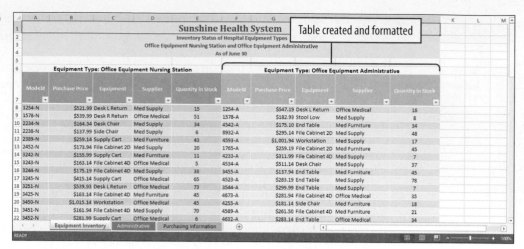

7 ▶ Save 🖫 your workbook.

Activity 10.14 | Sorting Side-by-Side Tables

1 ▶ Click any cell in the **Office Equipment Nursing Station** table on the left. On the **DATA tab**, click **Sort** to display the **Sort** dialog box.

2 ▶ In the **Sort** dialog box, under **Column**, click the **Sort by arrow**, and then click **Equipment**. Verify that **Sort On** indicates *Values* and **Order** indicates *A to Z*.

3 ▶ Click **Add Level**. Under **Column**, click the **Then by arrow**, and then click **Purchase Price**. Click the **Order arrow**, and set the sort order to **Largest to Smallest**. Compare your screen with Figure 10.37.

FIGURE 10.37

4 ▶ Click **OK**, and then compare your screen with Figure 10.38.

The Equipment column is sorted alphabetically, and within each equipment type, the items are sorted by Purchase Price from the highest to lowest.

FIGURE 10.38

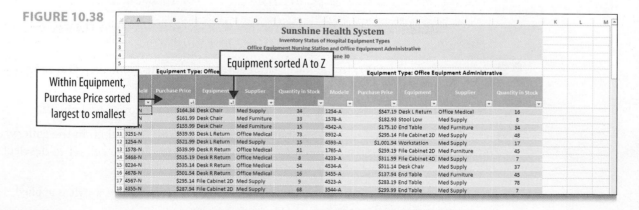

5 Using the same technique and sort orders, sort the **Office Equipment Administrative** table. Compare your screen with Figure 10.39.

By having the two tables side-by-side in the same worksheet, you can sort similar sets of data to make comparisons. Notice that the Administrative desk chairs are more expensive than the Nursing Station desk chairs.

FIGURE 10.39

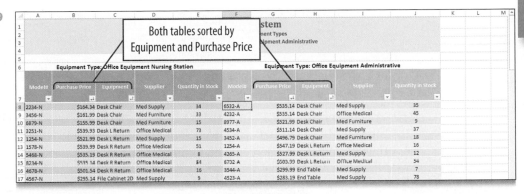

6 Save your workbook.

Objective 6   Apply Conditional Formatting to Side-by-Side Tables

Video E10-6

Recall that *conditional formatting* makes your data easier to interpret by changing the appearance of your data based on a condition; if the condition is true, the cell is formatted based on that condition, and if the condition is false, the cell is not formatted. *Icon sets* are sets of three, four, or five small graphic images that make your data visually easier to interpret. The icons are placed inside the cells. Their shape or color indicates the values in the cells relative to all other adjacent cells formatted using the same condition.

Activity 10.15 | Applying Icon Sets to Side-by-Side Tables

Mr. Shepard has learned that the hospital will be remodeling the East wing, and that an inventory of hospital office equipment is needed. In this activity, you will use icon sets as the conditional formatting to distinguish visually the Stock Level of the hospital office equipment.

1 Select the range **E8:E62**. On the **HOME tab**, in the **Styles group**, click **Conditional Formatting**.

2 Point to **Icon Sets**, and then under **Directional**, in the first row, click the first icon set—**3 Arrows (Colored)**. Click cell **E63** to deselect. Compare your screen with Figure 10.40.

In this icon set, a colored arrow provides the visual cue about the value of a cell relative to other cells. A green upward pointing arrow represents a higher value, a yellow sideways pointing arrow represents a mid-level value, and a red downward pointing arrow represents a lower value. Icon sets are useful to quickly identify higher and lower numbers within a large group of data, such as very high or very low levels of inventory.

FIGURE 10.40

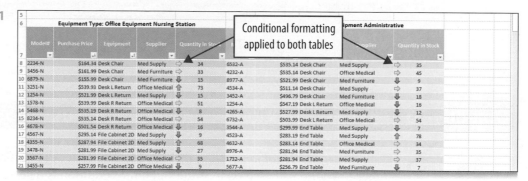

3 Select the range **J8:J57**. In the lower right corner of the selection, click **Quick Analysis** 📊, on the **FORMATTING** tab, click **Icon Sets**. Press Ctrl + Home to make cell **A1** the active cell, and then compare your screen with Figure 10.41.

FIGURE 10.41

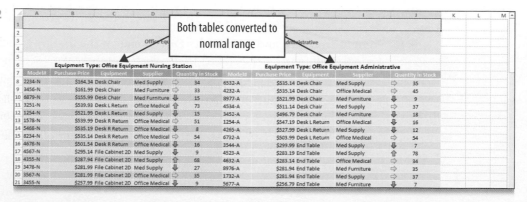

4 Click anywhere in the **Office Equipment Administrative** table to activate the table. Click the **DESIGN tab,** and then in the **Tools group**, click **Convert to Range**. In the message box, click **Yes** to convert the table to a normal range.

> The list arrows are removed from the column titles; the color and shading formats applied from the table style remain.

5 Using the same technique, convert the **Office Equipment Nursing Station** table into a range. Press Ctrl + Home to make cell **A1** the active cell, and then compare your screen with Figure 10.42.

FIGURE 10.42

6 **Save** 💾 your workbook.

Video E10-7

A **screenshot** is an image of an active window on your computer that you can insert into a worksheet. Screenshots are especially useful when you want to insert an image of a website into an Excel worksheet. You can insert a screenshot of any open window on your computer, and then print the worksheet with the inserted screenshot.

Activity 10.16 │ Inserting a Screenshot

The Sunshine Health System is enrolled in the government purchasing program for acquiring office furniture. In this activity, you will go to the U.S. General Services Administration website, and then insert the information into an Excel worksheet.

1 Display the third worksheet in the workbook—**Purchasing Information**.

2 In the **Purchasing Information** worksheet, click cell **A5**. Open your browser. In the **address bar**, type **www.gsa.gov** and press Enter to navigate to the site.

The U.S. General Services Administration webpage displays.

3 From the taskbar, redisplay your **Lastname_Firstname_10B_Purchasing_Information** workbook. On the **INSERT tab**, in the **Illustrations group**, click **Screenshot** ▦. In the gallery, point to the GSA screen to display the ScreenTip, and then compare your screen with Figure 10.43.

All of your open windows display in the Available Windows gallery and are available to insert into your worksheet.

FIGURE 10.43

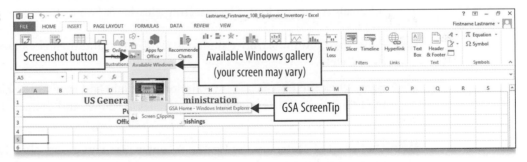

4 Click the **GSA** screenshot and notice that the screen image displays in your worksheet and is selected.

ALERT! **Hyperlink Your Screenshot Message**

If a *Would you like to automatically hyperlink your screenshot to the URL of the captured browser window?* message displays, click No.

---

5 On the **FORMAT tab**, in the **Size group**, change the **Shape Height** to **4.25"** and then compare your screen with Figure 10.44.

FIGURE 10.44

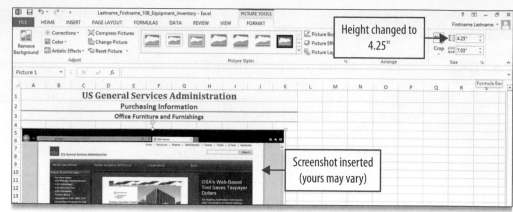

Height changed to 4.25"

Screenshot inserted (yours may vary)

6 ▶ **Save** 💾 your workbook.

Objective 8   Create Custom Headers and Footers

Video E10-8

You can create custom headers and footers to provide useful information about your worksheet. You can type your own text or insert header and footer elements such as pictures, page numbers, and the date and time.

Activity 10.17 | Creating Custom Headers and Footers

In this activity, you will create a custom header by inserting a logo, text, and the date and time. You will create a custom footer by inserting Header & Footer Elements.

1 ▶ Point to the **Administrative sheet tab**, right-click, and then click **Delete.** In the warning box, click **Delete.**

2 ▶ Right-click the **Purchasing Information sheet tab**, and then click **Select All Sheets**. On the **INSERT tab**, in the **Text group**, click **Header & Footer**, and then click in the **left header section** of the header.

3 ▶ On the **DESIGN tab**, in the **Header & Footer Elements group**, click **Picture**. In the **Insert Pictures** dialog box, click **From a file**. Navigate to your student files, click the file **e10B_Logo**, and then click **Insert**. Click above the header. Compare your screen with Figure 10.45.

A logo of the Sunshine Health System displays in the left section of the header.

FIGURE 10.45

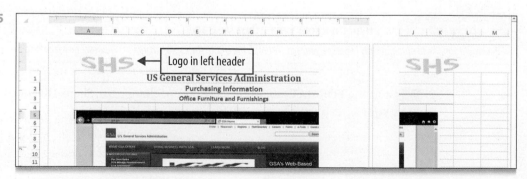

Logo in left header

4 Click in the **middle header section**, type **Created by Pat Shepard** and then press `Tab` to move to the **right header section**. On the **DESIGN tab**, in the **Header & Footer Elements group**, click **Current Date**, press `Spacebar`, and then click **Current Time**. Click above the header. Compare your screen with Figure 10.46.

In the header, the logo displays in the left section, text displays in the middle section, and the date and time display in the right section.

FIGURE 10.46

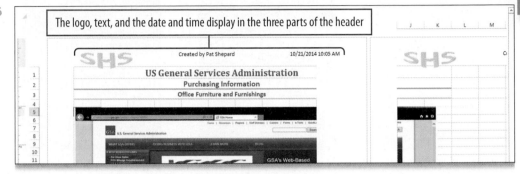

5 On the **INSERT tab**, in the **Text group**, click **Header & Footer**, and then, in the **Navigation group**, click **Go to Footer**.

6 Click in the **left section**, and then in the **Header & Footer Elements group** click **File Name**. Click in the **right section**, and then click **Sheet Name**. Click a cell just above the footer area to deselect, and then compare your screen with Figure 10.47.

In the footer, the file name displays in the left section and the sheet name displays in the right section.

FIGURE 10.47

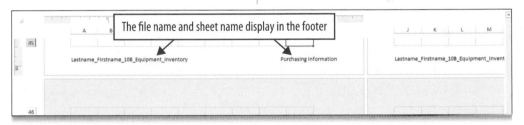

7 In the lower right corner of your screen, in the status bar, click **Normal** 🏢 to return to **Normal** view, and then press `Ctrl` + `Home` to display the top of your worksheet.

8 Be sure your two worksheets are still grouped—*[Group]* displays in the title bar. On the **PAGE LAYOUT tab**, set the **Orientation** to **Landscape**. Set the **Width** to **1 page** and the **Height** to **1 page**. **Center** the worksheets horizontally. Press `Ctrl` + `F2` to check the **Print Preview**, and then return to the workbook.

The first worksheet is slightly wider and taller than the normal margins, so scaling in this manner will keep all the information on one page.

9 Display the **document properties** and under **Related People**, if necessary, right-click the author name, click **Edit Property**, and then type your name. In the **Subject** box, type your course name and section number, and in the **Tags** box, type **office equipment, inventory**

10 Ungroup the worksheets, **Save** 💾 your workbook. Print or submit your workbook electronically. **Close** the workbook and **Close** Excel.

END | You have completed Project 10B

END OF CHAPTER

SUMMARY

Data can be imported into Excel from external sources such as webpages, databases, or text files. Cleaning up data includes removing duplicates, fixing spacing and case, and separating or merging fields.

A database is an organized collection of facts related to a specific topic or purpose. Excel's database functions such as DSUM, DAVERAGE, and DCOUNT can be used to perform calculations on the database.

You can insert a second table into a worksheet and sort data in side-by-side tables to compare data. Apply conditional formatting using icon sets to add visual emphasis to the conditional format of a list.

A screenshot of any open window can be inserted into a worksheet. Custom headers and footers can contain pictures, text, and fields such as file name, sheet name, page number, date, and time.

GO! LEARN IT ONLINE

Review the concepts and key terms in this chapter by completing these online challenges, which you can find at **www.pearsonhighered.com/go**.

Matching and Multiple Choice:
Answer matching and multiple choice questions to test what you learned in this chapter. MyITLab®

Crossword Puzzle:
Spell out the words that match the numbered clues, and put them in the puzzle squares.

Flipboard:
Flip through the definitions of the key terms in this chapter and match them with the correct term.

Your instructor may assign one or more of these projects to help you review the chapter and assess your mastery and understanding of the chapter.

	Review and Assessment Guide for Excel Chapter 10		
Project	**Apply Skills from These Chapter Objectives**	**Project Type**	**Project Location**
10C	Objectives 1–4 from Project 10A	**10C Skills Review** A guided review of the skills from Project 10A.	On the following pages
10D	Objectives 5–8 from Project 10B	**10D Skills Review** A guided review of the skills from Project 10B.	On the following pages
10E	Objectives 1–4 from Project 10A	**10E Mastery (Grader Project)** A demonstration of your mastery of the skills in Project 10A with extensive decision making.	In MyITLab and on the following pages
10F	Objectives 5–8 from Project 10B	**10F Mastery (Grader Project)** A demonstration of your mastery of the skills in Project 10B with extensive decision making.	In MyITLab and on the following pages
10G	Objectives 1–8 from Projects 10A and 10B	**10G Mastery (Grader Project)** A demonstration of your mastery of the skills in Projects 10A and 10B with extensive decision making.	In MyITLab and on the following pages
10H	Combination of Objectives from Projects 10A and 10B	**10H GO! Fix It** A demonstration of your mastery of the skills in Projects 10A and 10B by creating a correct result from a document that contains errors you must find.	Online
10I	Combination of Objectives from Projects 10A and 10B	**10I GO! Make It** A demonstration of your mastery of the skills in Projects 10A and 10B by creating a result from a supplied picture.	Online
10J	Combination of Objectives from Projects 10A and 10B	**10J GO! Solve It** A demonstration of your mastery of the skills in Projects 10A and 10B, your decision-making skills, and your critical thinking skills. A task-specific rubric helps you self-assess your result.	Online
10K	Combination of Objectives from Projects 10A and 10B	**10K GO! Solve It** A demonstration of your mastery of the skills in Projects 10A and 10B, your decision-making skills, and your critical thinking skills. A task-specific rubric helps you self-assess your result.	On the following pages
10L	Combination of Objectives from Projects 10A and 10B	**10L GO! Think** A demonstration of your understanding of the chapter concepts applied in a manner that you would outside of college. An analytic rubric helps you and your instructor grade the quality of your work by comparing it to the work an expert in the discipline would create.	On the following pages
10M	Combination of Objectives from Projects 10A and 10B	**10M GO! Think** A demonstration of your understanding of the chapter concepts applied in a manner that you would outside of college. An analytic rubric helps you and your instructor grade the quality of your work by comparing it to the work an expert in the discipline would create.	Online
10N	Combination of Objectives from Projects 10A and 10B	**10N You and GO!** A demonstration of your understanding of the chapter concepts applied in a manner that you would in a personal situation. An analytic rubric helps you and your instructor grade the quality of your work.	Online

GLOSSARY

GLOSSARY OF CHAPTER KEY TERMS

Arguments The values that an Excel function uses to perform calculations or operations.

Compound criteria The use of two or more criteria on the same row—all conditions must be met for the records to be included in the results.

CONCATENATE A text function used to join up to 255 strings of characters.

Conditional formatting A format that changes the appearance of a cell—for example, by adding cell shading or font color—based on a condition; if the condition is true, the cell is formatted based on that condition, and if the condition is false, the cell is not formatted.

Data Facts about people, events, things, or ideas.

Data connection A link to external data that automatically updates an Excel workbook from the original data whenever the original data source gets new information.

Database An organized collection of facts related to a specific topic or purpose.

DAVERAGE function A function that determines an average in a database that is limited by criteria set for one or more cells.

DCOUNT function A function that counts the number of occurrences of a specified condition in a database.

Delimited A text file in which the text is separated by commas or tabs.

DSUM function A function that sums a column of values in a database that is limited by criteria set for one or more cells.

Extensible Markup Language (XML) A language that structures data in text files so that it can be read by other systems, regardless of the hardware platform or operating system.

Field A specific type of data such as name, employee number, or social security number that is stored in columns.

Flash Fill An Excel feature that predicts how to alter data based upon the pattern you enter into the cell at the beginning of the column. The data must be in the adjacent column to use Flash Fill.

Function A predefined formula that performs calculations by using specific values, called arguments, in a particular order or structure.

Get External Data A group of commands that enable you to bring data from an Access database, from the web, from a text file, or from an XML file into Excel without repeatedly copying the data.

Icon set A set of three, four, or five small graphic images that make your data visually easier to interpret.

Information Data that has been organized in a useful manner.

LEFT A text function that returns the specified number of characters from the beginning (left) of a string of characters.

LOWER A text function that changes the case of the characters in a string, making all characters lowercase.

Microsoft Access A database program used to manage database files.

MID A text function that extracts a series of characters from a text string given the location of the beginning character.

PROPER A text function that capitalizes the first letter of each word.

Query A process of restricting records through the use of criteria conditions that will display records that will answer a question about the data.

Record All the categories of data pertaining to one database item such as a person, place, thing, event, or idea, stored in a horizontal row in a database.

RIGHT A text function that returns the specified number of characters from the end (right) of a string of characters.

Schema An XML file that contains the rules for what can and cannot reside in an XML data file.

Screenshot An image of an active window on your computer that you can insert into a worksheet.

Syntax The arrangement of the arguments in a function.

Table Data stored in a format of rows and columns.

Text function A function that can be used to combine or separate data, change case, and apply formatting to a string of characters.

TRIM A text function that removes extra blank spaces from a string of characters.

UPPER A text function that changes the case of the characters in a string, making all characters uppercase.

Wizard A feature in Microsoft Office programs that walks you step by step through a process.

Skills Review | Project 10C Lab Information

Apply 10A skills from these Objectives:

1 Get External Data into Excel
2 Cleanup and Manage Data
3 Create a Query and Use the Query Wizard to Sort and Filter
4 Use Database Functions

In the following Skills Review, you will import data about lab department technicians, hematologists, blood bank services, and lab suppliers into Excel, and query the database to locate information. Your completed worksheets will look similar to Figure 10.48.

PROJECT FILES

For Project 10C, you will need the following files:

e10C_Blood_Banks (Access database)
e10C_Hematologist_Information (Text Document)
e10C_Lab_Dept (Excel Workbook)
e10C_Lab_Seminars (HTML Document)
e10C_Lab_Supplies (XML Document)
e10C_Technician_Information (Access Database)

You will save your workbook as:

Lastname_Firstname_10C_Lab_Dept

PROJECT RESULTS

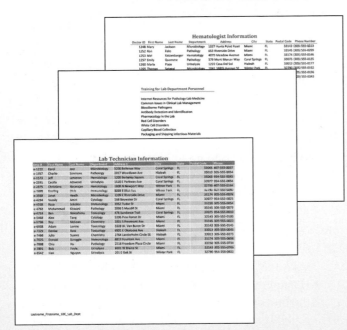

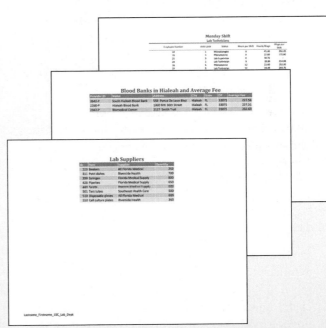

FIGURE 10.48

(Project 10C Lab Information continues on the next page)

CHAPTER REVIEW

1 Start Excel. From your student files, open the Excel file **e10C_Lab_Dept**. **Save** the file in your **Excel Chapter 10** folder as **Lastname_Firstname_10C_Lab_Dept**

a. On the **Lab Tech Information** worksheet, click in cell **A2**. On the **DATA tab**, in the **Get External Data group**, click **From Access**. In the **Select Data Source** dialog box, navigate to your student files, click the Access file **e10C_Technician_Information**, and then click **Open**.

b. In the **Import Data** dialog box, be sure that **Table** is selected, and then click **OK**. **Merge & Center** the text in cell **A1** across the range **A1:I1**, and then apply the **Title** cell style.

2 Display the **Lab Seminars** worksheet. Press Ctrl + F12 to display the **Open** dialog box. Navigate to your student files, right-click the HTML document **e10C_Lab_Seminars**, point to **Open with**, and then click **Internet Explorer** (or your Internet browser).

a. On your browser screen, point to the **address bar**, right-click, click **Copy**, and then **Close** the Internet browser window. **Close** the **Open** dialog box. Click in cell **A3**. On the **DATA tab**, in the **Get External Data group**, click **From Web**.

b. In the **New Web Query** dialog box, point to the **address bar**, right-click, click **Paste**, and then at the end of **address bar**, click **Go**. As necessary, drag the title bar of the **New Web Query** dialog box to the upper portion of your screen, and then in the lower right corner of the dialog box, drag the pointer as necessary to resize the dialog box and display the table on the webpage.

c. On the left side of the **Continuing Education Lab Seminars** table, click the **yellow arrow** to select the table. In the lower right corner of the dialog box, click **Import**, and then in the **Import Data** dialog box, verify that **Existing worksheet** and cell **$A$3** are selected. Click **OK**. Select cell **A1**, and then apply the **Heading 2** cell style.

3 Display the **Hematologist Information** worksheet. Click in cell **A9**. On the **DATA tab**, in the **Get External Data group**, click **From Text**. In the **Import Text File** dialog box, navigate to your student files, select the text file **e10C_Hematologist_Information** and then click **Import**. Click **Next**, click **Next** again, click **Finish**, and then click **OK**.

a. On the **DATA tab**, in the **Connections group**, click **Connections** to open the **Workbook Connections** dialog box. Verify the two connections exist in the workbook and then **Close** the **Workbook Connections** dialog box.

4 With the **Hematologist Information** worksheet active, on the **DATA tab**, in the **Data Tools group**, click **Remove Duplicates**.

a. Click **Unselect All**, verify that the *My data has headers box* is checked, check the **Doctor ID** and **Department** check boxes, and then click **OK**.

5 Notice the city, state, and zip are all in the same field in **column F**. Click the **column G** header, right-click, and then click **Insert** to insert a new column. Use the same method to insert two additional columns.

a. Click cell **G2**, type **City** and then press Tab. In cell **H2**, type **State** and press Tab, in cell **I2**, type **Zip** and then press Enter.

b. In cell **G3**, type **Miami** and press Enter. In cell **G4**, type **W** and then press Enter to Flash Fill the column.

c. Click cell **H3** and type **Fl** Use the **fill handle** to copy the text down through **H11**.

6 Click cell **I3**. Click the **FORMULAS tab**, in the **Function Library group**, click **Text**, and then click **RIGHT**.

a. With the insertion point in the **Text** box, click cell **F3**. Press Tab, and then, in the **Num_chars** box, type **5** Click **OK**. Drag the **fill handle** to copy the function down through cell **I11**.

b. Click cell **K3**, in the **Function Library**, click **Text**, scroll down as necessary and then click **UPPER**. With the insertion point in the **Text** box, click cell **H3** and then click **OK**. Drag the **fill handle** to copy the function down through cell **K11**. With the range **K3:K11** selected, right-click over the selection and then click **Copy**. Right-click over cell **H3** and, under **Paste Options**, click **Values (V)**. Click the **column K** heading and press Delete.

c. Click cell **K2** and type **Full Name** Click cell **K3**, on the **FORMULAS tab**, in the **Function Library group**, click **Text**, and then click **CONCATENATE**. With the insertion point in the **Text1** box, click cell **B3**. Press Tab, in the **Text2** box, type " press Spacebar and

(Project 10C Lab Information continues on the next page)

then type **"** Press [Tab] and in the **Text3** box, click **C3**. Click **OK**. Use the **fill handle** to copy the function down through cell **K11**.

d. Click cell **A1**. **Merge & Center** the text across the range **A1:K1** and apply the **Title** cell style. **AutoFit columns A:K**. Click the **column F** heading, right-click, and then click **Hide**.

7 ▶ Display the **Lab Suppliers** worksheet. Click in cell **A2**. On the **DATA tab**, in the **Get External Data group**, click **From Other Sources**, and then click **From XML Data Import**.

a. In the **Select Data Source** dialog box, navigate to your student files, click to select the XML file **e10C_Lab_Supplies**, and then click **Open**. Click **OK** to display the **Import Data** dialog box, and then click **OK**. **Merge & Center** the title in cell **A1** across the range **A1:D1**, and then apply the **Title** cell style.

8 ▶ Display the **Blood Bank Info** worksheet. Click in cell **A2**. On the **DATA tab**, in the **Get External Data group**, click **From Other Sources**. Click **From Microsoft Query**.

a. In the **Choose Data Source** dialog box, verify that the **Databases tab** is active and, at the bottom, the **Use the Query Wizard to create/edit queries** check box is selected. Click **MS Access Database***. Click **OK** to display the **Select Database** dialog box. Under **Directories**, be sure the folder containing your student files is selected—if necessary, scroll down to view and select the folder. Then, under **Database Name**, click **e10C_Blood_Banks.accdb**. Click **OK**.

b. Under **Available tables and columns**, to the left of **10C Blood Bank Services**, click **+** to expand the table and view the column names. Under **Available tables and columns**, click **Provider ID**, and then click **Add Field** to move the field to the **Columns in your query** list on the right. Double-click the **Name** field to add it to your query.

c. Using either **Add Field** or double-click, add the following fields to the **Columns in your query** list: **Address, City, State, ZIP, Average Fee**. In the lower right corner, click **Next**. Under **Column to filter**, click **ZIP**. Under **Only include rows where**, click in the **ZIP** box to display a list, and then click **equals**. In the box to the right, type **33075**

d. Click **Next**. In the **Query Wizard – Sort Order** dialog box, under **Sort by**, click the **arrow**, and then click **Average Fee**. Verify that **Ascending** is selected. In the lower right corner, click **Next**.

e. Be sure **Return Data to Microsoft Excel** is selected, and then click **Finish**. In the **Import Data** dialog box, verify that **Table** is selected, that **Existing worksheet** is selected, and that cell **$A$2** is indicated. Click **OK**. In cell **A1**, **Merge & Center** the title across the range **A1:G1**, and then apply the **Title** cell style.

9 ▶ In your **Blood Bank Info** worksheet, click any cell in the table data. On the **DESIGN tab**, in the **Tools group**, click **Convert to Range**. Click **OK**.

10 ▶ Display the **Lab Technicians** worksheet. In cell **A22**, type **Average Hourly Wage for Phlebotomists** and press [Tab]. **AutoFit column A**. Point to cell **C3**, right-click, and then click **Copy**. Scroll down, point to cell **C22**, right-click, and then click **Paste (P)**.

a. In cell **C23**, type **Phlebotomist** and press [Tab]. Click cell **B22**, and then to the left of the **Formula Bar**, click **Insert Function**. In the **Insert Function** dialog box, click the **Or select a category arrow**, and then from the list, click **Database**. In the **Select a function** box, click **DAVERAGE**, and then click **OK**.

b. In the **Database** box, click **Collapse Dialog Box**, and then select the range **A3:F20**. In the collapsed dialog box, click **Expand Dialog Box**. In the **Field** box, type **Hourly Wage** and press [Tab]. With the insertion point in the **Criteria** box, select the range **C22:C23**. Click **OK**. Right-click cell **B22**, and then from the mini toolbar, apply **Accounting Number Format**.

11 ▶ In cell **A25**, type **Wage per Shift for Lab Technicians** and press [Tab]. Select and then copy the range **C3:D3**. Point to cell **C25** and right-click, and then click **Paste (P)**. In cell **C26**, type **Lab Technician** and press [Tab]. In cell **D26**, type **>0** and then press [Enter].

a. Click cell **B25**, and then type **=dsum(** to begin the formula for the DSUM function. Select the range **A3:F20**, and then type **,** (a comma). Being sure to include the comma, type **"Wage per Shift"** to enter the second part of the argument. As indicated by *criteria* in the ScreenTip, type the criteria as **c31:d32** and then press [Enter]. Right-click cell **B25** and apply **Accounting Number Format**.

(Project 10C Lab Information continues on the next page)

CHAPTER REVIEW

12 In cell **A28**, type **Count Day Shift (Code 1, 3, 5)** and press [Tab]. Click cell **B3**, hold down [Ctrl] and click cell **D3**. Right-click either of the selected cells, and then click **Copy**. Scroll down, point to cell **C28**, right-click, and then click **Paste (P)**.

a. In cell **C29**, type **1** and press [Tab]. In cell **D29**, type **>0** and press [Enter]. In cell **C30**, type **3** and press [Tab]. In cell **D30**, type **>0** and press [Enter]. In cell **C31**, type **5** and press [Tab]. In cell **D31**, type **>0** and press [Enter].

b. Click cell **B28**. To the left of the **Formula Bar**, click **Insert Function**. Click the **Or select a category arrow**, and then click **Database**. In the **Select a function** box, click **DCOUNT**, and then click **OK**.

c. In the **Database** box, click **Collapse Dialog Box**. Move the collapsed box to the upper right corner of your screen. Scroll as necessary, and then select the range **A3:F20**. In the collapsed dialog box, click **Expand Dialog Box**.

d. In the **Field** box, type **Employee Number** and then press [Tab]. With the insertion point in the **Criteria** box, click **Collapse Dialog Box**, scroll as necessary,

and then select the range **C28:D31**. In the collapsed dialog box, click **Expand Dialog**. Click **OK**.

13 Display the first worksheet—**Lab Tech Information**. In the sheet tab area, point to any sheet tab, right-click, and then click **Select All Sheets**.

a. Insert a footer in the **left section** with the **File Name**, click above the footer area to deselect, and then return to **Normal** view. Make cell **A1** the active cell. Set the **Width** to **1 page** and the **Height** to **1 page**.

b. Display the **document properties** and under **Related People**, if necessary, right-click the author name, click **Edit Property,** and then type your name. In the **Subject** box, type your course name and section number, and in the **Tags** box, type **lab department information** Ungroup the worksheets and **Save** your workbook. Print or submit your workbook electronically. If required, print or create an electronic version of your worksheets with formulas displayed. **Close** the workbook and **Close** Excel.

END | You have completed Project 10C

Skills Review | Project 10D Medical Supplies

In the following Skills Review, you will edit a worksheet for Pat Shepard, Vice President of Operations, detailing the current inventory of two medical supply types—Medical Supplies, Hospital and Medical Supplies, Physician's Clinic. Your completed worksheets will look similar to Figure 10.49.

PROJECT FILES

For Project 10D, you will need the following files:

e10D_Logo

e10D_Medical_Supplies

You will save your workbook as:

Lastname_Firstname_10D_Medical_Supplies

PROJECT RESULTS

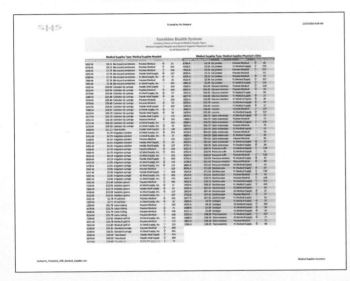

FIGURE 10.49

(Project 10D Medical Supplies continues on the next page)

CHAPTER REVIEW

1 Start Excel. From your student files, open the file **e10D_Medical_Supplies**. In your **Excel Chapter 10** folder, **Save** the file as **Lastname_Firstname_10D_Medical_Supplies**

a. On the **Medical Supplies Inventory** worksheet, select the range **A7:E62**, and then on the **INSERT tab**, in the **Tables group**, click **Table**. In the **Create Table** dialog box, verify that *=$A$7:$E$62* displays as the data range and that the **My table has headers** check box is selected. Click **OK**.

b. Display the **Physician's Clinic** worksheet, select the range **A1:E52**, right-click over the selection, and then, click **Copy**. Display the **Medical Supplies Inventory** worksheet, scroll up as necessary, point to cell **F6** and right-click, and then, under **Paste Options**, click **Paste (P)**. Click any cell to deselect.

c. Select the range **F7:J57**. In the lower right corner of the selection click **Quick Analysis**, click **TABLES**, and then click **Table**. On the **DESIGN tab**, in the **Table Styles group**, click **More** and then under **Medium**, click **Table Style Medium 13**.

2 Click any cell in the **Medical Supplies Hospital** table on the left. On the **DATA tab**, click **Sort** to display the **Sort** dialog box.

a. In the **Sort** dialog box, under **Column**, click the **Sort by arrow**, and then click **Item**. Be sure **Sort On** indicates *Values* and **Order** indicates *A to Z*. In the upper left corner, click **Add Level**. Under **Column**, click the **Then by arrow**, and then click **Purchase Price**. Click the **Order arrow** and set the sort order to **Largest to Smallest**. Click **OK**. Using the same technique and sort orders, sort the **Medical Supplies Physician's Clinic** table. AutoFit columns A:J.

3 Select the range **E8:E62**. On the **HOME tab**, in the **Styles group**, click **Conditional Formatting**. Point to **Icon Sets**, and then under **Directional**, in the first row, click the first icon set—**3 Arrows (Colored)**. Click any cell to deselect.

a. Select the range **J8:J57** and then in the lower right corner of the selection click **Quick Analysis**. Click **Icon Sets**.

b. Click anywhere in the **Medical Supplies Physician's Clinic** table to activate the table. Click the **DESIGN tab**, and then in the **Tools group**, click **Convert to Range**. In the message box, click **Yes** to convert

the table to a normal range. Convert the **Medical Supplies Hospital** table to a range.

4 Display the third worksheet in the workbook—**Medical Equipment Info**. In the **Medical Equipment Info** worksheet, click cell **A5**. Start your Internet browser. In the **address bar**, type **http://dseis.od.nih.gov** and press Enter to navigate to the site.

a. From the taskbar, redisplay your **10D_Medical_Supplies** workbook. On the **INSERT tab**, in the **Illustrations group**, click **Screenshot**. In the gallery, point to the *Division of Scientific Equipment and Instrumentation Services* screen to display the ScreenTip.

b. Click the **screenshot,** and notice that the screen image displays in your worksheet and is selected. Note: If a *Would you like to automatically hyperlink your screenshot to the URL of the captured browser window?* message displays, click **No**. Click the **FORMAT tab**, in the **Size group**, change the **Shape Height** to 4".

5 Point to the **Physician's Clinic sheet tab**, right-click, and then click **Delete**. Click **Delete** a second time to confirm the deletion. Right-click the **Medical Equipment Info** sheet tab, and then click **Select All Sheets**. On the **INSERT tab**, in the **Text group**, click **Header & Footer**, and then in the **Header**, click in the **left section**.

a. On the **DESIGN tab**, in the **Header & Footer Elements group**, click **Picture**, and then click **From a file**. From your student files, click the file **e10D_Logo**, and then click **Insert**. Click above the header to deselect the header area.

b. Click in the **middle header section**, type **Created by Pat Shepard** and then press Tab to move to the **right header section**. On the **DESIGN tab**, in the **Header & Footer Elements group**, click **Current Date**, press Spacebar, and then click **Current Time**. Click above the header.

c. On the **INSERT tab**, in the **Text group**, click **Header & Footer**, and then click **Go to Footer**. Click in the **left section**, and then in the **Header & Footer Elements group**, click **File Name**. Click in the **right section**, and then click **Sheet Name**. Click a cell just above the footer area to deselect. In the lower right corner of your screen, in the status bar, click **Normal**

(Project 10D Medical Supplies continues on the next page)

CHAPTER REVIEW

to return to **Normal** view, and then press Ctrl + Home to display the top of your worksheet.

6 Be sure your two worksheets are still grouped—*[Group]* displays in the title bar. On the **PAGE LAYOUT tab**, set the **Orientation** to **Landscape**.

a. In the **Scale to Fit group**, set the **Width** to **1 page** and the **Height** to **1 page**. **Center** the worksheets horizontally. Press Ctrl + F2 to check the **Print Preview**.

b. Display the **document properties** and under **Related People**, if necessary, right-click the author name, click **Edit Property**, and then type your name. In the **Subject** box, type your course name and section number, and in the **Tags** box, type **medical supplies, inventory**

c. Ungroup the worksheets and **Save** your workbook. Print or submit your workbook electronically. **Close** the workbook and **Close** Excel.

END | You have completed Project 10D

CONTENT-BASED ASSESSMENTS

Apply 10A skills from these Objectives:

1 Get External Data into Excel

2 Cleanup and Manage Data

3 Create a Query and Use the Query Wizard to Sort and Filter

4 Use Database Functions

In the following Mastering Excel project, you will import data about Emergency department technicians, ER doctors, paramedic services, and emergency suppliers into Excel, and query the database to locate information. Your completed worksheet will look similar to Figure 10.50.

PROJECT FILES

For Project 10E, you will need the following files:

e10E_Emergency_Training (HTML Document)

e10E_ER_Dept (Excel workbook)

e10E_ER_Doctors (Text Document)

e10E_ER_Staff (Access database)

e10E_Paramedic_Contacts (Access database)

You will save your workbook as:

Lastname_Firstname_10E_ER_Dept

PROJECT RESULTS

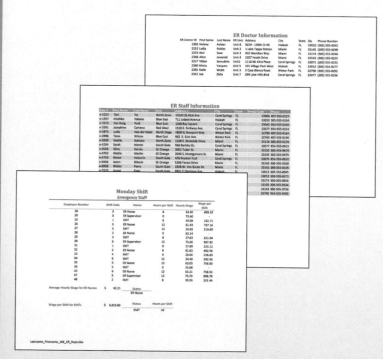

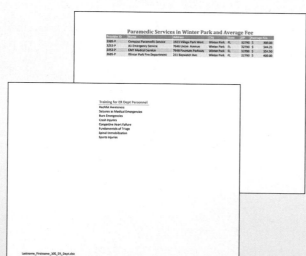

FIGURE 10.50

(Project 10E ER Department continues on the next page)

CONTENT-BASED ASSESSMENTS

1 ▶ Start Excel. From your student files, open the Excel workbook **e10E_ER_Dept**. **Save** the file in your **Excel Chapter 10** folder as **Lastname_Firstname_10E_ER_Dept** On the **Emergency Staff** worksheet, insert a **DAVERAGE** function in cell **B22**. As the **Database**, use the range **a3:f20** As the **Field**, type **Hourly Wage** and as the **Criteria**, use the range **c22:c23** Apply **Accounting Number Format** to the result.

2 ▶ In cell **B25**, enter a DSUM function using the database range **A3:F20**, type **"Wage per Shift"** as the field, and **c31:d32** as the criteria. Apply **Accounting Number Format** to the result.

3 ▶ Display the **ER Staff Information** worksheet, click cell **A2**. From your student files, import the data from the Access file **e10E_ER_Staff** as a table in the existing worksheet.

4 ▶ Display the **ER Doctors** worksheet; click cell **A6**. From your student files import the text file **e10E_ER_Doctors**. Remove duplicate doctors from each unit, and separate the **City, State, and Zip** fields. **AutoFit columns A:J**. Hide **column F**.

5 ▶ Display the **Emergency Training** worksheet. Display the **Open** dialog box, and then, from your student files, open the HTML file **e10E_Emergency_Training** with your browser. **Copy** the address from the browser **address bar**. Import the data from the **Emergency Training** table into cell **A2** of your worksheet.

6 ▶ Display the **Paramedic Services** worksheet. In cell **A2** import data from a **Microsoft Query**. As the data source, select the **MS Access Database e10E_Paramedic_Contacts.accdb**.

7 ▶ Expand the table, and then add *all* the fields to the **Columns in your query** list on the right. Filter the data to display only **ZIP 32790 Sort by** the **Average Fee** in **Ascending** order. Import the table into the existing workbook. Convert the table to a range, and then apply **Accounting Number Format** to the fees.

8 ▶ Select all the sheets, insert a footer in the **left section** with the **File Name,** set the **Orientation** to **Landscape,** set the **Width** to **1 page** and the **Height** to **1 page. Center** the worksheets horizontally. Return to **Normal** view, and then make cell **A1** the active cell. With the worksheets still grouped, display the **document properties** and under **Related People,** if necessary, right-click the author name, click **Edit Property,** and then type your name. In the **Subject** box, type your course name and section number, and in the **Tags** box, type **emergency department information** Ungroup the worksheets and **Save** your workbook. Print or submit your workbook electronically. If required, print or create an electronic version of your worksheets with formulas displayed. **Close** the workbook and **Close** Excel.

END | You have completed Project 10E

CONTENT-BASED ASSESSMENTS

| **Mastering Excel** | **Project 10F Beverage Supplies** |

In the following Mastering Excel project, you will edit a worksheet for Pat Shepard, Vice President of Operations, detailing the current inventory of two beverage supply types—Beverage Supplies Staff and Beverage Supplies Guests. Your completed worksheet will look similar to Figure 10.51.

Apply 10B skills from these Objectives:

5 Insert a Second Table into a Worksheet

6 Apply Conditional Formatting to Side-by-Side Tables

7 Insert a Screenshot

8 Create Custom Headers and Footers

PROJECT FILES

For Project 10F, you will need the following files:

e10F_Beverage_Supplies

e10F_Logo

You will save your workbook as:

Lastname_Firstname_10F_Beverage_Supplies

PROJECT RESULTS

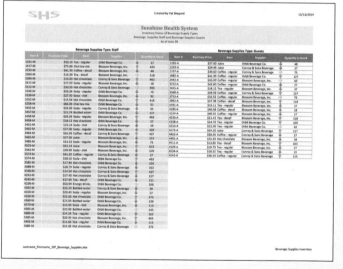

FIGURE 10.51

(Project 10F Beverage Supplies continues on the next page)

CONTENT-BASED ASSESSMENTS

Mastering Excel Project 10F Beverage Supplies (continued)

1 ▶ Start Excel. From your student files, open the file **e10F_Beverage_Supplies**, and then **Save** the file in your **Excel Chapter 10** folder as **Lastname_Firstname_10F_Beverage_Supplies** On the **Beverage Supplies Info** worksheet, click cell **A5. Start** your Internet browser and navigate to **http://www.ameribev.org** Redisplay your **10F_Beverage_Supplies** workbook and insert the American **Beverage Service Association** screenshot. Change the **Shape Height** to **4.5"**.

2 ▶ On the **Beverage Supplies Inventory** worksheet, insert a table in the range **A7:E47**. Display the **Guests** worksheet, copy the range **A1:E25**. Display the **Beverage Supplies Inventory** worksheet, and paste into cell **F6**. Insert a table in the range **F7:J30** and apply **Table Style Light 11**.

3 ▶ Sort the **Beverage Supplies Type: Staff** table by **Item #**. Sort on *Values* and *A to Z* order. Add a second level sort by **Purchase Price**, largest to smallest. Using the same sort orders, sort the **Beverage Supplies Type: Guests** table. **AutoFit columns A:J.**

4 ▶ Apply **conditional formatting** using the **3 Arrows (Colored)** icon set to the *Quantity in Stock* for both tables and convert both tables to a range.

5 ▶ Delete the **Guests** worksheet. Group the worksheets, and insert a header. In the **left header section** of the header, insert the picture **e10F_Logo** from your student data files. In the **middle header section**, type **Created by Pat Shepard** and then, in the **right header section**, insert the **Current Date**. Insert a footer, and in the **left section**, insert the **File Name**. In the **right section**, insert the **Sheet Name**. Return to **Normal** view, and return to cell **A1**.

6 ▶ With your two worksheets still grouped, set the **Orientation** to **Landscape**, set the **Width** to **1 page**, the **Height** to **1 page**, and center **horizontally**. Check the **Print Preview**. Display the **document properties** and under **Related People**, if necessary, right-click the author name, click **Edit Property**, and then type your name. In the **Subject** box, type your course name and section number, and in the **Tags** box, type **beverage supplies, inventory** Ungroup the worksheets and **Save** your workbook. Print or submit your workbook electronically. **Close** the workbook and **Close** Excel.

END | You have completed Project 10F

Mastering Excel Project 10G Pharmacy Department

In the following Mastering Excel project, you will import data about Pharmacy suppliers. You will edit a worksheet for Pat Shepard, Vice President of Operations, detailing the current inventory of two pharmacy supply types—Hospital and Physician's Clinic. Your completed worksheet will look similar to Figure 10.52.

PROJECT FILES

For Project 10G, you will need the following files:

e10G_Pharmacy_Suppliers (Access database)
e10G_Pharmacy_Supplies (Excel Workbook)

You will save your workbook as:

Lastname_Firstname_10G_Pharmacy_Supplies

PROJECT RESULTS

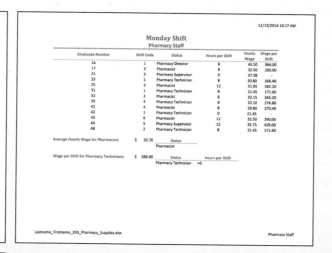

FIGURE 10.52

(Project 10G Pharmacy Department continues on the next page)

1   Start Excel. From your student files, open the file **e10G_Pharmacy_Supplies**. **Save** the file in your **Excel Chapter 10** folder as **Lastname_Firstname_10G_Pharmacy_Supplies** Display the **Pharmacy Suppliers Info** worksheet. Click in cell **A2**. From your student files, import the Access file **e10G_Pharmacy_Suppliers** as a table in the existing worksheet. Use the **UPPER** function to make the **State** field uppercase.

2   Display the **Pharmacy Staff** worksheet. Insert a **DAVERAGE** function in cell **B18** that calculates the average **Hourly Wage** for pharmacists using the criteria, in the range **C18:C19**. Insert a **DSUM** function in cell **B21** that calculates the **Wage per Shift** for pharmacy technicians using the criteria in cells **C21:D22**. Apply **Accounting Number Format** to cells **B18** and **B21**.

3   Display the **Pharmacy Supplies Inventory** worksheet. Insert a table in the range **A7:E42**. Display the **Physician's Clinic** worksheet and copy the range **A1:E32**. Display the **Pharmacy Supplies Inventory** worksheet, and paste the data into cell **F6**. Insert a table in the range **F7:J37** and apply **Table Style Medium 7**. Autofit columns **H:I**.

4   Apply **conditional formatting** to the range **E8:E42** using the **3 Traffic Lights (Rimmed)** icon set. Use **Quick Analysis** to apply the default icon set to indicate the *Quantity in Stock* for the **Pharmacy Supplies Type: Physician's Clinic**. Convert both tables to a range. **Delete** the **Physician's Clinic** worksheet.

5   Select all the sheets, insert a header in the **right section** that displays the current date and time. Insert a footer in the **left section**, insert the **File Name**, and in the **right section**, insert the **Sheet Name**. Return to **Normal** view, and then make cell **A1** the active cell. Set the **orientation** to landscape, set the **Width** to **1 page**, the **Height** to **1 page**, and **center horizontally**. Check the **Print Preview**. Display the **document properties** and under **Related People**, if necessary, right-click the author name, click **Edit Property**, and then type your name. In the **Subject** box, type your course name and section number, and in the **Tags** box, **pharmacy supplies, inventory** Ungroup the worksheets and **Save** your workbook. Print or submit your workbook electronically. If required, print or create an electronic version of your worksheets with formulas displayed. **Close** the workbook and **Close** Excel.

END | You have completed Project 10G

CONTENT-BASED ASSESSMENTS

| GO! Fix It | Project 10H Imaging Technicians | Online |

| GO! Make It | Project 10I Snack Supplies | Online |

| GO! Solve It | Project 10J Medical Imaging Suppliers | Online |

Apply a combination of the 10A and 10B skills.

| GO! Solve It | Project 10K Gift Shop Supplies |

PROJECT FILES

For Project 10K, you will need the following file:

e10K_Gift_Shop

You will save your workbook as:

Lastname_Firstname_10K_Gift_Shop

Open the file e10K_Gift_Shop and save it in your Excel chapter 10 folder as **Lastname_Firstname_10K_Gift_Shop** Insert a table to the Gift Shop Inventory worksheet for the range A7:E40. On the Clinic worksheet, remove duplicates, select and copy the remaining data, and then on the Gift Shop Inventory worksheet, paste it in the range beginning in cell F6. Insert a Table, and then apply Table Style Medium 13. AutoFit columns as necessary. Delete the Clinic worksheet. In each table's Quantity in Stock column, apply a different conditional formatting icon sets. Convert each table to a range. Insert the file name in the footer in the left section and the current date in the header right section. Set the orientation to landscape and center horizontally. Add appropriate information to the document properties including the tags **gift shop supplies, inventory** and submit as directed by your instructor.

Performance Level

Performance Criteria		Exemplary	Proficient	Developing
	Remove Duplicate Data	All duplicate data was removed.	Some duplicate data was removed.	Duplicate data was not removed.
	Insert a Second Table into a Worksheet	A second table is inserted into a worksheet, and tables display side-by-side.	A second table is inserted into a worksheet, but tables do not display side-by-side.	A second table was not inserted into a worksheet.
	Delete the Clinic Worksheet	Clinic worksheet was deleted.	N/A	Clinic worksheet was not deleted.
	Apply Conditional Formatting to Side-by-Side Tables	Conditional Formatting Icon Sets applied to the Quantity in Stock columns.	Conditional Formatting Icon Sets applied to one but not the other Quantity in Stock columns.	Conditional Formatting was not applied to the Quantity in Stock columns.
	Convert a Table to a Range	The tables are converted to a range.	One but not the other table is converted to a range.	The tables are not converted to a range.
	Header and Footer Information Inserted	Header and footer correctly inserted.	Header and footer inserted but missing some information.	Header and footer not inserted.

END | You have completed Project 10K

OUTCOMES-BASED ASSESSMENTS

RUBRIC

The following outcomes-based assessments are open-ended assessments. That is, there is no specific correct result; your result will depend on your approach to the information provided. Make Professional Quality your goal. Use the following scoring rubric to guide you in how to approach the problem and then to evaluate how well your approach solves the problem.

The *criteria*—Software Mastery, Content, Format and Layout, and Process—represent the knowledge and skills you have gained that you can apply to solving the problem. The *levels of performance*—Professional Quality, Approaching Professional Quality, or Needs Quality Improvements—help you and your instructor evaluate your result.

	Your completed project is of Professional Quality if you:	Your completed project is Approaching Professional Quality if you:	Your completed project Needs Quality Improvements if you:
1-Software Mastery	Choose and apply the most appropriate skills, tools, and features and identify efficient methods to solve the problem.	Choose and apply some appropriate skills, tools, and features, but not in the most efficient manner.	Choose inappropriate skills, tools, or features, or are inefficient in solving the problem.
2-Content	Construct a solution that is clear and well organized, contains content that is accurate, appropriate to the audience and purpose, and is complete. Provide a solution that contains no errors in spelling, grammar, or style.	Construct a solution in which some components are unclear, poorly organized, inconsistent, or incomplete. Misjudge the needs of the audience. Have some errors in spelling, grammar, or style, but the errors do not detract from comprehension.	Construct a solution that is unclear, incomplete, or poorly organized; contains some inaccurate or inappropriate content; and contains many errors in spelling, grammar, or style. Do not solve the problem.
3-Format & Layout	Format and arrange all elements to communicate information and ideas, clarify function, illustrate relationships, and indicate relative importance.	Apply appropriate format and layout features to some elements, but not others. Overuse features, causing minor distraction.	Apply format and layout that does not communicate information or ideas clearly. Do not use format and layout features to clarify function, illustrate relationships, or indicate relative importance. Use available features excessively, causing distraction.
4-Process	Use an organized approach that integrates planning, development, self-assessment, revision, and reflection.	Demonstrate an organized approach in some areas, but not others; or, use an insufficient process of organization throughout.	Do not use an organized approach to solve the problem.

OUTCOMES-BASED ASSESSMENTS

| GO! Think | Project 10L Facilities Pay |

PROJECT FILES

For Project 10L, you will need the following file:

e10L_Facilities_Pay

You will save your workbook as:

Lastname_Firstname_10L_Facilities_Pay

> **Apply a combination of the 9A and 9B skills.**

Open the file e10L_Facilities_Pay, and then save it in your Excel chapter 10 folder as **Lastname_Firstname_10L_Facilities_Pay** In this project, you will use a worksheet that contains payroll information for the facilities staff. You will calculate the average pay and count how many employees have worked for the hospital for over five years.

In rows 26–27, enter the criteria and a DAVERAGE function to determine the average wage for housekeeping. Apply Currency Style to the result. In rows 29–30, enter the criteria and a DCOUNT function to count the number of employees hired prior to 1/1/2010.

Insert the file name in the left section of the footer and the current date in the right section of the header. Set orientation to landscape and center horizontally. Set width and height to 1 page. Add appropriate information to the document properties, including the tags **facilities pay** and submit as directed by your instructor.

END | You have completed Project 10L

| GO! Think | Project 10M Institutes of Health | Online |

Build from Scratch

| You and GO! | Project 10N Budget | Online |

Collaborating with Others and Preparing a Workbook for Distribution

GO! to Work
Video E11

PROJECT 11A

OUTCOMES
Assemble changes from multiple sources to collaborate with others.

OBJECTIVES

1. Create a Shared Workbook
2. Track Changes Made to a Workbook
3. Merge Workbooks and Accept Changes

PROJECT 11B

OUTCOMES
Inspect a workbook, prepare a workbook for distribution, and store a workbook in the Cloud.

OBJECTIVES

4. Prepare a Final Workbook for Distribution
5. Upload a Workbook to SkyDrive

Tyler Olson/Fotolia

In This Chapter

In this chapter, you will assemble changes from multiple sources to collaborate with others. The process of collaborating typically involves sending a worksheet to others and asking each person to review the worksheet and make changes or add comments. Changes can be tracked and then accepted or rejected. Additionally, you will compare two different versions of a workbook and merge them together.

You will also prepare a final workbook for distribution, inspect the workbook for hidden information, add security by encrypting the workbook with a password, digitally sign the workbook, and upload the workbook to SkyDrive.

The projects in this chapter relate to **Capital Cities Community College**, which provides high-quality education and professional training to residents in the cities surrounding the nation's capital. Its five campuses serve over 50,000 students and offer more than 140 programs, including associate degrees, certifications, and continuing education courses. Over 1,700 faculty and staff make student success a top priority. Capital Cities Community College makes positive contributions to the community through cultural and athletic programs, health care, economic development activities, and partnerships with businesses and nonprofit organizations.

Summer Schedule

PROJECT ACTIVITIES

In Activities 11.01 through 11.10, you will create a shared workbook so that it can be reviewed by the different Department Chairs in the College's Business Division. Various individuals in the Business Division will be able to edit and comment on the information in the workbook. Your completed workbook will look similar to Figure 11.1.

PROJECT FILES

For Project 11A, you will need the following files:

e11A_Draft
e11A_Summer_Schedule

You will save your workbooks as:

Lastname_Firstname_11A_Summer_Schedule
Lastname_Firstname_11A_Summer_Schedule - Copy

PROJECT RESULTS

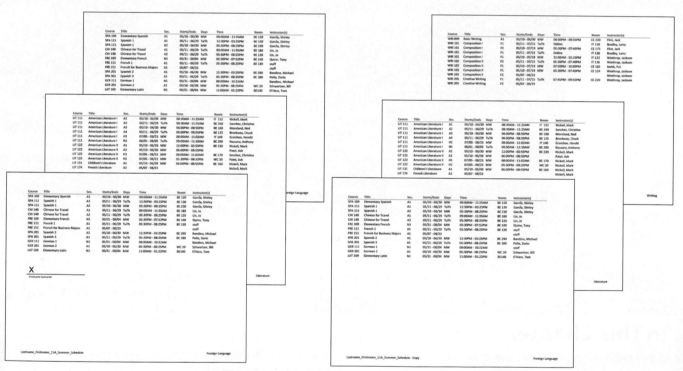

FIGURE 11.1 Project 11A Summer Schedule

NOTE   **If You Are Using a Touchscreen**

- Tap an item to click it.
- Press and hold for a few seconds to right-click; release when the information or command display.
- Touch the screen with two or more fingers and then pinch together to zoom in or stretch your fingers apart to zoom out.
- Slide your finger on the screen to scroll—slide left to scroll right and slide right to scroll left.
- Slide to rearrange—similar to dragging with a mouse.
- Swipe from edge: from right to display charms; from left to expose open apps, snap apps, or close apps; from top or bottom to show commands or close an app.
- Swipe to select—slide an item a short distance with a quick movement—to select an item and bring up commands, if any.

Objective 1 | Create a Shared Workbook

Video E11-1

In Excel, *collaboration* refers to the process of working jointly with others to review, comment on, and make necessary changes to a shared workbook. A *shared workbook* is a workbook set up to allow multiple users on a network to view and make changes to the workbook at the same time. Typically the users are on an *intranet*, which is a network within an organization and that uses Internet technologies. When the collaboration process is complete, as the owner of the shared workbook, you can accept or reject the input suggested by others.

Activity 11.01 | Locating and Modifying Workbook Properties

Every Excel workbook file has *properties*, which are details about a file that describe or identify the file, including the title, author name, subject, and tags that identify the file's topic or contents—also known as *metadata*. Properties also include the size and location of the file. You can change file properties before the file is distributed so that the recipients will know who distributed the file. Some property information displays when you point to a file in a list of files, such as in File Manager or in the Open dialog box.

1 Start Excel. From your student files, open the file **e11A_Summer_Schedule**. Display the **Save As** dialog box, navigate to the location where you are storing your files for this chapter, and then create a new folder named **Excel Chapter 11** Save the file in your **Excel Chapter 11** folder as **Lastname_Firstname_11A_Summer_Schedule**

This workbook contains three worksheets listing the proposed summer classes for three departments in the Liberal Arts Division.

2 Group the worksheets. Insert a footer with the file name in the **left section** and the sheet name in the **right section**, click above the footer area to deselect, and then return to **Normal** view. Set the **Orientation** to **Landscape**. Press Ctrl + Home to move to the top of the sheet.

3 Click the **FILE tab** to display **Backstage** view. On the **Info tab**, at the top of the screen, notice that the location of this file on your computer displays under the file name. On the right, notice that some of the more common properties for this file display, for example, the file *Size* and *Author*.

4 Under **Properties**, in the **Title** box, type **Proposed Summer Schedule** and then compare your screen with Figure 11.2.

Some of the properties displayed on the Info tab, such as Titles, Tags, and Categories, can be changed.

FIGURE 11.2

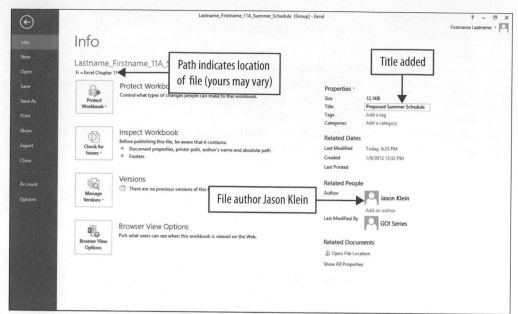

5 Under **Related People**, point to the text *Jason Klein*, who is the author, to display the **Contact Card**, and then compare your screen with Figure 11.3.

> In a networked environment, from this Contact Card you could send an email message to this individual, initiate an IM (Instant Messaging) session, schedule a meeting in Outlook, or look up contact information such as a phone number.

FIGURE 11.3

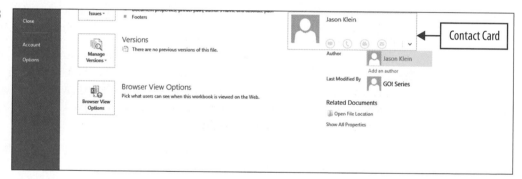

6 Move the mouse pointer away from the **Contact Card**. Near the top right of the **info** pane click the **Properties arrow**, click **Advanced Properties**, and then in the Properties dialog box, if necessary click the **General tab**.

> In the Properties dialog box for a file, there are additional properties that you can view and change. On the General tab you can see the date the file was last accessed. The Attributes area is dimmed because these properties cannot be changed while the file is open.

7 Click the **Summary tab**.

> The Author name *Jason Klein* was generated from the computer on which the file was originally created. If you receive a file from someone else, which you then modify and use, the original author's name remains with the file, even when you save the file with a new name. If you want your name, division, or company to be associated with the file, change the information located here. Information entered here can also be used by search engines to help locate files.

8 In the **Author** box, delete *Jason Klein,* type **Fred Nicholas** and then press `Tab`. In the **Manager** box, type **Dean Massaro, Liberal Arts Division** Compare your screen with Figure 11.4.

FIGURE 11.4

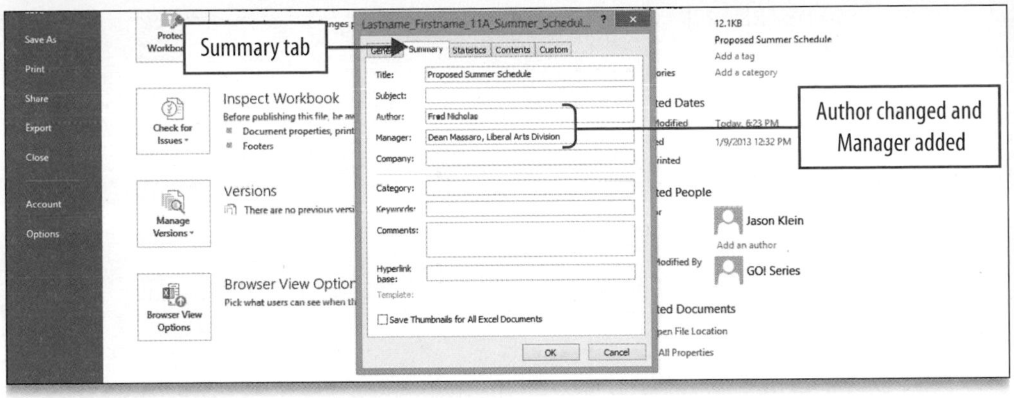

9 ▶ Click **OK**. Click **Save** to save your workbook and return to the worksheet.

More Knowledge **Read-Only Property**

One of the attributes that displays in the Properties dialog box is the Read-only property. When this property is selected, the file can be read or copied, but it cannot be changed or saved. This property cannot be set while the file is open. To change a file to Read-only, display the file list in File Explorer, right-click the file name, and then click Properties. In the Properties dialog box, select the Read-only attribute, and then click OK. When the file is opened, [Read-only] will display in the title bar, which indicates that the file cannot be changed or saved. If you need to use a Read-only file, you must save it with a new file name, which preserves the original file.

Activity 11.02 | **Making Edits in a Foreign Language and Inserting a Watermark Image**

When you share a workbook with others, it is helpful to include a watermark that indicates the document is draft. A **watermark** is a faded image or text used as a background of a document. Excel does not include a feature to add an automatic watermark, but you can create one by using an image as the worksheet background. Many of the instructors in the Foreign Language Department have names that use foreign characters. In the following activity, you will insert a background image in the workbook and use the Symbol dialog box to insert foreign characters into a cell. Both of these tasks must be done before you share the file, as inserting symbols and other objects is disabled in a shared file.

1 ▶ Point to the **Foreign Language sheet tab**, right-click, and then click **Ungroup Sheets**. With the **Foreign Language** worksheet active, on the **PAGE LAYOUT tab**, in the **Page Setup group**, click **Background**. In the **Insert Pictures** dialog box, click **From a File**.

2 ▶ In the **Sheet Background** dialog box, navigate to your student data files, click the file **e11A_Draft**, and then click **Insert**. Save 🔲 your workbook and compare your screen with Figure 11.5.

When you share a workbook with others, it is helpful to include a watermark that indicates the document is draft. The **background image** is behind, not in, the worksheet cells.

FIGURE 11.5

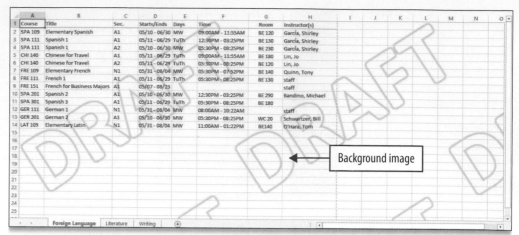

Background image

3 ▸ On the **Foreign Language** worksheet, click cell **H11**, type **Pe** On the **INSERT tab**, in the **Symbols group**, click **Symbol**. If necessary, drag the **Symbol** dialog box up so that cell **H11** is visible. In the **Symbol** dialog box, if necessary, click the Font arrow, and then click (normal text). Click the **Subset arrow**, and then click **Latin-1 Supplement**. Click the **scrollbar arrows** as necessary to locate the symbol ñ—*Latin Small Letter N With Tilde*. Click ñ and compare your screen with Figure 11.6.

FIGURE 11.6

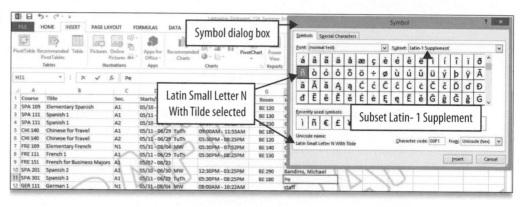

Symbol dialog box

Latin Small Letter N With Tilde selected

Subset Latin-1 Supplement

4 ▸ Click **Insert**, click **Close**, and then type **a, Dar** Display the **Symbol** dialog box, verify that the **Latin-1 Supplement** subset is selected, scroll up one row, and insert the symbol ì—*Latin Small Letter I With Grave*. **Close** the **Symbol** dialog box, type **o** and then press Enter. **Save** your workbook and then compare your screen with Figure 11.7.

The Symbol dialog box is used to insert symbols such as foreign language letters, currency symbols, and other special characters.

FIGURE 11.7

Peña, Darìo entered in cell H11

More Knowledge **Office Language Preferences**

If you regularly need to work in a foreign language in Excel, you can set the Office Language Preferences from the Excel Options dialog box Language tab. This sets the editing preferences for all of the installed Microsoft Office applications.

When you share a workbook with others, you control the collaboration process by using Excel's **Track Changes** feature, which logs details about workbook changes including insertions and deletions. When you activate the Track Changes feature, the workbook automatically becomes a shared workbook.

1 On the **REVIEW tab**, in the **Changes group**, click **Track Changes**, and then click **Highlight Changes**.

2 In the **Highlight Changes** dialog box, click to select the **Track changes while editing** check box, which activates the Track Changes feature and saves the file as a shared workbook.

3 Verify that the **When** check box is selected and indicates *All*. Select the **Who** check box and be sure *Everyone* is indicated. Verify that the **Highlight changes on screen** check box is selected, and then compare your screen with Figure 11.8.

> Use onscreen highlighting when there are minimal changes in the workbook or when you want to see, at a glance, what has changed.

FIGURE 11.8

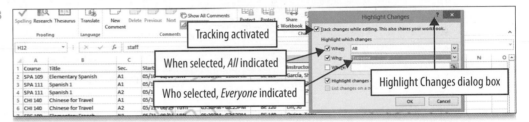

Tracking activated

When selected, *All* indicated

Who selected, *Everyone* indicated

Highlight Changes dialog box

4 Click **OK**.

> A message box displays, informing you that this action will save the workbook.

5 Click **OK** to continue.

> The workbook is saved, and *[Shared]* displays on the title bar. The file is ready to be shared by others who will make changes to the proposed summer schedule.

6 On the **FILE tab**, click **Close** to close the file and leave Excel open.

Objective 2 | Track Changes Made to a Workbook

Video E11-2

As others make changes to a shared workbook, you can view and track the changes they make by viewing the details in the *change history*—information that is maintained about changes made in past editing sessions. The information includes the name of the person who made each change, when the change was made, and what data was changed. After the changes are recorded, you can review the shared file and accept or reject the changes.

Activity 11.04 | Making a Copy of a Shared Workbook

For individuals who do not have access to the network, make a copy of the shared workbook and send it to them by email service. After changes are made to this copy of the shared workbook, it can be returned and merged with the original shared workbook. In this manner, you can view all the changes made by reviewers—even from reviewers who did not have access to the shared workbook. In the following activity, you will make a copy of the shared workbook for Kyle Messina, Chair of the Writing Department, because he will not have access to the college's network during the review period.

1 Press Ctrl + F12 to display the **Open** dialog box. Navigate to your **Excel Chapter 11** folder, point to your **Lastname_Firstname_11A_Summer_Schedule** file, right-click, and then click **Copy**.

2 Right-click in an empty space below the file list, and then click **Paste**. If necessary, point to the border between the **Name** and **Date modified columns** to display the ✛ pointer, and then, drag the border to the right to display the complete file names. Compare your screen with Figure 11.9.

A copy of the shared file is created and is named *Lastname_Firstname_11A_Summer_Schedule - Copy*

FIGURE 11.9

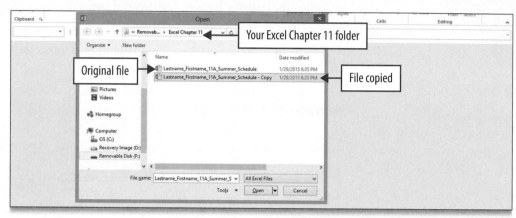

3 In the **Open** dialog box, click **Cancel**.

Activity 11.05 | Making Changes to a Shared Workbook

Each department's chairperson needs to review the summer schedule and make any necessary changes. In the following activity, you will open the file and make the changes for Ryan Woodward, Chair of the Literature Department and Claudette Fischer, Chair of the Language Department.

1 Press Ctrl + F12 to display the **Open** dialog box, and then open your **Lastname_Firstname_11A_Summer_Schedule** file—open the original, *not* the copy that you made.

Notice that the title bar displays *[Shared]* at the end of the file name.

2 On the **FILE tab**, click **Options**. In the **Excel Options** dialog box, on the left, verify that **General** is selected.

3 Under **Personalize your copy of Microsoft Office**, click in the **User name** box.

The Excel Options dialog box displays, and the *User name* assigned to your computer displays.

4 On a piece of paper, write down the User name that displays so that you can restore it later. Select the User name text, type **Ryan Woodward, Literature** to replace the selected User name text. Compare your screen with Figure 11.10.

From this point forward, any changes made to the file will display this User name until you change the User name again.

N O T E   **Changing the User Name**

Under normal circumstances, you would not change the User name. The person making changes would be using his or her own computer, which would already display their name in the User name box. In this project, you are changing the User name for instructional purposes.

FIGURE 11.10

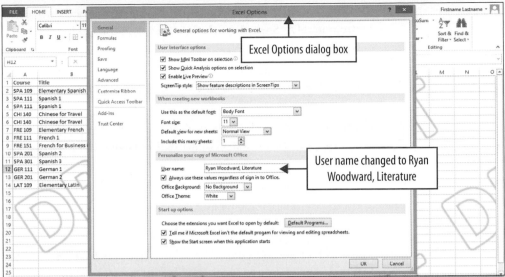

5 Click **OK** to close the **Excel Options** dialog box.

6 Display the **Literature** worksheet. Click cell **H10**, begin to type **Sanchez, Christina** and press Enter to accept the AutoComplete suggestion to change the name. In cell **H11**, change the name to **Patel, Ash** Press Ctrl + Home to move to cell **A1**, and then compare your screen with Figure 11.11. The instructor names for two literature courses are changed.

FIGURE 11.11

7 On the **REVIEW tab**, in the **Changes group**, click **Track Changes**, and then click **Highlight Changes**. In the **Highlight Changes** dialog box, click the **When arrow**, and then click **All**. Select the **Who** check box, and be sure that it indicates *Everyone*. Click **OK**.

> By activating Highlight Changes, the two cells changed by Ryan Woodward are outlined in blue with a Track Changes indicator shown in the upper left corner of each cell.

8 Point to cell **H11** to view the ScreenTip, which indicates the change that was made and the date and time the change was made. Compare your screen with Figure 11.12.

FIGURE 11.12

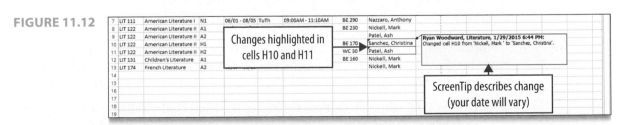

9 **Save** your workbook. On the **FILE tab** click **Close** to close the file and leave Excel open.

> To change the User name for the next set of changes, you must close and then reopen the file.

10 Press Ctrl + F12 to display the **Open** dialog box, and then reopen your **Lastname_Firstname_11A_Summer_Schedule** file—not the copy.

↻ **ANOTHER WAY**   On the FILE tab, click Open, and select the Lastname_Firstname_11A_Summer_Schedule file from the Recent files list.

11 On the **FILE tab**, click **Options** to display the **Excel Options** dialog box, and then using the technique you practiced, change the **User name** to **Claudette Fischer, Language** and then click **OK**.

12 Display the **Foreign Language** worksheet. Click cell **G9** and type **Permission** Click cell **H12** and type **Bandino, Michael** and then press Enter.

This completes the changes made by Ms. Fischer, Chair of the Language Department.

13 Press Ctrl + Home to make cell **A1** the active cell. **Save** 🖫 your workbook, and then on the **FILE tab,** click **Close** to close the file and leave Excel open.

Activity 11.06 | Making Changes to a Copy of the Shared Workbook

Recall that a copy of the shared workbook was prepared for Kyle Messina, Chair of the Writing Department. In this activity, you will make Mr. Messina's changes on his copy of the shared workbook.

1 Press Ctrl + F12 and open the **Lastname_Firstname_11A_Summer_Schedule - Copy** file that you created earlier.

Notice that the title bar displays *Copy [Shared]* at the end of the file name.

2 On the **FILE tab**, click **Options** to display the **Excel Options** dialog box, and then using the technique you practiced, change the **User name** to **Kyle Messina, Writing** and then click **OK**.

3 Display the **Writing** worksheet. Click cell **F3** and type **Online** Click cell **F5**, type **Online** and then press Enter. Press Ctrl + Home.

This completes the changes made by Mr. Messina.

4 **Save** 🖫 your workbook. On the **FILE tab,** click **Close** to close the file and leave Excel open.

Objective 3 | Merge Workbooks and Accept Changes

Video E11-3

After others make changes to the shared workbook, you can view and then accept or reject their changes. When more than one copy of the shared workbook contains marked changes, first merge the workbooks so that you can view everyone's changes in a single workbook.

Activity 11.07 | Merging Revisions

Recall that because he was not connected to the network, the Chair of the Writing Department made his changes on a separate copy of the shared workbook. In this activity, you will merge the two workbooks so that you can view everyone's changes in a single workbook.

1 On the **FILE tab**, click **Options** to display the **Excel Options** dialog box, and then change the **User name** to **Dean Massaro** Click **OK** to close the dialog box, and then open your **Lastname_Firstname_11A_Summer_Schedule** file.

The Dean of the Liberal Arts Division must review the changes before the file is submitted to the Vice President for final schedule preparation.

2 With the **Foreign Language** worksheet active, on the **REVIEW tab**, in the **Changes group**, click **Track Changes**, and then click **Highlight Changes**.

3 In the **Highlight Changes** dialog box, click the **When arrow**, and then click **All**. Click the **Who arrow**, and then click **Everyone but Me**. Click **OK**. Compare your screen with Figure 11.13.

By selecting *Everyone but Me*, you can accept or reject changes without your own actions being recorded as a change. A Track Changes indicator displays in the upper left corner of the cells that were changed on this worksheet, and the cells display a colored border.

FIGURE 11.13

Two changes highlighted on the Foreign Language worksheet

4 Display the **Literature** worksheet and notice the light blue borders around cells **H10** and **H11** indicating that changes have been made.

5 Display the **Writing** worksheet, and notice that no changes are indicated because changes for this department were made on another copy of the shared workbook.

6 On the **FILE tab**, click **Options** to display the **Excel Options** dialog box, and then on the left, click **Quick Access Toolbar**.

7 At the top of the dialog box, under **Customize the Quick Access Toolbar**, click the **Choose commands from arrow**, and then click **Commands Not in the Ribbon**. In the list below, scroll as necessary, click **Compare and Merge Workbooks**, in the center click **Add**, and then compare your screen with Figure 11.14.

ANOTHER WAY   To the right of the Quick Access Toolbar, click More, under Customize Quick Access Toolbar, click More commands to open the Excel Options dialog box.

FIGURE 11.14

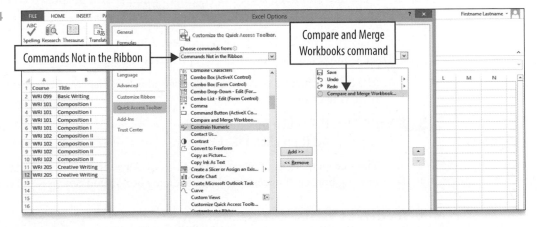

Commands Not in the Ribbon

Compare and Merge Workbooks command

8 Click **OK**. On the **Quick Access Toolbar**, click **Compare and Merge Workbooks** ◉. In the **Select Files to Merge Into Current Workbook** dialog box, if necessary, navigate to your **Excel Chapter 11** folder. Compare your screen with Figure 11.15.

Here you select the workbook to be merged into the open workbook.

FIGURE 11.15

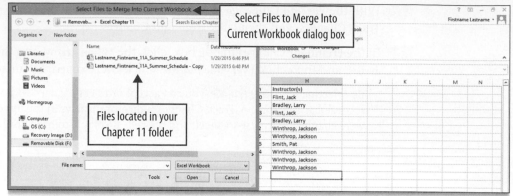

Select Files to Merge Into Current Workbook dialog box

Files located in your Chapter 11 folder

9 Locate your **Lastname_Firstname_11A_Summer_Schedule - Copy** file—if necessary, adjust the **Name column** to display the complete file name—and then click to select it. Click **OK**, and then compare your screen with Figure 11.16.

After a moment, a colored border displays around cells F3 and F5 on the Writing sheet, and the changes from the file Lastname_Firstname_11A_Summer_Schedule - Copy are merged into the original file.

FIGURE 11.16

Changes from merged file highlighted

Activity 11.08 | Accepting or Rejecting Tracked Changes

Now that each person's changes have been incorporated into one copy of the workbook, you can review each change and decide whether to accept the change and keep the new value or to reject the change and keep the cell's original value. After a proposed change is accepted or rejected, the tracking notation is removed from the cell.

1 Display the **Foreign Language** worksheet. On the **REVIEW tab**, in the **Changes group**, click **Track Changes**, and then click **Accept/Reject Changes**.

The Select Changes to Accept or Reject dialog box displays. Here you set the parameters for reviewing changes.

2 Verify that the **When** box indicates *Not yet reviewed*. Change the **Who** box to indicate *Everyone*, and then click **OK**. Compare your screen with Figure 11.17.

The Accept or Reject Changes dialog box displays, and the first changed cell is surrounded by a moving border. If necessary, drag the dialog box so you can view the changed cell.

FIGURE 11.17

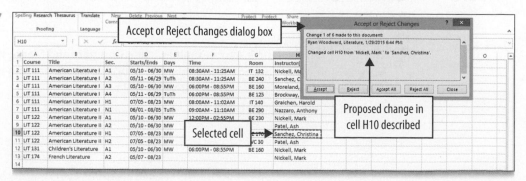

Accept or Reject Changes dialog box

Selected cell

Proposed change in cell H10 described

3 Click **Accept** to accept the change of instructor in cell **H10** to *Sanchez, Christina*.

The change is accepted and the next changed cell displays a moving border. The Accept or Reject Changes dialog box displays the information for the change in cell H11—from *Nickell, Mark* to *Patel, Ash*.

4 Click **Accept**. Compare your screen with Figure 11.18.

The change is accepted and the next change is selected. This is the third of six changes that were made to the shared workbook.

FIGURE 11.18

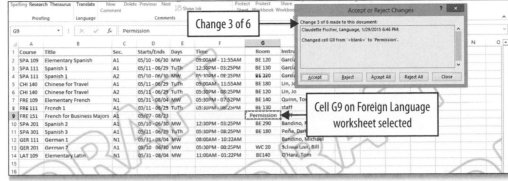

5 Click **Reject** to reject the change in cell **G9**.

The change is rejected, and the cell returns to its former value—a blank cell. The next change is selected.

6 **Accept** the next change—change 4 of 6—a change in instructor to *Bandino, Michael*.

The change is accepted. The next change, in cell F3, which was changed to *Online*, is selected on the Writing worksheet.

7 Click **Accept**, and then **accept** the last change—a change in cell **F5** to *Online*.

All the changes have been reviewed, and the Accept or Reject Changes dialog box closes.

8 Display the **Writing** worksheet, click cell **F3**, and then press Delete. Press Tab and in cell **G3**, type **Online** Click cell **F5** and press Delete. Press Tab and in cell **G5**, type **Online** and press Enter. Compare your screen with Figure 11.19.

The classes taught by Larry Bradley are online classes, so the Time column is left blank and *Online* is entered in the Room column.

FIGURE 11.19

	Course	Title	Sec.	Starts/Ends	Days	Time	Room	Instructor(s)		
1										
2	WRI 099	Basic Writing	A1	05/10 - 06/30	MW	08:00PM - 09:55PM	CE 220			
3	WRI 101	Composition I	F1	05/11 - 07/15	TuTh		Online			
4	WRI 101	Composition I	F2	05/10 - 07/19	MW	05:30PM - 07:45PM	CE 173			
5	WRI 101	Composition I	F1	05/11 - 07/15	TuTh		Online			
6	WRI 101	Composition I	F1	05/10 - 07/19	MW	11:00AM - 01:15PM	IT 122			
7	WRI 102	Composition II	F2	05/11 - 07/15	TuTh	05:30PM - 07:40PM	IT 116	Winthrop, Jackson		
8	WRI 102	Composition II	F1	05/10 - 07/19	MW	07:50PM - 10:05PM	CE 165	Smith, Pat		
9	WRI 102	Composition II	F1	05/10 - 07/19	MW	05:30PM - 07:45PM	CE 124	Winthrop, Jackson		
10	WRI 102	Composition II	F2	05/07 - 08/23				Winthrop, Jackson		
11	WRI 205	Creative Writing	F1	05/11 - 07/15	TuTh	07:45PM - 09:55PM	CE 220	Winthrop, Jackson		
12	WRI 205	Creative Writing	F2	05/07 - 08/23						
13										

Cells F3 and F5 blank: G3 and G5 indicate Online

9 **Save** 🖫 your workbook.

Activity 11.09 | **Removing the Shared Designation, Resetting the User Name, and Removing a Command from the Quick Access Toolbar**

After the changes have been reviewed and before the workbook is published, the Shared designation must be removed from the workbook. Removing the Shared designation will also turn off the Track Changes feature and remove the tracking indicators. Because you changed the User name for this project, you will also restore your computer's original User name.

1 On the **REVIEW tab**, in the **Changes group**, click **Share Workbook**. Compare your screen with Figure 11.20.

The Share Workbook dialog box displays and indicates the name of the person who is currently using the file—*Dean Massaro*.

FIGURE 11.20

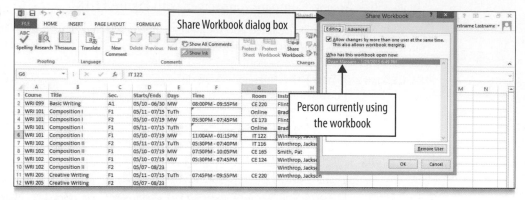

2 Clear the **Allow changes by more than one user at the same time** check box, and then click **OK**. In the **Microsoft Excel** information box, click **Yes**.

The dialog box closes, *[Shared]* no longer displays on the title bar, and the tracking indicators are removed from the changed cells.

3 In the **FILE tab**, click **Options** to display the **Excel Options** dialog box, click in the **User name** box.

4 Select the text *Dean Massaro*, and then type the name that you wrote down in Activity 11.05 to replace the selected User name text, and then click **OK**.

The original User name is restored.

5 On the **Quick Access Toolbar**, right-click **Compare and Merge Workbooks** ⊙, and then click **Remove from Quick Access Toolbar**.

More Knowledge | **Change History**

In a shared workbook, information that is maintained about changes made in past editing sessions is called the change history. The change history includes the name of the person who made each change, when the change was made, and what data was changed. When this feature is enabled, Excel creates a history worksheet detailing the changes made to the shared workbook. To enable change history, in the Highlight Changes dialog box, enable track changes, and then select the List changes on a new sheet check box. The resulting worksheet is inserted after the last worksheet in the workbook. Formatting changes are not recorded in the change history. The history worksheet displays only when a worksheet is in shared mode. The worksheet does not display when you turn off change tracking. If you subsequently restart a shared workbook session, the history begins anew, and any changes recorded in previous sharing sessions are no longer available. To keep track of the change history after discontinuing the sharing session, copy the contents of the locked history worksheet and paste them into another worksheet, copy the worksheet, or print the worksheet.

Activity 11.10 | **Adding a Signature Line**

A *digital signature* is an electronic, encrypted, stamp of authentication. A digital signature is a means of proving identity and authenticity that ensures that a file originated from the signer and has not been changed.

You must have a current *digital certificate*, which proves identity, to digitally sign an Office document. You can obtain a digital certificate from a *certificate authority*, which is a commercial organization that issues digital certificates, keeps track of who is assigned to a certificate, signs certificates to verify their validity, and tracks which certificates are revoked or expired. Institutions, governments, and corporations can also issue their own digital certificates. A digital certificate works by providing a cryptographic key pair that is associated with a digital signature.

A digital certificate authenticates—verifies that people and products are who and what they claim to be—the digital signature. A digital signature helps to assure that the signer is who they claim to be, helps to assure that the document content has not been changed or tampered with since it was digitally signed, and helps to prove to all parties the origin of the signed content. It cannot be repudiated—the signer cannot deny association with the signed content.

A digital signature may be visible or invisible. In either case, the digital signature references a digital certificate, which authenticates the source of the signature. When you create your own certificate, it is referred to as a *self-signed* project. Certificates you create yourself are considered unauthenticated; however, self-signed projects are considered safer to open than those with no certificates at all. In this activity, you will create a digital signature line for the Summer Schedule workbook.

1 ▶ Display the **Foreign Language** worksheet, and then click cell **A16**. On the **INSERT tab**, in the **Text group**, click the **Add a Signature Line arrow** , and then click **Microsoft Office Signature Line**. Compare your screen with Figure 11.21.

The Signature Setup dialog box displays. A *signature line* specifies the individual who must sign the document. Inserting an actual digital signature requires that you obtain a digital ID.

FIGURE 11.21

2 ▶ In the **Signature Setup** dialog box, in the **Suggested signer** box, *using your own name*, type **Firstname Lastname** and then click **OK**. Compare your screen with Figure 11.22.

The signature line with a large X displays on the worksheet. *Firstname Lastname* displays below the signature line.

FIGURE 11.22

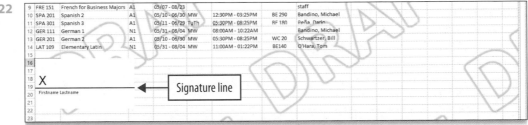

3 ▶ Right-click the **Foreign Language sheet tab**, and then click **Select All Sheets**. On the **PAGE LAYOUT tab**, set the **Width** to **1 page**. Center the worksheets horizontally on the page. Display the **document properties** and under **Related People**, right-click the author name, click **Edit Property**, and then type your name. In the **Subject** box, type your course name and section #, and in the **Tags** box, type **summer courses**

4 ▶ Display and check the **Print Preview**, make any necessary corrections, and then ungroup the worksheets. **Save** your workbook, and then **print** or submit your workbook electronically as directed. **Close** Excel.

END | You have completed Project 11A

PROJECT ACTIVITIES

In Activities 11.11 through 11.16, you will assist Justin Mitrani, Vice President of Academic Affairs, in distributing a workbook to the Instructional Deans at the college. Your completed workbook will look similar to Figure 11.23.

PROJECT FILES

For Project 11B, you will need the following file:

e11B_Courses

You will save your workbooks as:

Lastname_Firstname_11B_Courses
Lastname_Firstname_11B_Courses_Compatibility
Lastname_Firstname_11B_Courses_Encrypted

PROJECT RESULTS

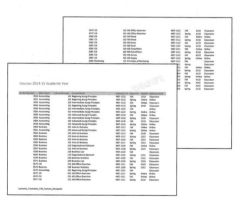

FIGURE 11.23 Project 11B Distributed Workbook

Video E11-4

Before distributing Excel workbooks to others, review the contents of the workbook to ensure that it does not contain sensitive or personal information that you do not want to share with other people. Such information might be stored in the document itself or in the document properties.

Activity 11.11 | Ensuring Accessibility in a Workbook

To ensure that an Excel 2013 workbook is accessible and can be read by individuals with disabilities, you can run the Accessibility Checker. The **Accessibility Checker** finds any potential accessibility issues and creates a report so that you can resolve the issues to make your file easier for those with disabilities to use. In this activity, you will run the Accessibility Checker and correct three problems.

1 ▶ Start Excel. From your student files, open the file **e11B_Courses**. **Save** the file in your **Excel Chapter 11** folder as **Lastname_Firstname_11B_Courses** On the **FILE tab** click **Check for Issues**, and then click **Check Accessibility**. Compare your screen with Figure 11.24.

The Accessibility Checker pane displays and the Inspection Results displays one error and two warnings that you should address. Errors are more severe than warnings.

FIGURE 11.24

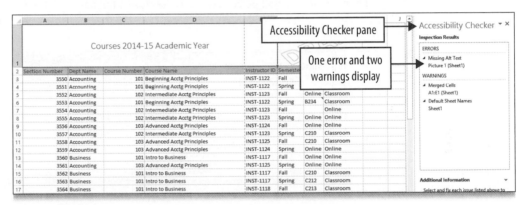

2 ▶ In the **Accessibility Checker** pane, under **ERRORS** click **Picture 1 (Sheet1)**. Under **Additional Information**, read the information under **Why Fix**. Scroll down and read **How To Fix**.

Alt text is used in documents and webpages to provide a text description of an image.

3 ▶ Right-click the selected image in cells **F1:H1**. Click **Format Picture**, on the **Format Picture** pane, click **Size & Properties**, and then, click to expand **ALT TEXT**. In the **Title** box, type **DRAFT** Notice the error no longer displays in the **Accessibility Checker** pane.

4 ▶ **Close** ✖ the **Format Picture** pane. In the **Accessibility Checker** pane, under **WARNINGS**, under **Merged Cells**, click **A1:E1 (Sheet1)**. Read the *Why Fix* and *How To Fix* sections. On the **HOME tab**, in the **Alignment group**, click **Merge & Center** to split the merged cells.

Merged cells can make a spreadsheet structure difficult to understand and navigate.

5 ▶ In the **Accessibility Checker** pane, under **WARNINGS**, under **Default Sheet Names**, click **Sheet1**. Read the *Why Fix* and *How To Fix* sections. Right-click the **Sheet1 sheet tab**, click **Rename**, type **Courses** and then press Enter.

Sheet names make it easier to understand and navigate a workbook.

6 ▶ Notice that the **Accessibility Checker** indicates there are no accessibility issues found. **Close** ✖ the **Accessibility Checker** pane.

7 Display the **document properties** and under **Related People**, be sure that your name displays as the author. If necessary, right-click the author name, click **Edit Property**, and then type your name. In the **Subject** box, type your course name and section #, in the **Tags** box, type **accessibility** and then **Save** 💾 your workbook.

Activity 11.12 | Ensuring Backward-Compatibility in a Workbook

To ensure that an Excel 2013 workbook does not have compatibility issues that cause a loss of functionality or fidelity in an earlier version of Excel, you can run the Compatibility Checker. The **Compatibility Checker** finds any potential compatibility issues and creates a report so that you can resolve the issues. When you work on a workbook in **Compatibility Mode**, where the workbook is in Excel 97-2003 file format (.xls) instead of the newer XML-based file format (.xlsx), the Compatibility Checker runs automatically when you save a workbook. In this activity, you will run the Compatibility Checker to identify features in the workbook that cannot be transferred to earlier versions of Excel.

1 On the **FILE tab** click **Check for Issues**, and then click **Check Compatibility**. Compare your screen with Figure 11.25.

> The Microsoft Excel - Compatibility Checker dialog box displays. The Compatibility Checker displays one minor loss of fidelity issue with formatting styles. The formats—cell title fill and font Theme Colors—will be converted to the closest format available when the worksheet is saved in an earlier version of Excel.

FIGURE 11.25

2 Click **OK**.

3 Display the **document properties**. In the **Tags** box, delete *accessibility* and type **compatibility**

4 Click **Save As**, and then click **Browse** to display the **Save As** dialog box. At the bottom of the dialog box, click the **Save as type arrow**, and then near the top of the list, click **Excel 97-2003 Workbook**. **Save** the file in your **Excel Chapter 11** folder as **Lastname_Firstname_11B_Courses_Compatibility**

> The Microsoft Excel - Compatibility Checker dialog box displays.

5 In the **Microsoft Excel - Compatibility Checker** dialog box, click **Continue**.

> The file is saved in an earlier version of Excel—Excel 97-2003.

6 On the **FILE tab** click **Close** to close the workbook. Leave Excel open for the next activity.

Activity 11.13 | Inspecting a Document

The **Document Inspector** is an Excel feature that can find and remove hidden properties and personal information in a workbook. In this activity, you will inspect the workbook and review the results that the Document Inspector finds to determine what information, if any, should be removed. Because some information is not needed by the distribution recipients of the Courses document, Justin Mitrani, Vice President of Academic Affairs, has asked you to remove some information.

1 Press Ctrl + F12, and then open your **Lastname_Firstname_11B_Courses** workbook.

2 On the **FILE tab**, click **Check for Issues**, and then, click **Inspect Document**. Compare your screen with Figure 11.26.

The Document Inspector dialog box displays and lists the various types of content that will be checked. By default, all the check boxes are selected.

FIGURE 11.26

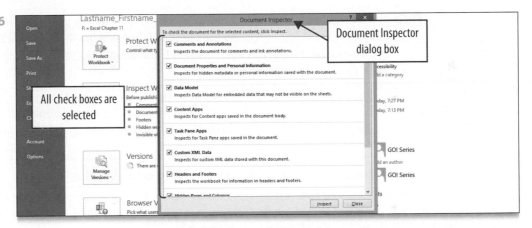

3 In the lower right corner of the **Document Inspector** dialog box, click **Inspect**. Compare your screen with Figure 11.27.

The Document Inspector indicates four categories that contain sensitive or personal information. A red exclamation point and a Remove All button display in the inspection results for these four categories. In this workbook, the Document Inspector found comments, document properties, footers, and a hidden worksheet.

FIGURE 11.27

4 **Close** the **Document Inspector** dialog box, and then click ⊙ to return to the worksheet.

5 Click cell **G6**, and notice the comment that displays.

6 On the **FILE tab**, click **Show All Properties**. Notice that in the **Status** box, *DRAFT* displays.

7 Click ⊖ to return to the worksheet. Right-click the **Courses sheet tab**, and then click **Unhide**. In the **Unhide** dialog box, with *Instructors* selected, click **OK**.

> The Instructors worksheet, which was hidden, displays.

8 Right-click the **Instructors sheet tab**, and then click **Hide**.

> The Instructors worksheet is once again hidden.

9 Save 🖫 your workbook. On the **FILE tab**, click **Check for Issues**, and then click **Inspect Document**.

10 In the **Document Inspector** dialog box, click **Inspect**.

> You have now examined three of the four items flagged by the Document Inspector—the comment regarding the new podium, the subject DRAFT in the document properties, and the hidden worksheet with instructor names and email addresses.

11 To the right of **Comments and Annotations**, click **Remove All**. To the right of **Headers and Footers**, click **Remove All**. To the right of **Hidden Worksheets**, click **Remove All**. Do not remove the **Document Properties and Personal Information**. Scroll to the top of the list and compare your screen with Figure 11.28.

> The comments, footer, and hidden worksheet are removed from the file. This information is not needed by the distribution recipients of the Courses document. If you remove the hidden worksheet, you are losing this data, so if you want to keep it, make a copy elsewhere.

> **NOTE** — **Removing Document Properties and Personal Information**
>
> When you remove document properties and personal information using the Document Inspector, it applies a setting that automatically removes properties and personal information whenever you save the document. To add properties such as author or tags to such a file, on the FILE tab, enter the properties and then, under Inspect Workbook, click *Allow this information to be saved in your file.*

FIGURE 11.28

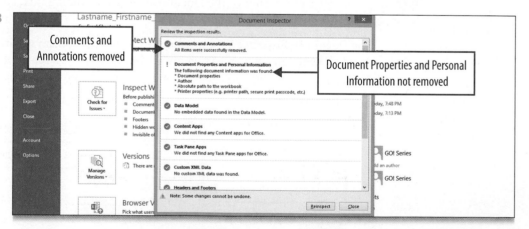

12 In the lower right corner of the **Document Inspector** dialog box, click **Close**.

13 Return to the worksheet. Set the **Orientation** to **Landscape**, the **Width** to **1 page**, and center the worksheet horizontally. Insert a footer in the **left section** that includes the file name, return to **Normal** ▦ view, make cell **A1** the active cell, and then click **Save** 🖫.

Activity 11.14 | Encrypting a Workbook

You can provide another level of security for your workbook by adding encryption. *Encryption* is the process by which a file is encoded so that it cannot be opened without the proper password. Encryption is more than simple password protection—the process digitally obscures information to make it unreadable without a proper key to decode it. Passwords prevent users from editing a worksheet or the entire workbook. Encryption is different—it prevents users from opening the file. In this activity, you will apply encryption to your workbook.

1 With your **Lastname_Firstname_11B_Courses** workbook open, press F12 to display the **Save As** dialog box, and then **Save** the file in your **Excel Chapter 11** folder as **Lastname_Firstname_11B_Courses_Encrypted** Display the **document properties**. In the **Tags** box, delete *accessibility*, and then type **encrypted**

2 Click **Protect Workbook**, and then, click **Encrypt with Password**. Compare your screen with Figure 11.29.

> The Encrypt Document dialog box displays. A box in which to type the password and a note of caution about entering passwords displays.

FIGURE 11.29

3 In the **Encrypt Document** dialog box, in the **Password** box, type **goseries** and then click **OK**. In the **Reenter password** box, type **goseries** and then click **OK**.

More **Knowledge** | **Making Passwords More Secure**

The Windows Help system has the following suggestions for secure passwords: "A more secure or strong password is one that's difficult for others to determine by guessing or by using automated programs. Strong passwords contain 7–16 characters, do not include common words or names, and combine uppercase letters, lowercase letters, numbers, and symbols."

---

4 **Save** and **Close** the workbook. Leave Excel open.

5 On the **FILE tab**, on the **Open tab**, click **Computer,** and then click **Browse** to display the **Open** dialog box. Navigate to your **Excel Chapter 11** folder, and then open your **Lastname_Firstname_11B_Courses_Encrypted** file.

> The Password dialog box displays. The workbook cannot be opened without the password.

ANOTHER WAY   Click Open and the click the Lastname_Firstname_11B_Courses_Encrypted file in the Recent Workbooks list.

6 Type **goseries** and then click **OK**.

> Your Lastname_Firstname_11B_Courses_Encrypted workbook opens.

Activity 11.15 | Marking a Workbook as Final

Before you share a workbook, you can apply the Mark as Final command, which makes the document read-only. The **Mark as Final command** prevents additional changes to the document and disables typing, editing comments, and proofing marks. When the document is opened by others, the user will be notified by Microsoft Excel that the document has been *Marked as Final*. In this activity, you will mark the workbook as final.

1 ▶ With your **Lastname_Firstname_11B_Courses_Encrypted** workbook open, on the **FILE tab**, click **Protect Workbook**, and then click **Mark as Final**.

The Microsoft Excel dialog box displays and indicates that the workbook will be marked as final and then saved.

2 ▶ Click **OK**. Read the message box, and then click **OK**, and then compare your screen with Figure 11.30.

The workbook is marked as final. The title bar displays *[Read-Only]* to indicate the file can be read but not edited. A yellow bar displays below the ribbon tabs, indicating that *An author has marked this workbook as final to discourage editing*. If someone opening the file clicks Edit Anyway, the workbook will no longer be *Marked as Final* and will not be a Read-Only file.

FIGURE 11.30

3 ▶ Click any cell and type a number or text to confirm the workbook cannot be edited. **Close** Excel.

More Knowledge   **Mark as Final Feature**

The Mark as Final command is not a security feature. Anyone can edit a document that has been marked as final by removing the Mark as Final status from the document, editing the file, and then reapplying the Mark as Final status. To ensure that a workbook cannot be edited, you must password protect the workbook. Mark as Final signifies the intent of the author that the document is final in content.

Video E11-5

Cloud storage is online storage of data so that you can access your data from different places and devices. Microsoft offers *SkyDrive*, a free cloud storage for anyone with a free Microsoft account. You can upload files and then access them from any computer with Internet access and a web browser such as Internet Explorer. SkyDrive enables you to engage in a form of *cloud computing*, which means applications and services that are accessed over the Internet, rather than applications that are installed on your local computer.

SkyDrive uses a Microsoft account for security to control access to your files. Online file storage is helpful for keeping files in one location rather than on multiple devices or in several locations. It is also useful for sharing files with others who can access your information with a web browser. In SkyDrive, you can share files or keep them private. *Synchronization*, or just *syncing*, is the process of updating computer files that are in two or more locations according to specific rules. When you connect multiple devices, such as your laptop, tablet, and desktop computers, to your SkyDrive, the files on these devices are automatically synced based upon the rules or settings that you apply.

More Knowledge **The World of Cloud Computing Is Fast Changing**

Because these tools are growing rapidly as individuals move more and more to cloud computing, the steps and screens in Activity 11.16 may work differently than described here.

Activity 11.16 | Uploading a Workbook to SkyDrive

In this activity, you will navigate to the SkyDrive site, and then sign in to access the SkyDrive file storage and file sharing services.

ALERT! **You Must Be Signed in to Office with a Microsoft Account to Complete This Activity**

If you do not have a Microsoft account, refer to Activity 1.21 of the Office Features chapter to create one by using Microsoft's new outlook.com email service, which includes free SkyDrive cloud storage.

---

1 Start your web browser. Click in the **address bar**, and then replace the existing text by typing **http://skydrive.com** Press Enter.

The SkyDrive page displays. If you are currently logged into Windows using your Microsoft account, your SkyDrive displays. If you are not logged in to a Microsoft account, the SkyDrive home page displays.

2 If necessary, sign in to display the SkyDrive page.

3 At the top of the page, on the blue menu bar, click **Create** and compare your screen with Figure 11.31.

FIGURE 11.31

4 ▸ Click **Folder**. As the **Name,** type **Chapter 11** and press Enter. Click the new folder and on the blue menu bar, click **Sharing**. On the left, under **Share**, click the **Get a Link tab** and then click **Make public** and compare your screen with Figure 11.32.

> The public link can be shared with others, such as your instructor or classmates, to give them access to your folder.

N O T E   **Shortening the URL**

To make the URL more user-friendly and easier to use, click the Shorten button in the Share dialog box.

FIGURE 11.32

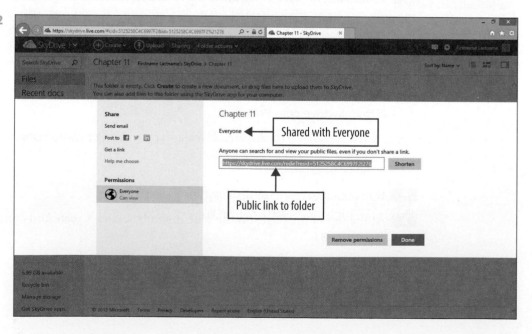

5 Click **Done**. On the menu bar, click **Upload** to display the **Choose File to Upload** dialog box. Navigate to your **Excel Chapter 11** folder, and then select your **Lastname_Firstname_11B_ Courses_Encrypted** file. Click **Open**. Compare your screen with Figure 11.33.

> A copy of your Lastname_Firstname_11B_Courses_Encrypted file is saved and displays in the Chapter 11 SkyDrive storage location.

ANOTHER WAY You can simply drag files from your computer to the browser window to upload one or more files.

FIGURE 11.33

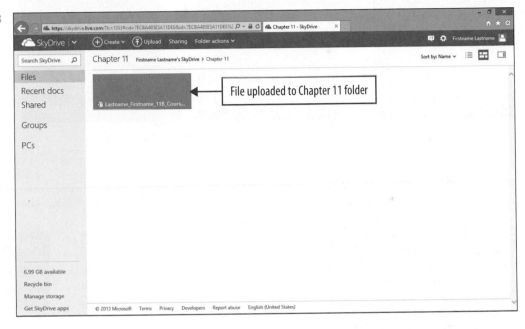

File uploaded to Chapter 11 folder

6 If directed by your instructor, use the Windows Snipping Tool to create a snip of your screen showing your uploaded file to your SkyDrive account or provide your instructor with the public link to your folder. In the upper right corner of the screen, click your name, and then click **Sign out** to exit SkyDrive. **Close** the browser. **Print** the three workbooks, or submit your workbooks electronically as directed.

More **Knowledge**   **Syncing SkyDrive with Your Computer**

The SkyDrive app allows you to save files on your computer in a special SkyDrive folder that is automatically synced with SkyDrive, so you do not have to upload files to your SkyDrive.

END | You have completed Project 11B

END OF CHAPTER

SUMMARY

Collaboration is the process of working jointly with others to review, comment on, and make changes to a shared workbook. This includes comparing different versions of a workbook and merging them together.

Changes to documents by different individuals can be tracked and then accepted or rejected. A file can be signed with a digital signature to ensure that it originated from the signer and has not been altered.

Preparing a final workbook for distribution, includes inspecting the workbook for hidden information, encrypting a workbook with a password, and checking for compatibility and accessibility issues.

Cloud storage is online storage of data so that you can access your data from different places and devices. Microsoft offers SkyDrive, a free cloud storage for anyone with a free Microsoft account.

GO! LEARN IT ONLINE

Review the concepts and key terms in this chapter by completing these online challenges, which you can find at **www.pearsonhighered.com/go**.

Matching and Multiple Choice:
Answer matching and multiple choice questions to test what you learned in this chapter. MyITLab®

Crossword Puzzle:
Spell out the words that match the numbered clues, and put them in the puzzle squares.

Flipboard:
Flip through the definitions of the key terms in this chapter and match them with the correct term.

END OF CHAPTER

REVIEW AND ASSESSMENT GUIDE FOR EXCEL CHAPTER 11

Your instructor may assign one or more of these projects to help you review the chapter and assess your mastery and understanding of the chapter.

	Review and Assessment Guide for Excel Chapter 11		
Project	**Apply Skills from These Chapter Objectives**	**Project Type**	**Project Location**
11C	Objectives 1–3 from Project 11A	**11C Skills Review** A guided review of the skills from Project 11A.	On the following pages
11D	Objectives 4 and 5 from Project 11B	**11D Skills Review** A guided review of the skills from Project 11B.	On the following pages
11E	Objectives 1–3 from Project 11A	**11E Mastery (Grader Project)** A demonstration of your mastery of the skills in Project 11A with extensive decision making.	In MyITLab and on the following pages
11F	Objectives 4 and 5 from Project 11B	**11F Mastery (Grader Project)** A demonstration of your mastery of the skills in Project 11B with extensive decision making.	In MyITLab and on the following pages
11G	Objectives 1–5 from Projects 11A and 11B	**11G Mastery (Grader Project)** A demonstration of your mastery of the skills in Projects 11A and 11B with extensive decision making.	In MyITLab and on the following pages
11H	Combination of Objectives from Projects 11A and 11B	**11H GO! Fix It** A demonstration of your mastery of the skills in Projects 11A and 11B by creating a correct result from a document that contains errors you must find.	Online
11I	Combination of Objectives from Projects 11A and 11B	**11I GO! Make It** A demonstration of your mastery of the skills in Projects 11A and 11B by creating a result from a supplied picture.	Online
11J	Combination of Objectives from Projects 11A and 11B	**11J GO! Solve It** A demonstration of your mastery of the skills in Projects 11A and 11B, your decision-making skills, and your critical thinking skills. A task-specific rubric helps you self-assess your result.	Online
11K	Combination of Objectives from Projects 11A and 11B	**11K GO! Solve It** A demonstration of your mastery of the skills in Projects 11A and 11B, your decision-making skills, and your critical thinking skills. A task-specific rubric helps you self-assess your result.	On the following pages
11L	Combination of Objectives from Projects 11A and 11B	**11L GO! Think** A demonstration of your understanding of the chapter concepts applied in a manner that you would outside of college. An analytic rubric helps you and your instructor grade the quality of your work by comparing it to the work an expert in the discipline would create.	On the following pages
11M	Combination of Objectives from Projects 11A and 11B	**11M GO! Think** A demonstration of your understanding of the chapter concepts applied in a manner that you would outside of college. An analytic rubric helps you and your instructor grade the quality of your work by comparing it to the work an expert in the discipline would create.	Online
11N	Combination of Objectives from Projects 11A and 11B	**11N You and GO!** A demonstration of your understanding of the chapter concepts applied in a manner that you would in a personal situation. An analytic rubric helps you and your instructor grade the quality of your work.	Online

GLOSSARY

GLOSSARY OF CHAPTER KEY TERMS

Accessibility Checker An Excel tool that finds any potential accessibility issues and creates a report so that you can resolve the issues to make your file easier for those with disabilities to use.

Alt text Text used in documents and webpages to provide a text description of an image.

Background image An image inserted in a worksheet that is behind, not in, the worksheet cells.

Certificate authority A commercial organization that issues digital certificates, keeps track of who is assigned to a certificate, signs certificates to verify their validity, and tracks which certificates are revoked or expired.

Change history Information that is maintained about changes made in past editing sessions.

Cloud computing Refers to applications and services that are accessed over the Internet, rather than to applications that are installed on your local computer.

Cloud storage Online storage of data so that you can access your data from different places and devices.

Collaboration In Excel, the process of working jointly with others to review, comment on, and make necessary changes to a shared workbook.

Compatibility Checker An Excel tool that finds any potential compatibility issues that might cause a significant loss of

functionality or a minor loss of fidelity in an earlier version of Excel, and creates a report so that you can resolve the issues.

Compatibility Mode Using a workbook in Excel 97-2003 file format (.xls) instead of the newer XML-based file format (.xlsx).

Digital certificate An electronic means of proving identity issued by a certificate authority.

Digital signature An electronic, encrypted, stamp of authentication. A means of proving identity and authenticity that ensures that a file originated from the signer and has not been changed.

Document Inspector An Excel feature that can find and remove hidden properties and personal information in a workbook.

Encryption The process by which a file is encoded so that it cannot be opened without the proper password.

Intranet A network within an organization and that uses Internet technologies.

Mark as Final command Prevents additional changes to the document and disables typing, editing comments, and proofing marks.

Metadata The details about a file that describe or identify the file, including the title, author name, subject, and tags that identify the file's topic or contents. Also known as properties.

Properties The details about a file that describe or identify the file, including the title, author name, subject, and tags that identify the file's topic or contents. Also known as metadata.

Self-signed A project signed with a certificate that you create yourself.

Shared workbook A workbook set up to allow multiple users on a network to view and make changes to the workbook at the same time.

Signature line Specifies the individual who must sign the document.

SkyDrive Microsoft's free cloud storage for anyone with a free Microsoft account.

Synchronization The process of updating computer files that are in two or more locations according to specific rules—also called syncing.

Syncing The process of updating computer files that are in two or more locations according to specific rules—also called synchronization.

Track Changes An Excel feature that logs details about workbook changes including insertions and deletions.

Watermark A faded image or text used as a background of a document.

Apply 11A skills from these Objectives:

1 Create a Shared Workbook

2 Track Changes Made to a Workbook

3 Merge Workbooks and Accept Changes

Skills Review | Project 11C Fall Schedule

In the following Skills Review, you will create a shared workbook so that it can be reviewed by the different Department Chairpersons in the College's Liberal Arts Division. Various individuals in the Liberal Arts Division will be able to edit and comment on the information in the workbook. Your completed worksheets will look similar to Figure 11.34.

Build from Scratch

PROJECT FILES

For Project 11C, you will need the following files:

e11C_Draft
e11C_Fall_Schedule

You will save your workbooks as:

Lastname_Firstname_11C_Fall_Schedule
Lastname_Firstname_11C_Fall_Schedule - Copy

PROJECT RESULTS

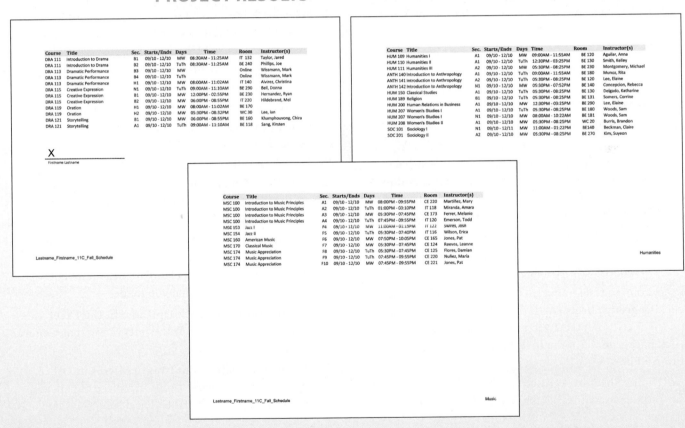

FIGURE 11.34

(Project 11C Fall Schedule continues on the next page)

CHAPTER REVIEW

1 ▶ Start Excel. From your student files, open the file **e11C_Fall_Schedule**. Display the **Save As** dialog box, navigate to the location where you are storing your files for this chapter, and then **Save** the file in your **Excel Chapter 11** folder as **Lastname_Firstname_11C_Fall_Schedule**

a. Group the worksheets. Insert a footer with the file name in the **left section** and the sheet name in the **right section**, click above the footer area to deselect, and then return to **Normal** view. Set the **Orientation** to **Landscape**. Press Ctrl + Home to move to the top of the sheet.

b. Click the **FILE tab** to display **Backstage** view. On the **Info tab**, at the top of the screen, notice that the location of this file on your computer displays under the file name. On the right, notice that some of the more common properties for this file display, for example, the file *Size* and *Author*.

c. Under **Properties**, in the **Title** box, type **Proposed Fall Schedule** Under **Related People**, point to the text *Molly Morton*, who is the author to view the **Contact Card**.

d. Move the mouse pointer away from the **Contact Card**, near the top right of the **Info** pane click the **Properties arrow**, and then click **Advanced Properties**. Click the **Summary tab**. In the **Author** box, delete *Molly Morton*, type **Kelly Clinton** and then press Tab. In the **Manager** box, type **Dean Massaro, Liberal Arts Division**

e. Click **OK**. Click **Save** to save your workbook and return to the worksheet.

2 ▶ Point to the **Drama sheet tab**, right-click, and then click **Ungroup Sheets**. With the **Drama** worksheet active, on the **PAGE LAYOUT tab** in the **Page Setup group**, click **Background**. In the **Insert Pictures** dialog box, click **From a File**.

a. In the **Sheet Background** dialog box, navigate to your student data files, click the file **e11C_Draft** and then click **Insert**. **Save** your workbook.

b. On the **Music** worksheet, click cell **H11**, type **Nu** On the **INSERT tab**, in the **Symbols group**, click **Symbol**. If necessary, drag the **Symbol** dialog

box up so that cell **H11** is visible. In the **Symbol** dialog box, click the **Subset arrow**, and then click **Latin-1 Supplement**. Click the **scrollbar arrows** as necessary to locate the symbol ñ—*Latin Small Letter N With Tilde*. Click **Insert**, click **Close**, and then type **ez, Mar** Display the **Symbol** dialog box, verify that the **Latin-1 Supplement** subset is selected, scroll up one row, and then insert the symbol í—*Latin Small Letter I With Acute*. **Close** the **Symbol** dialog box, type **a** and then press Enter. **Save** your workbook.

3 ▶ On the **REVIEW tab**, in the **Changes group**, click **Track Changes**, and then click **Highlight Changes**. In the **Highlight Changes** dialog box, click to select the **Track changes while editing** check box. Verify that the **When** check box is selected and indicates *All*. Select the **Who** check box and be sure *Everyone* is indicated. Verify that the **Highlight changes on screen** check box is selected, and then click **OK**.

a. Click **OK**. On the **FILE tab**, click **Close** to close the file and leave Excel open.

4 ▶ Press Ctrl + F12 to display the **Open** dialog box. Navigate to your **Excel Chapter 11** folder, point to your **Lastname_Firstname_11C_Fall_Schedule** file, right-click, and then click **Copy**.

a. Right-click in an empty space below or to the right of the file list, and then click **Paste**. In the **Open** dialog box click **Cancel**.

5 ▶ Press Ctrl + F12 to display the **Open** dialog box, navigate to your **Excel Chapter 11** folder, and then open your **Lastname_Firstname_11C_Fall_Schedule** file—open the original, *not* the copy that you made.

a. On the **FILE tab**, click **Options**. In the **Excel Options** dialog box, on the left, verify that **General** is selected.

b. Under **Personalize your copy of Microsoft Office**, click in the **User name** box. On a piece of paper, write down the User name that displays so that you can restore it later. Select the User name text, type **Andy Koch, Humanities** to replace the selected User name text. Click **OK**.

(Project 11C Fall Schedule continues on the next page)

c. Display the **Humanities** worksheet. Click cell **H10**, begin to type **Lee, Elaine** and press Enter to accept the AutoComplete suggestion to change the name. In cell **H12**, change the name to **Woods, Sam** Press Ctrl + Home to move to cell **A1**.

d. On the **REVIEW tab**, in the **Changes group**, click **Track Changes**, and then click **Highlight Changes**. In the **Highlight Changes** dialog box, click the **When arrow**, and then click **All**. Click the **Who** check box, and be sure that it indicates *Everyone*. Click **OK**. Point to each of the changed cells to view the ScreenTip, which indicates the change that was made and the date and time the change was made. **Save** your workbook, and then on the **FILE tab**, click **Close** to close the file and leave Excel open.

e. Press Ctrl + F12 to display the **Open** dialog box. Navigate to and then reopen your **Lastname_Firstname_11C_Fall_Schedule** file—not the copy. On the **FILE tab**, click **Options** to display the **Excel Options** dialog box change the **User name** to **Jan Clarke, Music** and then click **OK**.

f. Display the **Music** worksheet. Click cell **G9** and type **Permission** Click cell **H12** and type **Jones, Pat** then press Enter. Press Ctrl + Home to make cell **A1** the active cell. **Save** your workbook, and then on the **FILE tab** click **Close** to close the file and leave Excel open.

6 ▶ Press Ctrl + F12 and open the **Lastname_Firstname_11C_Fall_Schedule - Copy** file that you created earlier.

a. On the **FILE tab**, click **Options** to display the **Excel Options** dialog box, change the **User name** to **Kate Sparks, Drama** and then click **OK**.

b. Display the **Drama** worksheet. Click cell **F4** and type **Online** Click cell **F5**, type **Online** and then press Enter. Press Ctrl + Home. **Save** your workbook, and then on the **FILE tab**, click **Close** to close the file and leave Excel open.

7 ▶ On the **FILE tab**, click **Options** to display the **Excel Options** dialog box, and then change the **User name** to **Dean Massaro** Click **OK** to close the dialog box, and then open your **Lastname_Firstname_11C_Fall_Schedule** file.

a. With the **Music** worksheet active, on the **REVIEW tab**, in the **Changes group**, click **Track Changes**,

and then click **Highlight Changes**. In the **Highlight Changes** dialog box, click the **When arrow**, and then click **All**. Click the **Who arrow**, and then click **Everyone but Me**. Click **OK**.

b. Display the **Humanities** worksheet and notice the borders around cells **H10** and **H12** indicating that changes have been made. Display the **Drama** worksheet, and notice that no changes are indicated because changes for this department were made on another copy of the shared workbook.

c. On the **FILE tab**, click **Options** to display the **Excel Options** dialog box, and then on the left, click **Quick Access Toolbar**. At the top of the dialog box, under **Customize the Quick Access Toolbar**, click the **Choose commands from arrow**, and then click **Commands Not in the Ribbon**. In the list below, scroll as necessary, click **Compare and Merge Workbooks**, in the center click **Add**. Click **OK**.

d. On the **Quick Access Toolbar**, click **Compare and Merge Workbooks**. In the **Select Files to Merge Into Current Workbook** dialog box, if necessary, navigate to your **Excel Chapter 11** folder. Locate your **Lastname_Firstname_11C_Fall_Schedule - Copy** file—if necessary, widen the **Name column** to display the complete file name—and then click to select it. Click **OK**.

8 ▶ Display the **Humanities** worksheet. On the **REVIEW tab**, in the **Changes group**, click **Track Changes**, and then click **Accept/Reject Changes**.

a. Verify that the **When** box indicates *Not yet reviewed*. Change the **Who** box to indicate *Everyone*, and then click **OK**.

b. Click **Accept** to accept the change of instructor in cell **H10** to *Lee, Elaine*. Click **Accept**. Click **Reject** to reject the change in cell **G9**. **Accept** the next change—change 4 of 6—a change in instructor to *Jones, Pat*.

c. Click **Accept**, and then **Accept** the last change—a change in cell **F5** to *Online*.

d. Display the **Drama** worksheet, click cell **F4**, and then press Delete. Press Tab and in cell **G4**, type **Online** Click cell **F5** and press Delete. Press Tab and in cell **G5**, type **Online** and press Enter. **Save** your workbook.

(Project 11C Fall Schedule continues on the next page)

CHAPTER REVIEW

9 On the **REVIEW tab**, in the **Changes group**, click **Share Workbook**. Clear the **Allow changes by more than one user at the same time** check box, and then click **OK**. On the **Microsoft Excel** information box, click **Yes**.

a. On the **FILE tab**, click **Options** to display the **Excel Options** dialog box, and then click in the **User name** box. Select the text *Dean Massaro*, type the name that you wrote down previously to replace the selected User name text, and then click **OK**.

b. On the **Quick Access Toolbar**, right-click **Compare and Merge Workbooks**, and then click **Remove from Quick Access Toolbar**.

10 Display the **Drama** worksheet, and then click cell **A15**. On the **INSERT tab**, in the **Text group**, click the **Add Signature Line arrow**, and then click **Microsoft Office Signature Line**.

a. In the **Signature Setup** dialog box, in the **Suggested signer** box, using your own name, type **Firstname Lastname** and then click **OK**.

b. Right-click the **Drama sheet tab**, and then click **Select All Sheets**. On the **PAGE LAYOUT tab**, set the **Width** to **1 page**. Center the worksheets horizontally on the page. Display the **document properties** and under **Related People**, right-click the author name, click **Edit Property**, type your name and then press Enter. In the **Subject** box, type your course name and section #, and in the **Tags** box, type **fall classes**

c. Display and check the **Print Preview**, make any necessary corrections, and then ungroup the worksheets. **Save** your workbook, and then **print** or submit your workbook electronically as directed. **Close** Excel.

END | You have completed Project 11C

CHAPTER REVIEW

Skills Review | Project 11D Distributed Class Workbook

Apply 11B skills from these Objectives:

4   Prepare a Final Workbook for Distribution

5   Upload a Workbook to SkyDrive

In the following Skills Review, you will assist Justin Mitrani, Vice President of Academic Affairs, in distributing a workbook for social science classes to the instructional deans at the college. Your completed worksheets will look similar to Figure 11.35.

PROJECT FILES

Build from Scratch

For Project 11D, you will need the following file:

e11D_Classes

You will save your workbooks as:

Lastname_Firstname_11D_Classes

Lastname_Firstname_11D_Classes_Compatibility

Lastname_Firstname_11D_Classes_Encrypted

PROJECT RESULTS

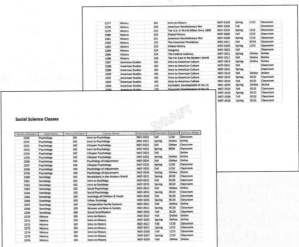

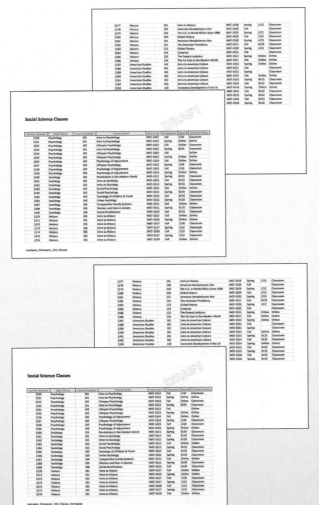

FIGURE 11.35

(Project 11D Distributed Class Workbook continues on the next page)

CHAPTER REVIEW

1 ▶ Start Excel. From your student files, open the file **e11D_Classes** and then **Save** the file in your **Excel Chapter 11** folder as **Lastname_Firstname_11D_Classes**

a. On the **FILE tab**, click **Check for Issues**, and then click **Check Accessibility**.

b. In the **Accessibility Checker** pane, under **ERRORS** click **Picture 1 (Sheet1)**. Right-click the selected image in cells **E1:H1**. Click **Format Picture**, on the **Format Picture** pane, click **Size & Properties**, and then, if necessary, click to expand **ALT TEXT**. In the **Title** box, type **DRAFT** Notice that the error no longer displays in the **Accessibility Checker** pane. **Close** the **Format Picture** pane.

c. In the **Accessibility Checker** pane, under **WARNINGS**, under **Merged Cells**, click **A1:G1 (Sheet1)**. On the **HOME tab**, in the **Alignment** group, click **Merge & Center** to split the merged cells.

d. In the **Accessibility Checker** pane, under **WARNINGS**, under **Default Sheet Names**, click **Sheet1**. Read the Right-click the **Sheet1 sheet tab**, click **Rename**, type **Courses** and then press Enter . Notice that the **Accessibility Checker** indicates there are no accessibility issues found. **Close** the **Accessibility Checker** pane.

e. Display the **document properties** and under **Related People**, be sure that your name displays as the author. If necessary, right-click the author name, click **Edit Property**, and then type your name. In the **Subject** box, type your course name and section #, in the **Tags** box, type **accessibility** and then **Save** your workbook.

2 ▶ On the **FILE tab**, click **Check for Issues**, and then click **Check Compatibility**. Click **OK**.

a. Display the **document properties**. In the **Tags** box, delete *accessibility* and type **compatibility**

b. Click **Save As** and then click **Browse** to display the **Save As** dialog box. At the bottom of the dialog box, click the **Save as type arrow**, click **Excel 97-2003 Workbook**. **Save** the file in your **Excel Chapter 11** folder as **Lastname_Firstname_11D_Classes_ Compatibility** In the **Microsoft Excel - Compatibility Checker** dialog box, click **Continue**. On the **FILE tab**,

click **Close** to close the workbook. Leave Excel open for the next activity.

3 ▶ Press Ctrl + F12 to display the **Open** dialog box. Navigate to your **Excel Chapter 11** folder and open your **Lastname_Firstname_11D_Classes** workbook.

a. On the **FILE tab**, click **Check for Issues**, and then, click **Inspect Document**. In the lower right corner of the dialog box, click **Inspect**. **Close** the **Document Inspector** dialog box, and then return to the worksheet.

b. Click cell **G6**, and notice the comment that displays. On the **FILE tab**, click **Show All Properties**. Notice that in the **Status** box, *DRAFT* displays. Return to the worksheet. Right-click the **Courses sheet tab**, and then click **Unhide**. In the **Unhide** dialog box, with *Instructors* selected, click **OK**. Right-click the **Instructors sheet tab**, and then click **Hide**.

c. **Save** your workbook. On the **FILE tab**, click **Check for Issues**, and then click **Inspect Document**. In the **Document Inspector** dialog box, click **Inspect**. To the right of **Comments and Annotations**, click **Remove All**. To the right of **Headers and Footers**, click **Remove All**. To the right of **Hidden Worksheets**, click **Remove All**.

d. In the lower right corner of the **Document Inspector** dialog box, click **Close**. Return to the worksheet. Set the **Orientation** to **Landscape**, the **Width** to **1 page**, and center the worksheet horizontally. Insert a footer in the **left section** that includes the file name, return to **Normal** view, make cell **A1** the active cell, and then click **Save**.

4 ▶ With your **Lastname_Firstname_11D_Classes** file open, press F12 to display the **Save As** dialog box, and then **Save** the file in your **Excel Chapter 11** folder as **Lastname_Firstname_11D_Classes_Encrypted** Display the **document properties**, in the **Tags** box, delete *accessibility,* and then type **encrypted**

a. Click **Protect Workbook**, and then click **Encrypt with Password**. In the **Encrypt Document** dialog box, in the **Password** box, type **goseries** and then click **OK**. In the **Reenter password** box, type **goseries** and then click **OK**.

(Project 11D Distributed Class Workbook continues on the next page)

CHAPTER REVIEW

b. **Save** and **Close** the workbook. Leave Excel open. On the **FILE tab**, click **Open**, click **Computer**, and then click **Browse** to display the **Open** dialog box. Navigate to your **Excel Chapter 11** folder, and then open your **Lastname_Firstname_11D_Classes_ Encrypted** file. Type **goseries** and then click **OK**.

5 With the **Lastname_Firstname_11D_Classes_ Encrypted** file open, on the **FILE tab**, click **Protect Workbook**, and then click **Mark as Final**. Click **OK**. Read the message box, and then click **OK**. Click any cell in the worksheet and type a number or text to confirm that you cannot edit the workbook. **Close** the workbook and **Close** Excel.

6 Start your web browser. Click in the **address bar**, and then replace the existing text by typing **http://skydrive.com** Press Enter.

a. If necessary, sign in to display the SkyDrive page. If you do not have a Microsoft account, refer to Activity 1.21 of the Office Features chapter to create one.

b. If necessary, at the top of the page, on the blue menu bar, click **Create**. Click **Folder**. As the Name, type **Chapter 11** and press Enter. Click the new folder and on the blue menu bar, click **Sharing**. On the left, under **Share**, click the **Get a Link tab** and then click **Make public**. Click **Done**.

c. If necessary, click the **Chapter 11** folder to open it. On the menu bar, click **Upload** to display the **Choose File to Upload** dialog box. Navigate to your **Excel Chapter 11** folder, and then select your **Lastname_ Firstname_11D_Classes_Encrypted** file. Click **Open**. If directed by your instructor, use the Windows Snipping Tool to create a snip of your screen showing your uploaded file to your new SkyDrive or provide your instructor with the public link to your folder. In the upper right corner of the screen, click your name and then click **Sign out**.

7 **Close** the browser. **Print** the three workbooks or submit electronically as directed.

END | You have completed Project 11D

CONTENT-BASED ASSESSMENTS

MyITLab® grader

Mastering Excel | Project 11E Scholarship Classes

Apply 11A skills from these Objectives:

1. Create a Shared Workbook
2. Track Changes Made to a Workbook
3. Merge Workbooks and Accept Changes

In the following Mastering Excel project, you will create a shared workbook, change the User name, and then make changes to the workbook for the Continuing Education Division of Capital Cities Community College. Capital Cities Community College offers a selection of free (scholarship) classes to nonprofit agencies. The class list from the previous semester must be updated for the upcoming semester. Then you will review the changes that were made and accept or reject the changes. Your completed worksheet will look similar to Figure 11.36.

PROJECT FILES

Build from Scratch

For Project 11E, you will need the following file:

e11E_Scholarship_Classes

You will save your workbook as:

Lastname_Firstname_11E_Scholarship_Classes

PROJECT RESULTS

Scholarship Classes for Nonprofit Agencies

Fall

Title	Dates	Time	Class Number
Introduction to Access	Sept 17 & 24	8 AM-12 PM	OS 325
Intermediate Access	Oct 1 & 8	8 AM-12 PM	OS 326
Introduction to Excel	Oct 15 & 22	1-5 PM	OS 322
Intermediate Excel	Oct 29 & Nov 5	8 AM-12 PM	OS 310
Introduction to PowerPoint	Oct 15 & 22	8 AM-12 PM	OS 328
Introduction to Word	Nov 12 & 19	1-5 PM	OS 319
Intermediate Word	Dec 3 & 10	1-5 PM	OS 320
MS Publisher	Nov 12 & 19	8 AM-12 PM	OS 345

Lastname_Firstname_11E_Scholarship_Classes.xlsx

FIGURE 11.36

(Project 11E Scholarship Classes continues on the next page)

CONTENT-BASED ASSESSMENTS

1 Start Excel. From your student files, open the Excel workbook **e11E_Scholarship_Classes**. **Save** the file in your **Excel Chapter 11** folder as **Lastname_Firstname_11E_Scholarship_Classes** Insert a footer in the **left section** with the **File Name**. Display the **document properties**. In the **Subject** box, type your course name and section #, type **scholarship classes** as the tags and **Fall Nonprofit Classes** as the title.

2 On the **NonProfits** worksheet, in cell **A3**, type **Fall** On the **REVIEW tab**, in the **Changes group**, click the **Track Changes arrow**, and then click **Highlight Changes**. In the **Highlight Changes** dialog box, select the **Track changes while editing** check box. Be sure the **When** check box is selected and indicates *All* and that the **Who** check box is selected and indicates *Everyone*.

3 **Close** the file and then reopen it. Display the **Excel Options** dialog box, verify that **General** is selected. Under **Personalize your copy of Microsoft Office**, write down the name that displays in the **User name** box so that you can restore it later, and then change the name to **Kimberly Phillips**

4 Delete the text in the range **B6:B13**. In **column B**, starting in cell **B6** enter the following dates:

Sept 17 & 24
Oct 1 & 8
Oct 15 & 22
Oct 29 & Nov 5
Oct 15 & 22
Nov 12 & 19
Dec 3 & 10
Nov 12 & 19

5 Return to cell **A1**. **Save** the file, and then **Close** it. Open your **Lastname_Firstname_11E_Scholarship_Classes** file again, display the **Excel Options** dialog box, and change the **User name** to **Jo Marzetti**

6 On the **REVIEW tab**, in the **Changes group**, click the **Track Changes arrow**, and then click **Accept/Reject Changes**. In the **Select Changes to Accept or Reject** dialog box, be sure the **When** check box is selected and that it indicates *Not yet reviewed*. Be sure the **Who** check box is selected, click its arrow, and then click **Everyone but Me**. The first date that was changed is surrounded by a border. Click **Accept**. The first change is accepted, and the second change is indicated. Click **Accept**, and then click **Accept All**.

7 **Save** your workbook. **Print** or submit your workbook electronically. **Close** the workbook. Display the **Excel Options** dialog box, and change the **User name** to the name that you wrote down in Step 3 to restore the original setting. **Close** Excel.

END | You have completed Project 11E

CONTENT-BASED ASSESSMENTS

Apply 11B skills from these Objectives:

4 Prepare a Final Workbook for Distribution

5 Upload a Workbook to SkyDrive

In the following Mastering Excel project, you will assist Stephen Brown, Associate Dean of Music, in distributing a workbook of musical instruments inventory to the music faculty at the college. Your completed worksheets will look similar to Figure 11.37.

PROJECT FILES

For Project 11F, you will need the following file:

e11F_Music

You will save your workbooks as:

Lastname_Firstname_11F_Music
Lastname_Firstname_11F_Music_Compatibility
Lastname_Firstname_11F_Music_Encrypted

PROJECT RESULTS

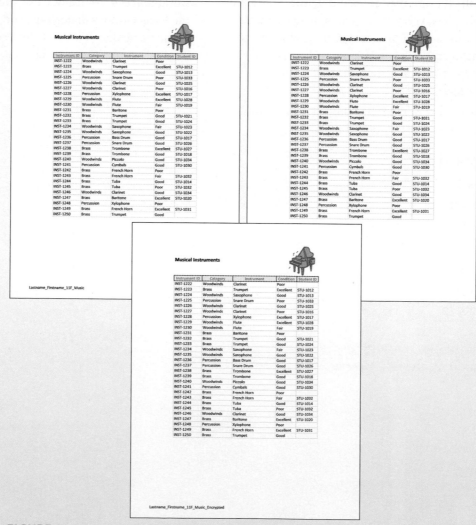

FIGURE 11.37

(Project 11F Instruments Distributed Workbook continues on the next page)

1 Start Excel. From your student files, open the file **e11F_Music**. **Save** the file in your **Excel Chapter 11** folder as **Lastname_Firstname_11F_Music** Check the workbook for accessibility and correct the three problems identified. Use the alt text **piano** and the sheet name **Instruments**.

2 Run the **Document Inspector** and then return to the worksheet. Click cell **D6**, and notice the comment that displays. **Unhide** the **Music Instructors** worksheet to verify that it exists and then hide the worksheet.

3 **Save** your workbook, and then run the **Document Inspector**. Remove the **Comments and Annotations** and **Hidden Worksheets**, identified by the document inspector. Insert a footer in the **left section** that includes the file name. Display the **document properties**. In the **Author** box, type your firstname and lastname, in the **Subject** box, type your course name and section #, and in the **Tags** box, type **musical instruments** Save your workbook.

4 With your **Lastname_Firstname_11F_Music** file open, **Save** the file in your **Excel Chapter 11** folder as **Lastname_Firstname_11F_Music_Encrypted** In the **Tags** box, type **musical instruments, encrypted** Encrypt the workbook with the password **goseries Close** and then reopen the workbook and verify that the password will open the file.

5 Mark the **Lastname_Firstname_11F_Music_Encrypted** as final. **Close** the workbook.

6 From your student files, open the file **e11F_Music**. Check the workbook for compatibility. Display the **document properties**. In the **Author** box, type your firstname and lastname, in the **Subject** box, type your course name and section #, and in the **Tags** box, type **musical instruments, compatibility** Insert a footer in the **left section** that includes the file name and **Save** the file in your **Excel Chapter 11** folder as an **Excel 97-2003 Workbook** with the name **Lastname_Firstname_11F_Music_Compatibility Close** your workbook.

7 Start your web browser. Go to **http://skydrive.com**. If necessary, create a new folder named **Chapter 11** share the folder, and then click **Make public**. Upload your **Lastname_Firstname_11F_Music_Encrypted** file. If directed by your instructor, use the Windows Snipping Tool to create a snip of your screen showing your uploaded file to your new SkyDrive or provide your instructor with the public link to your folder. Sign out of SkyDrive.

8 **Close** the browser. **Print** the three workbooks or submit electronically as directed.

END | You have completed Project 11F

Apply 11A and 11B skills from these Objectives:

1 Create a Shared Workbook

2 Track Changes Made to a Workbook

3 Merge Workbooks and Accept Changes

4 Prepare a Final Workbook for Distribution

5 Upload a Workbook to SkyDrive

In the following Mastering Excel project, you will assist Eric Marks, Athletic Director, in distributing a workbook of sports equipment inventory to the sports coaches at the college. You will also create a shared workbook that the Athletics Department will use to review proposed salary changes. Your completed worksheet will look similar to Figure 11.38.

PROJECT FILES

For Project 11G, you will need the following files:

e11G_Salary

e11G_Sports

You will save your workbooks as:

Lastname_Firstname_11G_Salary

Lastname_Firstname_11G_Sports

Build from Scratch

PROJECT RESULTS

Salary Budget

Last Name	First Name	Present Grade	Present Salary	Anticipated Grade	Proposed Salary
Anderson	Nancy	17	$ 51,480	17	$ 53,000
Carlton	Elaine	18	56,100	18	57,222
Desprez	Jan	16	50,050	17	56,000
Hernandez	Jose	19	61,688	19	62,922
Mandala	Eduardo	17	51,700	17	52,734
Philips	Matt	17	53,900	17	54,978
Thomas	Doris	16	46,200	16	47,124
Wagner	John	18	57,255	18	58,500
			$ 428,373		$ 442,480

Sports Equipment Inventory

Equipment ID	Category	Equipment	Condition	Student ID
SPORTS-1777	Baseball	Catcher's Mit	Poor	
SPORTS-1773	Tennis	Tennis Racket	Excellent	STU-3032
SPORTS-1774	Baseball	Catcher's Facemask	Good	STU-3033
SPORTS-1775	Tennis	Tennis Racket	Poor	STU-3033
SPORTS-1776	Baseball	Bat	Good	STU-3025
SPORTS-1777	Baseball	Catcher's Mit	Poor	STU-3036
SPORTS-1778	Basketball	Basketball	Excellent	STU-3037
SPORTS-1779	Baseball	Catcher's Mit	Excellent	STU-3028
SPORTS-1730	Tennis	Tennis Racket	Fair	STU-3039
SPORTS-1731	Basketball	Basketball	Poor	
SPORTS-1737	Tennis	Tennis Racket	Good	STU-3023
SPORTS-1733	Tennis	Tennis Racket	Good	STU-3024
SPORTS-1734	Baseball	Bat	Fair	STU-3023
SPORTS-1735	Baseball	Catcher's Mit	Good	STU-3022
SPORTS-1736	Basketball	Basketball	Good	STU-3037
SPORTS-1737	Basketball	Basketball	Good	STU-3026

Salary Ranges

Grade	Beginning	Midpoint	Ending
16	$45,650	$48,400	$51,150
17	$50,050	$52,525	$55,000
18	$53,900	$56,375	$58,850
19	$57,750	$60,225	$62,700
20	$61,600	$64,075	$66,550
21	$65,450	$67,925	$70,400
22	$69,300	$71,775	$74,250
23	$73,150	$75,625	$78,100
24	$77,000	$79,475	$81,950
25	$80,850	$83,325	$85,800
26	$84,700	$87,175	$89,650
27	$88,550	$91,025	$93,500
28	$92,400	$94,875	$97,350
29	$96,250	$98,725	$101,200
30	$100,100	$102,575	$105,050

Salary Budget

Last Name	First Name	Present Grade	Present Salary	Anticipated Grade	Proposed Salary
Applebee	Linda	20	$ 63,800	20	$ 65,076
Matthews	Chuck	19	62,150	20	63,393
McIntrye	Allison	17	51,700	17	52,734
Patel	Asad	18	54,010	18	56,000
Randolph	Thomas	20	63,800	20	65,076
Reid	James	16	47,300	17	49,000
Ricciardo	Geoff	19	58,575	19	59,747
Williams	George	19	59,180	19	60,364
Zelnik	Charles	18	53,570	18	54,000
			$ 514,085		$ 525,389

Lastname_Firstname_11G_Salary

Lastname_Firstname_11G_Salary

FIGURE 11.38

(Project 11G Sports Distributed Workbook continues on the next page)

CONTENT-BASED ASSESSMENTS

1 Start Excel. From your student files, open the file **e11G_Sports**. Open the file **e11G_Sports** and then **Save** the file in your **Excel Chapter 11** folder as **Lastname_Firstname_11G_Sports**

2 Run the **Document Inspector**. Click cell **D6**, and notice the comment that displays. Verify that the **Coaches** worksheet is hidden. Run the **Document Inspector**. Remove the **Comments and Annotations** and **Hidden Worksheets** identified by the document inspector.

3 Run the **Accessibility Checker** and correct the error indicated. Insert a footer in the **left section** that includes the file name. Center the worksheet horizontally. Display the **document properties**. In the **Author** box, type your firstname and lastname, in the **Subject** box, type your course name and section #, in the **Tags** box, type **sports equipment** and then **Save** the workbook.

4 Mark the workbook as final. **Close** the workbook and **Close** Excel.

5 Start your web browser. Go to **http://skydrive.com**. If necessary, create a new public folder named **Chapter 11** Upload your **Lastname_Firstname_11G_Sports** file. If directed by your instructor, use the Windows Snipping Tool to create a snip of your screen showing your uploaded file to your SkyDrive or provide your instructor with the public link to your folder. Sign out of SkyDrive. **Close** the Internet browser.

6 From your student files, open the file **e11G_Salary**. **Save** the file in your **Excel Chapter 11** folder as **Lastname_Firstname_11G_Salary** Group the sheets and insert a footer in the **left section** that includes the file name. Ungroup the worksheets.

Take a moment to examine the worksheet. The **Salary Ranges** sheet shows selected salary grades at the college. Examine the other two sheets. Each sheet contains a list of employees, their current grade and salary, and their proposed grade and salary. Within the Athletics Department, this information will be sent to the Chairs of the Aquatics and Sports Departments to review and adjust.

7 Display the **Highlight Changes** dialog box. Select the **Track changes while editing** check box, and be sure **When** indicates *All*, and **Who** is selected and indicates *Everyone*. **Close** the file, and then open it again. Display

the **Excel Options** dialog box. Write down the current User name, and then change the **User name** to **Grace Johnson**

8 On the **Aquatics** worksheet change the following proposed salaries and anticipated grade for Desprez:

Last Name	Anticipated Grade	Proposed Salary
Anderson		53000
Desprez	17	56000
Wagner		58500

9 **Save** the file and **Close** it. Reopen the file and change the **User name** to **Ken Saito** On the **Sports** worksheet change the following proposed salaries and anticipated grade for Reid:

Last Name	Anticipated Grade	Proposed Salary
Matthews		63000
Patel		56000
Reid	17	49000
Zelnik		54000

10 **Save** the file and **Close** it. Reopen the file and change the **User name** to **Dean Angelo** the Dean of Athletics, who will accept or reject the changes. Display the **Highlight Changes** dialog box, change **When** to *All*, and be sure **Who** is selected and displays *Everyone*. Click each new salary in **column F**.

11 Display the **Select Changes to Accept or Reject** dialog box and **Save** if prompted. Review changes for **Everyone but Me**. Accept all changes except the change for *Matthews* in the Sports Department. After reviewing the changes, change Matthews's **Anticipated Grade** to **20** Turn off Sharing.

12 Display the **document properties**. In the **Author** box, type your firstname and lastname, in the **Subject** box, type your course name and section #, and in the **Tags** box, type **salary Save** your workbook. **Print** or submit your workbooks electronically. Display the **Excel Options** dialog box and change the **User name** back to the User name that you wrote down in Step 7. **Close** the workbook and **Close** Excel.

END | You have completed Project 11G

CONTENT-BASED ASSESSMENTS

Apply a combination of the 11A and 11B skills.

GO! Fix It	Project 11H Fall Schedule	Online
GO! Make It	Project 11I Fall Sports	Online
GO! Solve It	Project 11J Weekend Classes	Online
GO! Solve It	Project 11K Scholarships	

PROJECT FILES

For Project 11K, you will need the following file:

e11K_Scholarships

You will save your workbook as:

Lastname_Firstname_11K_Scholarships

Open the file e11K_Scholarships and save it as **Lastname_Firstname_11K_Scholarships** Inspect the document and remove the hidden worksheet. Encrypt the workbook with the password **goseries** Insert the file name in the footer in the left section. Add appropriate information to the document properties including the tag **scholarships** Mark the workbook as Final. Submit as directed by your instructor.

Performance Level

Performance Criteria		Exemplary: You consistently applied the relevant skills.	Proficient: You sometimes, but not always, applied the relevant skills.	Developing: You rarely or never applied the relevant skills.
	Inspect a Document	The document has been inspected for a hidden worksheet.	Not applicable.	The document has not been inspected for a hidden worksheet.
	Encrypt a Workbook	The document has been encrypted with goseries as the password.	Not applicable.	The document has not been encrypted with a password.
	Mark a Workbook as Final	The document has been marked as Final.	Not applicable.	The document has not been marked as Final.

END | You have completed Project 11K

OUTCOMES-BASED ASSESSMENTS

RUBRIC

The following outcomes-based assessments are open-ended assessments. That is, there is no specific correct result; your result will depend on your approach to the information provided. Make Professional Quality your goal. Use the following scoring rubric to guide you in how to approach the problem and then to evaluate how well your approach solves the problem.

The *criteria*—Software Mastery, Content, Format and Layout, and Process—represent the knowledge and skills you have gained that you can apply to solving the problem. The *levels of performance*—Professional Quality, Approaching Professional Quality, or Needs Quality Improvements—help you and your instructor evaluate your result.

	Your completed project is of Professional Quality if you:	Your completed project is Approaching Professional Quality if you:	Your completed project Needs Quality Improvements if you:
1-Software Mastery	Choose and apply the most appropriate skills, tools, and features and identify efficient methods to solve the problem.	Choose and apply some appropriate skills, tools, and features, but not in the most efficient manner.	Choose inappropriate skills, tools, or features, or are inefficient in solving the problem.
2-Content	Construct a solution that is clear and well organized, contains content that is accurate, appropriate to the audience and purpose, and is complete. Provide a solution that contains no errors in spelling, grammar, or style.	Construct a solution in which some components are unclear, poorly organized, inconsistent, or incomplete. Misjudge the needs of the audience. Have some errors in spelling, grammar, or style, but the errors do not detract from comprehension.	Construct a solution that is unclear, incomplete, or poorly organized; contains some inaccurate or inappropriate content; and contains many errors in spelling, grammar, or style. Do not solve the problem.
3-Format & Layout	Format and arrange all elements to communicate information and ideas, clarify function, illustrate relationships, and indicate relative importance.	Apply appropriate format and layout features to some elements, but not others. Overuse features, causing minor distraction.	Apply format and layout that does not communicate information or ideas clearly. Do not use format and layout features to clarify function, illustrate relationships, or indicate relative importance. Use available features excessively, causing distraction.
4-Process	Use an organized approach that integrates planning, development, self-assessment, revision, and reflection.	Demonstrate an organized approach in some areas, but not others; or, use an insufficient process of organization throughout.	Do not use an organized approach to solve the problem.

OUTCOMES-BASED ASSESSMENTS

Apply a combination of the 11A and 11B skills.

Build from Scratch

GO! Think   Project 11L Budget

PROJECT FILES

For Project 11L, you will need the following file:

e11L_Budget

You will save your workbooks as:

Lastname_Firstname_11L_Budget
Lastname_Firstname_11L_Budget - Copy

Open the file e11L_Budget, and then save it in your Excel Chapter 11 folder as **Lastname_Firstname_11L_Budget**

Group the worksheets, insert a footer, and in the left section, add the file name. Add appropriate information to the document properties including the tag **budget** Create a shared file and a copy of the workbook so that it can be completed by the various department chairs who need to do so. Open the original Lastname_Firstname_11L_Budget file. Write down the User name that displays in Excel Options to restore it later. Change the User name to **Melissa Dever, Nursing** Be sure the Nursing sheet tab is displayed. In column F, starting in cell F6, enter the budget figures that reflect a modest increase from the previous years. Save and close the file.

Open the Lastname_Firstname_11L_Budget - Copy file. Change the User name to **Richard Wyatt, Radiology**. Click the Radiology sheet tab. In column F enter budget figures that reflect a modest increase from the previous years, and then save and close the file.

Open the Lastname_Firstname_11L_Budget file. Change the User name to **Dean Peale** so that you can review all the various changes for the Division Dean. Compare and merge the workbooks. Review the Nursing worksheet. Because the total budget and individual items seem reasonable, no changes are needed for the Nursing budget. Click the Radiology sheet tab. Because the total budget and individual items seem reasonable, no changes are needed for the Radiology budget. Accept all changes in the file and stop sharing the workbook.

Submit as directed by your instructor. Restore the original User name to the name that you wrote down earlier, and remove the Compare and Merge Workbooks button from the Quick Access Toolbar.

> **END | You have completed Project 11L**

GO! Think   Project 11M Purchase Orders   Online

You and GO!   Project 11N Digital Signature   Online

Glossary

3-D The shortened term for *three-dimensional*, which refers to an image that appears to have all three spatial dimensions—length, width, and depth.

Absolute cell reference A cell reference that refers to cells by their fixed position in a worksheet; an absolute cell reference remains the same when the formula is copied.

Accessibility Checker An Excel tool that finds any potential accessibility issues and creates a report so that you can resolve the issues to make your file easier for those with disabilities to use.

Accounting Number Format The Excel number format that applies a thousand comma separator where appropriate, inserts a fixed U.S. dollar sign aligned at the left edge of the cell, applies two decimal places, and leaves a small amount of space at the right edge of the cell to accommodate a parenthesis for negative numbers.

Active cell The cell, surrounded by a black border, ready to receive data or be affected by the next Excel command.

ActiveX control Graphic object, such as a check box or button, that you place on a form to display or enter data, perform an action, or make the form easier to read. When the person filling in the form clicks the ActiveX control, VBA code runs that automates a task or offers options.

Add-in An optional command or feature that is not immediately available; you must first install and/or activate an add-in to use it.

Additive The term that describes the behavior of a filter when each additional filter that you apply is based on the current filter, and that further reduces the number of records displayed.

Address bar (Internet Explorer) The area at the top of the Internet Explorer window that displays and where you can type a URL—Uniform Resource Locator—which is an address that uniquely identifies a location on the Internet.

Address bar (Windows) The bar at the top of a folder window with which you can navigate to a different folder or library, or go back to a previous one.

Advanced Filter A filter that can specify three or more criteria for a particular column, apply complex criteria to two or more columns, or specify computed criteria.

Alignment The placement of text or objects relative to the left and right margins.

Alignment guides Green lines that display when you move an object to assist in alignment.

Alt text Text used in documents and webpages to provide a text description of an image.

And comparison operator The comparison operator that requires each and every one of the comparison criteria to be true.

AND function A logical function that can be used to develop compound logical tests using up to 255 arguments. The function returns a result of TRUE if ALL of the conditions are met.

App The term that commonly refers to computer programs that run from the device software on a smartphone or a tablet computer—for example, iOS, Android, or Windows Phone—or computer programs that run from the browser software on a desktop PC or laptop PC—for example, Internet Explorer, Safari, Firefox, or Chrome.

App for Office A webpage that works within one of the Office applications, such as Excel, and that you download from the Office Store.

Apps for Office 2013 and SharePoint 2013 A collection of downloadable apps that enable you to create and view information within your familiar Office programs.

Arguments The values that an Excel function uses to perform calculations or operations.

Arithmetic operators The symbols +, -, *, /, %, and ^ used to denote addition, subtraction (or negation), multiplication, division, percentage, and exponentiation in an Excel formula.

Arrange All The command that tiles all open program windows on the screen.

Ascending The term that refers to the arrangement of text that is sorted alphabetically from A to Z, numbers sorted from lowest to highest, or dates and times sorted from earliest to latest.

Associated PivotTable report The PivotTable report in a workbook that is graphically represented in a PivotChart.

Auditing The process of examining a worksheet for errors in formulas.

Auto Fill An Excel feature that generates and extends values into adjacent cells based on the values of selected cells.

AutoCalculate A feature that displays three calculations in the status bar by default—Average, Count, and Sum—when you select a range of numerical data.

AutoComplete A feature that speeds your typing and lessens the likelihood of errors; if the first few characters you type in a cell match an existing entry in the column, Excel fills in the remaining characters for you.

AutoFilter menu A drop-down menu from which you can filter a column by a list of values, by a format, or by criteria.

AutoFit An Excel feature that adjusts the width of a column to fit the cell content of the widest cell in the column.

AutoSum A button that provides quick access to the SUM function.

AVERAGE function An Excel function that adds a group of values, and then divides the result by the number of values in the group.

Axis A line that serves as a frame of reference for measurement and that borders the chart plot area.

Background image An image inserted in a worksheet that is behind, not in the worksheet cells.

Backstage tabs The area along the left side of Backstage view with tabs to display screens with related groups of commands.

Backstage view A centralized space for file management tasks; for example, opening, saving, printing, publishing, or sharing a file. A navigation pane displays along the left side with tabs that group file-related tasks together.

Base The starting point when you divide the amount of increase by it to calculate the rate of increase.

Bevel A shape effect that uses shading and shadows to make the edges of a shape appear to be curved or angled.

Break-even point The point at which a company starts to make a profit.

Business Intelligence tools Tools that can be used to perform data analysis and create sophisticated charts and reports.

Canvas The area of a Power View worksheet that contains data visualizations.

Category axis The area along the bottom of a chart that identifies the categories of data; also referred to as the x-axis.

Category labels The labels that display along the bottom of a chart to identify the categories of data; Excel uses the row titles as the category names.

Cell The intersection of a column and a row.

Cell address Another name for a cell reference.

Cell content Anything typed into a cell.

Cell reference The identification of a specific cell by its intersecting column letter and row number.

Cell style A defined set of formatting characteristics, such as font, font size, font color, cell borders, and cell shading.

Center alignment The alignment of text or objects that is centered horizontally between the left and right margins.

Certificate authority A commercial organization that issues digital certificates, keeps track of who is assigned to a certificate, signs certificates to verify their validity, and tracks which certificates are revoked or expired.

Change history Information that is maintained about changes made in past editing sessions.

Chart The graphic representation of data in a worksheet; data presented as a chart is usually easier to understand than a table of numbers.

Chart area The entire chart and all of its elements.

Chart elements Objects that make up a chart.

Chart Elements button A button that enables you to add, remove, or change chart elements such as the title, legend, gridlines, and data labels.

Chart Filters button A button that enables you to change which data displays in the chart.

Chart layout The combination of chart elements that can be displayed in a chart such as a title, legend, labels for the columns, and the table of charted cells.

Chart sheet A workbook sheet that contains only a chart.

Chart style The overall visual look of a chart in terms of its graphic effects, colors, and backgrounds; for example, you can have flat or beveled columns, colors that are solid or transparent, and backgrounds that are dark or light.

Chart Styles button A button that enables you to set a style and color scheme for your chart.

Chart Styles gallery A group of predesigned chart styles that you can apply to an Excel chart.

Chart types Various chart formats used in a way that is meaningful to the reader; common examples are column charts, pie charts, and line charts.

Check box A type of ActiveX control that the person filling in the form can select to indicate a choice.

Circular reference An Excel error that occurs when a formula directly or indirectly refers to itself.

Clear Filter A button that removes a filter.

Click The action of pressing and releasing the left button on a mouse pointing device one time.

Clip art Downloadable predefined graphics available online from Office.com and other sites.

Clipboard A temporary storage area that holds text or graphics that you select and then cut or copy.

Cloud computing Refers to applications and services that are accessed over the Internet, rather than to applications that are installed on your local computer.

Cloud storage Online storage of data so that you can access your data from different places and devices.

Collaborate To work with others as a team in an intellectual endeavor to complete a shared task or to achieve a shared goal.

Collaboration In Excel, the process of working jointly with others to review, comment on, and make necessary changes to a shared workbook.

Column A vertical group of cells in a worksheet.

Column chart A chart in which the data is arranged in columns and that is useful for showing data changes over a period of time or for illustrating comparisons among items.

Column heading The letter that displays at the top of a vertical group of cells in a worksheet; beginning with the first letter of the alphabet, a unique letter or combination of letters identifies each column.

COLUMNS area An area to position fields that you want to display as columns in the PivotTable report. Field names placed here become column titles, and the data is grouped in columns by these titles.

Comma delimited file A file type that saves the contents of the cells by placing commas between them and an end-of-paragraph mark at the end of each row; also referred to as a CSV (comma separated values) file.

Comma Style The Excel number format that inserts thousand comma separators where appropriate and applies two decimal places; Comma Style also leaves space at the right to accommodate a parenthesis when negative numbers are present.

Commands An instruction to a computer program that causes an action to be carried out.

Common dialog boxes The set of dialog boxes that includes Open, Save, and Save As, which are provided by the Windows programming interface, and which display and operate in all of the Office programs in the same manner.

Comparison operators Symbols that evaluate each value to determine if it is the same (=), greater than (>), less than (<), or in between a range of values as specified by the criteria.

Compatibility Checker An Excel tool that finds any potential compatibility issues that might cause a significant loss of functionality or a minor loss of fidelity in an earlier version of Excel, and creates a report so that you can resolve the issues.

Compatibility Mode Using a workbook in Excel 97-2003 file format (.xls) instead of the newer XML-based file format (.xlsx).

Compound criteria The use of two or more criteria on the same row—all conditions must be met for the records to be included in the results.

Compound filter A filter that uses more than one condition—and one that uses comparison operators.

Compressed file A file that has been reduced in size and thus takes up less storage space and can be transferred to other computers quickly.

Compressed folder A folder that has been reduced in size and thus takes up less storage space and can be transferred to other computers quickly; also called a *zipped* folder.

CONCATENATE A text function used to join up to 255 strings of characters.

Conditional format A format that changes the appearance of a cell—for example, by adding cell shading or font color—based on a condition; if the condition is true, the cell is formatted based on that condition, and if the condition is false, the cell is *not* formatted.

Constant value Numbers, text, dates, or times of day that you type into a cell.

Constraint In Solver, a condition or restriction that must be met.

Constraint cell In Solver, a cell that contains a value that limits or restricts the outcome.

Context menus Menus that display commands and options relevant to the selected text or object; also called *shortcut menus*.

Context sensitive A command associated with the currently selected or active object; often activated by right-clicking a screen item.

Context-sensitive commands Commands that display on a shortcut menu that relate to the object or text that you right-clicked.

Contextual tabs Tabs that are added to the ribbon automatically when a specific object, such as a picture, is selected, and that contain commands relevant to the selected object.

Copy A command that duplicates a selection and places it on the Clipboard.

COUNT A statistical function that counts the number of cells in a range that contain numbers.

COUNTIF function A statistical function that counts the number of cells within a range that meet the given condition and that has two arguments— the range of cells to check and the criteria.

COUNTIFS function A logical function that counts the cells that meet specific criteria in multiple ranges.

Criteria Conditions that you specify in a logical function or filter.

Criteria range An area on your worksheet where you define the criteria for the filter, and that indicates how the displayed records are filtered.

CSV (comma separated values) file A file type in which the cells in each row are separated by commas and an end-of-paragraph mark at the end of each row; also referred to as a comma delimited file.

Custom filter A filter with which you can apply complex criteria to a single column.

Custom list A sort order that you can define.

Cut A command that removes a selection and places it on the Clipboard.

Cycle A category of SmartArt graphics that illustrates a continual process.

Data Facts about people, events, things, or ideas. Data is represented by text or numbers in a cell.

Data bar A cell format consisting of a shaded bar that provides a visual cue to the reader about the value of a cell relative to other cells; the length of the bar represents the value in the cell—a longer bar represents a higher value and a shorter bar represents s lower value.

Data connection A link to external data that automatically updates an Excel workbook from the original data whenever the original data source gets new information.

Data labels Labels that display the value, percentage, and/or category of each particular data point and can contain one or more of the choices listed—Series name, Category name, Value, or Percentage.

Data marker A column, bar, area, dot, pie slice, or other symbol in a chart that represents a single data point; related data points form a data series.

Data Model A method of incorporating data from multiple, related tables into an Excel worksheet.

Data point A value that originates in a worksheet cell and that is represented in a chart by a data marker.

Data series Related data points represented by data markers; each data series has a unique color or pattern represented in the chart legend.

Data table A range of cells that shows how changing certain values in your formulas affect the results of those formulas and that makes it easy to calculate multiple versions in one operation.

Data validation A technique by which you can control the type of data or the values that are entered into a cell by limiting the acceptable values to a defined list.

Database An organized collection of facts related to a specific topic or purpose.

DAVERAGE function A function that determines an average in a database that is limited by criteria set for one or more cells.

DCOUNT function A function that counts the number of occurrences of a specified condition in a database.

Decision variable In Solver, a cell in which the value will change to achieve the desired results.

Default The term that refers to the current selection or setting that is automatically used by a computer program unless you specify otherwise.

Defined name A word or string of characters in Excel that represents a cell, a range of cells, a formula, or a constant value; also referred to as simply a *name*.

Delimited A text file in which the text is separated by commas or tabs.

Dependent cells Cells that contain formulas that refer to other cells.

Descending The term that refers to the arrangement of text that is sorted alphabetically from Z to A, numbers sorted from highest to lowest, or dates and times sorted from latest to earliest.

Deselect The action of canceling the selection of an object or block of text by clicking outside of the selection.

Design mode An Excel mode or view in which you can work with ActiveX controls.

Desktop In Windows, the screen that simulates your work area.

Desktop app The term that commonly refers to a computer program that is installed on your computer and requires a computer operating system like Microsoft Windows or Apple OS to run.

Detail data The subtotaled rows that are totaled and summarized; typically adjacent to and either above or to the left of the summary data.

Detail sheets The worksheets that contain the details of the information summarized on a summary sheet.

Dialog box A small window that contains options for completing a task.

Dialog Box Launcher A small icon that displays to the right of some group names on the ribbon, and which opens a related dialog box or pane providing additional options and commands related to that group.

Digital certificate An electronic means of proving identity issued by a certificate authority.

Digital signature An electronic, encrypted, stamp of authentication. A means of proving identity and authenticity that ensures that a file originated from the signer and has not been changed.

Displayed value The data that displays in a cell.

Document Inspector An Excel feature that can find and remove hidden properties and personal information in a workbook.

Document properties Details about a file that describe or identify it, including the title, author name, subject, and keywords that identify the document's topic or contents; also known as *metadata*.

Drag The action of holding down the left mouse button while moving your mouse.

Drag and drop The action of moving a selection by dragging it to a new location.

DSUM function A function that sums a column of values in a database that is limited by criteria set for one or more cells.

Dual-axis chart A chart that has one series plotted on a secondary axis. Useful when comparing data series that use different scales or different types of measurements.

Edit The process of making changes to text or graphics in an Office file.

Ellipsis A set of three dots indicating incompleteness; an ellipsis following a command name indicates that a dialog box will display if you click the command.

Embed The action of inserting something created in one program into another program.

Embedded chart A chart that is inserted into the same worksheet that contains the data used to create the chart.

Encryption The process by which a file is encoded so that it cannot be opened without the proper password.

Enhanced ScreenTip A ScreenTip that displays more descriptive text than a normal ScreenTip.

Enterprise fund A municipal government fund that reports income and expenditures related to municipal services for which a fee is charged in exchange for goods or services.

Error Checking command A command that checks for common errors that occur in formulas.

Error value The result of a formula that Excel cannot evaluate correctly.

Event The action that causes a program or macro to run, such as clicking a button or a command or pressing a combination of keys.

Excel pointer An Excel window element with which you can display the location of the pointer.

Excel table A series of rows and columns that contains related data that is managed independently from the data in other rows and columns in the worksheet.

Expand Formula Bar button An Excel window element with which you can increase the height of the Formula Bar to display lengthy cell content.

Expand horizontal scroll bar button An Excel window element with which you can increase the width of the horizontal scroll bar.

Explode The action of pulling out one or more pie slices from a pie chart for emphasis.

Extensible Markup Language (XML) A language that structures data in text files so that it can be read by other systems, regardless of the hardware platform or operating system.

Extract The process of pulling out multiple sets of data for comparison purposes. Or, to decompress, or pull out, files from a compressed form.

Extract area The location to which you copy records when extracting filtered rows.

Field A specific type of data such as name, employee number, or social security number that is stored in columns.

Field button A button on a PivotChart with an arrow to choose a filter, and thus change the data that is displayed in the chart.

Field names The column titles from source data that form the categories of data for a PivotTable.

Field section The upper portion of the PivotTable Fields pane containing the fields—column titles—from your source data; use this area to add fields to and remove fields from the PivotTable.

File A collection of information stored on a computer under a single name, for example, a Word document or a PowerPoint presentation.

File Explorer The program that displays the files and folders on your computer, and which is at work anytime you are viewing the contents of files and folders in a window.

Fill The inside color of an object.

Fill handle The small black square in the lower right corner of a selected cell.

Filter The process of displaying only a portion of the data based on matching a specific value to show only the data that meets the criteria that you specify.

FILTER area An area in the lower portion of the PivotTable Fields pane to position fields by which you want to filter the PivotTable report, enabling you to display a subset of data in the PivotTable report.

Filtering A process in which only the rows that meet the criteria display; rows that do not meet the criteria are hidden.

Filtering button A button on a slicer which you use to select the item by which to filter.

Financial functions Pre-built formulas that perform common business calculations such as calculating a loan payment on a vehicle or calculating how much to save each month to buy something; financial functions commonly involve a period of time such as months or years.

Find A command that finds and selects specific text or formatting.

Find and replace A command that searches the cells in a worksheet—or in a selected range—for matches and then replaces each match with a replacement value of your choice.

Fixed expense Expense that remains the same each month regardless of the amount of activity.

Flash Fill An Excel feature that predicts how to alter data based upon the pattern you enter into the cell at the beginning of the column. The data must be in the adjacent column to use Flash Fill. Use it to split data from two or more cells or to combine data from two cells.

Folder A container in which you store files.

Folder window In Windows, a window that displays the contents of the current folder, library, or device, and contains helpful parts so that you can navigate the Windows file structure.

Font A set of characters with the same design and shape.

Font styles Formatting emphasis such as bold, italic, and underline.

Footer A reserved area for text or graphics that displays at the bottom of each page in a document.

Forecast A prediction of the future, often based on past performances.

Form An Excel worksheet or object that contains fields and controls that enable a user to easily enter or edit data.

Form control A graphic object that does not require VBA code. A Form control is compatible with versions of Excel that do not support ActiveX.

Format Changing the appearance of cells and worksheet elements to make a worksheet attractive and easy to read.

Formatting The process of establishing the overall appearance of text, graphics, and pages in an Office file—for example, in a Word document.

Formatting marks Characters that display on the screen, but do not print, indicating where the Enter key, the Spacebar, and the Tab key were pressed; also called *nonprinting characters*.

Formula An equation that performs mathematical calculations on values in a worksheet.

Formula Auditing Tools and commands accessible from the Formulas tab that help you check your worksheet for errors.

Formula AutoComplete An Excel feature that, after typing an = (equal sign) and the beginning letter or letters of a function name, displays a list of function names that match the typed letter(s), and from which you can insert the function by pointing to its name and pressing the Tab key or double-clicking.

Formula Bar An element in the Excel window that displays the value or formula contained in the active cell; here you can also enter or edit values or formulas.

Freeze Panes A command that enables you to select one or more rows or columns and freeze (lock) them into place so that they remain on the screen while you scroll; the locked rows and columns become separate panes.

Function A predefined formula—a formula that Excel has already built for you—that performs calculations by using specific values in a particular order or structure.

Fund A sum of money set aside for a specific purpose.

Future value (Fv) The value at the end of the time periods in an Excel function; the cash balance you want to attain after the last payment is made—usually zero for loans.

Gallery An Office feature that displays a list of potential results instead of just the command name.

General format The default format that Excel applies to numbers; this format has no specific characteristics—whatever you type in the cell will display, with the exception that trailing zeros to the right of a decimal point will not display.

General fund The term used to describe money set aside for the normal operating activities of a government entity such as a city.

Get External Data A group of commands that enables you to bring data from an Access database, from the web, from a text file, or from an XML file into Excel without repeatedly copying the data.

Go To A command that moves to a specific cell or range of cells that you specify.

Go To Special A command that moves to cells that have special characteristics, for example, to cells that are blank or to cells that contain constants, as opposed to formulas.

Goal Seek One of Excel's What-If Analysis tools that provides a method to find a specific value for a cell by adjusting the value of one other cell—find the right input when you know the result you want.

Google Docs Google's free web-based word processor, spreadsheet, slide show, and form service, that along with free data storage, is known as Google Drive.

Google Drive Google's free web-based word processor, spreadsheet, slide show, and form service, that includes free data storage.

Gradient fill A fill effect in which one color fades into another.

Gridlines Lines in the plot area that aid the eye in determining the plotted values.

Groups On the Office ribbon, the sets of related commands that you might need for a specific type of task.

Header A reserved area for text or graphics that displays at the top of each page in a document.

Hierarchy A category of SmartArt graphics used to create an organization chart or show a decision tree.

HLOOKUP An Excel function that looks up values that are displayed horizontally in a row.

Horizontal Category axis (x-axis) The area along the bottom of a chart that identifies the categories of data; also referred to as the x-axis.

HTML (Hypertext Markup Language) A language web browsers can interpret.

Hyperlink Text or graphics that, when clicked, take you to another location in the worksheet, to another file, or to a webpage on the Internet or on your organization's intranet.

Icon set A set of three, four, or five small graphic images that make your data visually easier to interpret.

IF function A function that uses a logical test to check whether a condition is met, and then returns one value if true, and another value if false.

Info tab The tab in Backstage view that displays information about the current file.

Information Data that has been organized in a useful manner.

Insertion point A blinking vertical line that indicates where text or graphics will be inserted.

Integer A whole number.

Interest The amount charged for the use of borrowed money.

Interval The number of cells to include in the average.

Intranet A network within an organization that uses Internet technologies.

Iterative calculation When Excel recalculates a formula over and over because of a circular reference.

Keyboard shortcut A combination of two or more keyboard keys, used to perform a task that would otherwise require a mouse.

KeyTip The letter that displays on a command in the ribbon and that indicates the key you can press to activate the command when keyboard control of the ribbon is activated.

Keywords Custom file properties in the form of words that you associate with a document to give an indication of the document's content; used to help find and organize files. Also called *tags*.

Label Another name for a text value, and which usually provides information about number values. Or, column and row headings that describe the values and help the reader understand the Chart.

Landscape orientation A page orientation in which the paper is wider than it is tall.

Layout Options A button that displays when an object is selected and that has commands to choose how the object interacts with surrounding text.

Layout section The lower portion of the PivotTable Fields pane containing the four areas for layout; use this area to rearrange and reposition fields in the PivotTable.

LEFT A text function that returns the specified number of characters from the beginning (left) of a string of characters.

Left alignment The cell format in which characters align at the left edge of the cell; this is the default for text entries and is an example of formatting information stored in a cell.

Legend A chart element that identifies the patterns or colors that are assigned to the categories in the chart.

Lettered column headings The area along the top edge of a worksheet that identifies each column with a unique letter or combination of letters.

Line charts A chart type that is useful to display trends over time; time displays along the bottom axis and the data point values are connected with a line.

List A category of SmartArt graphics used to show non-sequential information. Or, a series of rows that contains related data that you can group by adding subtotals.

Live Preview A technology that shows the result of applying an editing or formatting change as you point to possible results—*before* you actually apply it.

Location Any disk drive, folder, or other place in which you can store files and folders.

Locked [cells] In a protected worksheet, data cannot be inserted, modified, deleted, or formatted in these cells.

Logical function A function that tests for specific conditions.

Logical functions A group of functions that test for specific conditions and that typically use conditional tests to determine whether specified conditions are true or false.

Logical test Any value or expression that can be evaluated as being true or false.

LOOKUP An Excel function that looks up values in either a one-row or one-column range.

Lookup functions A group of Excel functions that look up a value in a defined range of cells located in another part of the workbook to find a corresponding value.

LOWER A text function that changes the case of the characters in a string, making all characters lowercase.

Macro An action or a set of actions with which you can automate tasks by grouping a series of commands into a single command.

Macro virus Unauthorized programming code in a macro that erases or damages files.

Major sort A term sometimes used to refer to the first sort level in the Sort dialog box.

Major unit The value in a chart's value axis that determines the spacing between tick marks and between the gridlines in the plot area.

Major unit value A number that determines the spacing between tick marks and between the gridlines in the plot area.

Mark as Final command Prevents additional changes to the document and disables typing, editing comments, and proofing marks.

Matrix A category of SmartArt graphics used to show how parts relate to a whole.

MAX function An Excel function that determines the largest value in a selected range of values.

MEDIAN function An Excel function that finds the middle value that has as many values above it in the group as are below it; it differs from AVERAGE in that the result is not affected as much by a single value that is greatly different from the others.

Merge & Center A command that joins selected cells in an Excel worksheet into one larger cell and centers the contents in the merged cell.

Metadata Details about a file that describe or identify it, including the title, author name, subject, and keywords that identify the document's topic or contents; also known as *document properties*.

Microsoft Access A database program used to manage database files.

MID A text function that extracts a series of characters from a text string given the location of the beginning character.

MIN function An Excel function that determines the smallest value in a selected range of values.

Mini toolbar A small toolbar containing frequently used formatting commands that displays as a result of selecting text or objects.

Module The programming code written in VBA when you record a new macro; the place where the VBA code is stored.

Moving average A sequence of averages computed from parts of a data series.

MRU Acronym for *most recently used*, which refers to the state of some commands that retain the characteristic most recently applied; for example, the Font Color button retains the most recently used color until a new color is chosen.

Name A word or string of characters in Excel that represents a cell, a range of cells, a formula, or a constant value; also referred to as *a defined name*.

Name Box An element of the Excel window that displays the name of the selected cell, table, chart, or object.

Navigate The process of exploring within the organizing structure of Windows. Or, the process of moving within a worksheet or workbook.

Navigation pane In a folder window, the area on the left in which you can navigate to, open, and display favorites, libraries, folders, saved searches, and an expandable list of drives.

Nested function A function that is contained inside another function. The inner function is evaluated first and the result becomes the argument for the outer function.

Nonprinting characters Characters that display on the screen, but do not print, indicating where the Enter key, the Spacebar, and the Tab key were pressed; also called *formatting marks*.

Normal view A screen view that maximizes the number of cells visible on your screen and keeps the column letters and row numbers close to the columns and rows.

NOT function A logical function that takes only one argument and is used to test one condition. If the condition is true, the function returns the logical opposite false. If the condition is false, true is returned.

Notification bar An area at the bottom of an Internet Explorer window that displays information about pending downloads, security issues, add-ons, and other issues related to the operation of your computer.

NOW function An Excel function that retrieves the date and time from your computer's calendar and clock and inserts the information into the selected cell.

Nper The abbreviation for *number of time periods* in various Excel functions.

Number format A specific way in which Excel displays numbers in a cell.

Number values Constant values consisting of only numbers.

Numbered row headings The area along the left edge of a worksheet that identifies each row with a unique number.

Object A text box, picture, table, or shape that you can select and then move and resize.

Objective cell In Solver, a cell that contains a formula for the results you are trying to determine.

Office Web Apps The free online companions to Microsoft Word, Excel, PowerPoint, Access, and OneNote.

One-variable data table A data table that changes the value in only one cell.

Open dialog box A dialog box from which you can navigate to, and then open on your screen, an existing file that was created in that same program.

Operators The symbols with which you can specify the type of calculation you want to perform in an Excel formula.

Option button In a dialog box, a round button that enables you to make one choice among two or more options.

Options dialog box A dialog box within each Office application where you can select program settings and other options and preferences.

Or comparison operator The comparison operator that requires only one of the two comparison criteria that you specify to be true.

OR function A logical function that can be used to develop compound logical tests using up to 255 arguments. The function returns a value of TRUE if ANY of the conditions are met.

Order of operations The mathematical rules for performing multiple calculations within a formula.

Organization chart A type of graphic that is useful to depict reporting relationships within an organization.

Page Layout view A screen view in which you can use the rulers to measure the width and height of data, set margins for printing, hide or display the numbered row headings and the lettered column headings, and change the page orientation; this view is useful for preparing your worksheet for printing.

Pane A portion of a worksheet window bounded by and separated from other portions by vertical and horizontal bars.

Paragraph symbol The symbol ¶ that represents the end of a paragraph.

Password An optional element of a template added to prevent someone from disabling a worksheet's protection.

Paste The action of placing cell contents that have been copied or moved to the Clipboard into another location.

Paste area The target destination for data that has been cut or copied using the Office Clipboard.

Paste Options gallery A gallery of buttons that provides a Live Preview of all the Paste options available in the current context.

Path A sequence of folders that leads to a specific file or folder.

PDF The acronym for Portable Document Format, which is a file format that creates an image that preserves the look of your file; this is a popular format for sending documents electronically because the document will display on most computers.

PDF (Portable Document Format) A file format developed by Adobe Systems that creates a representation of electronic paper that displays your data on the screen as it would look when printed, but that cannot be easily changed.

Percent for new value = base percent + percent of increase The formula for calculating a percentage by which a value increases by adding the base percentage—usually 100%—to the percent increase.

Percentage rate of increase The percent by which one number increases over another number.

Picture A category of SmartArt graphics that is used to display pictures in a diagram.

Picture element A point of light measured in dots per square inch on a screen; 64 pixels equals 8.43 characters, which is the average number of characters that will fit in a cell in an Excel worksheet using the default font.

Pie chart A chart that shows the relationship of each part to a whole.

PivotChart report A graphical representation of the data in a PivotTable report.

PivotTable An interactive Excel report that summarizes and analyzes large amounts of data.

PivotTable Fields pane A window that lists, at the top, all of the fields—column titles—from the source data for use in the PivotTable report and at the bottom, an area in which you can arrange the fields in the PivotTable.

Pixel The abbreviated name for a picture element.

Plot area The area bounded by the axes of a chart, including all the data series.

PMT function An Excel function that calculates the payment for a loan based on constant payments and a constant interest rate.

Point The action of moving your mouse pointer over something on your screen.

Point and click method The technique of constructing a formula by pointing to and then clicking cells; this method is convenient when the referenced cells are not adjacent to one another.

Pointer Any symbol that displays on your screen in response to moving your mouse.

Points A measurement of the size of a font; there are 72 points in an inch.

Portable Document Format A file format that creates an image that preserves the look of your file, but that cannot be easily changed; a popular format for sending documents electronically, because the document will display on most computers.

Portrait orientation A page orientation in which the paper is taller than it is wide.

Power View An Excel BI tool that allows you to create and interact with multiple charts, slicers, and other data visualizations in a single sheet.

PowerPivot An Excel BI tool that allows you to analyze data from multiple sources, work with multiple data tables, and create relationships between tables.

Precedent cells Cells that are referred to by a formula in another cell.

Present value (Pv) The total amount that a series of future payments is worth now; also known as the *principal*.

Principal The total amount that a series of future payments is worth now; also known as the *Present value (Pv)*.

Print Preview A view of a document as it will appear when you print it.

Print Titles An Excel command that enables you to specify rows and columns to repeat on each printed page.

Procedure A named sequence of statements in a computer program that performs an action.

Process A category of SmartArt graphics that is used to show steps in a process or timeline.

Progress bar In a dialog box or taskbar button, a bar that indicates visually the progress of a task such as a download or file transfer.

PROPER A text function that capitalizes the first letter of each word.

Properties The details about a file that describe or identify the file, including the title, author name, subject, and tags that identify the file's topic or contents. Also known as *metadata*.

Protected View A security feature in Office 2013 that protects your computer from malicious files by opening them in a restricted environment until you enable them; you might encounter this feature if you open a file from an email or download files from the Internet.

Protection This prevents anyone from altering the formulas or changing other template components.

pt The abbreviation for *point*; for example, when referring to a font size.

Pyramid A category of SmartArt graphics that uses a series of pictures to show relationships.

Query A process of restricting records through the use of criteria conditions that will display records that will answer a question about the data.

Quick Access Toolbar In an Office program window, the small row of buttons in the upper left corner of the screen from which you can perform frequently used commands.

Quick Analysis tool A tool that displays in the lower right corner of a selected range with which you can analyze your data by using Excel tools such as charts, color-coding, and formulas.

Quick Explore A tool that allows you to drill down through PivotTable data with a single click.

Range Two or more selected cells on a worksheet that are adjacent or nonadjacent; because the range is treated as a single unit, you can make the same changes or combination of changes to more than one cell at a time.

Range finder An Excel feature that outlines cells in color to indicate which cells are used in a formula; useful for verifying which cells are referenced in a formula.

Rate In the Excel PMT function, the term used to indicate the interest rate for a loan.

Rate = amount of increase/base The mathematical formula to calculate a rate of increase.

Read-Only A property assigned to a file that prevents the file from being modified or deleted; it indicates that you cannot save any changes to the displayed document unless you first save it with a new name.

Recommended Charts An Excel feature that displays a customized set of charts that, according to Excel's calculations, will best fit your data based on the range of data that you select.

Record All the categories of data pertaining to one database item such as a person, place, thing, event, or idea, stored in a horizontal row in a database.

Record Macro A command that records your actions in Visual Basic for Applications (VBA).

Refresh The command to update a worksheet to reflect the new data.

Relationship A category of SmartArt graphics that is used to illustrate connections.

Relationship An association between tables that share a common field.

Relative cell reference In a formula, the address of a cell based on the relative positions of the cell that contains the formula and the cell referred to in the formula.

Ribbon A user interface in both Office 2013 and File Explorer that groups the commands for performing related tasks on tabs across the upper portion of the program window.

RIGHT A text function that returns the specified number of characters from the end (right) of a string of characters.

Right-click The action of clicking the right mouse button one time.

Rotation handle A circle that displays on the top side of a selected object used to rotate the object up to 360 degrees.

Rounding A procedure in which you determine which digit at the right of the number will be the last digit displayed and then increase it by one if the next digit to its right is 5, 6, 7, 8, or 9.

Row A horizontal group of cells in a worksheet.

Row heading The numbers along the left side of an Excel worksheet that designate the row numbers.

ROWS area An area to position fields that you want to display as rows in the PivotTable report. Field names placed here become row titles, and the data is grouped by these row titles.

Sans serif font A font design with no lines or extensions on the ends of characters.

Scale The range of numbers in the data series that controls the minimum, maximum, and incremental values on the value axis.

Scale to Fit Excel commands that enable you to stretch or shrink the width, height, or both, of printed output to fit a maximum number of pages.

Scaling The group of commands by which you can reduce the horizontal and vertical size of the printed data by a percentage or by the number of pages that you specify.

Scenario A set of values that Excel saves and can substitute automatically in your worksheet.

Scenario Manager A what-if analysis tool that compares alternatives.

Schema An XML file that contains the rules for what can and cannot reside in an XML data file.

Scope The location within which a defined name is recognized without qualification—usually either to a specific worksheet or to the entire workbook.

Screenshot An image of an active window on your computer that you can insert into a worksheet.

ScreenTip A small box that displays useful information when you perform various mouse actions such as pointing to screen elements or dragging.

Scroll bar A vertical or horizontal bar in a window or a pane to assist in bringing an area into view, and which contains a scroll box and scroll arrows.

Scroll box The box in the vertical and horizontal scroll bars that can be dragged to reposition the contents of a window or pane on the screen.

Select All box A box in the upper left corner of the worksheet grid that, when clicked, selects all the cells in a worksheet.

Selecting Highlighting, by dragging with your mouse, areas of text or data or graphics, so that the selection can be edited, formatted, copied, or moved.

Self-signed A project signed with a certificate that you create yourself.

Series A group of things that come one after another in succession; for example, January, February, March, and so on.

Serif font A font design that includes small line extensions on the ends of the letters to guide the eye in reading from left to right.

Shared workbook A workbook set up to allow multiple users on a network to view and make changes to the workbook at the same time.

SharePoint Collaboration software with which people in an organization can set up team sites to share information, manage documents, and publish reports for others to see.

Sheet tab scrolling buttons Buttons to the left of the sheet tabs used to display Excel sheet tabs that are not in view; used when there are more sheet tabs than will display in the space provided.

Sheet tabs The labels along the lower border of the Excel window that identify each worksheet.

Shortcut menu A menu that displays commands and options relevant to the selected text or object; also called a *context menu*.

Show Formulas A command that displays the formula in each cell instead of the resulting value.

Signature line Specifies the individual who must sign the document.

Sizing handles Small squares that indicate a picture or object is selected.

SkyDrive Microsoft's free cloud storage for anyone with a free Microsoft account.

Slicer Easy-to-use filtering control with buttons that enable you to drill down through large amounts of data.

Slicer header The top of a slicer that indicates the category of the slicer items.

SmartArt graphic A visual representation of information and ideas.

Solver A what-if analysis tool with which you can find an optimal (maximum or minimum) value for a formula in one cell—referred to as the objective cell—subject to constraints, or limits, on the values of other formula cells on a worksheet.

Sort The process of arranging data in a specific order based on the value in each field.

Sort dialog box A dialog box in which you can sort data based on several criteria at once, and that enables a sort by more than one column or row.

Source data The data for a PivotTable, formatted in columns and rows, which can be located in an Excel worksheet or an external source.

Sparkline A tiny chart in the background of a cell that gives a visual trend summary alongside your data; makes a pattern more obvious.

Split The command that enables you to view separate parts of the same worksheet on your screen; splits the window into multiple resizable panes to view distant parts of the worksheet at one time.

Split button A button divided into two parts and in which clicking the main part of the button performs a command and clicking the arrow opens a menu with choices.

Spreadsheet Another name for a worksheet.

Standardization All forms created within the organization will have a uniform appearance; the data will always be organized in the same manner.

Start search The search feature in Windows 8 in which, from the Start screen, you can begin to type and by default, Windows 8 searches for apps; you can adjust the search to search for files or settings.

Statistical functions Excel functions, including the AVERAGE, MEDIAN, MIN, and MAX functions, which are useful to analyze a group of measurements.

Status bar The area along the lower edge of the Excel window that displays, on the left side, the current cell mode, page number, and worksheet information; on the right side, when numerical data is selected, common calculations such as Sum and Average display.

Style A group of formatting commands, such as font, font size, font color, paragraph alignment, and line spacing that can be applied to a paragraph with one command.

Sub Short for a sub procedure.

Sub procedure A unit of computer code that performs an action.

Subfolder A folder within a folder.

Subtotal command The command that totals several rows of related data together by automatically inserting subtotals and totals for the selected cells.

SUM function A predefined formula that adds all the numbers in a selected range of cells.

SUMIF function A logical function that contains one logic test—it will add values in a specified range that meet certain conditions or criteria.

SUMIFS function A logical function that will add values in multiple ranges that meet multiple criteria.

Summary sheet A worksheet where totals from other worksheets are displayed and summarized.

Switch Row/Column A charting command to swap the data over the axis—data being charted on the vertical axis will move to the horizontal axis and vice versa.

Synchronization The process of updating computer files that are in two or more locations according to specific rules—also called syncing.

Syncing The process of updating computer files that are in two or more locations according to specific rules—also called synchronization.

Syntax The arrangement of the arguments in a function.

Tab delimited text file A file type in which cells are separated by tabs; this type of file can be readily exchanged with various database programs.

Table Data stored in a format of rows and columns.

Table array A defined range of cells, arranged in a column or a row, used in a VLOOKUP or HLOOKUP function.

Tabs (ribbon) On the Office ribbon, the name of each activity area.

Tags Custom file properties in the form of words that you associate with a document to give an indication of the document's content; used to help find and organize files. Also called *keywords*.

Taskbar The area along the lower edge of the desktop that displays buttons representing programs.

Template A special workbook that may include formatting, formulas, and other elements, and that is used as a pattern for creating other workbooks.

Text function A function that can be used to combine or separate data, change case, and apply formatting to a string of characters.

Text pane The pane that displays to the left of the graphic, is populated with placeholder text, and is used to build a graphic by entering and editing text.

Text values Constant values consisting of only text, and which usually provide information about number values; also referred to as labels.

Theme A predesigned set of colors, fonts, lines, and fill effects that look good together and that can be applied to your entire document or to specific items.

Tick mark labels Identifying information for a tick mark generated from the cells on the worksheet used to create the chart.

Tick marks The short lines that display on an axis at regular intervals.

Title bar The bar at the top edge of the program window that indicates the name of the current file and the program name.

Toggle button A button that can be turned on by clicking it once, and then turned off by clicking it again.

Toolbar In a folder window, a row of buttons with which you can perform common tasks, such as changing the view of your files and folders or burning files to a CD.

Trace Dependents command A command that displays arrows that indicate what cells are affected by the value of the currently selected cell.

Trace Error command A tool that helps locate and resolve an error by tracing the selected error value.

Trace Precedents command A command that displays arrows to indicate what cells affect the value of the cell that is selected.

Tracer arrow An indicator that shows the relationship between the active cell and its related cell.

Track Changes An Excel feature that logs details about workbook changes including insertions and deletions.

Transpose To switch the data in rows and columns.

Trendline A graphic representation of trends in a data series, such as a line sloping upward to represent increased sales over a period of months.

TRIM A text function that removes extra blank spaces from a string of characters.

Triple-click The action of clicking the left mouse button three times in rapid succession.

Trusted Documents A security feature in Office that remembers which files you have already enabled; you might encounter this feature if you open a file from an email or download files from the Internet.

Two-variable data table A data table that changes the values in two cells.

Type argument An optional argument in the PMT function that assumes that the payment will be made at the end of each time period.

Underlying formula The formula entered in a cell and visible only on the Formula Bar.

Underlying value The data that displays in the Formula Bar.

Uniform Resource Locator An address that uniquely identifies a location on the Internet.

Unlocked [cells] Cells in a protected worksheet that may be filled in.

UPPER A text function that changes the case of the characters in a string, making all characters uppercase.

URL The acronym for Uniform Resource Locator, which is an address that uniquely identifies a location on the Internet.

USB flash drive A small data storage device that plugs into a computer USB port.

Validation list A list of values that are acceptable for a group of cells; only values in the list are valid and any value *not* in the list is considered invalid.

Value Another name for a constant value.

Value after increase = base x percent for new value The formula for calculating the value after an increase by multiplying the original value—the base—by the percent for new value (see the *Percent for new value* formula).

Value axis A numerical scale on the left side of a chart that shows the range of numbers for the data points; also referred to as the Y-axis.

VALUES area An area to position fields that contain data that is summarized in a PivotTable report or PivotChart report. The data placed here is usually numeric or financial in nature and the data is summarized—summed. You can also perform other basic calculations such as finding the average, the minimum, or the maximum.

Variable cell In Solver, a cell in which the value will change to achieve the desired results.

Variable expense Expense that varies depending on the amount of sales.

VBA The abbreviation for the Visual Basic for Applications programming language.

VBA construct An instruction that enables a macro to perform multiple operations on a single object.

Vertical Value axis (y-axis) A numerical scale on the left side of a chart that shows the range of numbers for the data points; also referred to as the y-axis.

Visual Basic Editor The window in which you can view and edit Visual Basic code.

Visual Basic for Applications The programming language used to write computer programs in the Microsoft Windows environment.

VLOOOKUP An Excel function that looks up values that are displayed vertically in a column.

Volatile A term used to describe an Excel function that is subject to change each time the workbook is reopened; for example the NOW function updates itself to the current date and time each time the workbook is opened.

Walls and floor The areas surrounding a 3-D chart that give dimension and boundaries to the chart.

Watch Window A window that displays the results of specified cells.

Watermark A faded image or text used as a background of a document.

What-If Analysis The process of changing the values in cells to see how those changes affect the outcome of formulas in a worksheet.

Wildcard A character, for example the asterisk or question mark, used to search a field when you are uncertain of the exact value or when you want to widen the search to include more records.

Window A rectangular area on a computer screen in which programs and content appear, and which can be moved, resized, minimized, or closed.

Wizard A feature in Microsoft Office programs that walks you step by step through a process.

WordArt A feature with which you can insert decorative text in your document.

Workbook An Excel file that contains one or more worksheets.

Workbook-level buttons Buttons at the far right of the ribbon tabs that minimize or restore a displayed workbook.

Worksheet The primary document that you use in Excel to work with and store data, and which is formatted as a pattern of uniformly spaced horizontal and vertical lines.

Worksheet grid area A part of the Excel window that displays the columns and rows that intersect to form the worksheet's cells.

X-axis Another name for the horizontal (category) axis.

.xlsx file name extension The default file format used by Excel 2013 to save an Excel workbook.

XML Paper Specification A Microsoft file format that creates an image of your document and that opens in the XPS viewer.

XPS The acronym for XML Paper Specification—a Microsoft file format that creates an image of your document and that opens in the XPS viewer.

XPS (XML Paper Specification) A file type, developed by Microsoft, which creates a representation of electronic paper that displays your data on the screen as it would look when printed.

Y-axis Another name for the vertical (value) axis.

Zipped folder A folder that has been reduced in size and thus takes up less storage space and can be transferred to other computers quickly; also called a *compressed* folder.

Zoom The action of increasing or decreasing the size of the viewing area on the screen.

Index